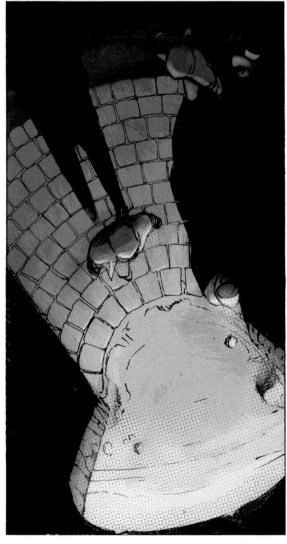

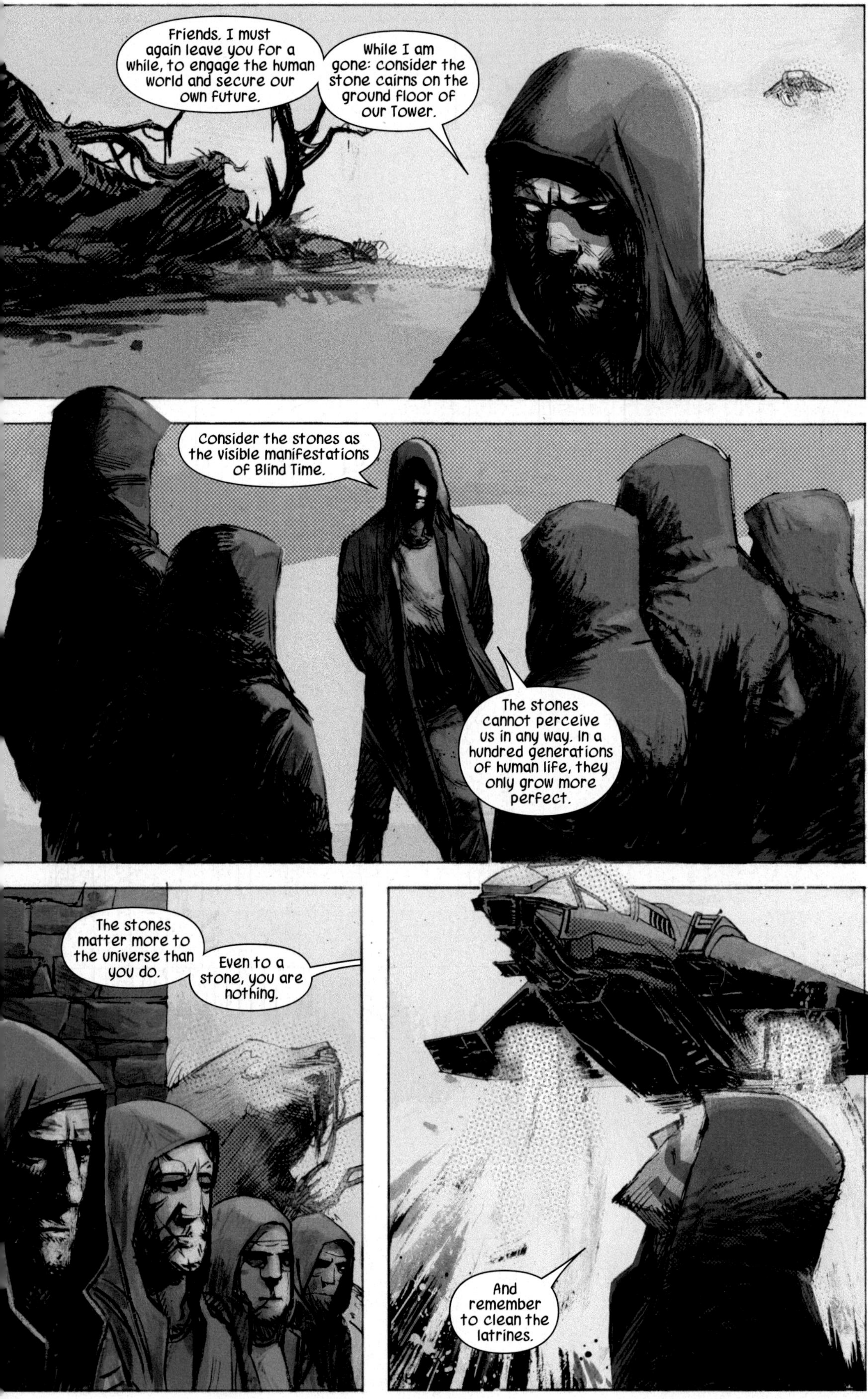
Friends. I must again leave you for a while, to engage the human world and secure our own future.
While I am gone: consider the stone cairns on the ground floor of our Tower.
Consider the stones as the visible manifestations of Blind Time.
The stones cannot perceive us in any way. In a hundred generations of human life, they only grow more perfect.
The stones matter more to the universe than you do.
Even to a stone, you are nothing.
And remember to clean the latrines.

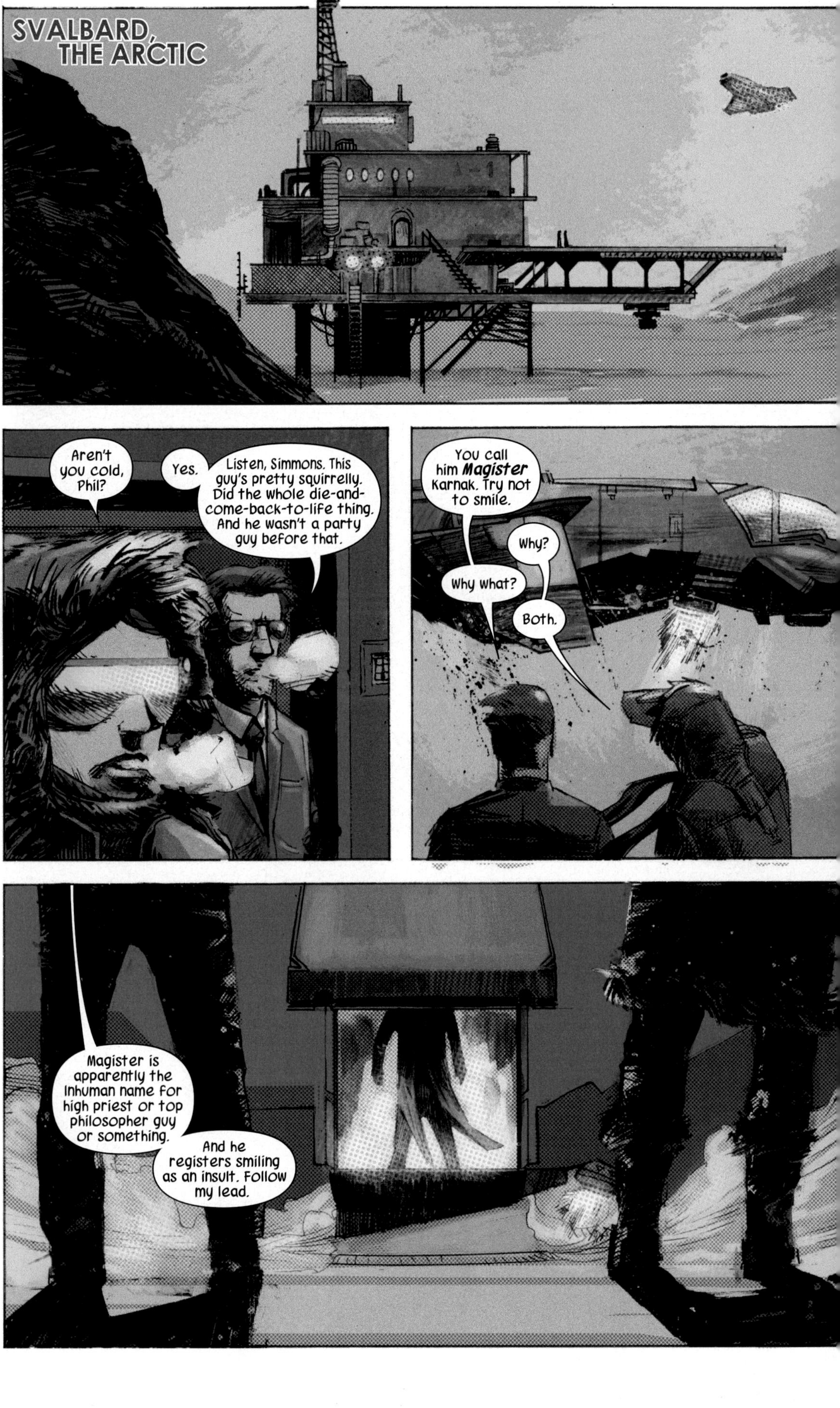
SVALBARD, THE ARCTIC
Aren't you cold, Phil?
Yes.
Listen, Simmons. This guy's pretty squirrelly. Did the whole die-and-come-back-to-life thing. And he wasn't a party guy before that.
You call him Magister Karnak. Try not to smile.
Why?
Why what?
Both.
Magister is apparently the Inhuman name for high priest or top philosopher guy or something.
And he registers smiling as an insult. Follow my lead.

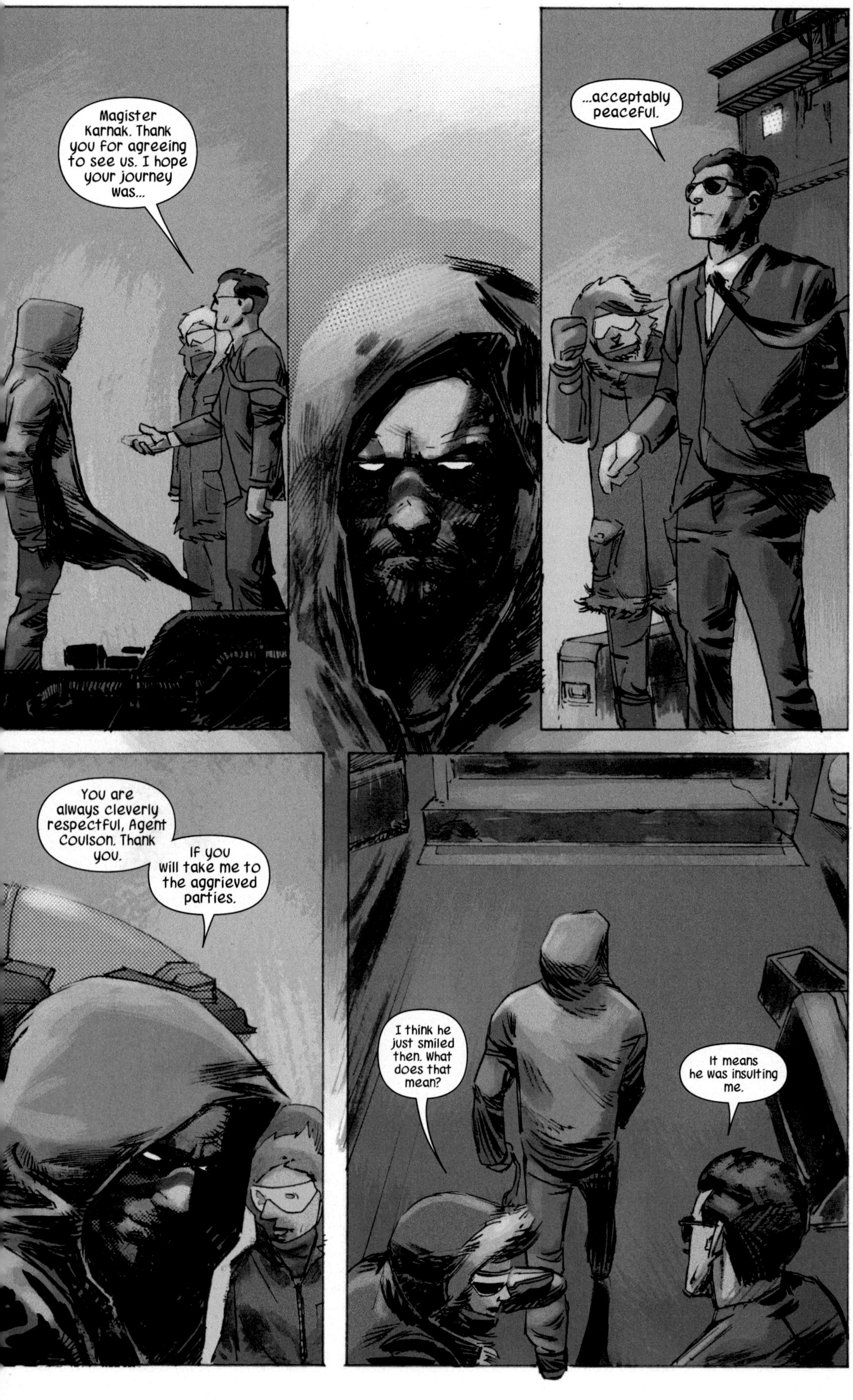
Magister Karnak. Thank you for agreeing to see us. I hope your journey was...
...acceptably peaceful.
You are always cleverly respectful, Agent Coulson. Thank you.
If you will take me to the aggrieved parties.
I think he just smiled then. What does that mean?
It means he was insulting me.

Where are we, Agent Coulson?

One of S.H.I.E.L.D.'s older substations. We've had some security issues lately, so we're reviving some places off the grid.

I meant the geographical location.

Svalbard. The Arctic Ocean.

Ah. Attilan, the seat of Inhumanity, was once located in the North Atlantic. It was a little like this. Bleak. Isolated. Cold.

It is pleasing to me.

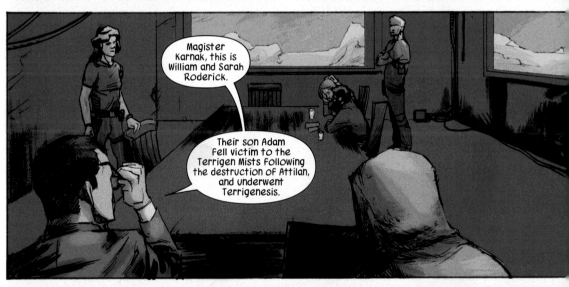

Magister Karnak, this is William and Sarah Roderick.

Their son Adam fell victim to the Terrigen Mists following the destruction of Attilan, and underwent Terrigenesis.

I can comprehend the relative difficulty of your lives.

I, ah...thank you?

What was the nature of his transformation?

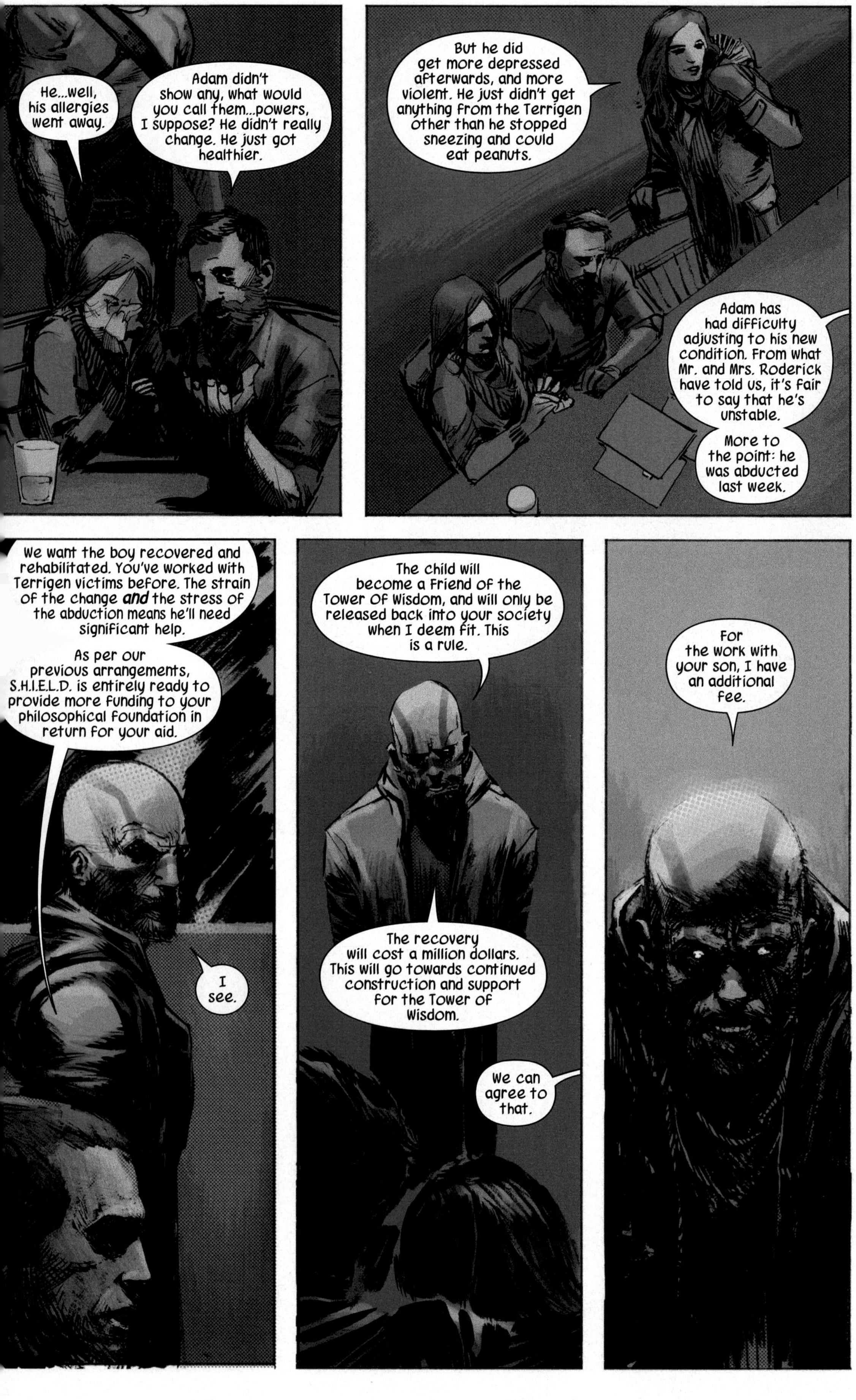

He...well, his allergies went away.
Adam didn't show any, what would you call them...powers, I suppose? He didn't really change. He just got healthier.
But he did get more depressed afterwards, and more violent. He just didn't get anything from the Terrigen other than he stopped sneezing and could eat peanuts.
Adam has had difficulty adjusting to his new condition. From what Mr. and Mrs. Roderick have told us, it's fair to say that he's unstable.
More to the point: he was abducted last week.
We want the boy recovered and rehabilitated. You've worked with Terrigen victims before. The strain of the change *and* the stress of the abduction means he'll need significant help.
As per our previous arrangements, S.H.I.E.L.D. is entirely ready to provide more funding to your philosophical foundation in return for your aid.
I see.
The child will become a Friend of the Tower Of Wisdom, and will only be released back into your society when I deem fit. This is a rule.
The recovery will cost a million dollars. This will go towards continued construction and support for the Tower of Wisdom.
We can agree to that.
For the work with your son, I have an additional fee.

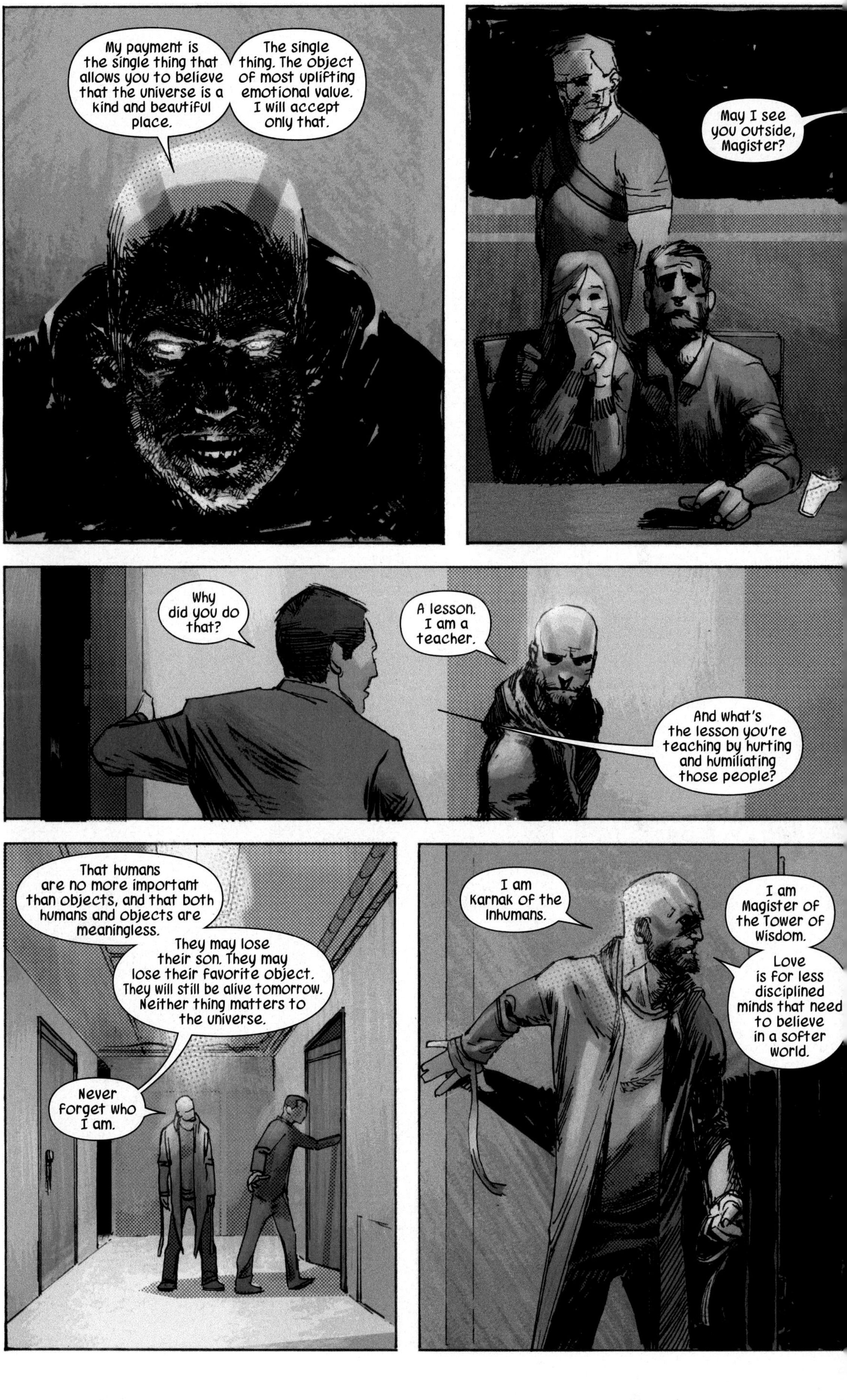
My payment is the single thing that allows you to believe that the universe is a kind and beautiful place.
The single thing. The object of most uplifting emotional value. I will accept only that.
May I see you outside, Magister?
Why did you do that?
A lesson. I am a teacher.
And what's the lesson you're teaching by hurting and humiliating those people?
That humans are no more important than objects, and that both humans and objects are meaningless.
They may lose their son. They may lose their favorite object. They will still be alive tomorrow. Neither thing matters to the universe.
Never forget who I am.
I am Karnak of the Inhumans.
I am Magister of the Tower of Wisdom.
Love is for less disciplined minds that need to believe in a softer world.

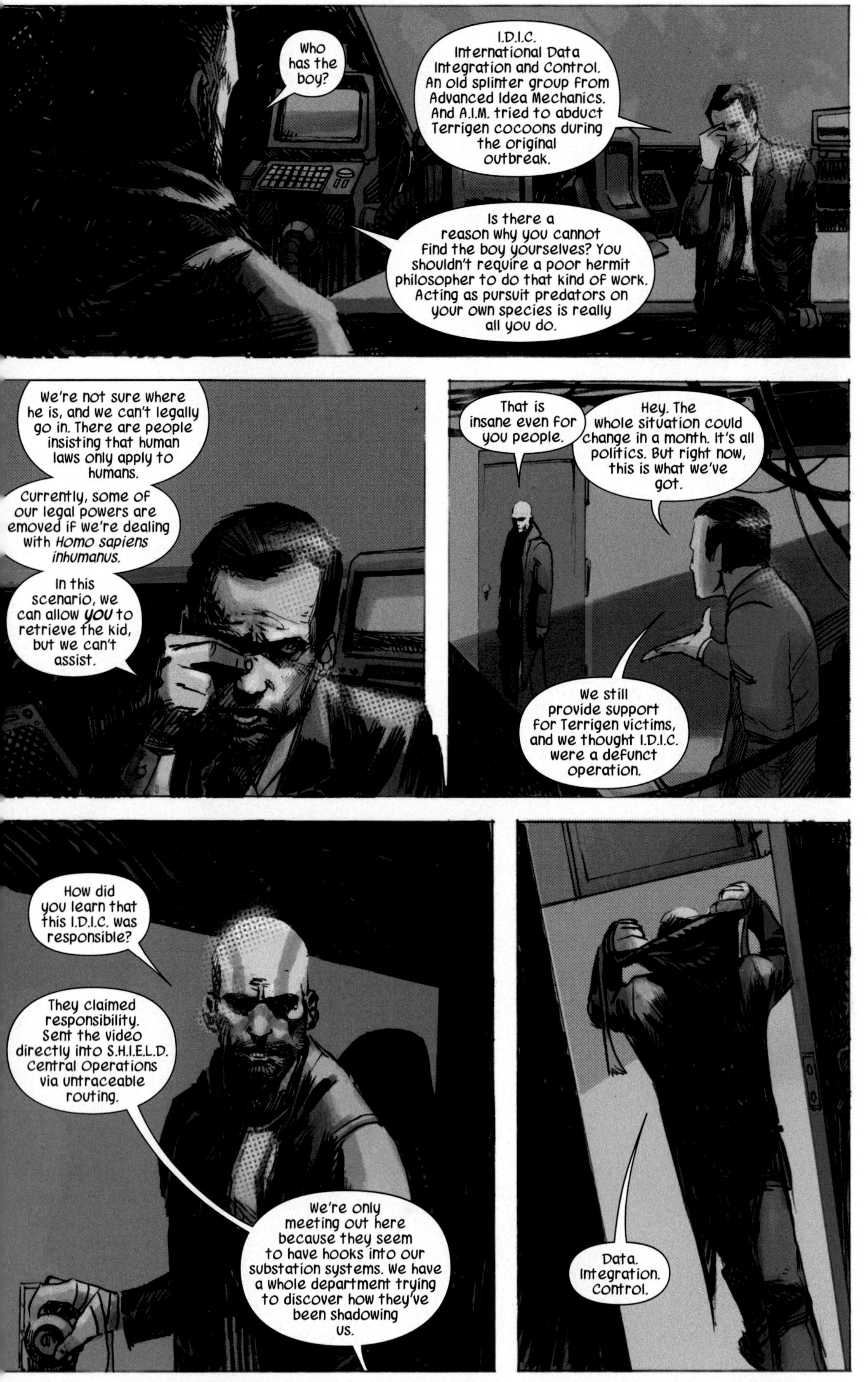
Who has the boy?
I.D.I.C. International Data Integration and Control. An old splinter group from Advanced Idea Mechanics. And A.I.M. tried to abduct Terrigen cocoons during the original outbreak.
Is there a reason why you cannot find the boy yourselves? You shouldn't require a poor hermit philosopher to do that kind of work. Acting as pursuit predators on your own species is really all you do.
We're not sure where he is, and we can't legally go in. There are people insisting that human laws only apply to humans.
Currently, some of our legal powers are emoved if we're dealing with *Homo sapiens inhumanus.*
In this scenario, we can allow **YOU** to retrieve the kid, but we can't assist.
That is insane even for you people.
Hey. The whole situation could change in a month. It's all politics. But right now, this is what we've got.
We still provide support for Terrigen victims, and we thought I.D.I.C. were a defunct operation.
How did you learn that this I.D.I.C. was responsible?
They claimed responsibility. Sent the video directly into S.H.I.E.L.D. Central Operations via untraceable routing.
We're only meeting out here because they seem to have hooks into our substation systems. We have a whole department trying to discover how they've been shadowing us.
Data. Integration. Control.

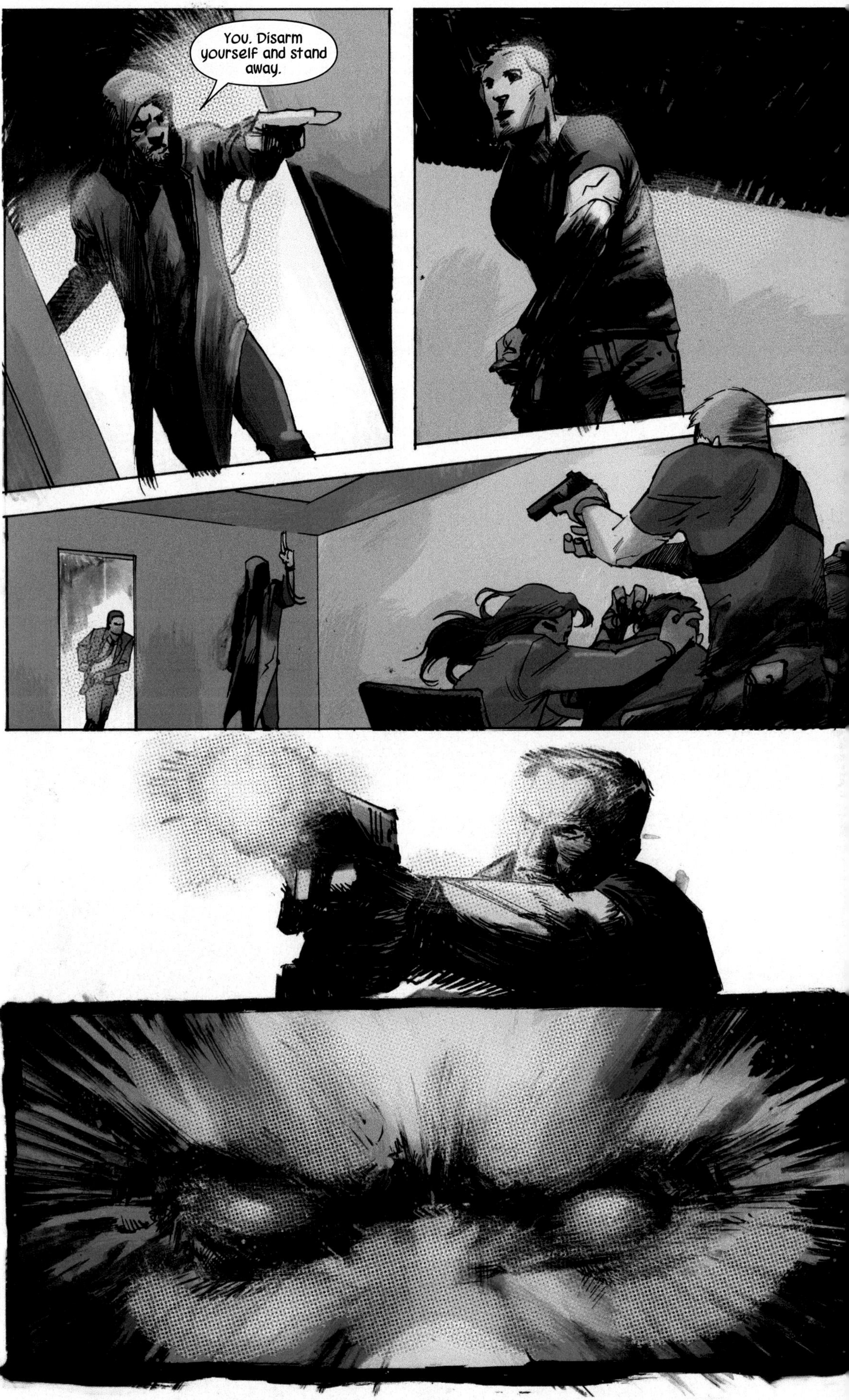
You. Disarm yourself and stand away.

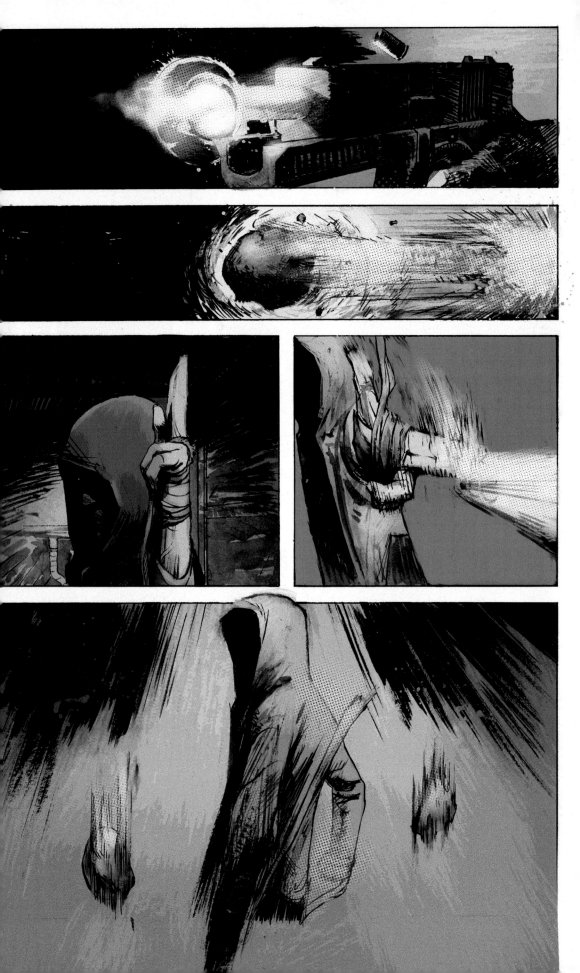

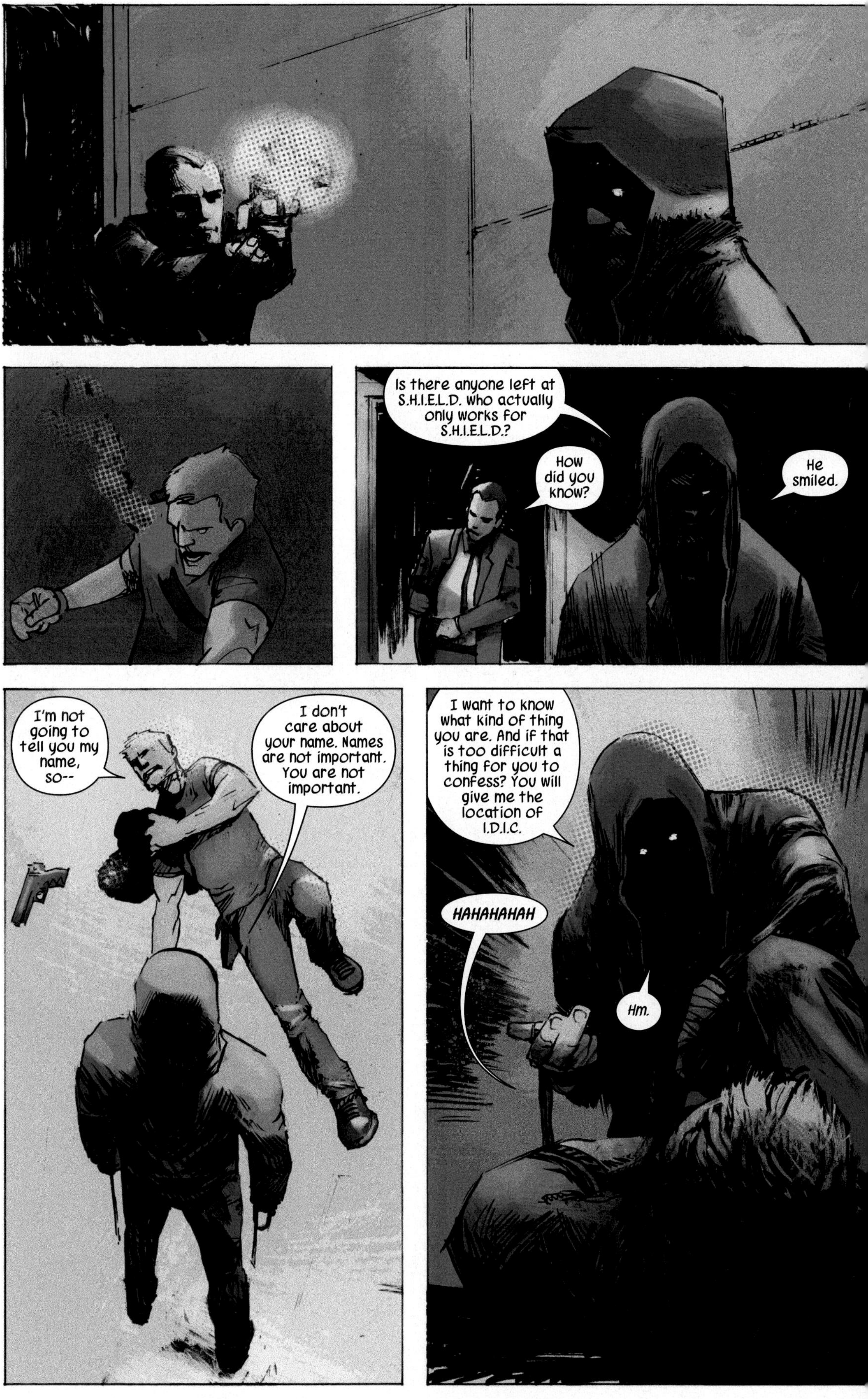
Is there anyone left at S.H.I.E.L.D. who actually only works for S.H.I.E.L.D.?
How did you know?
He smiled.
I'm not going to tell you my name, so--
I don't care about your name. Names are not important. You are not important.
I want to know what kind of thing you are. And if that is too difficult a thing for you to confess? You will give me the location of I.D.I.C.
HAHAHAHAH
Hm.

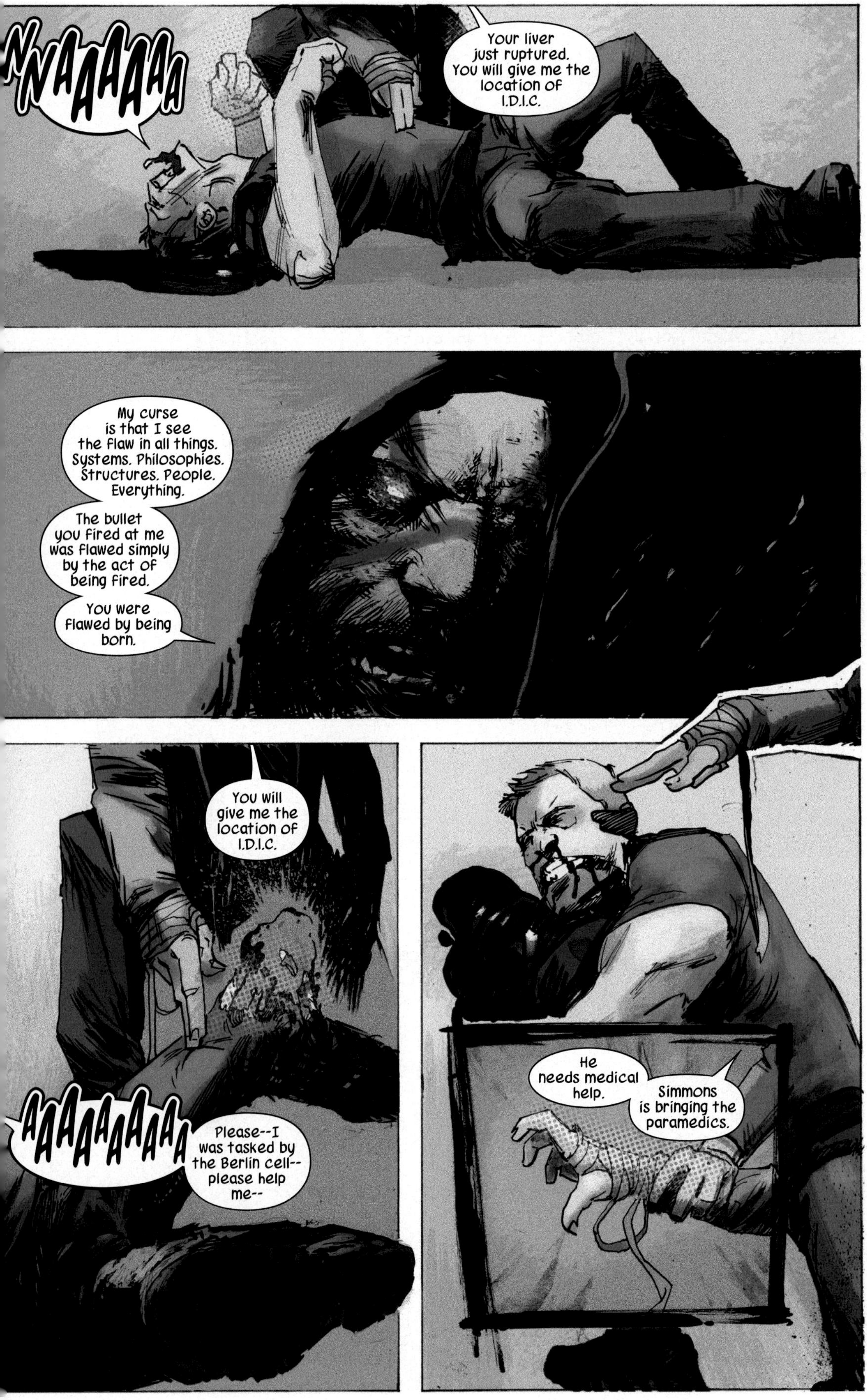
NNAAAAAAA
Your liver just ruptured. You will give me the location of I.D.I.C.
My curse is that I see the flaw in all things. Systems. Philosophies. Structures. People. Everything.
The bullet you fired at me was flawed simply by the act of being fired.
You were flawed by being born.
You will give me the location of I.D.I.C.
AAAAAAAAAA
Please--I was tasked by the Berlin cell--please help me--
He needs medical help.
Simmons is bringing the paramedics.

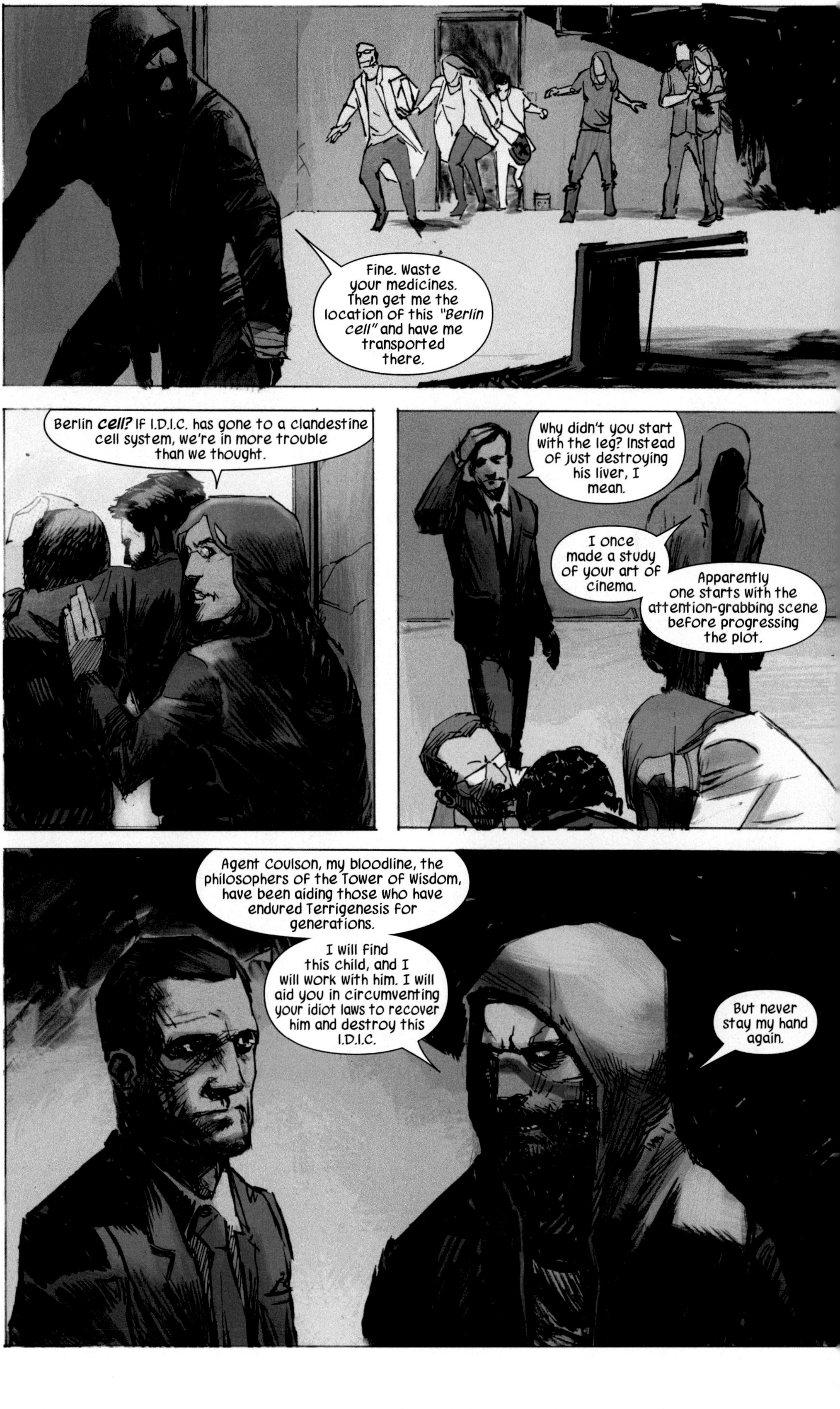
Fine. Waste your medicines. Then get me the location of this "Berlin cell" and have me transported there.
Berlin **cell?** If I.D.I.C. has gone to a clandestine cell system, we're in more trouble than we thought.
Why didn't you start with the leg? Instead of just destroying his liver, I mean.
I once made a study of your art of cinema.
Apparently one starts with the attention-grabbing scene before progressing the plot.
Agent Coulson, my bloodline, the philosophers of the Tower of Wisdom, have been aiding those who have endured Terrigenesis for generations.
I will find this child, and I will work with him. I will aid you in circumventing your idiot laws to recover him and destroy this I.D.I.C.
But never stay my hand again.

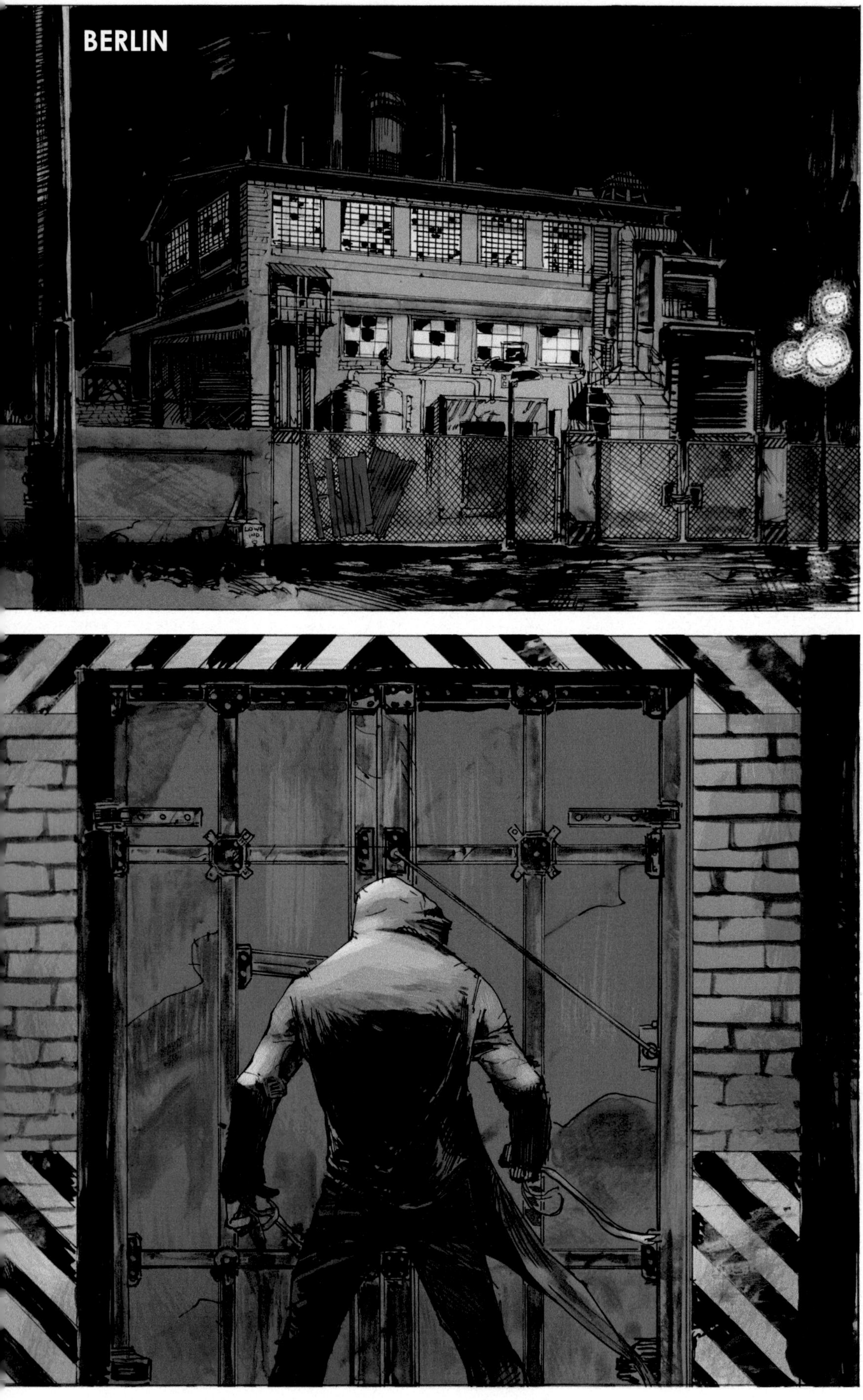
BERLIN
LOWE IND.

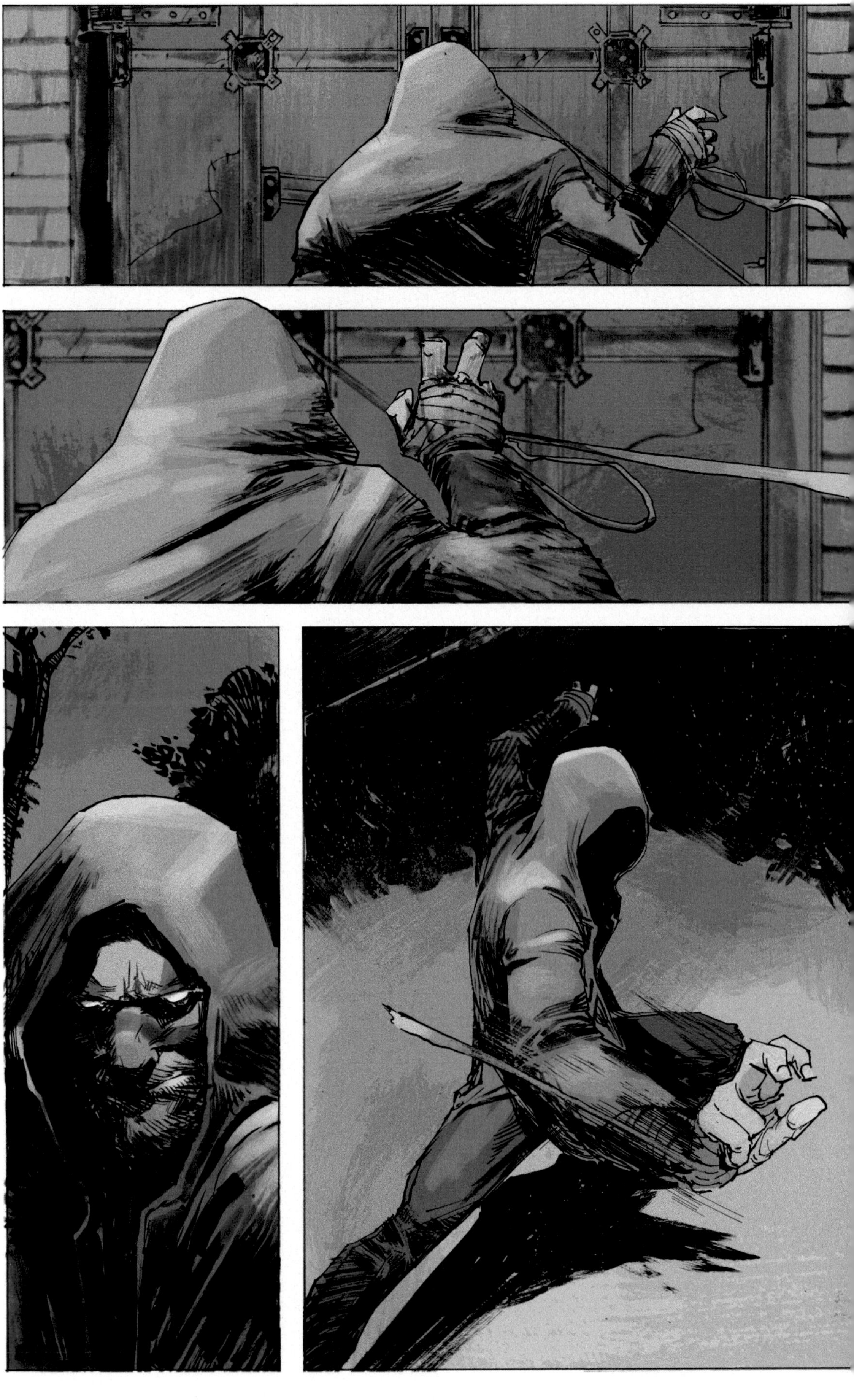

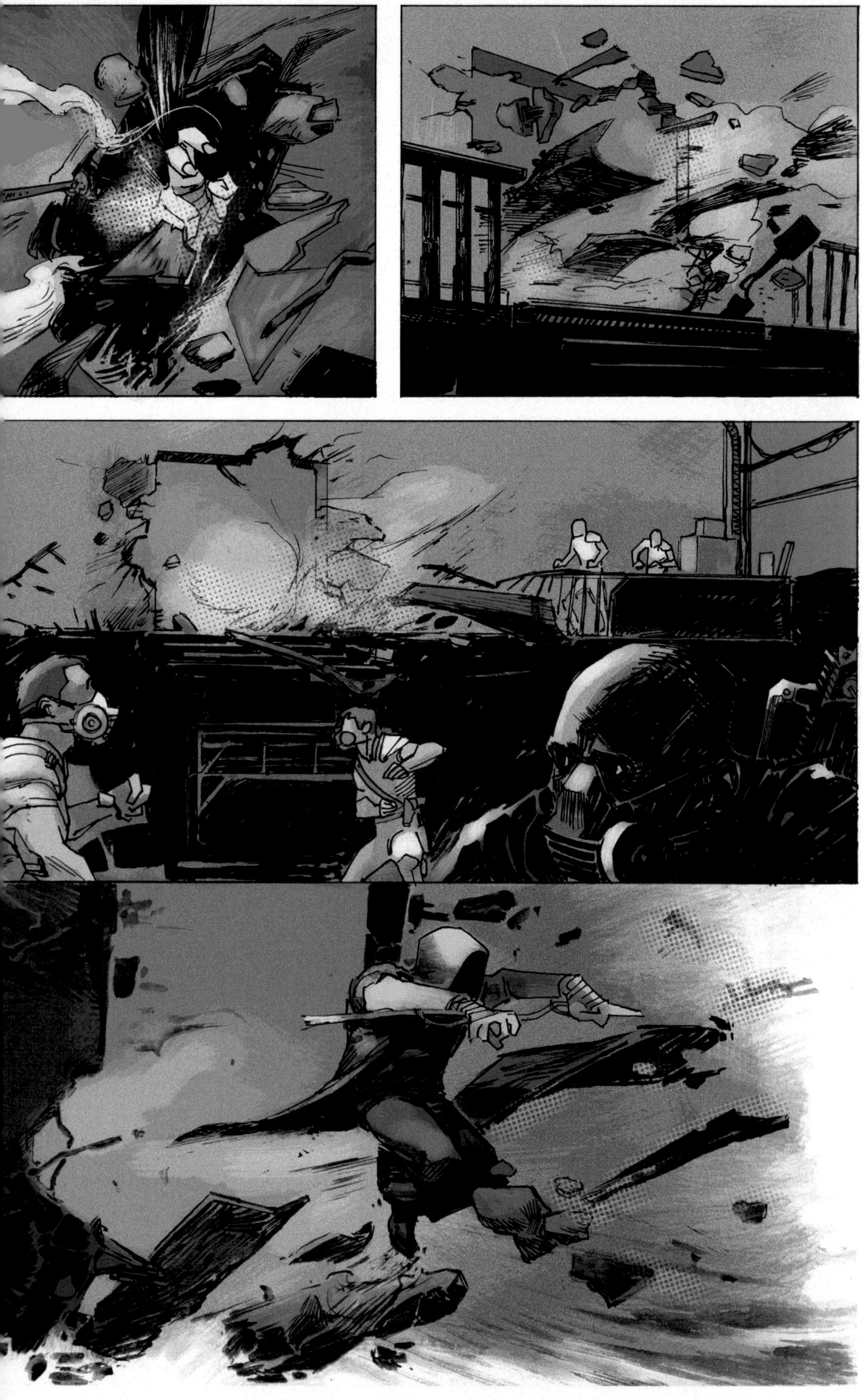

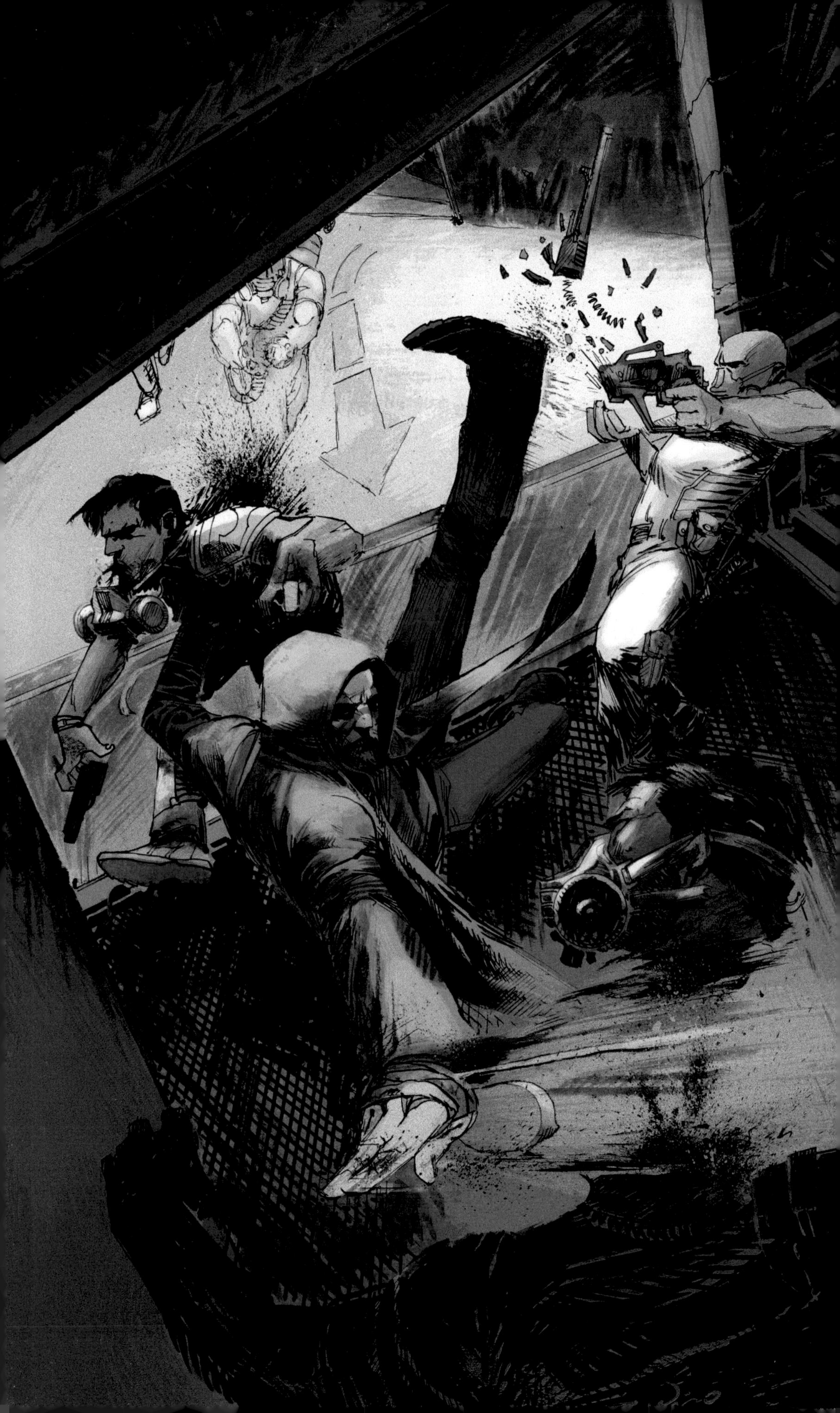

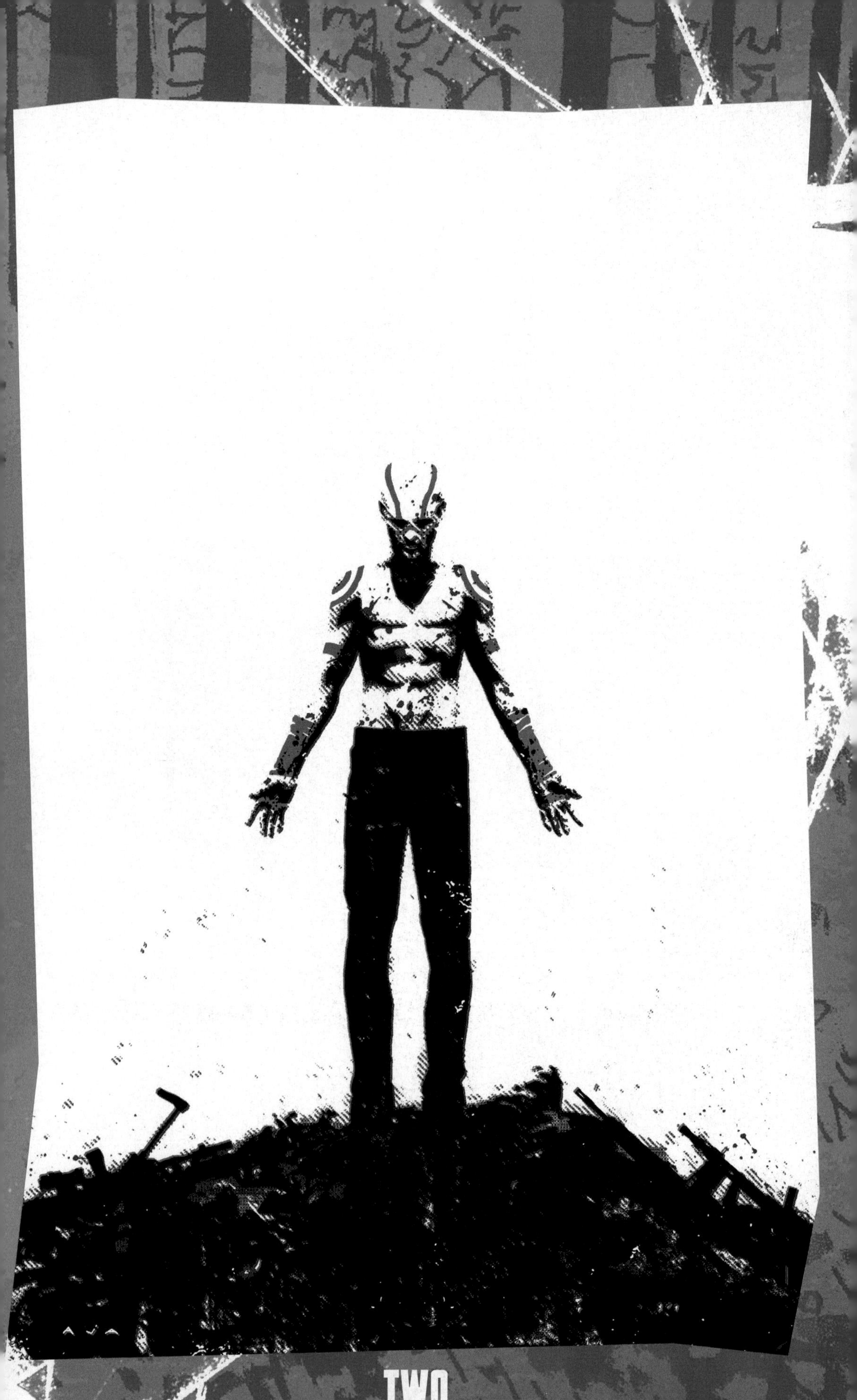

TWO

We are **not** exposing Karnak to the Terrigen Mists.

We don't understand why you'd deny your second child Terrigen.

Really? Go and visit his older brother. In the water. Where he has to live now.

Karnak will not suffer the same fate.

Then what use to Inhuman society is he?

He will join me in the Tower of Wisdom here in Attilan. He will study. He will train.

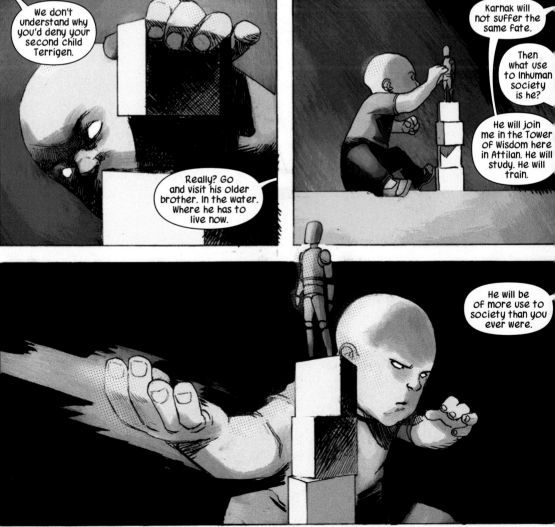

He will be of more use to society than you ever were.

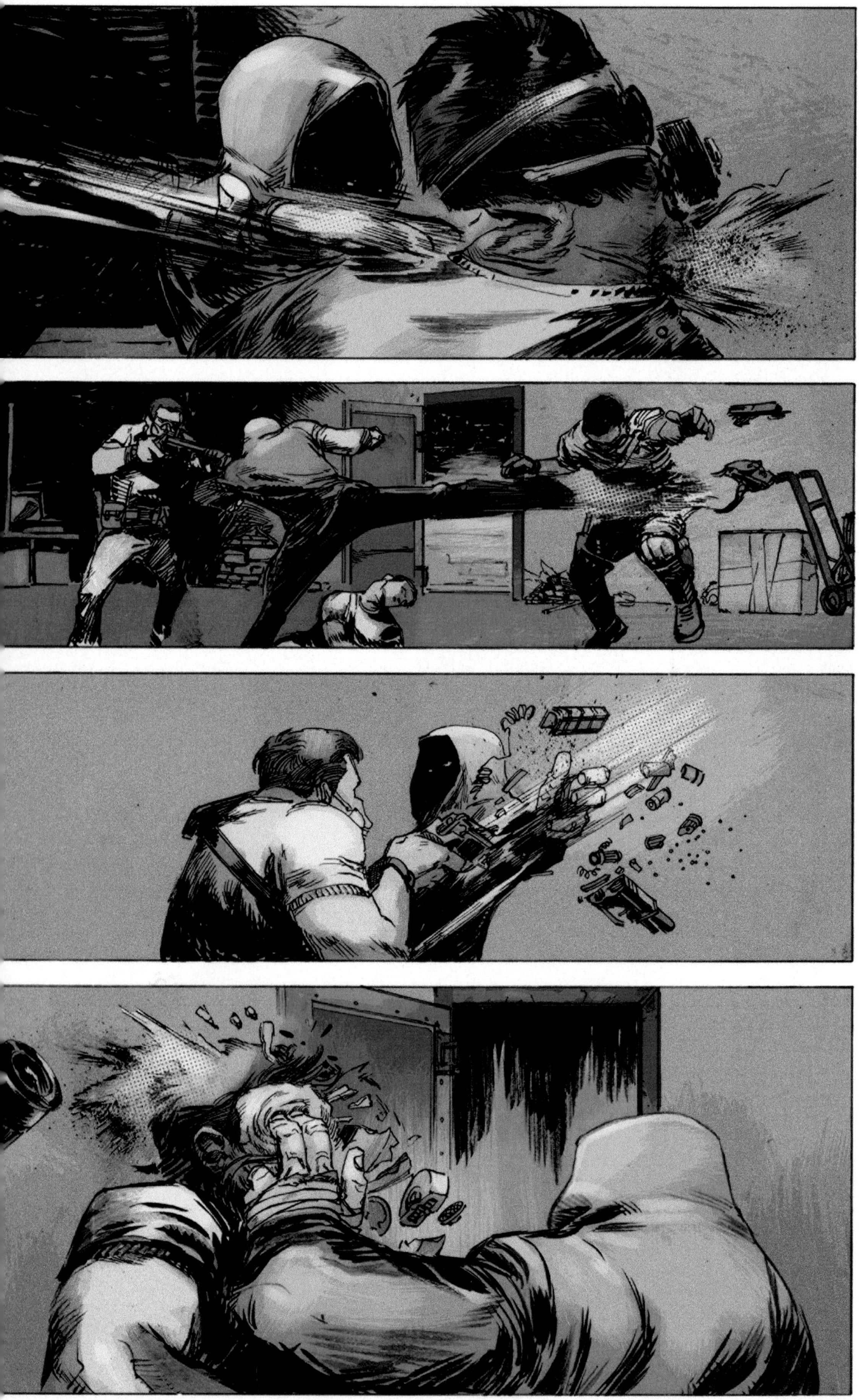

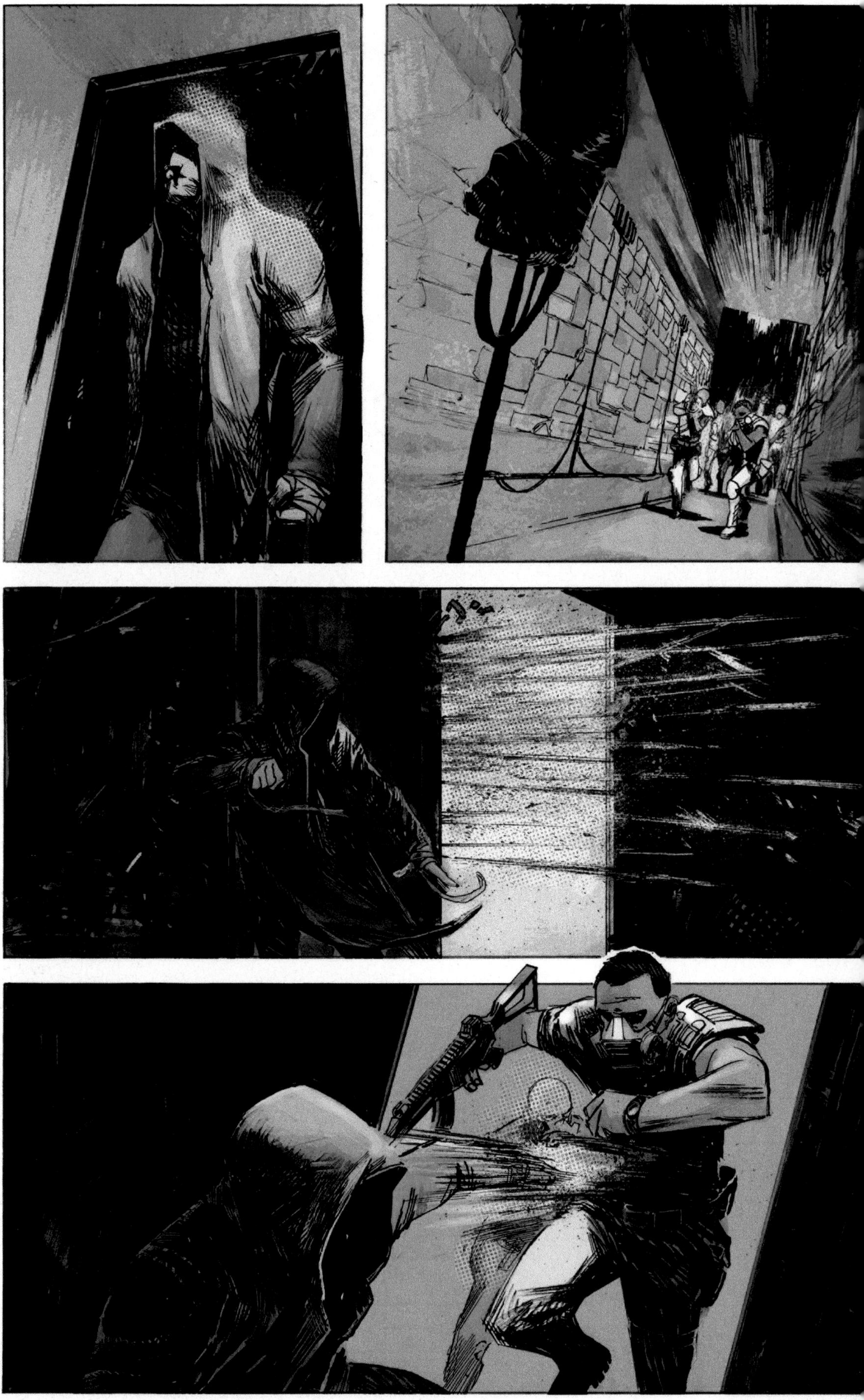

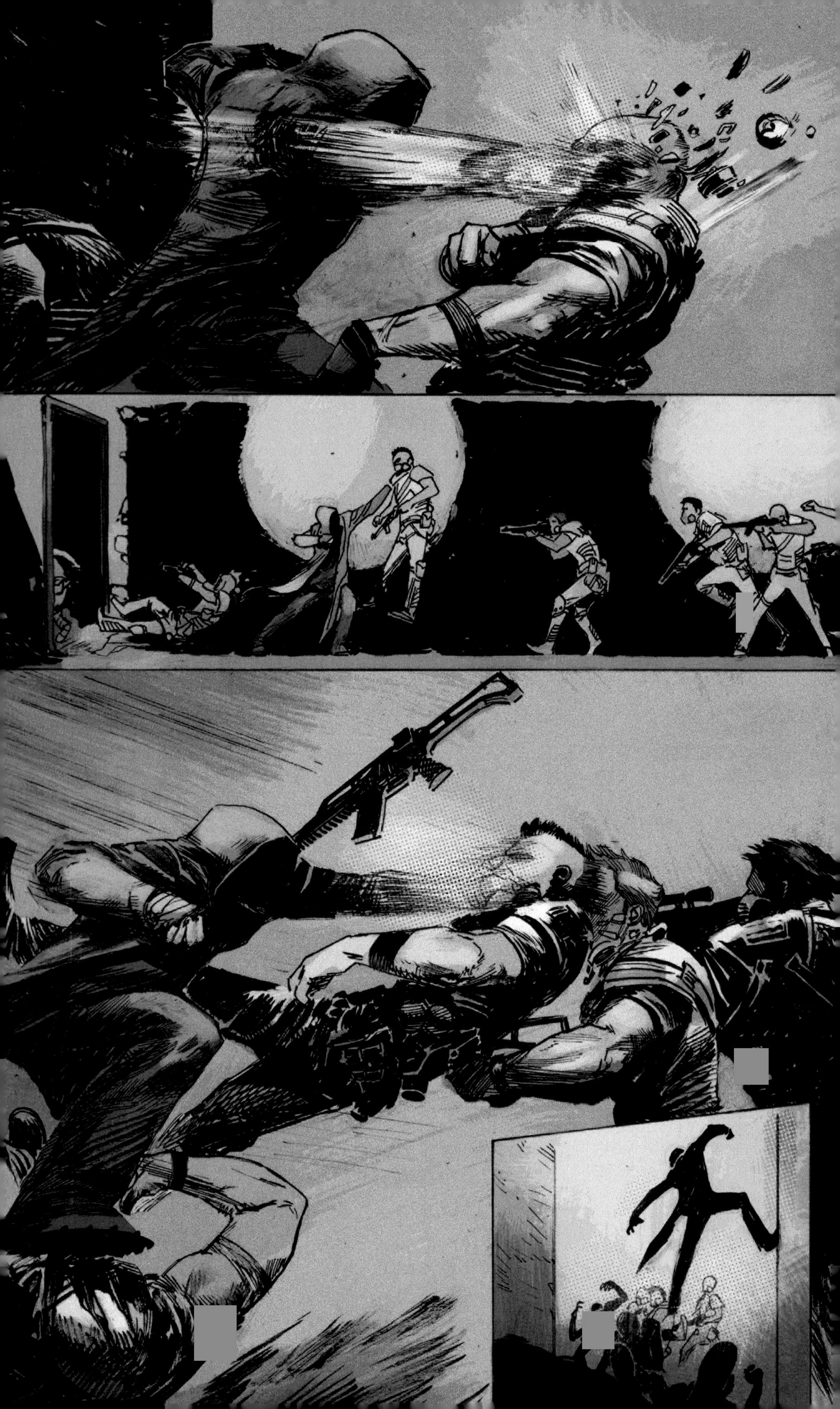

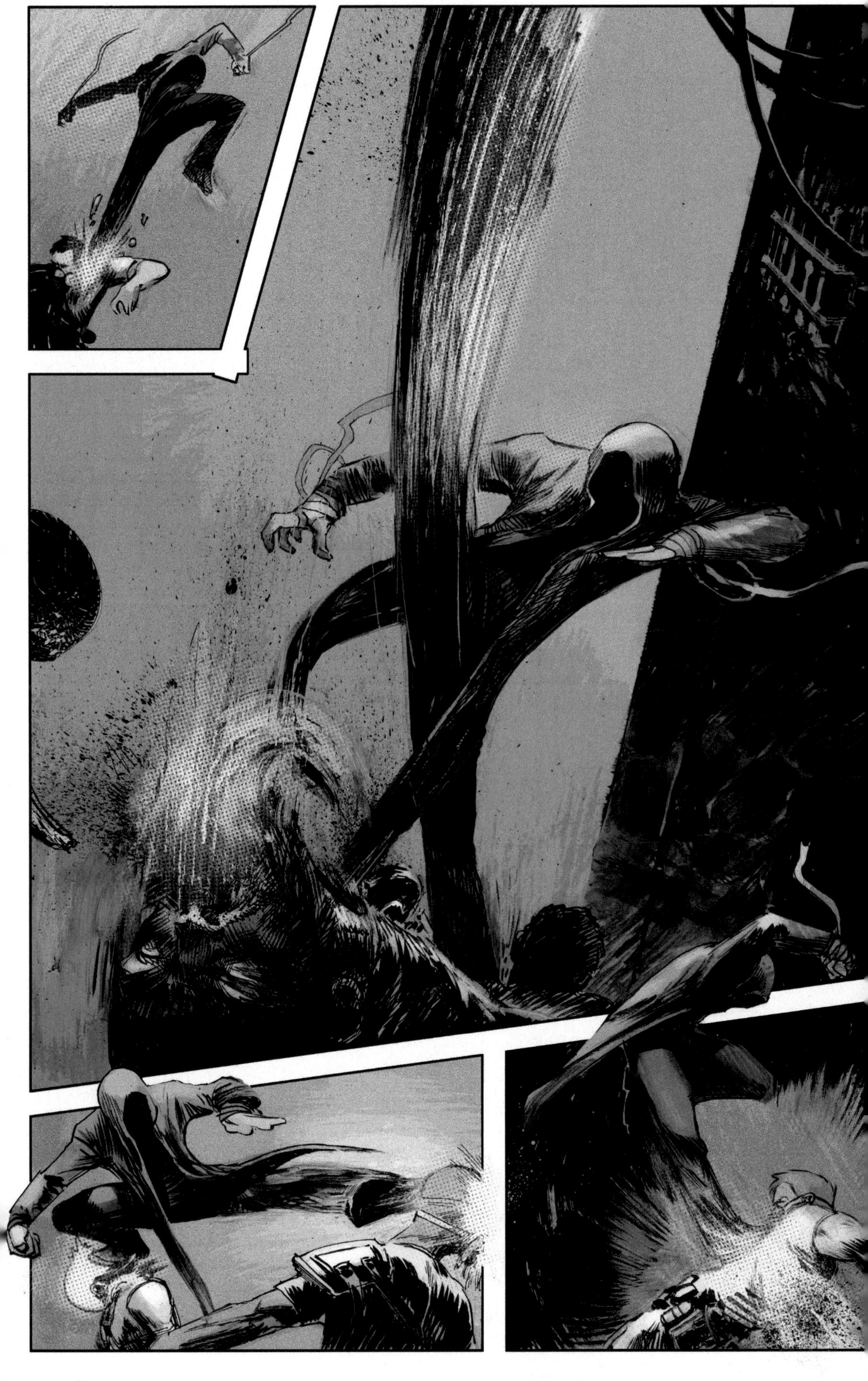

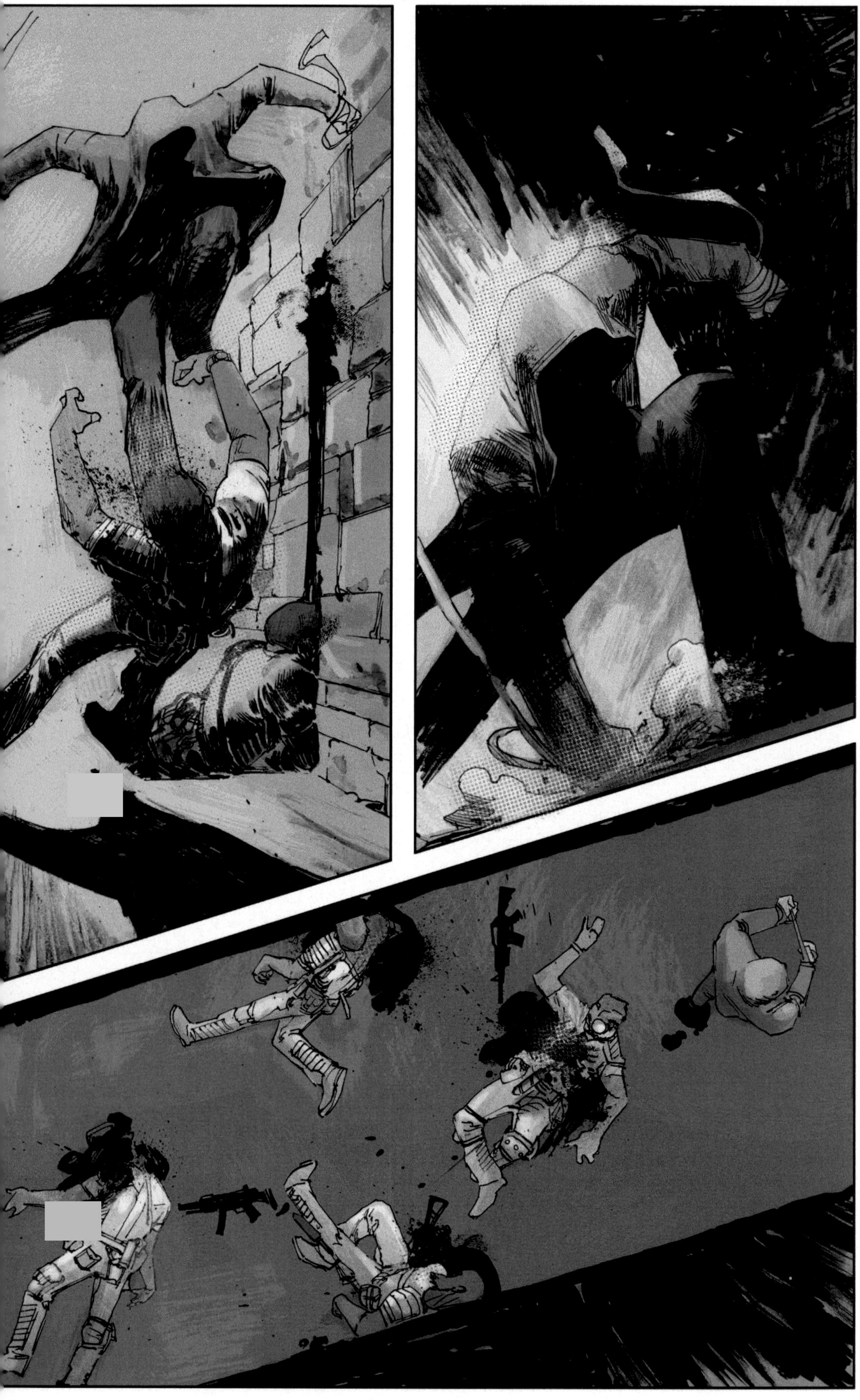

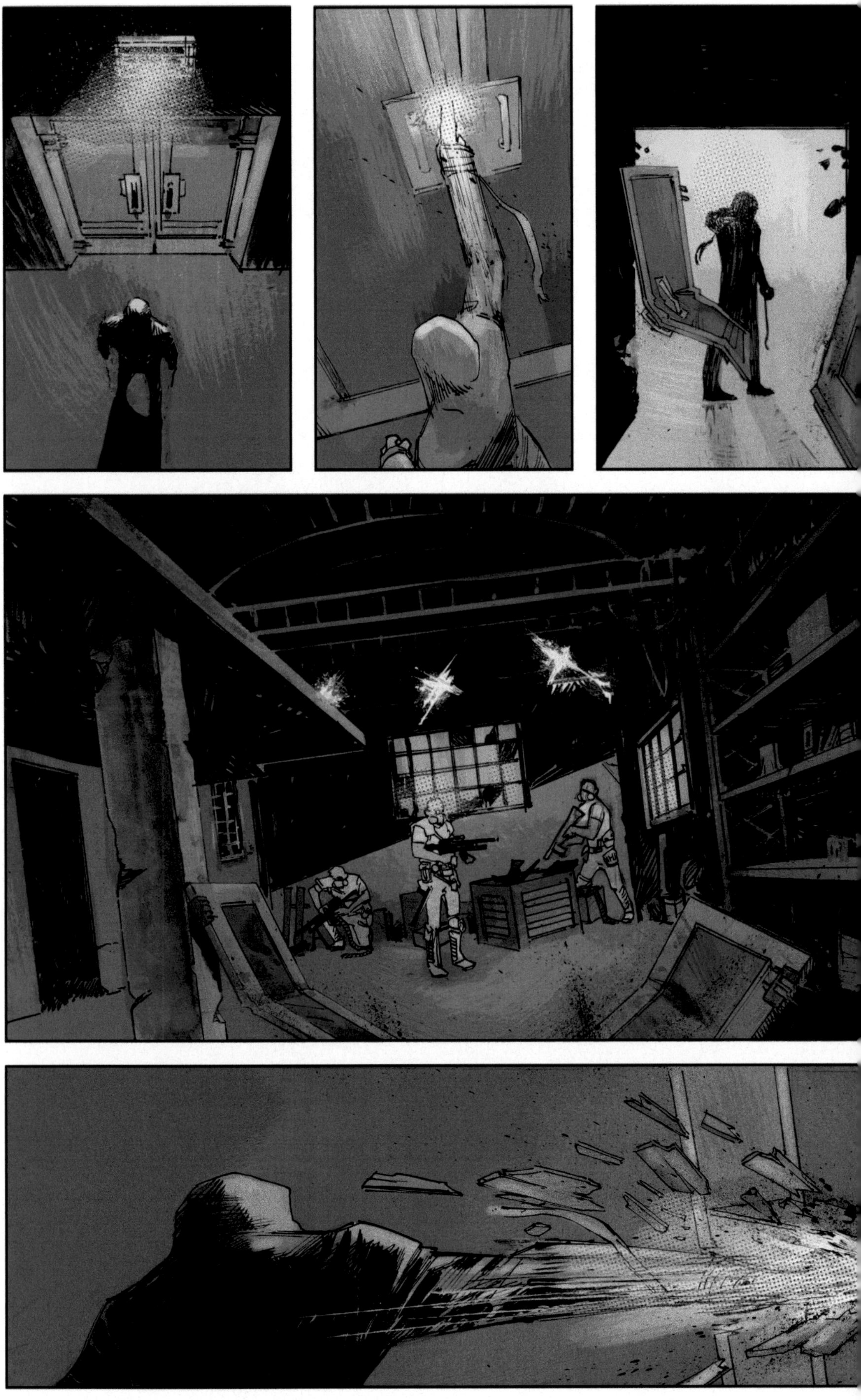

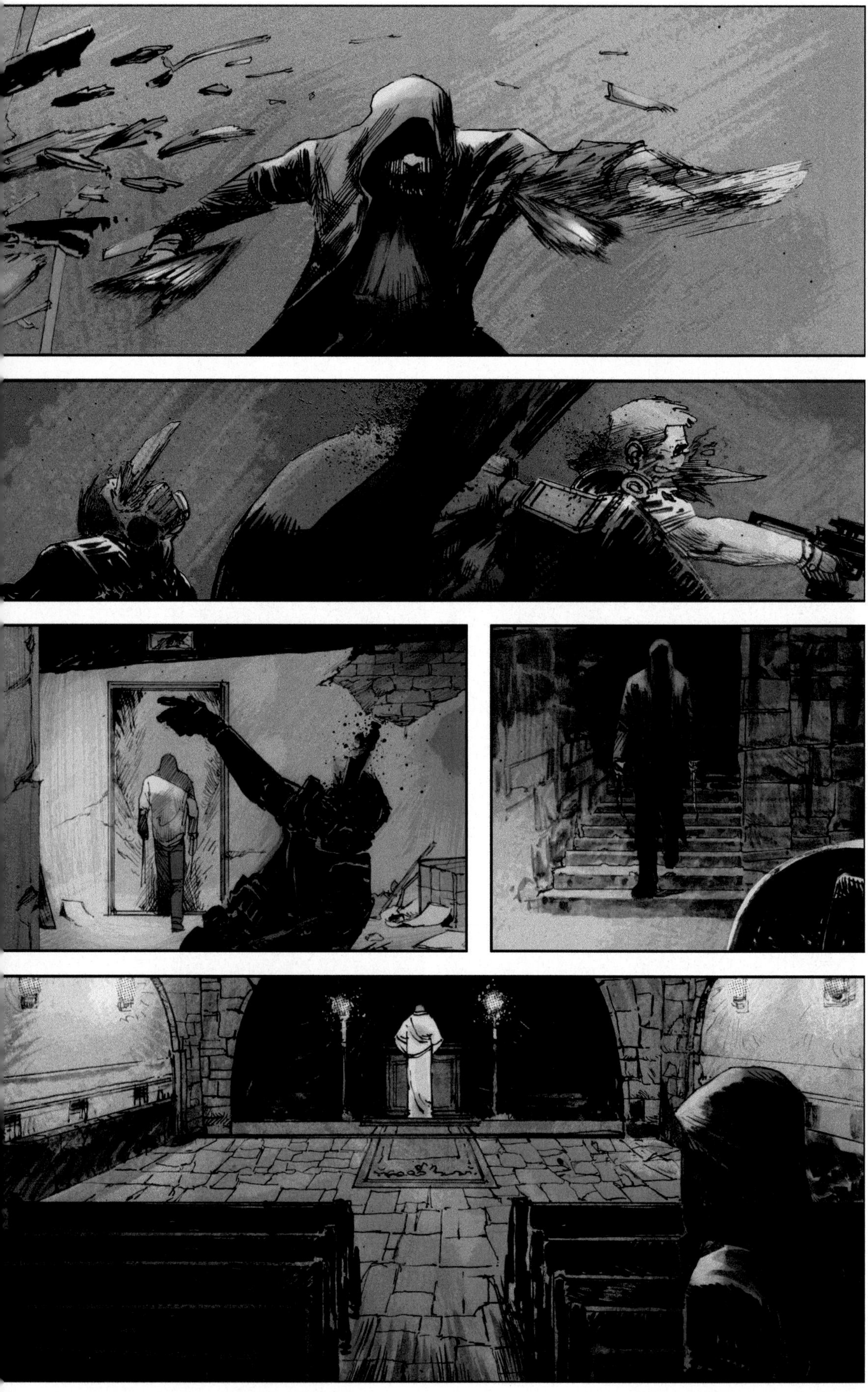

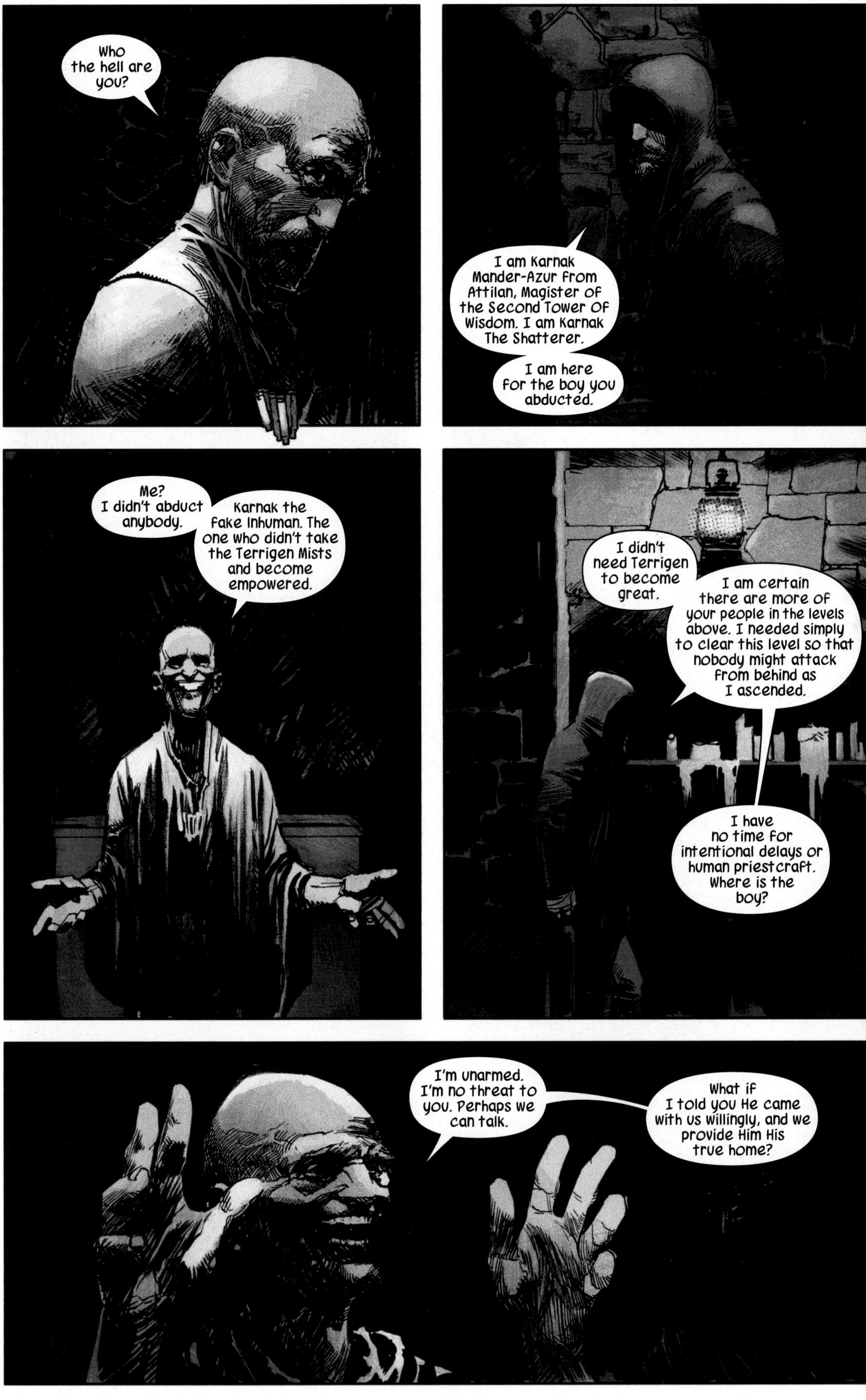

Who the hell are you?
I am Karnak Mander-Azur from Attilan, Magister of the Second Tower of Wisdom. I am Karnak The Shatterer.
I am here for the boy you abducted.
Me? I didn't abduct anybody.
Karnak the fake Inhuman. The one who didn't take the Terrigen Mists and become empowered.
I didn't need Terrigen to become great.
I am certain there are more of your people in the levels above. I needed simply to clear this level so that nobody might attack from behind as I ascended.
I have no time for intentional delays or human priestcraft. Where is the boy?
I'm unarmed. I'm no threat to you. Perhaps we can talk.
What if I told you He came with us willingly, and we provide Him His true home?

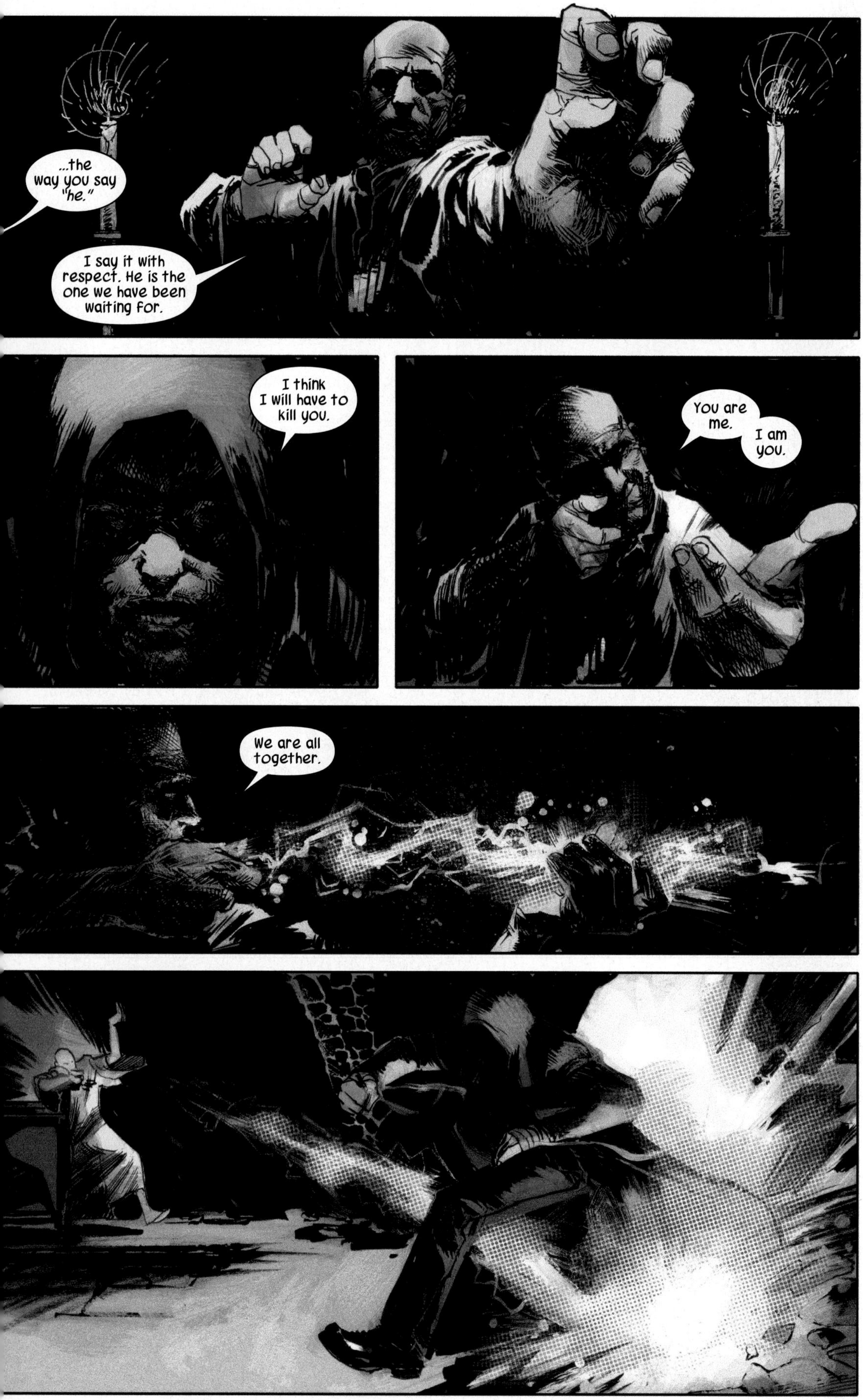

...the way you say "he."
I say it with respect. He is the one we have been waiting for.
I think I will have to kill you.
You are me.
I am you.
We are all together.

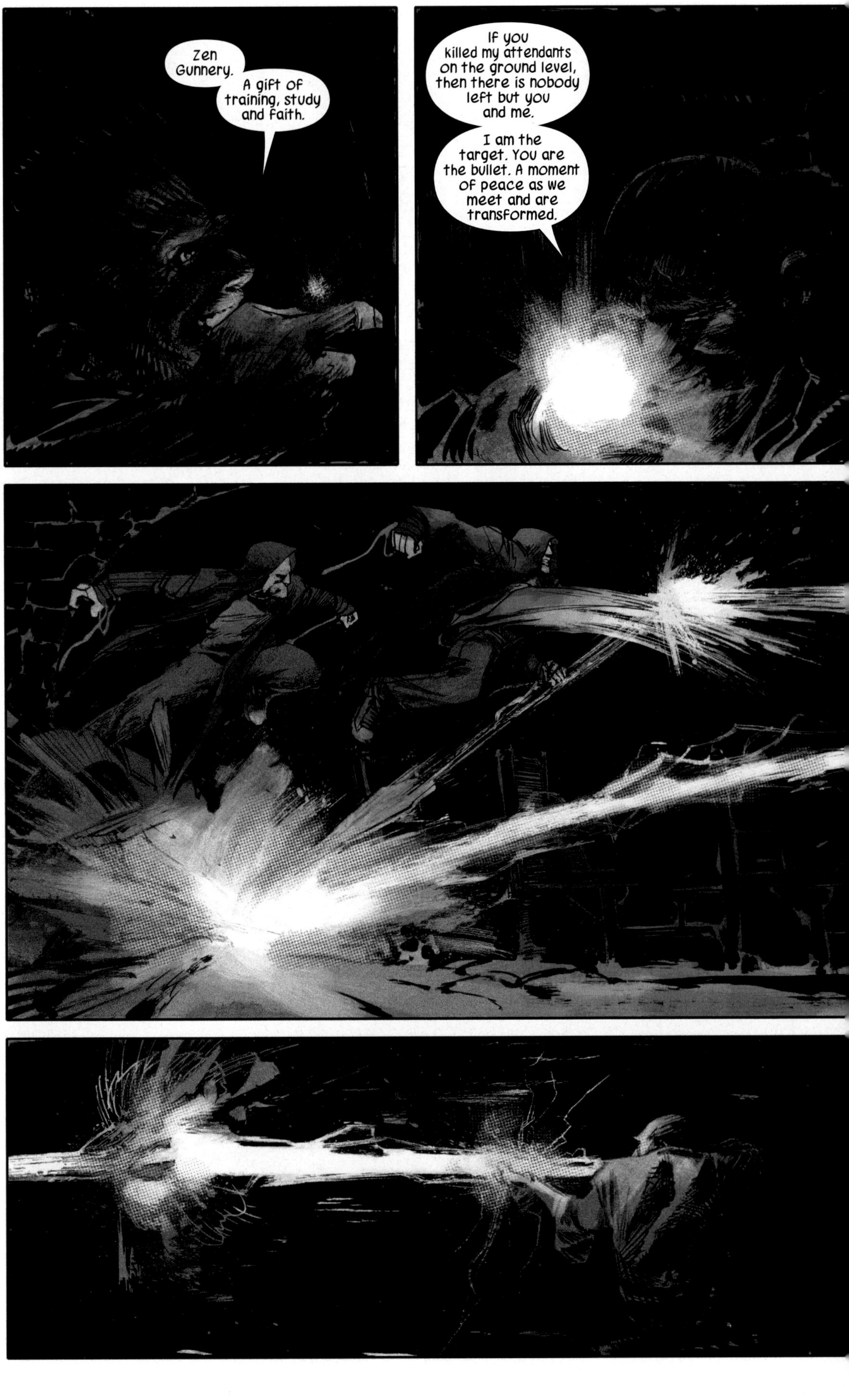
Zen Gunnery.
A gift of training, study and faith.
If you killed my attendants on the ground level, then there is nobody left but you and me.
I am the target. You are the bullet. A moment of peace as we meet and are transformed.

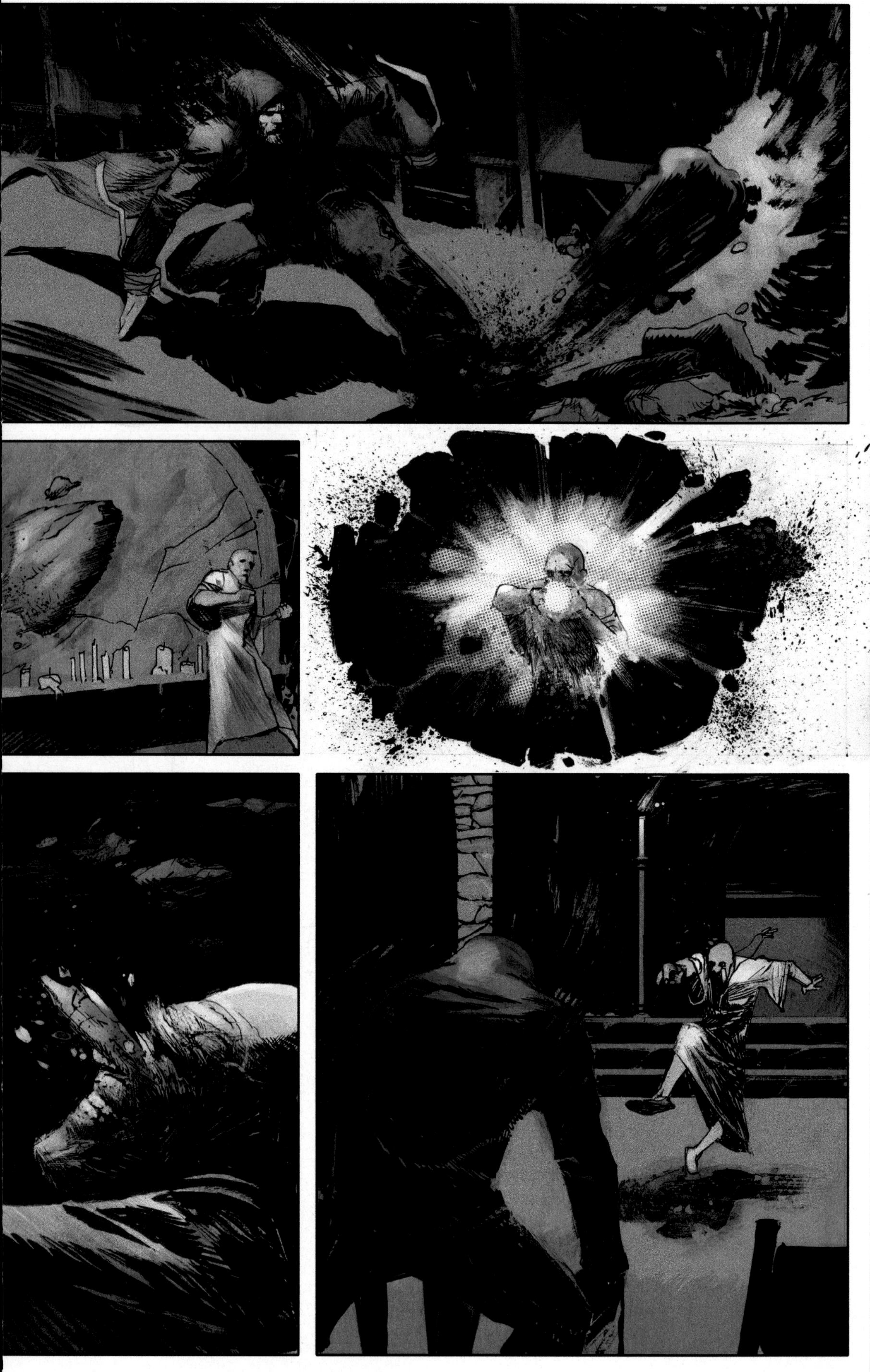

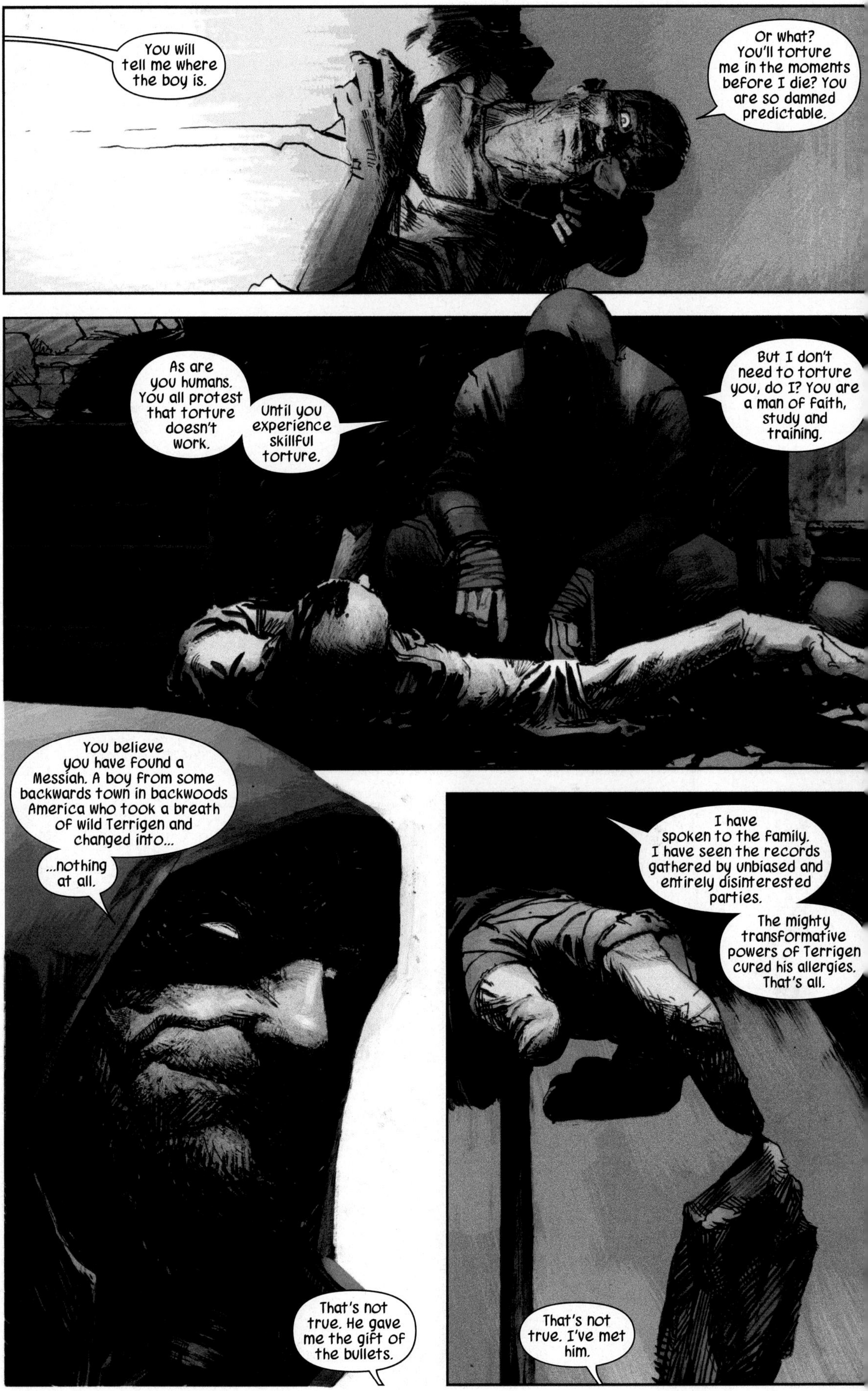
You will tell me where the boy is.
Or what? You'll torture me in the moments before I die? You are so damned predictable.
As are you humans. You all protest that torture doesn't work.
Until you experience skillful torture.
But I don't need to torture you, do I? You are a man of faith, study and training.
You believe you have found a Messiah. A boy from some backwards town in backwoods America who took a breath of wild Terrigen and changed into...
...nothing at all.
I have spoken to the family. I have seen the records gathered by unbiased and entirely disinterested parties.
The mighty transformative powers of Terrigen cured his allergies. That's all.
That's not true. He gave me the gift of the bullets.
That's not true. I've met him.

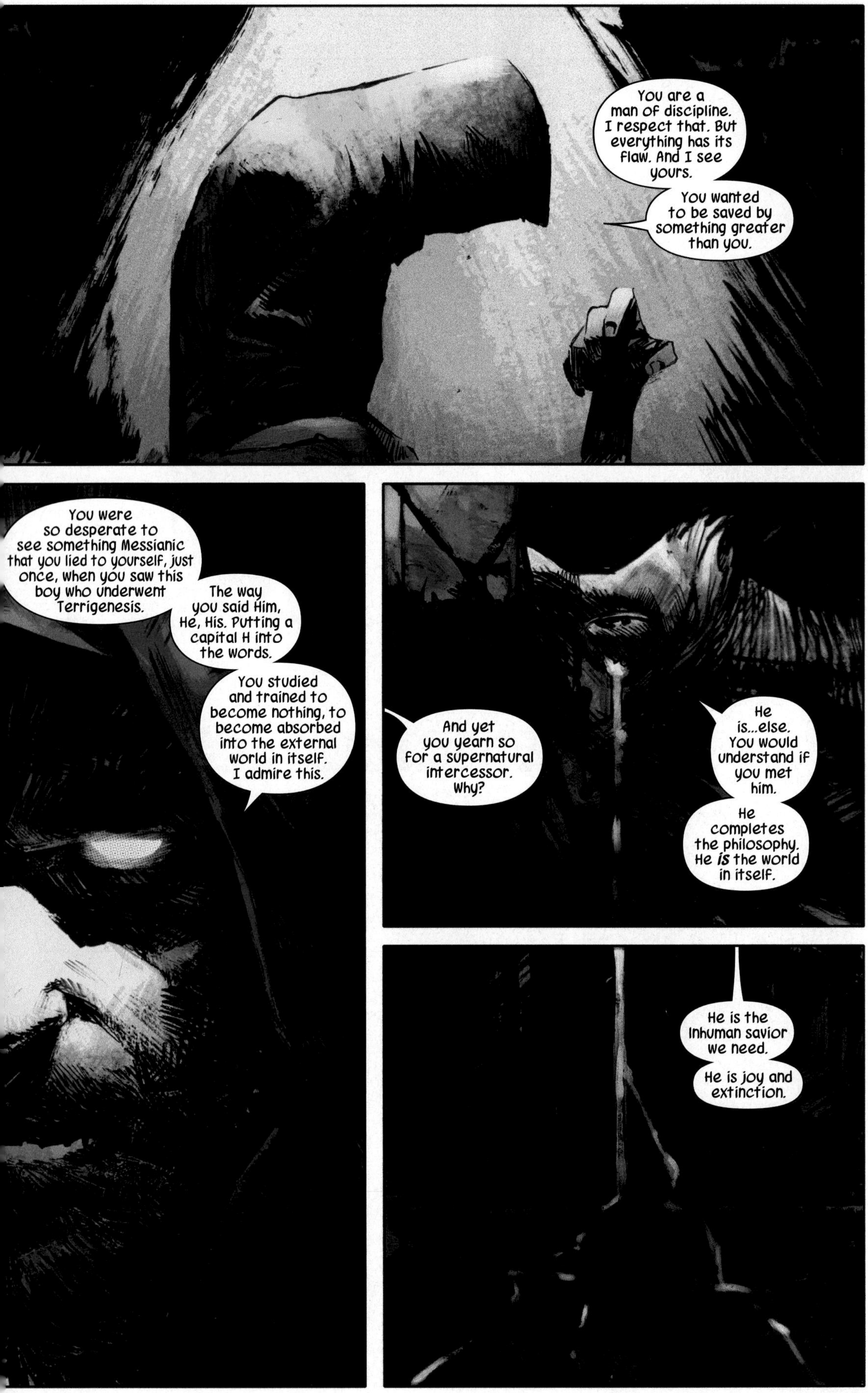
You are a man of discipline. I respect that. But everything has its flaw. And I see yours.
You wanted to be saved by something greater than you.
You were so desperate to see something Messianic that you lied to yourself, just once, when you saw this boy who underwent Terrigenesis.
The way you said Him, He, His. Putting a capital H into the words.
You studied and trained to become nothing, to become absorbed into the external world in itself. I admire this.
And yet you yearn so for a supernatural intercessor. Why?
He is...else. You would understand if you met him.
He completes the philosophy. He *is* the world in itself.
He is the Inhuman savior we need.
He is joy and extinction.

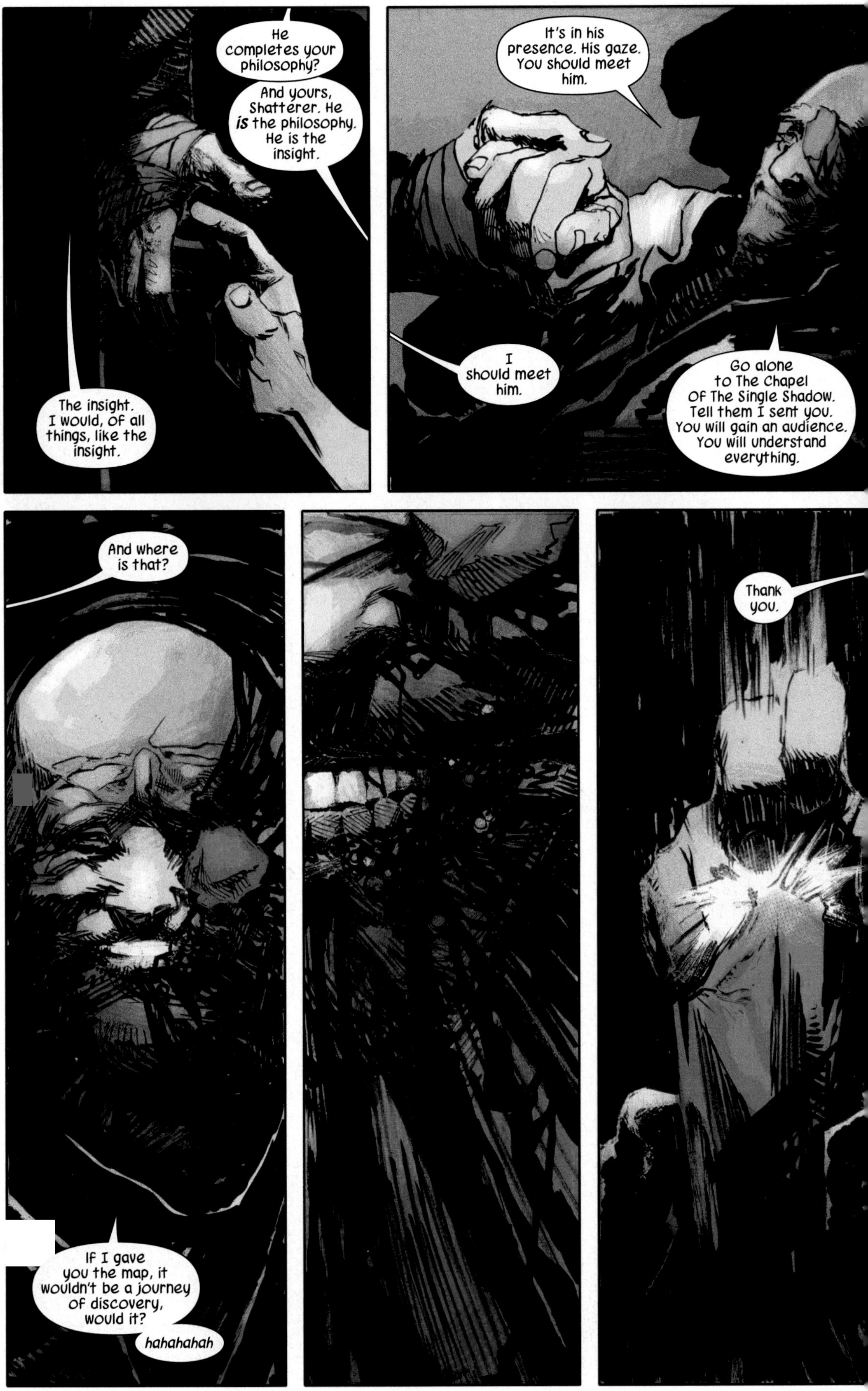
He completes your philosophy?
And yours, Shatterer. He *is* the philosophy. He is the insight.
The insight. I would, of all things, like the insight.
It's in his presence. His gaze. You should meet him.
I should meet him.
Go alone to The Chapel Of The Single Shadow. Tell them I sent you. You will gain an audience. You will understand everything.
And where is that?
If I gave you the map, it wouldn't be a journey of discovery, would it?
hahahahah
Thank you.

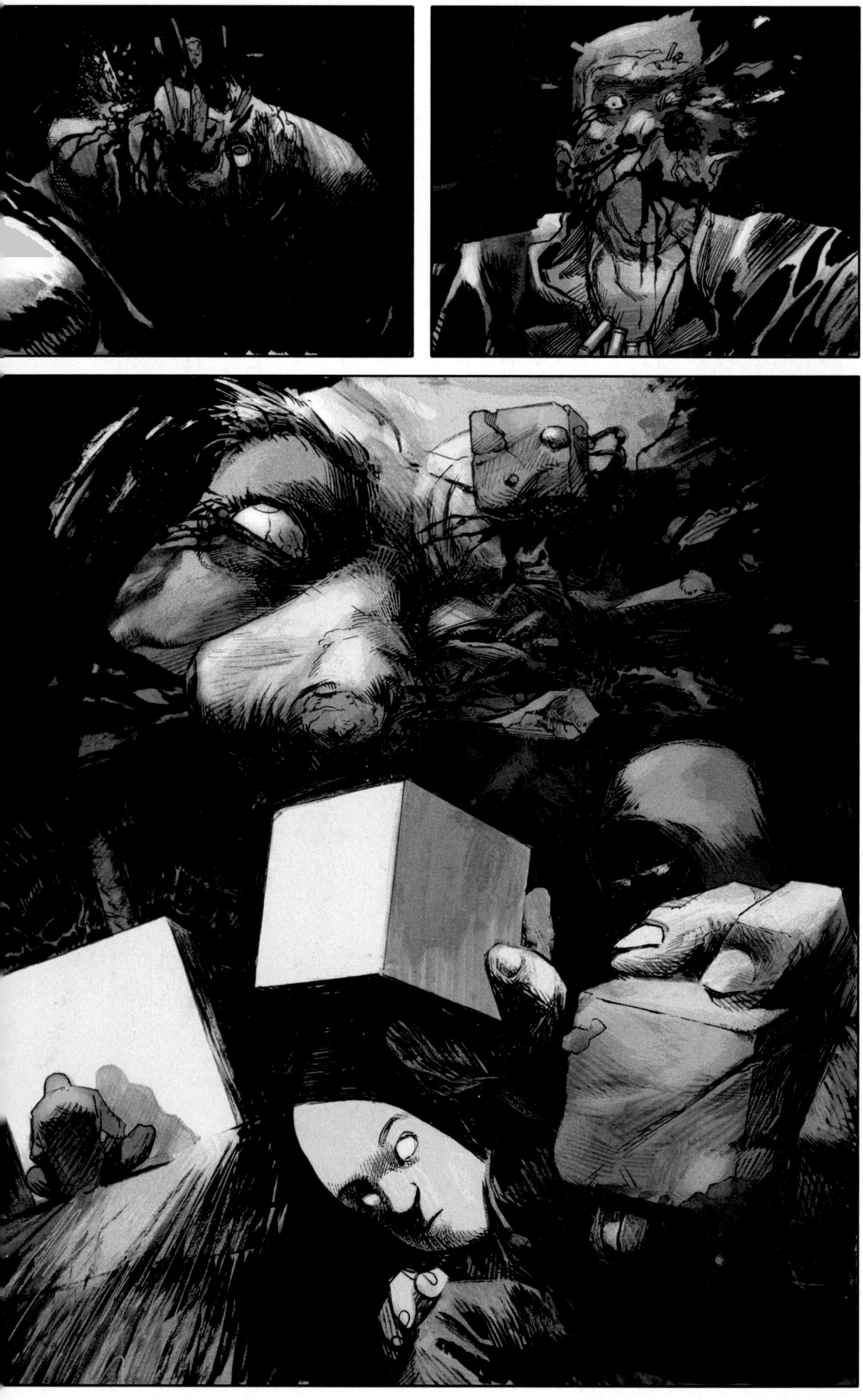

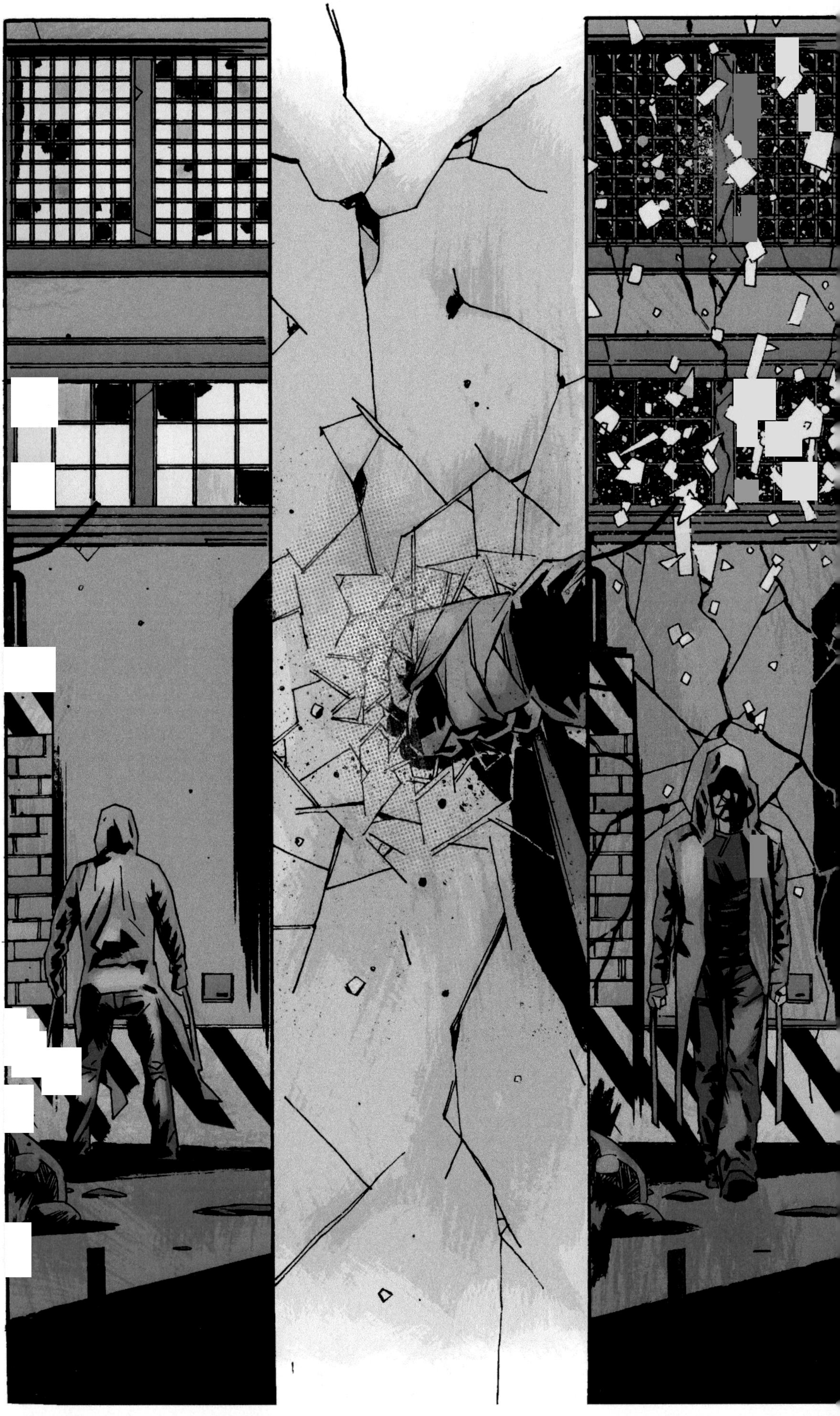

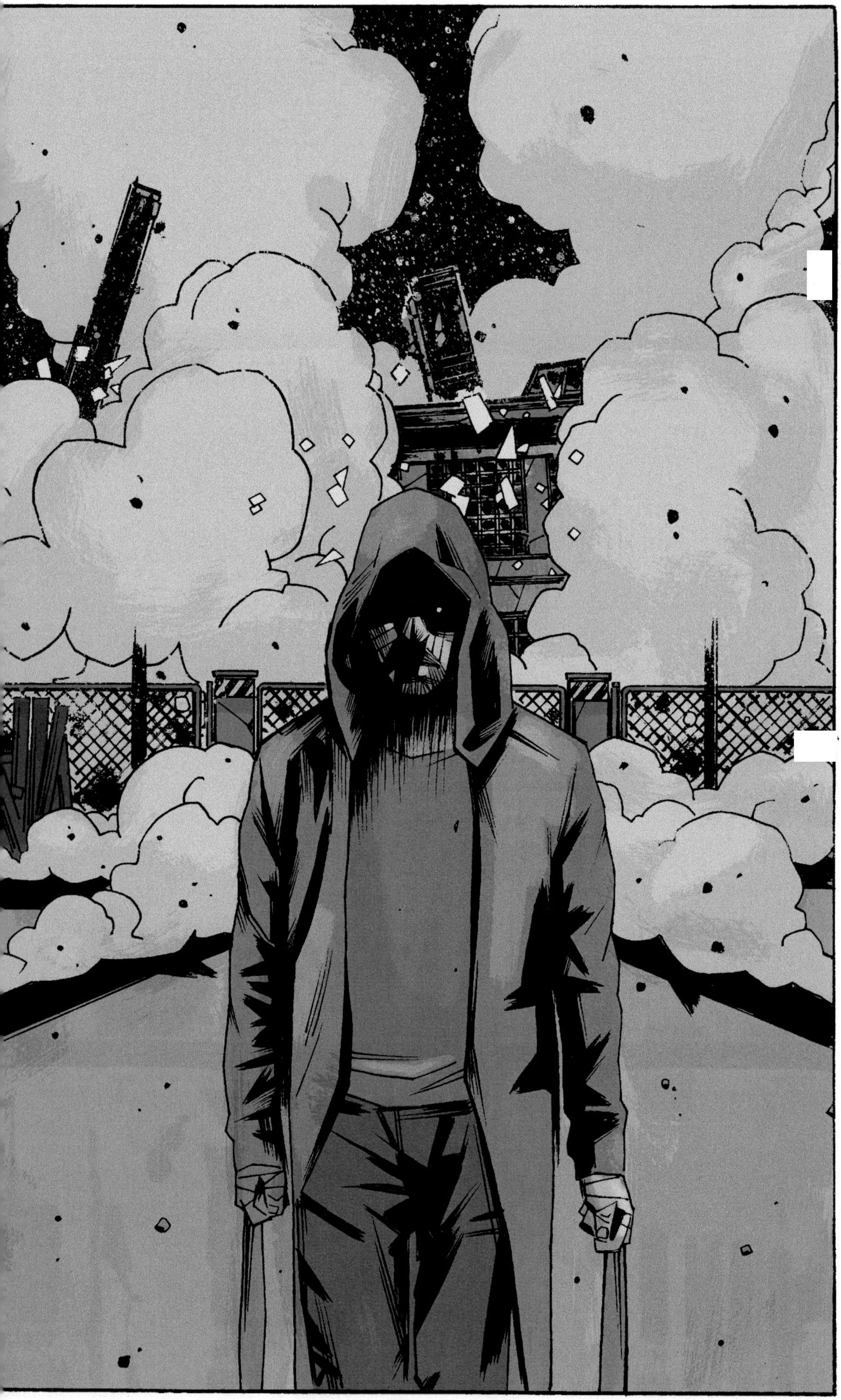

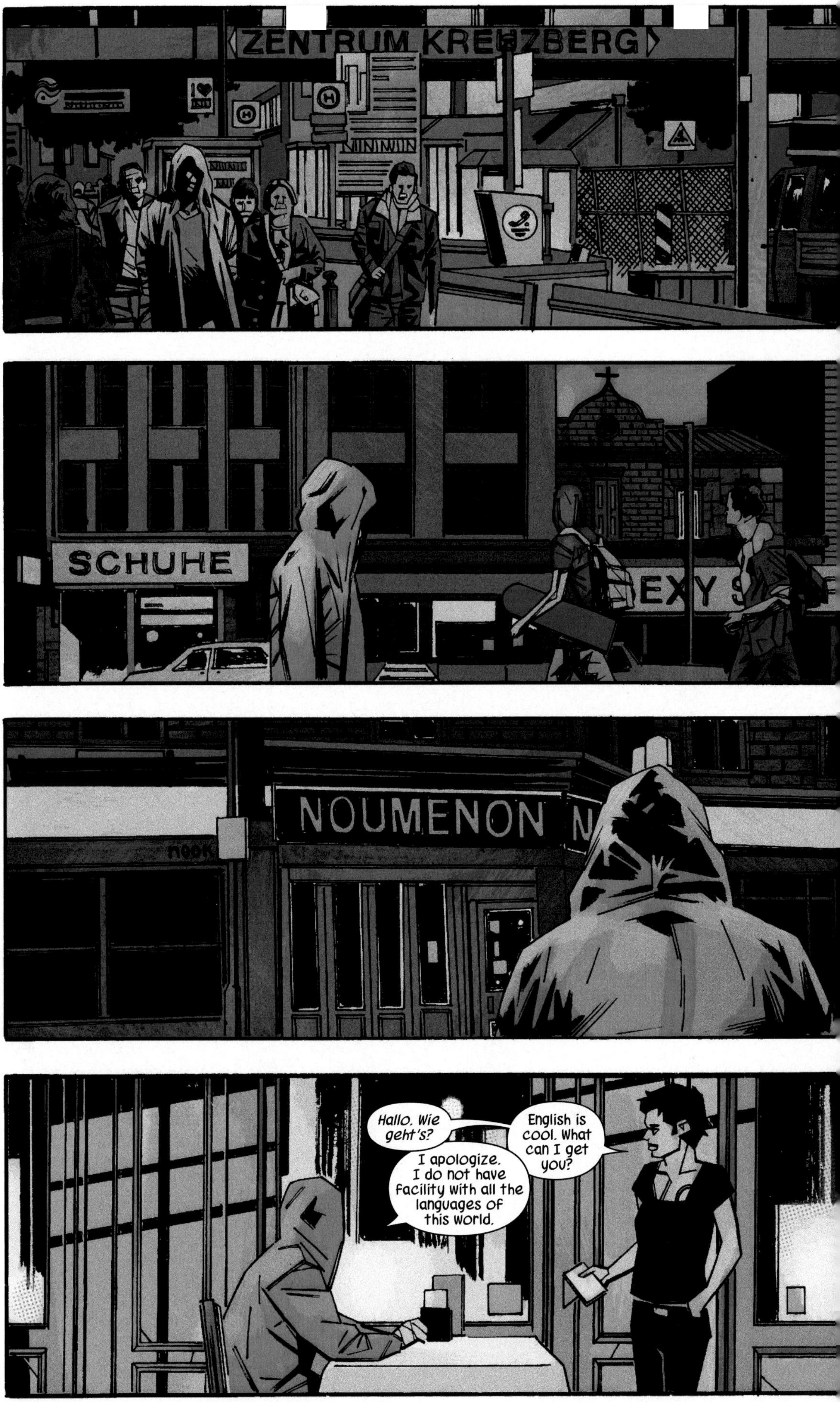
ZENTRUM KREUZBERG
SCHUHE
NOUMENON
Hallo. Wie geht's?
English is cool. What can I get you?
I apologize. I do not have facility with all the languages of this world.

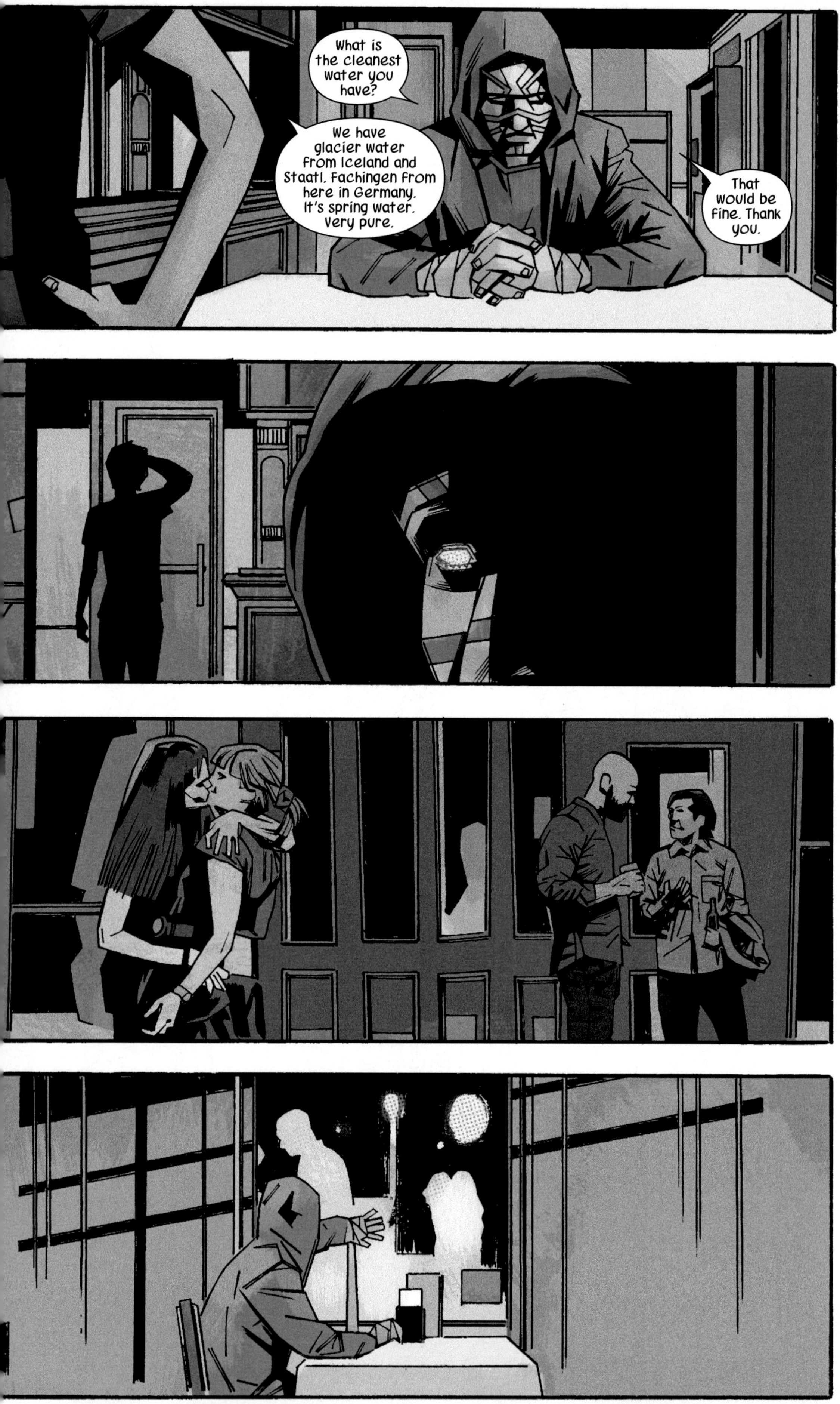
What is the cleanest water you have?
We have glacier water from Iceland and Staatl. Fachingen from here in Germany. It's spring water. Very pure.
That would be fine. Thank you.

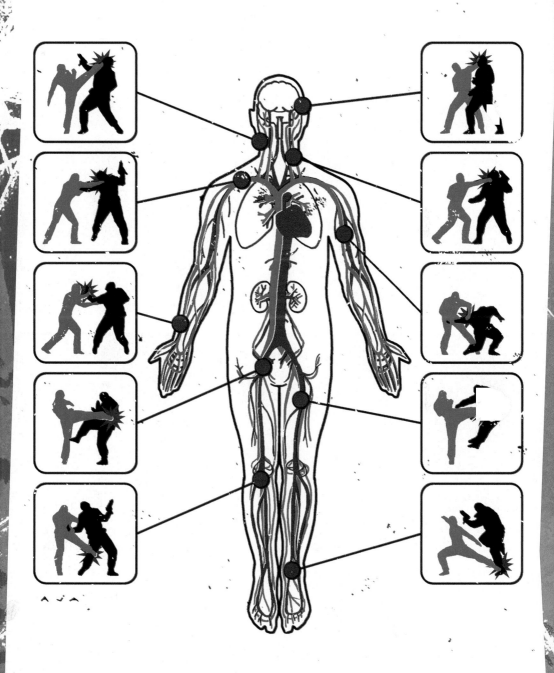

THREE

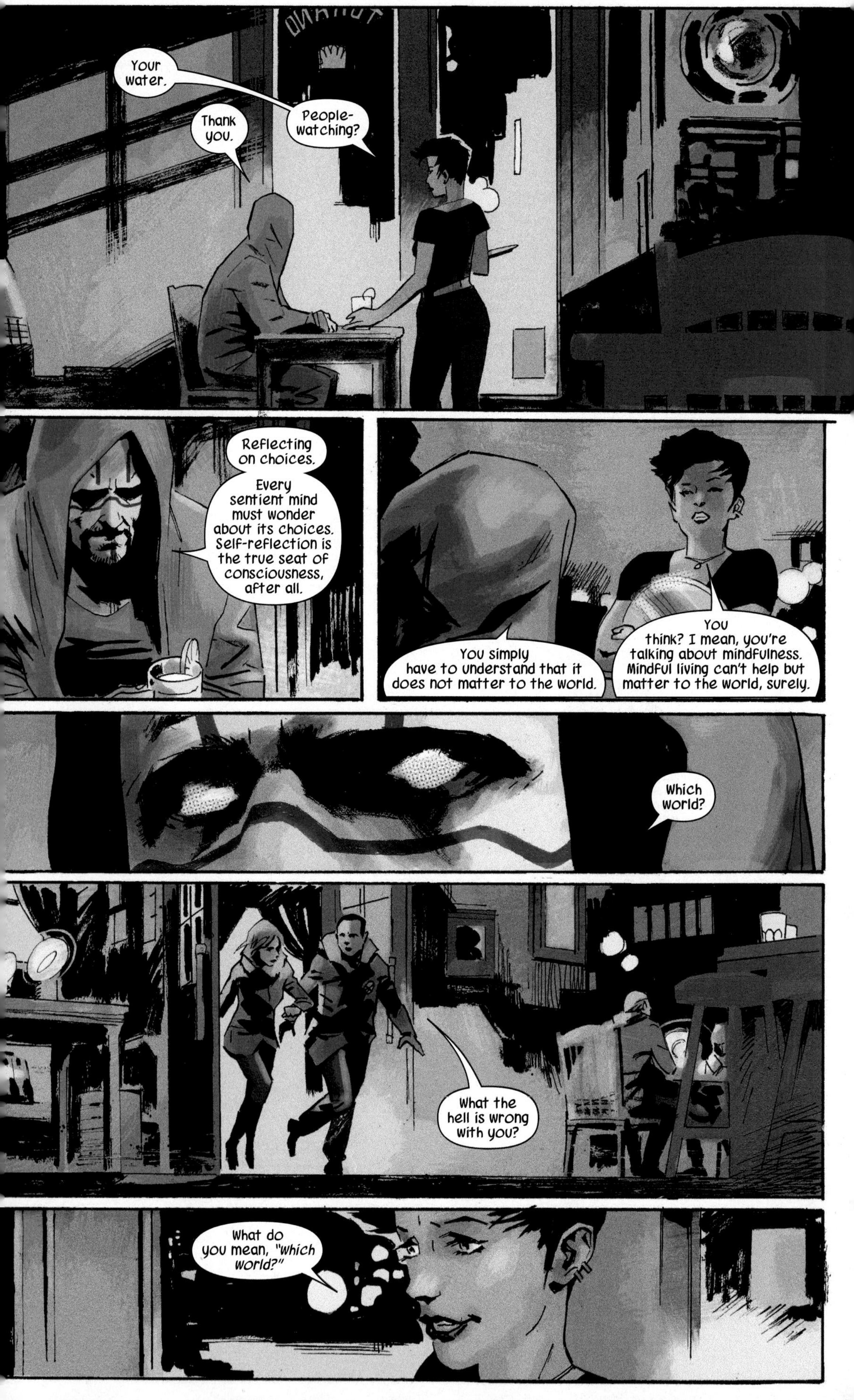
Your water.
Thank you.
People-watching?
Reflecting on choices.
Every sentient mind must wonder about its choices. Self-reflection is the true seat of consciousness, after all.
You think? I mean, you're talking about mindfulness. Mindful living can't help but matter to the world, surely.
You simply have to understand that it does not matter to the world.
Which world?
What the hell is wrong with you?
What do you mean, "which world?"

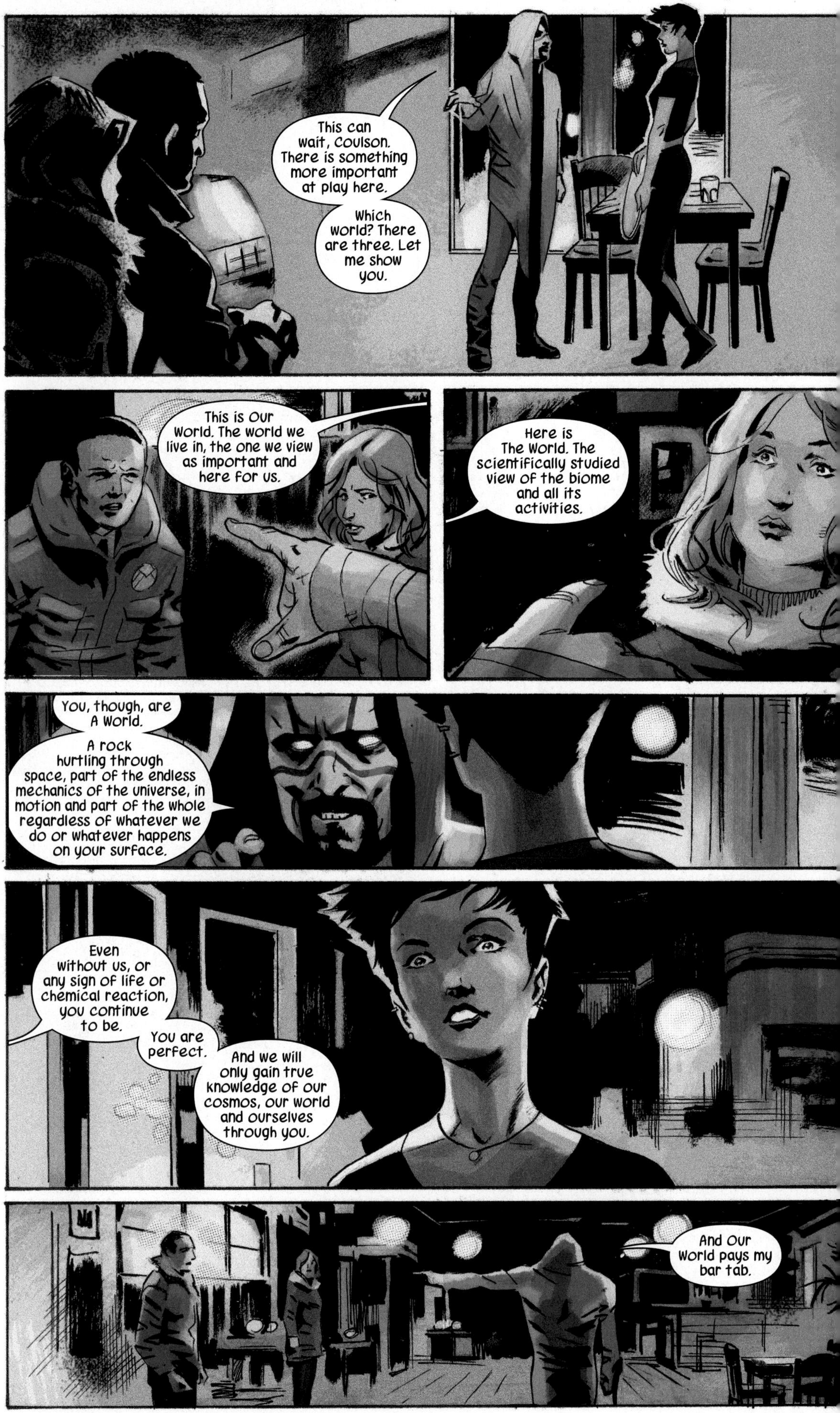
This can wait, Coulson. There is something more important at play here.
Which world? There are three. Let me show you.
This is Our World. The world we live in, the one we view as important and here for us.
Here is The World. The scientifically studied view of the biome and all its activities.
You, though, are A World.
A rock hurtling through space, part of the endless mechanics of the universe, in motion and part of the whole regardless of whatever we do or whatever happens on your surface.
Even without us, or any sign of life or chemical reaction, you continue to be.
You are perfect.
And we will only gain true knowledge of our cosmos, our world and ourselves through you.
And Our World pays my bar tab.

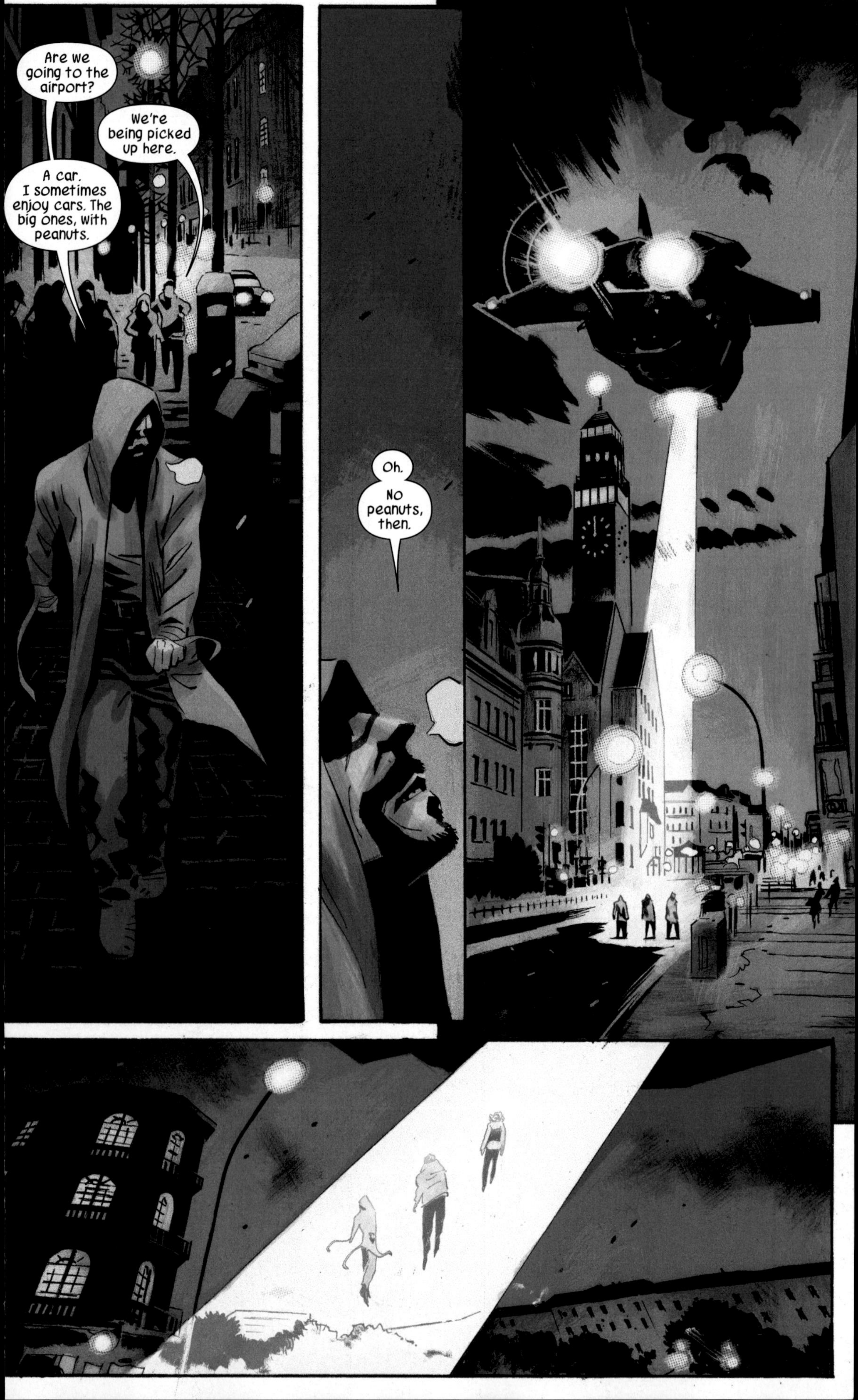
Are we going to the airport?
We're being picked up here.
A car. I sometimes enjoy cars. The big ones, with peanuts.
Oh.
No peanuts, then.

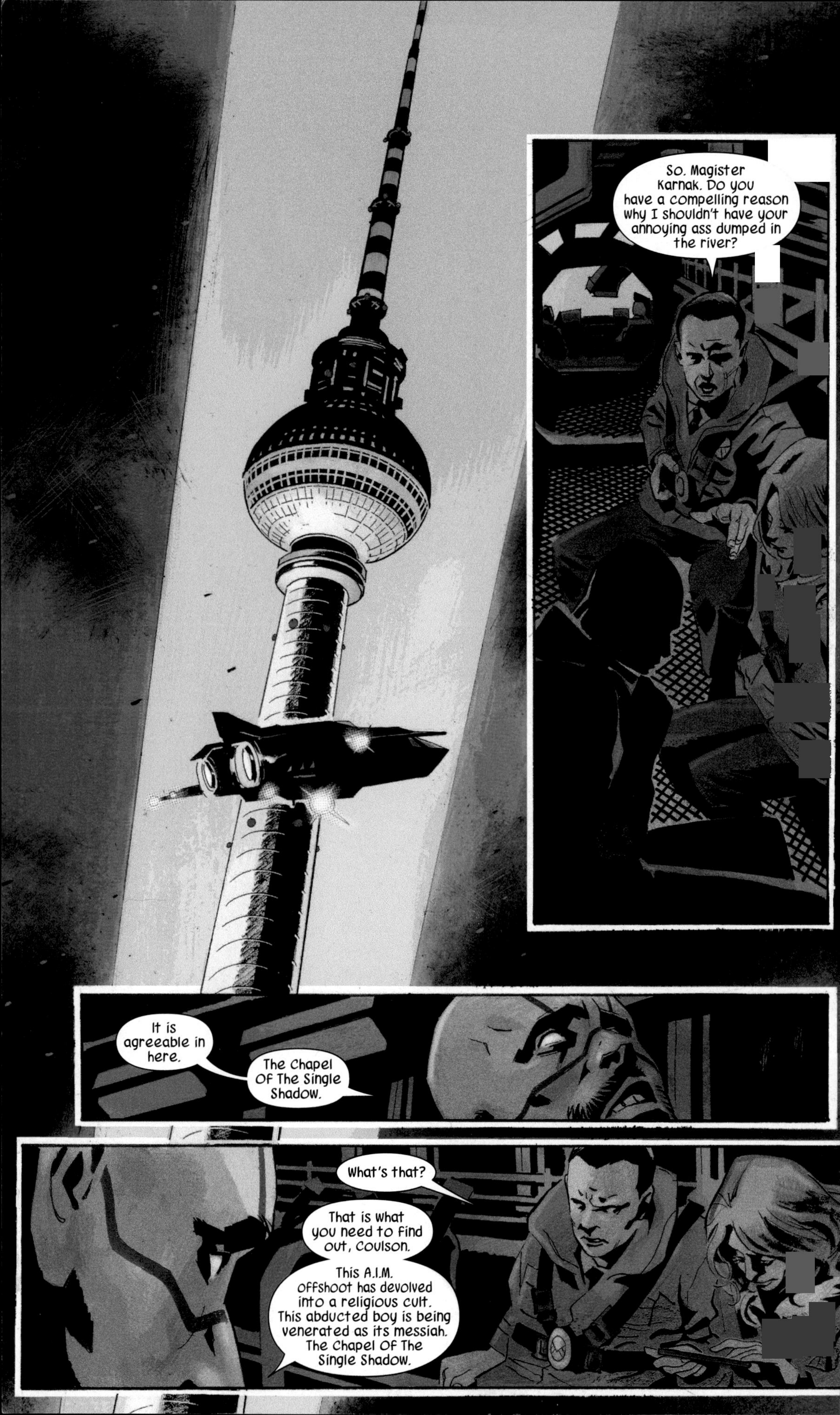
So. Magister Karnak. Do you have a compelling reason why I shouldn't have your annoying ass dumped in the river?
It is agreeable in here.
The Chapel Of The Single Shadow.
What's that?
That is what you need to find out, Coulson.
This A.I.M. Offshoot has devolved into a religious cult. This abducted boy is being venerated as its messiah. The Chapel Of The Single Shadow.

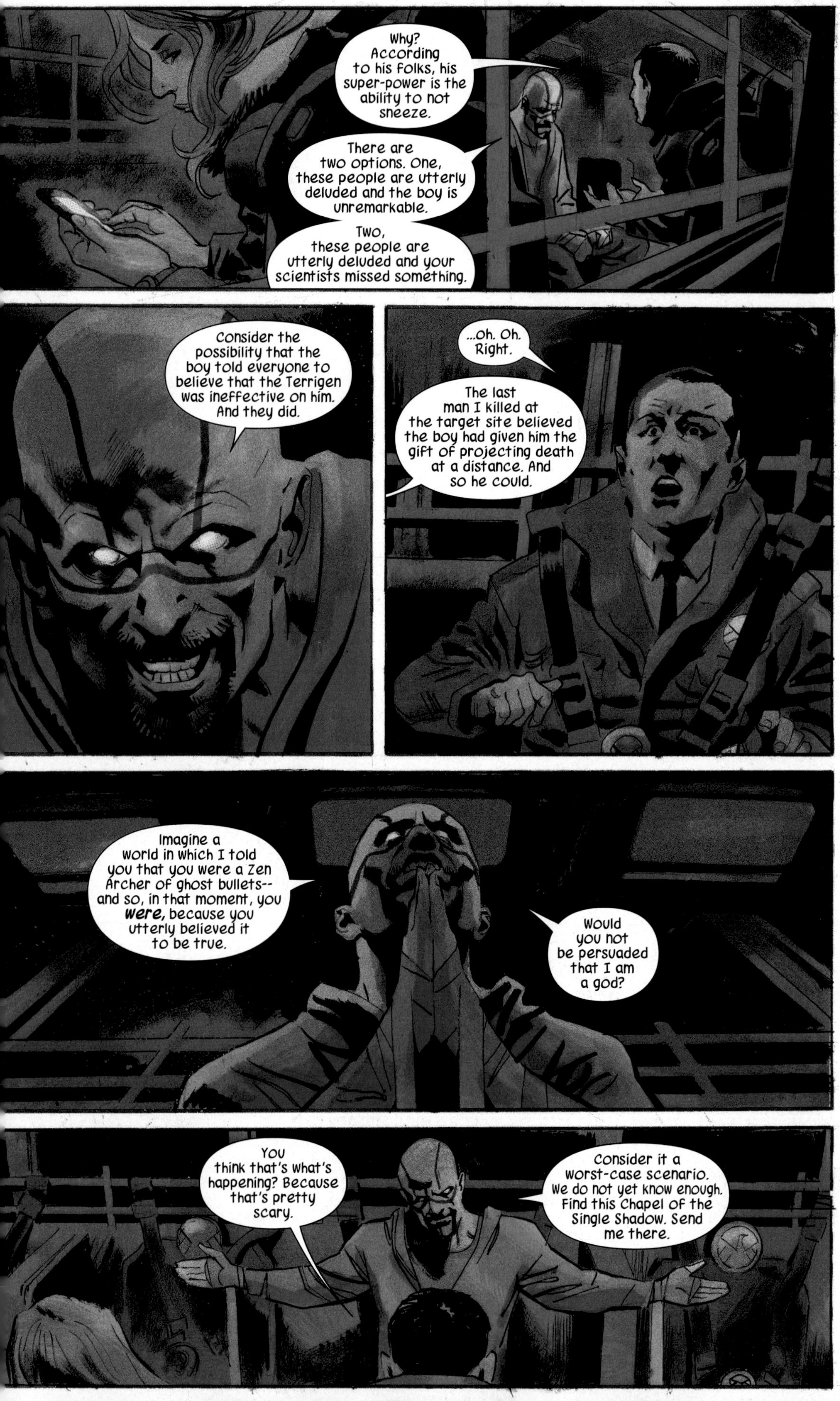
Why? According to his folks, his super-power is the ability to not sneeze.
There are two options. One, these people are utterly deluded and the boy is unremarkable.
Two, these people are utterly deluded and your scientists missed something.
Consider the possibility that the boy told everyone to believe that the Terrigen was ineffective on him. And they did.
...Oh. Oh. Right.
The last man I killed at the target site believed the boy had given him the gift of projecting death at a distance. And so he could.
Imagine a world in which I told you that you were a Zen Archer of ghost bullets--and so, in that moment, you *were,* because you utterly believed it to be true.
Would you not be persuaded that I am a god?
You think that's what's happening? Because that's pretty scary.
Consider it a worst-case scenario. We do not yet know enough. Find this Chapel of the Single Shadow. Send me there.

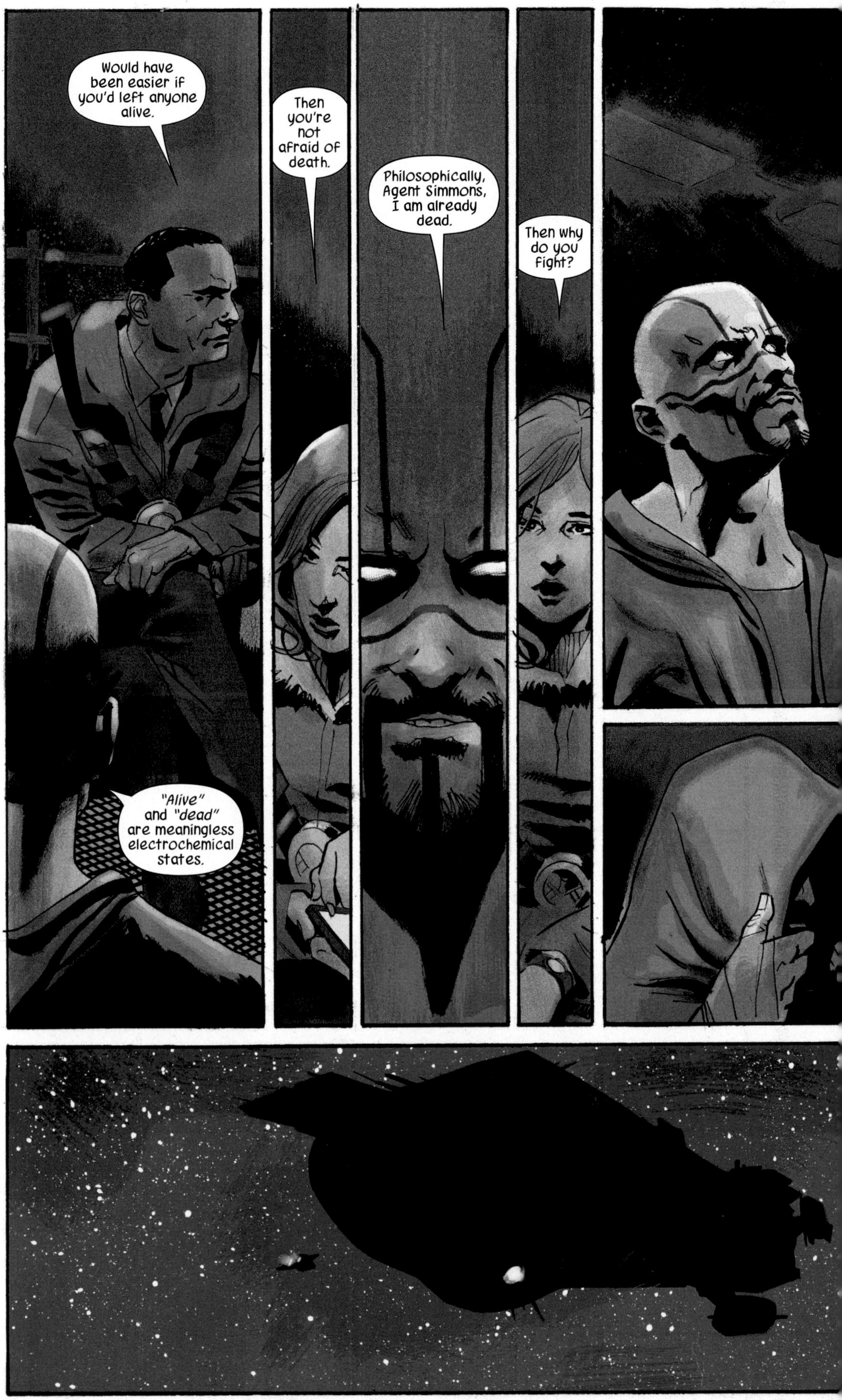
Would have been easier if you'd left anyone alive.
"Alive" and "dead" are meaningless electrochemical states.
Then you're not afraid of death.
Philosophically, Agent Simmons, I am already dead.
Then why do you fight?

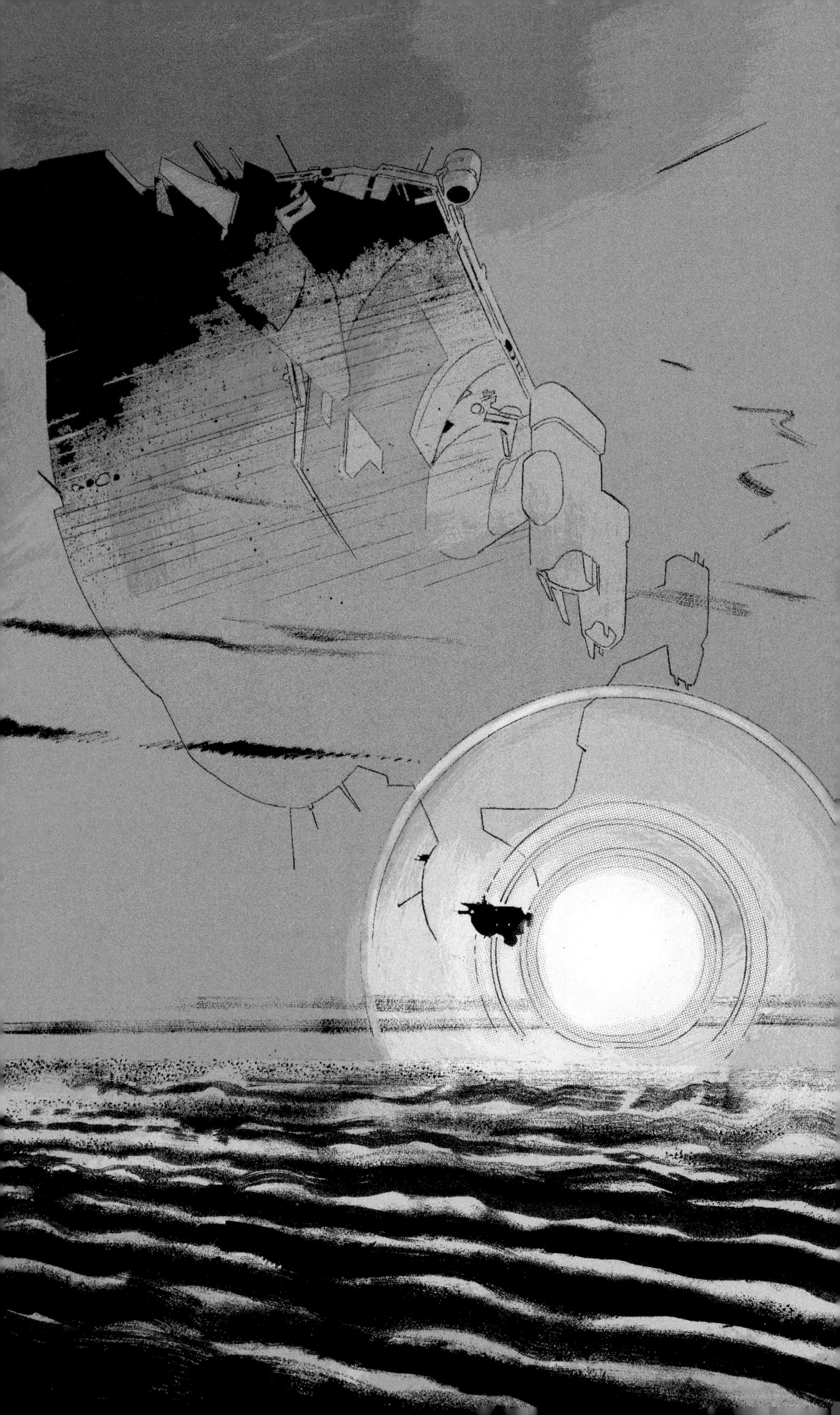

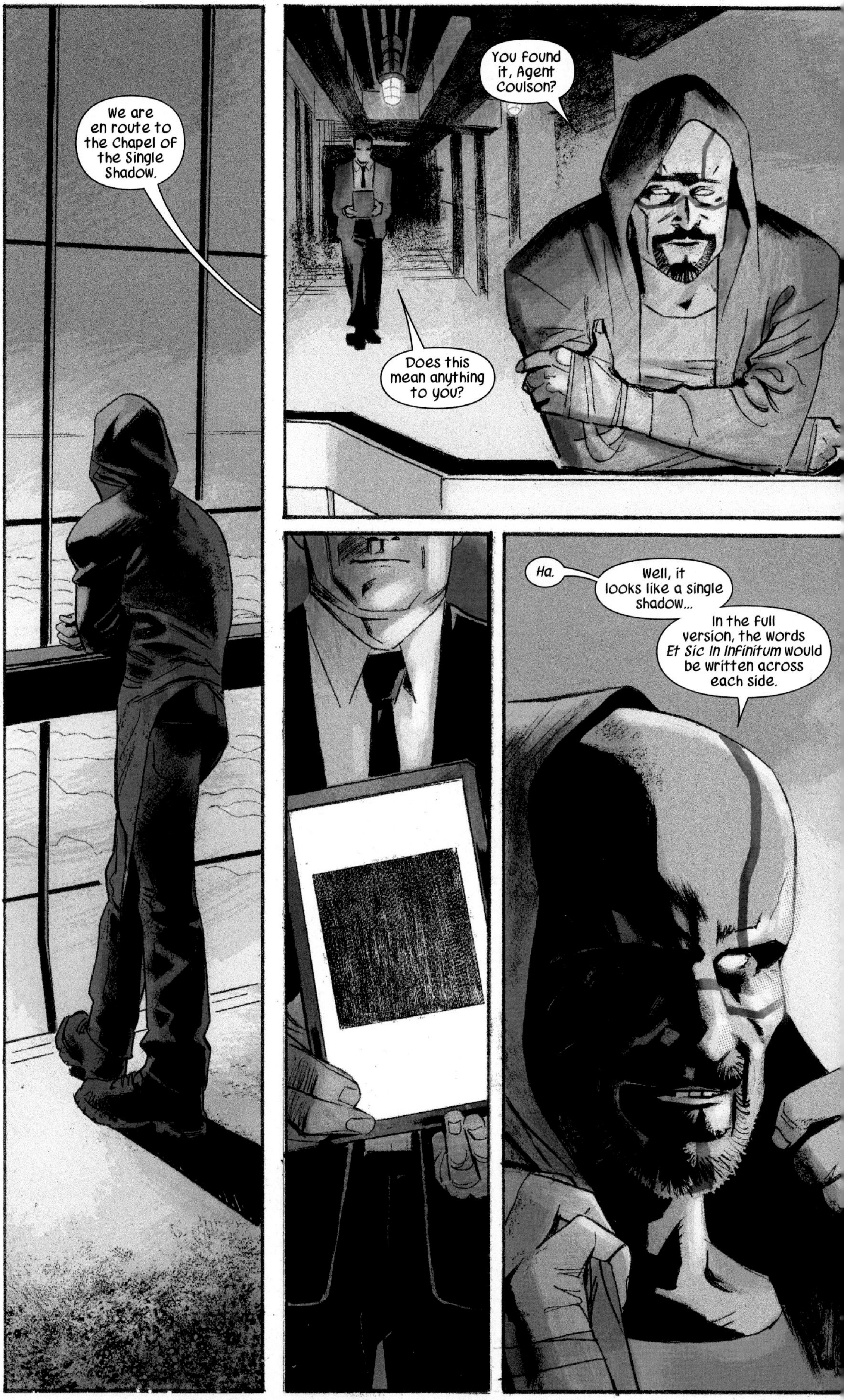
We are en route to the Chapel of the Single Shadow.
You found it, Agent Coulson?
Does this mean anything to you?
Ha.
Well, it looks like a single shadow...
In the full version, the words *Et Sic In Infinitum* would be written across each side.

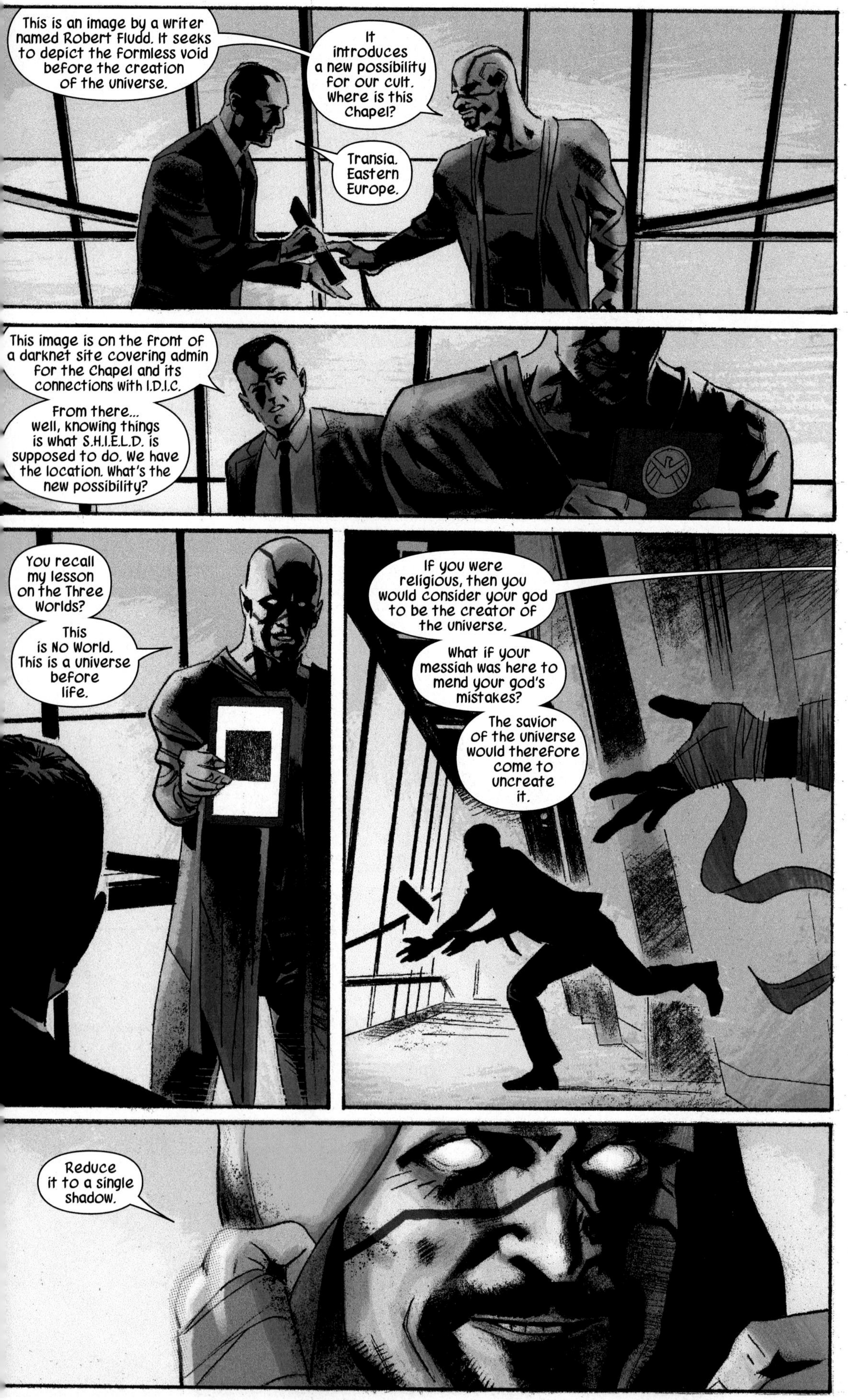
This is an image by a writer named Robert Fludd. It seeks to depict the formless void before the creation of the universe.
It introduces a new possibility for our cult. Where is this Chapel?
Transia. Eastern Europe.
This image is on the front of a darknet site covering admin for the Chapel and its connections with I.D.I.C.
From there... well, knowing things is what S.H.I.E.L.D. is supposed to do. We have the location. What's the new possibility?
You recall my lesson on the Three Worlds?
This is No World. This is a universe before life.
If you were religious, then you would consider your god to be the creator of the universe.
What if your messiah was here to mend your god's mistakes?
The savior of the universe would therefore come to uncreate it.
Reduce it to a single shadow.

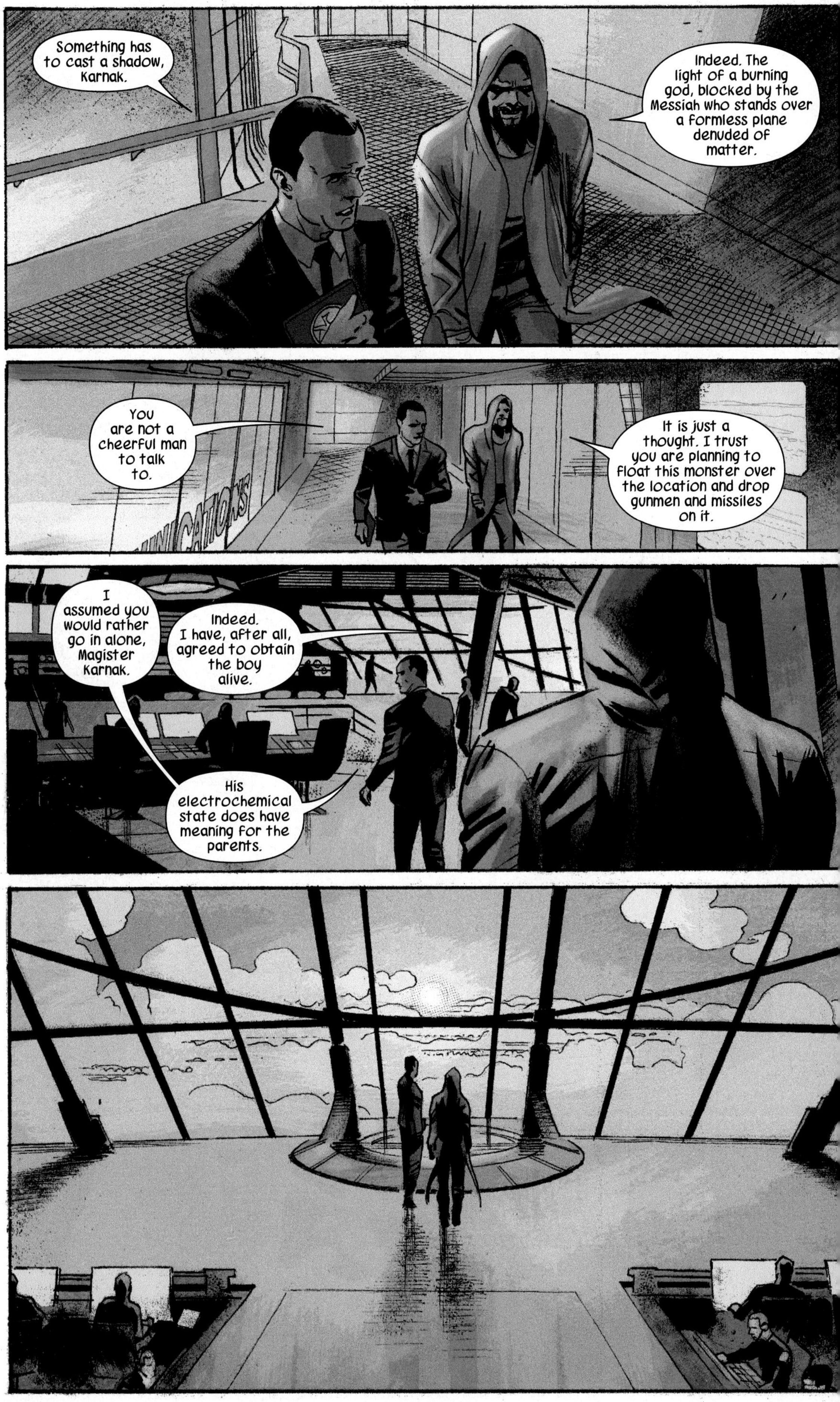
Something has to cast a shadow, Karnak.
Indeed. The light of a burning god, blocked by the Messiah who stands over a formless plane denuded of matter.
You are not a cheerful man to talk to.
It is just a thought. I trust you are planning to float this monster over the location and drop gunmen and missiles on it.
I assumed you would rather go in alone, Magister Karnak.
Indeed. I have, after all, agreed to obtain the boy alive.
His electrochemical state does have meaning for the parents.

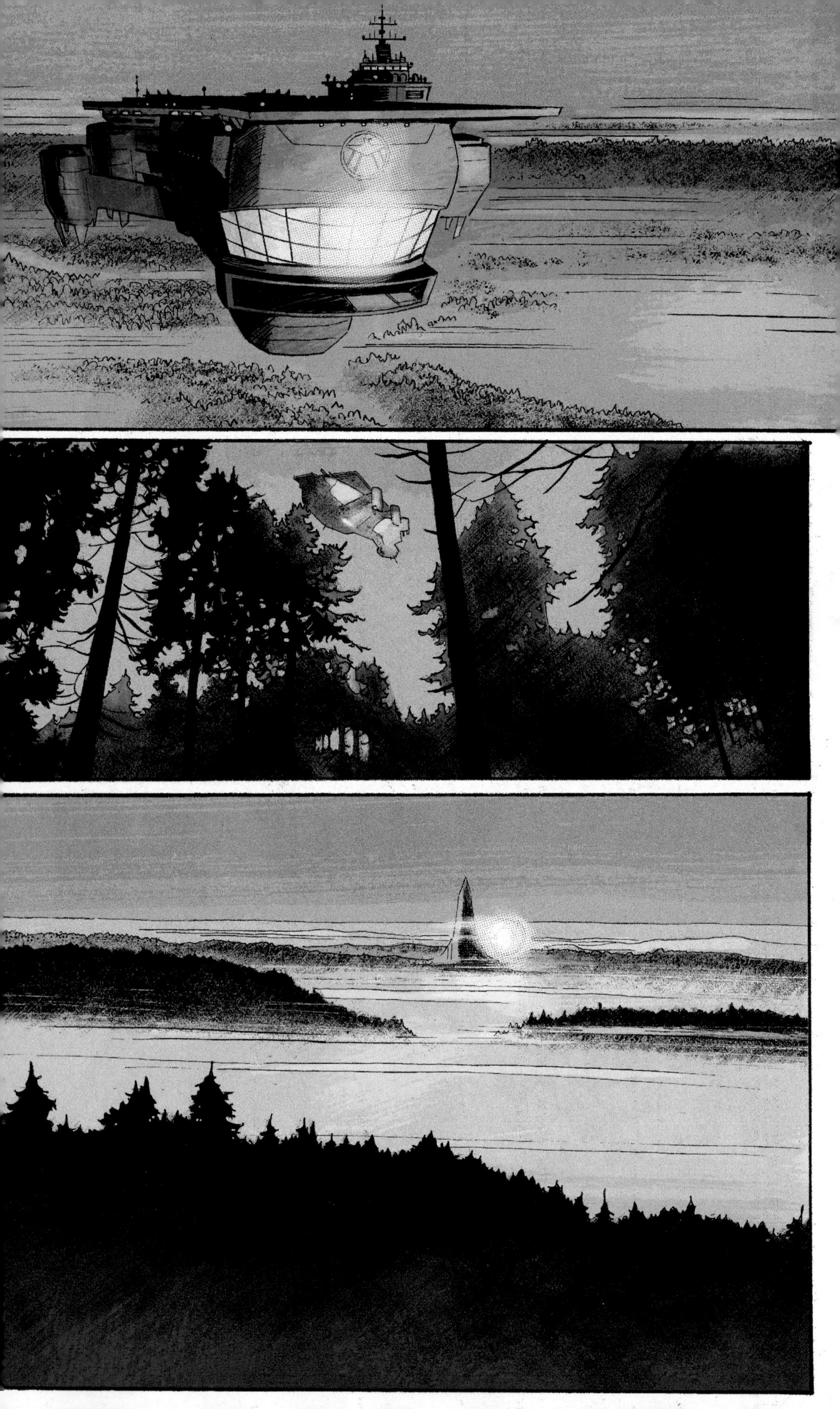

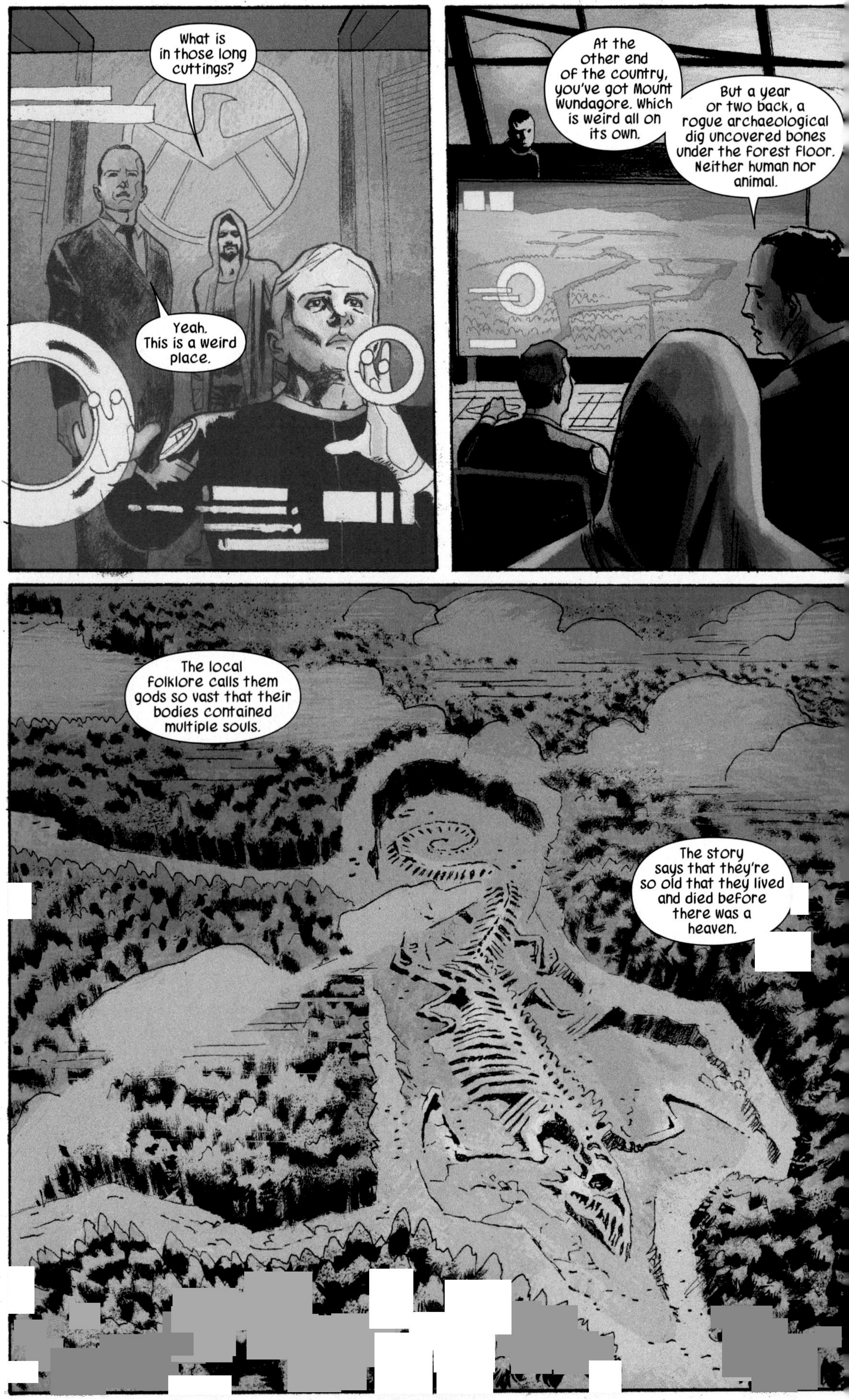
What is in those long cuttings?
Yeah. This is a weird place.
At the other end of the country, you've got Mount Wundagore. Which is weird all on its own.
But a year or two back, a rogue archaeological dig uncovered bones under the forest floor. Neither human nor animal.
The local folklore calls them gods so vast that their bodies contained multiple souls.
The story says that they're so old that they lived and died before there was a heaven.

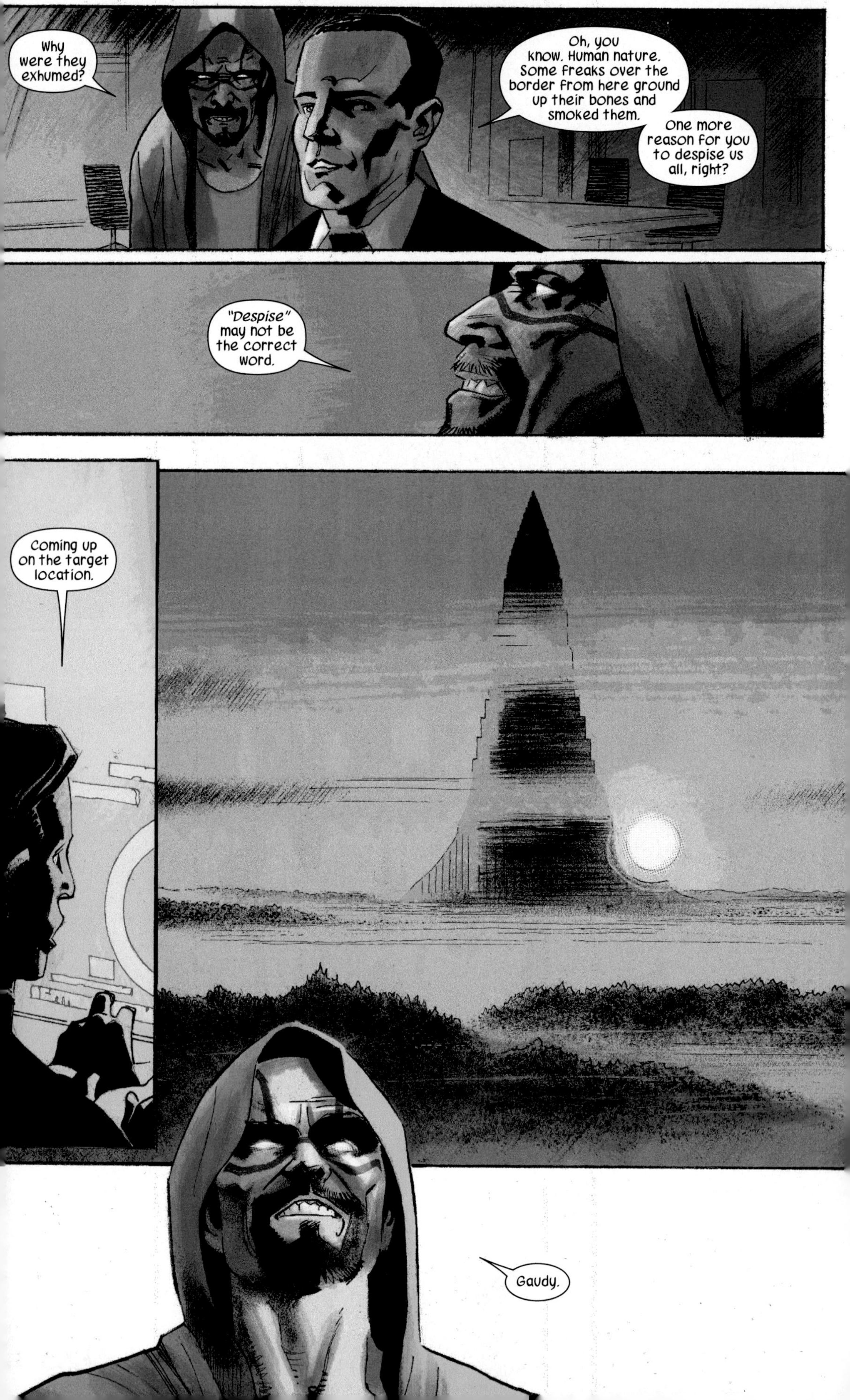
Why were they exhumed?
Oh, you know. Human nature. Some freaks over the border from here ground up their bones and smoked them.
One more reason for you to despise us all, right?
"Despise" may not be the correct word.
Coming up on the target location.
Gaudy.

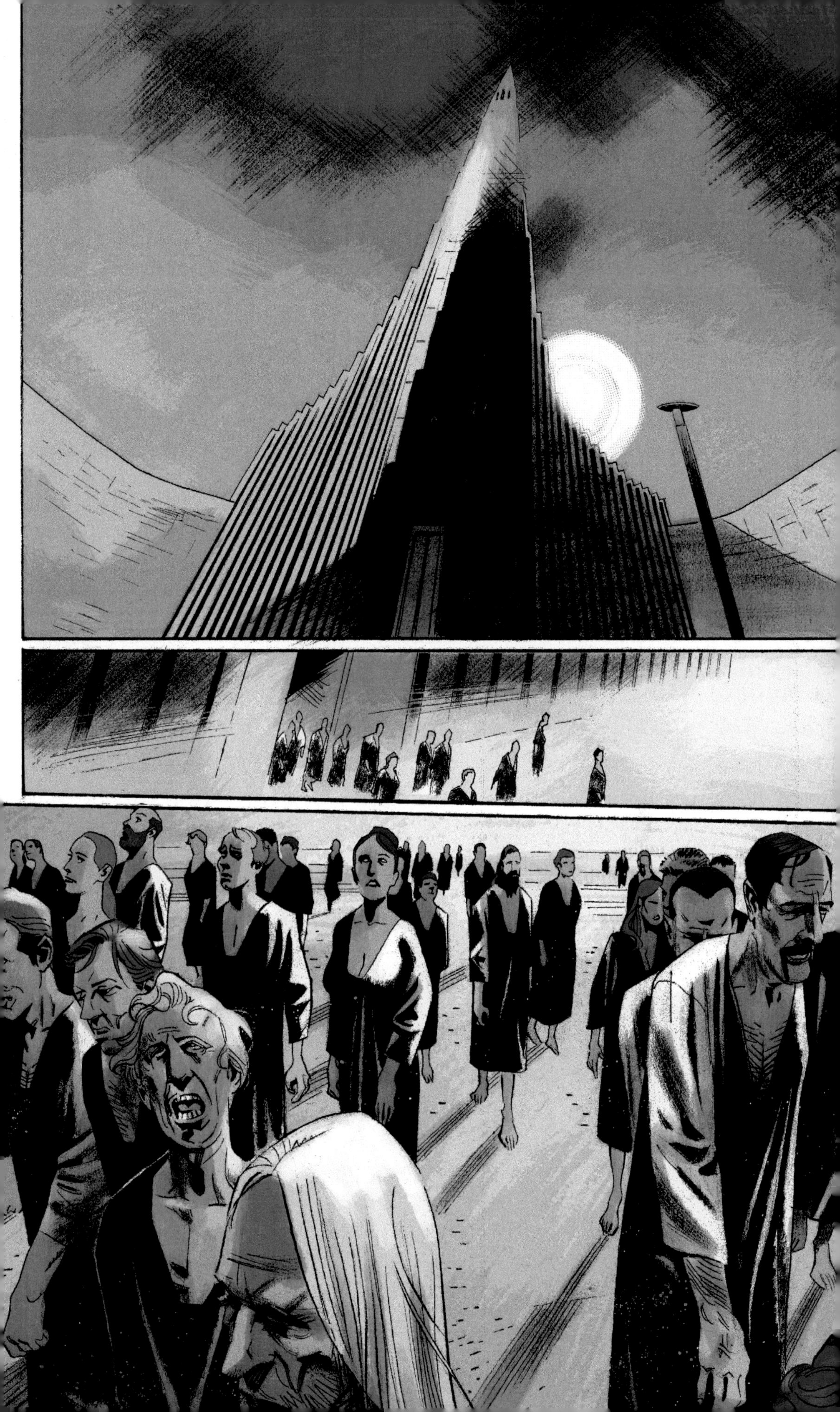

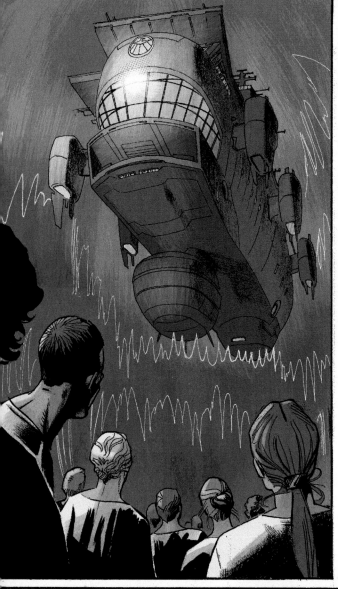

What an appalling noise.

I imagine it takes a lot of training for humans to sound like sick cats being put through one of those document-shredder things.

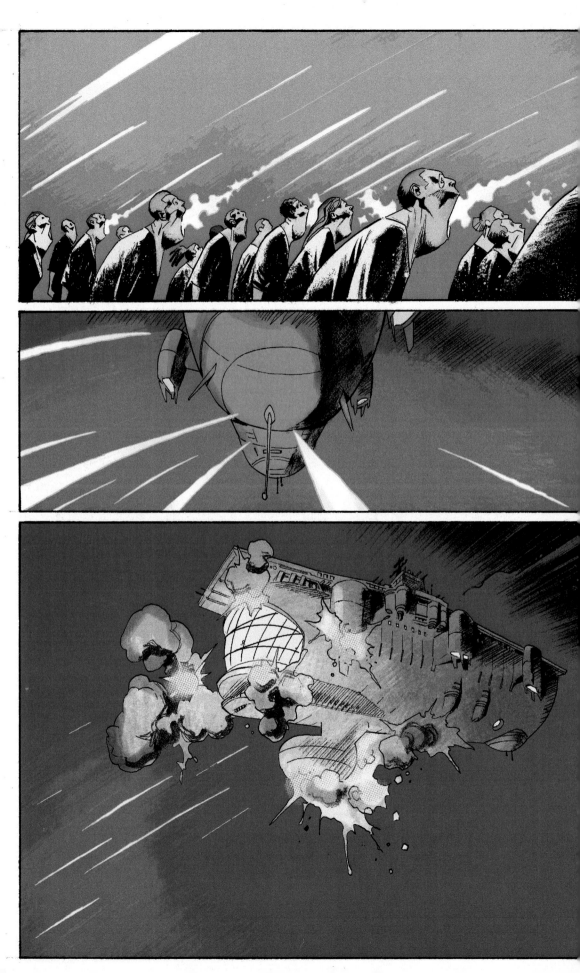

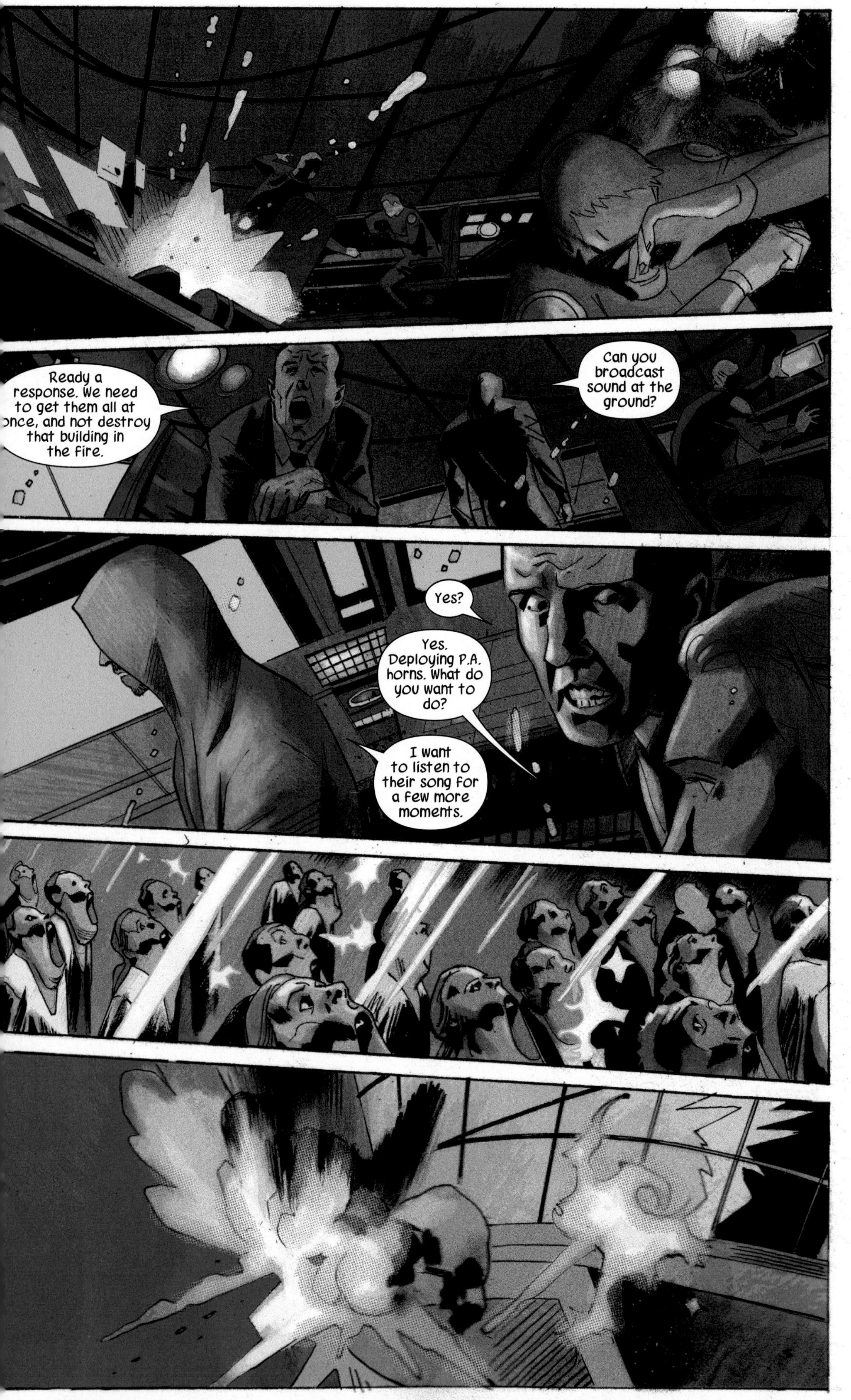
Ready a response. We need to get them all at once, and not destroy that building in the fire.
Can you broadcast sound at the ground?
Yes?
Yes. Deploying P.A. horns. What do you want to do?
I want to listen to their song for a few more moments.

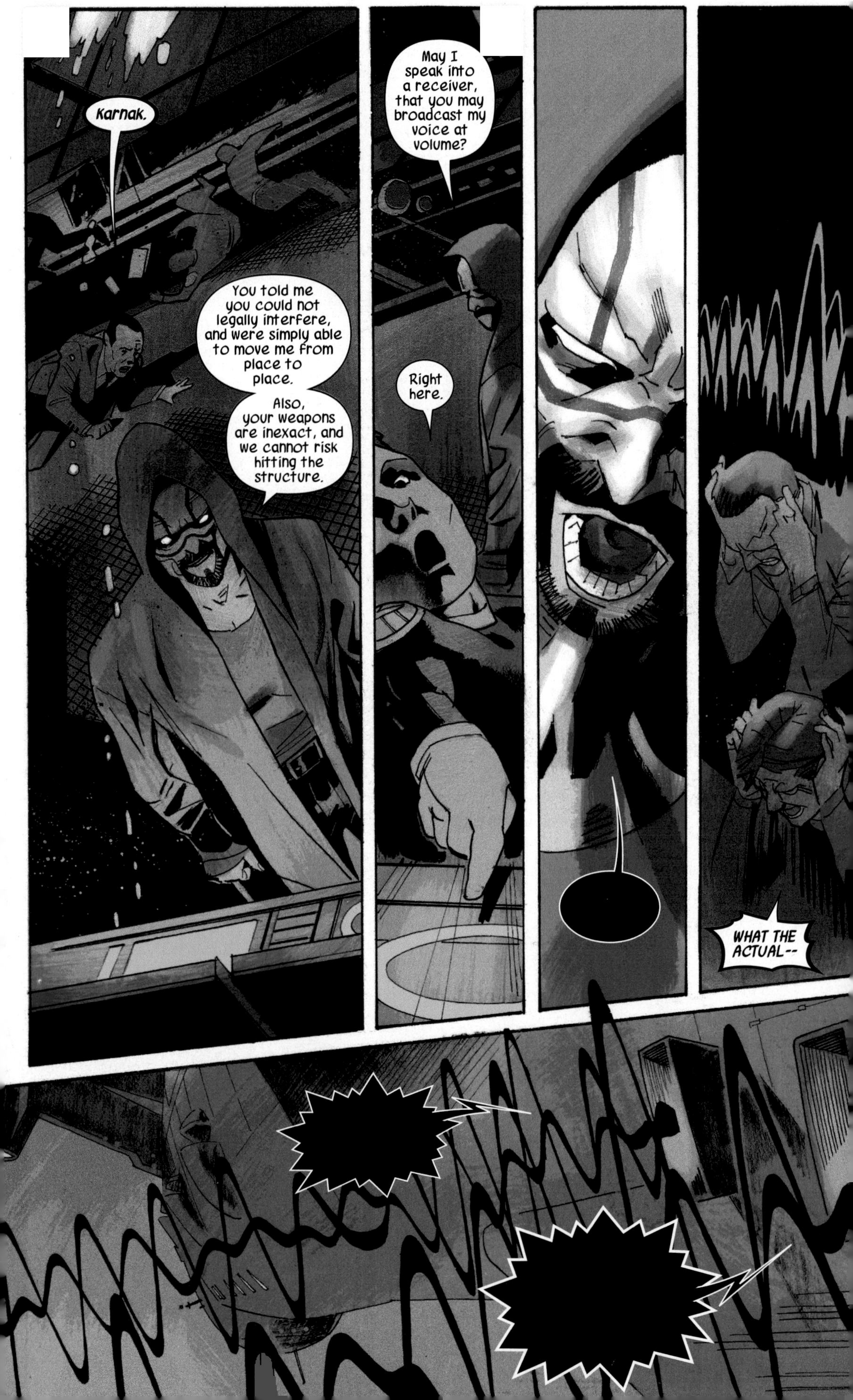
Karnak.
You told me you could not legally interfere, and were simply able to move me from place to place.
Also, your weapons are inexact, and we cannot risk hitting the structure.
May I speak into a receiver, that you may broadcast my voice at volume?
Right here.
WHAT THE ACTUAL--

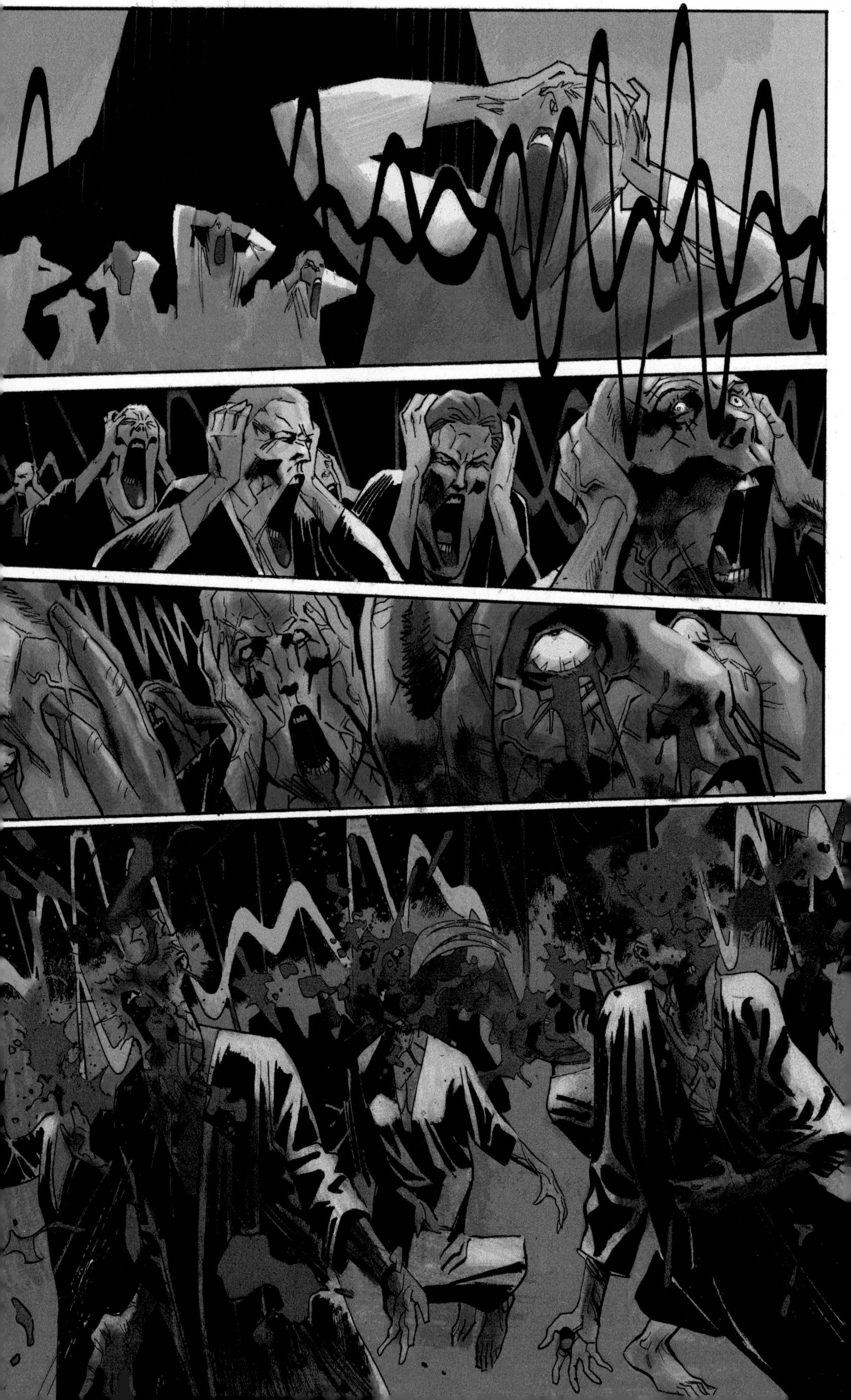

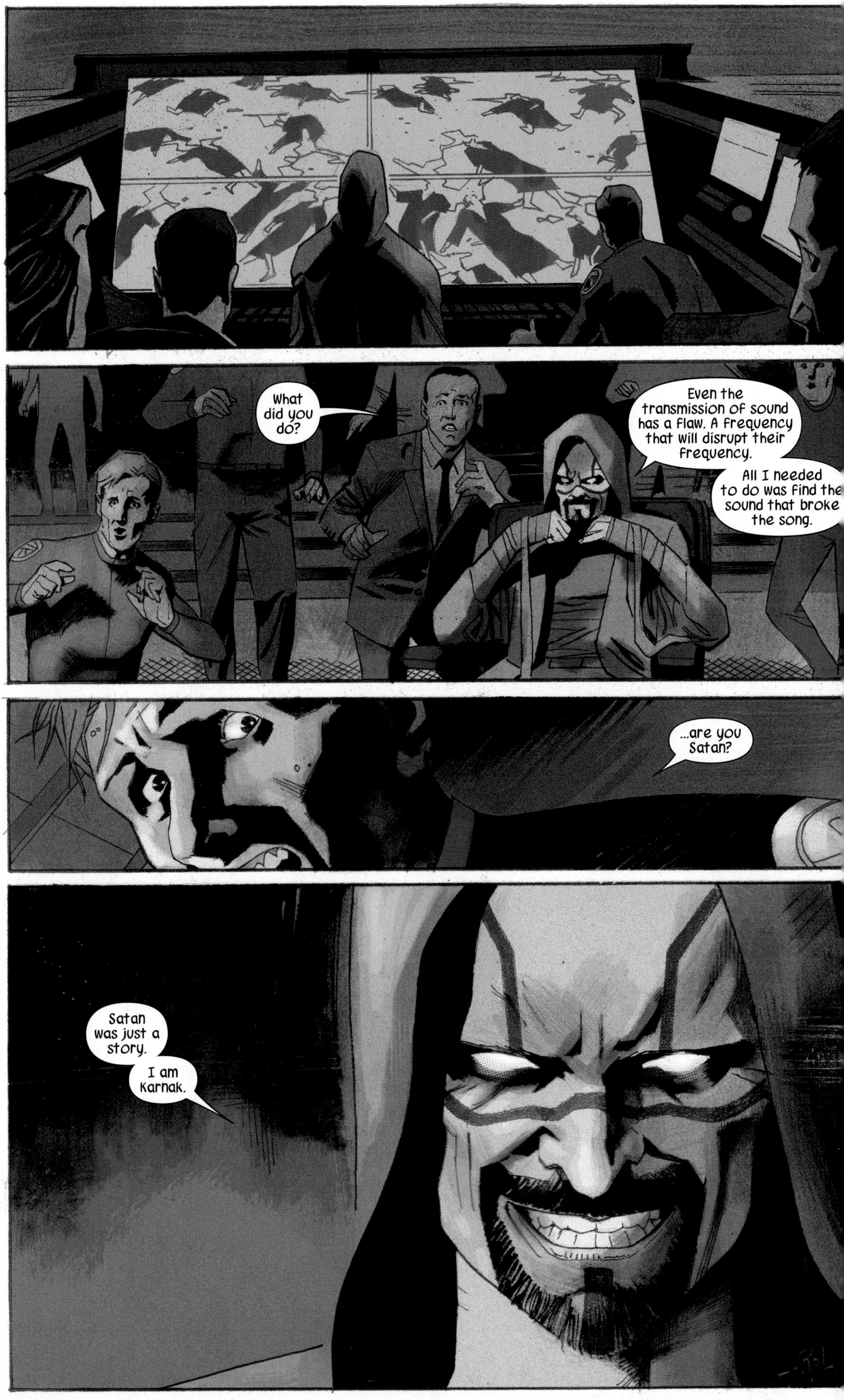
What did you do?
Even the transmission of sound has a flaw. A frequency that will disrupt their frequency.
All I needed to do was find the sound that broke the song.
...are you Satan?
Satan was just a story.
I am Karnak.

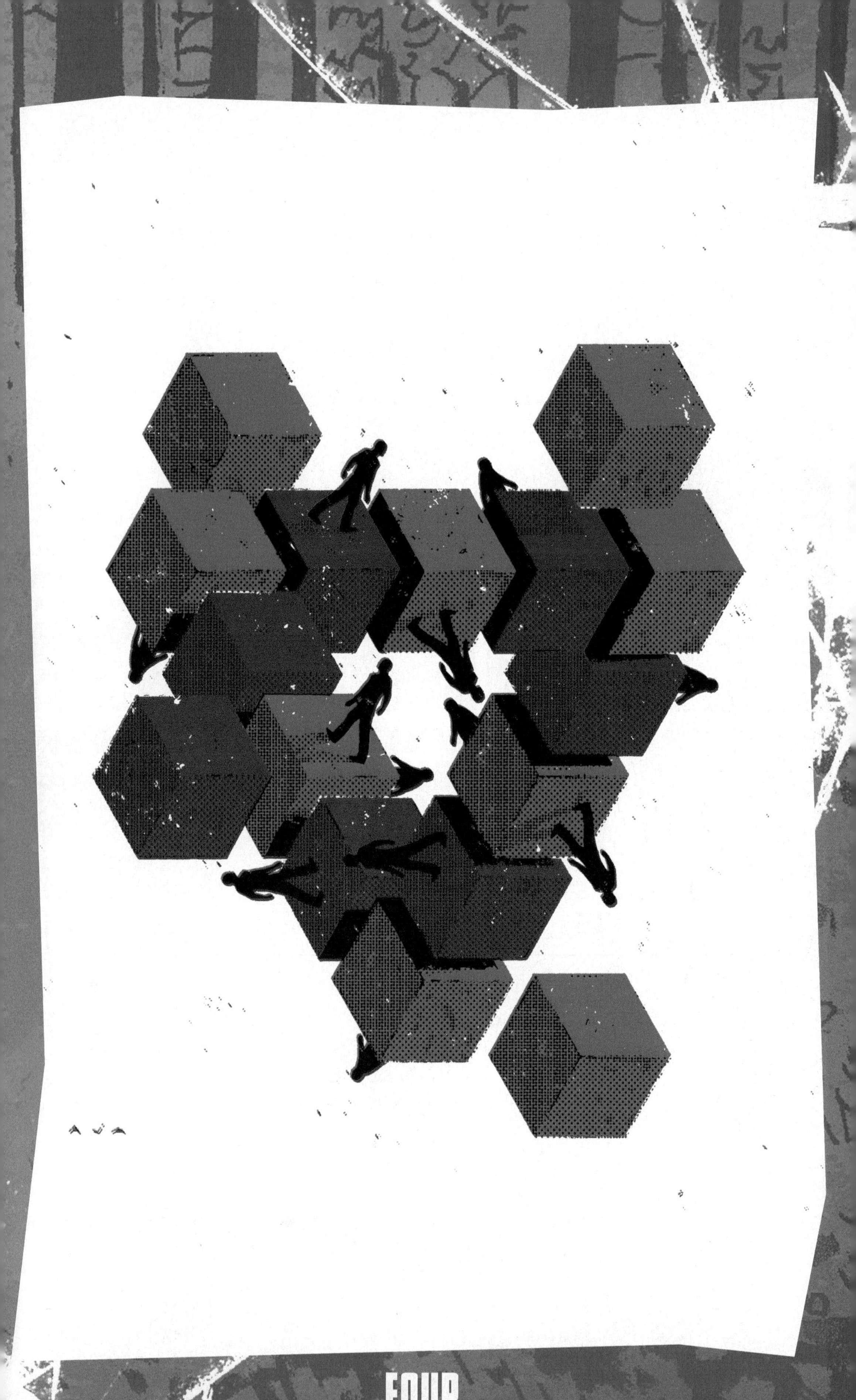

# FOUR

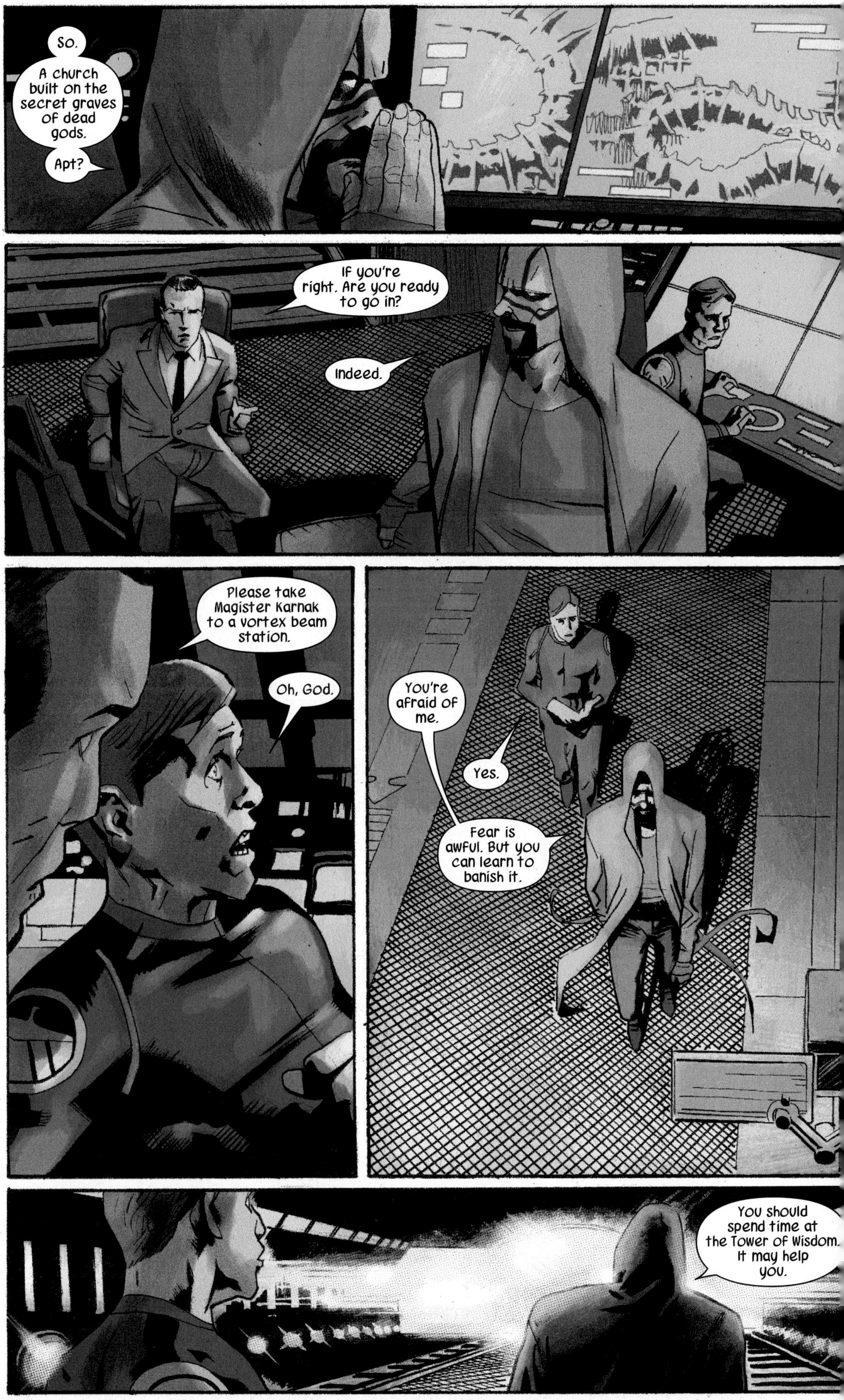
So.
A church built on the secret graves of dead gods.
Apt?
If you're right. Are you ready to go in?
Indeed.
Please take Magister Karnak to a vortex beam station.
Oh, God.
You're afraid of me.
Yes.
Fear is awful. But you can learn to banish it.
You should spend time at the Tower of Wisdom. It may help you.

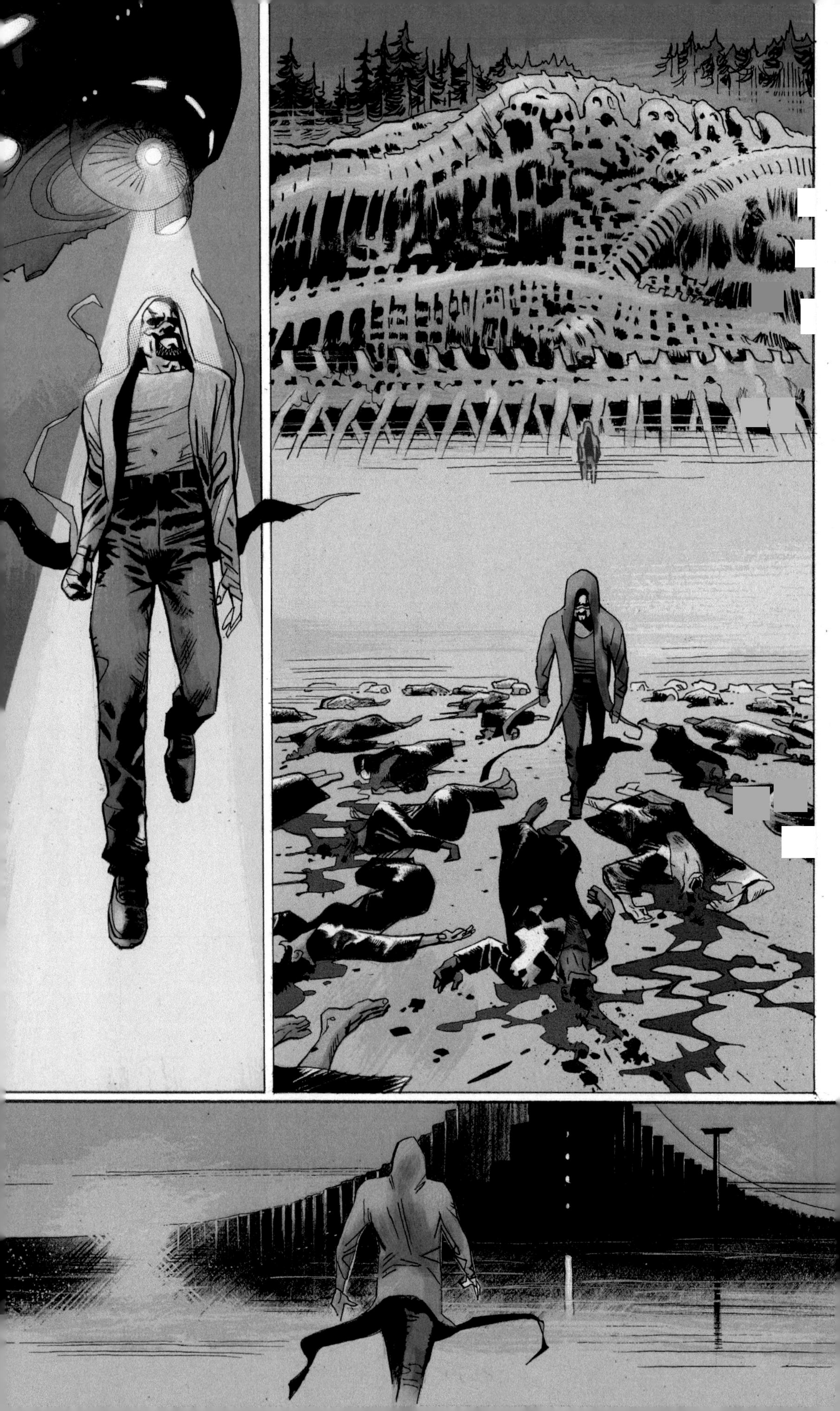

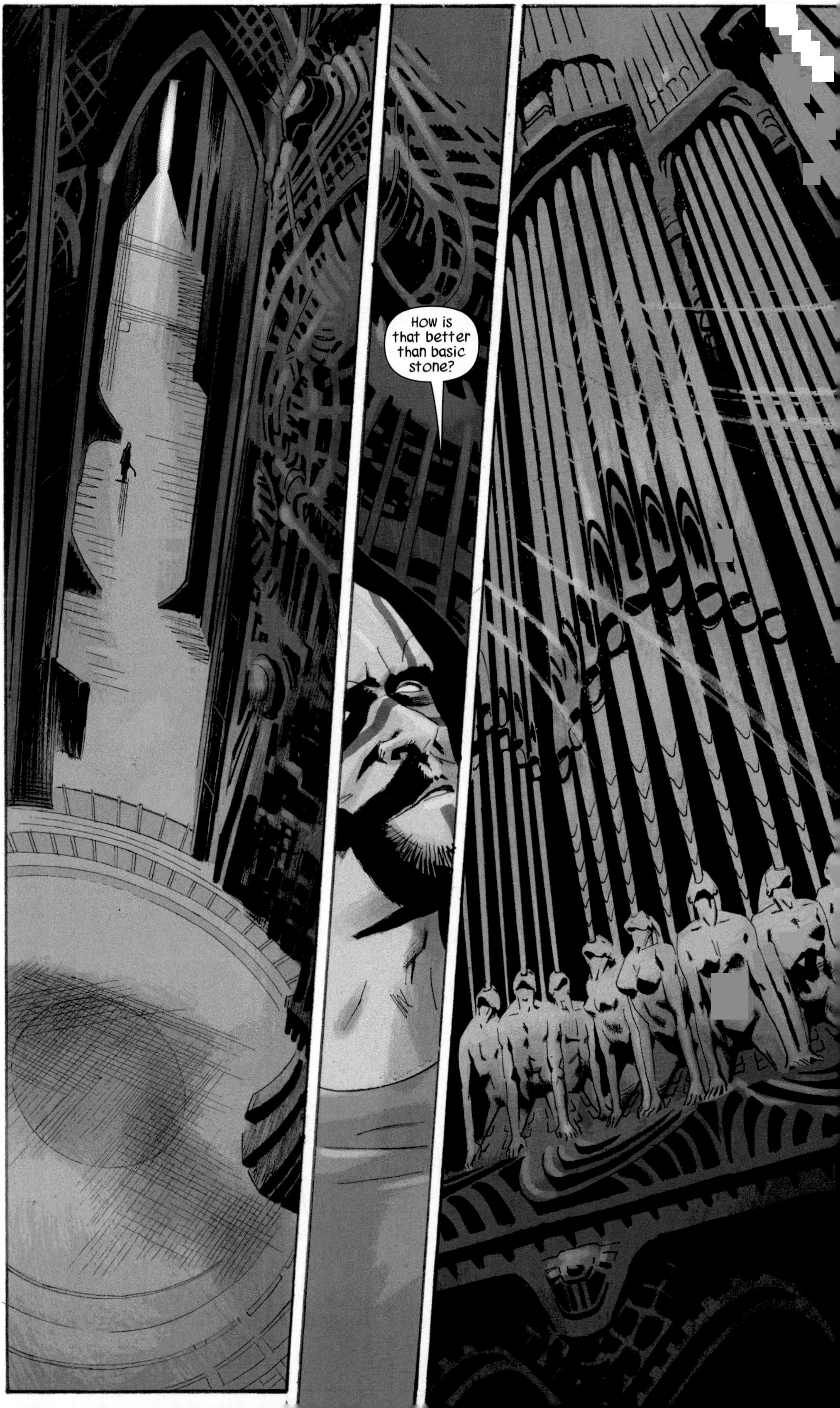
How is that better than basic stone?

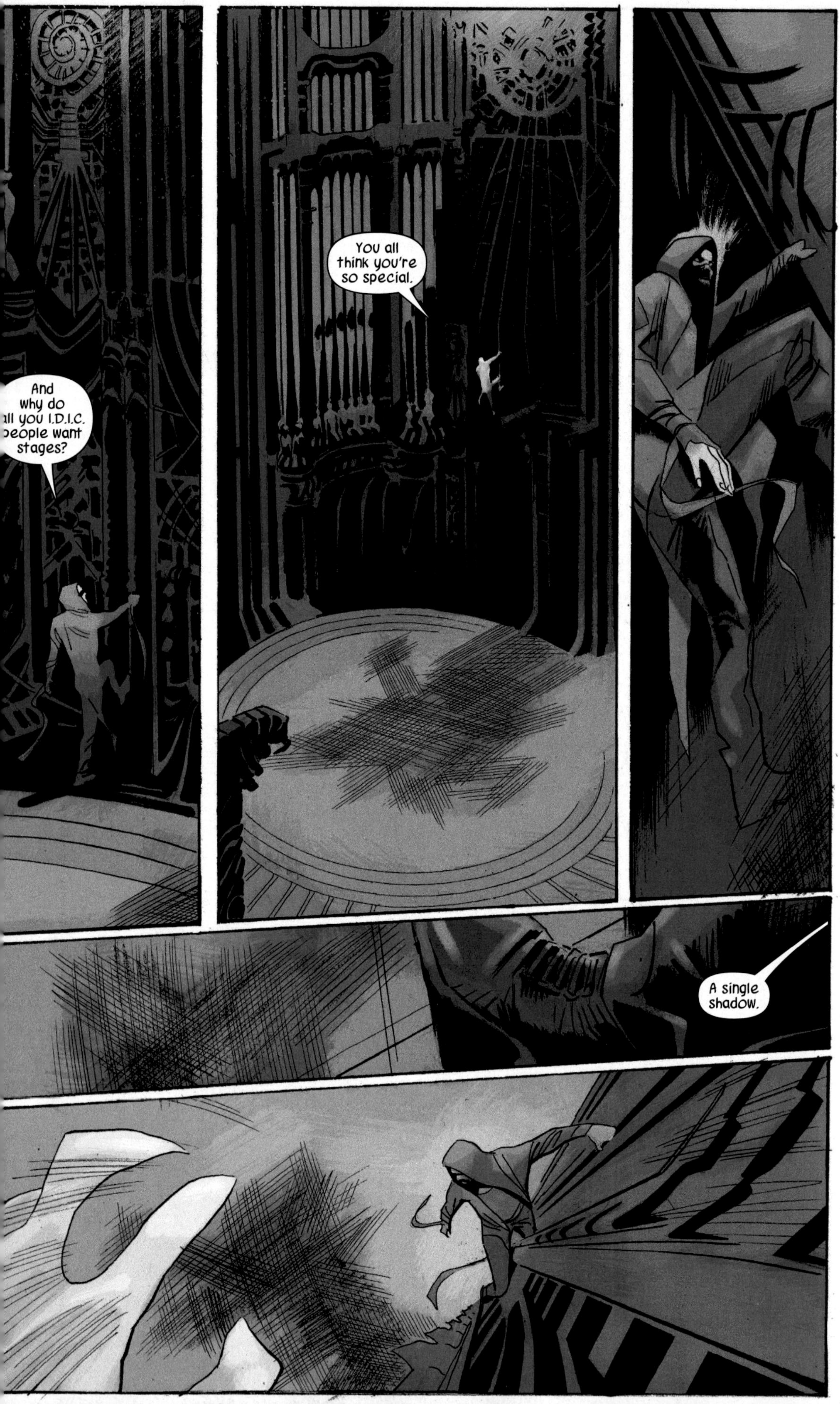
And why do all you I.D.I.C. people want stages?
You all think you're so special.
A single shadow.

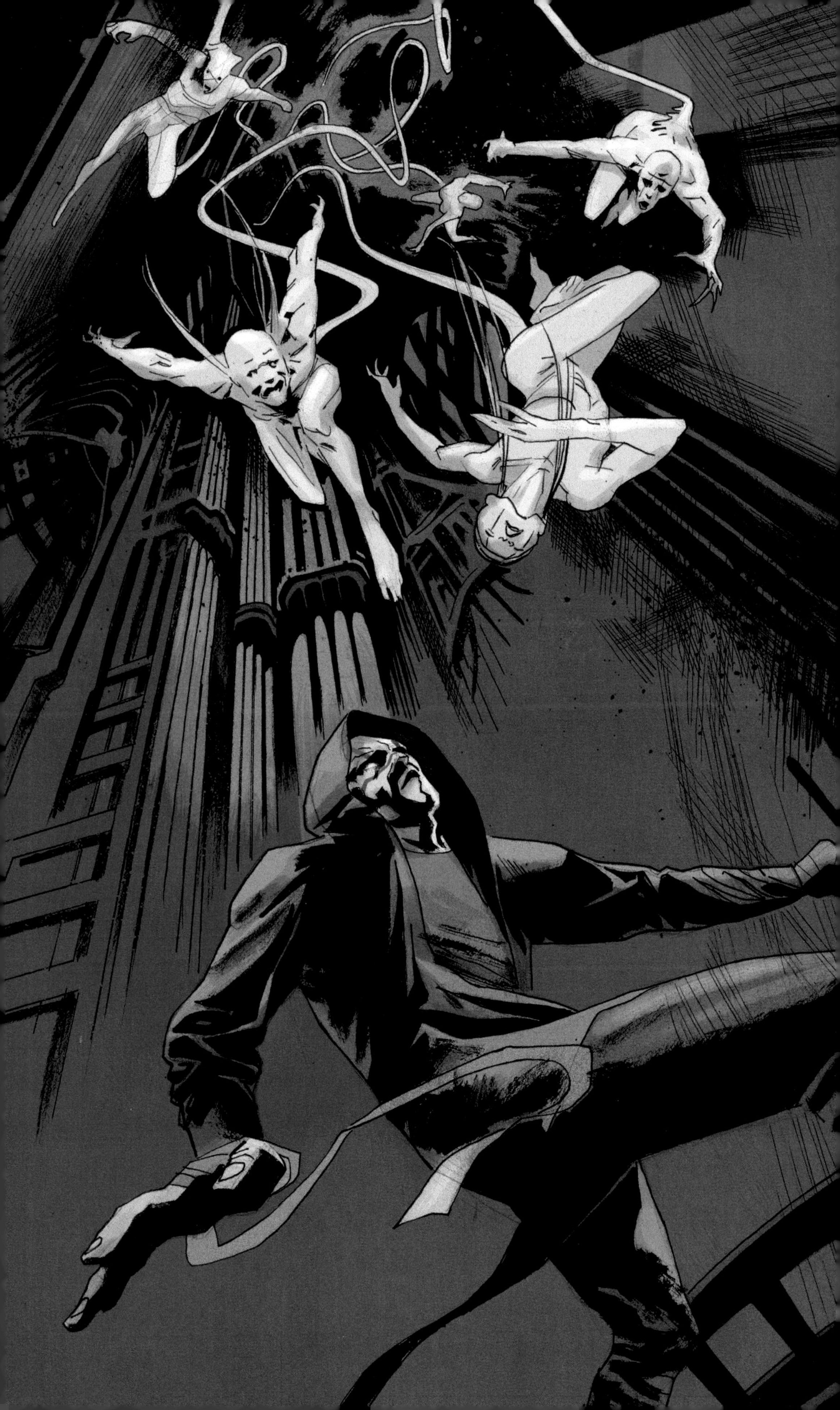

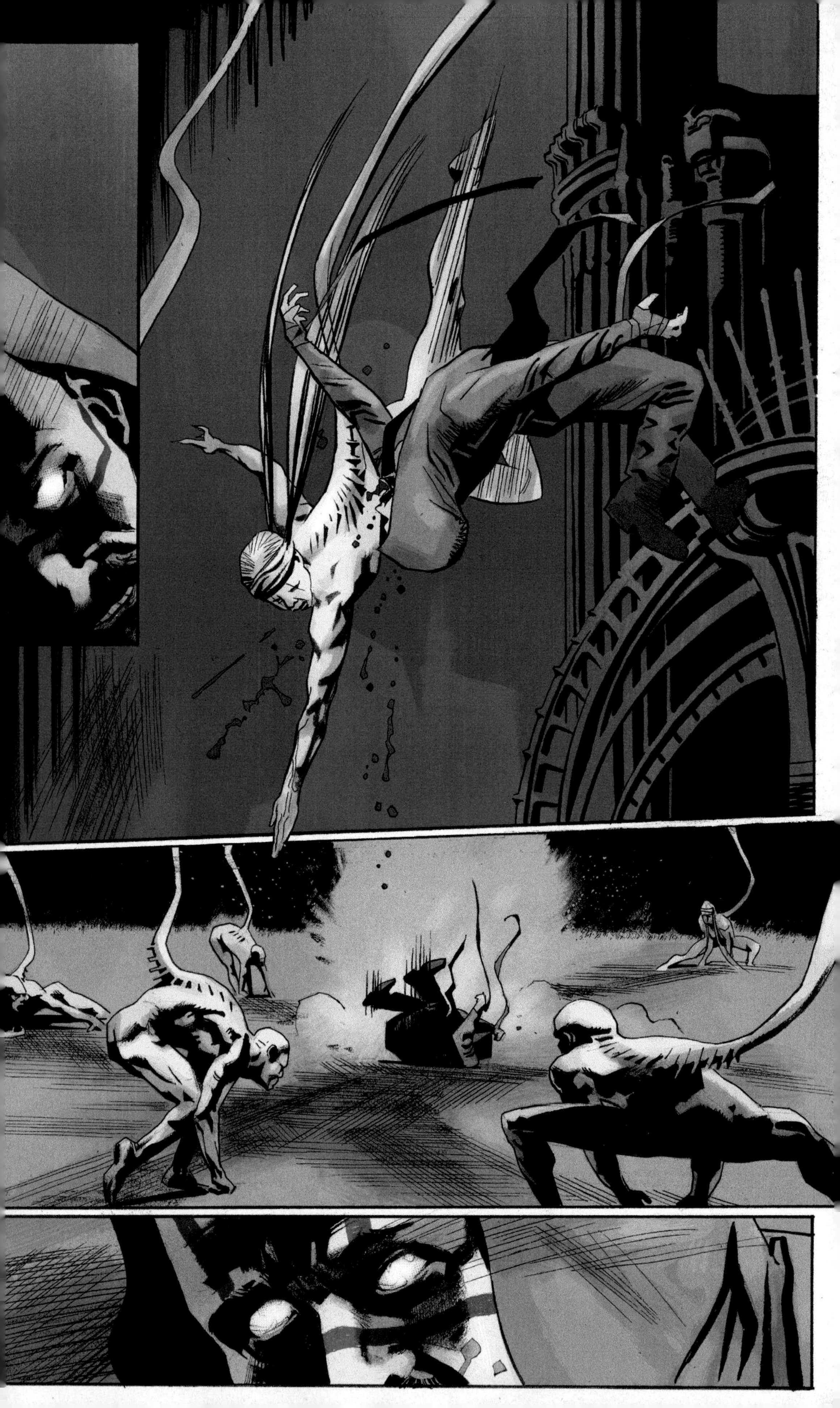

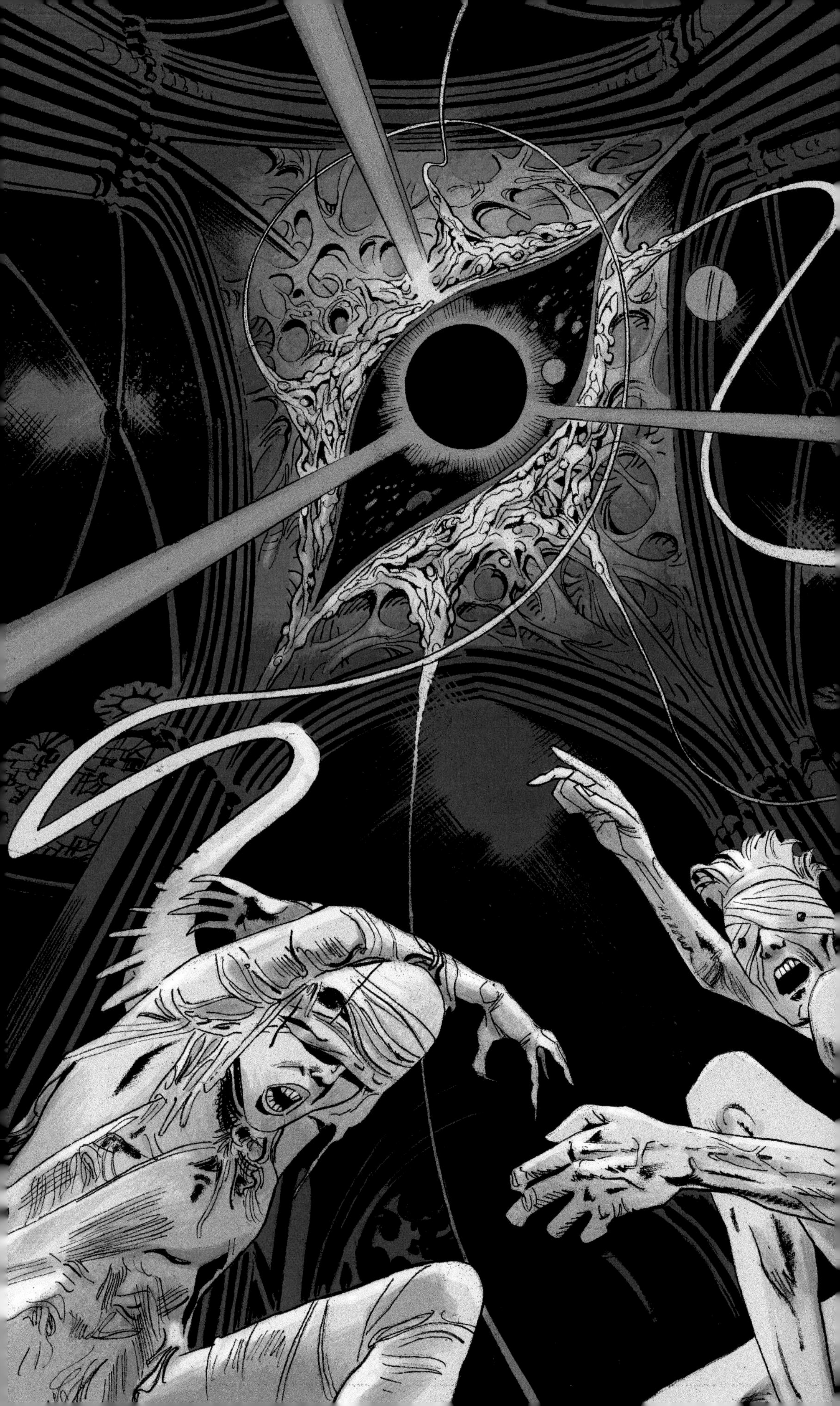

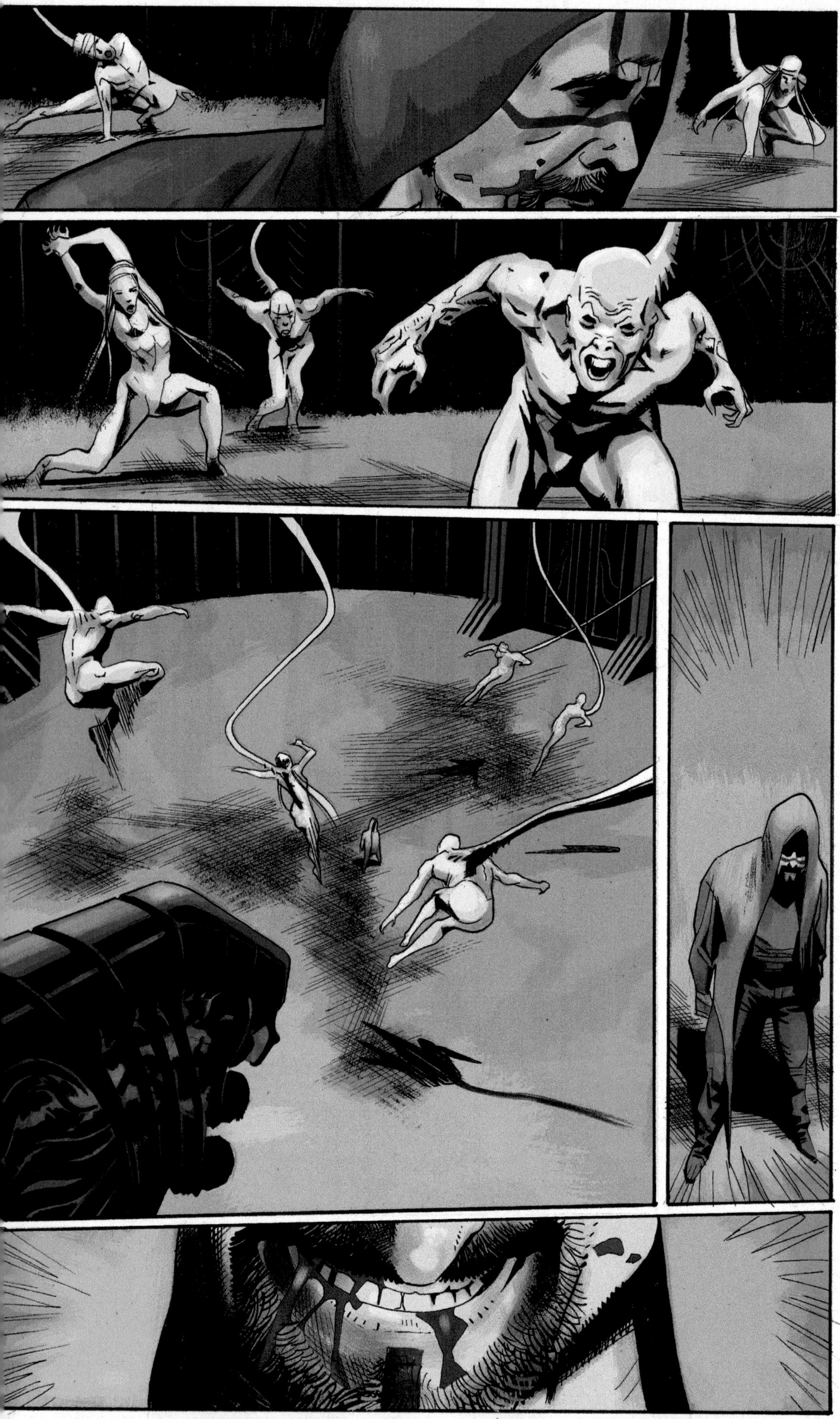

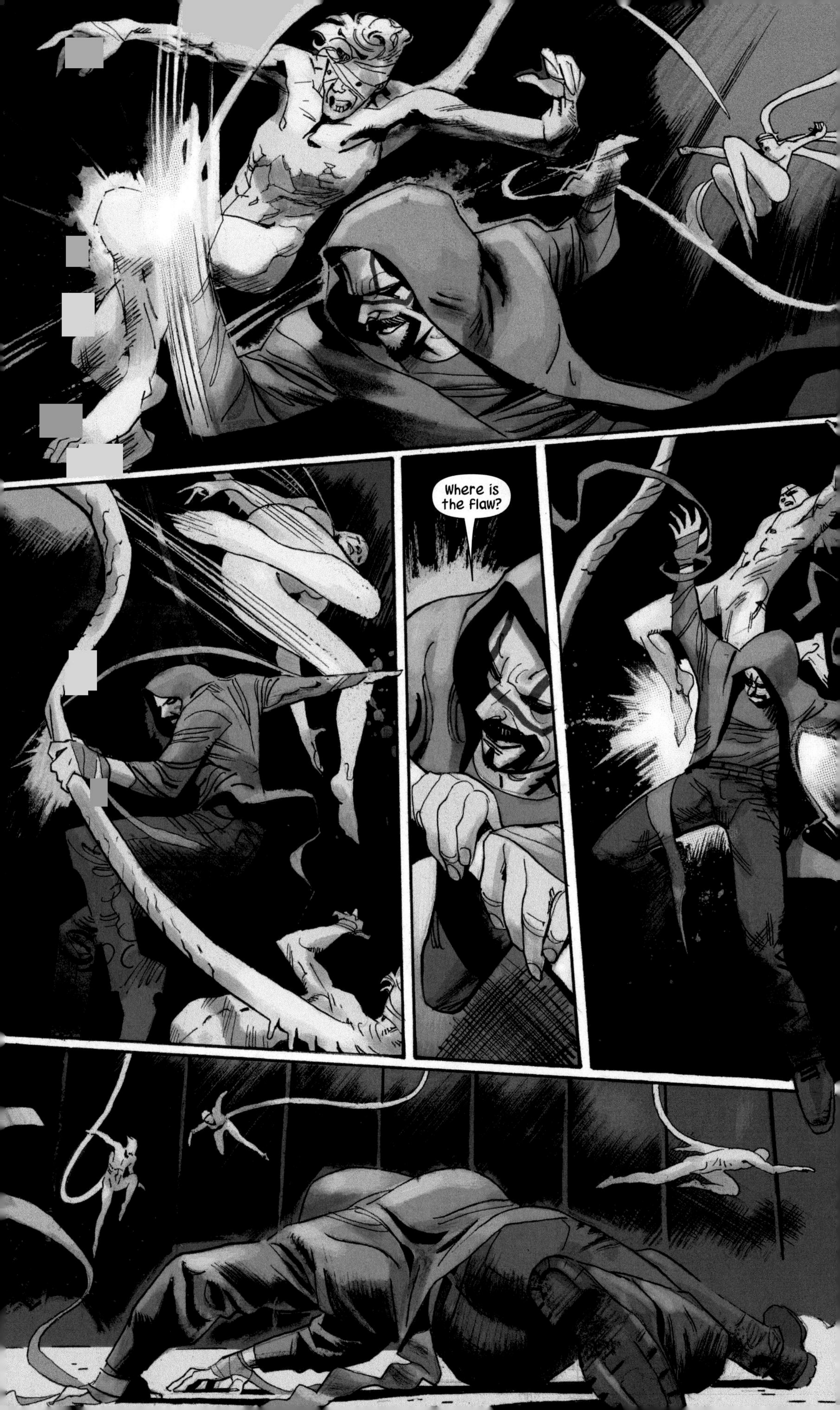
Where is the flaw?

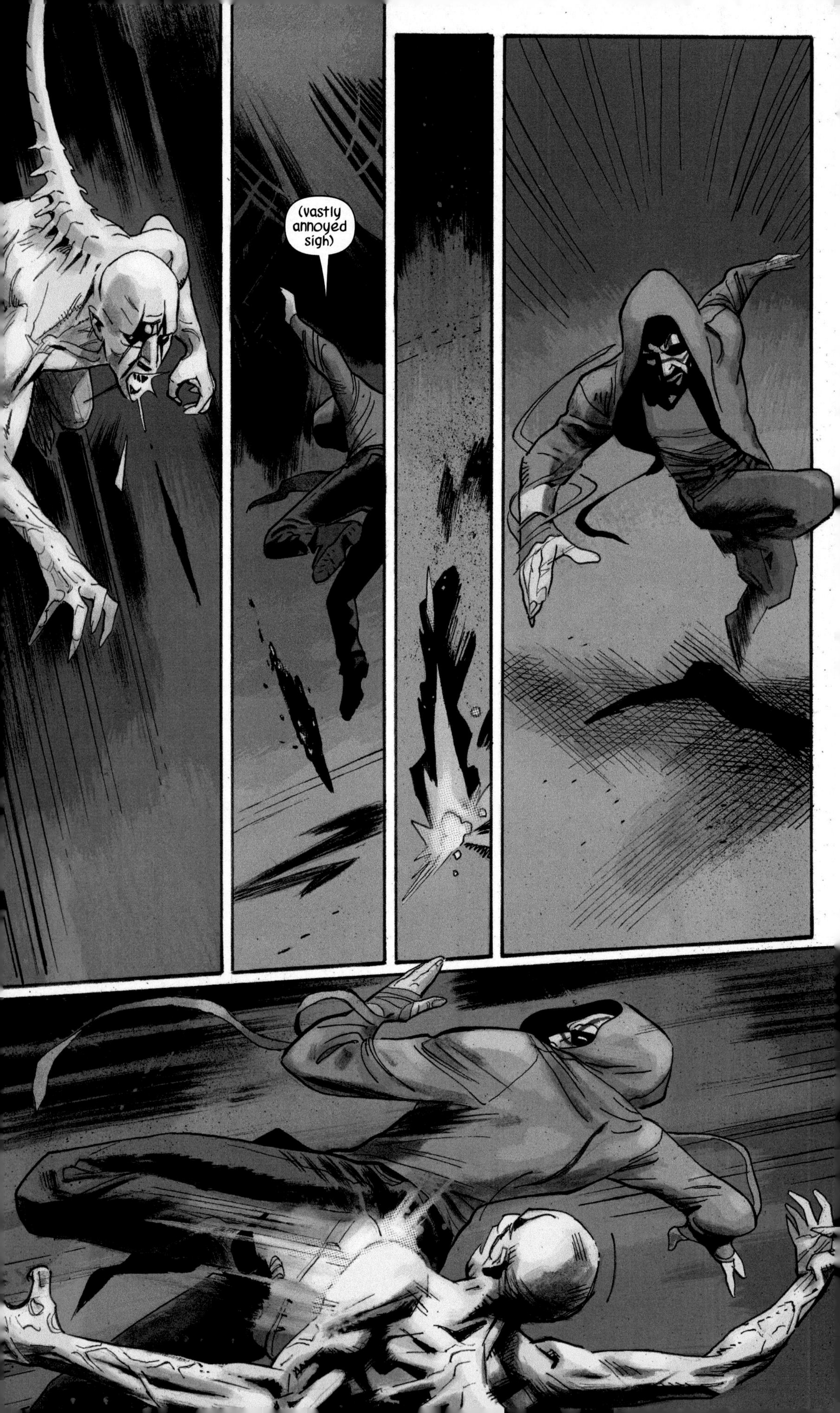
(vastly annoyed sigh)

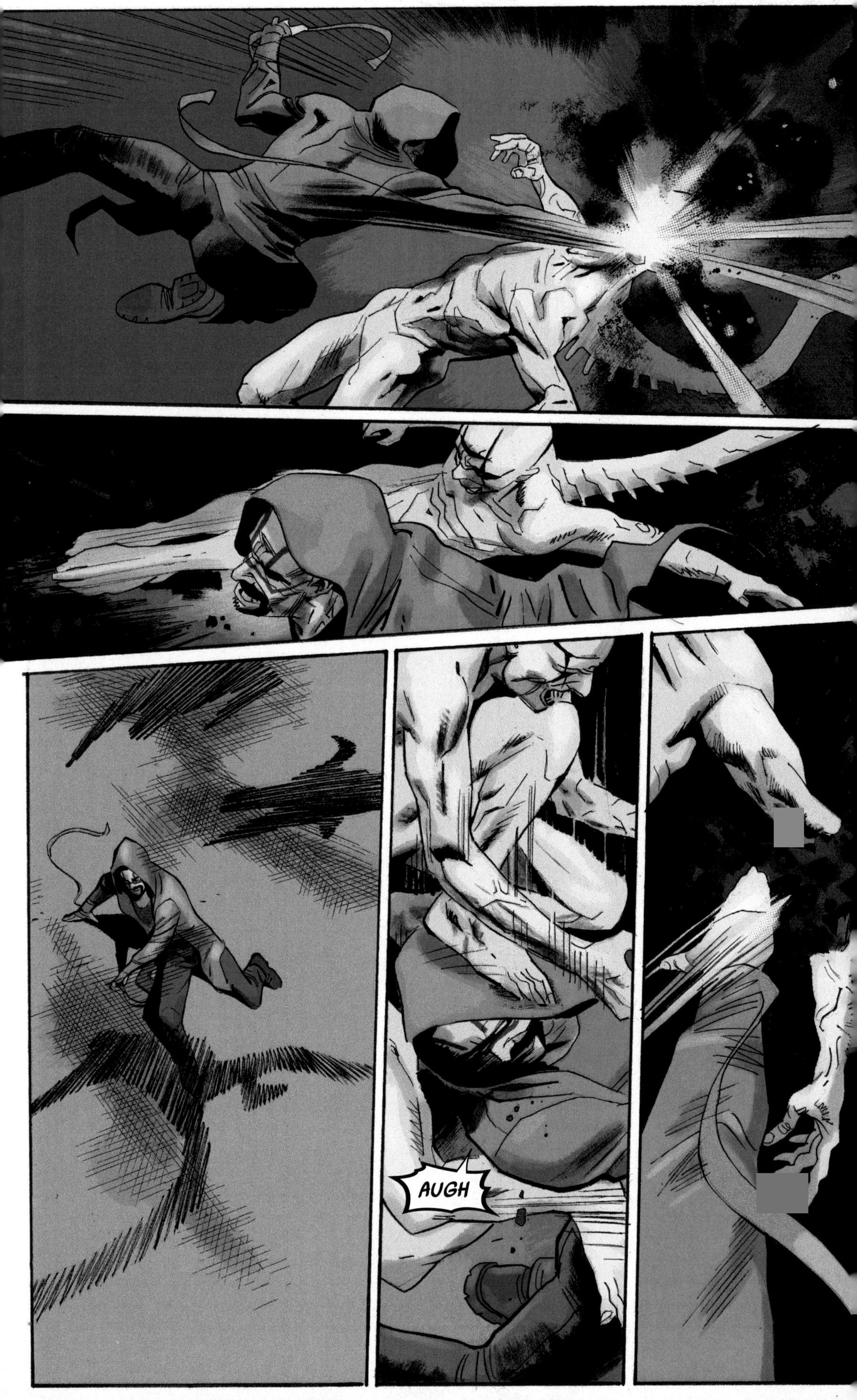
AUGH

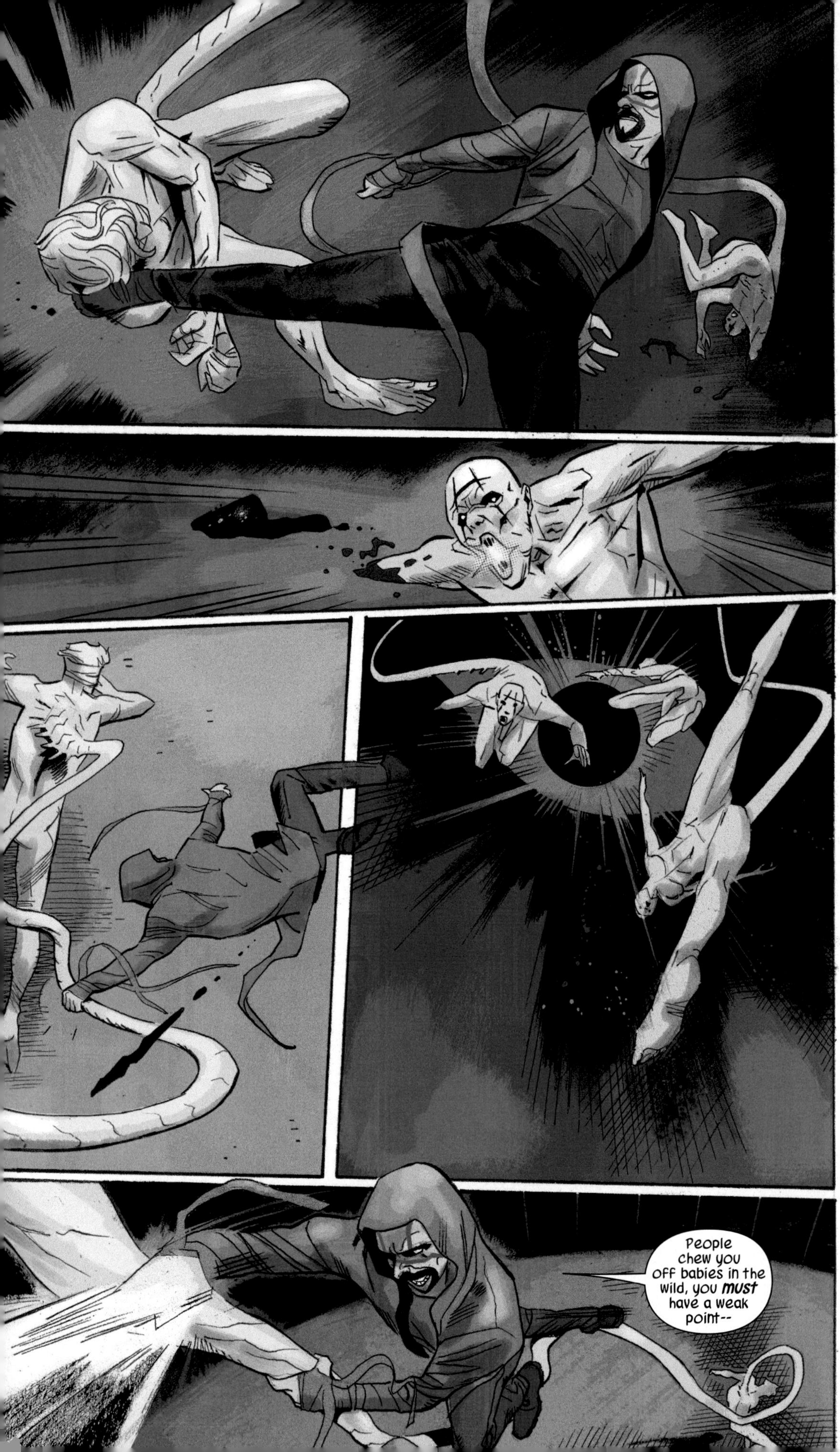
People chew you off babies in the wild, you *MUST* have a weak point--

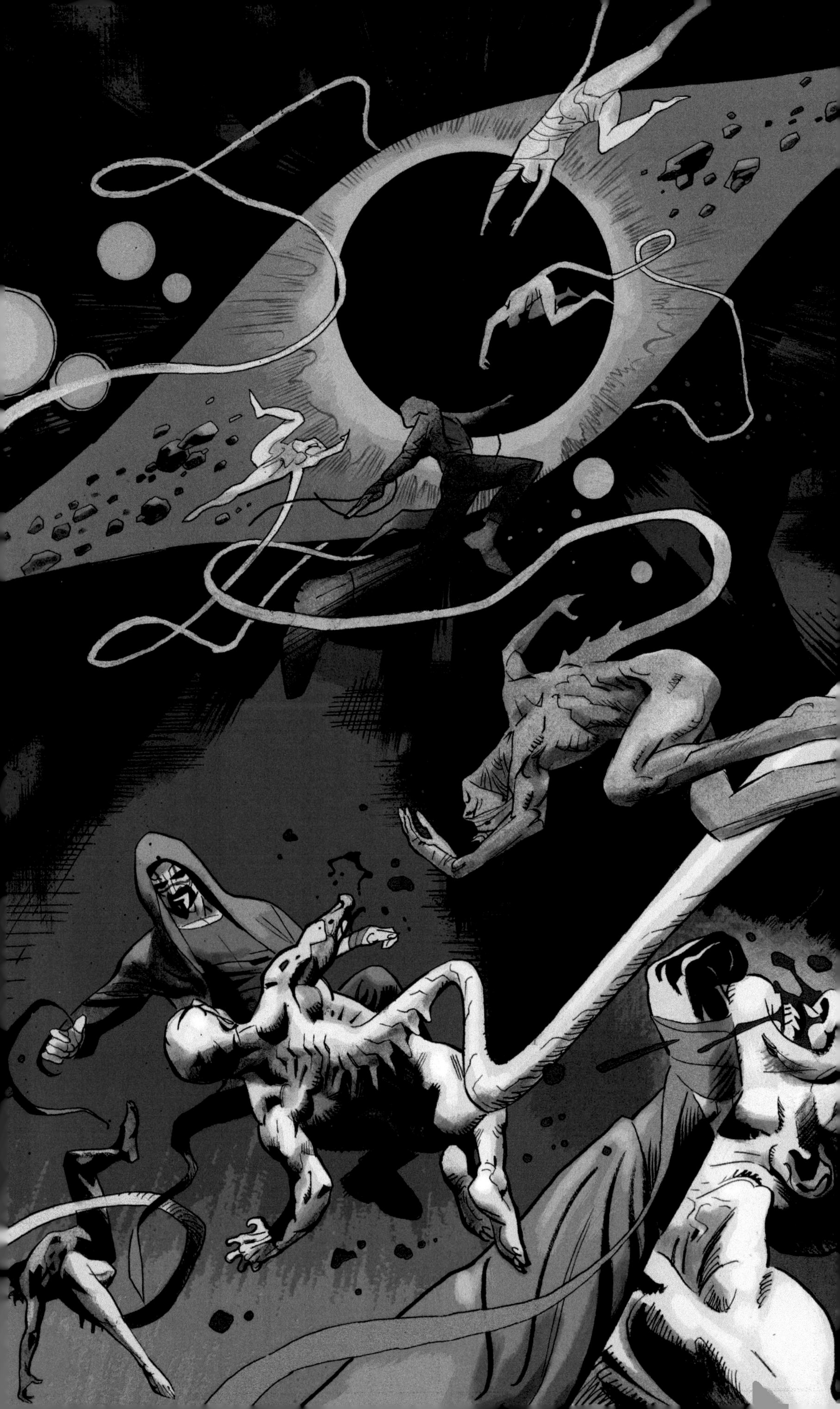

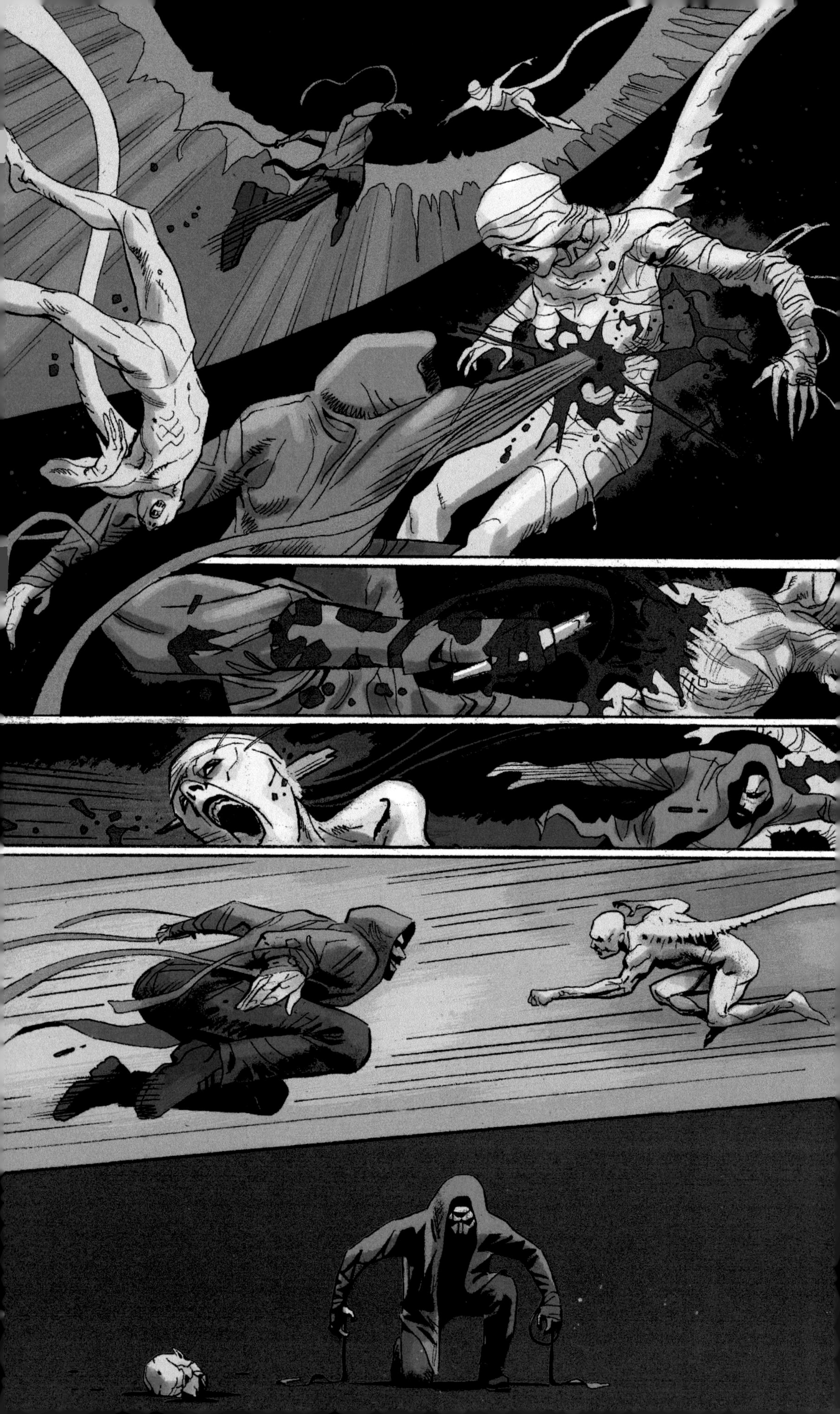

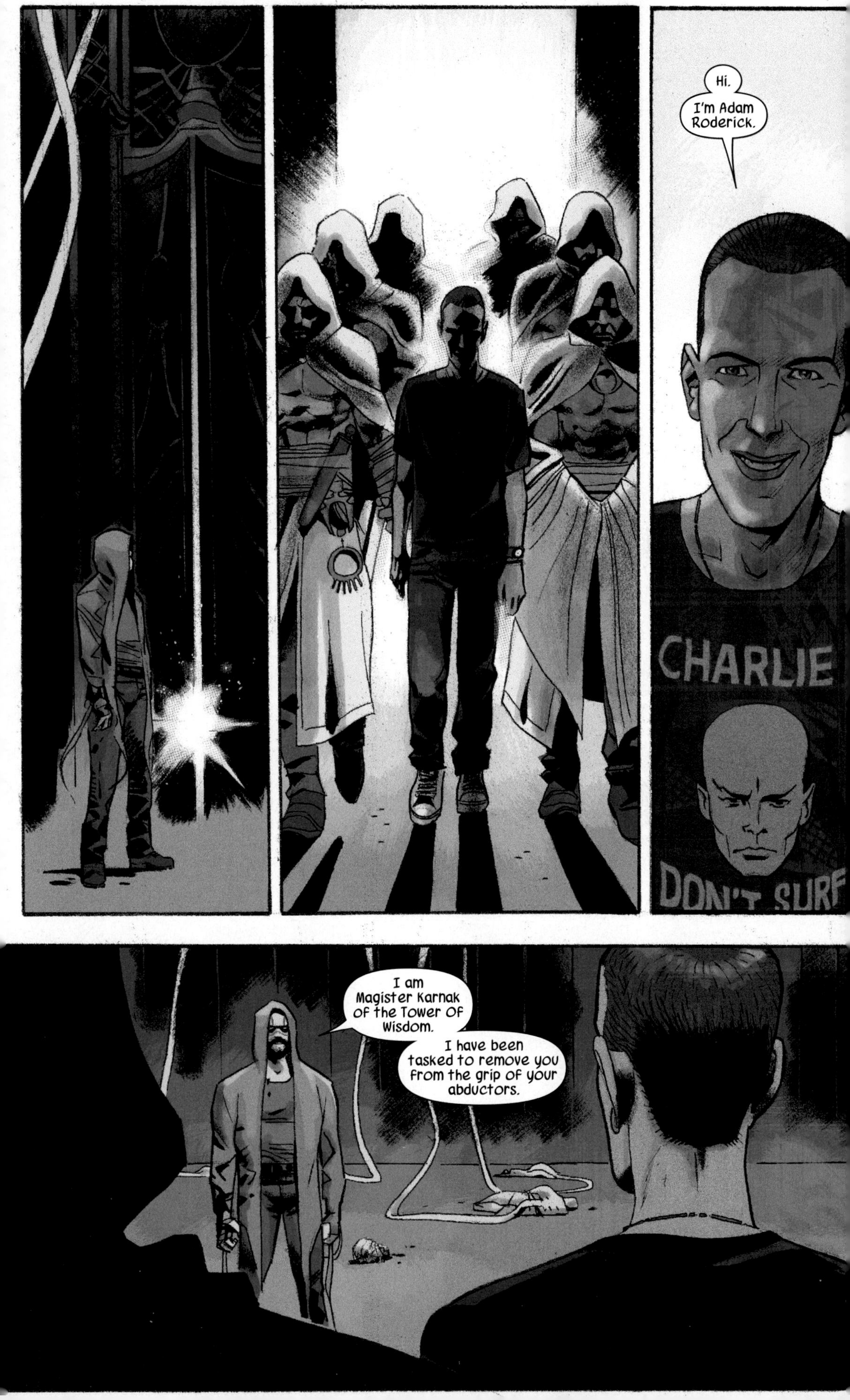
Hi.
I'm Adam Roderick.
CHARLIE
DON'T SURF
I am Magister Karnak of the Tower Of Wisdom.
I have been tasked to remove you from the grip of your abductors.

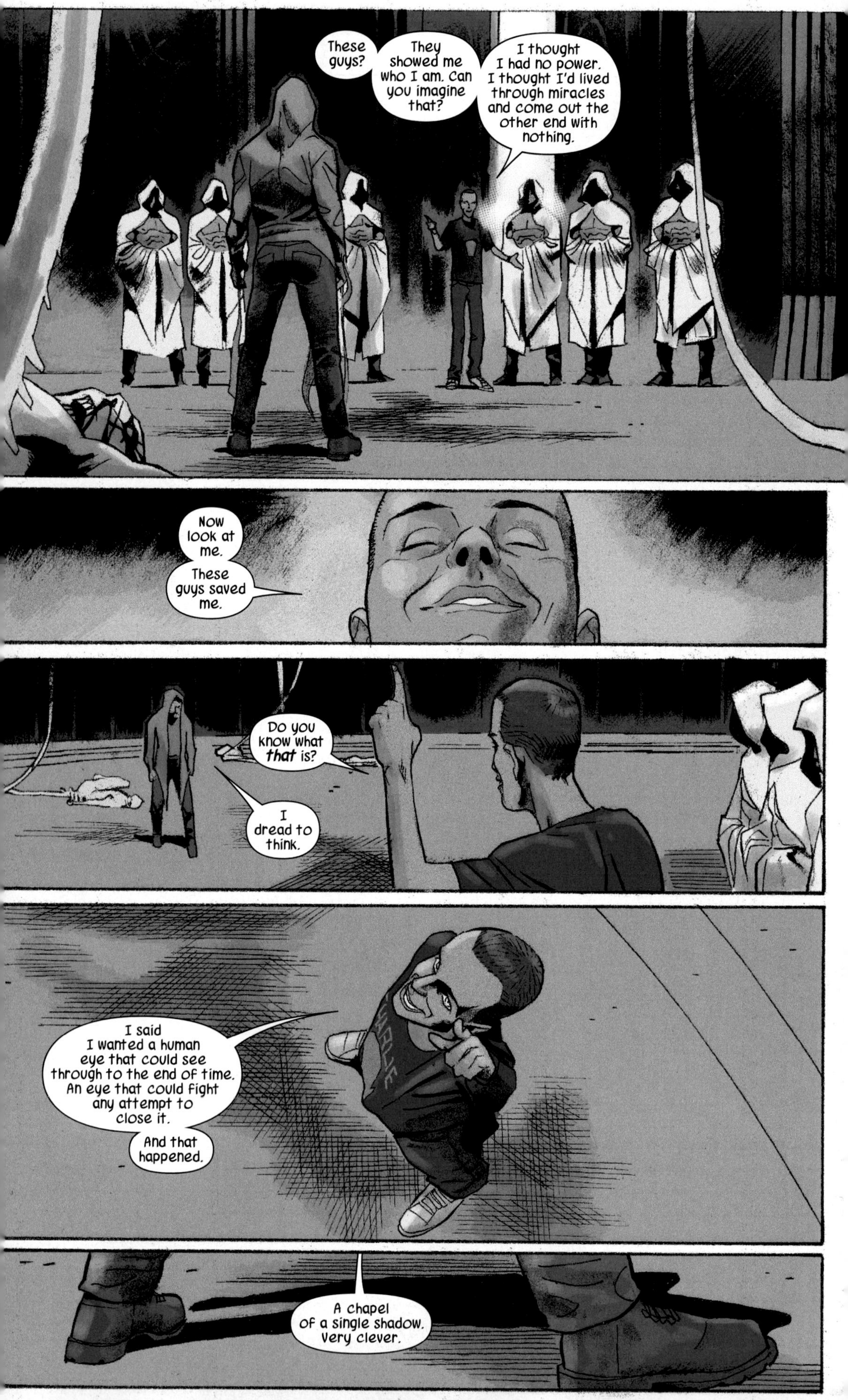
These guys?
They showed me who I am. Can you imagine that?
I thought I had no power. I thought I'd lived through miracles and come out the other end with nothing.
Now look at me.
These guys saved me.
Do you know what *that* is?
I dread to think.
I said I wanted a human eye that could see through to the end of time. An eye that could fight any attempt to close it.
And that happened.
A chapel of a single shadow. Very clever.

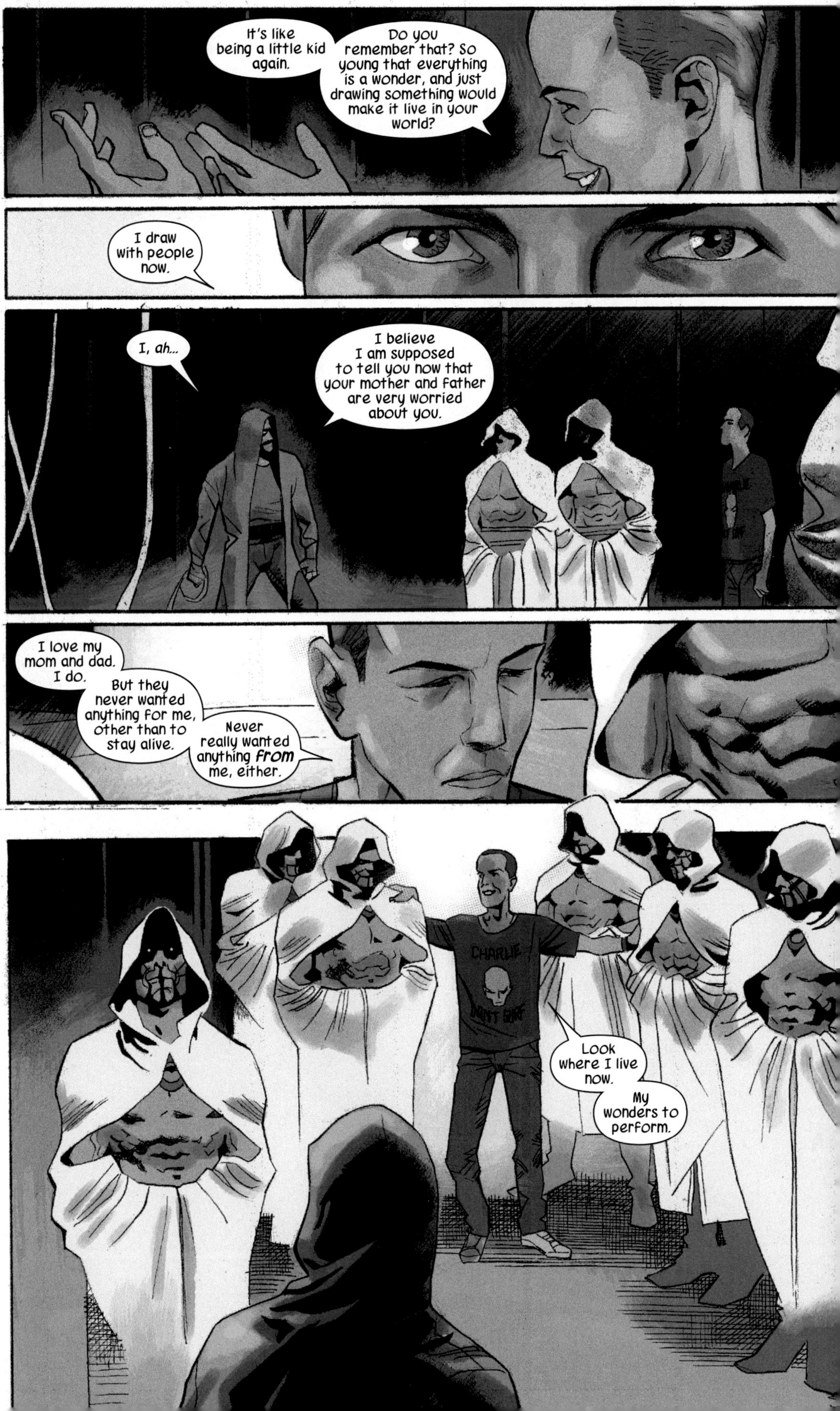
It's like being a little kid again.
Do you remember that? So young that everything is a wonder, and just drawing something would make it live in your world?
I draw with people now.
I, ah...
I believe I am supposed to tell you now that your mother and father are very worried about you.
I love my mom and dad. I do.
But they never wanted anything for me, other than to stay alive.
Never really wanted anything *from* me, either.
CHARLIE
Look where I live now.
My wonders to perform.

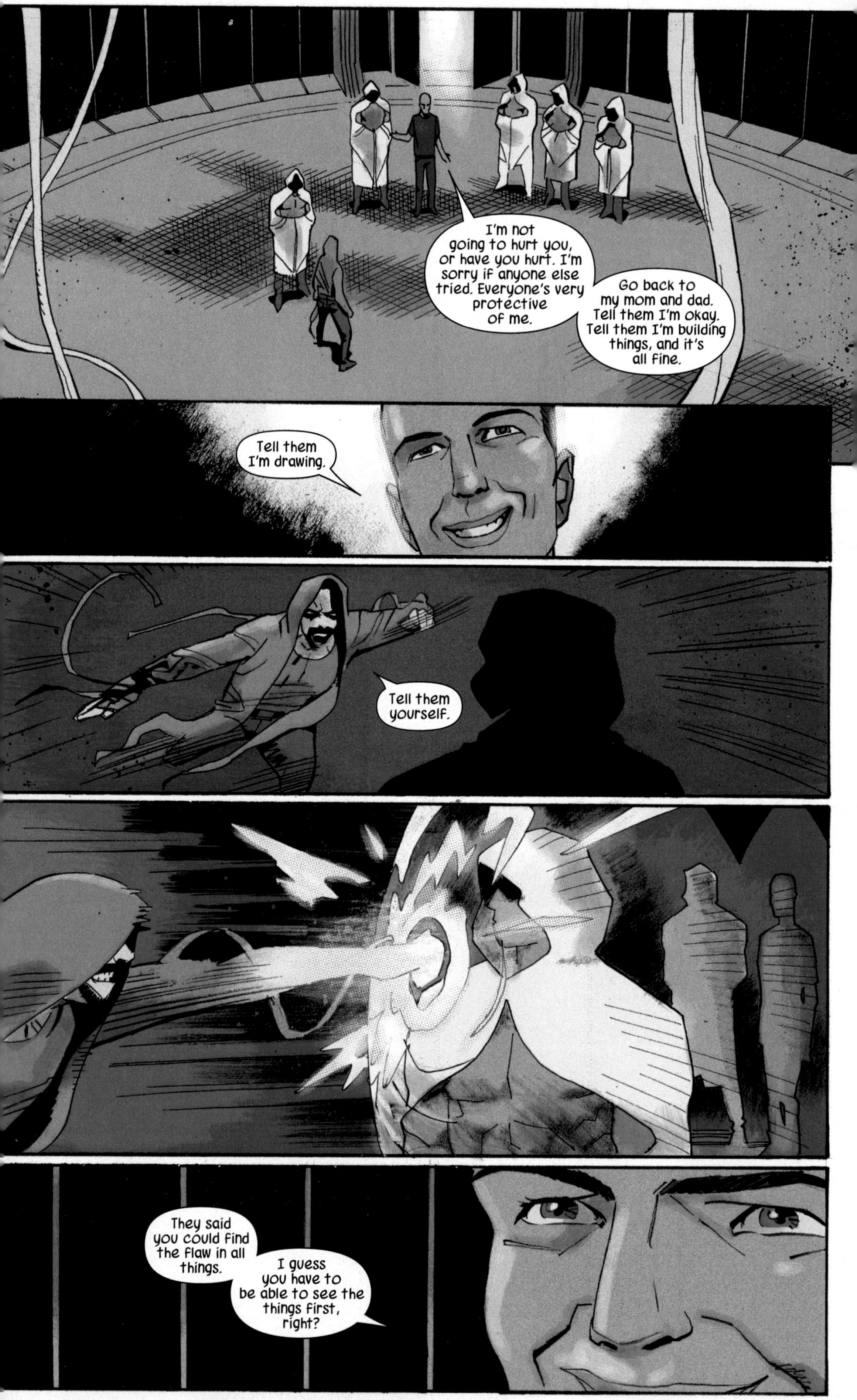
I'm not going to hurt you, or have you hurt. I'm sorry if anyone else tried. Everyone's very protective of me.
Go back to my mom and dad. Tell them I'm okay. Tell them I'm building things, and it's all fine.
Tell them I'm drawing.
Tell them yourself.
They said you could find the flaw in all things.
I guess you have to be able to see the things first, right?

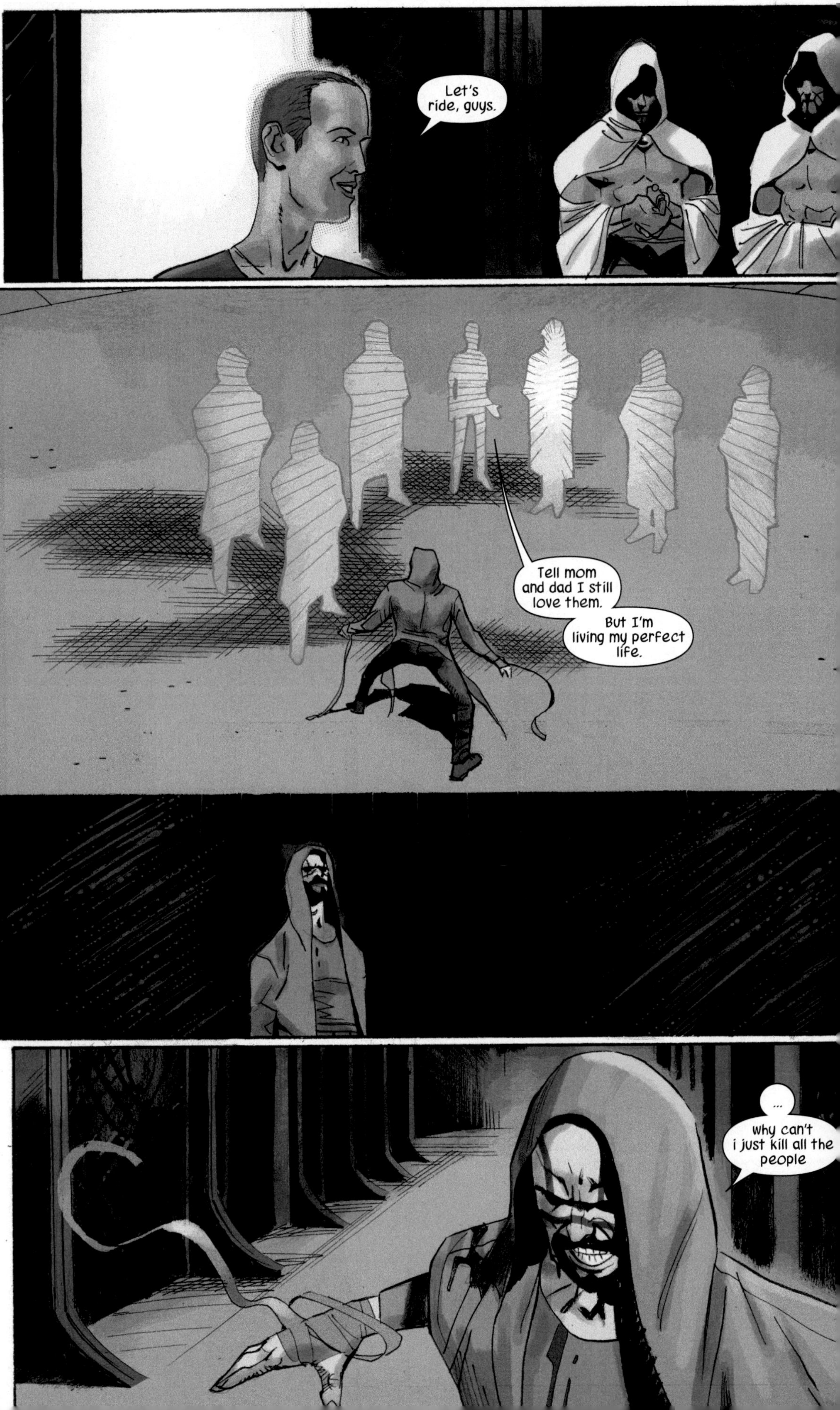
Let's ride, guys.
Tell mom and dad I still love them.
But I'm living my perfect life.
...
why can't i just kill all the people

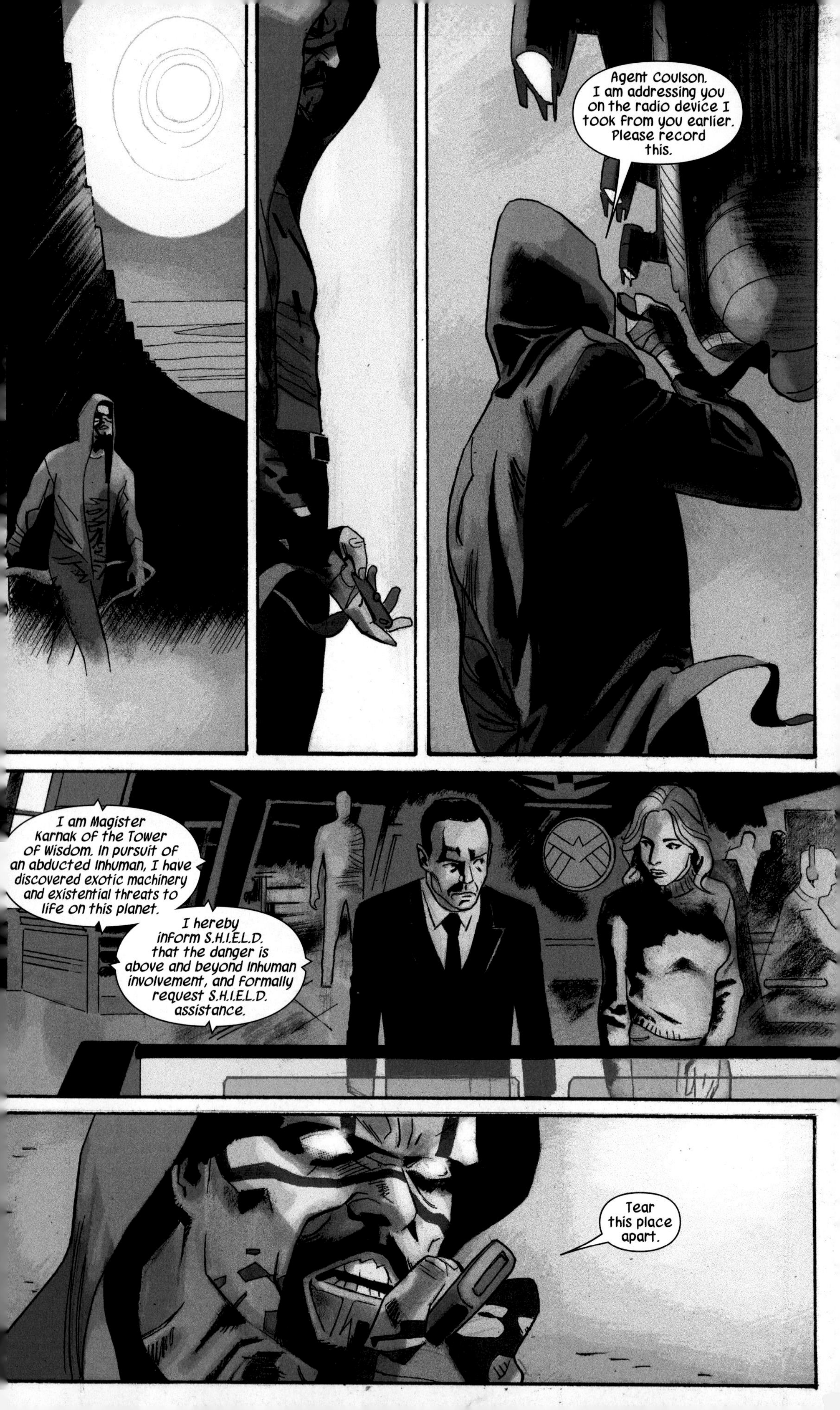

Agent Coulson. I am addressing you on the radio device I took from you earlier. Please record this.
I am Magister Karnak of the Tower of Wisdom. In pursuit of an abducted Inhuman, I have discovered exotic machinery and existential threats to life on this planet.
I hereby inform S.H.I.E.L.D. that the danger is above and beyond Inhuman involvement, and formally request S.H.I.E.L.D. assistance.
Tear this place apart.

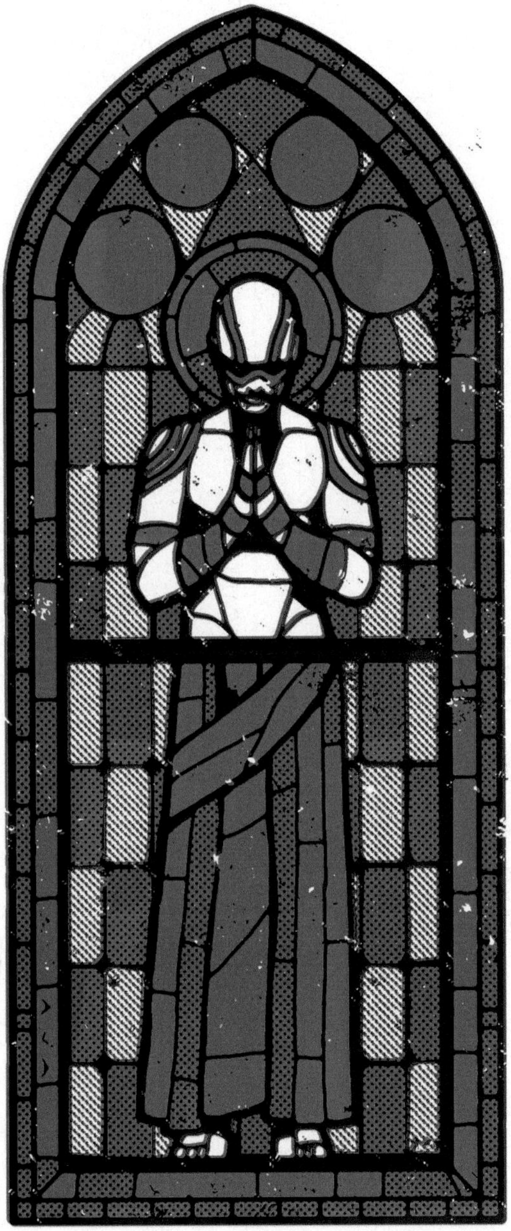

# FIVE

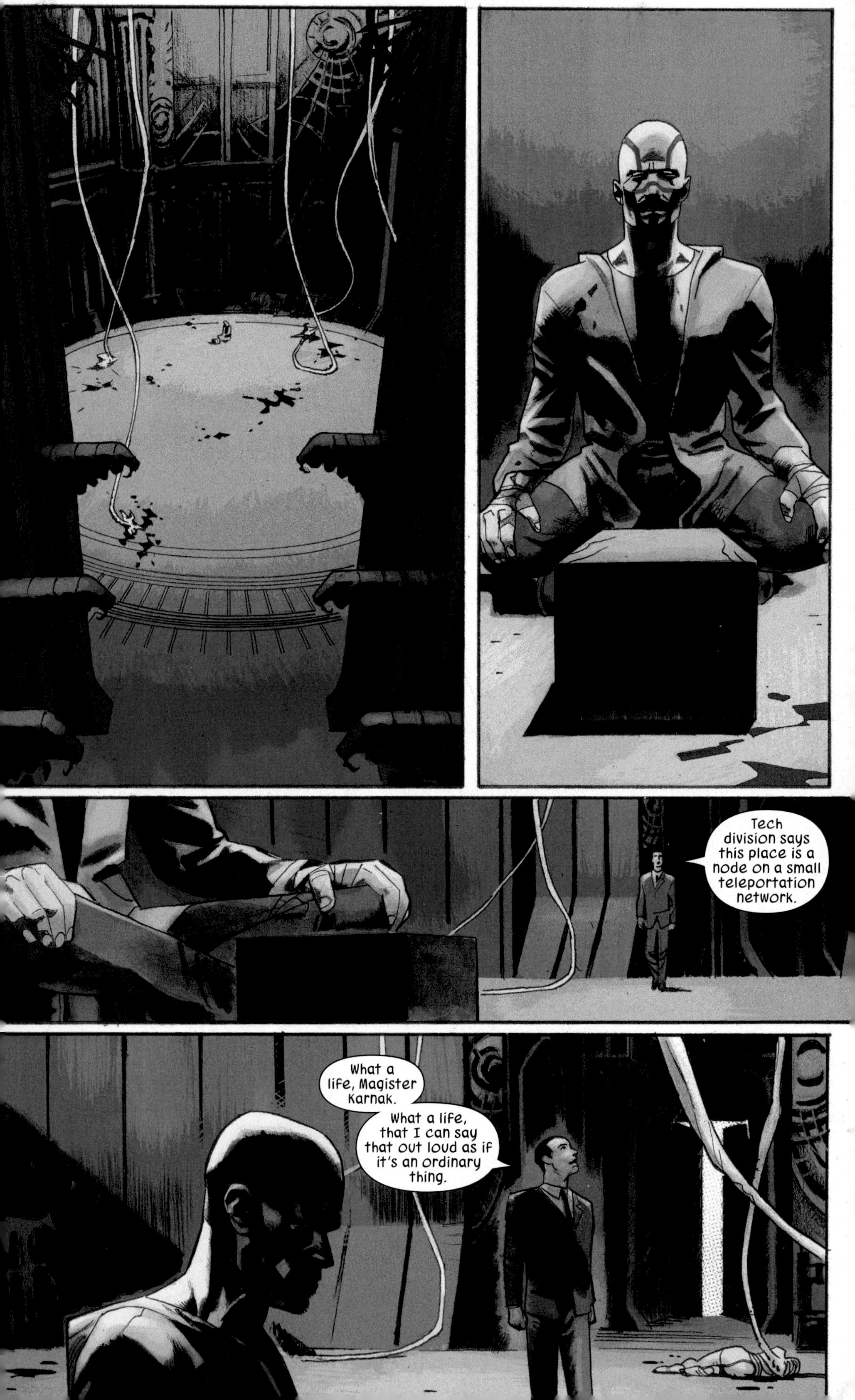
Tech division says this place is a node on a small teleportation network.
What a life, Magister Karnak.
What a life, that I can say that out loud as if it's an ordinary thing.

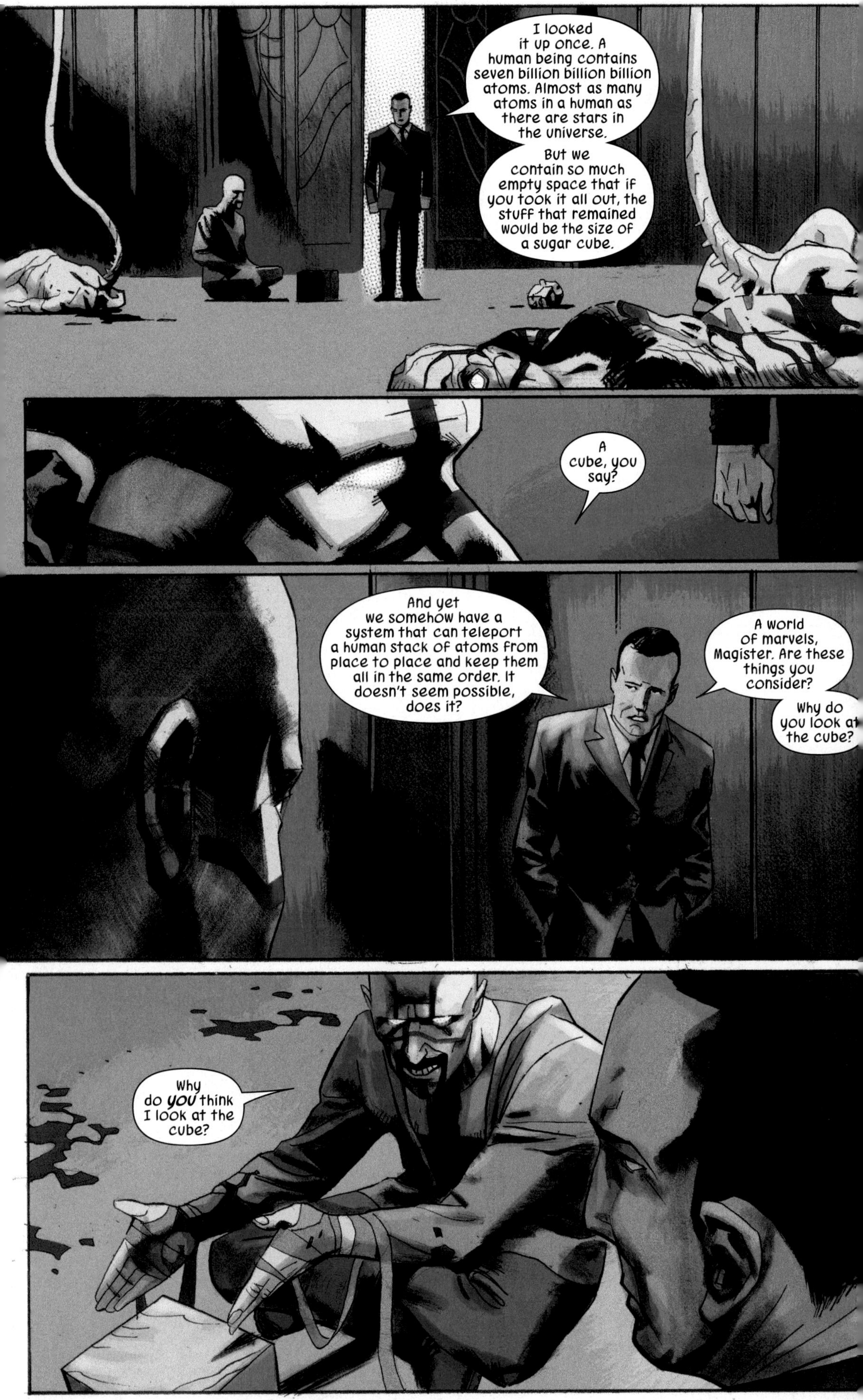
I looked it up once. A human being contains seven billion billion billion atoms. Almost as many atoms in a human as there are stars in the universe.
But we contain so much empty space that if you took it all out, the stuff that remained would be the size of a sugar cube.
A cube, you say?
And yet we somehow have a system that can teleport a human stack of atoms from place to place and keep them all in the same order. It doesn't seem possible, does it?
A world of marvels, Magister. Are these things you consider?
Why do you look at the cube?
Why do *you* think I look at the cube?

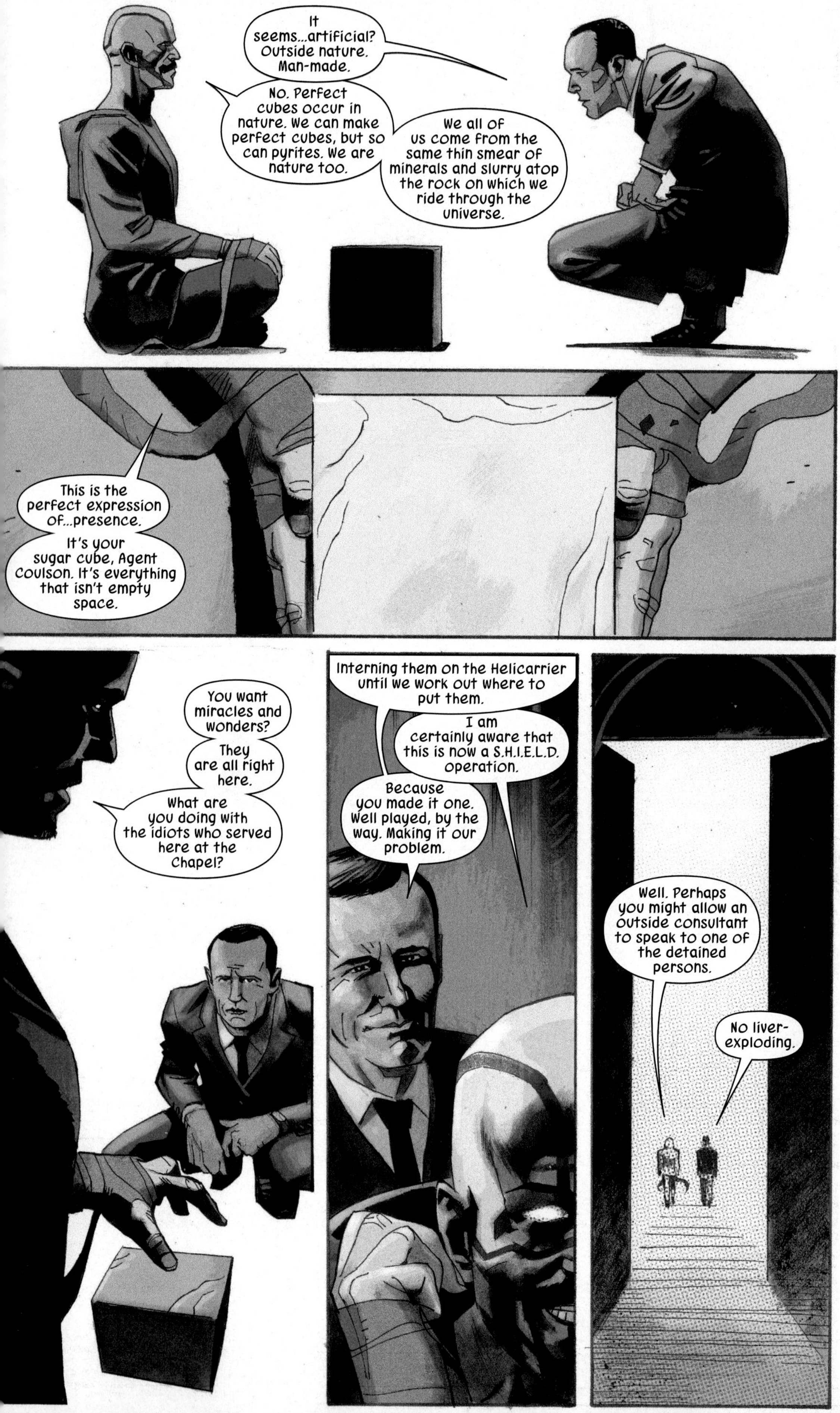
It seems...artificial? Outside nature. Man-made.
No. Perfect cubes occur in nature. We can make perfect cubes, but so can pyrites. We are nature too.
We all of us come from the same thin smear of minerals and slurry atop the rock on which we ride through the universe.
This is the perfect expression of...presence.
It's your sugar cube, Agent Coulson. It's everything that isn't empty space.
You want miracles and wonders?
They are all right here.
What are you doing with the idiots who served here at the Chapel?
Interning them on the Helicarrier until we work out where to put them.
I am certainly aware that this is now a S.H.I.E.L.D. operation.
Because you made it one. Well played, by the way. Making it our problem.
Well. Perhaps you might allow an outside consultant to speak to one of the detained persons.
No liver-exploding.

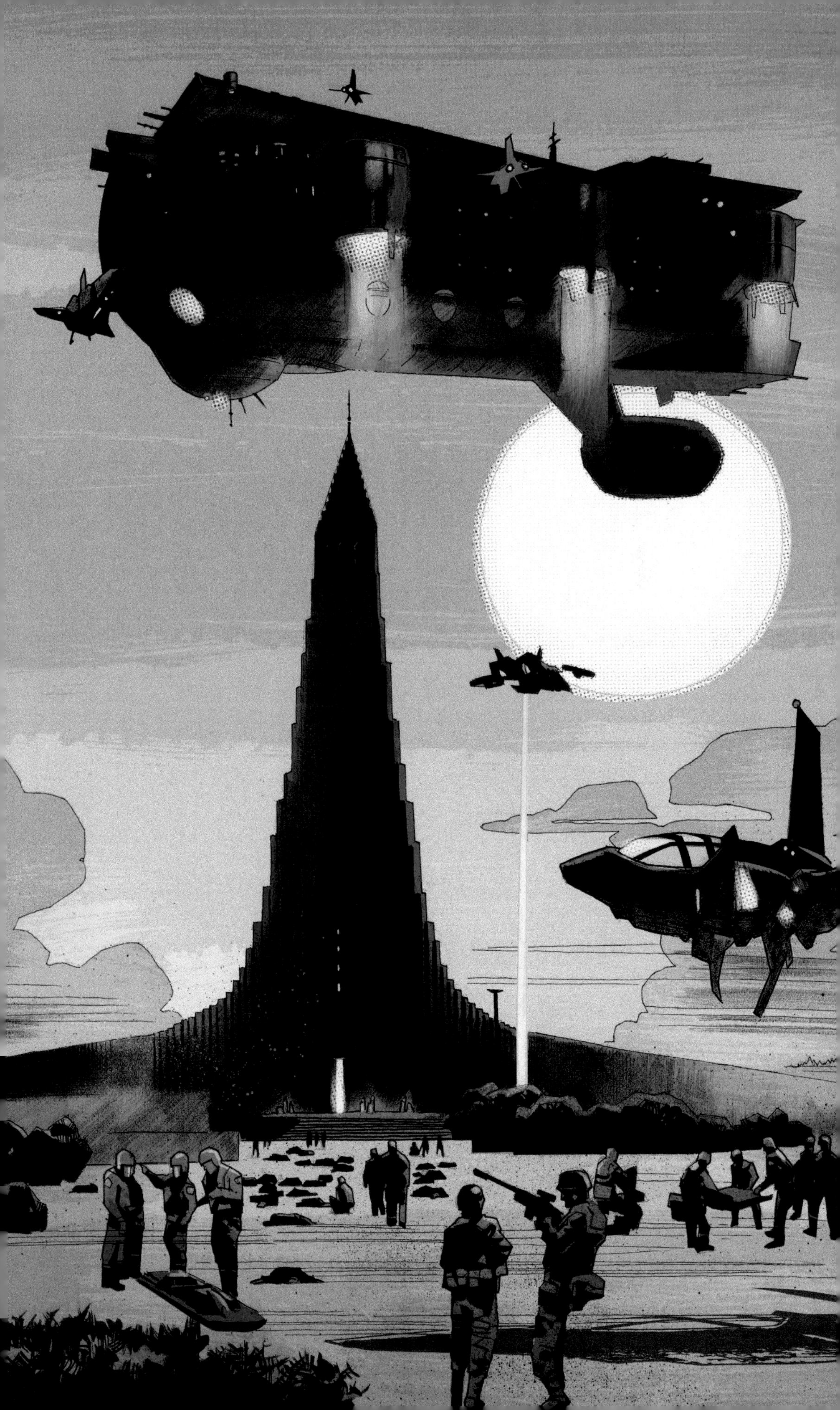

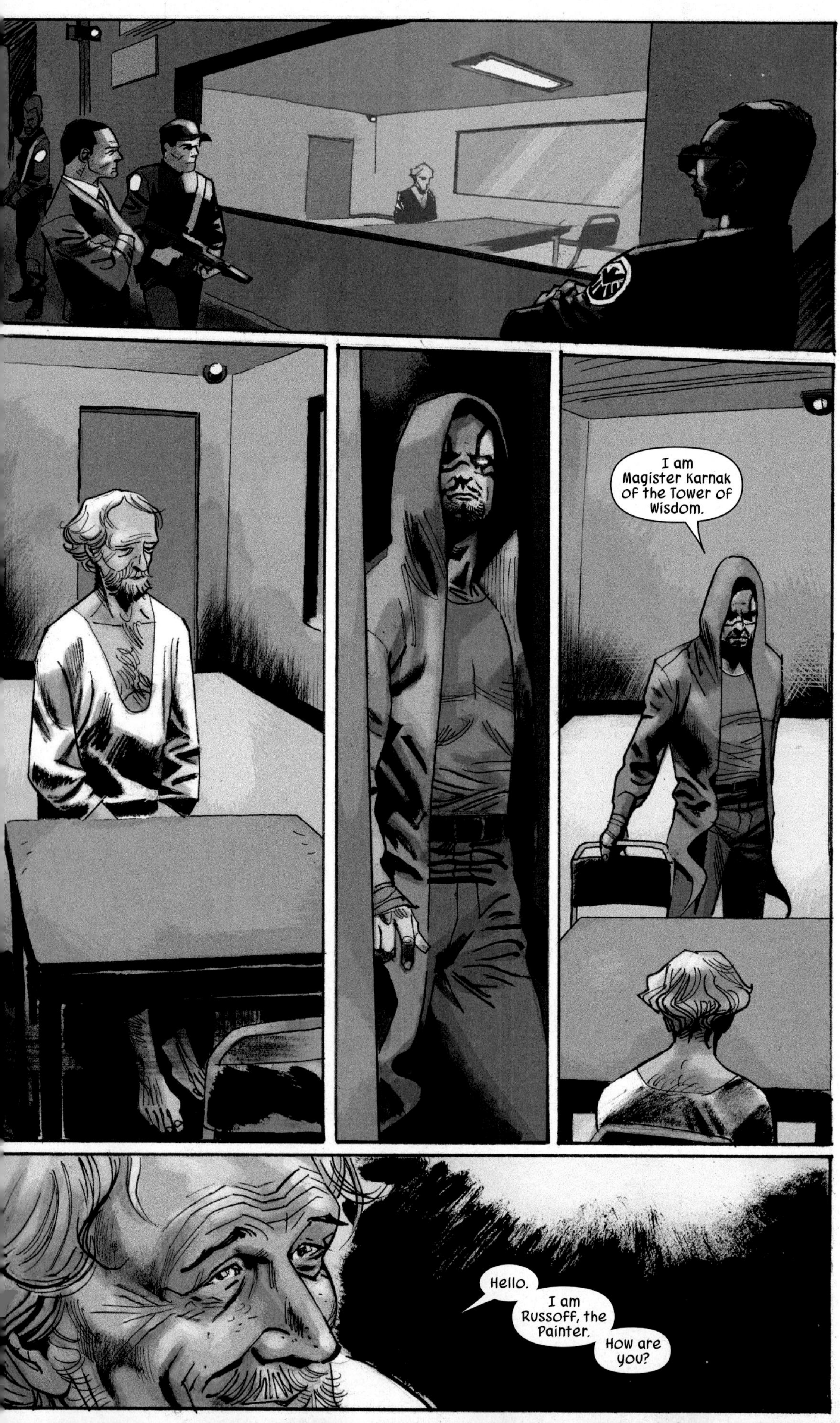
I am Magister Karnak of the Tower of Wisdom.
Hello.
I am Russoff, the Painter.
How are you?

I am...a little disturbed.

You were found in the bowels of a church evidently dedicated to the incarceration of a confused young Inhuman.

I heard you speaking to Adam in the great hall. You know he wasn't being held against his will.

But he was certainly abducted in the first instance.

NO, no. He was invited. He chose to come with us.

So you all keep saying. Were you involved, or was this just the story you were told?

This is the story Adam told me, on the day he made me the Painter.

And how did he make you a painter? Did that require magical powers?

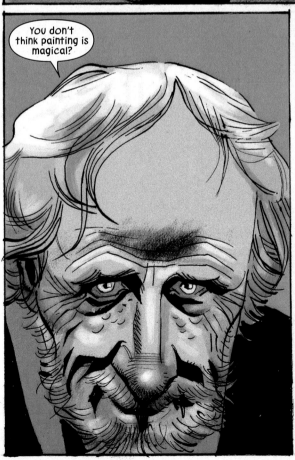

You don't think painting is magical?

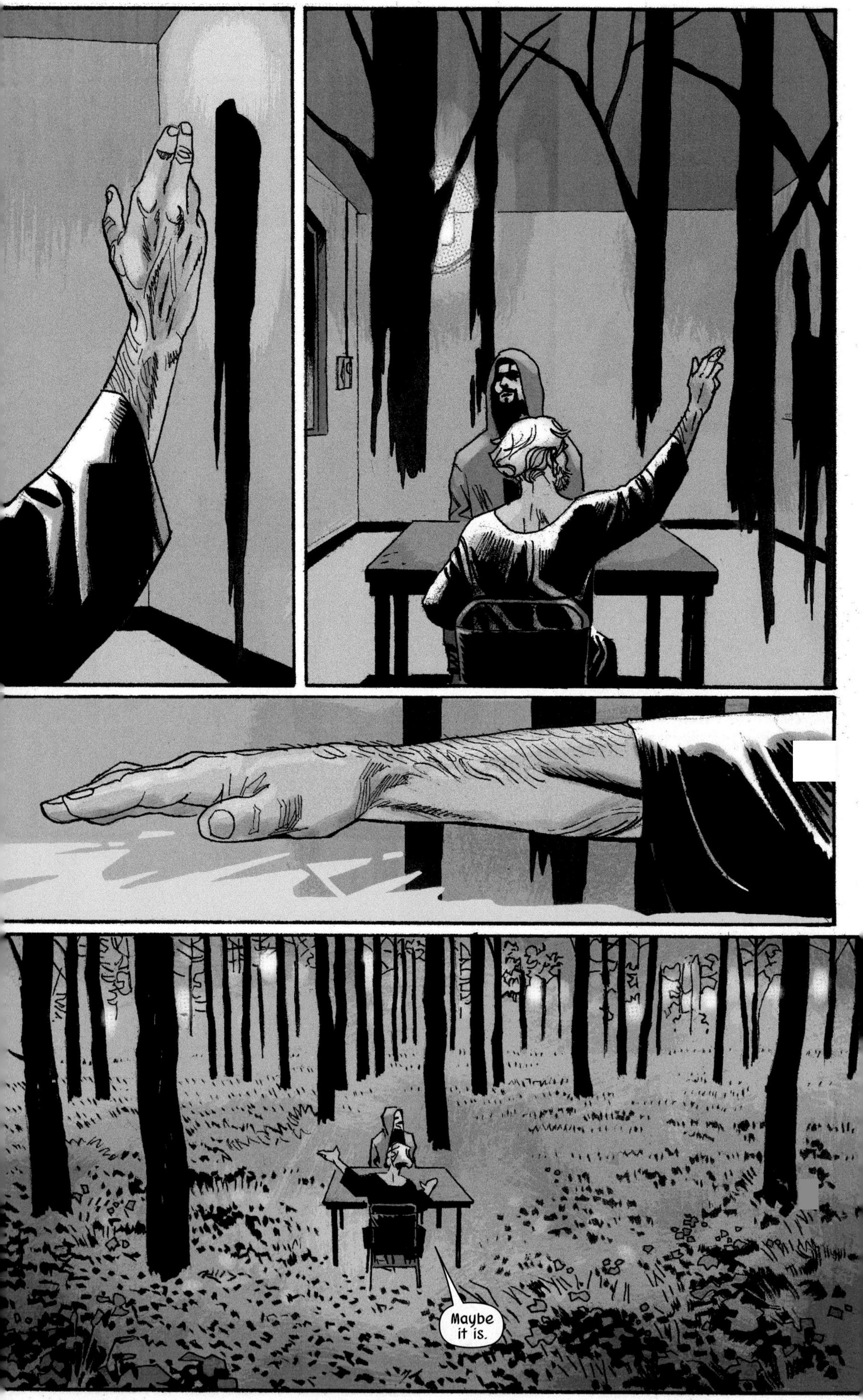
Maybe
it is.

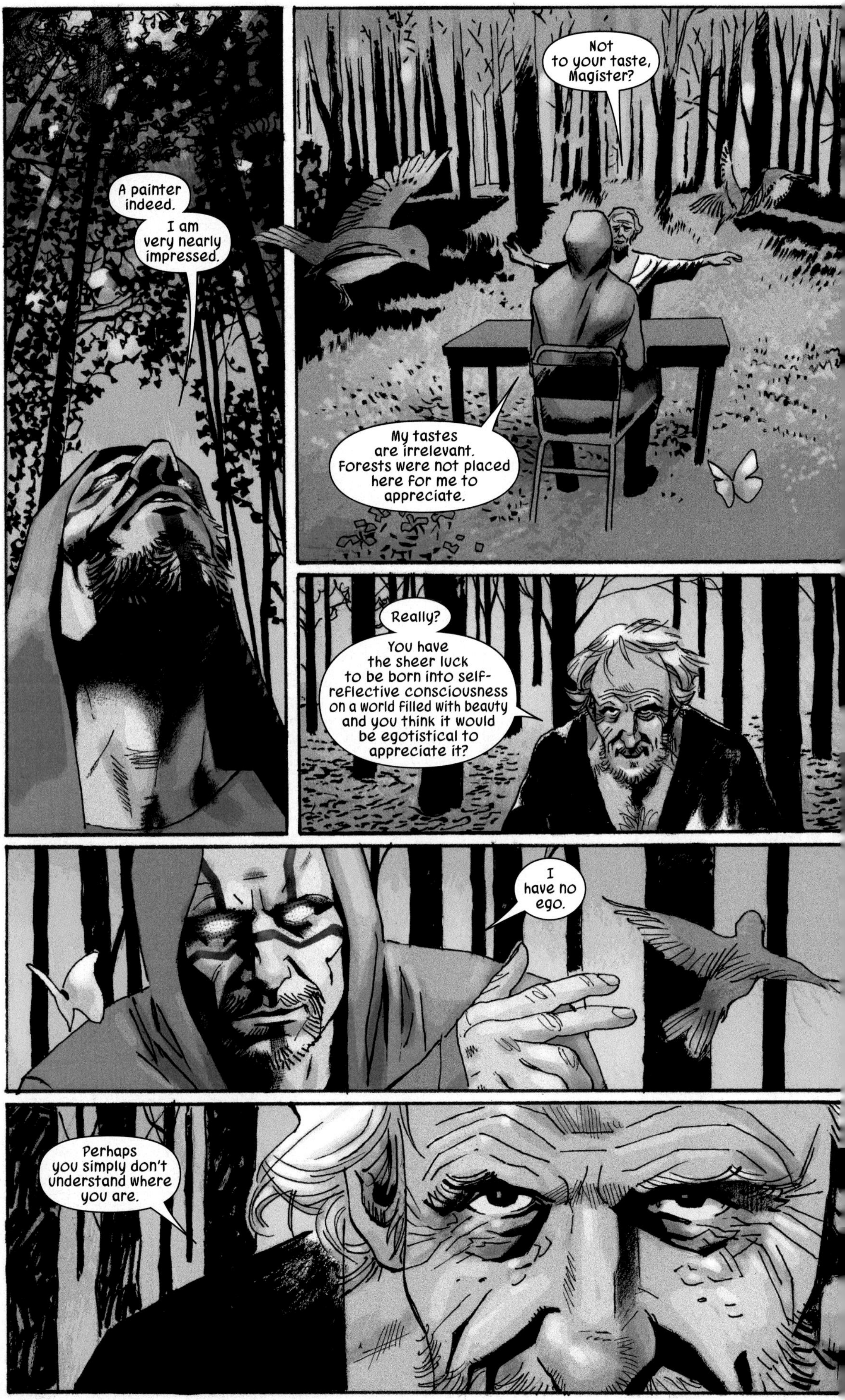
A painter indeed.
I am very nearly impressed.
Not to your taste, Magister?
My tastes are irrelevant. Forests were not placed here for me to appreciate.
Really?
You have the sheer luck to be born into self-reflective consciousness on a world filled with beauty and you think it would be egotistical to appreciate it?
I have no ego.
Perhaps you simply don't understand where you are.

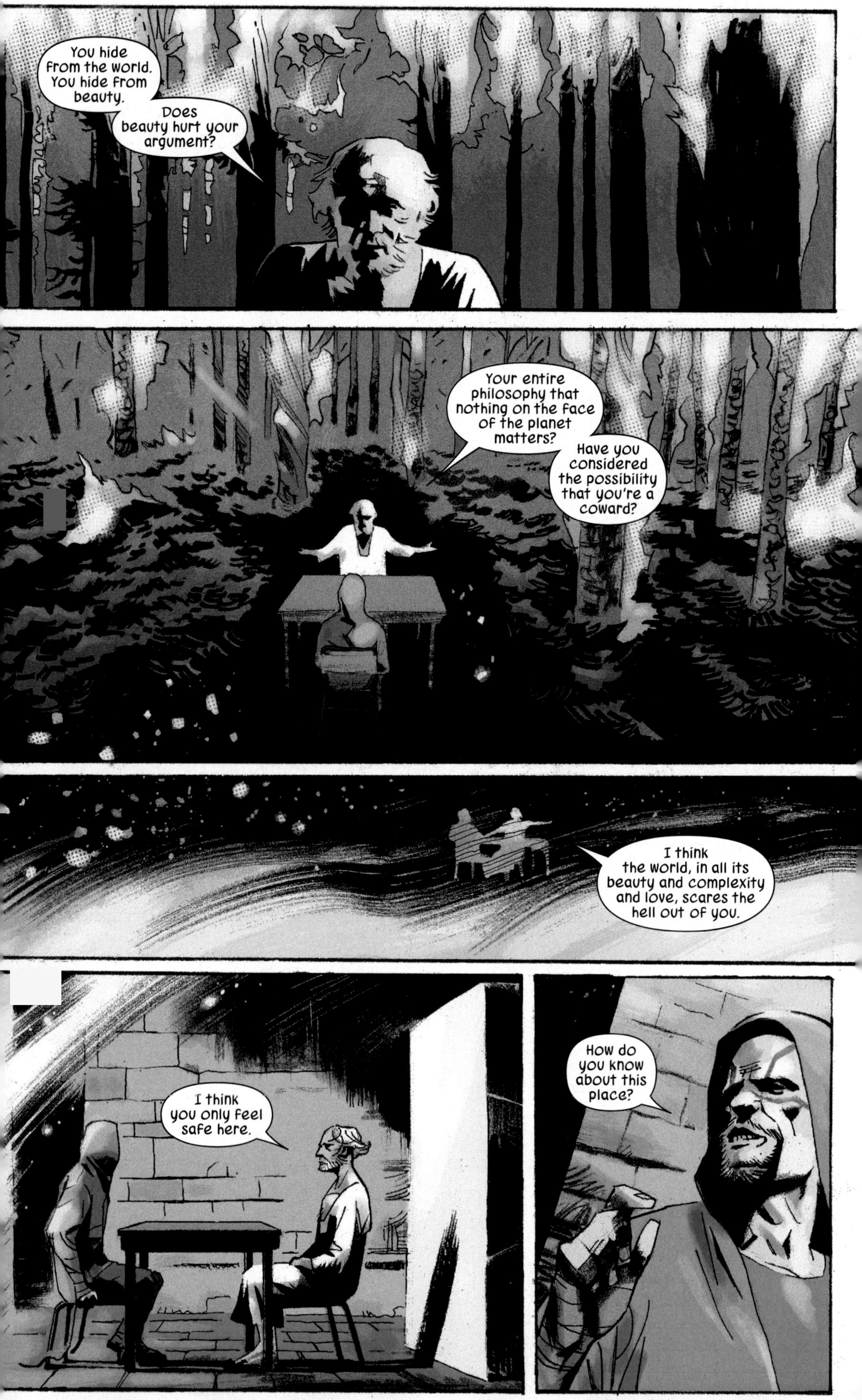
You hide from the world. You hide from beauty.
Does beauty hurt your argument?
Your entire philosophy that nothing on the face of the planet matters?
Have you considered the possibility that you're a coward?
I think the world, in all its beauty and complexity and love, scares the hell out of you.
I think you only feel safe here.
How do you know about this place?

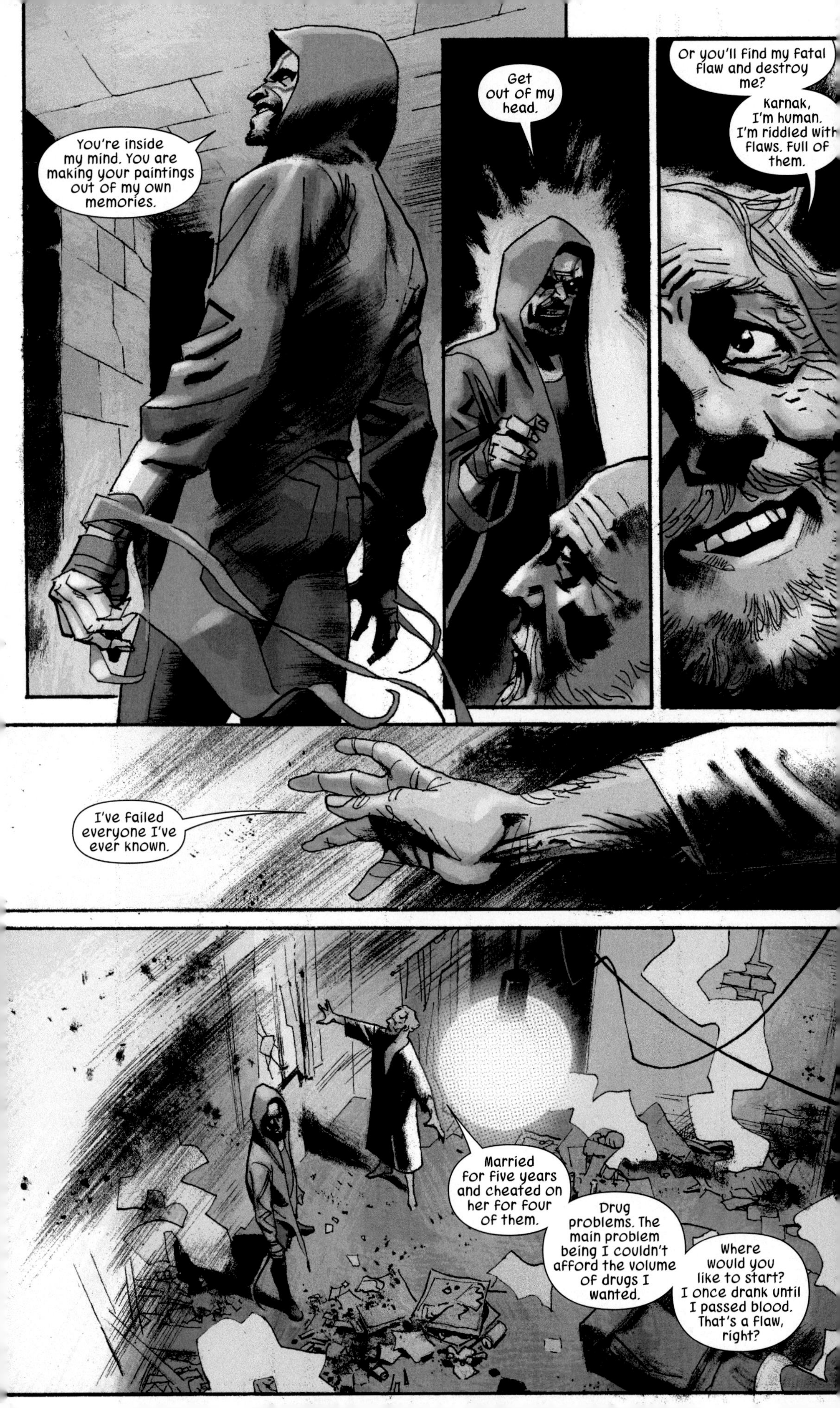
You're inside my mind. You are making your paintings out of my own memories.
Get out of my head.
Or you'll find my fatal flaw and destroy me?
Karnak, I'm human. I'm riddled with flaws. Full of them.
I've failed everyone I've ever known.
Married for five years and cheated on her for four of them.
Drug problems. The main problem being I couldn't afford the volume of drugs I wanted.
Where would you like to start? I once drank until I passed blood. That's a flaw, right?

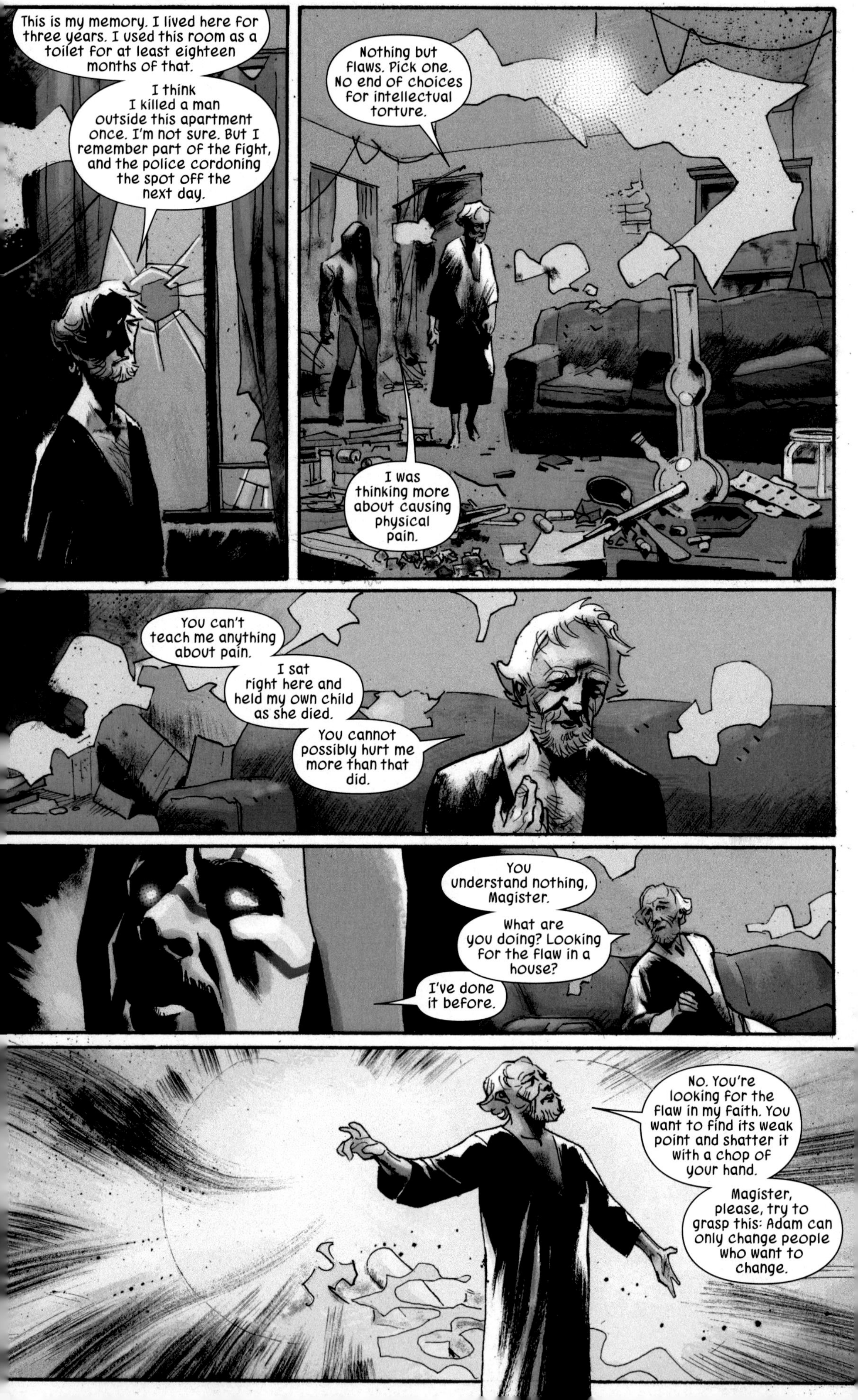

This is my memory. I lived here for three years. I used this room as a toilet for at least eighteen months of that.
I think I killed a man outside this apartment once. I'm not sure. But I remember part of the fight, and the police cordoning the spot off the next day.
Nothing but flaws. Pick one. No end of choices for intellectual torture.
I was thinking more about causing physical pain.
You can't teach me anything about pain.
I sat right here and held my own child as she died.
You cannot possibly hurt me more than that did.
You understand nothing, Magister.
What are you doing? Looking for the flaw in a house?
I've done it before.
No. You're looking for the flaw in my faith. You want to find its weak point and shatter it with a chop of your hand.
Magister, please, try to grasp this: Adam can only change people who want to change.

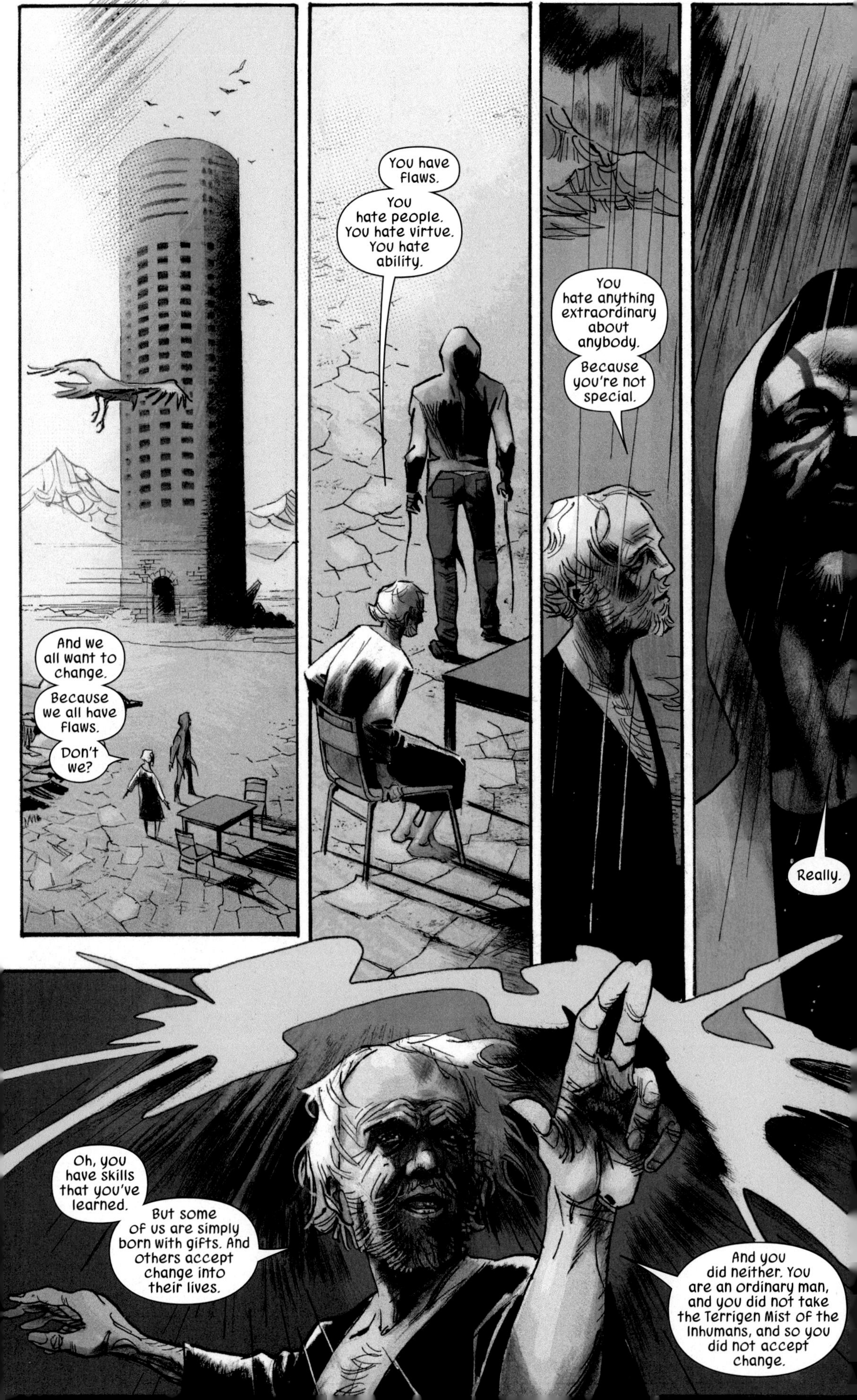

And we all want to change.
Because we all have flaws.
Don't we?
You have flaws.
You hate people. You hate virtue. You hate ability.
You hate anything extraordinary about anybody.
Because you're not special.
Really.
Oh, you have skills that you've learned.
But some of us are simply born with gifts. And others accept change into their lives.
And you did neither. You are an ordinary man, and you did not take the Terrigen Mist of the Inhumans, and so you did not accept change.

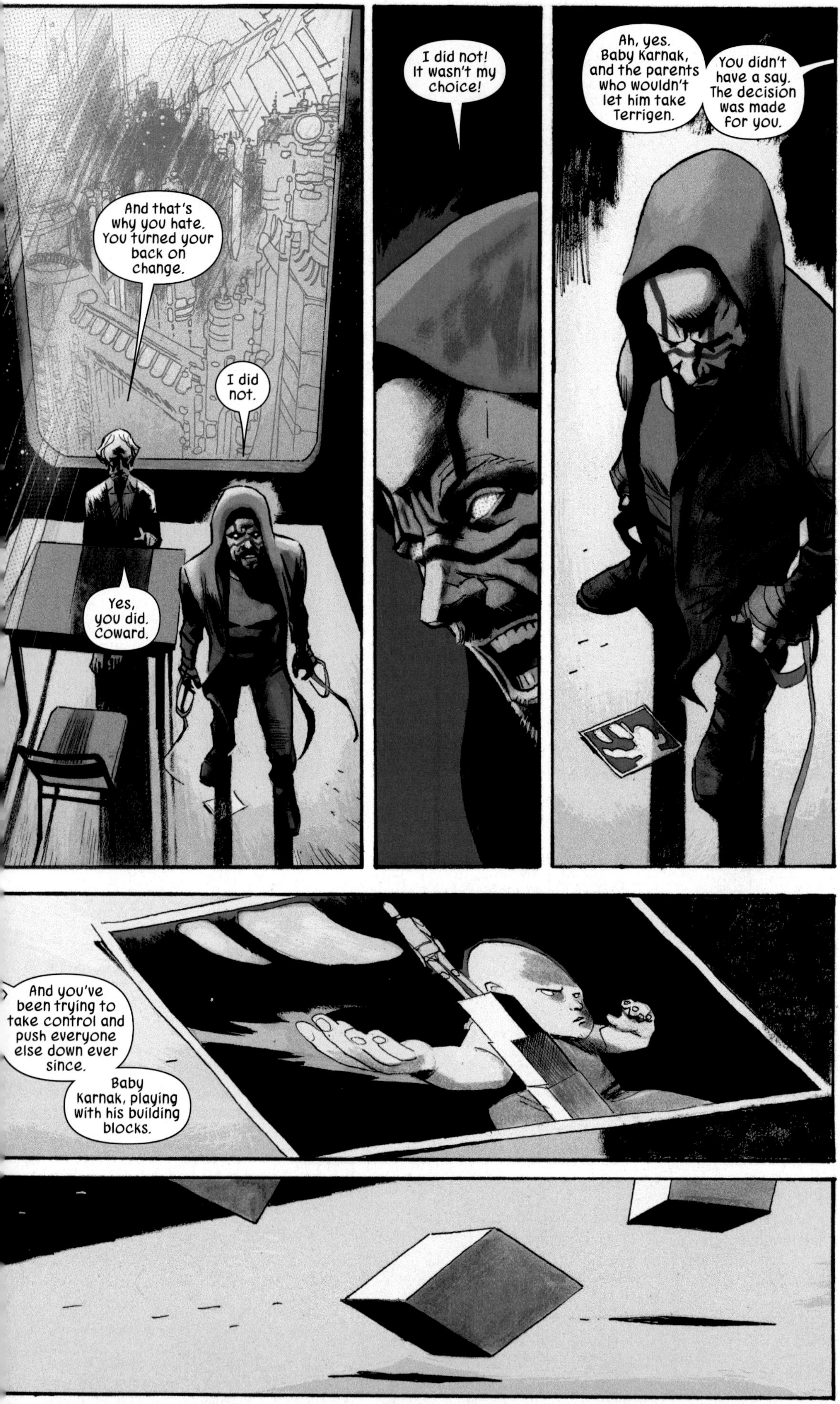

And that's why you hate. You turned your back on change.
I did not.
Yes, you did. Coward.
I did not! It wasn't my choice!
Ah, yes. Baby Karnak, and the parents who wouldn't let him take Terrigen.
You didn't have a say. The decision was made for you.
And you've been trying to take control and push everyone else down ever since.
Baby Karnak, playing with his building blocks.

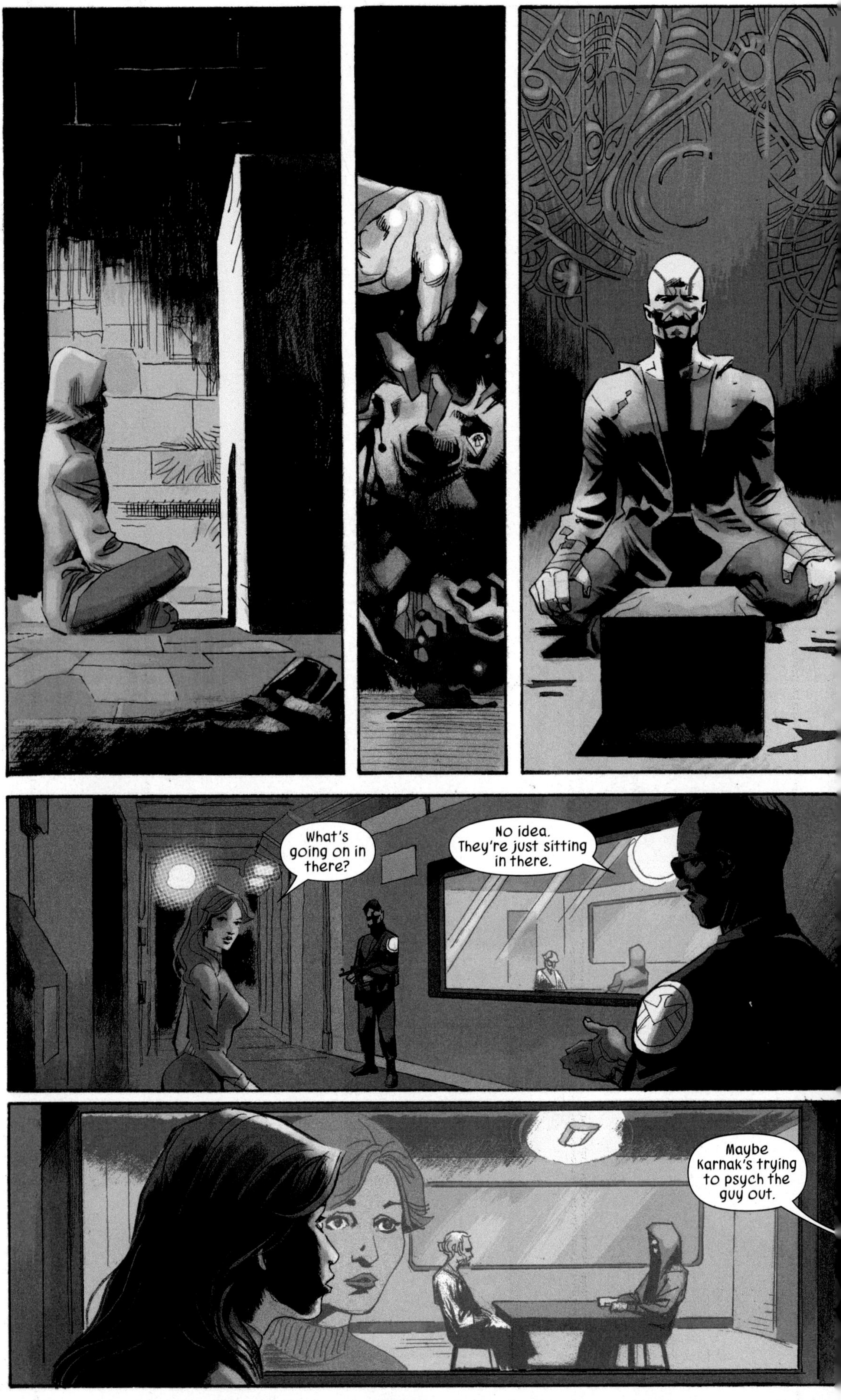
What's going on in there?
No idea. They're just sitting in there.
Maybe Karnak's trying to psych the guy out.

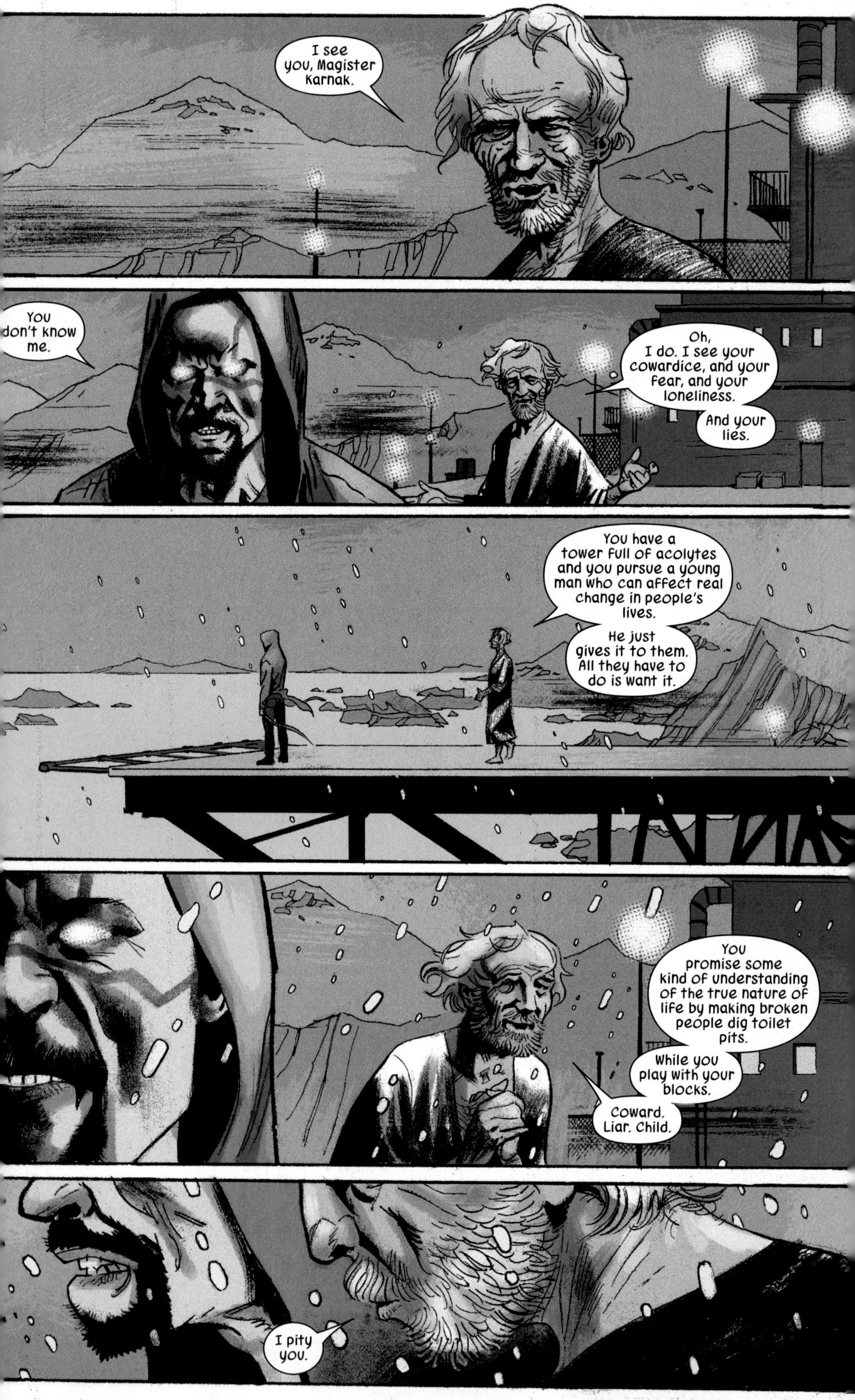
I see you, Magister Karnak.
You don't know me.
Oh, I do. I see your cowardice, and your fear, and your loneliness.
And your lies.
You have a tower full of acolytes and you pursue a young man who can affect real change in people's lives.
He just gives it to them. All they have to do is want it.
You promise some kind of understanding of the true nature of life by making broken people dig toilet pits.
While you play with your blocks.
Coward. Liar. Child.
I pity you.

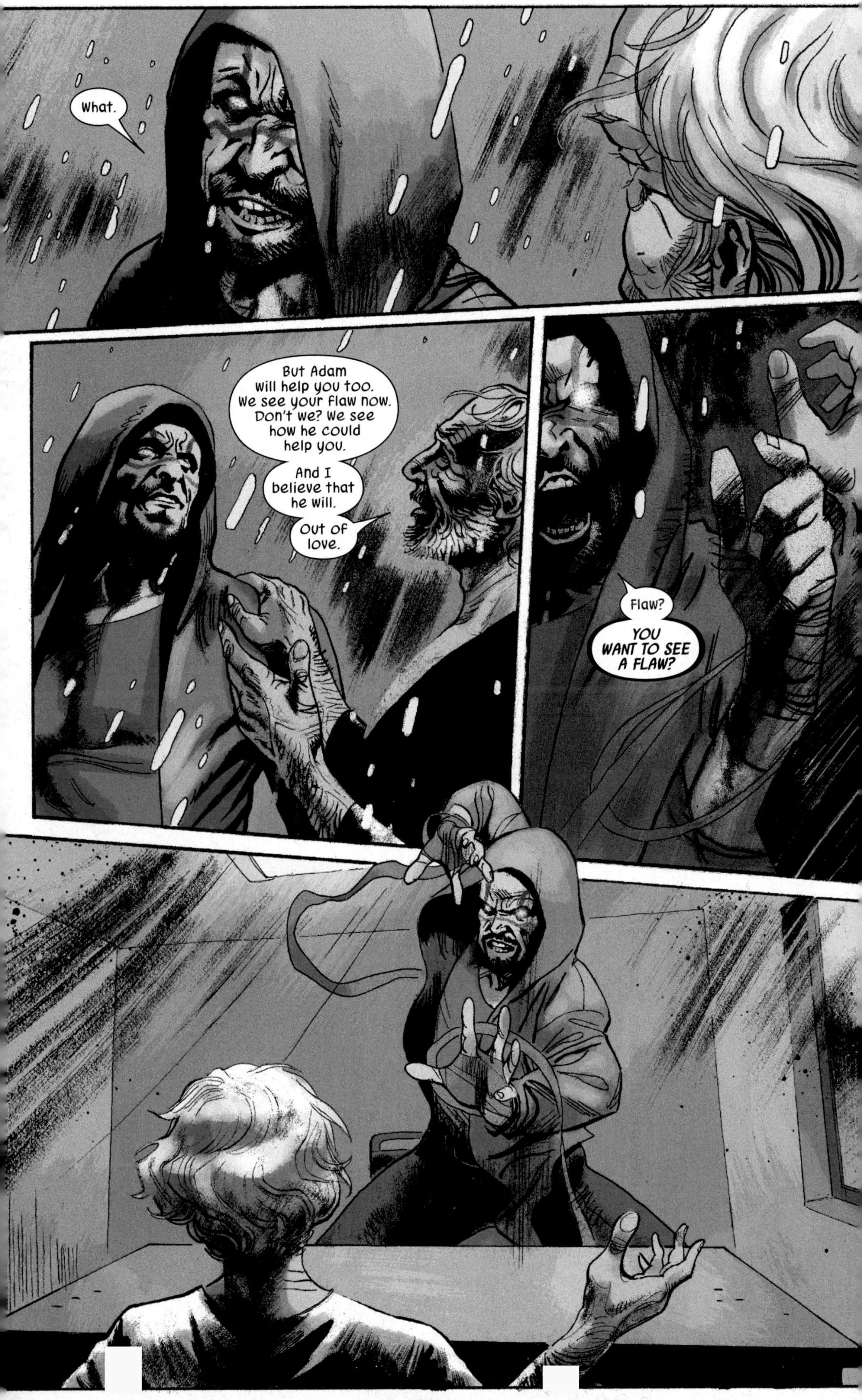
What.
But Adam will help you too. We see your flaw now. Don't we? We see how he could help you.
And I believe that he will.
Out of love.
Flaw?
YOU WANT TO SEE A FLAW?

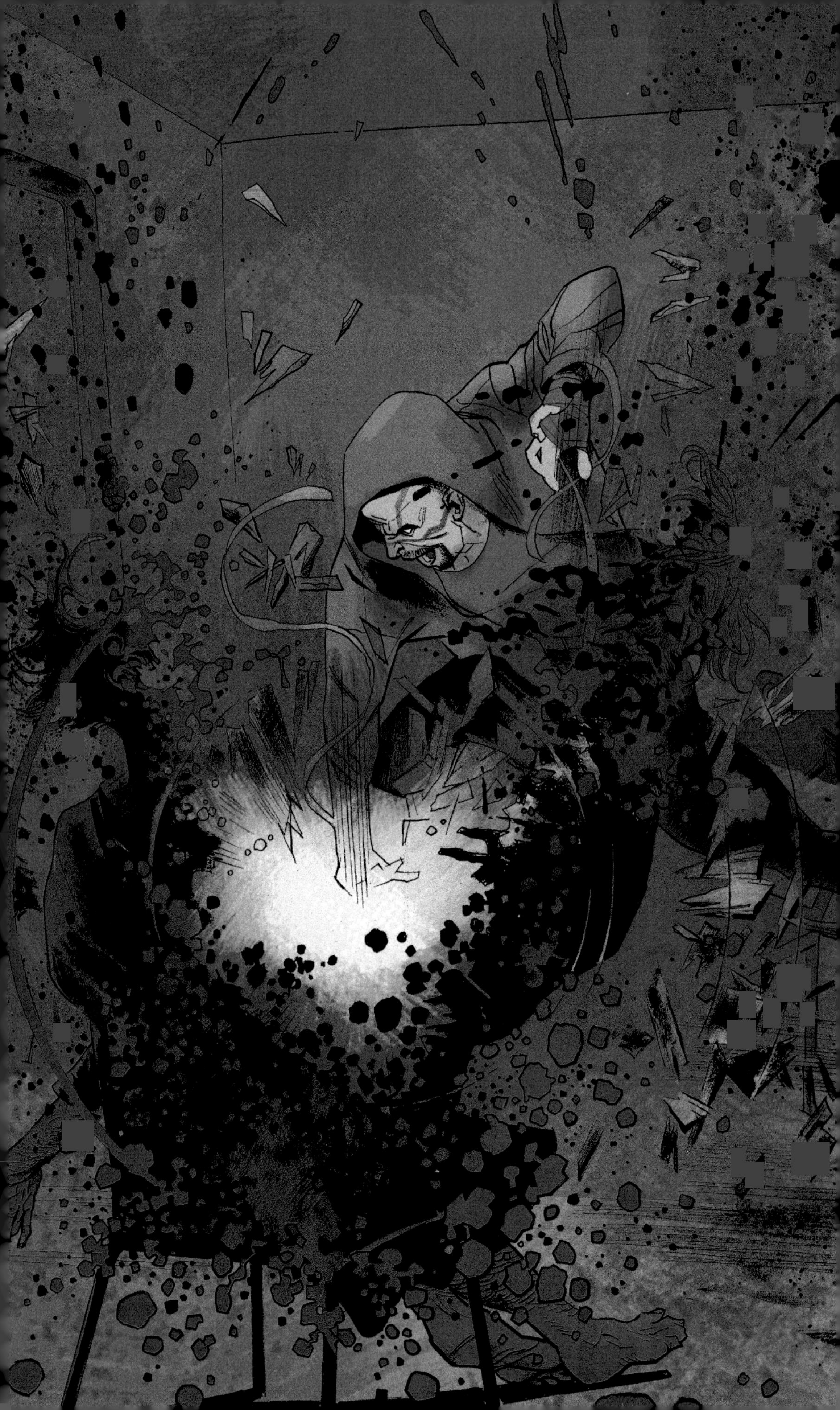

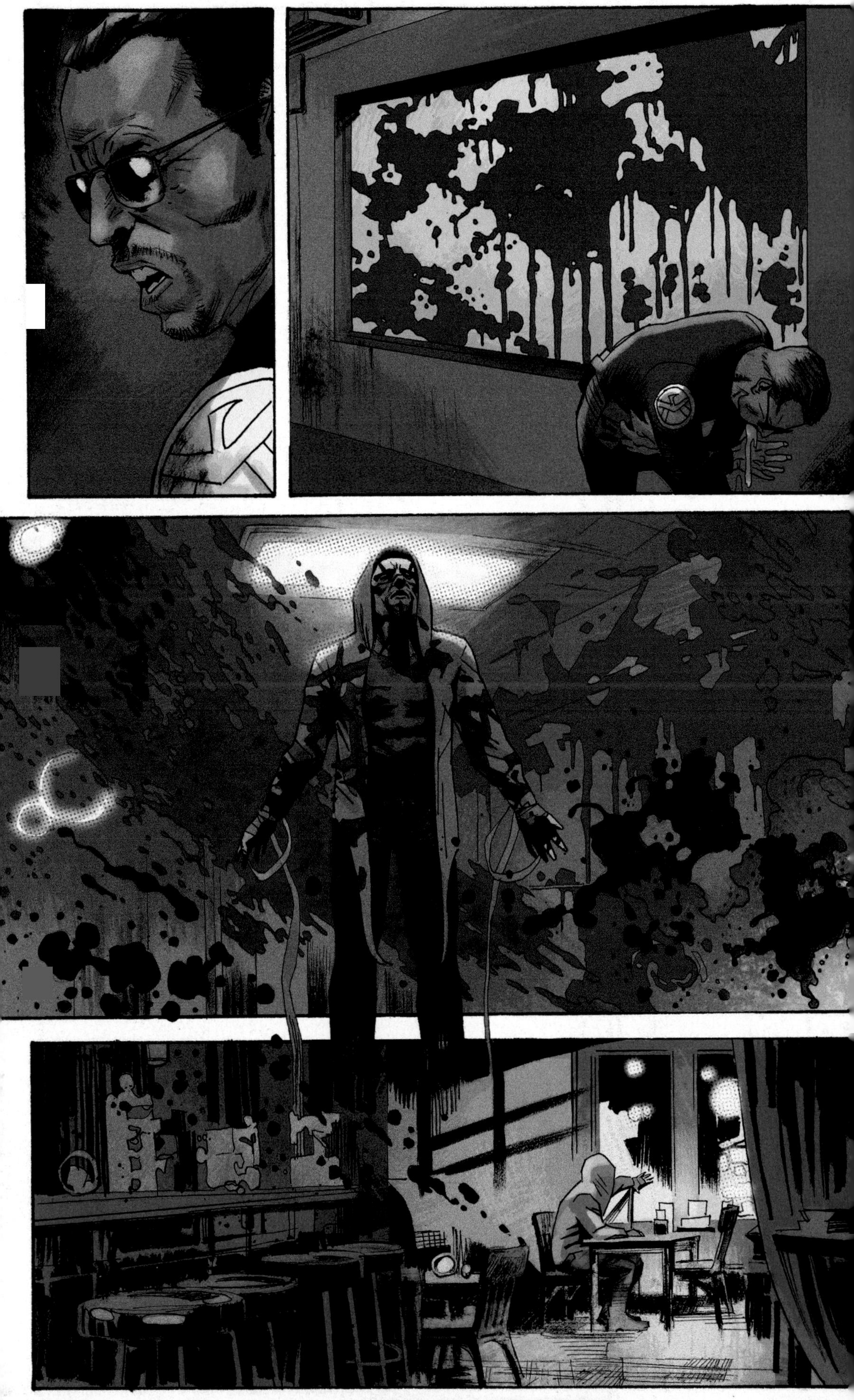

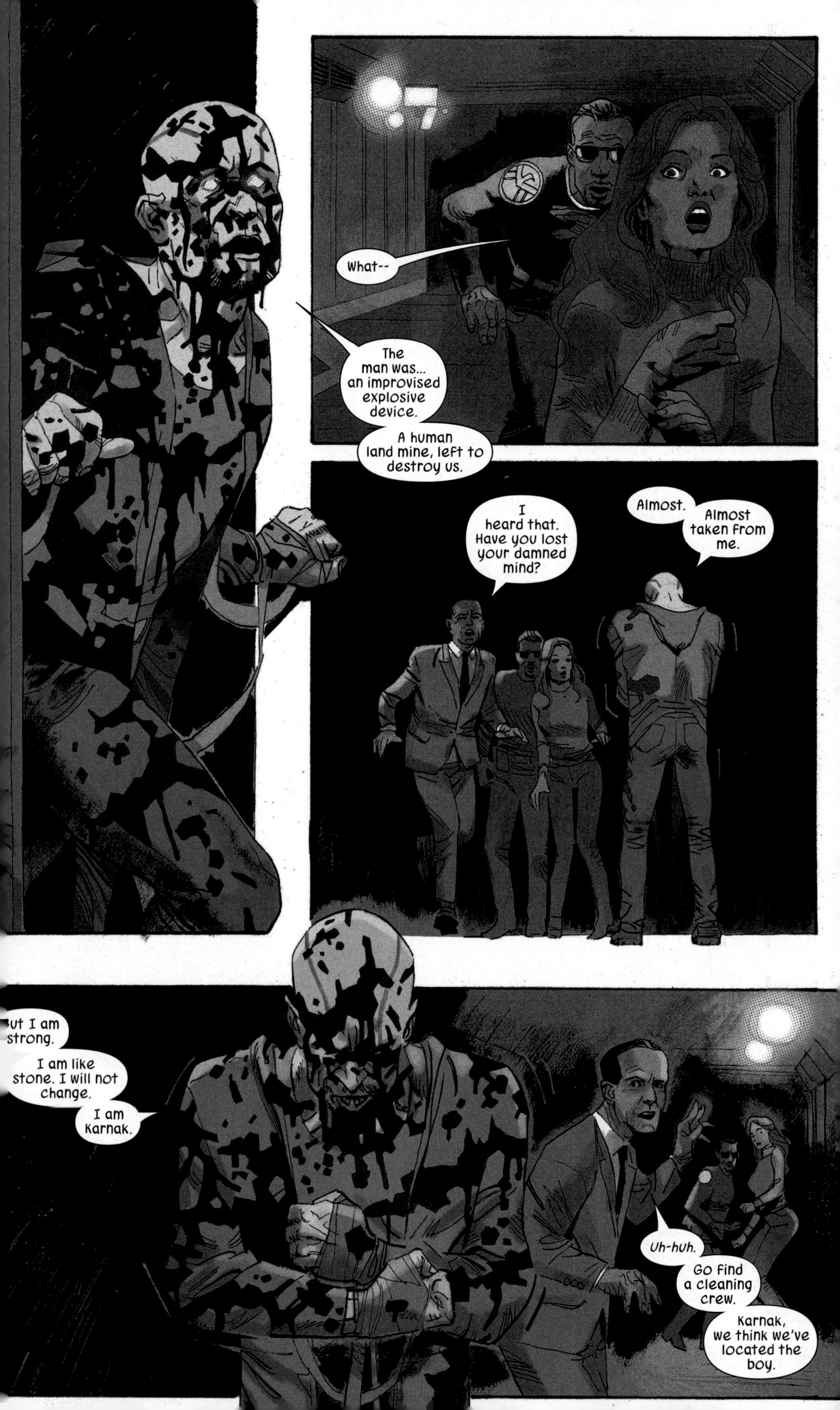
What--
The man was... an improvised explosive device.
A human land mine, left to destroy us.
I heard that. Have you lost your damned mind?
Almost.
Almost taken from me.
strong.
I am like stone. I will not change.
I am Karnak.
Uh-huh.
Go find a cleaning crew.
Karnak, we think we've located the boy.

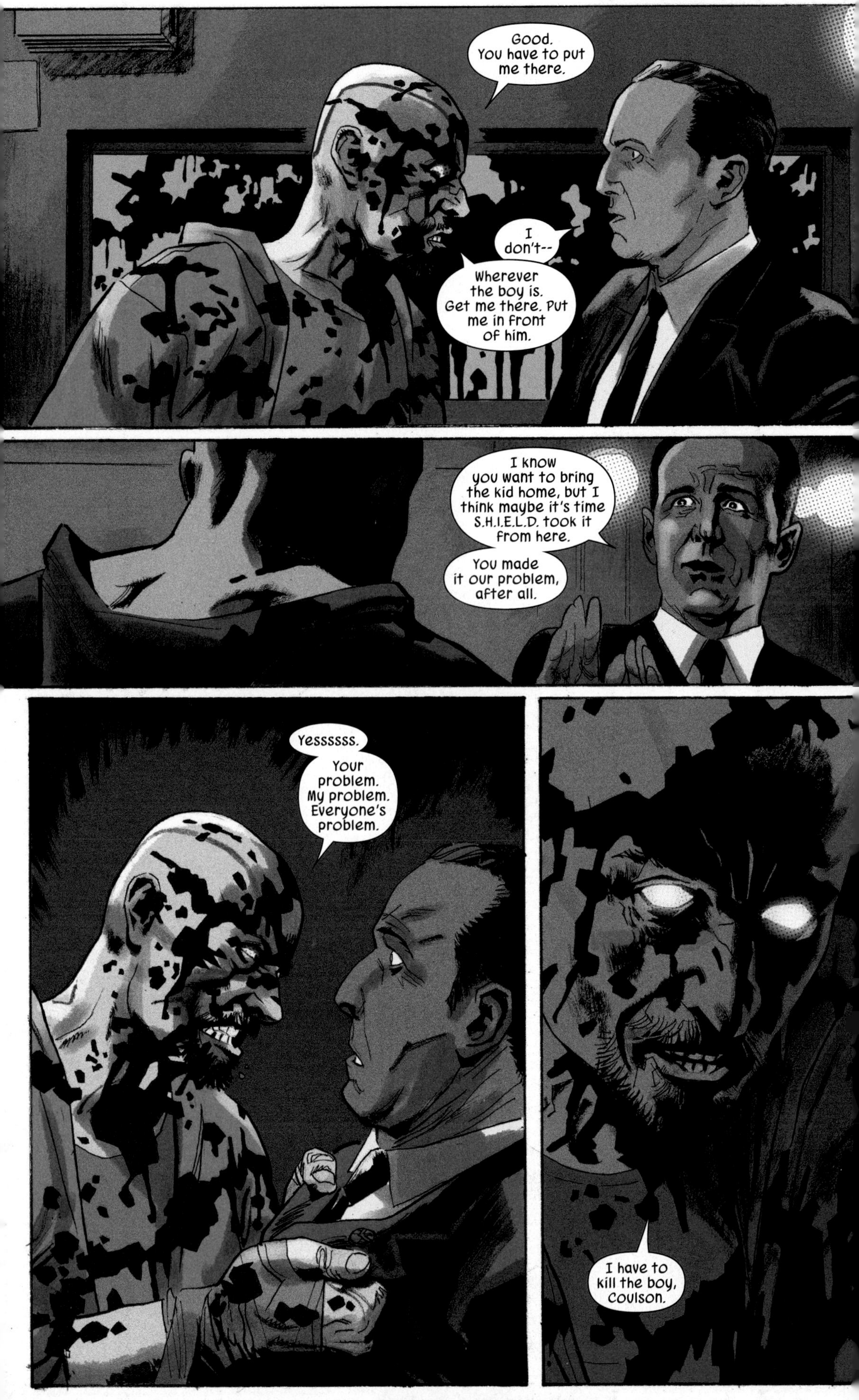
Good. You have to put me there.
I don't--
Wherever the boy is. Get me there. Put me in front of him.
I know you want to bring the kid home, but I think maybe it's time S.H.I.E.L.D. took it from here.
You made it our problem, after all.
Yesssssss.
Your problem. My problem. Everyone's problem.
I have to kill the boy, Coulson.

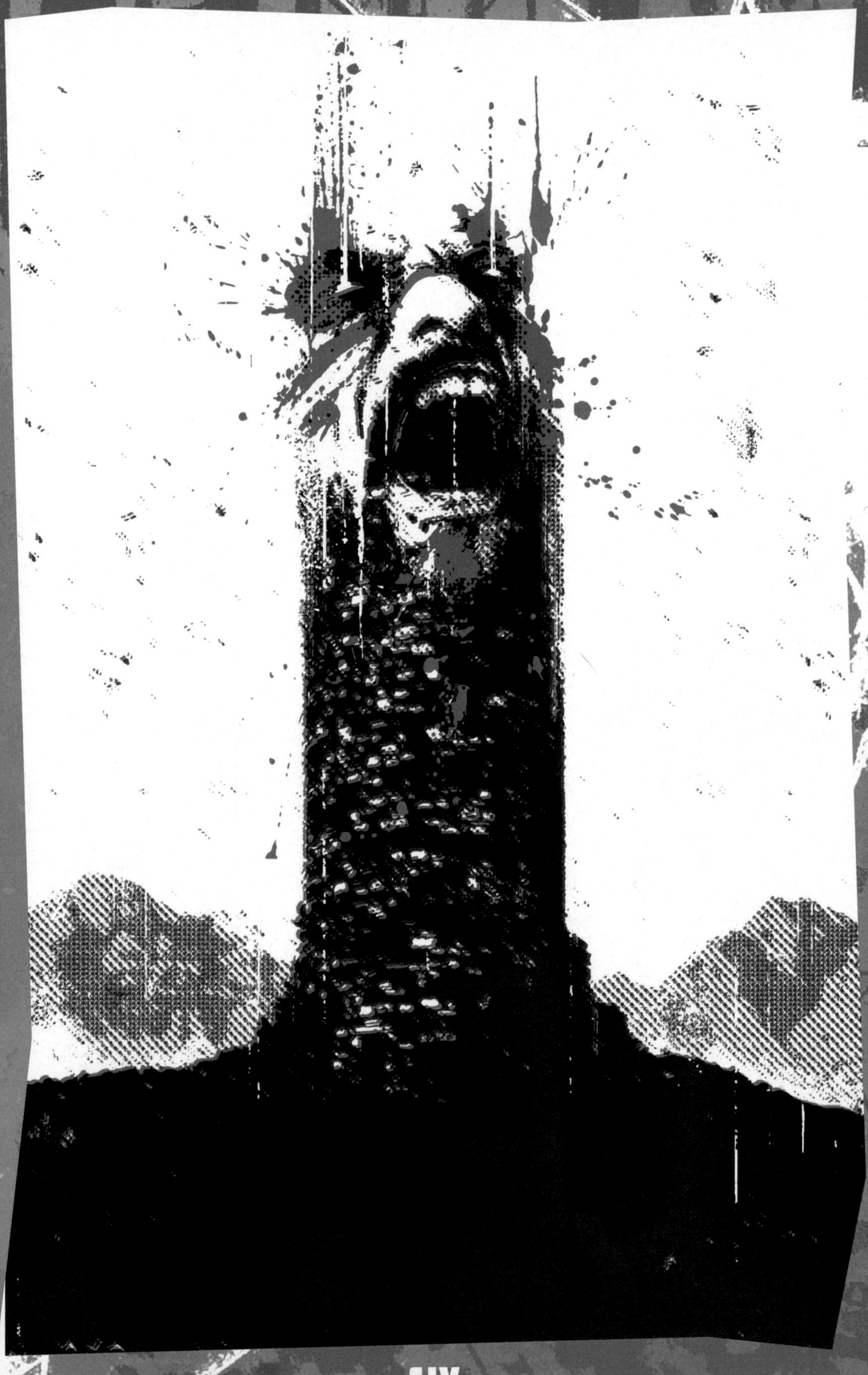

# SIX

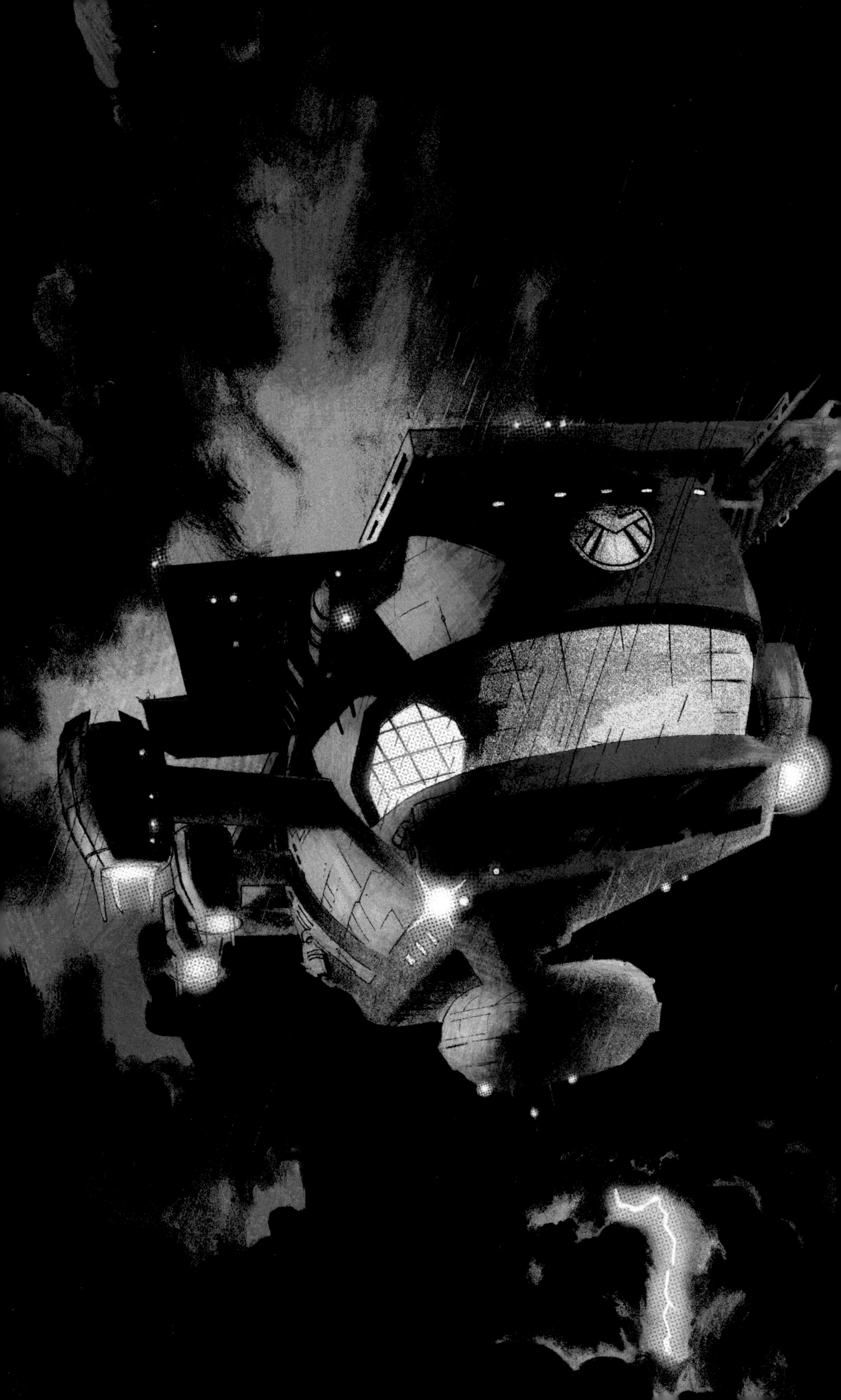

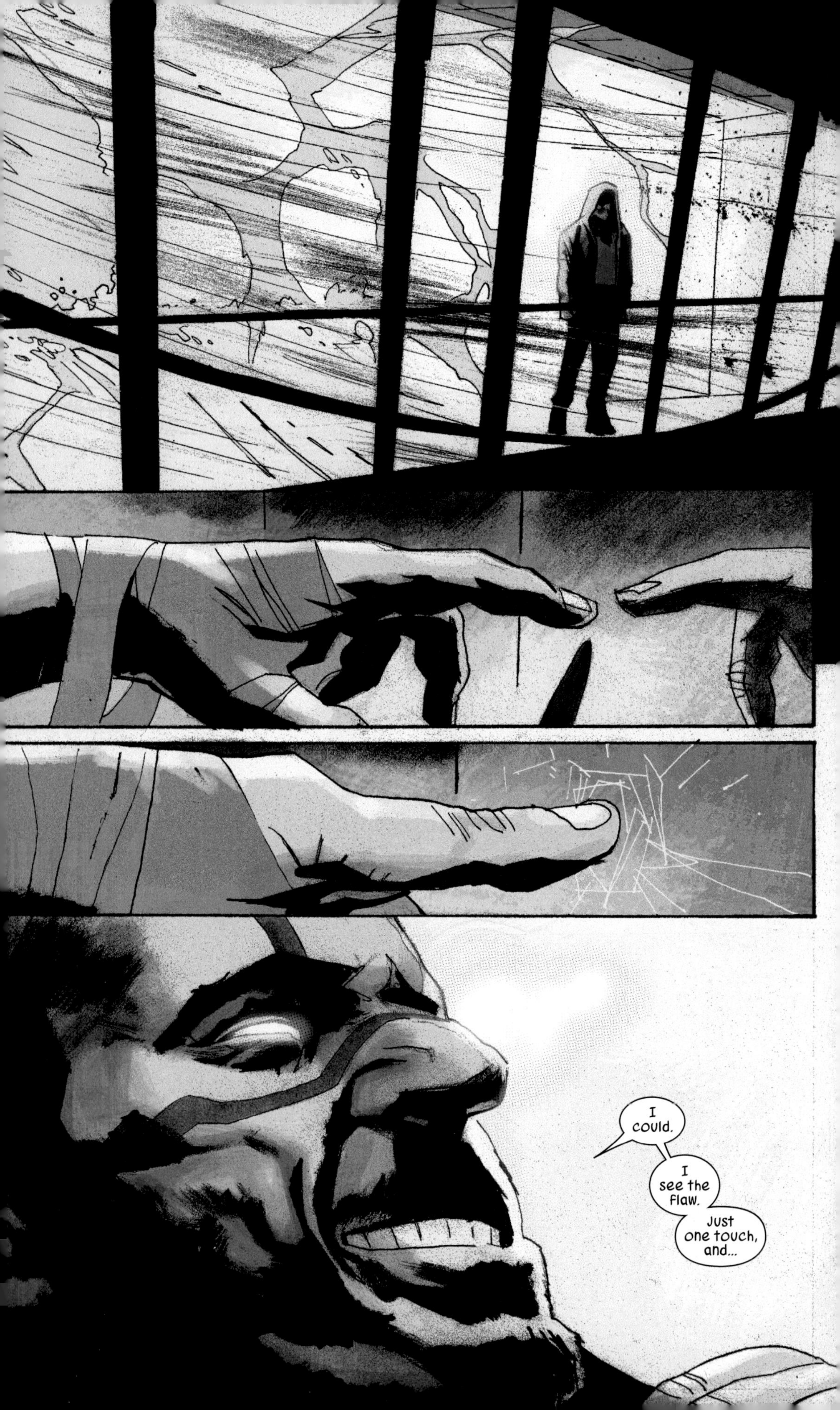
I could.
I see the flaw.
Just one touch, and...

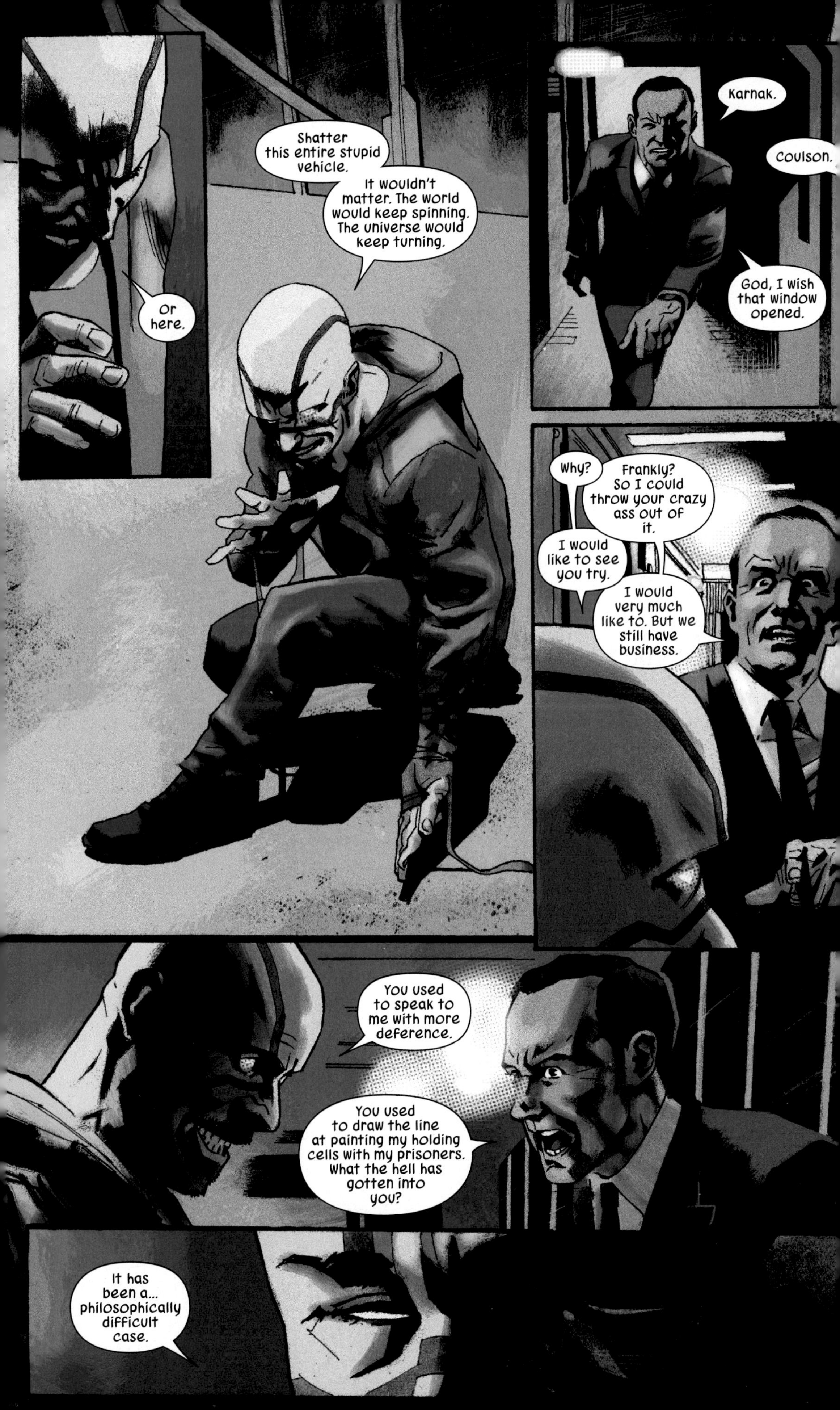
Or here.
Shatter this entire stupid vehicle.
It wouldn't matter. The world would keep spinning. The universe would keep turning.
Karnak.
Coulson.
God, I wish that window opened.
Why?
Frankly? So I could throw your crazy ass out of it.
I would like to see you try.
I would very much like to. But we still have business.
You used to speak to me with more deference.
You used to draw the line at painting my holding cells with my prisoners. What the hell has gotten into you?
It has been a... philosophically difficult case.

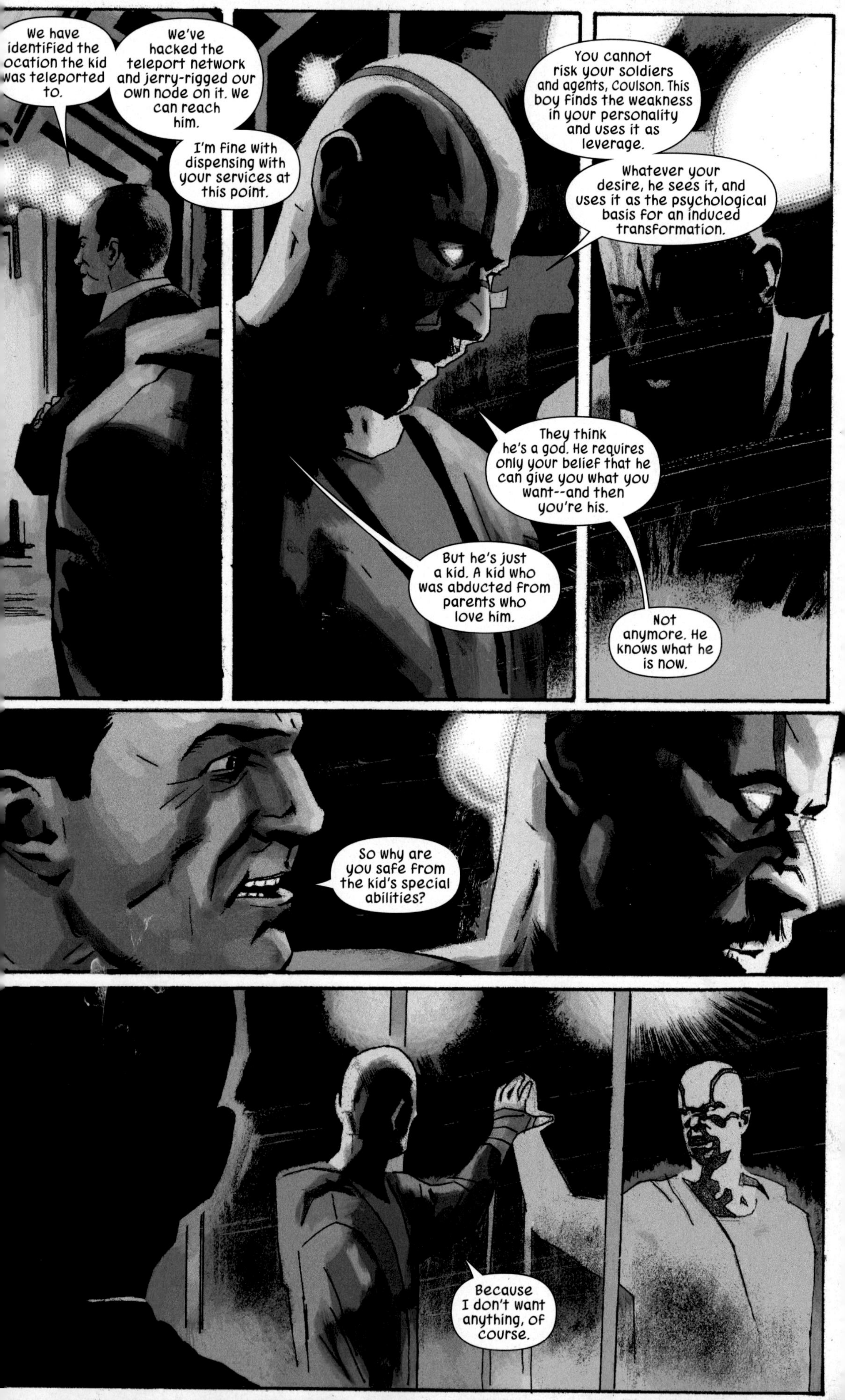
We have identified the ocation the kid was teleported to.
We've hacked the teleport network and jerry-rigged our own node on it. We can reach him.
I'm fine with dispensing with your services at this point.
You cannot risk your soldiers and agents, Coulson. This boy finds the weakness in your personality and uses it as leverage.
Whatever your desire, he sees it, and uses it as the psychological basis for an induced transformation.
They think he's a god. He requires only your belief that he can give you what you want--and then you're his.
But he's just a kid. A kid who was abducted from parents who love him.
Not anymore. He knows what he is now.
So why are you safe from the kid's special abilities?
Because I don't want anything, of course.

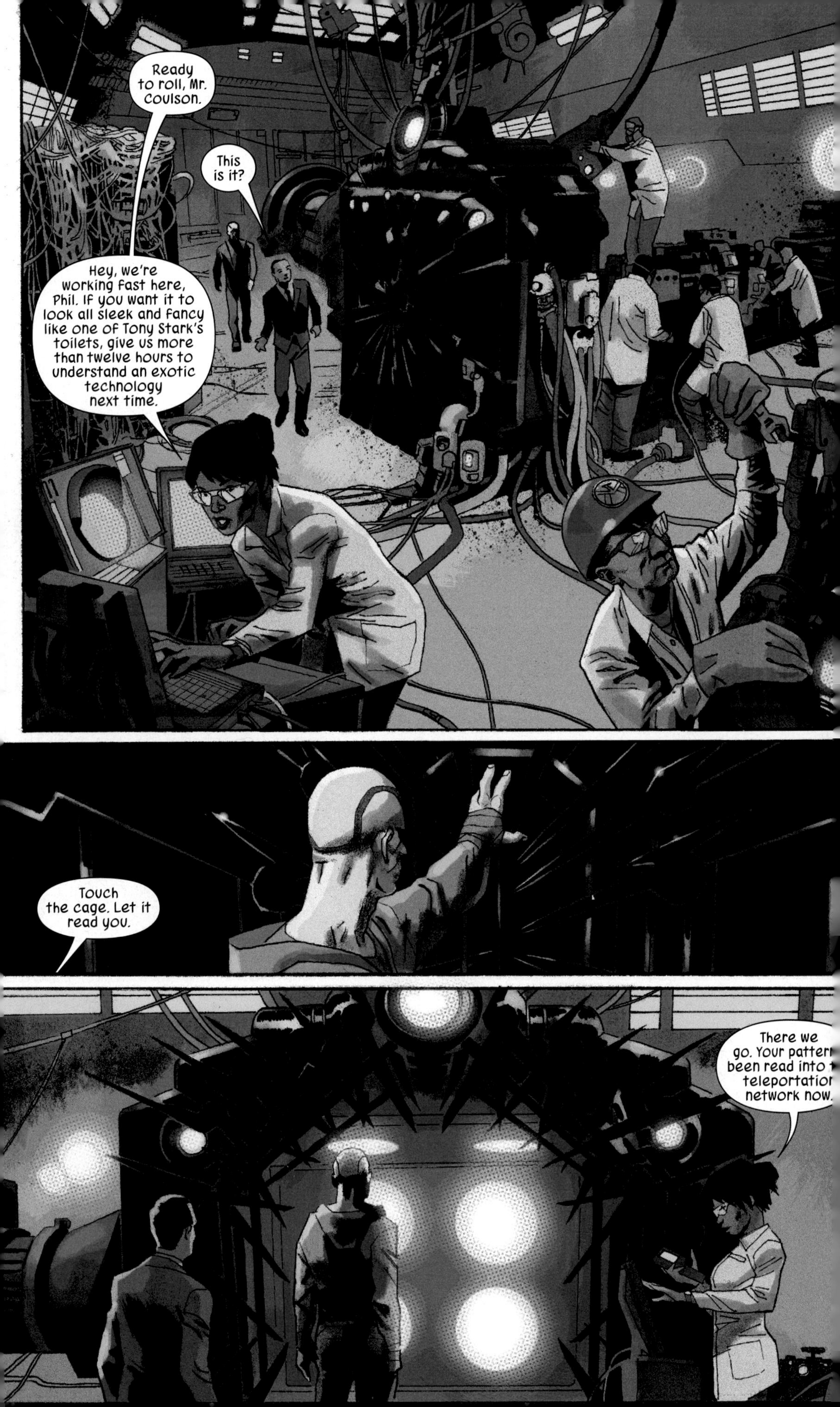
Ready to roll, Mr. Coulson.
This is it?
Hey, we're working fast here, Phil. If you want it to look all sleek and fancy like one of Tony Stark's toilets, give us more than twelve hours to understand an exotic technology next time.
Touch the cage. Let it read you.
There we go. Your pattern been read into the teleportation network now.

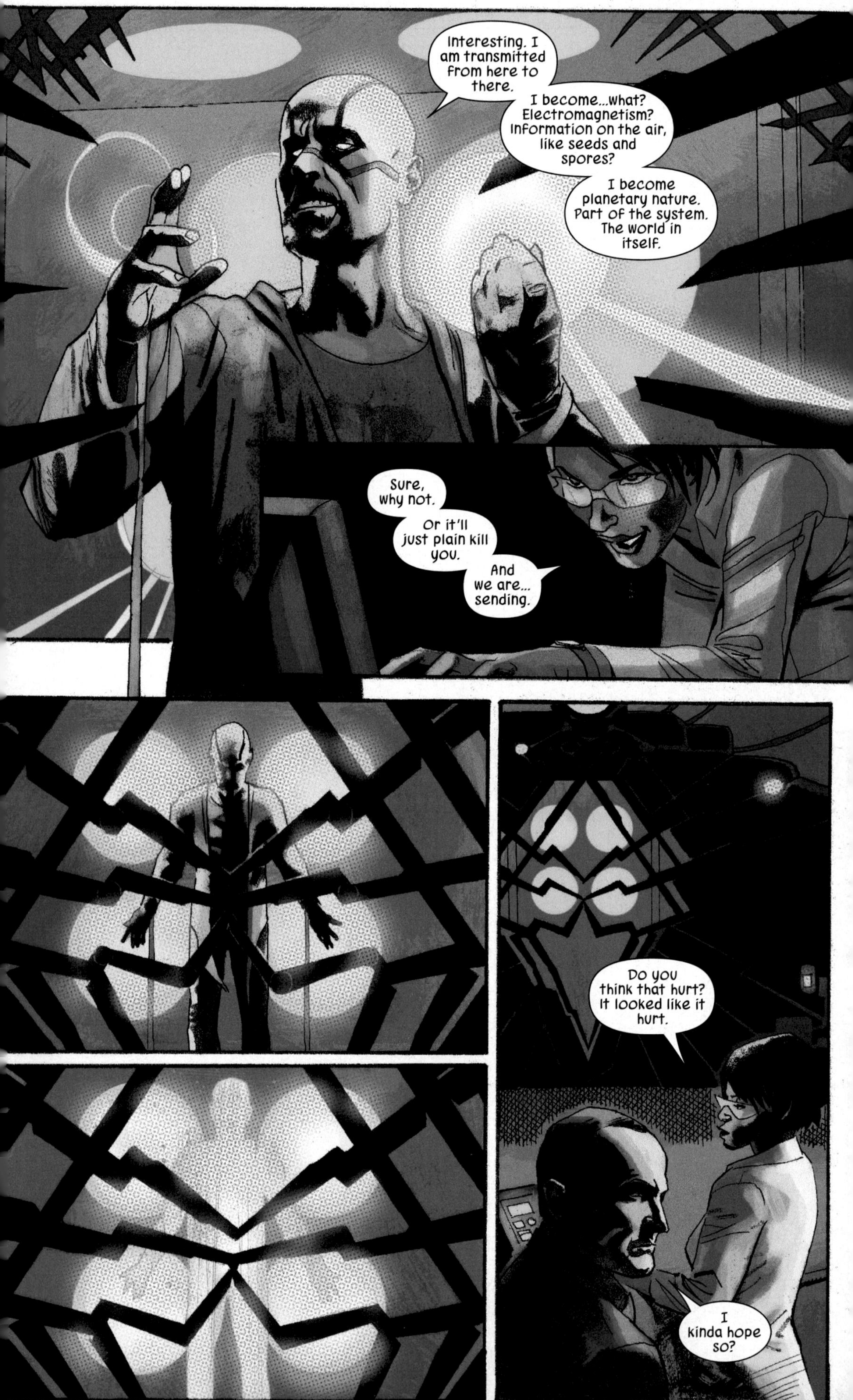
Interesting. I am transmitted from here to there.
I become...what? Electromagnetism? Information on the air, like seeds and spores?
I become planetary nature. Part of the system. The world in itself.
Sure, why not.
Or it'll just plain kill you.
And we are... sending.
Do you think that hurt? It looked like it hurt.
I kinda hope so?

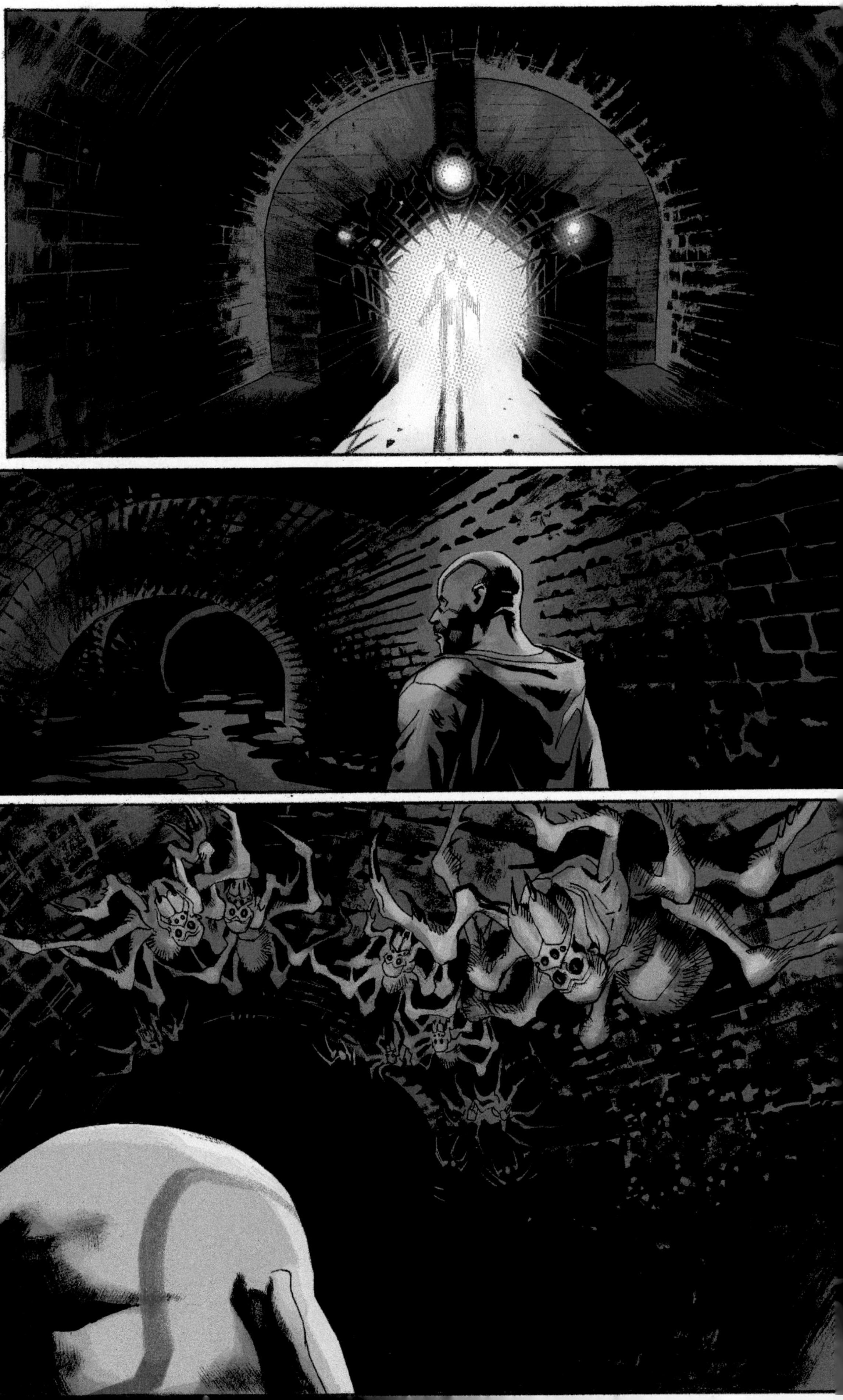

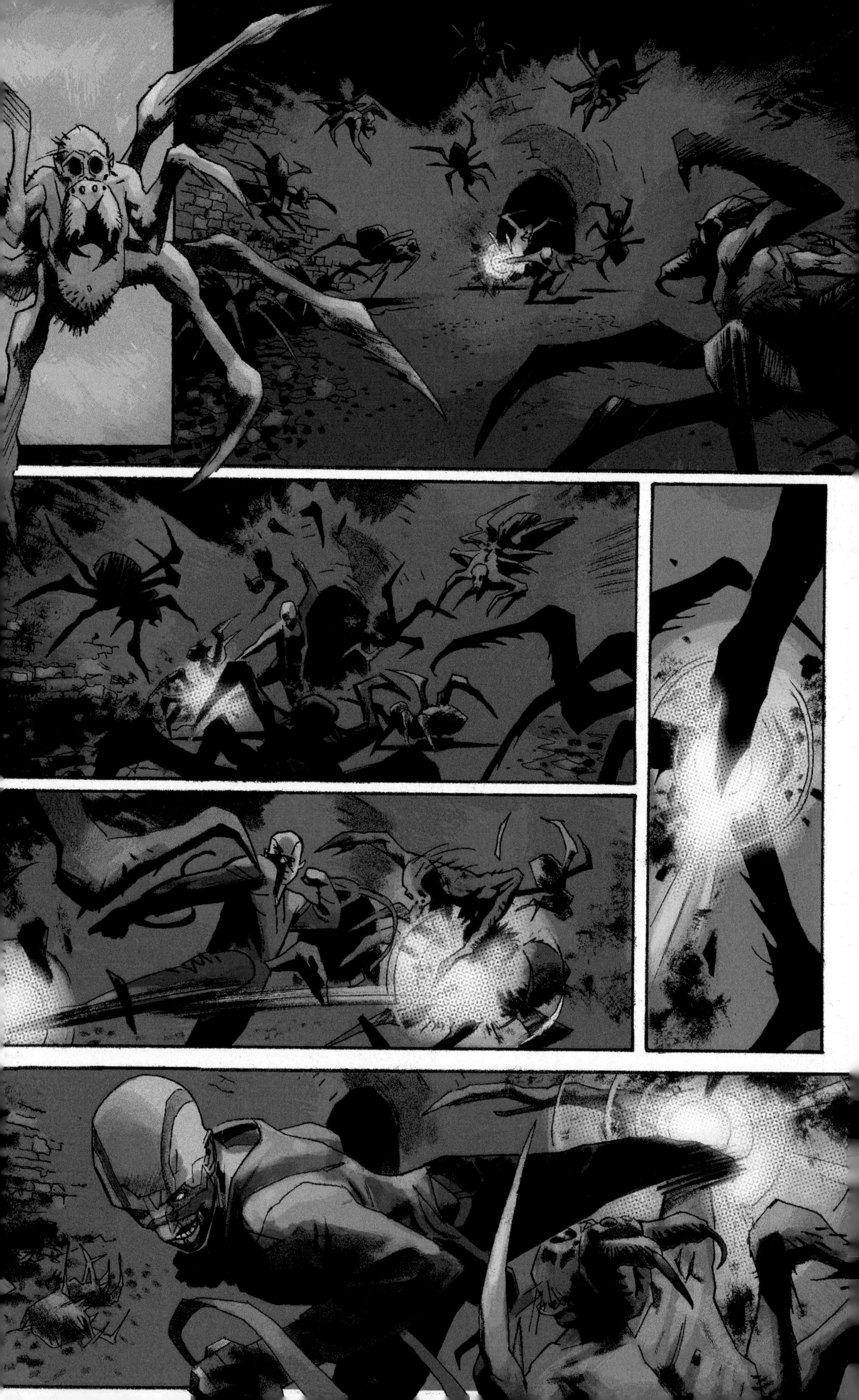

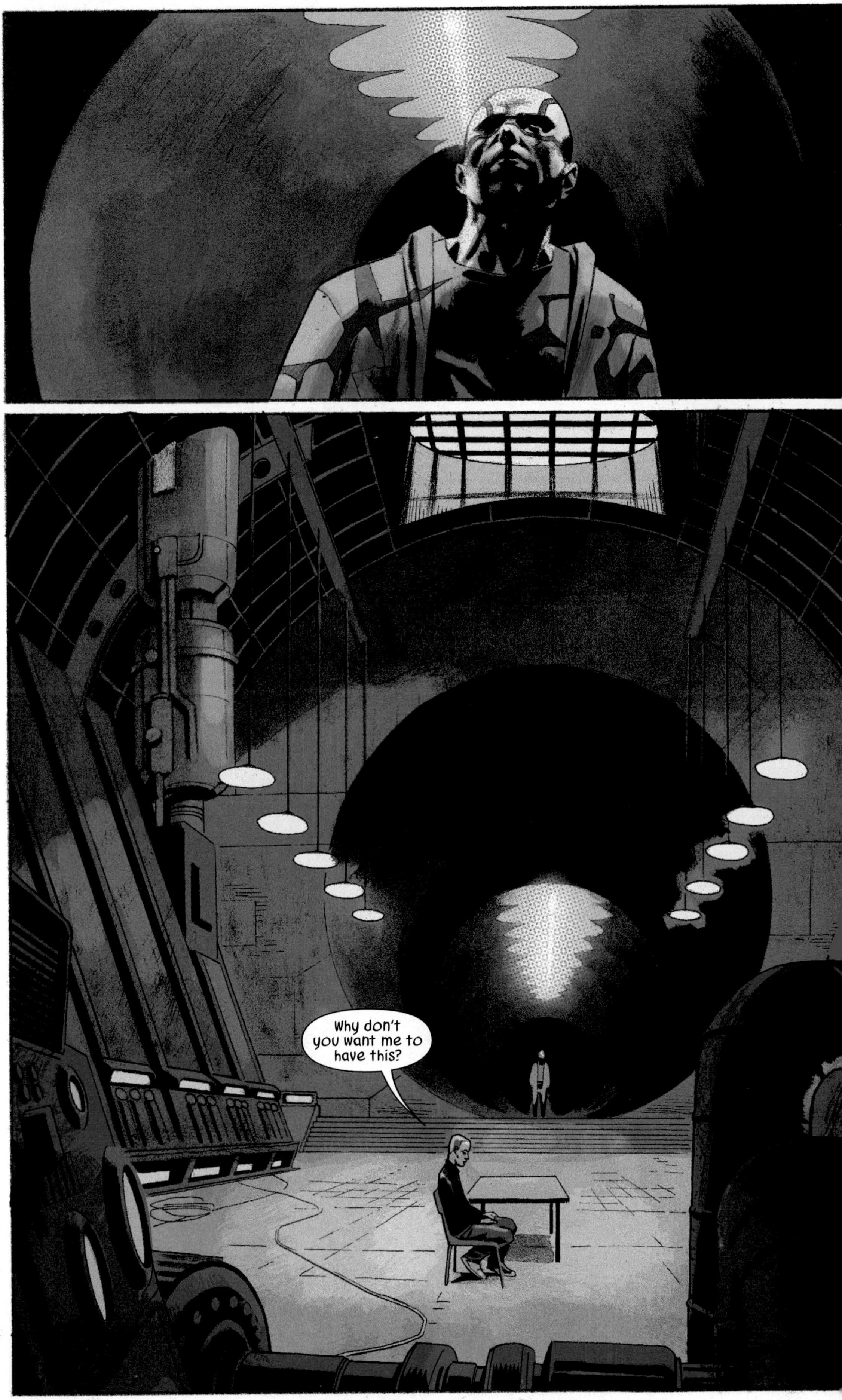
Why don't you want me to have this?

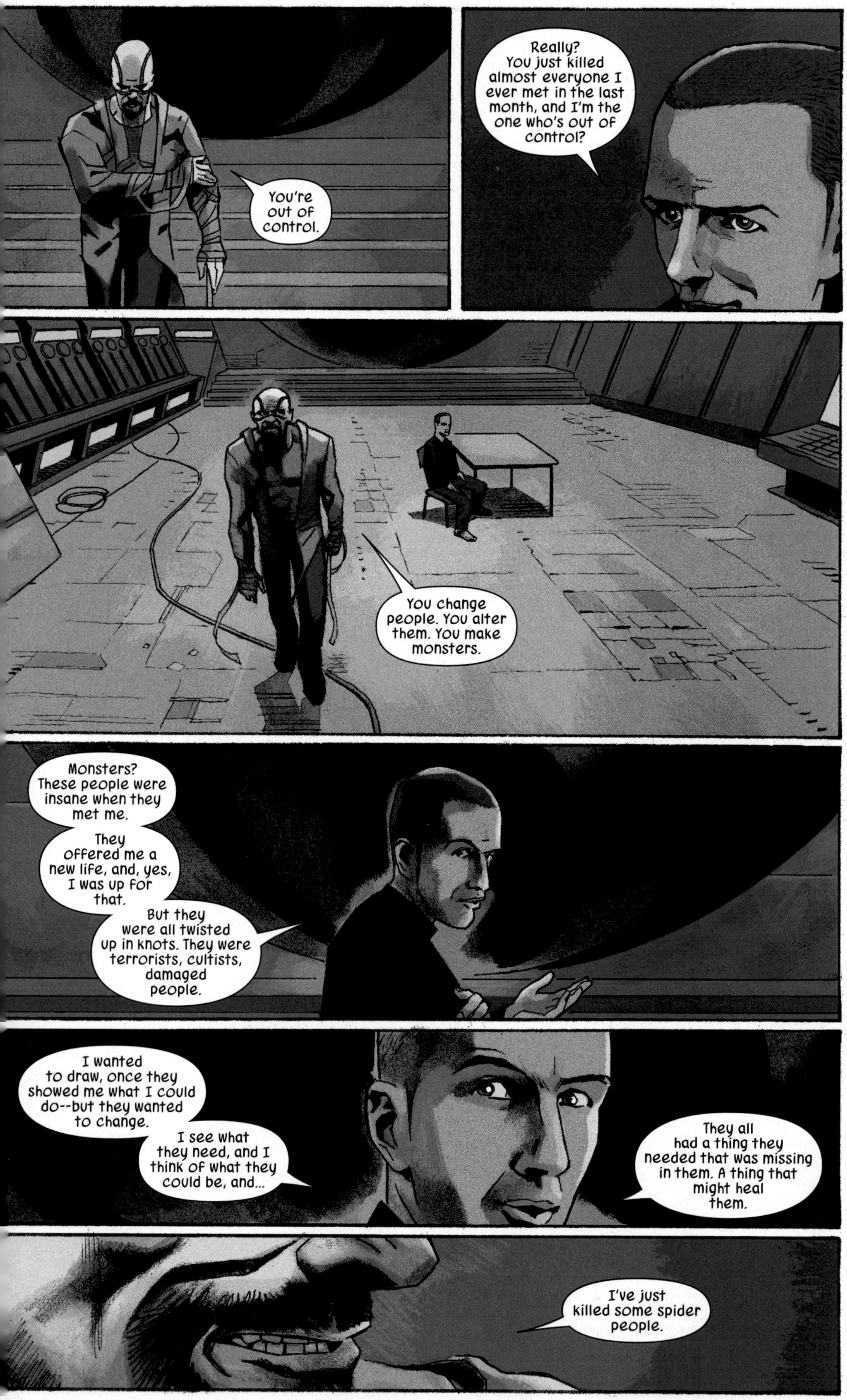

You're out of control.
Really? You just killed almost everyone I ever met in the last month, and I'm the one who's out of control?
You change people. You alter them. You make monsters.
Monsters? These people were insane when they met me.
They offered me a new life, and, yes, I was up for that.
But they were all twisted up in knots. They were terrorists, cultists, damaged people.
I wanted to draw, once they showed me what I could do--but they wanted to change.
I see what they need, and I think of what they could be, and...
They all had a thing they needed that was missing in them. A thing that might heal them.
I've just killed some spider people.

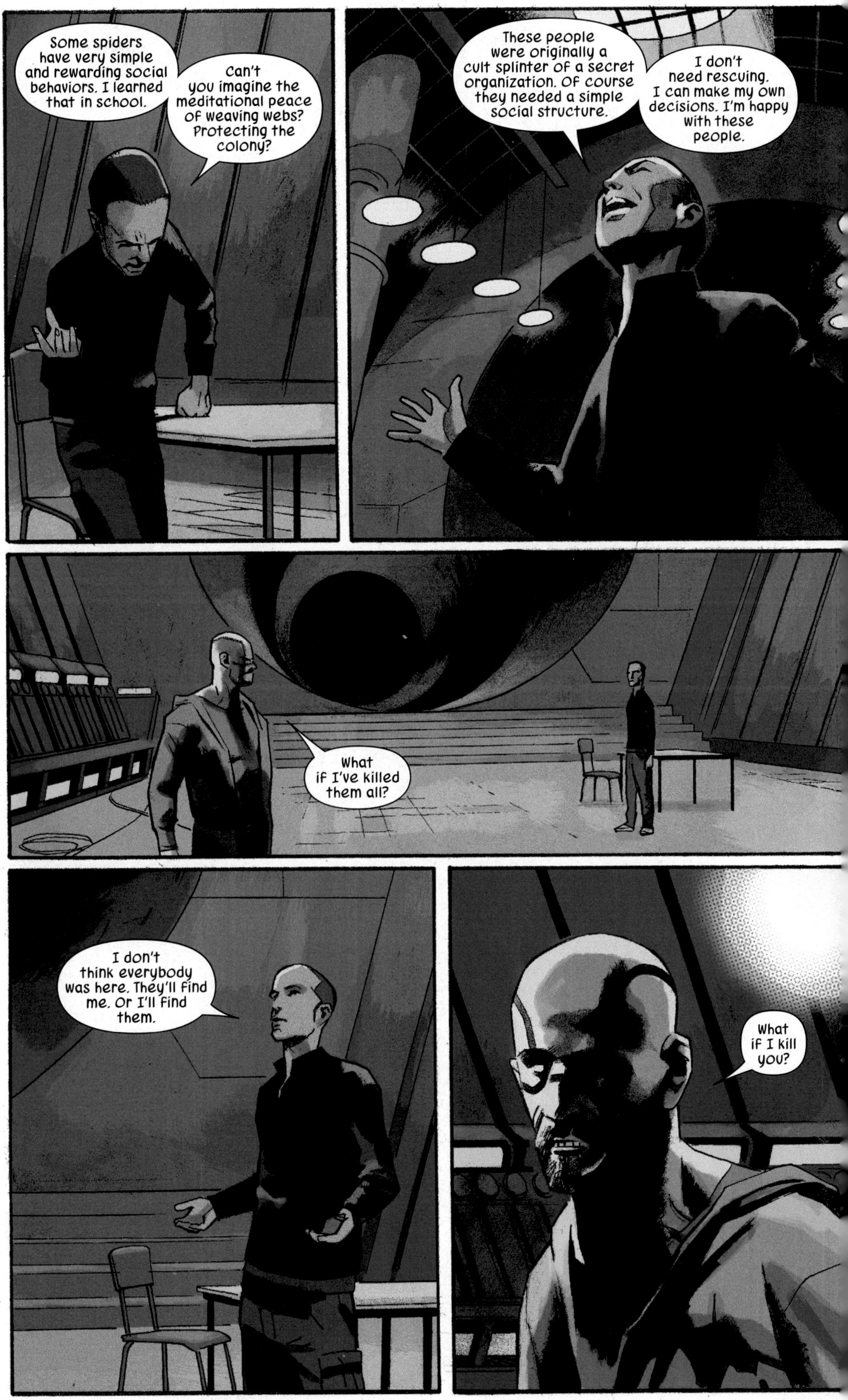

Some spiders have very simple and rewarding social behaviors. I learned that in school.
Can't you imagine the meditational peace of weaving webs? Protecting the colony?
These people were originally a cult splinter of a secret organization. Of course they needed a simple social structure.
I don't need rescuing. I can make my own decisions. I'm happy with these people.
What if I've killed them all?
I don't think everybody was here. They'll find me. Or I'll find them.
What if I kill you?

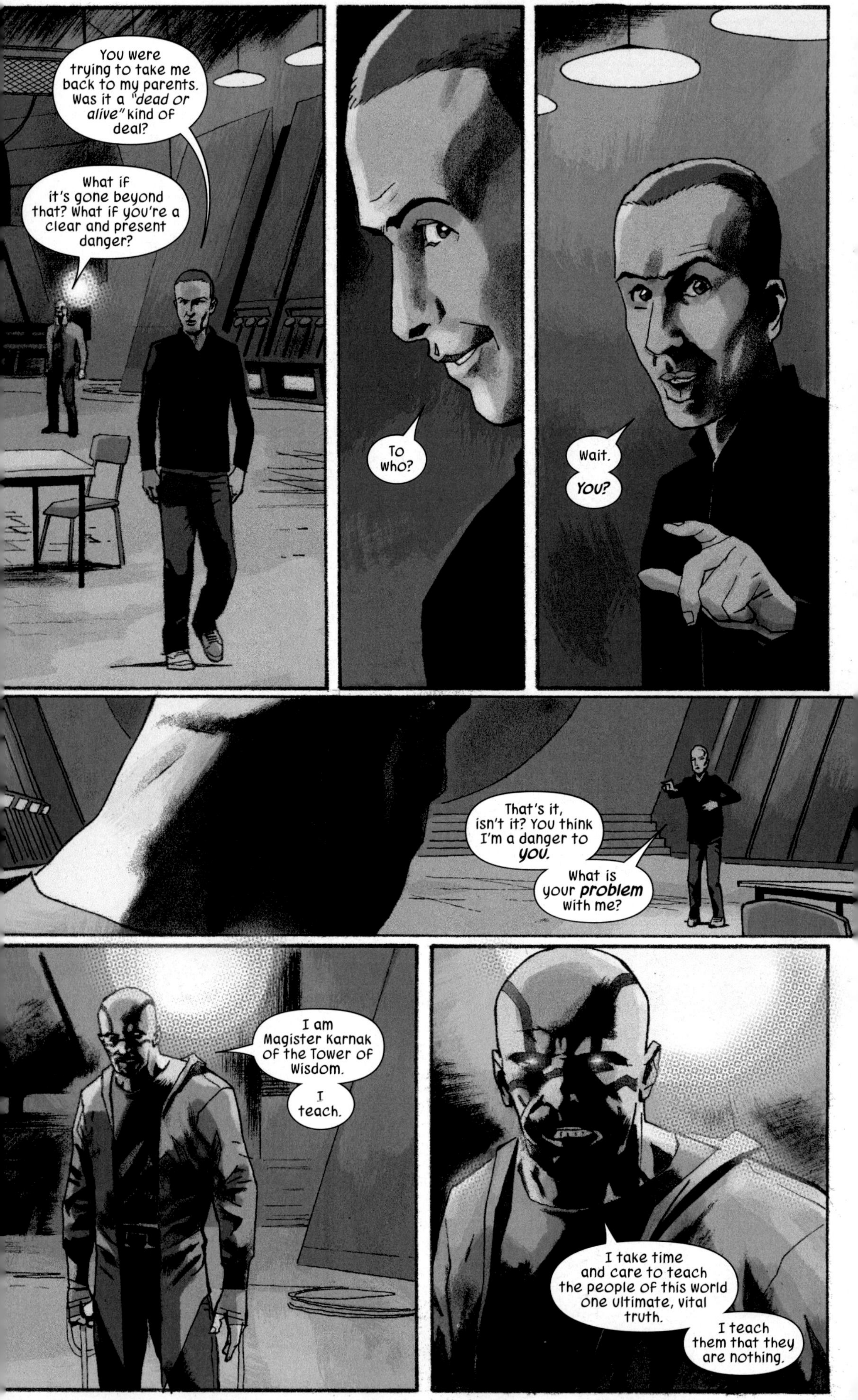
You were trying to take me back to my parents. Was it a "dead or alive" kind of deal?
What if it's gone beyond that? What if you're a clear and present danger?
To who?
Wait.
YOU?
That's it, isn't it? You think I'm a danger to YOU.
What is your problem with me?
I am Magister Karnak of the Tower of Wisdom.
I teach.
I take time and care to teach the people of this world one ultimate, vital truth.
I teach them that they are nothing.

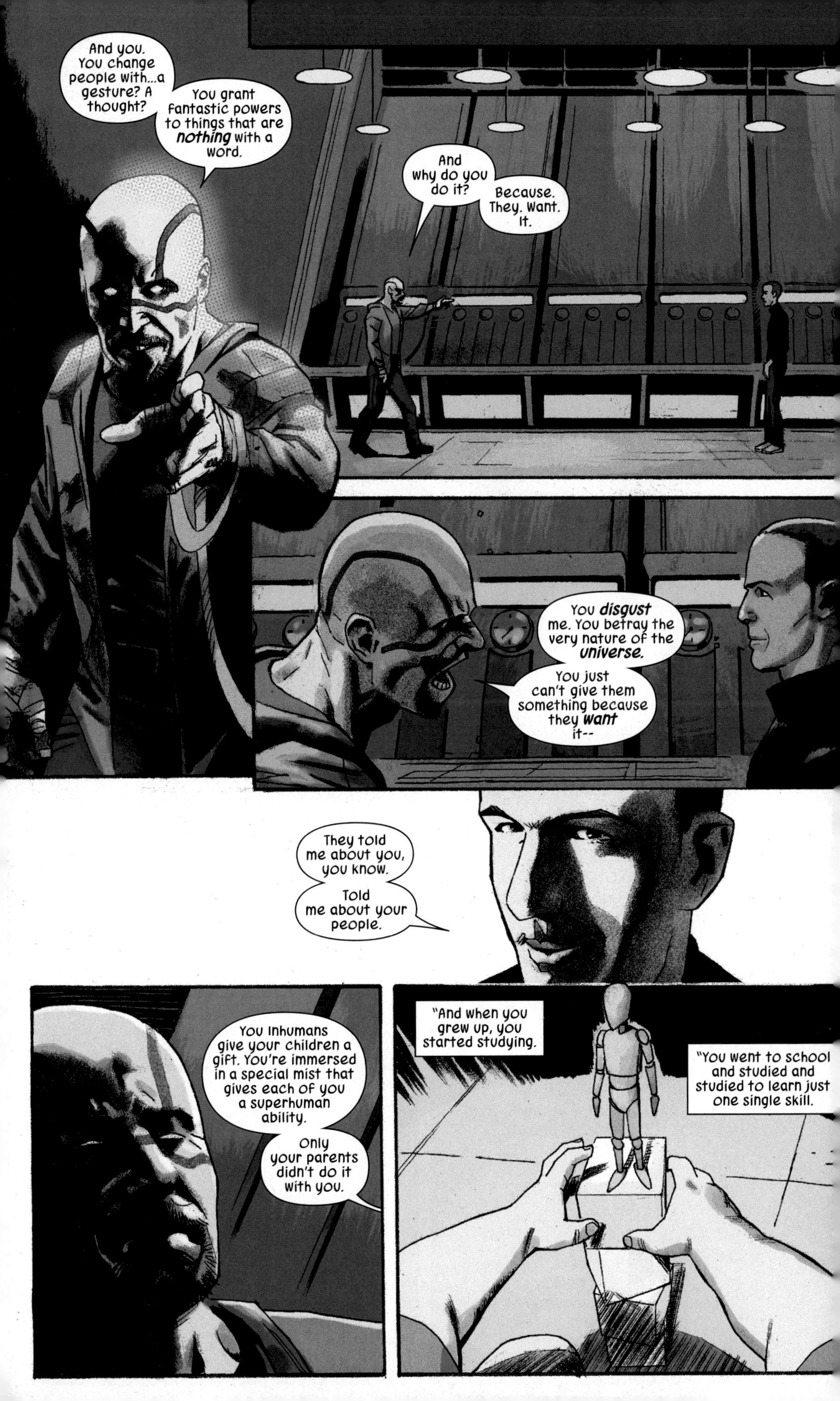
And you. You change people with...a gesture? A thought?
You grant fantastic powers to things that are *nothing* with a word.
And why do you do it?
Because. They. Want. It.
You *disgust* me. You betray the very nature of the *universe.*
You just can't give them something because they *want* it--
They told me about you, you know.
Told me about your people.
You Inhumans give your children a gift. You're immersed in a special mist that gives each of you a superhuman ability.
Only your parents didn't do it with you.
"And when you grew up, you started studying.
"You went to school and studied and studied to learn just one single skill.

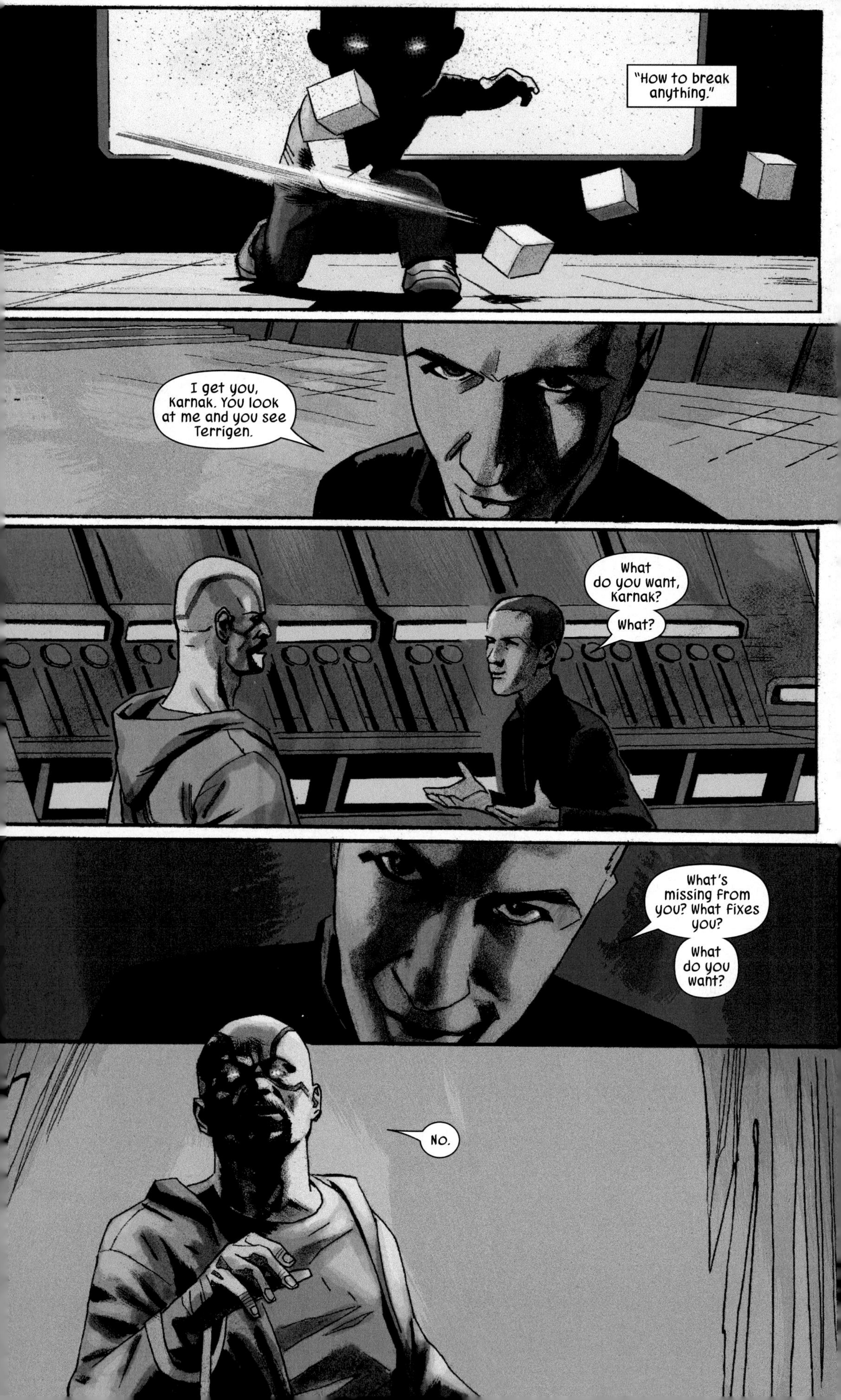
"How to break anything."
I get you, Karnak. You look at me and you see Terrigen.
What do you want, Karnak?
What?
What's missing from you? What fixes you?
What do you want?
No.

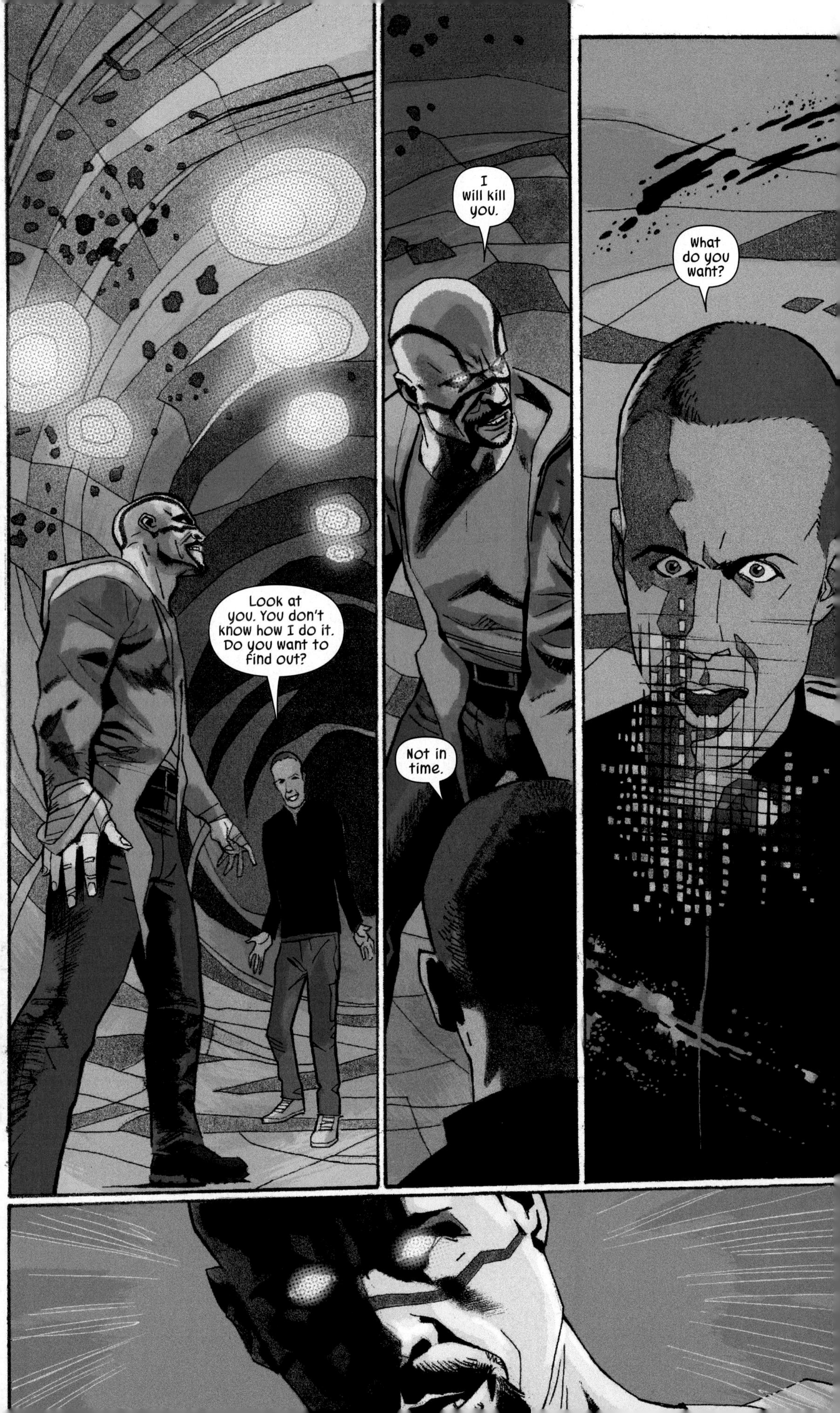

Look at you. You don't know how I do it. Do you want to find out?
I will kill you.
Not in time.
What do you want?

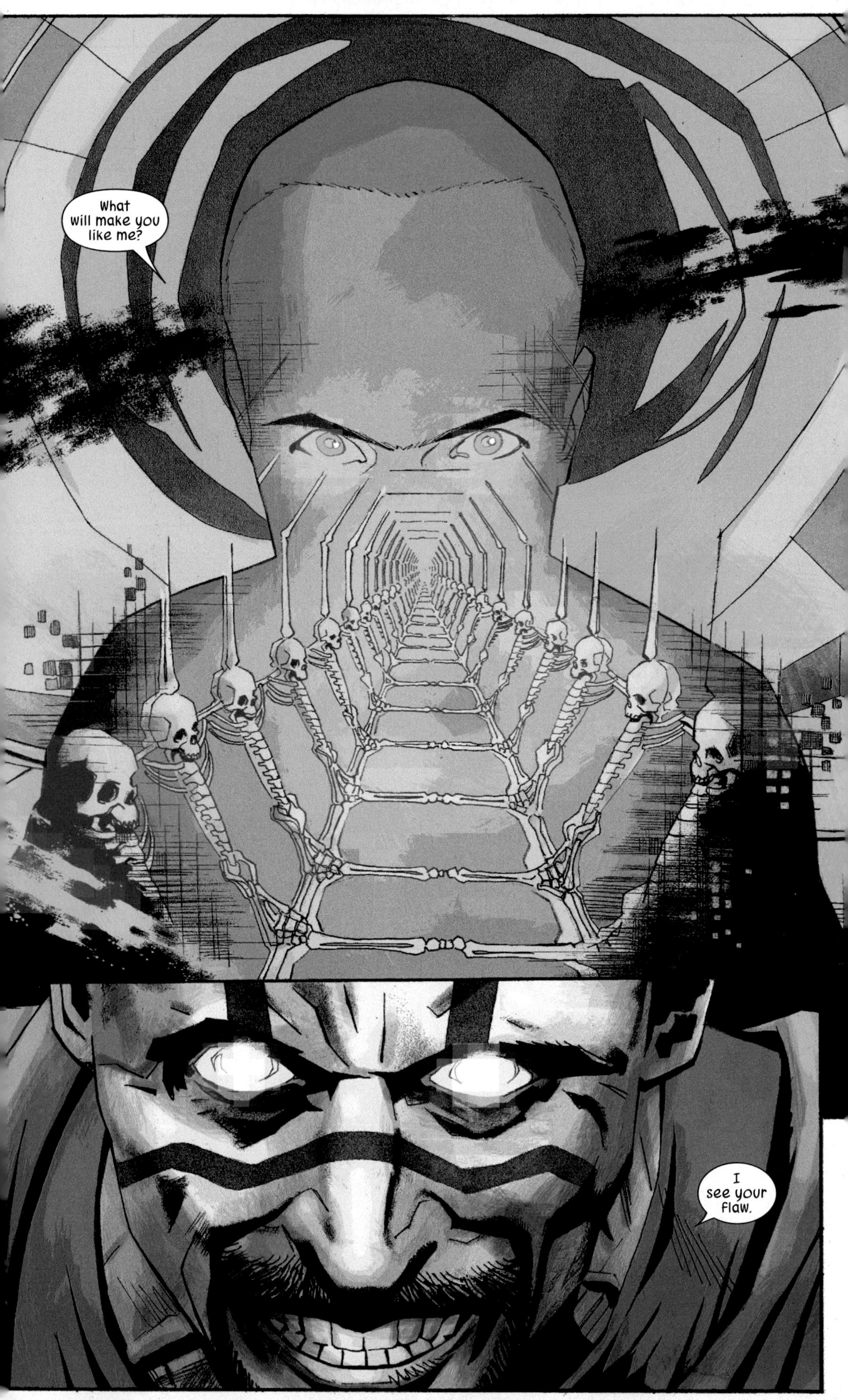
What will make you like me?
I see your flaw.

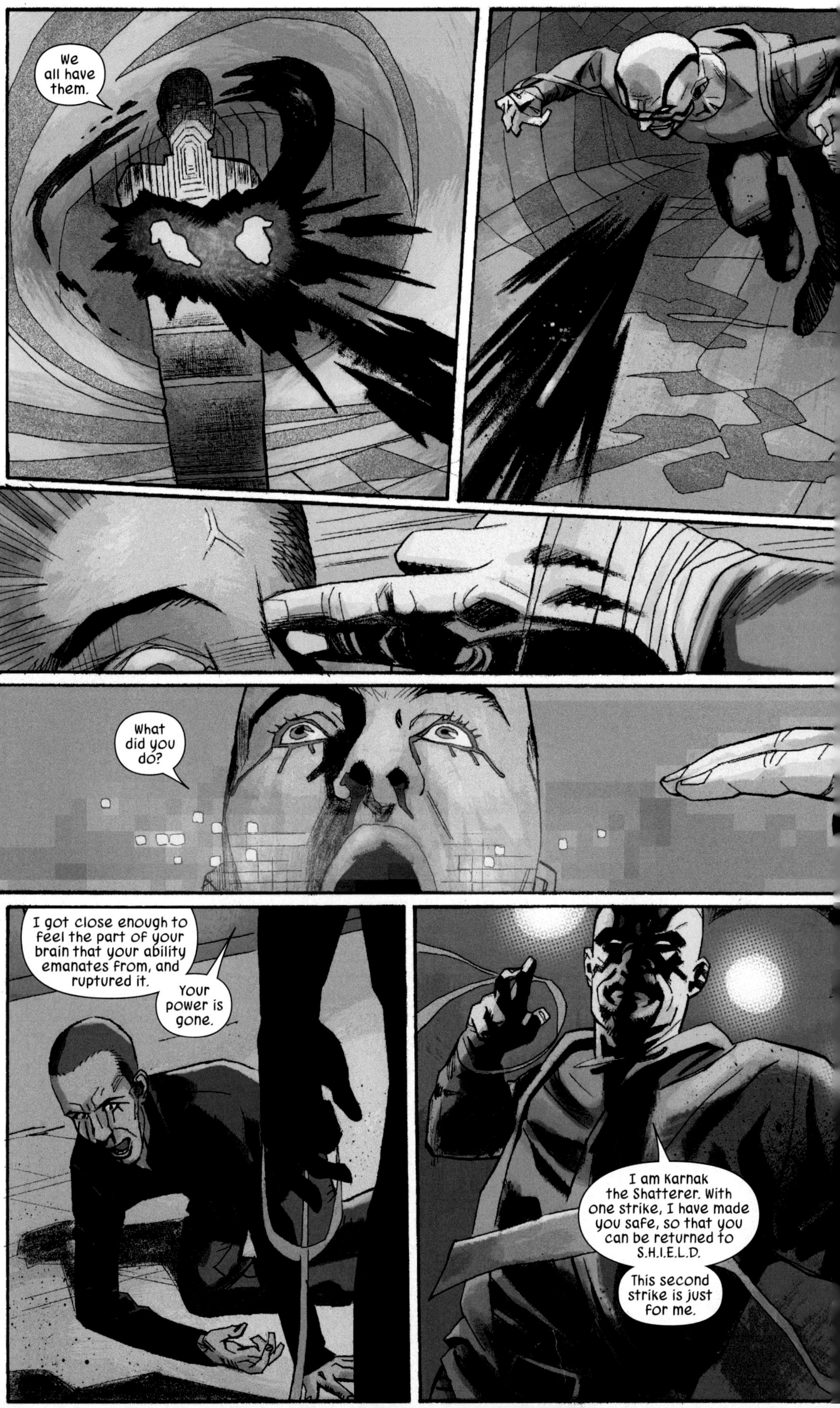
We all have them.
What did you do?
I got close enough to feel the part of your brain that your ability emanates from, and ruptured it.
Your power is gone.
I am Karnak the Shatterer. With one strike, I have made you safe, so that you can be returned to S.H.I.E.L.D.
This second strike is just for me.

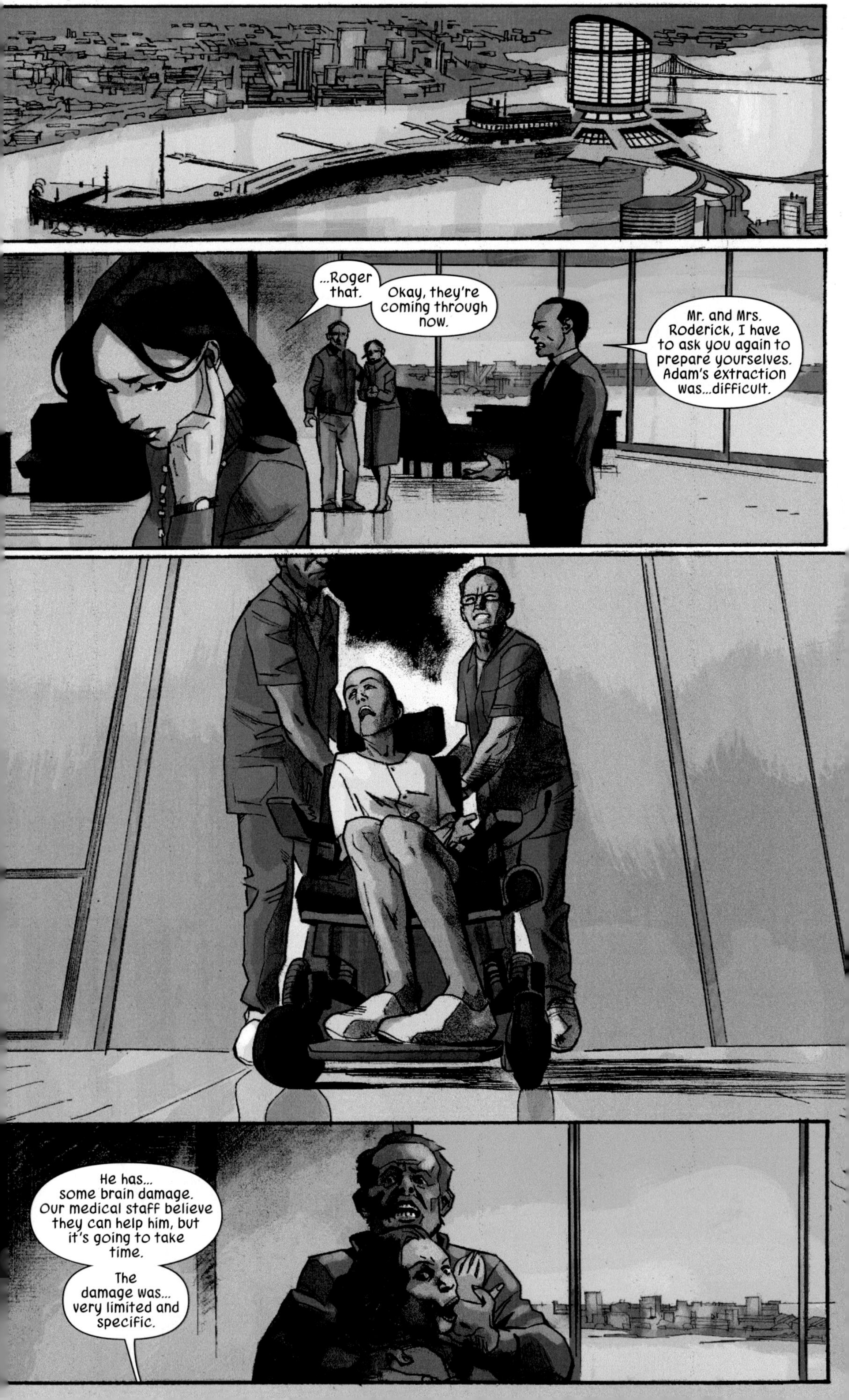
...Roger that.
Okay, they're coming through now.
Mr. and Mrs. Roderick, I have to ask you again to prepare yourselves. Adam's extraction was...difficult.
He has... some brain damage. Our medical staff believe they can help him, but it's going to take time.
The damage was... very limited and specific.

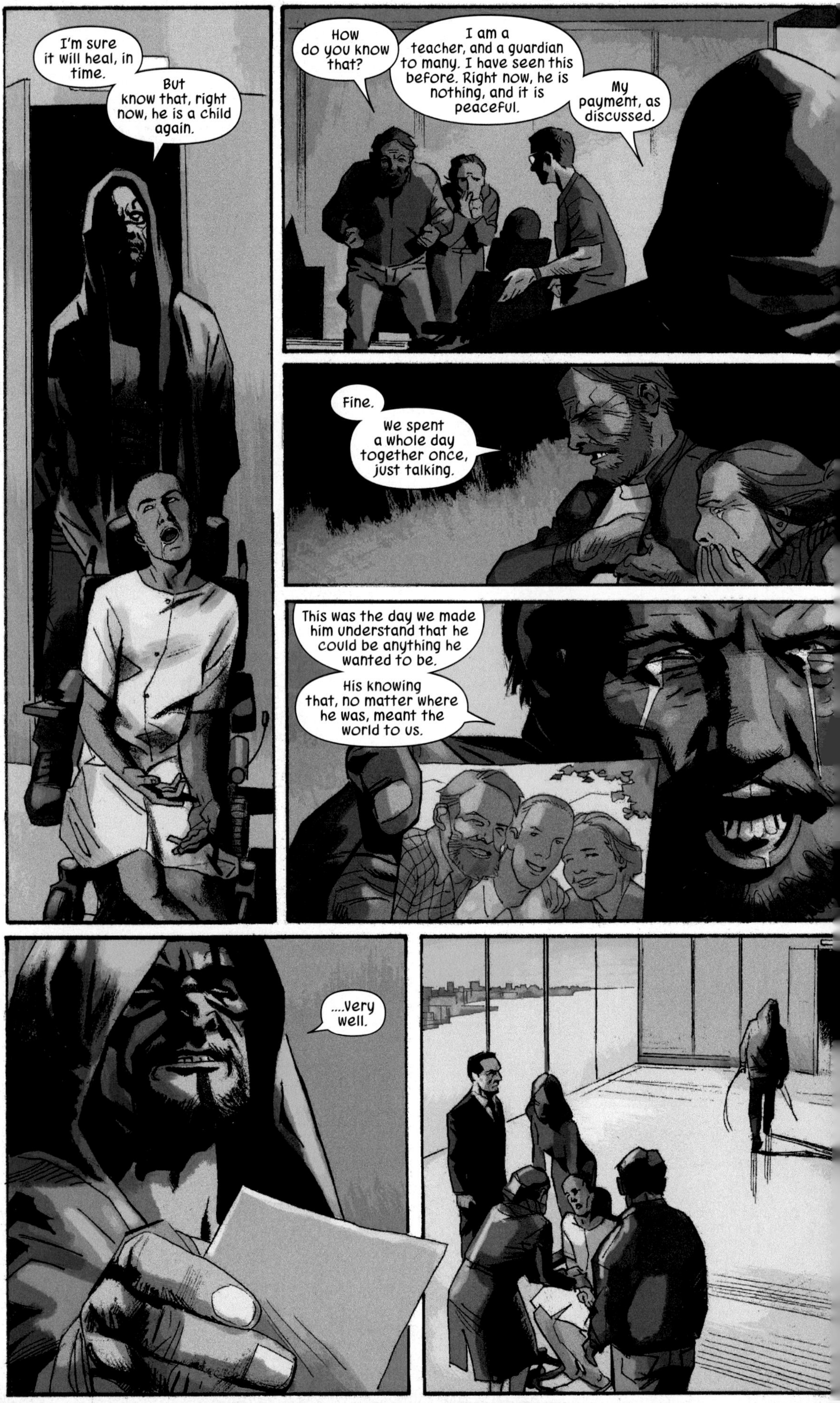

I'm sure it will heal, in time.
But know that, right now, he is a child again.
How do you know that?
I am a teacher, and a guardian to many. I have seen this before. Right now, he is nothing, and it is peaceful.
My payment, as discussed.
Fine.
We spent a whole day together once, just talking.
This was the day we made him understand that he could be anything he wanted to be.
His knowing that, no matter where he was, meant the world to us.
...Very well.

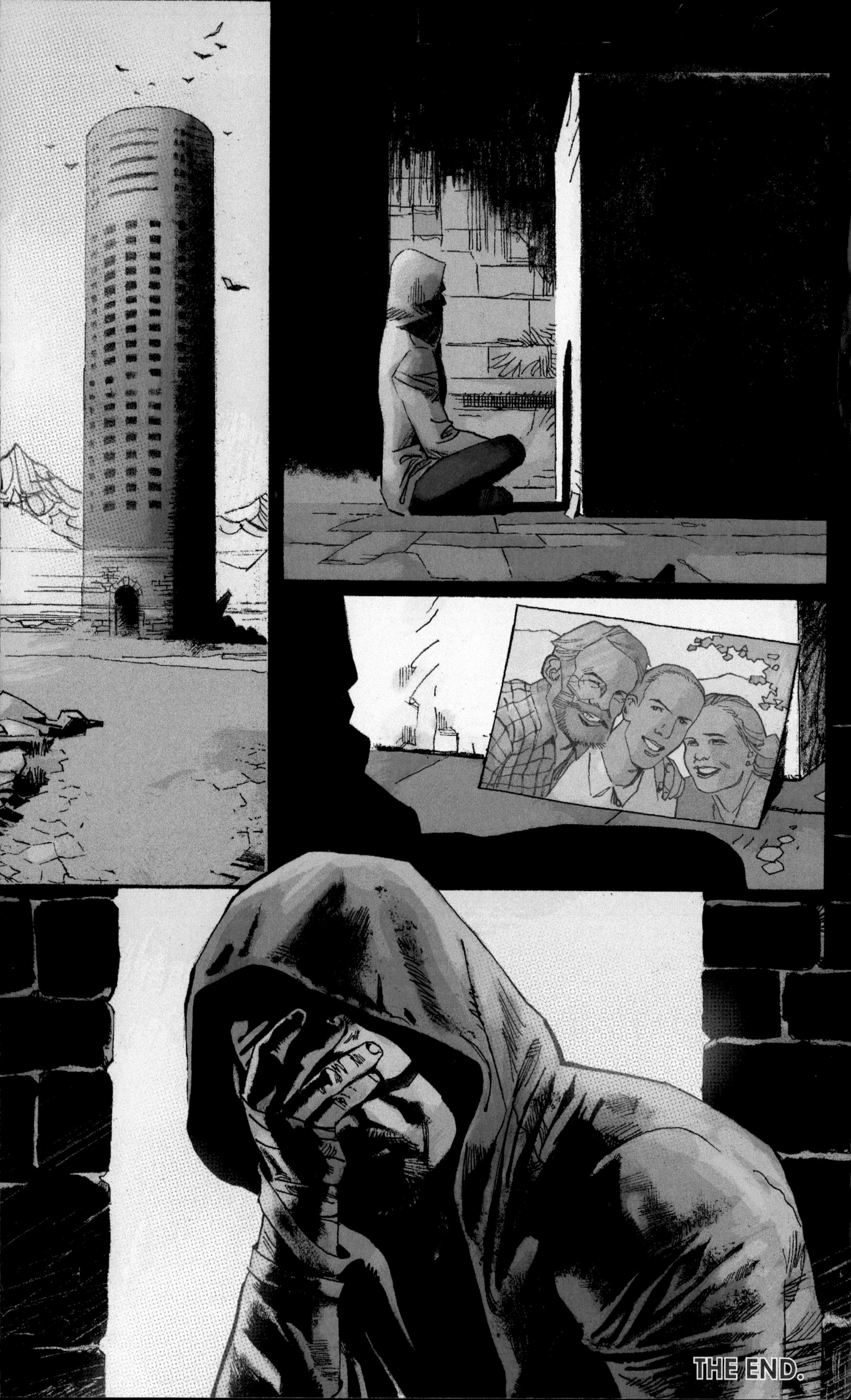
THE END.

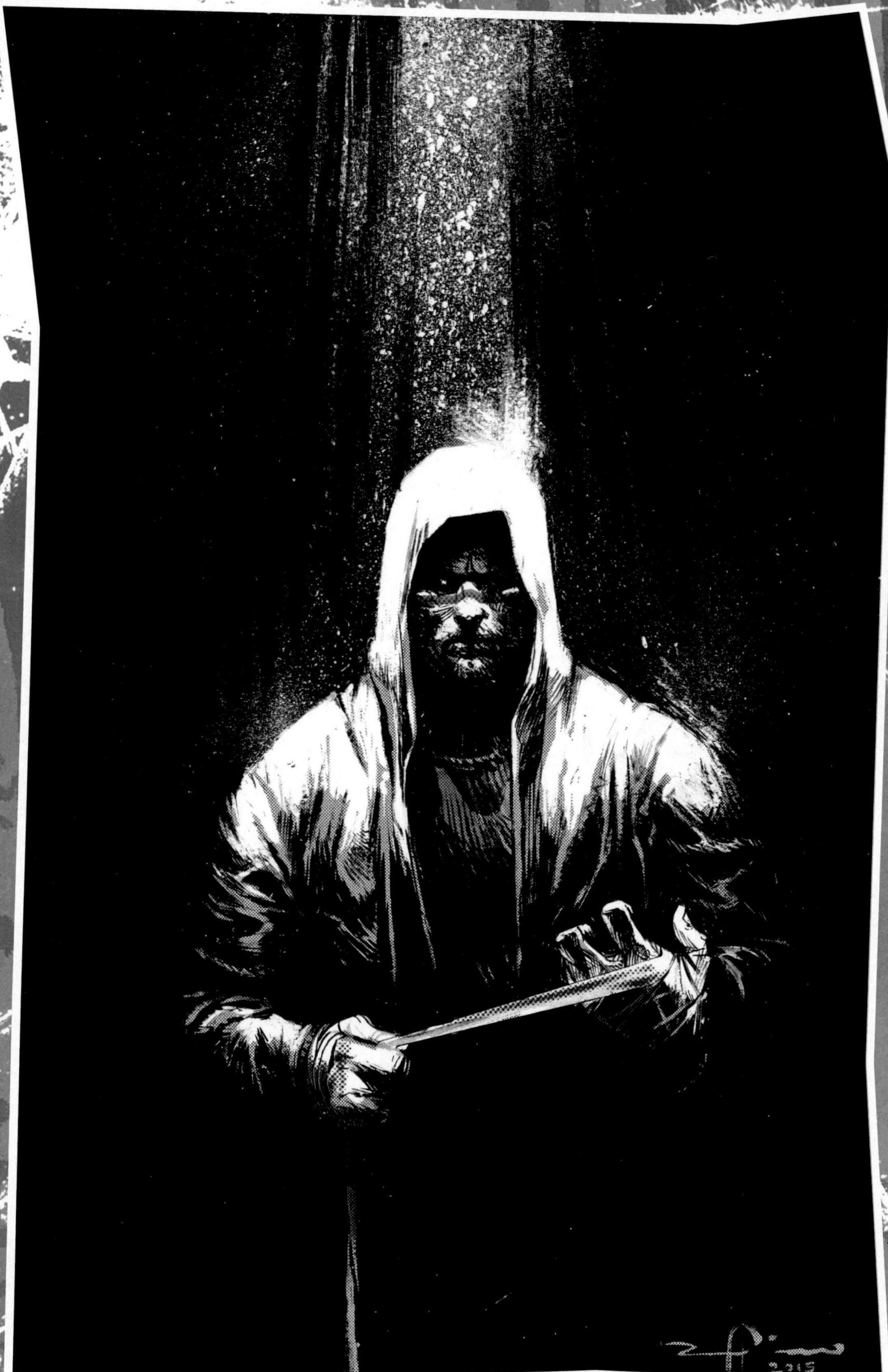

#1 VARIANT BY **GERARDO ZAFFINO**

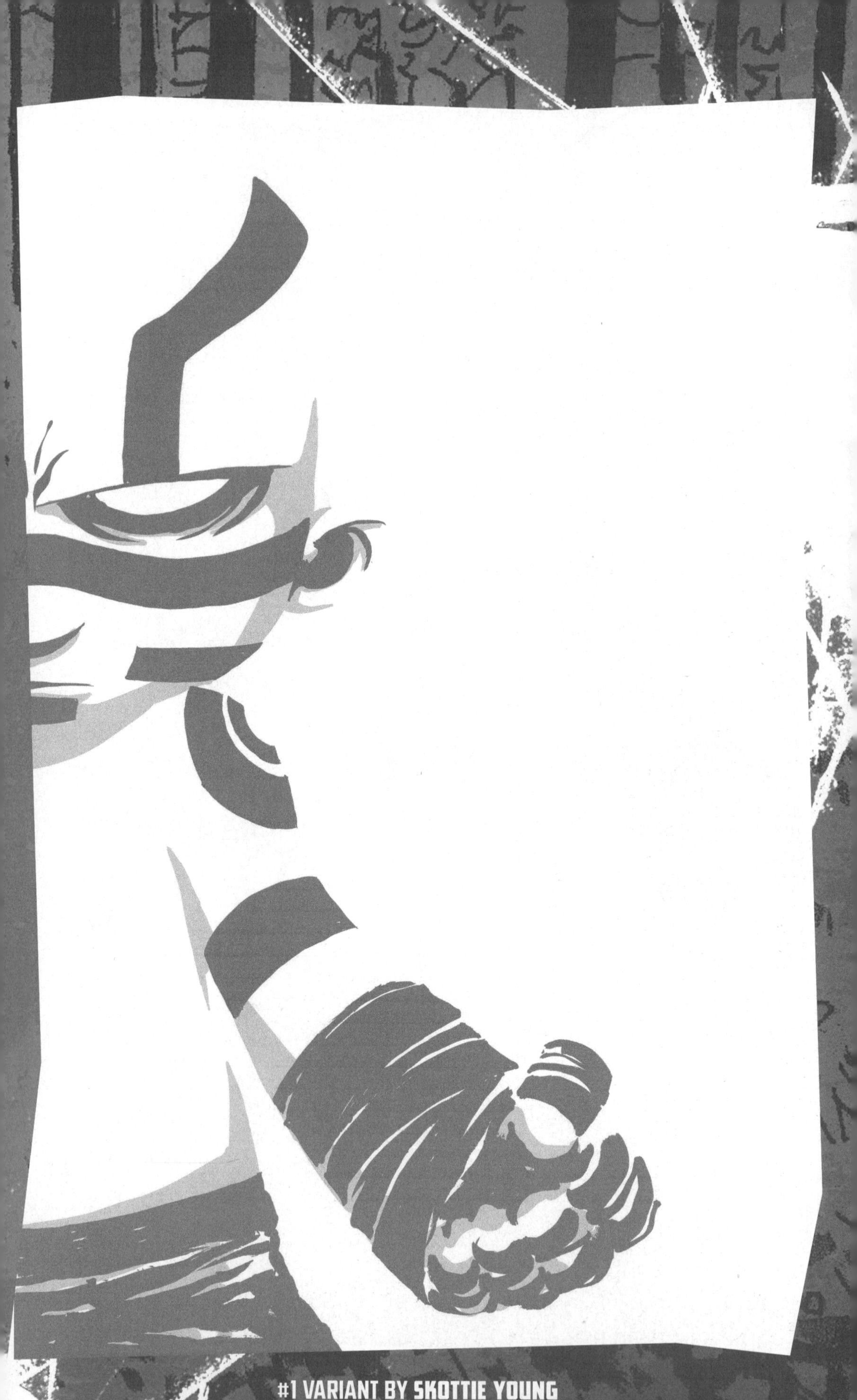

#1 VARIANT BY SKOTTIE YOUNG

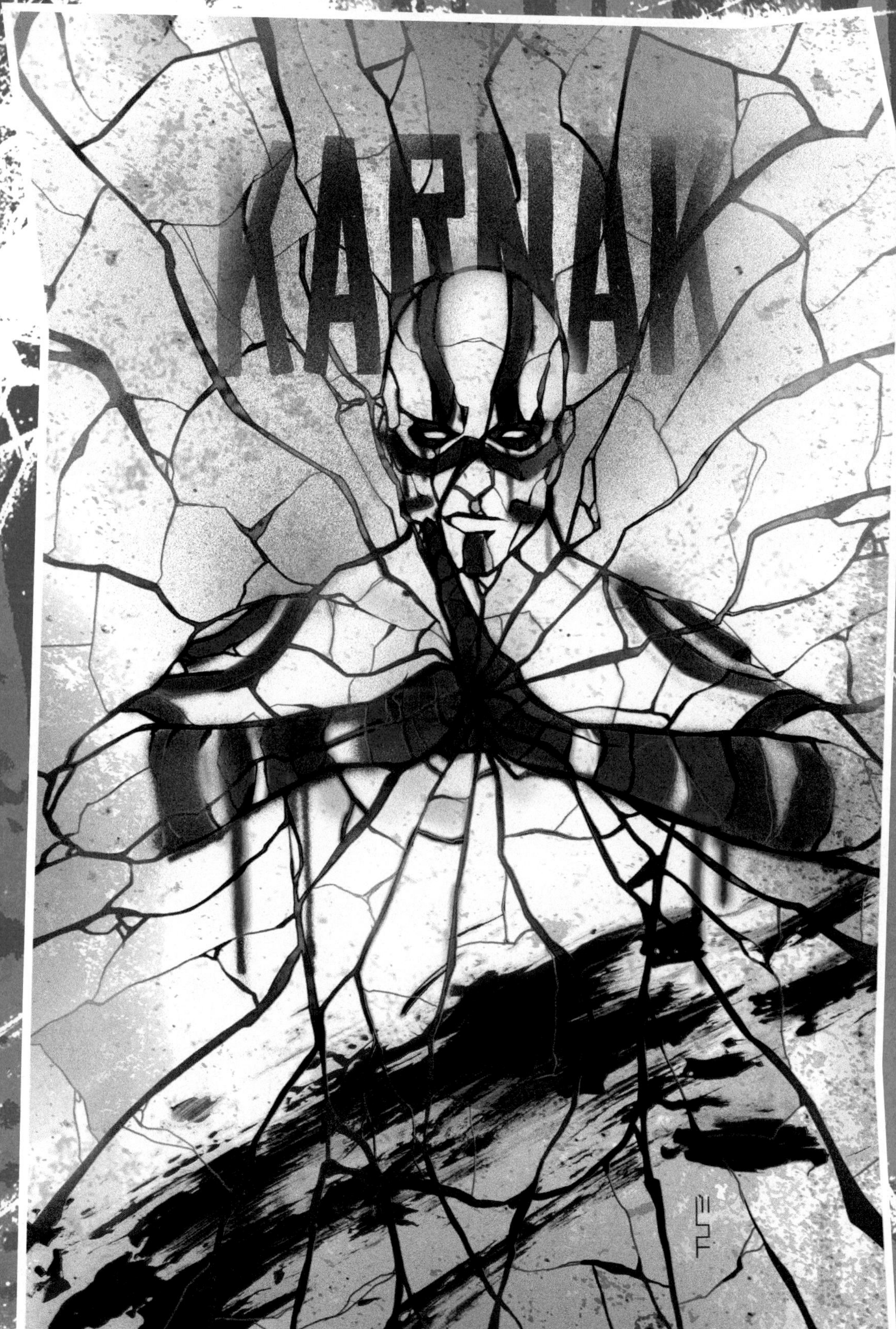
KARNAK

#1 VARIANT BY W. SCOTT FORBES

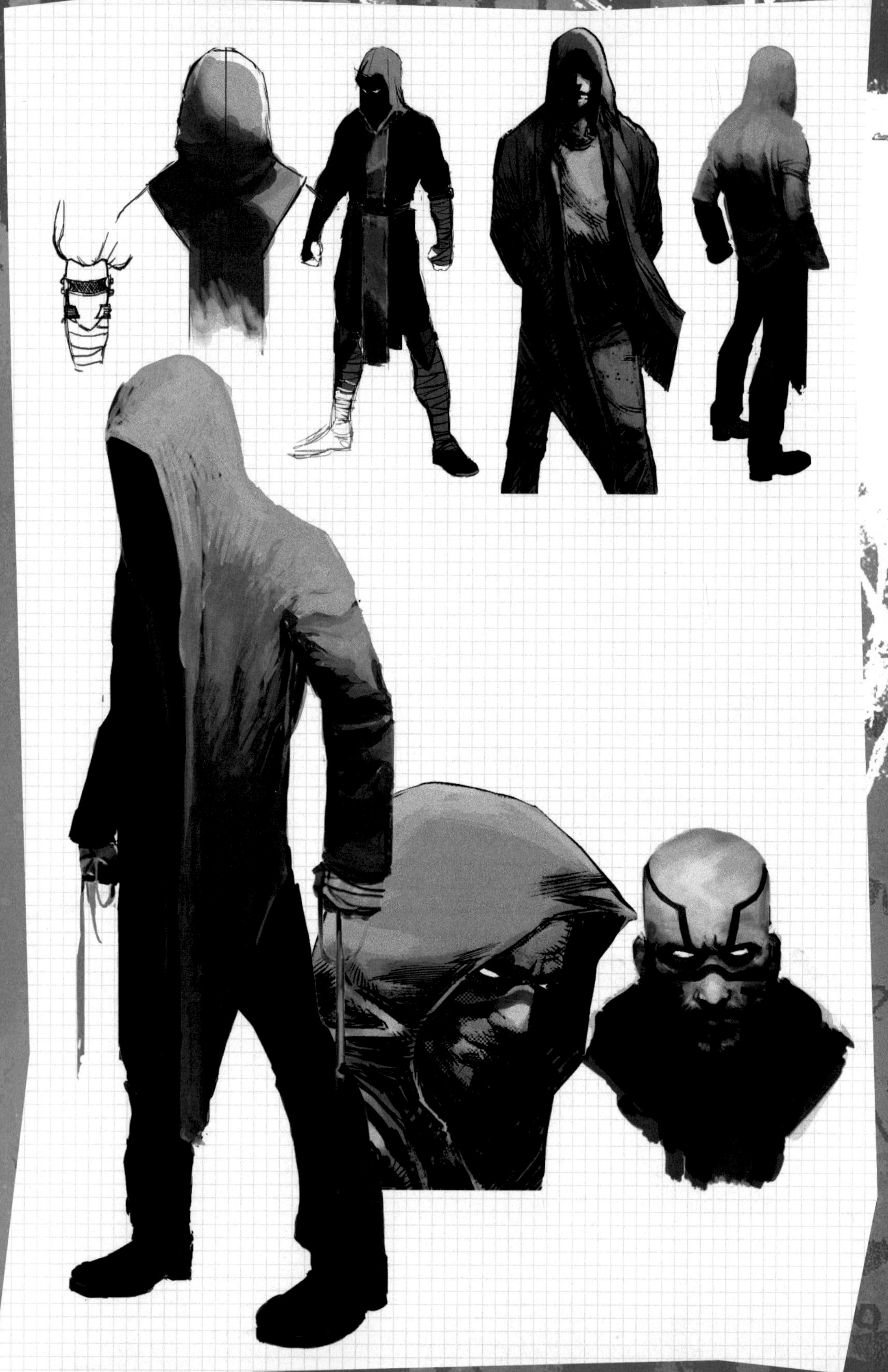

#1 DESIGN VARIANT BY **GERARDO ZAFFINO**

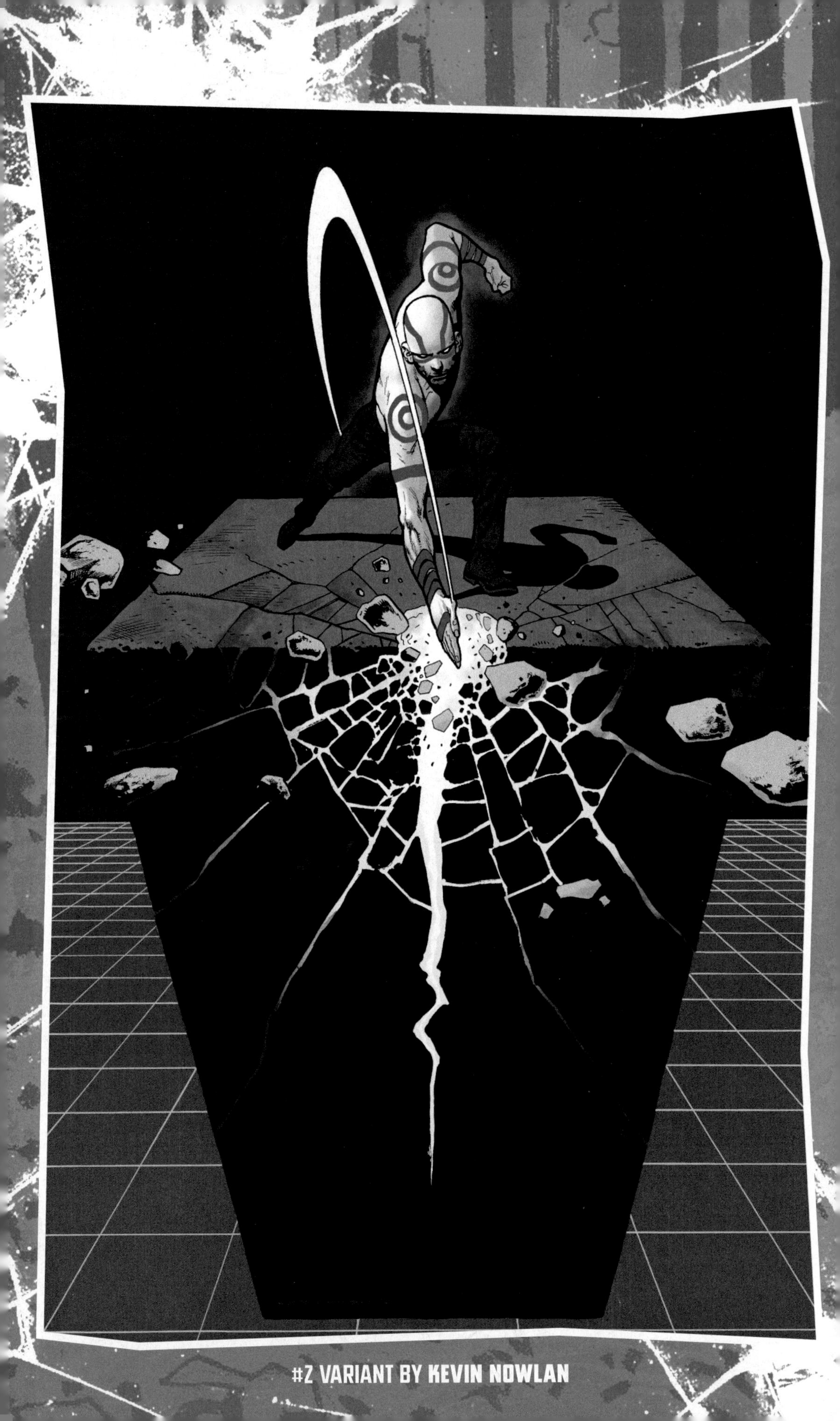

#2 VARIANT BY KEVIN NOWLAN

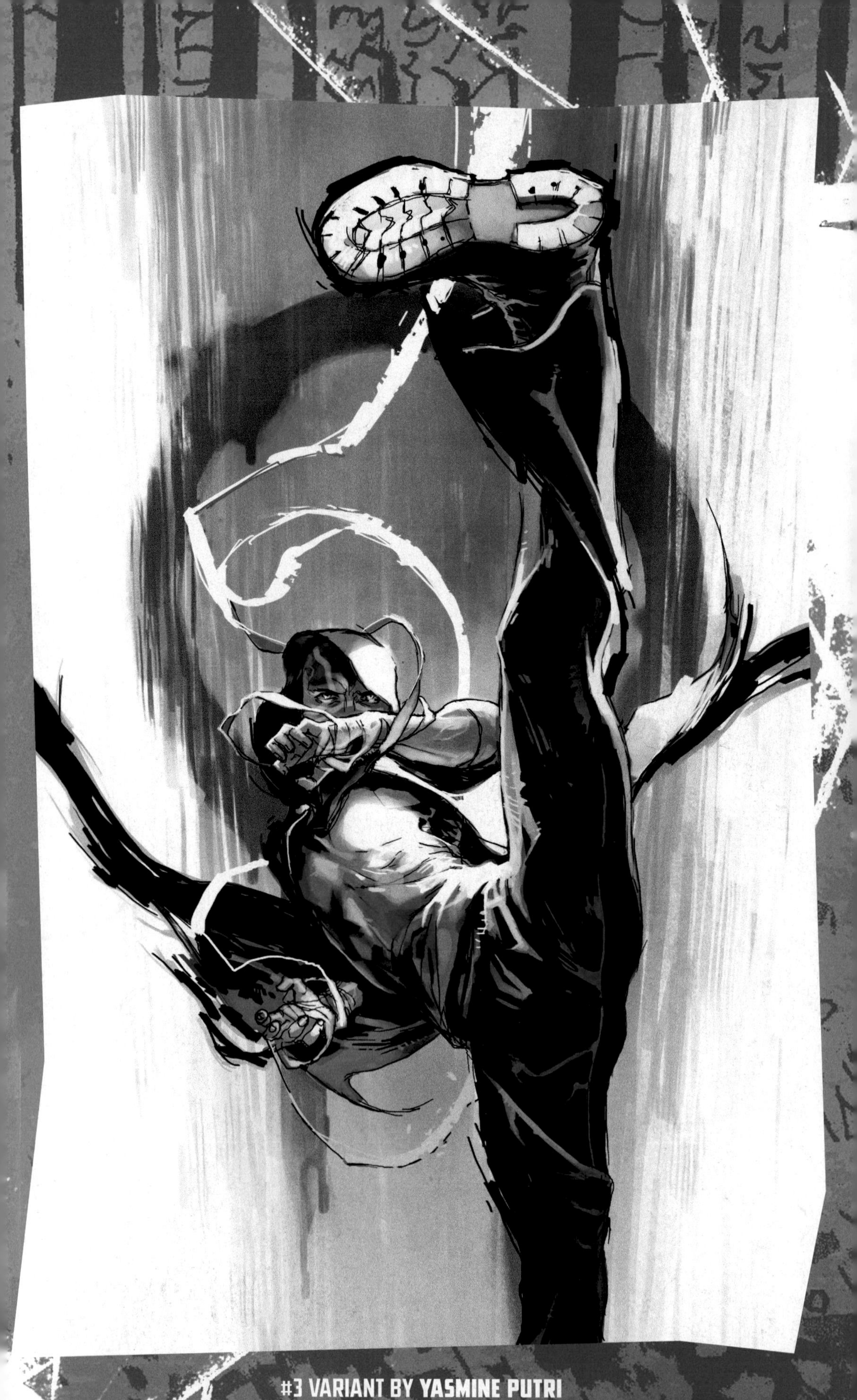

#3 VARIANT BY **YASMINE PUTRI**

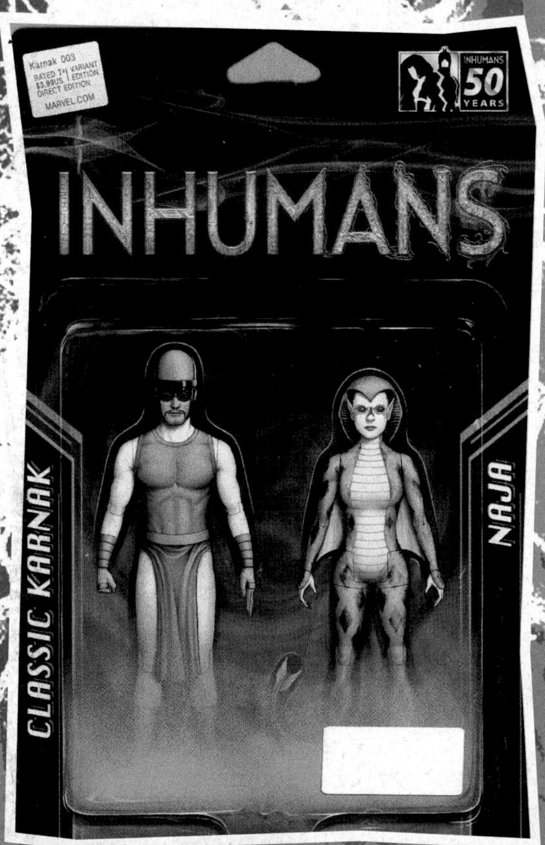
INHUMANS 50 YEARS
INHUMANS
CLASSIC KARNAK
NAJA

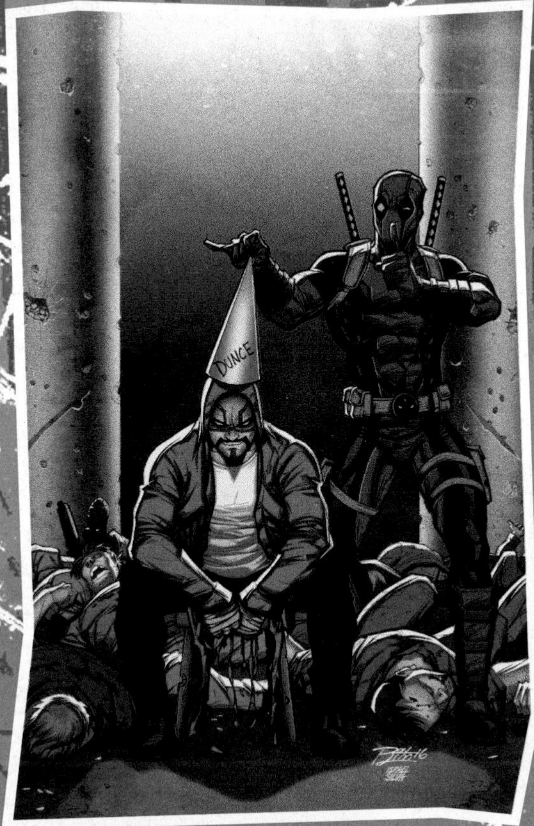
DUNCE

#3 ACTION FIGURE VARIANT
BY JOHN TYLER CHRISTOPHER

#4 DEADPOOL VARIANT
BY RON LIM & ISRAEL SILVA

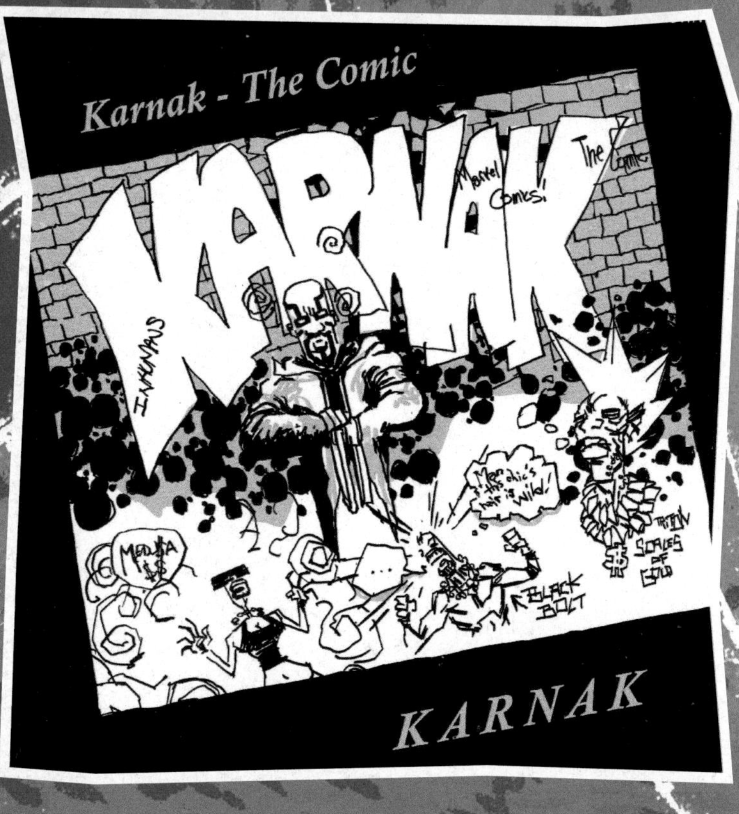
Karnak - The Comic
KARNAK
KARNAK

#1 HIP-HOP VARIANT BY KAARE ANDREWS

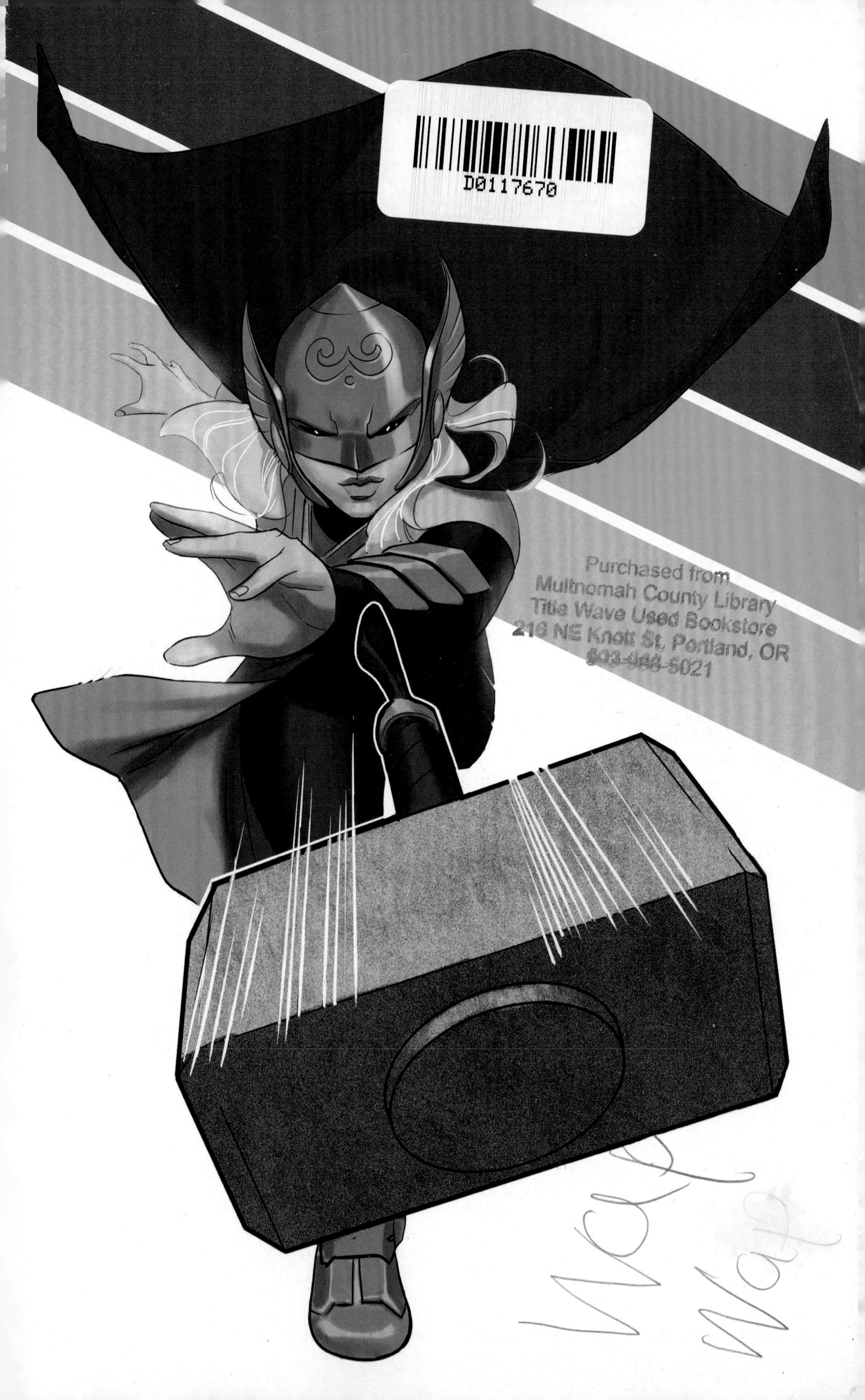

## A-FORCE PRESENTS

### BLACK WIDOW (2014) #5
writer NATHAN EDMONDSON
artist PHIL NOTO
letterer VC's CLAYTON COWLES
cover art PHIL NOTO
editor ELLIE PYLE

### SHE-HULK (2014) #5
writer CHARLES SOULE
artist RON WIMBERLY
color artist RICO RENZI
letterer VC's CLAYTON COWLES
cover art KEVIN WADA
assistant editor FRANKIE JOHNSON
editors JEANINE SCHAEFER
& TOM BRENNAN

### CAPTAIN MARVEL (2014) #5
writer KELLY SUE DeCONNICK
artist DAVID LOPEZ
color artist LEE LOUGHRIDGE
letterer VC's JOE CARAMAGNA
cover art DAVID LOPEZ
assistant editor DEVIN LEWIS
editor SANA AMANAT
senior editor NICK LOWE

### MS. MARVEL (2014) #5
writer G. WILLOW WILSON
artist ADRIAN ALPHONA
color artist IAN HERRING
letterer VC's JOE CARAMAGNA
cover art JAMIE McKELVIE &
MATTHEW WILSON
assistant editor DEVIN LEWIS
editor SANA AMANAT
senior editor NICK LOWE

### THOR (2014) #5
writer JASON AARON
artist/colorist JORGE MOLINA
letterer VC's JOE SABINO
cover art RUSSELL DAUTERMAN &
MATTHEW WILSON
assistant editor JON MOISAN
editor WIL MOSS

### THE UNBEATABLE
SQUIRREL GIRL (2015A) #5
writer RYAN NORTH
artist ERICA HENDERSON
color artist RICO RENZI &
ERICA HENDERSON
letterer VC's CLAYTON COWLES
cover art ERICA HENDERSON
assistant editor JON MOISAN
editor WIL MOSS
executive editor TOM BREVOORT

collection editor JENNIFER GRÜNWALD
associate editor SARAH BRUNSTAD
associate managing editor ALEX STARBUCK
editor, special projects MARK D. BEAZLEY
vp, production & special projects JEFF YOUNGQUIST
svp print, sales & marketing DAVID GABRIEL
book designer ADAM DEL RE

editor in chief AXEL ALONSO
chief creative officer JOE QUESADA
publisher DAN BUCKLEY
executive producer ALAN FINE

A-FORCE PRESENTS VOL. 5. Contains material originally published in magazine form as BLACK WIDOW #5, CAPTAIN MARVEL #5, MS. MARVEL #5, SHE-HULK #5, THOR #5 AND THE UNBEATABLE SQUIRREL GIRL #5. First printing 2016. ISBN# 978-1-302-90193-6. Published by MARVEL WORLDWIDE, INC., a subsidiary of MARVEL ENTERTAINMENT, LLC. OFFICE OF PUBLICATION: 135 West 50th Street, New York, NY 10020. Copyright © 2016 MARVEL No similarity between any of the names, characters, persons, and/or institutions in this magazine with those of any living or dead person or institution is intended, and any such similarity which may exist is purely coincidental. **Printed in Canada.** ALAN FINE, President, Marvel Entertainment; DAN BUCKLEY, President, TV, Publishing & Brand Management; JOE QUESADA, Chief Creative Officer; TOM BREVOORT, SVP of Publishing; DAVID BOGART, SVP of Business Affairs & Operations, Publishing & Partnership; C.B. CEBULSKI, VP of Brand Management & Development, Asia; DAVID GABRIEL, SVP of Sales & Marketing, Publishing; JEFF YOUNGQUIST, VP of Production & Special Projects; DAN CARR, Executive Director of Publishing Technology; ALEX MORALES, Director of Publishing Operations; SUSAN CRESPI, Production Manager; STAN LEE, Chairman Emeritus. For information regarding advertising in Marvel Comics or on Marvel.com, please contact Vit DeBellis, Integrated Sales Manager, at vdebellis@marvel.com. For Marvel subscription inquiries, please call 888-511-5480. **Manufactured between 5/20/2016 and 7/4/2016 by SOLISCO PRINTERS, SCOTT, QC, CANADA.**

COLLECTION EDITOR: **JENNIFER GRÜNWALD**
ASSISTANT EDITOR: **CAITLIN O'CONNELL**
ASSOCIATE MANAGING EDITOR: **KATERI WOODY**
EDITOR, SPECIAL PROJECTS: **MARK D. BEAZLEY**
VP PRODUCTION & SPECIAL PROJECTS: **JEFF YOUNGQUIST**
SVP PRINT, SALES & MARKETING: **DAVID GABRIEL**
BOOK DESIGNER: **JAY BOWEN**

EDITOR IN CHIEF: **AXEL ALONSO**
CHIEF CREATIVE OFFICER: **JOE QUESADA**
PUBLISHER: **DAN BUCKLEY**
EXECUTIVE PRODUCER: **ALAN FINE**

**KARNAK: THE FLAW IN ALL THINGS.** Contains material originally published in magazine form as KARNAK #1-6. First printing 2016. ISBN# 978-0-7851-9848-2. Published by MARVEL WORLDWIDE, INC., a subsidiary of MARVEL ENTERTAINMENT, LLC. OFFICE OF PUBLICATION: 135 West 50th Street, New York, NY 10020. Copyright © 2017 MARVEL No similarity between any of the names, characters, persons, and/or institutions in this magazine with those of any living or dead person or institution is intended, and any such similarity which may exist is purely coincidental. **Printed in the U.S.A.** ALAN FINE, President, Marvel Entertainment; DAN BUCKLEY, President, TV, Publishing & Brand Management; JOE QUESADA, Chief Creative Officer; TOM BREVOORT, SVP of Publishing; DAVID BOGART, SVP of Business Affairs & Operations, Publishing & Partnership; C.B. CEBULSKI, VP of Brand Management & Development, Asia; DAVID GABRIEL, SVP of Sales & Marketing, Publishing; JEFF YOUNGQUIST, VP of Production & Special Projects; DAN CARR, Executive Director of Publishing Technology; ALEX MORALES, Director of Publishing Operations; SUSAN CRESPI, Production Manager; STAN LEE, Chairman Emeritus. For information regarding advertising in Marvel Comics or on Marvel.com, please contact Vit DeBellis, Integrated Sales Manager, at vdebellis@marvel.com. For Marvel subscription inquiries, please call 888-511-5480. **Manufactured between 1/6/17 and 2/13/17 by QUAD/GRAPHICS WASECA, WASECA, MN, USA.**

10 9 8 7 6 5 4 3 2 1

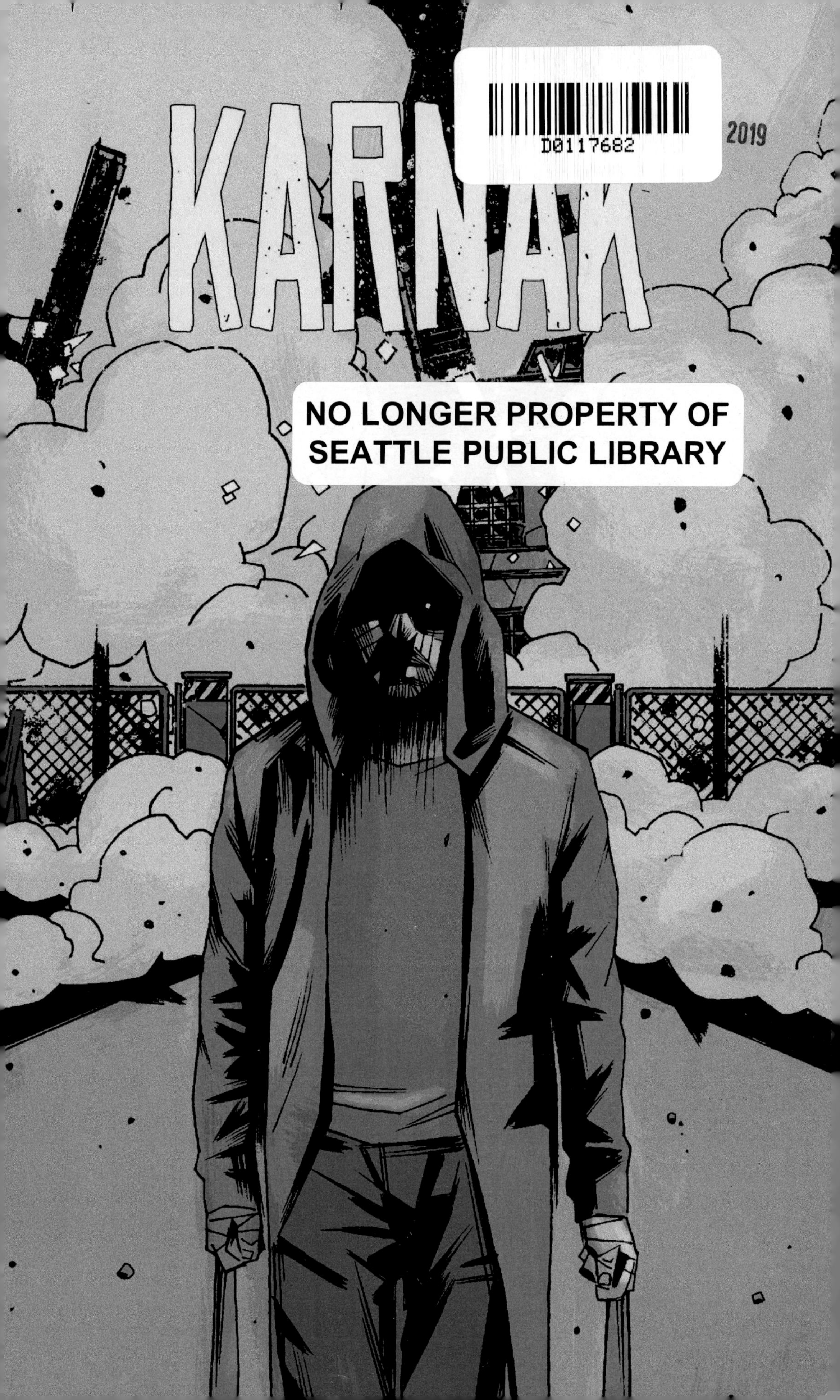
KARNAK
2019

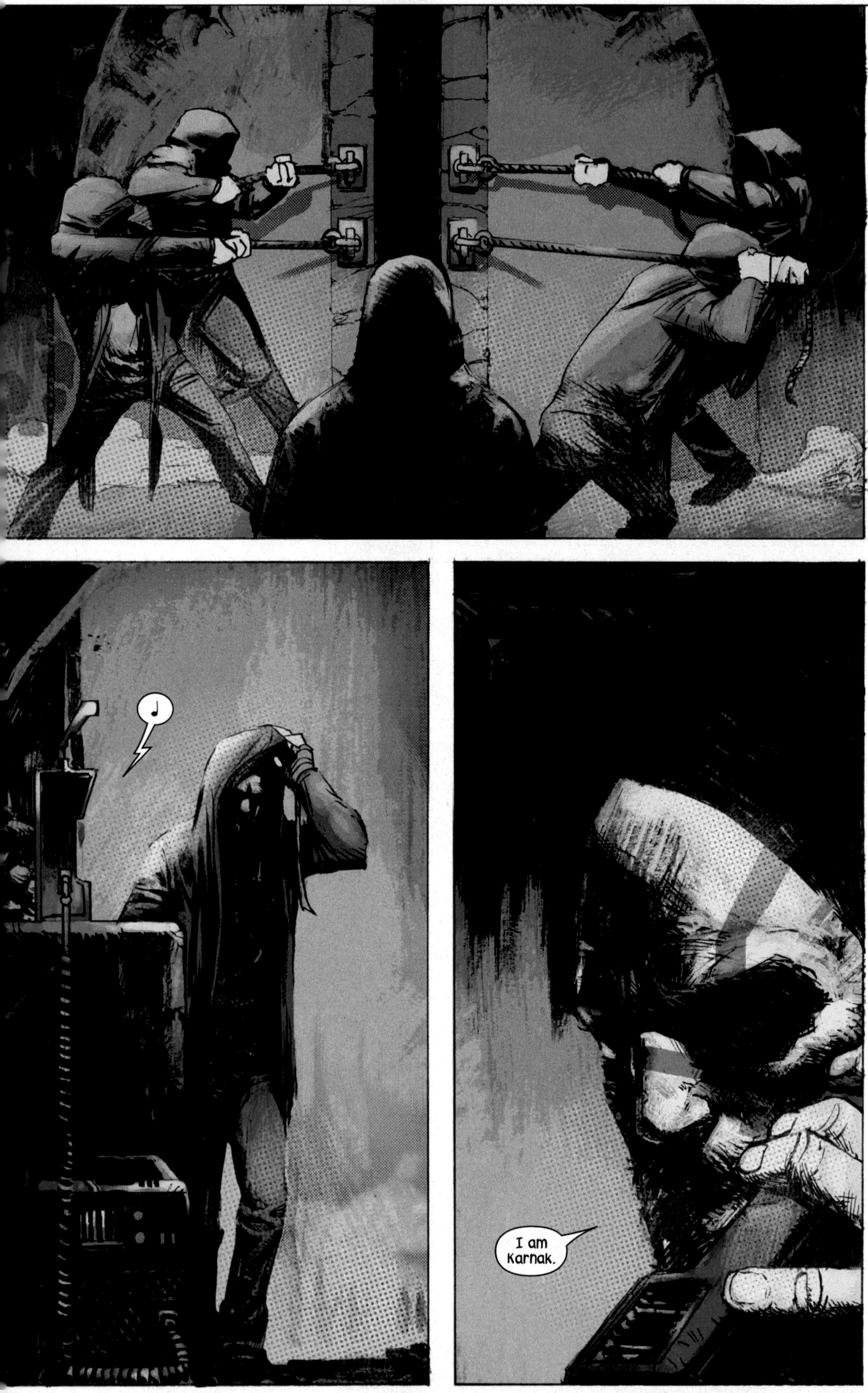
♩
I am Karnak.

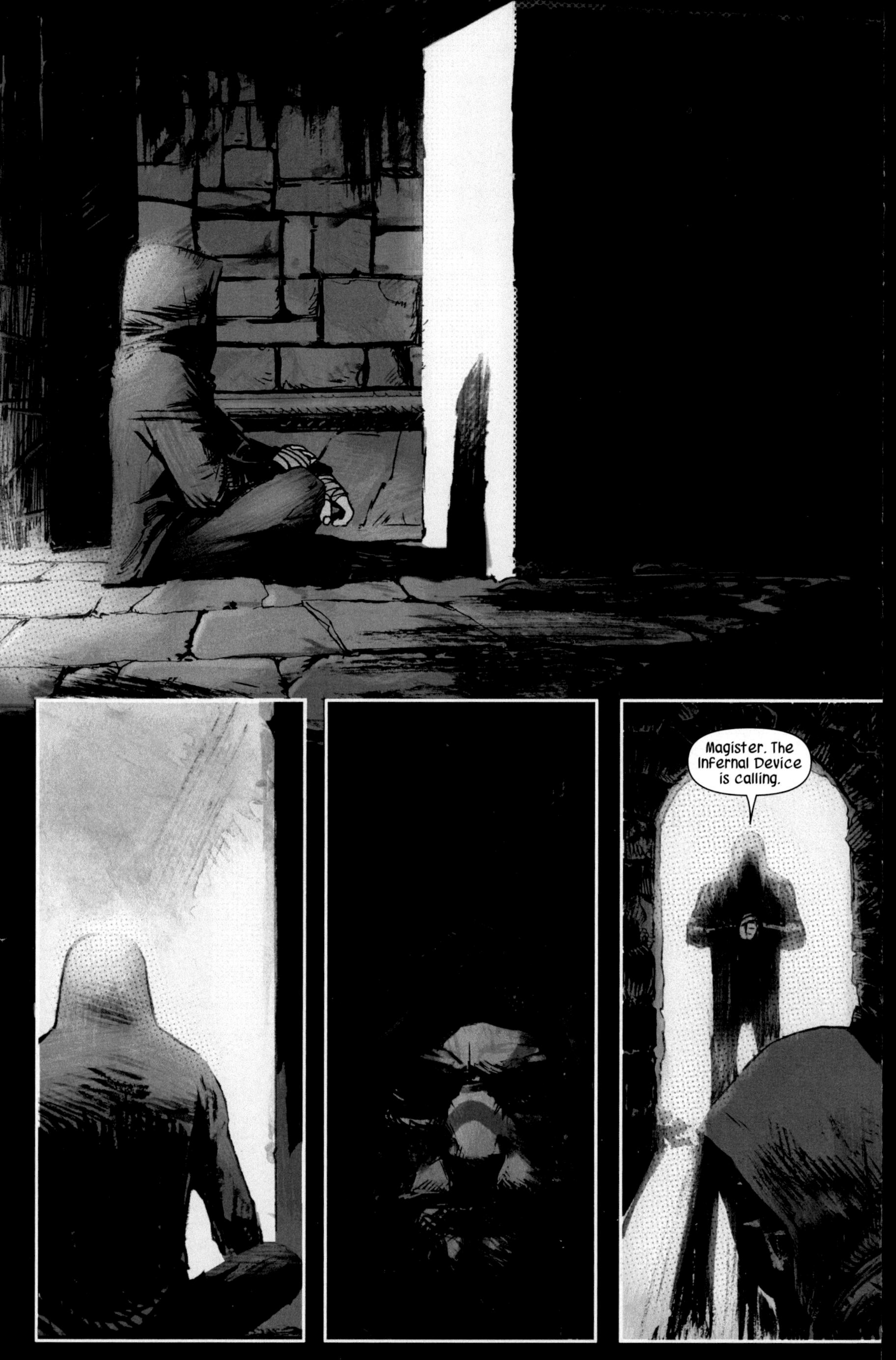
Magister. The Infernal Device is calling.

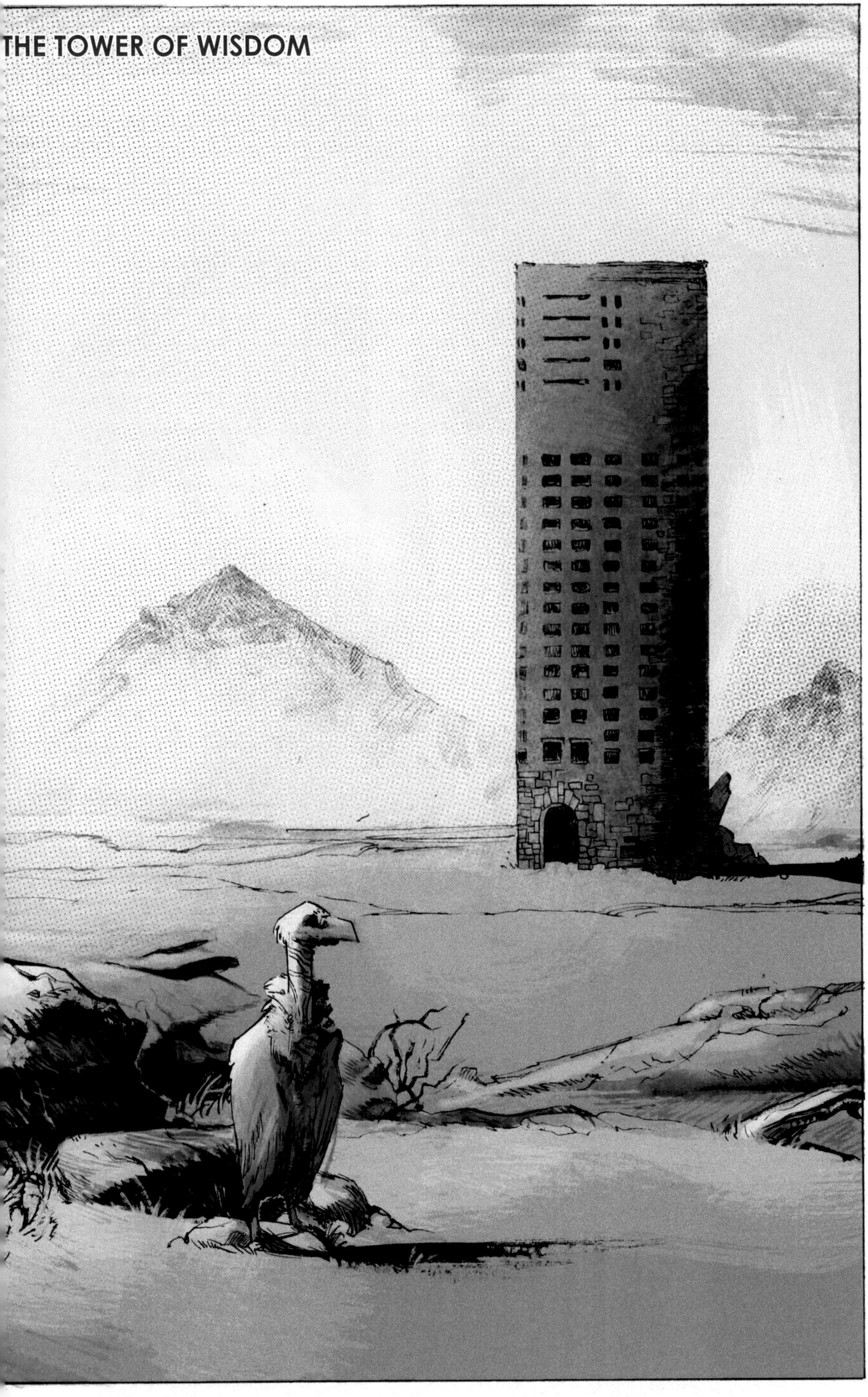
THE TOWER OF WISDOM

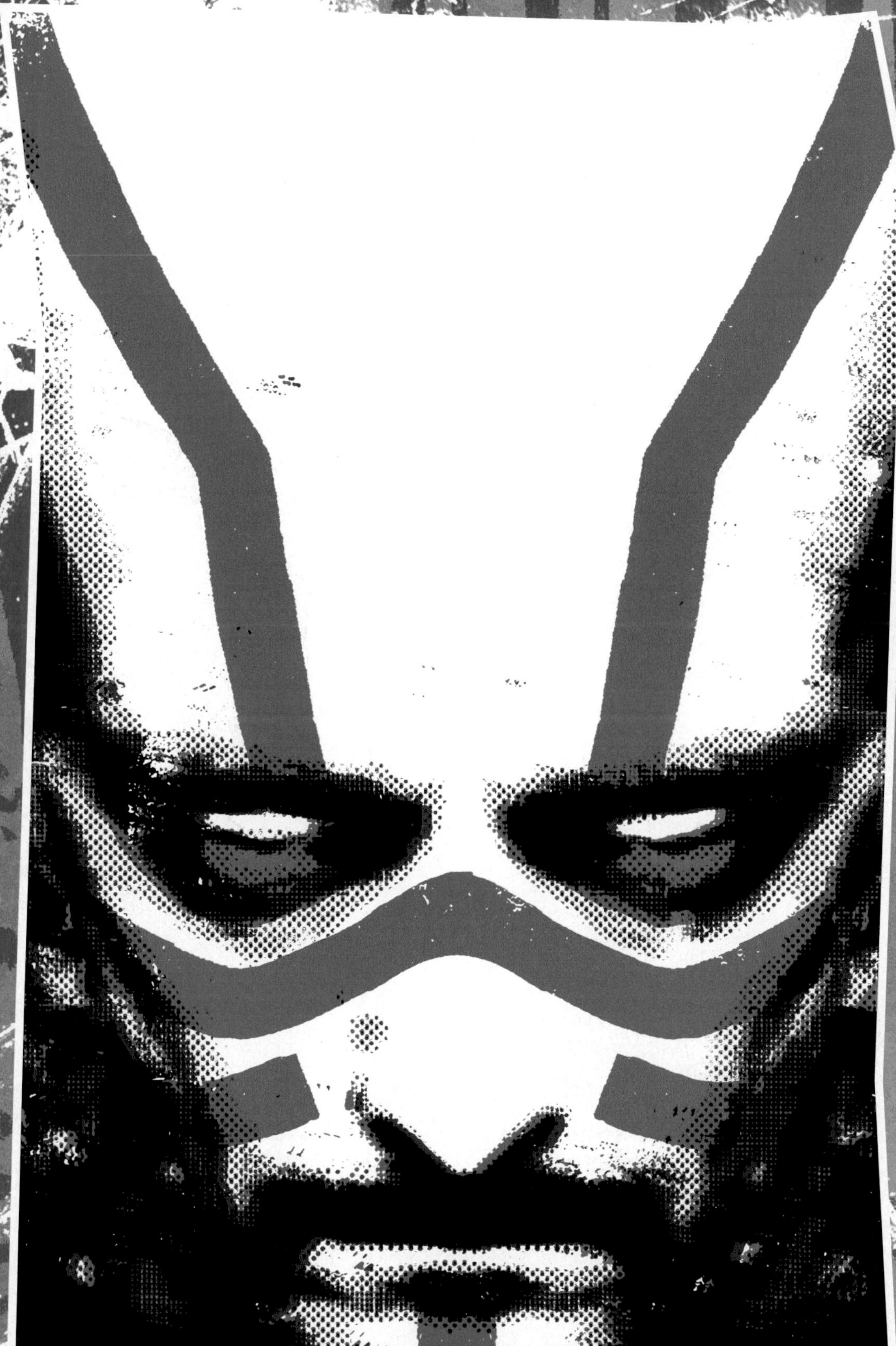

# ONE

# KARNAK
## THE FLAW IN ALL THINGS

**WARREN ELLIS**
WRITER

**GERARDO ZAFFINO** [#1-2]
**& ROLAND BOSCHI** [#3-6]
WITH **ANTONIO FUSO** [#2]
ARTISTS

**DAN BROWN**
COLOR ARTIST

**VC's CLAYTON COWLES**
WITH JOE CARAMAGNA [#2]
LETTERERS

**DAVID AJA**
COVER ART

**CHARLES BEACHAM**
ASSISTANT EDITOR

**DARREN SHAN**
ASSOCIATE EDITOR

**NICK LOWE**
EDITOR

KARNAK CREATED BY **STAN LEE & JACK KIRBY**

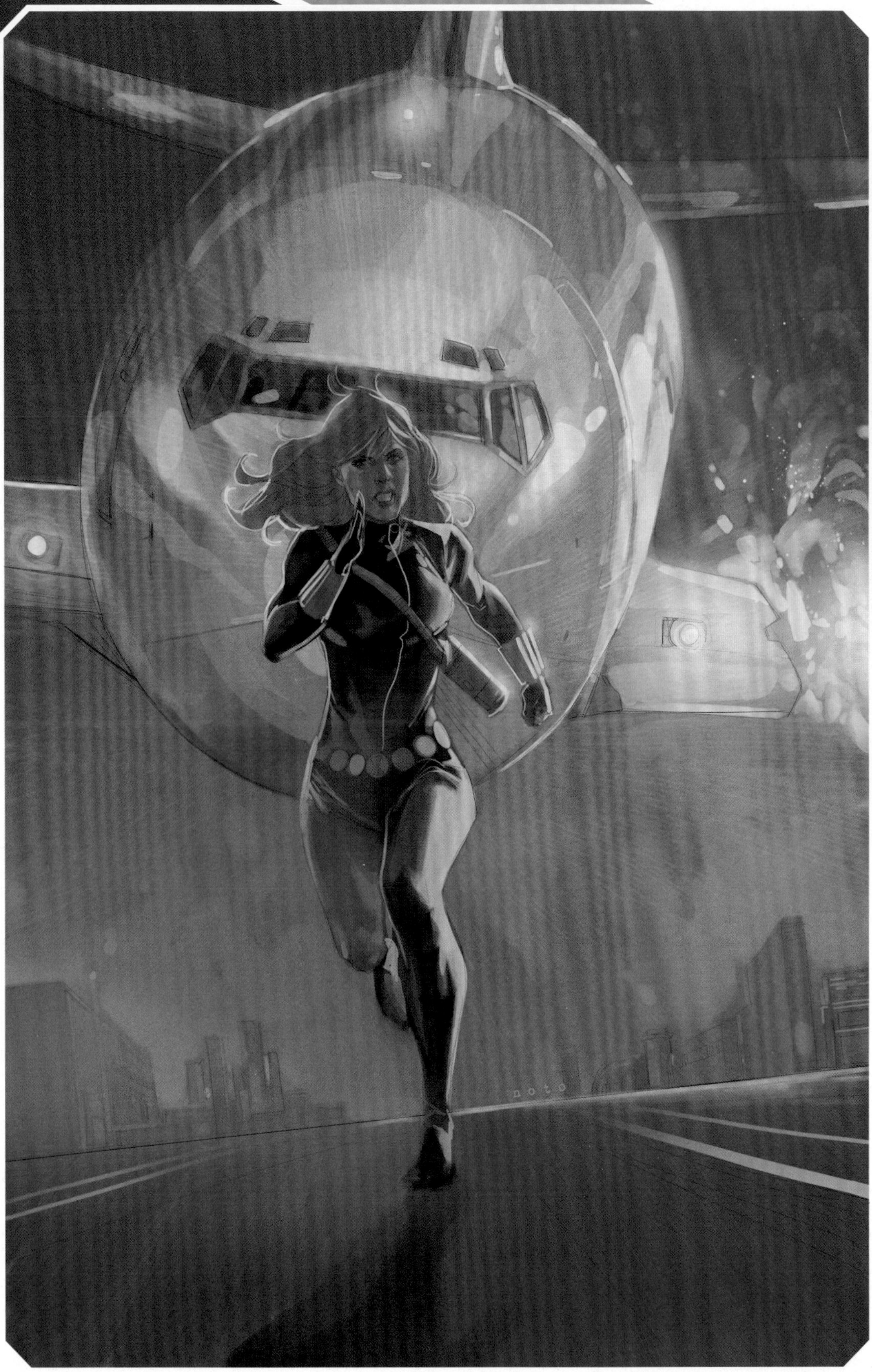

BLACK WIDOW #5

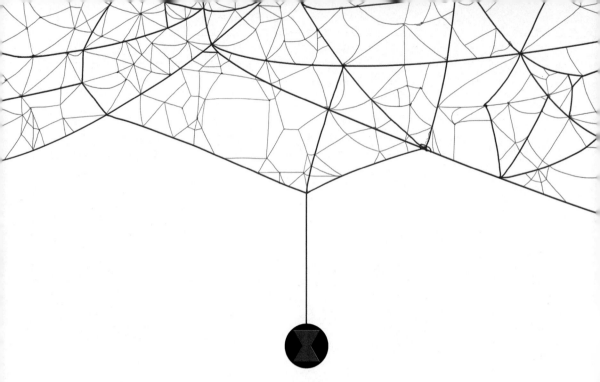

NATASHA ROMANOVA IS AN AVENGER, AN AGENT OF S.H.I.E.L.D. AND AN EX-KGB ASSASSIN, BUT ON HER OWN TIME, SHE USES HER UNIQUE SKILL SET TO ATONE FOR HER PAST. SHE IS:

# BLACK WIDOW

WHILE ON A MISSION FOR S.H.I.E.L.D., NATASHA ROMANOVA WITNESSED AN EMBASSY BOMBING. SHE CHASED DOWN THE MAD MONK RESPONSIBLE TWICE, BUT BOTH TIMES THIS SELF-TITLED "HAMMER OF GOD" WAS ABLE TO ESCAPE BY KNOCKING HER UNCONSCIOUS. SHE DOES NOT LIKE LOSING.

## "FOR THE BIRDS"

**NATHAN EDMONDSON**
WRITER

**PHIL NOTO**
ARTIST

**VC's CLAYTON COWLES**
LETTERER & PRODUCTION

**ELLIE PYLE**
EDITOR

**AXEL ALONSO**
EDITOR IN CHIEF

**JOE QUESADA**
CHIEF CREATIVE OFFICER

**DAN BUCKLEY**
PUBLISHER

**ALAN FINE**
EXEC. PRODUCER

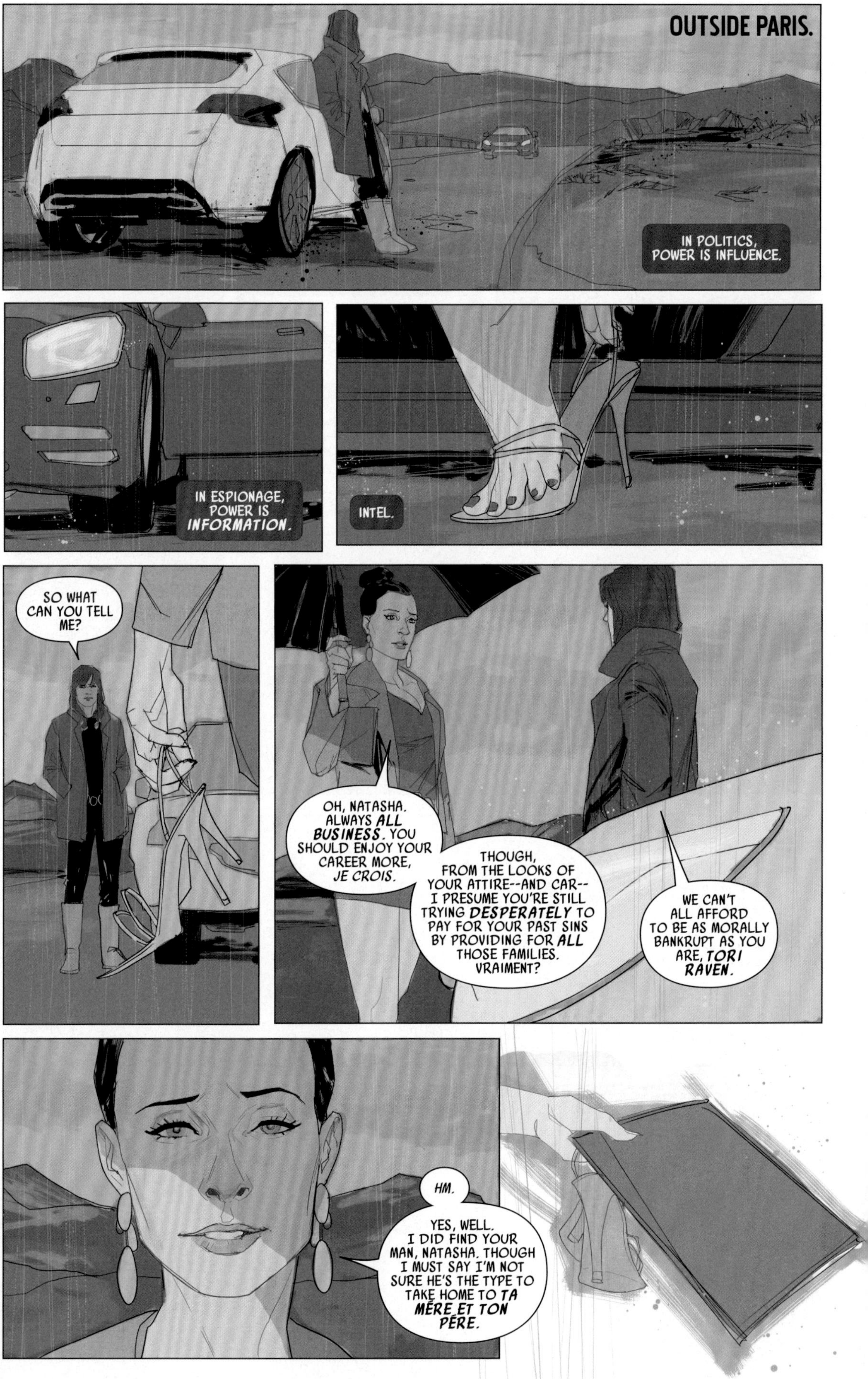
OUTSIDE PARIS.
IN POLITICS, POWER IS INFLUENCE.
IN ESPIONAGE, POWER IS INFORMATION.
INTEL.
SO WHAT CAN YOU TELL ME?
OH, NATASHA. ALWAYS ALL BUSINESS. YOU SHOULD ENJOY YOUR CAREER MORE, JE CROIS.
THOUGH, FROM THE LOOKS OF YOUR ATTIRE--AND CAR-- I PRESUME YOU'RE STILL TRYING DESPERATELY TO PAY FOR YOUR PAST SINS BY PROVIDING FOR ALL THOSE FAMILIES. VRAIMENT?
WE CAN'T ALL AFFORD TO BE AS MORALLY BANKRUPT AS YOU ARE, TORI RAVEN.
HM.
YES, WELL. I DID FIND YOUR MAN, NATASHA. THOUGH I MUST SAY I'M NOT SURE HE'S THE TYPE TO TAKE HOME TO TA MÉRE ET TON PÉRE.

HIS NAME IS MOLOT BOGA, OR *"HAMMER OF GOD."*

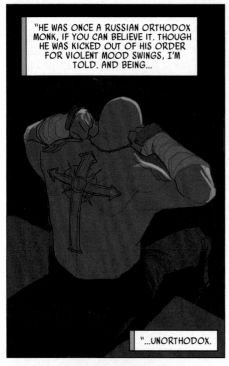

"HE WAS ONCE A RUSSIAN ORTHODOX MONK, IF YOU CAN BELIEVE IT. THOUGH HE WAS KICKED OUT OF HIS ORDER FOR VIOLENT MOOD SWINGS, I'M TOLD. AND BEING...

"...UNORTHODOX.

"HE'S DEVOUT BUT ABOUT AS THEOLOGICALLY CORRECT AS A TEMPLAR KNIGHT. USES HIS *DEVOTION* TO FUEL ACTS OF VENGEANCE AND VIOLENCE...

"APPARENTLY ALL MOTIVATED BY SOME TRAUMA FROM HIS YOUTH, FAMILY KILLED OR SOMETHING, BLAH BLAH BLAH--"

YOU KNOW? YOU TWO MIGHT BE GOOD FOR EACH OTHER AFTER ALL. A LOT IN COMMON.

DO YOU KNOW WHO HE'S WORKING FOR? OR WHERE HE IS?

WHO HE'S WORKING FOR...NOW THAT'S THE TRICKY ONE. CAN'T ANSWER THAT ONE FOR YOU.

BUT AS FOR WHERE HE IS?

IN ABOUT TWO HOURS HE'LL BE BLOWING UP AN AIRLINER AT GATWICK AIRPORT.

HURRY ALONG, LITTLE SPIDER...

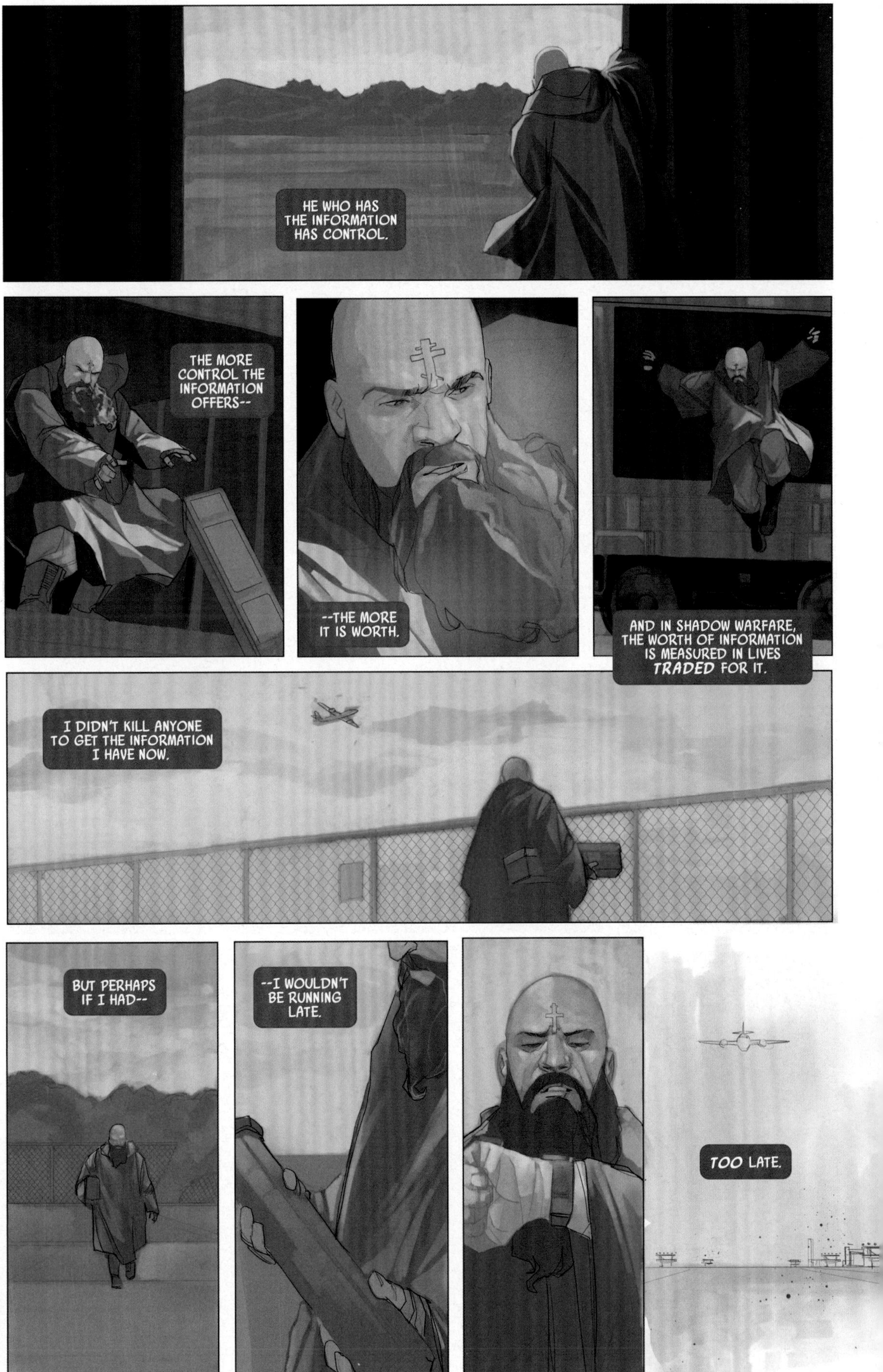
HE WHO HAS THE INFORMATION HAS CONTROL.
THE MORE CONTROL THE INFORMATION OFFERS--
--THE MORE IT IS WORTH.
AND IN SHADOW WARFARE, THE WORTH OF INFORMATION IS MEASURED IN LIVES *TRADED* FOR IT.
I DIDN'T KILL ANYONE TO GET THE INFORMATION I HAVE NOW.
BUT PERHAPS IF I HAD--
--I WOULDN'T BE RUNNING LATE.
*TOO* LATE.

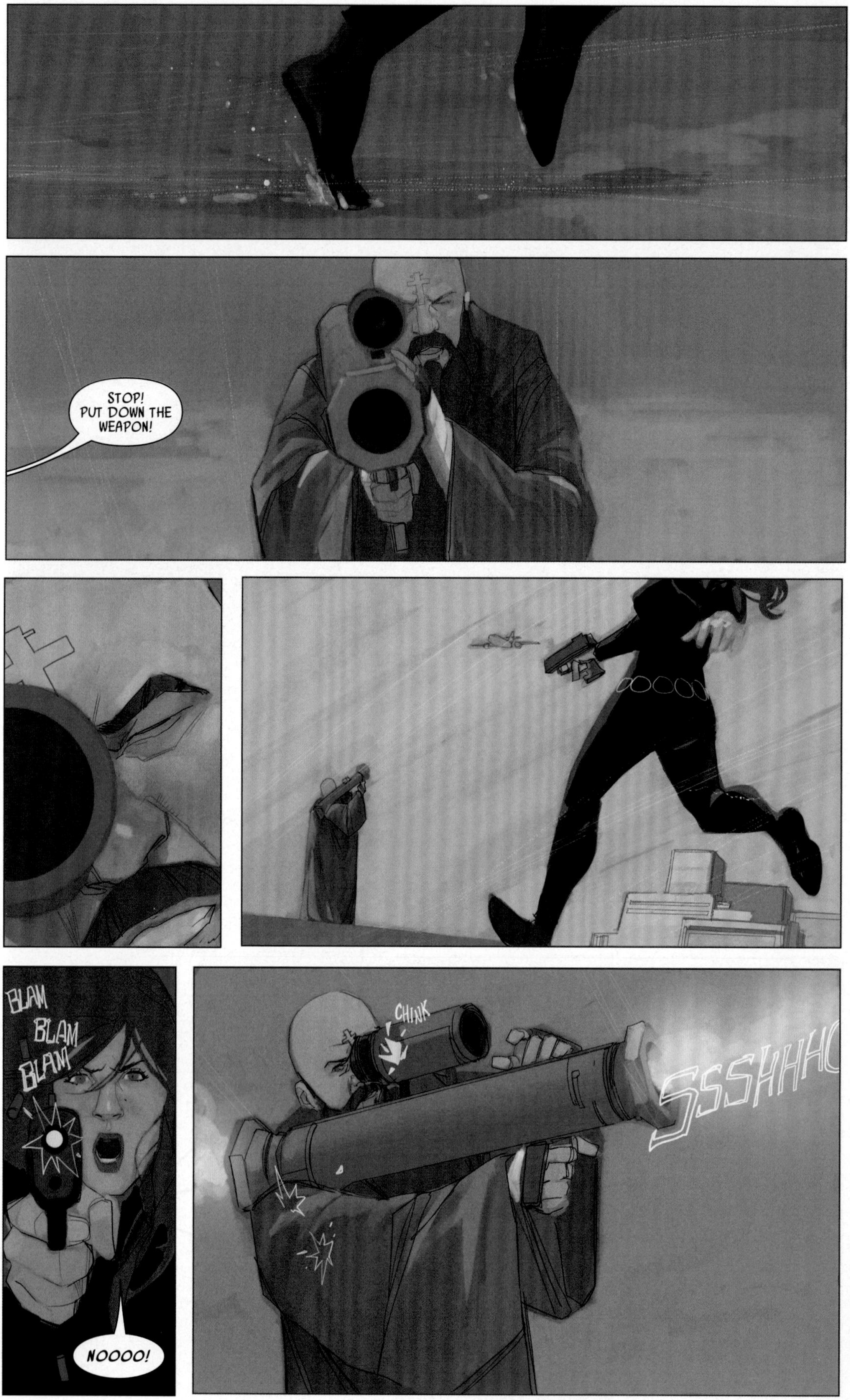
STOP! PUT DOWN THE WEAPON!
BLAM
BLAM
BLAM
NOOOO!
CHINK
SSSHHHO

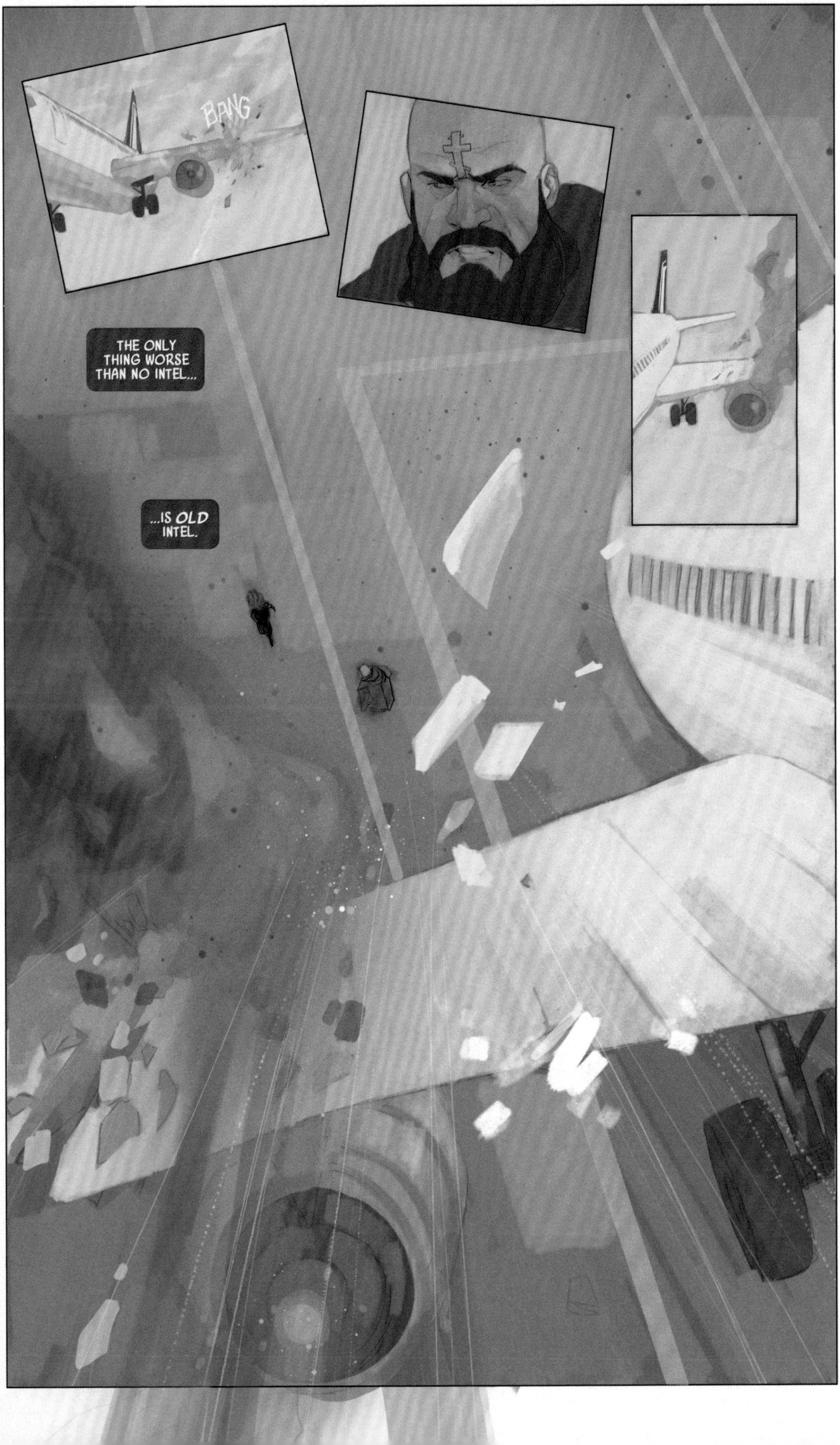
BANG
THE ONLY THING WORSE THAN NO INTEL...
...IS *OLD* INTEL.

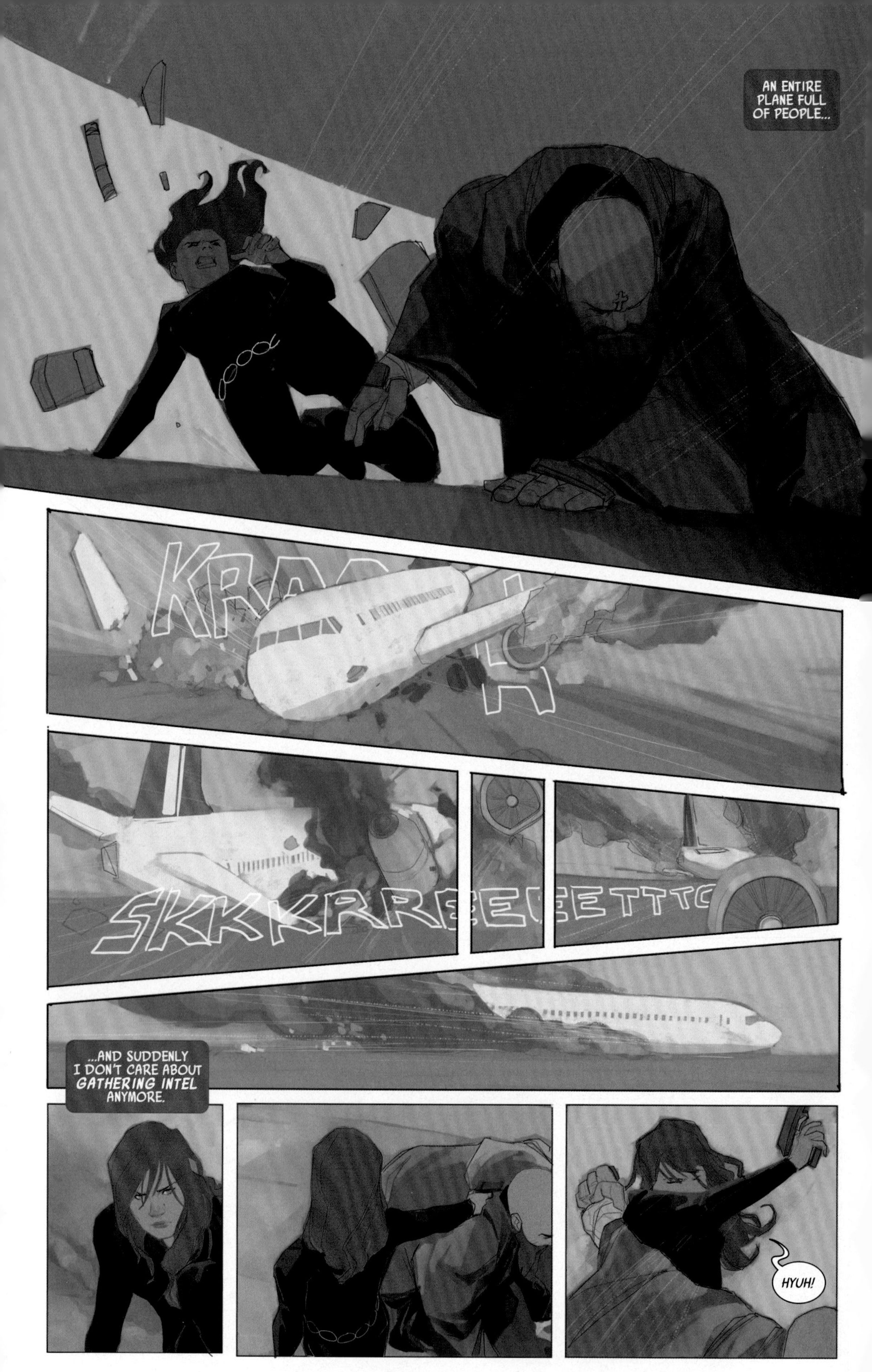
AN ENTIRE PLANE FULL OF PEOPLE...
SKKRREEEEETTTC
...AND SUDDENLY I DON'T CARE ABOUT GATHERING INTEL ANYMORE.
HYUH!

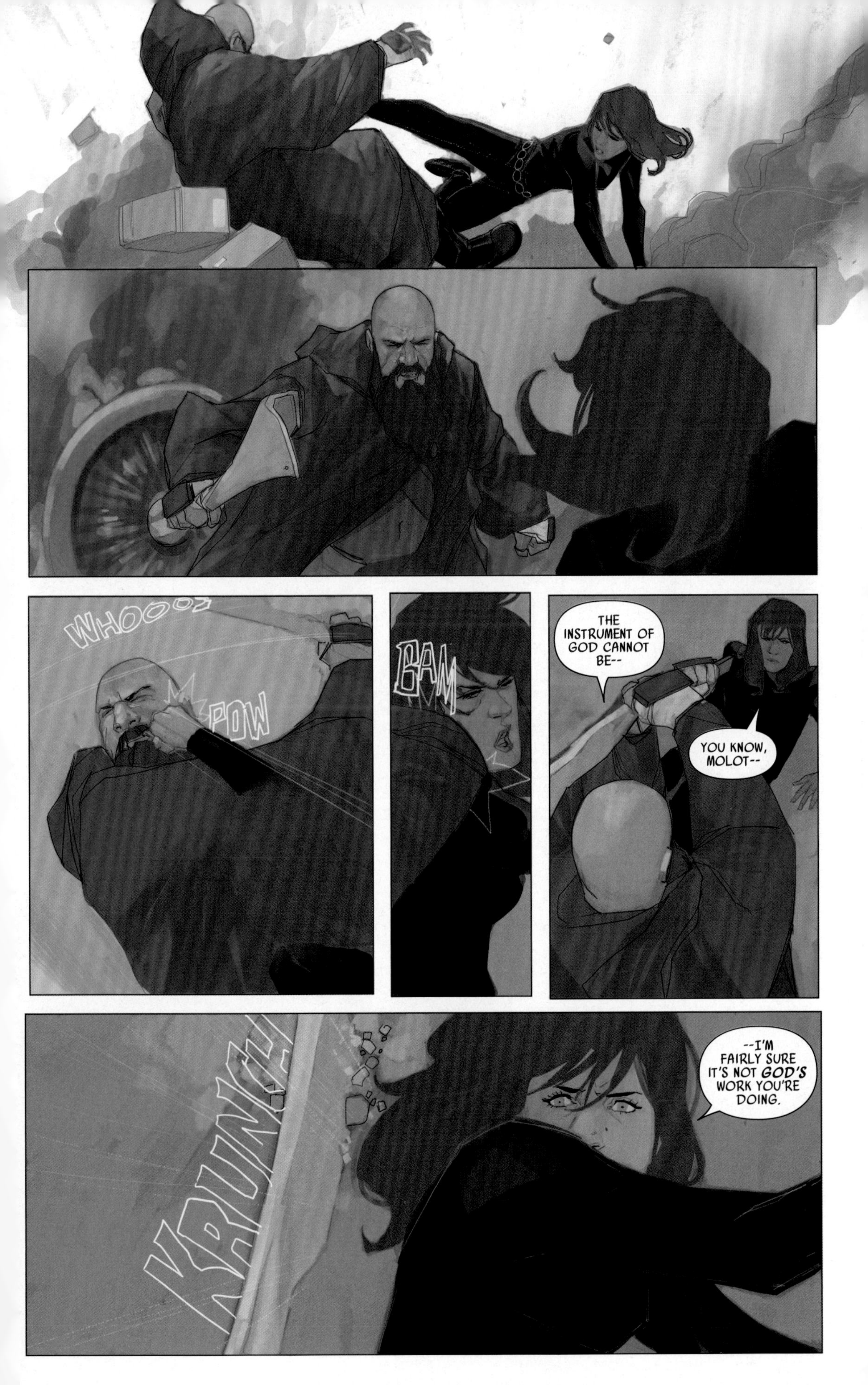
WHOOOO
POW
BAM
THE INSTRUMENT OF GOD CANNOT BE--
YOU KNOW, MOLOT--
KRUNCH
--I'M FAIRLY SURE IT'S NOT GOD'S WORK YOU'RE DOING.

THEY MUST BE PUNISHED FOR THEIR SINS.

PRO TIP: (OFTEN LEARNED TOO LATE) DON'T ARGUE WITH CRAZY.

JUST EXPECT CRAZY...

BAMM

BAMM

...TO BE &@#$%&# INSANE.

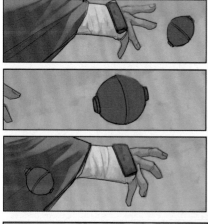

BCOOM

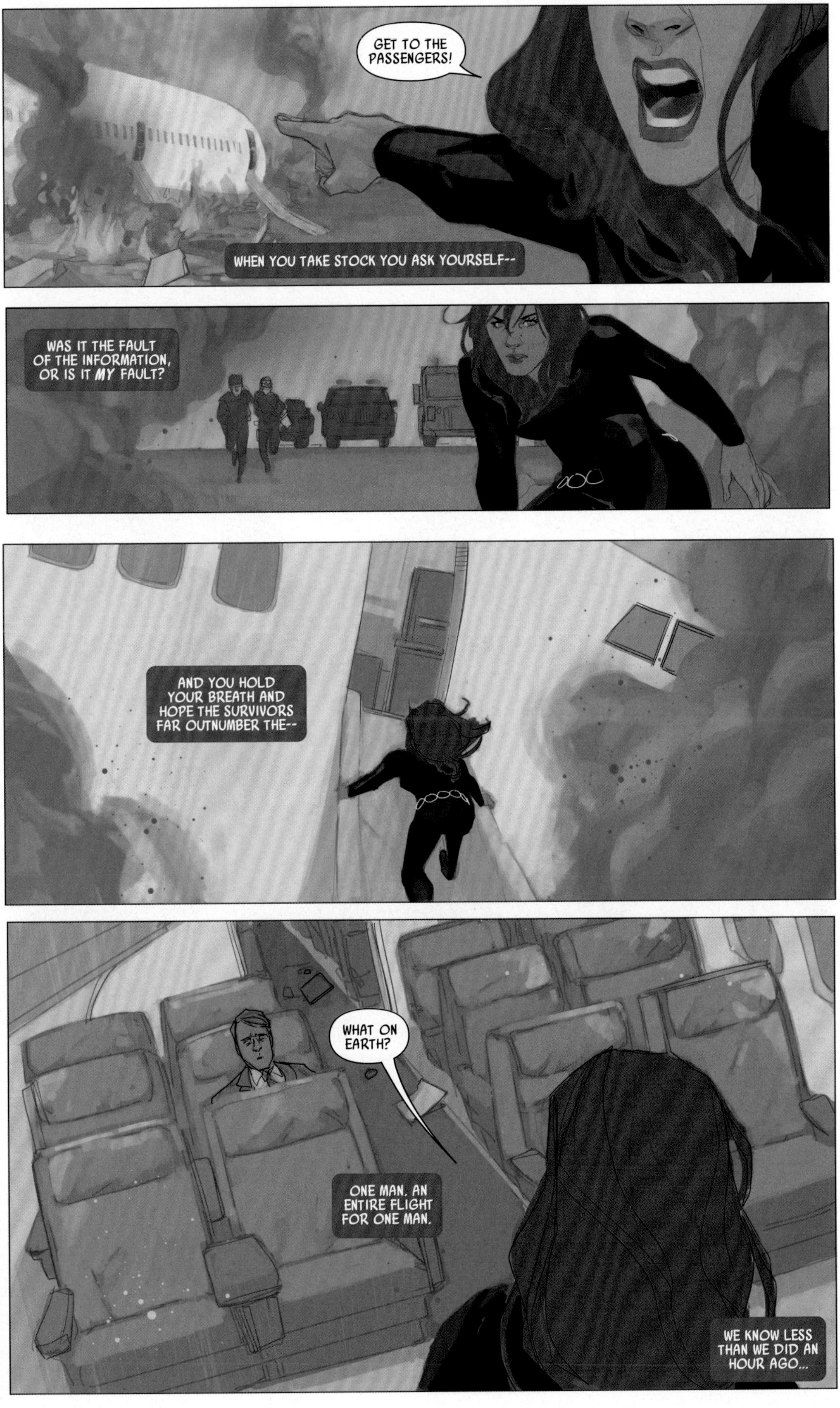
GET TO THE PASSENGERS!
WHEN YOU TAKE STOCK YOU ASK YOURSELF--
WAS IT THE FAULT OF THE INFORMATION, OR IS IT *MY* FAULT?
AND YOU HOLD YOUR BREATH AND HOPE THE SURVIVORS FAR OUTNUMBER THE--
WHAT ON EARTH?
ONE MAN. AN ENTIRE FLIGHT FOR ONE MAN.
WE KNOW LESS THAN WE DID AN HOUR AGO...

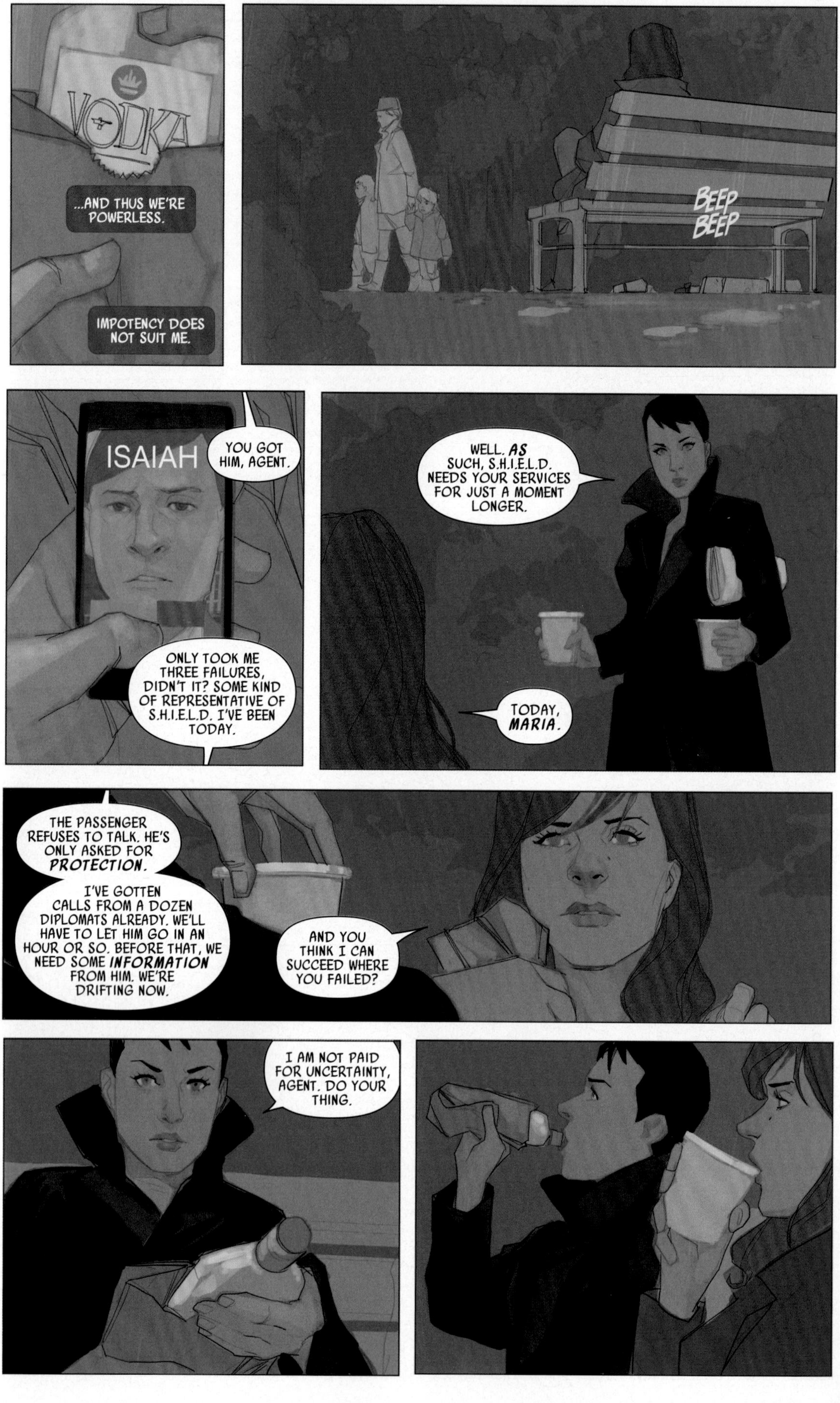

VODKA
...AND THUS WE'RE POWERLESS.
IMPOTENCY DOES NOT SUIT ME.
BEEP BEEP
ISAIAH
YOU GOT HIM, AGENT.
ONLY TOOK ME THREE FAILURES, DIDN'T IT? SOME KIND OF REPRESENTATIVE OF S.H.I.E.L.D. I'VE BEEN TODAY.
WELL. AS SUCH, S.H.I.E.L.D. NEEDS YOUR SERVICES FOR JUST A MOMENT LONGER.
TODAY, MARIA.
THE PASSENGER REFUSES TO TALK. HE'S ONLY ASKED FOR PROTECTION.
I'VE GOTTEN CALLS FROM A DOZEN DIPLOMATS ALREADY. WE'LL HAVE TO LET HIM GO IN AN HOUR OR SO. BEFORE THAT, WE NEED SOME INFORMATION FROM HIM. WE'RE DRIFTING NOW.
AND YOU THINK I CAN SUCCEED WHERE YOU FAILED?
I AM NOT PAID FOR UNCERTAINTY, AGENT. DO YOUR THING.

IS SOMEONE COMING TO--

QUIET, PLEASE.

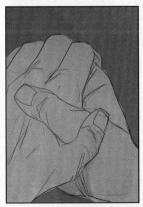

IS SOMEONE COMING FOR ME? I HAVE TO LEAVE SOON. I'M NOT *SAFE.*

WHAT PART OF *QUIET* IS UNCLEAR?

YOU MUST LET ME GO.

IS THAT SO?

HE WILL *COME* FOR ME.

YOU MEAN COMRADE GROUND BEEF? NOT LIKELY. HE WAS STRONG, BUT A *737* TURBINE...YIKES.

YOU FOOL. THE MONK WAS BUT A FINGER OF THE HAND!

THIS PLACE IS NOT SAFE FROM *HIM!* HE'S INDESTRUCTIBLE!

WHO IS *HE,* THEN?

CAN YOU STOP HIM?

YES, I CAN.

NO, YOU CAN'T.

WHAT-- NO--

HELP! GET US SOME HELP IN HERE!

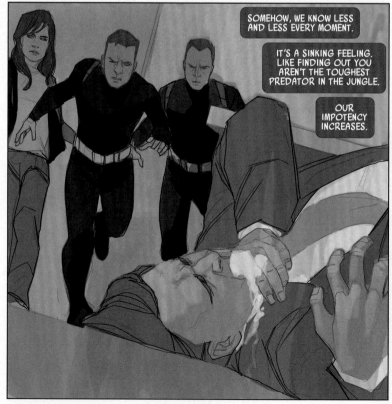

SOMEHOW, WE KNOW LESS AND LESS EVERY MOMENT.

IT'S A SINKING FEELING, LIKE FINDING OUT YOU AREN'T THE TOUGHEST PREDATOR IN THE JUNGLE.

OUR IMPOTENCY INCREASES.

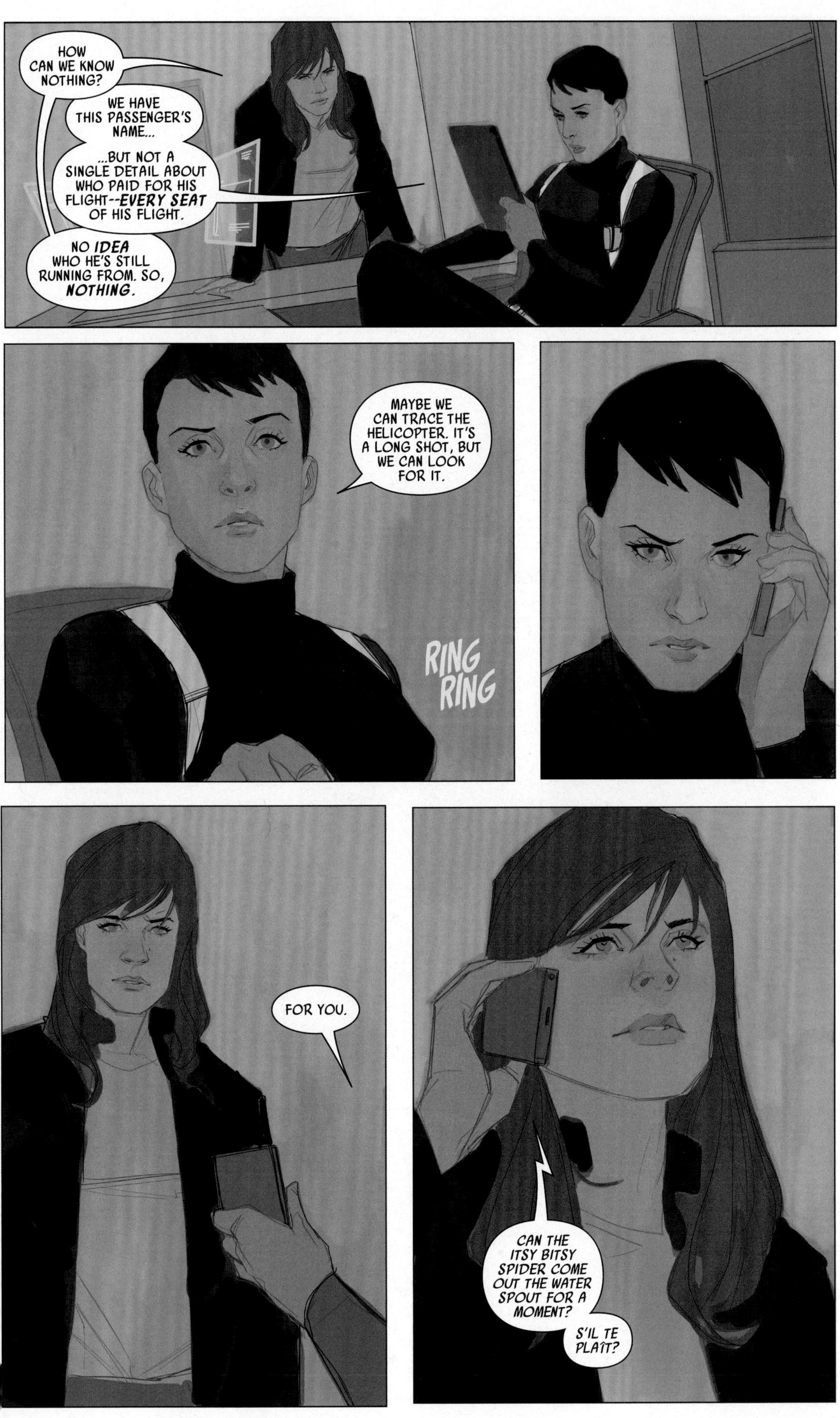
HOW CAN WE KNOW NOTHING?
WE HAVE THIS PASSENGER'S NAME...
...BUT NOT A SINGLE DETAIL ABOUT WHO PAID FOR HIS FLIGHT--EVERY SEAT OF HIS FLIGHT.
NO IDEA WHO HE'S STILL RUNNING FROM. SO, NOTHING.
MAYBE WE CAN TRACE THE HELICOPTER. IT'S A LONG SHOT, BUT WE CAN LOOK FOR IT.
RING RING
FOR YOU.
CAN THE ITSY BITSY SPIDER COME OUT THE WATER SPOUT FOR A MOMENT?
S'IL TE PLAÎT?

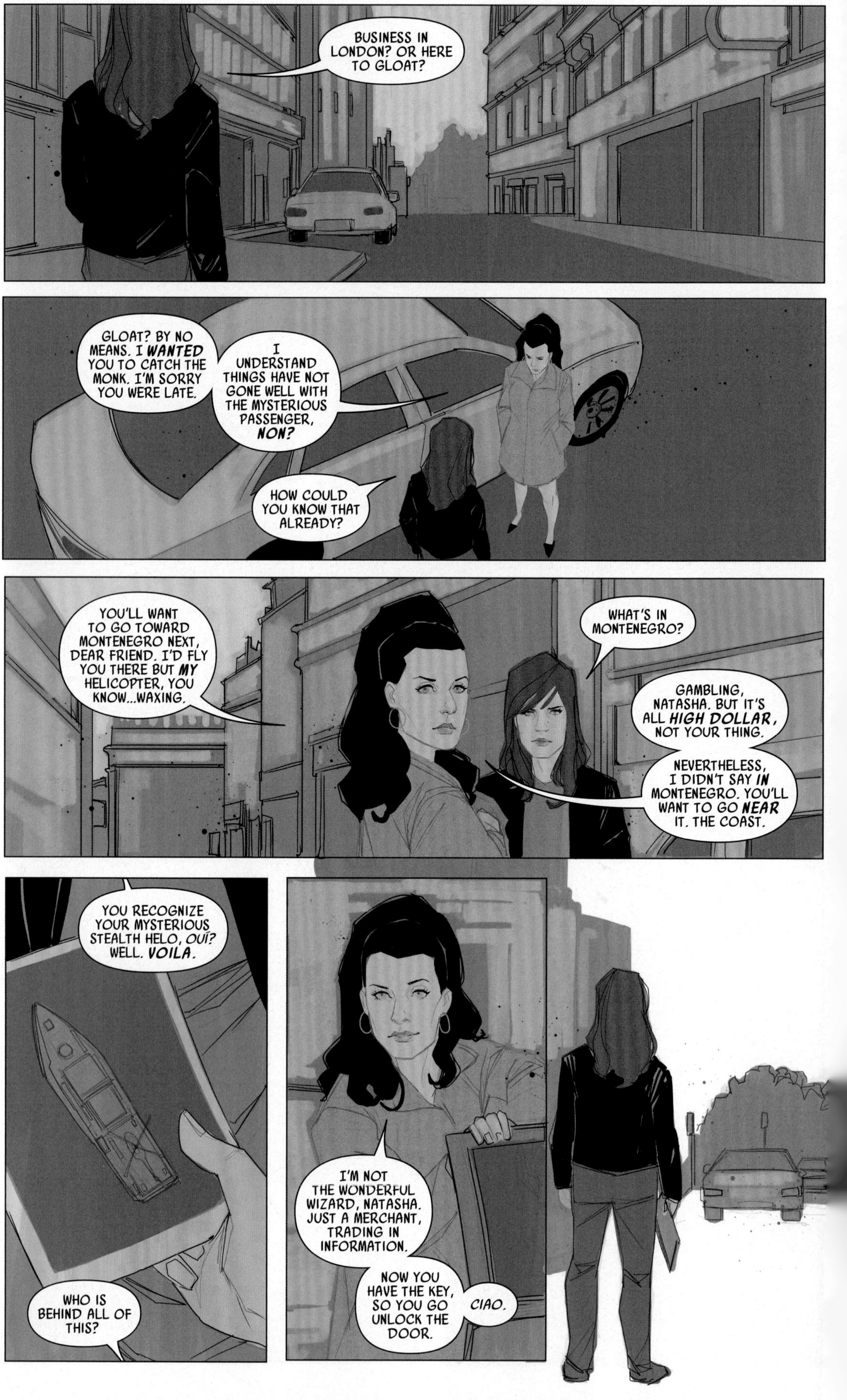
BUSINESS IN LONDON? OR HERE TO GLOAT?
GLOAT? BY NO MEANS. I WANTED YOU TO CATCH THE MONK. I'M SORRY YOU WERE LATE.
I UNDERSTAND THINGS HAVE NOT GONE WELL WITH THE MYSTERIOUS PASSENGER, NON?
HOW COULD YOU KNOW THAT ALREADY?
YOU'LL WANT TO GO TOWARD MONTENEGRO NEXT, DEAR FRIEND. I'D FLY YOU THERE BUT MY HELICOPTER, YOU KNOW...WAXING.
WHAT'S IN MONTENEGRO?
GAMBLING, NATASHA. BUT IT'S ALL HIGH DOLLAR, NOT YOUR THING.
NEVERTHELESS, I DIDN'T SAY IN MONTENEGRO. YOU'LL WANT TO GO NEAR IT. THE COAST.
YOU RECOGNIZE YOUR MYSTERIOUS STEALTH HELO, OUI? WELL. VOILA.
WHO IS BEHIND ALL OF THIS?
I'M NOT THE WONDERFUL WIZARD, NATASHA. JUST A MERCHANT, TRADING IN INFORMATION.
NOW YOU HAVE THE KEY, SO YOU GO UNLOCK THE DOOR.
CIAO.

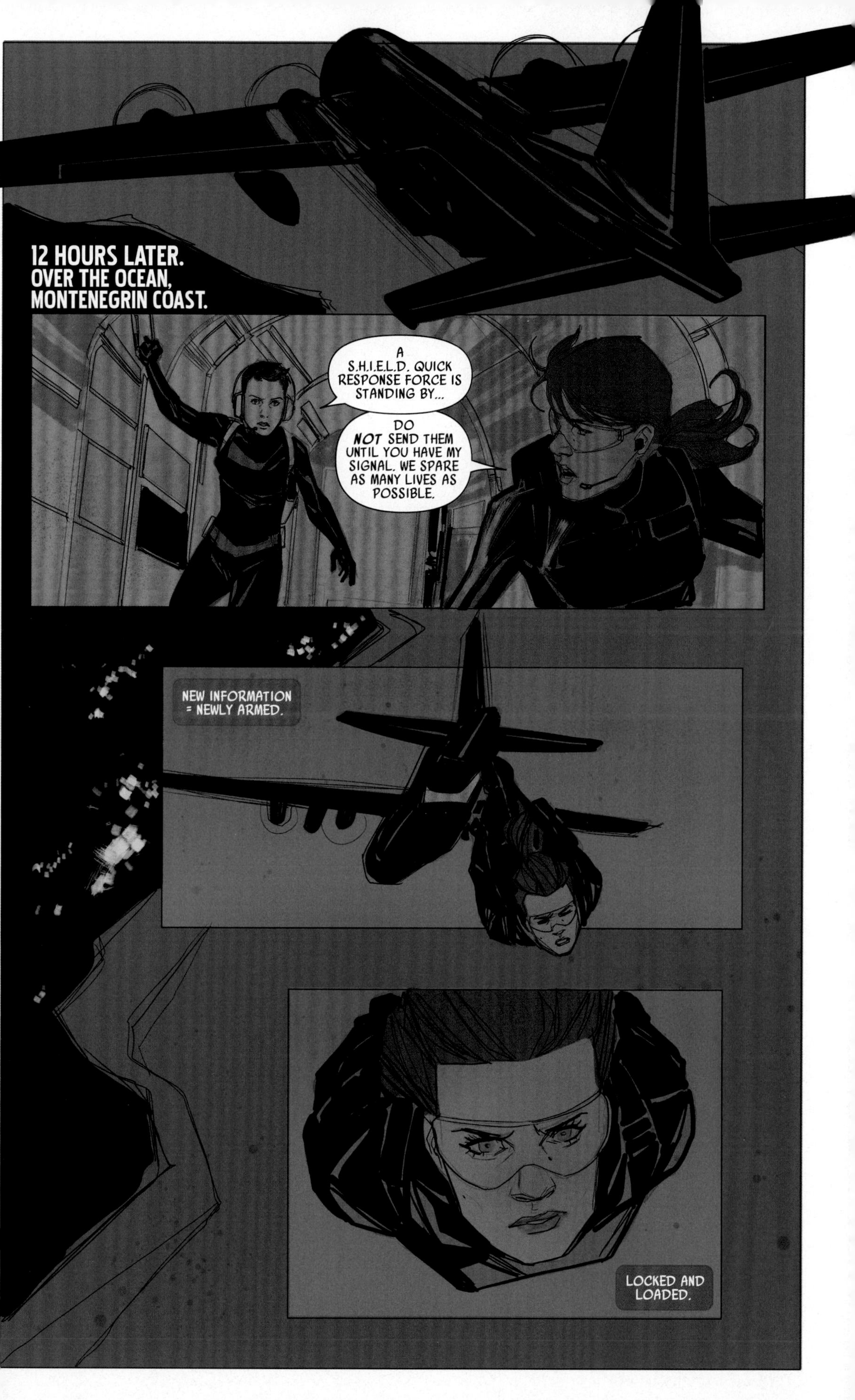
12 HOURS LATER. OVER THE OCEAN, MONTENEGRIN COAST.
A S.H.I.E.L.D. QUICK RESPONSE FORCE IS STANDING BY...
DO NOT SEND THEM UNTIL YOU HAVE MY SIGNAL. WE SPARE AS MANY LIVES AS POSSIBLE.
NEW INFORMATION = NEWLY ARMED.
LOCKED AND LOADED.

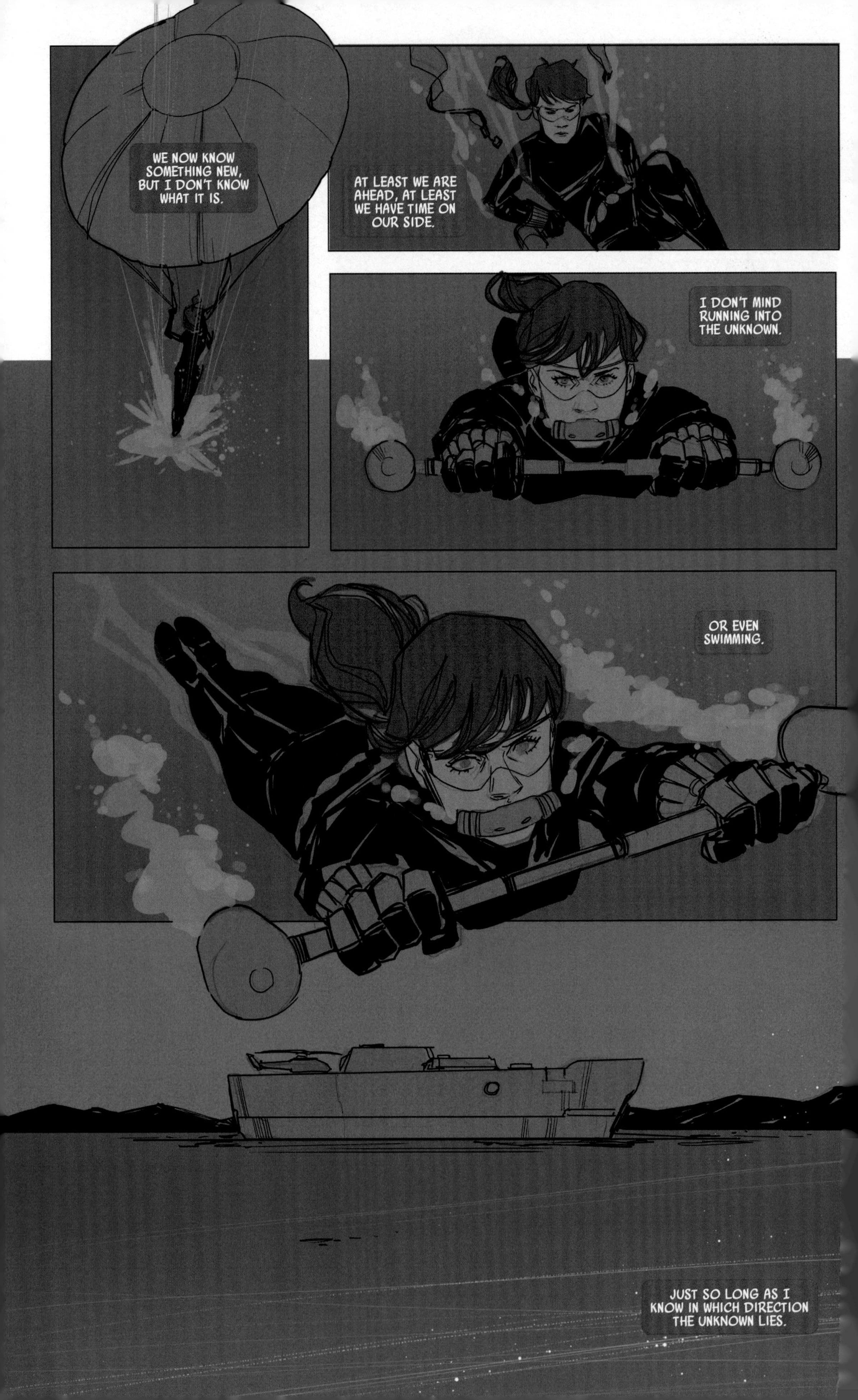
WE NOW KNOW SOMETHING NEW, BUT I DON'T KNOW WHAT IT IS.
AT LEAST WE ARE AHEAD, AT LEAST WE HAVE TIME ON OUR SIDE.
I DON'T MIND RUNNING INTO THE UNKNOWN.
OR EVEN SWIMMING.
JUST SO LONG AS I KNOW IN WHICH DIRECTION THE UNKNOWN LIES.

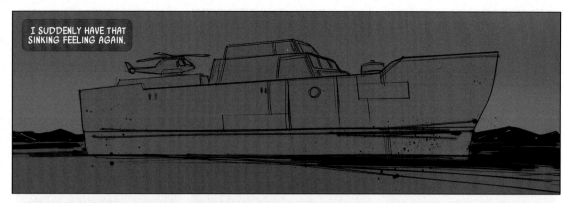

I SUDDENLY HAVE THAT SINKING FEELING AGAIN.

YEAH...

BLIND INTELLIGENCE IS LIKE AN UNPROVEN WEAPON.

IT SOMETIMES LEAVES YOU S.O.L.

IF YOU TRY TO MOVE, YOU WILL DIE.

THESE LASERS CAN HIT SOMETHING FIFTY FEET BELOW THE SURFACE.

COME ON. THE BOSS WILL DECIDE WHAT TO DO WITH YOU.

NATALIA ROMANOVA, IS IT?

NOW SOMETHING BECOMES CLEAR...

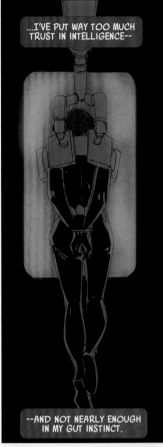

...I'VE PUT WAY TOO MUCH TRUST IN INTELLIGENCE--

--AND NOT NEARLY ENOUGH IN MY GUT INSTINCT.

I'M IN OVER MY HEAD, AND I HAVE NO ONE TO BLAME BUT MYSELF.

MISS NATASHA, YOU COME HERE, I HOPE, WITH SOME NEWS FOR ME.

DAMON DRAN?

YES, OLD FRIEND.

AND YOU HAVE ENDANGERED MY LIFE COMING HERE, BLACK WIDOW.

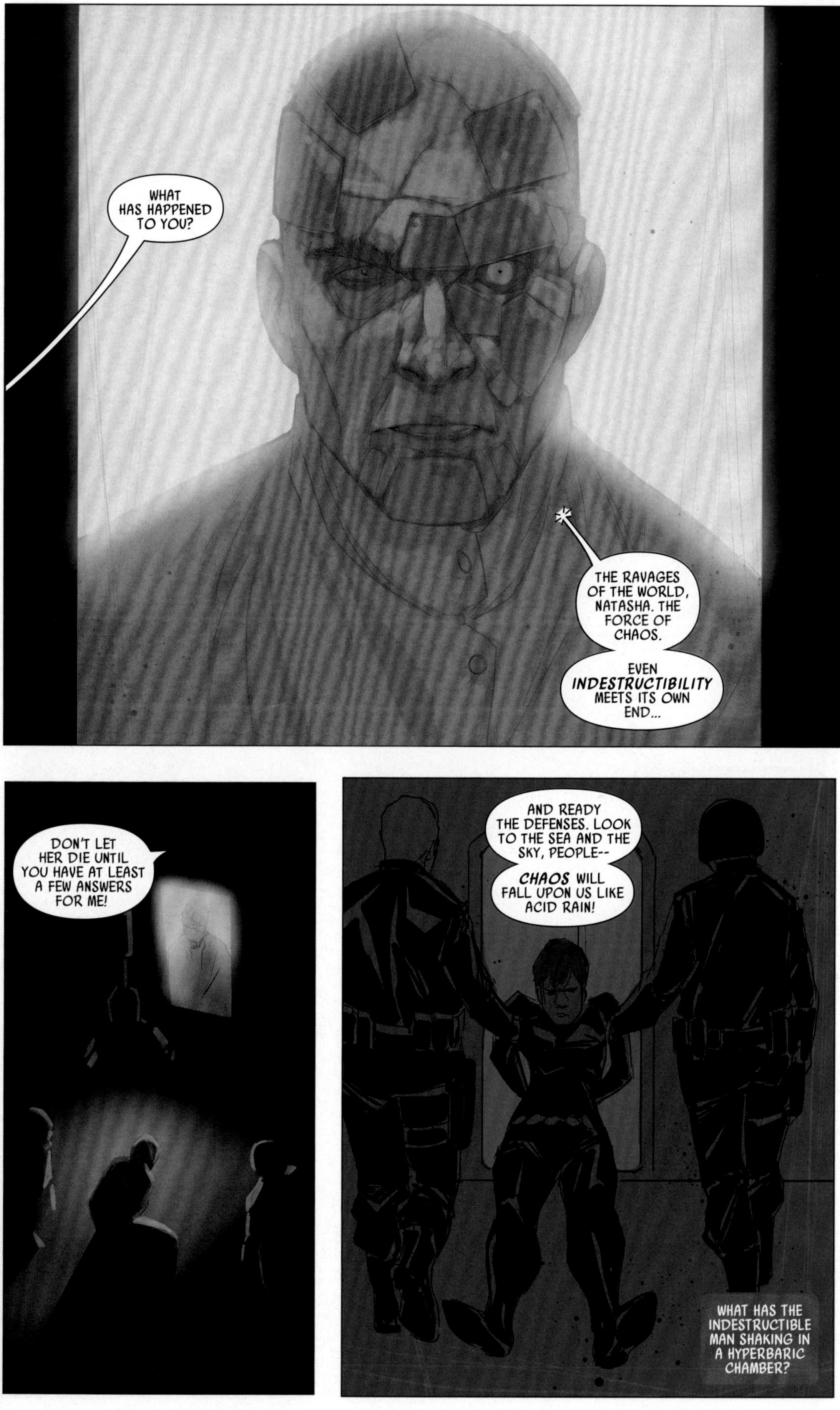
WHAT HAS HAPPENED TO YOU?
THE RAVAGES OF THE WORLD, NATASHA. THE FORCE OF CHAOS.
EVEN INDESTRUCTIBILITY MEETS ITS OWN END...
DON'T LET HER DIE UNTIL YOU HAVE AT LEAST A FEW ANSWERS FOR ME!
AND READY THE DEFENSES. LOOK TO THE SEA AND THE SKY, PEOPLE--
CHAOS WILL FALL UPON US LIKE ACID RAIN!
WHAT HAS THE INDESTRUCTIBLE MAN SHAKING IN A HYPERBARIC CHAMBER?

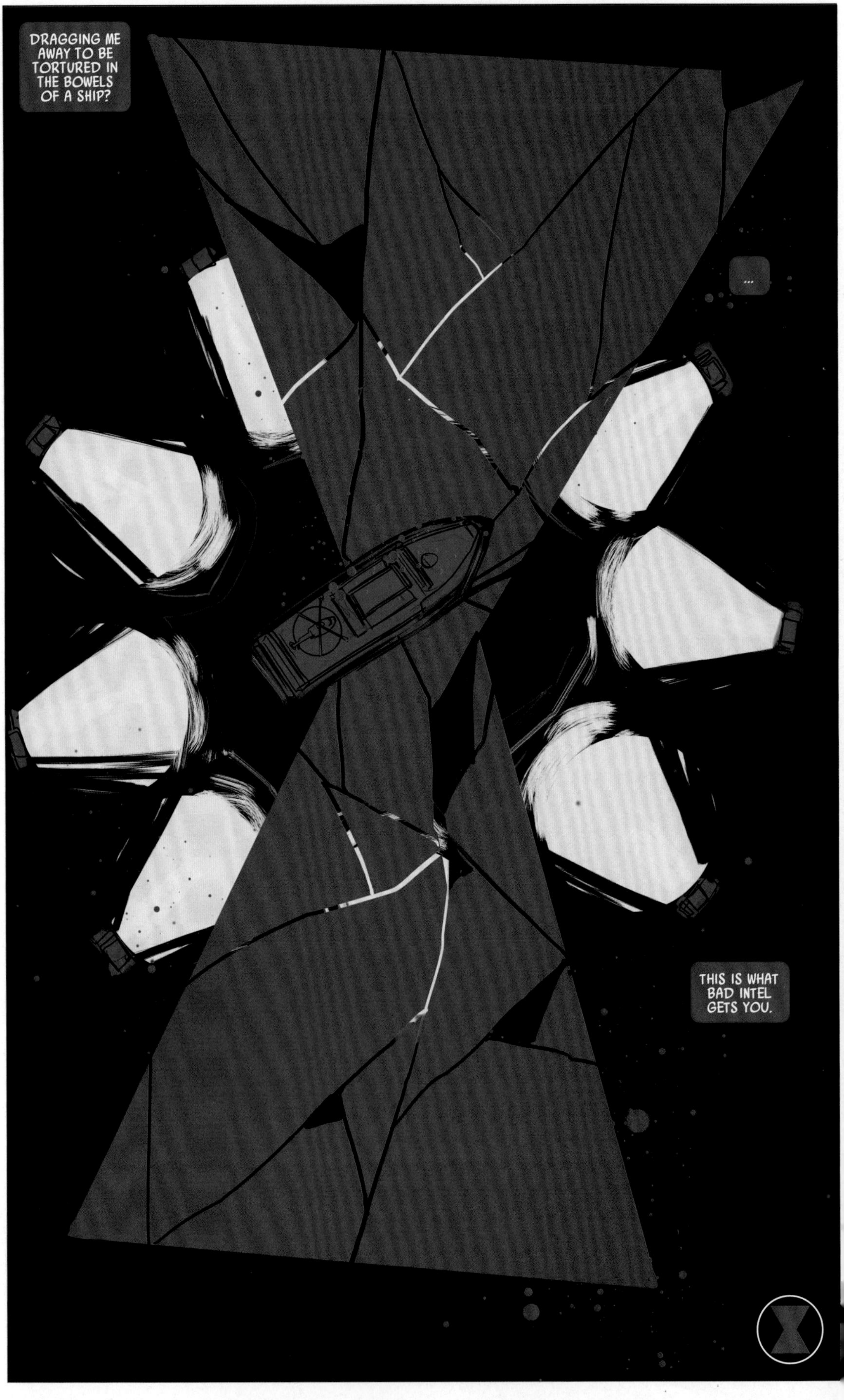
DRAGGING ME AWAY TO BE TORTURED IN THE BOWELS OF A SHIP?
...
THIS IS WHAT BAD INTEL GETS YOU.

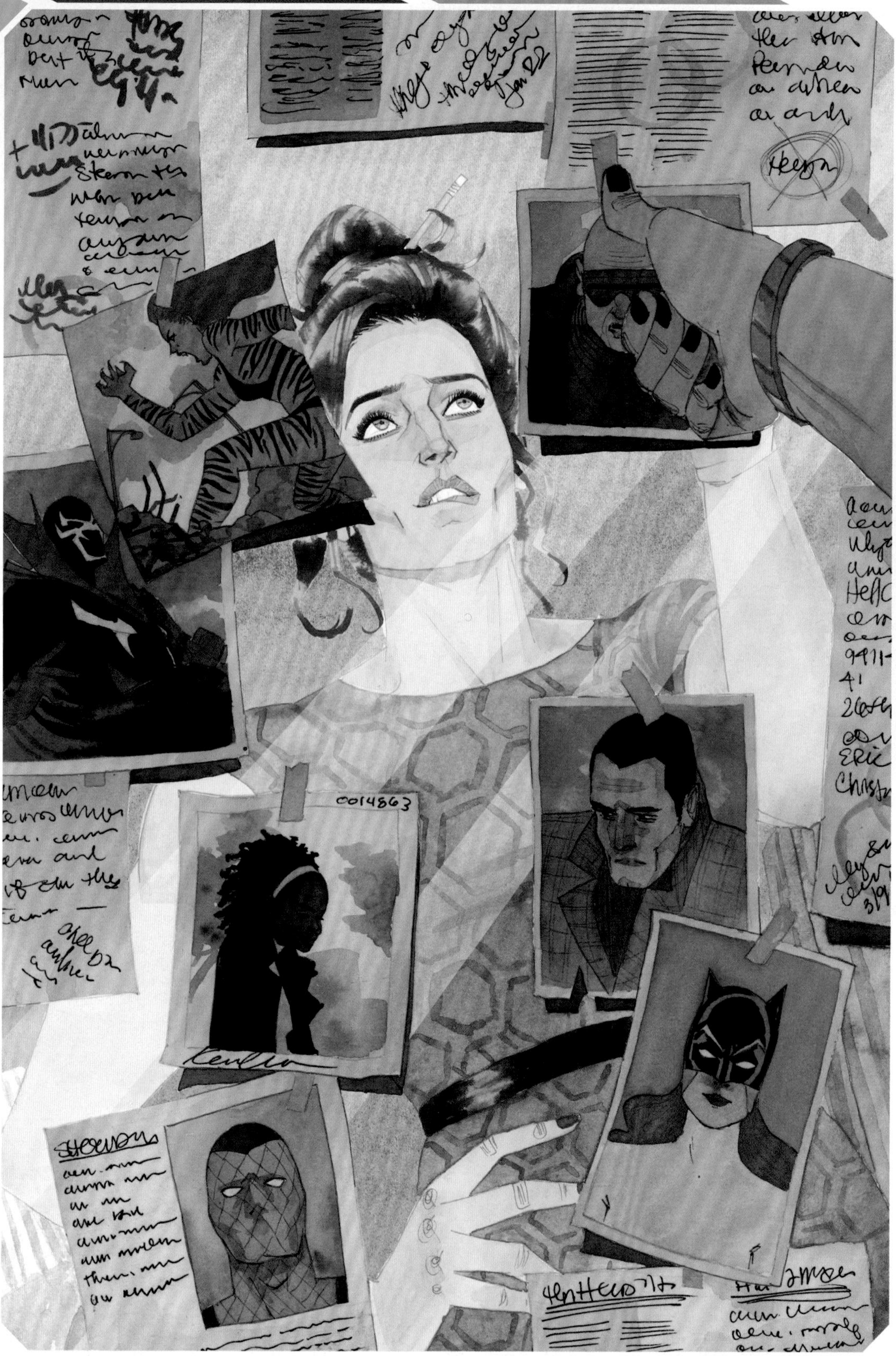
0014863

**SHE-HULK #5**

Jennifer Walters was a shy attorney, good at her job and quiet in her life, when she found herself gunned down by criminals. A gamma-irradiated blood transfusion from her cousin, Dr. Bruce Banner, a.k.a. the Incredible Hulk, didn't just give her a second chance at life, it gave her super strength and bulletproof green skin. Wherever justice is threatened, you'll find the Sensational...

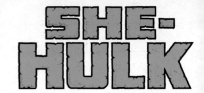

# SHE-HULK

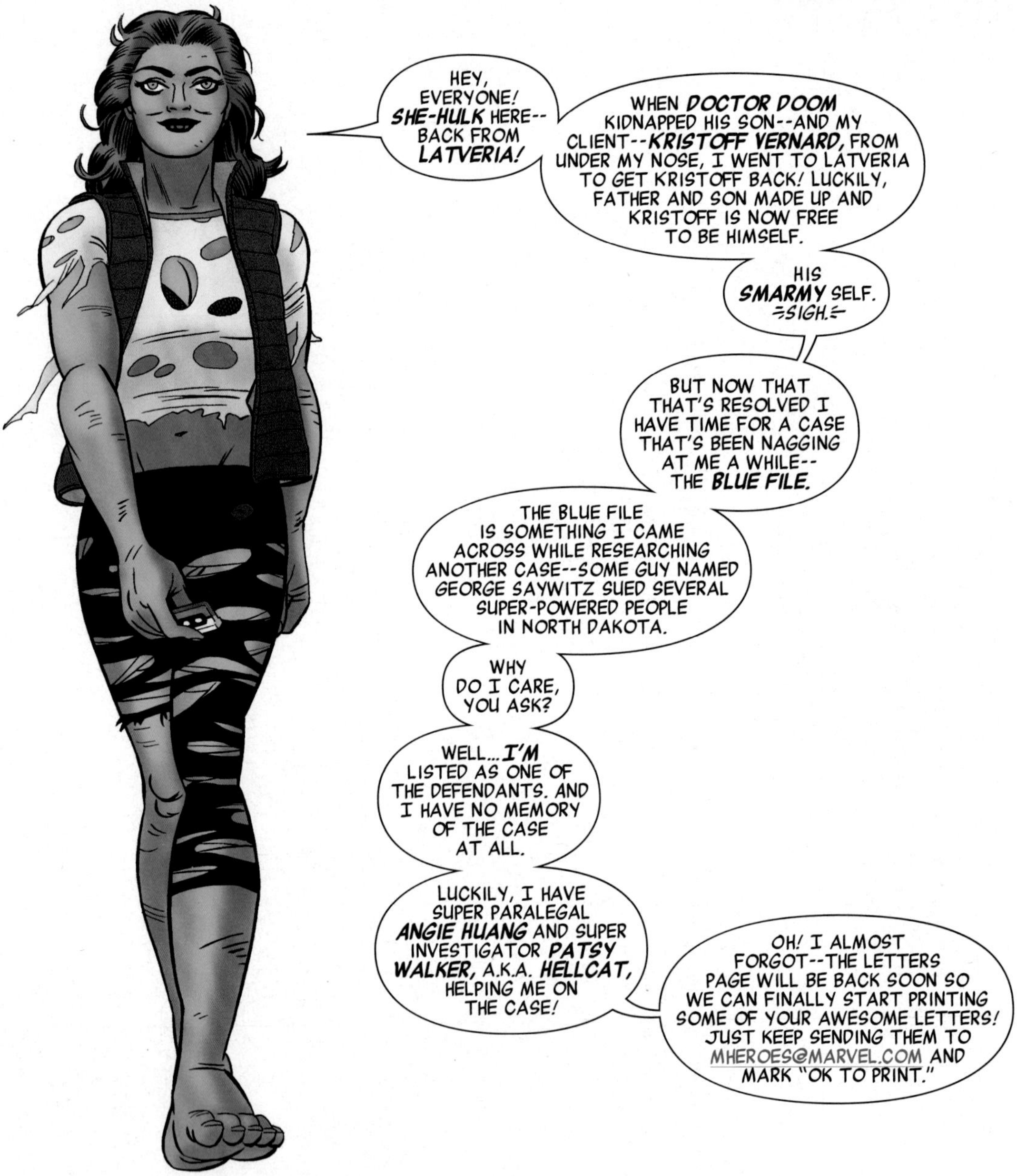
HEY, EVERYONE! SHE-HULK HERE--BACK FROM LATVERIA!
WHEN DOCTOR DOOM KIDNAPPED HIS SON--AND MY CLIENT--KRISTOFF VERNARD, FROM UNDER MY NOSE, I WENT TO LATVERIA TO GET KRISTOFF BACK! LUCKILY, FATHER AND SON MADE UP AND KRISTOFF IS NOW FREE TO BE HIMSELF.
HIS SMARMY SELF. =SIGH.=
BUT NOW THAT THAT'S RESOLVED I HAVE TIME FOR A CASE THAT'S BEEN NAGGING AT ME A WHILE--THE BLUE FILE.
THE BLUE FILE IS SOMETHING I CAME ACROSS WHILE RESEARCHING ANOTHER CASE--SOME GUY NAMED GEORGE SAYWITZ SUED SEVERAL SUPER-POWERED PEOPLE IN NORTH DAKOTA.
WHY DO I CARE, YOU ASK?
WELL...I'M LISTED AS ONE OF THE DEFENDANTS. AND I HAVE NO MEMORY OF THE CASE AT ALL.
LUCKILY, I HAVE SUPER PARALEGAL ANGIE HUANG AND SUPER INVESTIGATOR PATSY WALKER, A.K.A. HELLCAT, HELPING ME ON THE CASE!
OH! I ALMOST FORGOT--THE LETTERS PAGE WILL BE BACK SOON SO WE CAN FINALLY START PRINTING SOME OF YOUR AWESOME LETTERS! JUST KEEP SENDING THEM TO MHEROES@MARVEL.COM AND MARK "OK TO PRINT."

**CHARLES SOULE** writer

**RON WIMBERLY** artist

**RICO RENZI** color artist

**VC's CLAYTON COWLES** letterer

**KEVIN WADA** cover artist

**FRANKIE JOHNSON** assistant editor

**JEANINE SCHAEFER & TOM BRENNAN** editors

**AXEL ALONSO** editor in chief

**JOE QUESADA** chief creative officer

**DAN BUCKLEY** publisher

**ALAN FINE** exec. producer

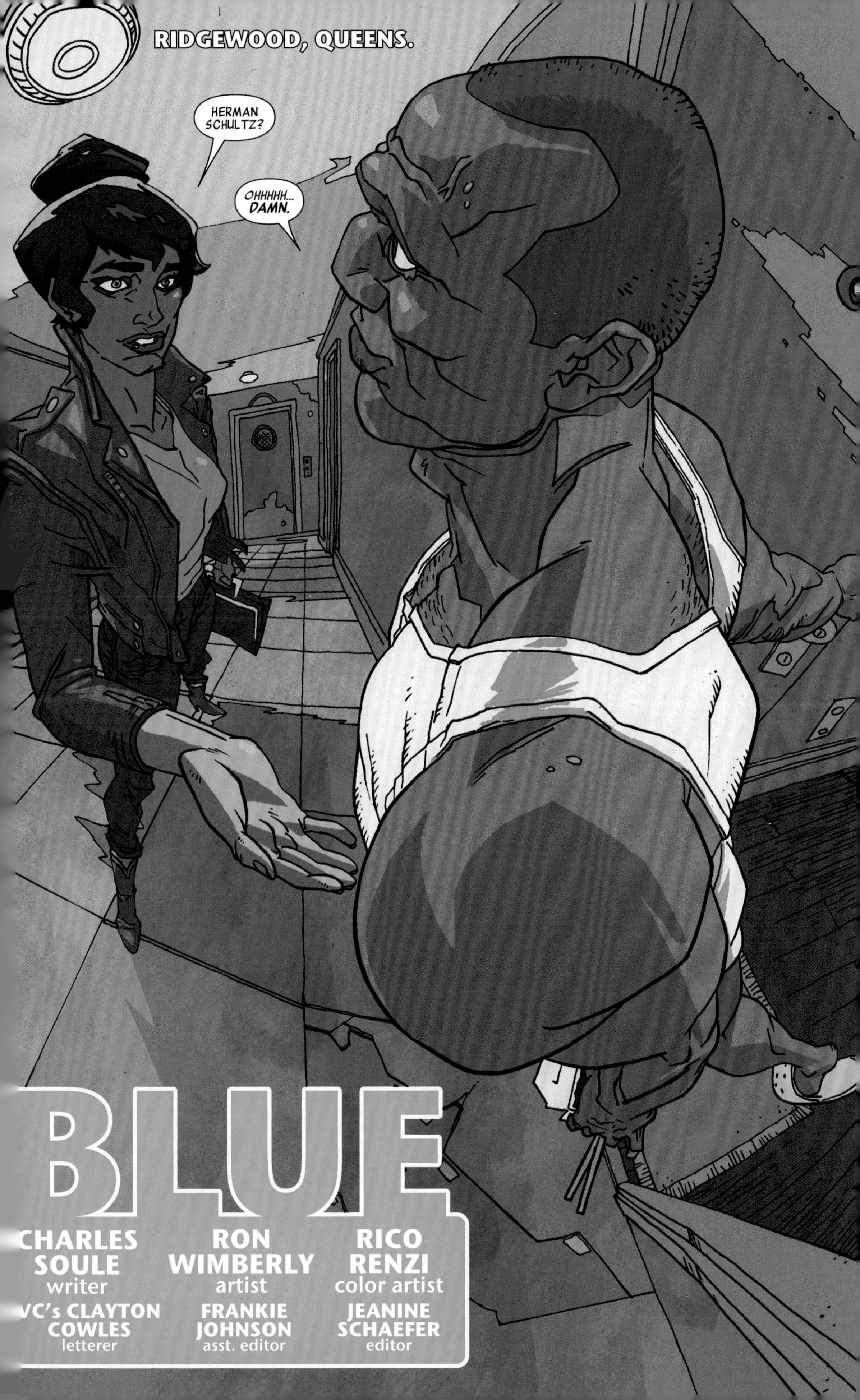
RIDGEWOOD, QUEENS.
HERMAN SCHULTZ?
OHHHHH... DAMN.
BLUE
CHARLES SOULE writer
RON WIMBERLY artist
RICO RENZI color artist
VC's CLAYTON COWLES letterer
FRANKIE JOHNSON asst. editor
JEANINE SCHAEFER editor

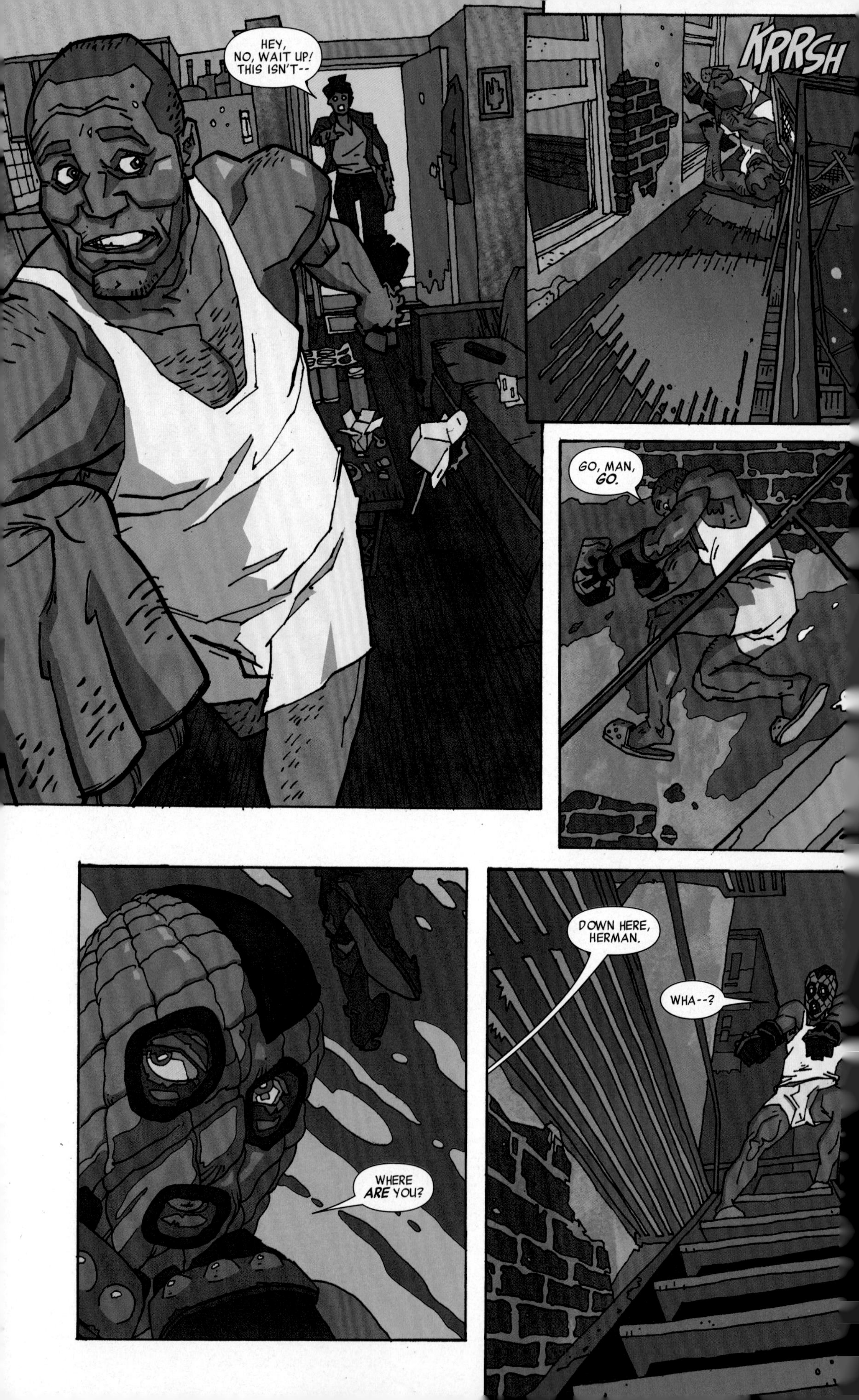
HEY, NO, WAIT UP! THIS ISN'T--
KRRSH
GO, MAN, GO.
WHERE ARE YOU?
DOWN HERE, HERMAN.
WHA--?

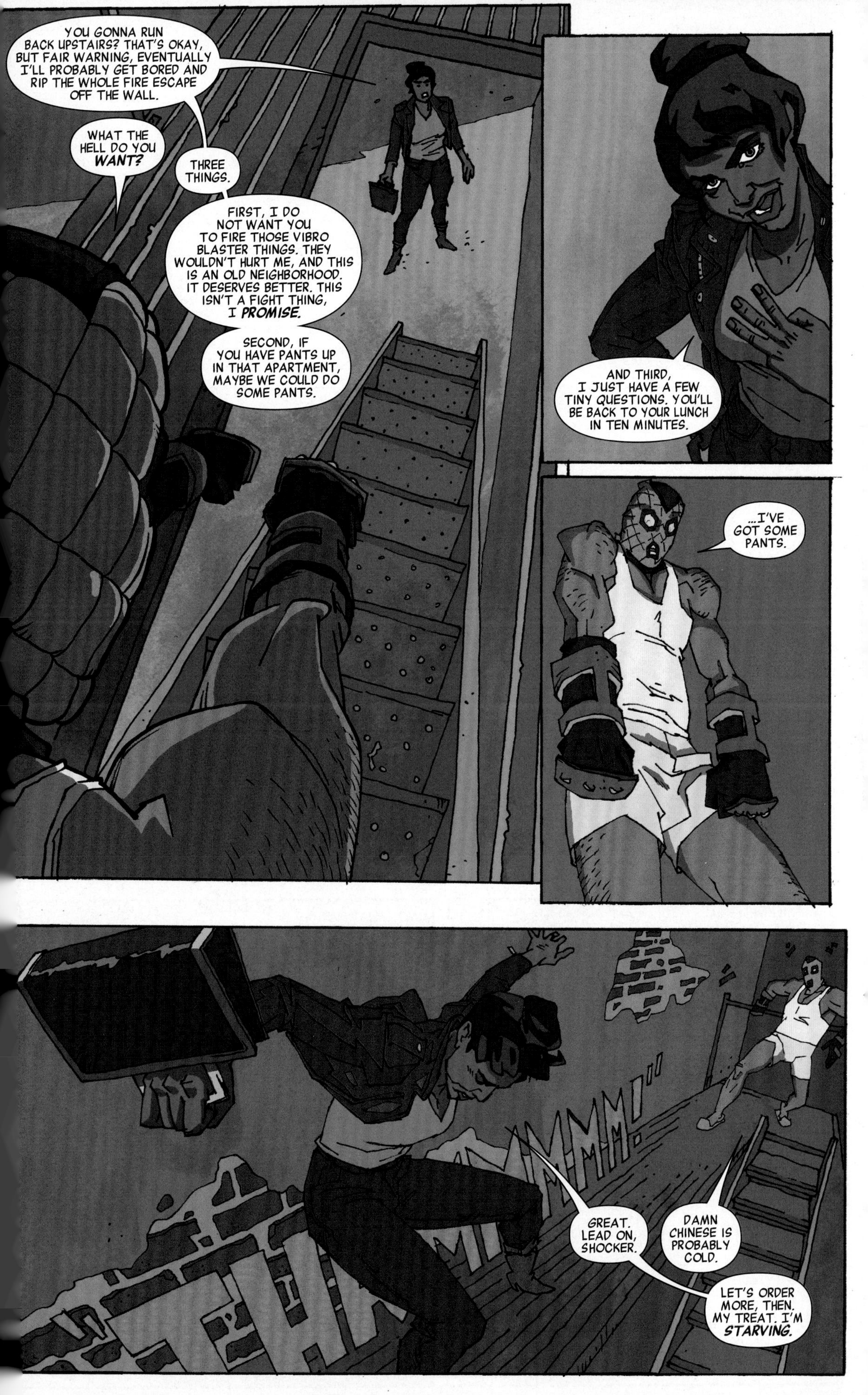
YOU GONNA RUN BACK UPSTAIRS? THAT'S OKAY, BUT FAIR WARNING, EVENTUALLY I'LL PROBABLY GET BORED AND RIP THE WHOLE FIRE ESCAPE OFF THE WALL.
WHAT THE HELL DO YOU *WANT?*
THREE THINGS.
FIRST, I DO NOT WANT YOU TO FIRE THOSE VIBRO BLASTER THINGS. THEY WOULDN'T HURT ME, AND THIS IS AN OLD NEIGHBORHOOD. IT DESERVES BETTER. THIS ISN'T A FIGHT THING, I *PROMISE.*
SECOND, IF YOU HAVE PANTS UP IN THAT APARTMENT, MAYBE WE COULD DO SOME PANTS.
AND THIRD, I JUST HAVE A FEW TINY QUESTIONS. YOU'LL BE BACK TO YOUR LUNCH IN TEN MINUTES.
...I'VE GOT SOME PANTS.
MMMMM!
GREAT. LEAD ON, SHOCKER.
DAMN CHINESE IS PROBABLY COLD.
LET'S ORDER MORE, THEN. MY TREAT. I'M *STARVING.*

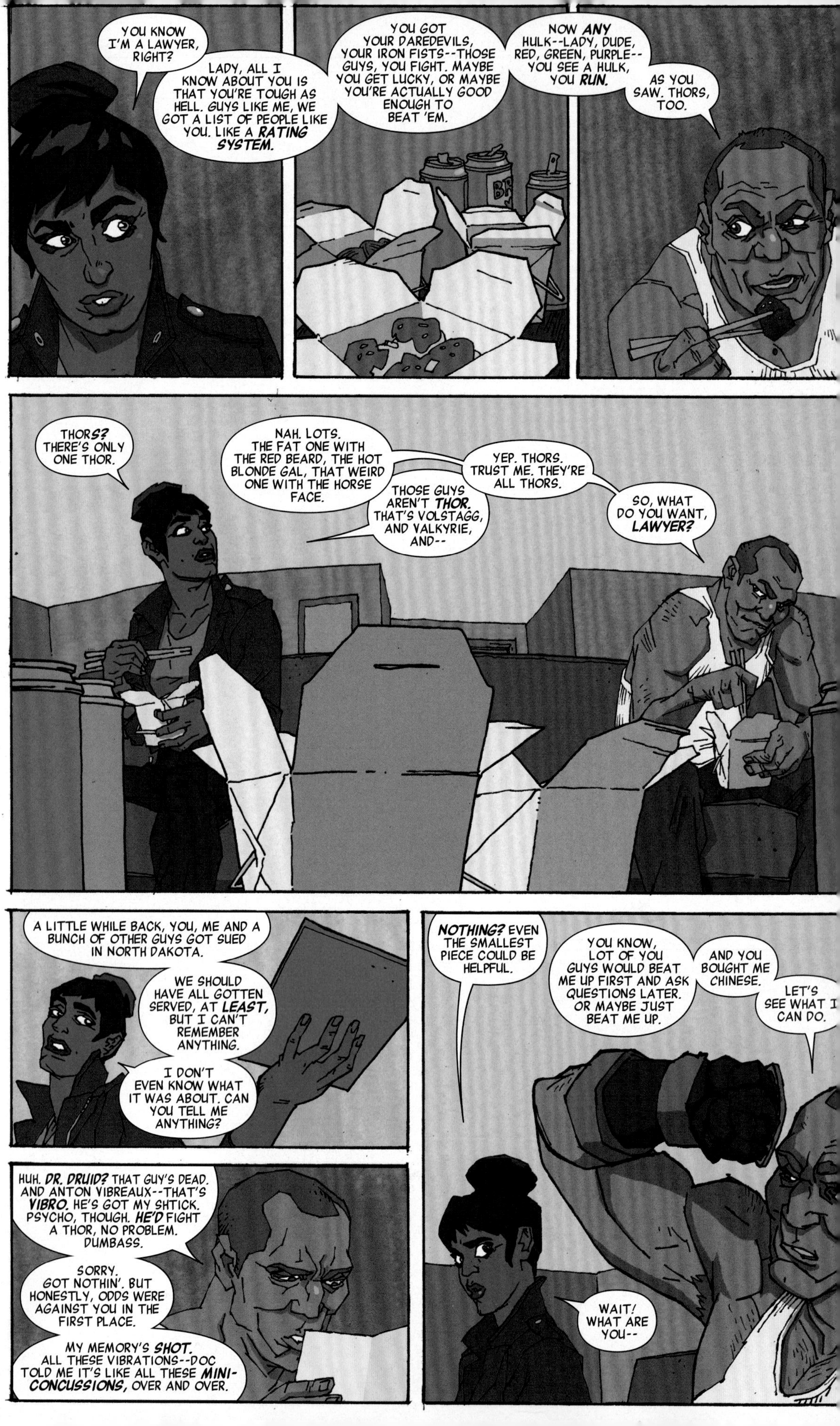

YOU KNOW I'M A LAWYER, RIGHT?
LADY, ALL I KNOW ABOUT YOU IS THAT YOU'RE TOUGH AS HELL. GUYS LIKE ME, WE GOT A LIST OF PEOPLE LIKE YOU. LIKE A RATING SYSTEM.
YOU GOT YOUR DAREDEVILS, YOUR IRON FISTS--THOSE GUYS, YOU FIGHT. MAYBE YOU GET LUCKY, OR MAYBE YOU'RE ACTUALLY GOOD ENOUGH TO BEAT 'EM.
NOW ANY HULK--LADY, DUDE, RED, GREEN, PURPLE--YOU SEE A HULK, YOU RUN.
AS YOU SAW. THORS, TOO.
THORS? THERE'S ONLY ONE THOR.
NAH. LOTS. THE FAT ONE WITH THE RED BEARD, THE HOT BLONDE GAL, THAT WEIRD ONE WITH THE HORSE FACE.
THOSE GUYS AREN'T THOR. THAT'S VOLSTAGG, AND VALKYRIE, AND--
YEP. THORS. TRUST ME. THEY'RE ALL THORS.
SO, WHAT DO YOU WANT, LAWYER?
A LITTLE WHILE BACK, YOU, ME AND A BUNCH OF OTHER GUYS GOT SUED IN NORTH DAKOTA.
WE SHOULD HAVE ALL GOTTEN SERVED, AT LEAST, BUT I CAN'T REMEMBER ANYTHING.
I DON'T EVEN KNOW WHAT IT WAS ABOUT. CAN YOU TELL ME ANYTHING?
HUH. DR. DRUID? THAT GUY'S DEAD. AND ANTON VIBREAUX--THAT'S VIBRO. HE'S GOT MY SHTICK. PSYCHO, THOUGH. HE'D FIGHT A THOR, NO PROBLEM. DUMBASS.
SORRY. GOT NOTHIN'. BUT HONESTLY, ODDS WERE AGAINST YOU IN THE FIRST PLACE.
MY MEMORY'S SHOT. ALL THESE VIBRATIONS--DOC TOLD ME IT'S LIKE ALL THESE MINI-CONCUSSIONS, OVER AND OVER.
NOTHING? EVEN THE SMALLEST PIECE COULD BE HELPFUL.
YOU KNOW, LOT OF YOU GUYS WOULD BEAT ME UP FIRST AND ASK QUESTIONS LATER. OR MAYBE JUST BEAT ME UP.
AND YOU BOUGHT ME CHINESE.
LET'S SEE WHAT I CAN DO.
WAIT! WHAT ARE YOU--

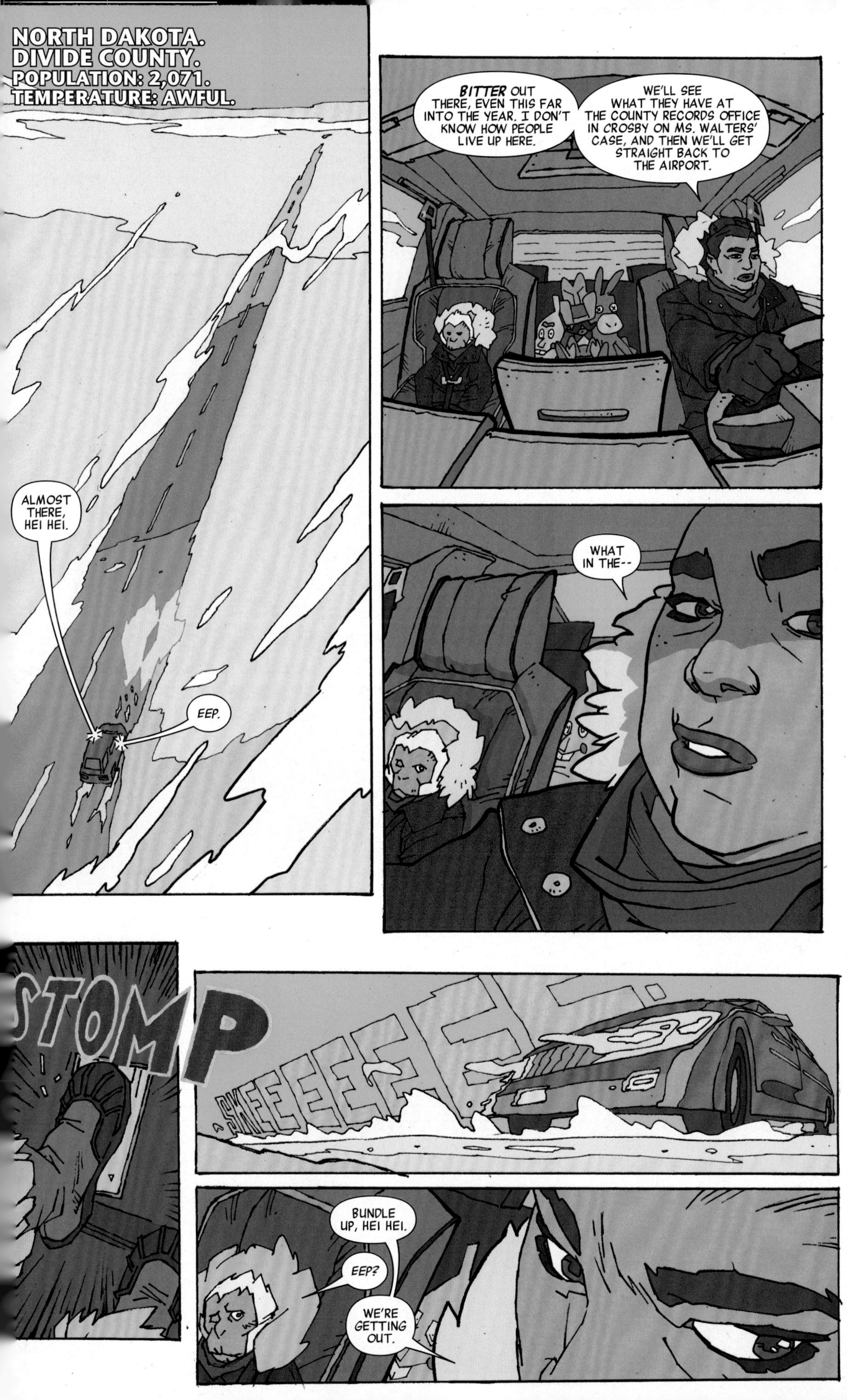
NORTH DAKOTA.
DIVIDE COUNTY.
POPULATION: 2,071.
TEMPERATURE: AWFUL.
ALMOST THERE, HEI HEI.
EEP.
BITTER OUT THERE, EVEN THIS FAR INTO THE YEAR. I DON'T KNOW HOW PEOPLE LIVE UP HERE.
WE'LL SEE WHAT THEY HAVE AT THE COUNTY RECORDS OFFICE IN CROSBY ON MS. WALTERS' CASE, AND THEN WE'LL GET STRAIGHT BACK TO THE AIRPORT.
WHAT IN THE--
STOMP
SKREEEEEE
BUNDLE UP, HEI HEI.
EEP?
WE'RE GETTING OUT.

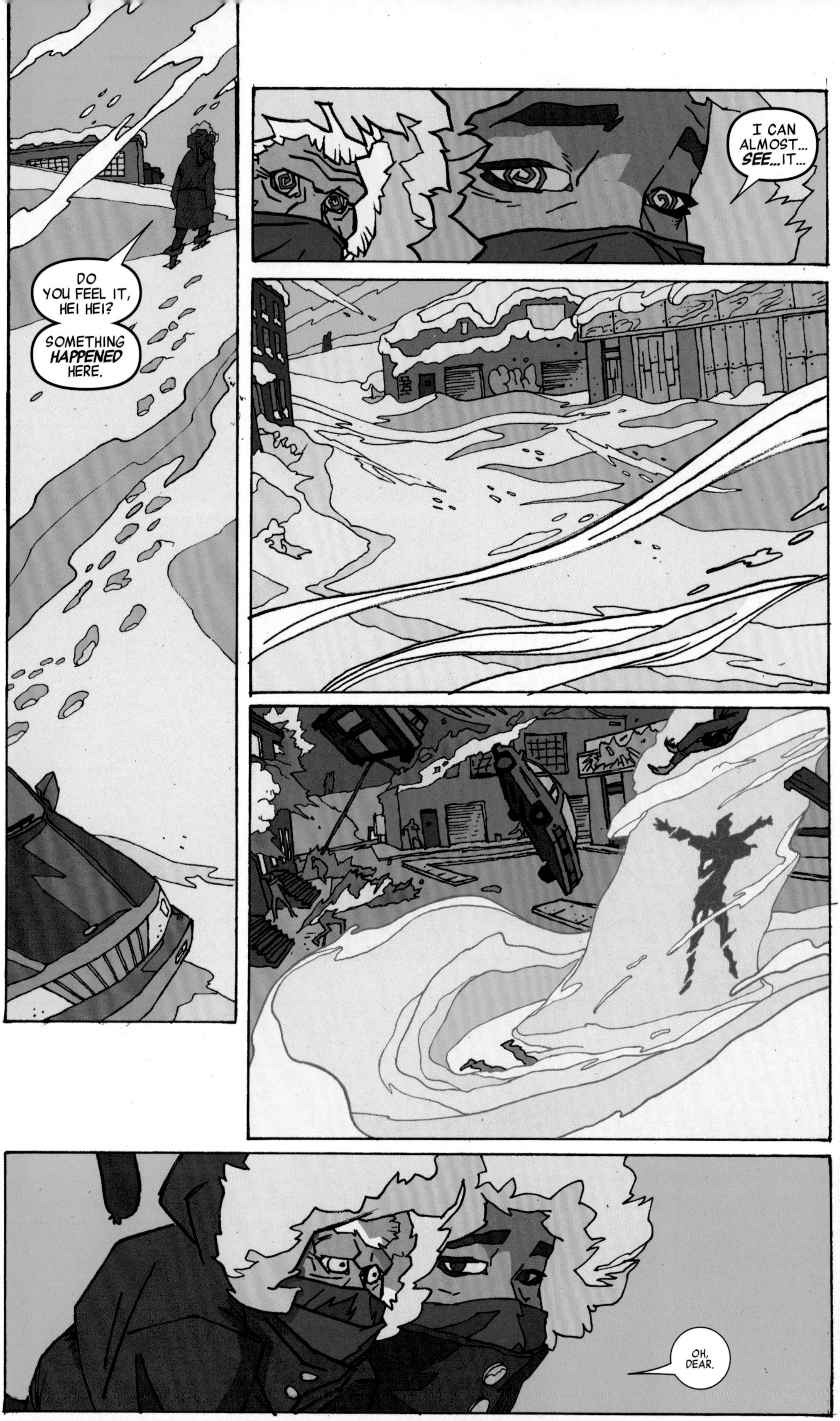
DO YOU FEEL IT, HEI HEI?
SOMETHING HAPPENED HERE.
I CAN ALMOST... SEE... IT...
OH, DEAR.

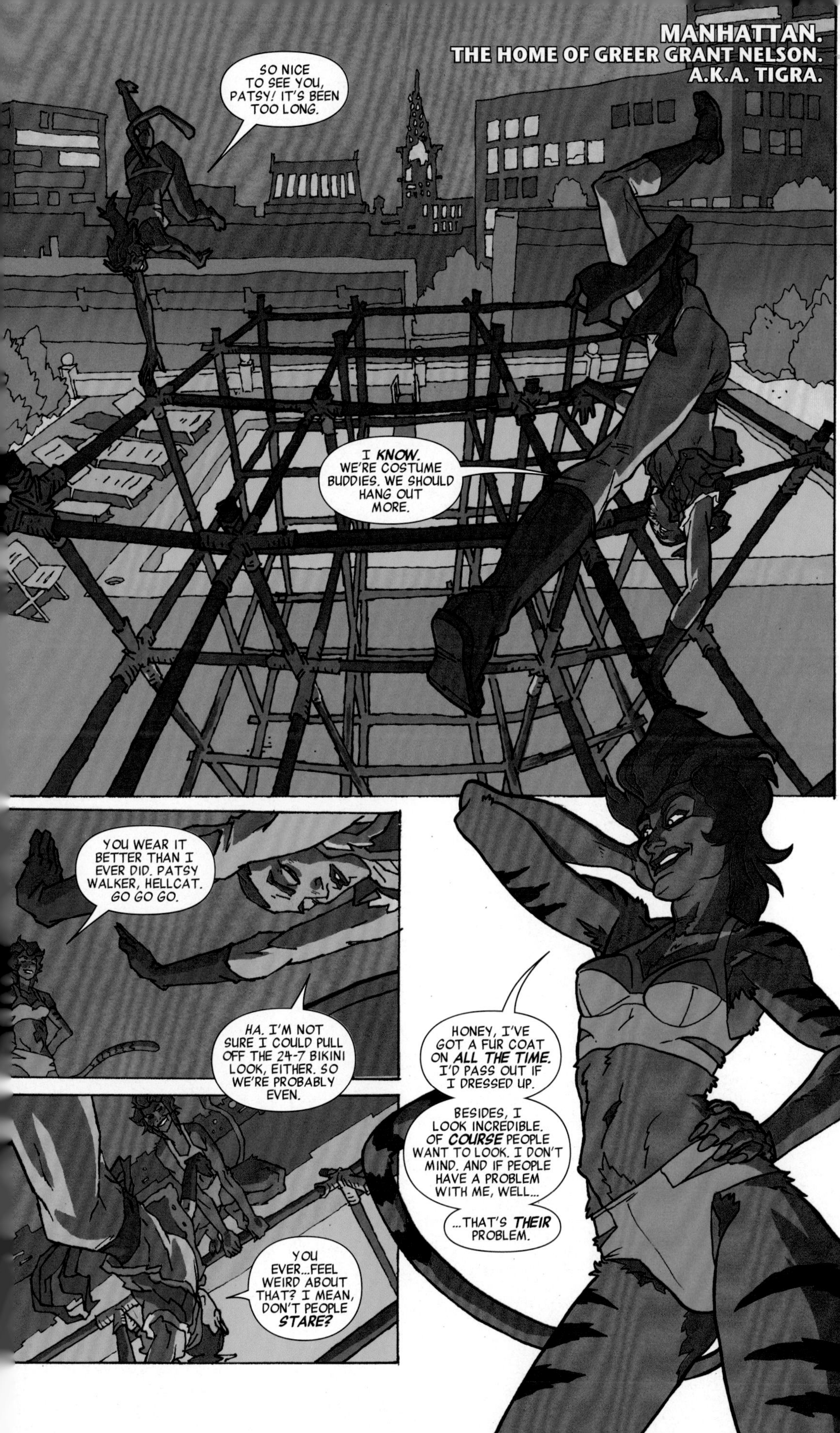
MANHATTAN.
THE HOME OF GREER GRANT NELSON.
A.K.A. TIGRA.
SO NICE TO SEE YOU, PATSY! IT'S BEEN TOO LONG.
I KNOW. WE'RE COSTUME BUDDIES. WE SHOULD HANG OUT MORE.
YOU WEAR IT BETTER THAN I EVER DID. PATSY WALKER, HELLCAT. GO GO GO.
HA. I'M NOT SURE I COULD PULL OFF THE 24-7 BIKINI LOOK, EITHER. SO WE'RE PROBABLY EVEN.
YOU EVER...FEEL WEIRD ABOUT THAT? I MEAN, DON'T PEOPLE STARE?
HONEY, I'VE GOT A FUR COAT ON ALL THE TIME. I'D PASS OUT IF I DRESSED UP.
BESIDES, I LOOK INCREDIBLE. OF COURSE PEOPLE WANT TO LOOK. I DON'T MIND. AND IF PEOPLE HAVE A PROBLEM WITH ME, WELL...
...THAT'S THEIR PROBLEM.

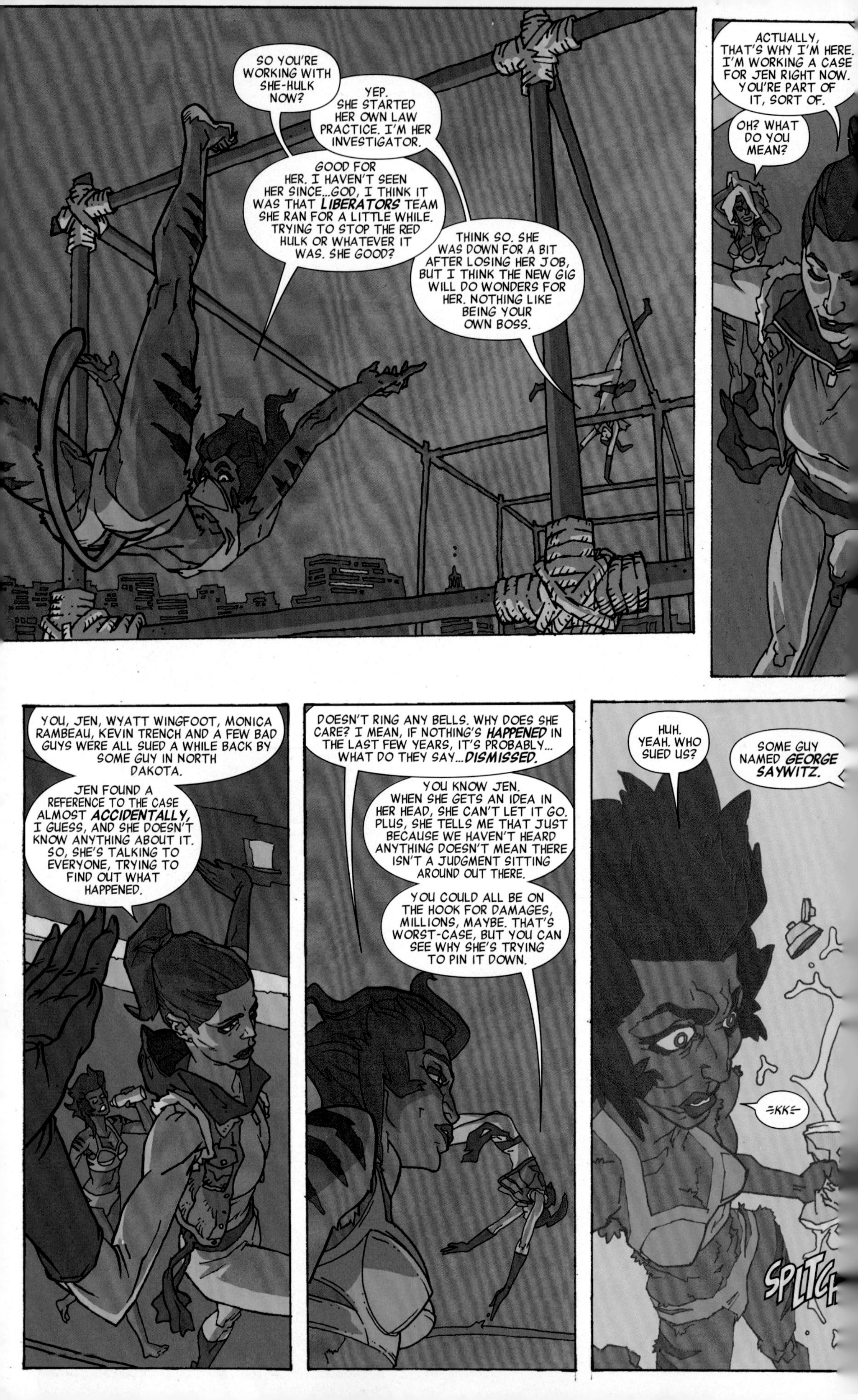

SO YOU'RE WORKING WITH SHE-HULK NOW?
YEP. SHE STARTED HER OWN LAW PRACTICE. I'M HER INVESTIGATOR.
GOOD FOR HER. I HAVEN'T SEEN HER SINCE...GOD, I THINK IT WAS THAT LIBERATORS TEAM SHE RAN FOR A LITTLE WHILE. TRYING TO STOP THE RED HULK OR WHATEVER IT WAS. SHE GOOD?
THINK SO. SHE WAS DOWN FOR A BIT AFTER LOSING HER JOB, BUT I THINK THE NEW GIG WILL DO WONDERS FOR HER. NOTHING LIKE BEING YOUR OWN BOSS.
ACTUALLY, THAT'S WHY I'M HERE. I'M WORKING A CASE FOR JEN RIGHT NOW. YOU'RE PART OF IT, SORT OF.
OH? WHAT DO YOU MEAN?
YOU, JEN, WYATT WINGFOOT, MONICA RAMBEAU, KEVIN TRENCH AND A FEW BAD GUYS WERE ALL SUED A WHILE BACK BY SOME GUY IN NORTH DAKOTA.
JEN FOUND A REFERENCE TO THE CASE ALMOST ACCIDENTALLY, I GUESS, AND SHE DOESN'T KNOW ANYTHING ABOUT IT. SO, SHE'S TALKING TO EVERYONE, TRYING TO FIND OUT WHAT HAPPENED.
DOESN'T RING ANY BELLS. WHY DOES SHE CARE? I MEAN, IF NOTHING'S HAPPENED IN THE LAST FEW YEARS, IT'S PROBABLY... WHAT DO THEY SAY...DISMISSED.
YOU KNOW JEN. WHEN SHE GETS AN IDEA IN HER HEAD, SHE CAN'T LET IT GO. PLUS, SHE TELLS ME THAT JUST BECAUSE WE HAVEN'T HEARD ANYTHING DOESN'T MEAN THERE ISN'T A JUDGMENT SITTING AROUND OUT THERE.
YOU COULD ALL BE ON THE HOOK FOR DAMAGES, MILLIONS, MAYBE. THAT'S WORST-CASE, BUT YOU CAN SEE WHY SHE'S TRYING TO PIN IT DOWN.
HUH. YEAH. WHO SUED US?
SOME GUY NAMED GEORGE SAYWITZ.
KK
SPLITCH

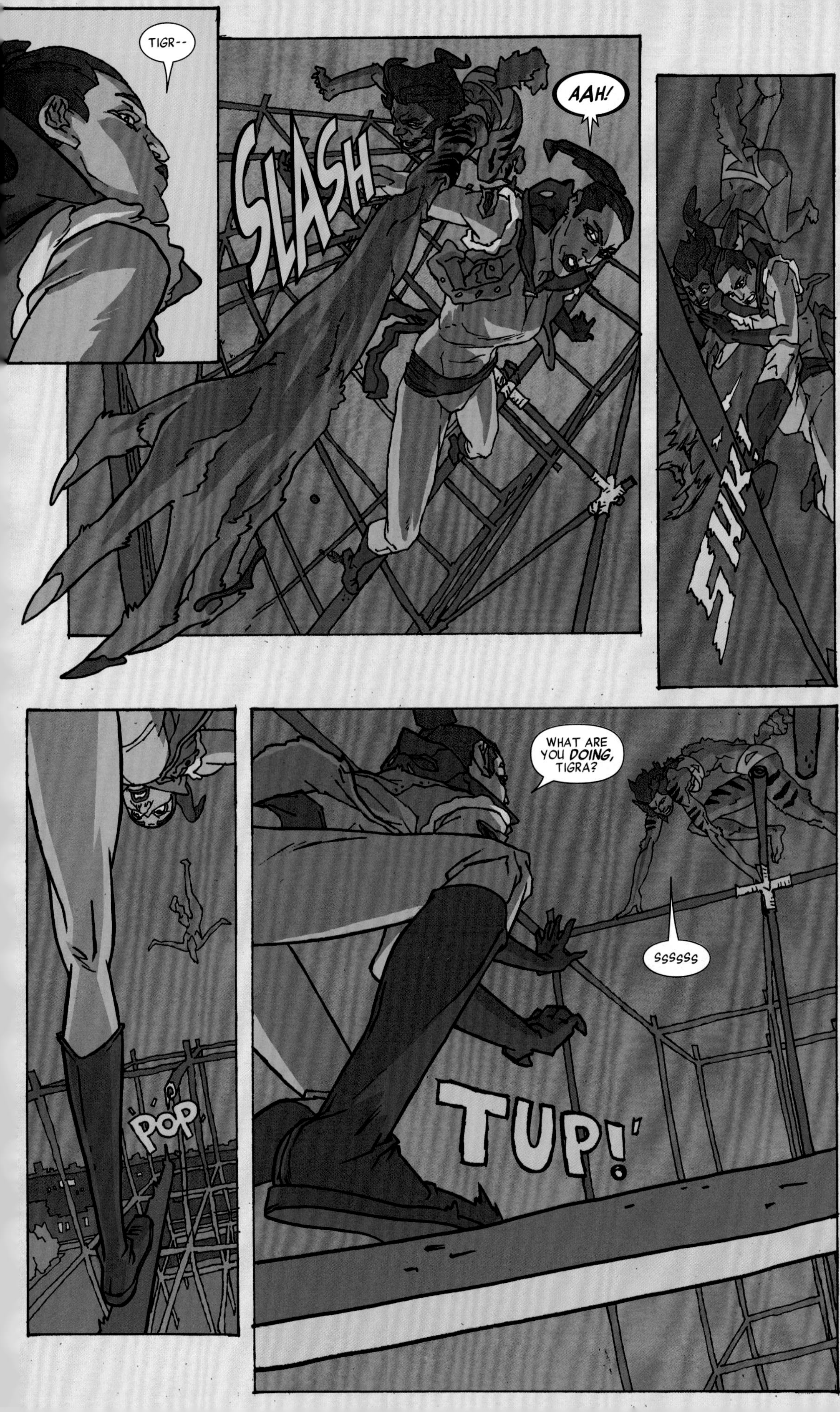
TIGR--
SLASH
AAH!
SHK!
WHAT ARE YOU DOING, TIGRA?
SSSSSS
POP
TUP!

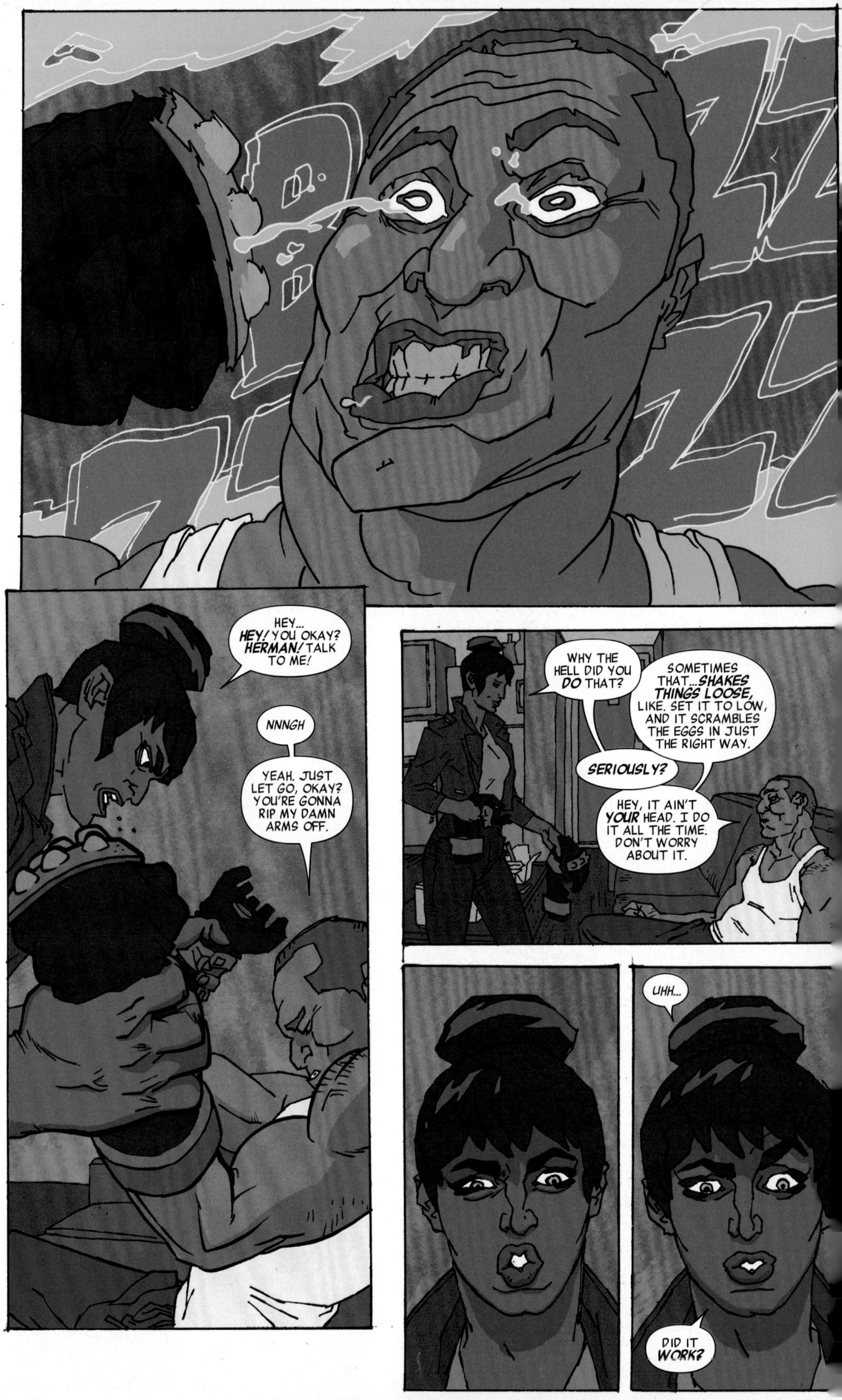
HEY... **HEY!** YOU OKAY? **HERMAN!** TALK TO ME!
NNNGH
YEAH. JUST LET GO, OKAY? YOU'RE GONNA RIP MY DAMN ARMS OFF.
WHY THE HELL DID YOU **DO** THAT?
SOMETIMES THAT... **SHAKES THINGS LOOSE,** LIKE. SET IT TO LOW, AND IT SCRAMBLES THE EGGS IN JUST THE RIGHT WAY.
**SERIOUSLY?**
HEY, IT AIN'T **YOUR** HEAD. I DO IT ALL THE TIME. DON'T WORRY ABOUT IT.
UHH...
DID IT **WORK?**

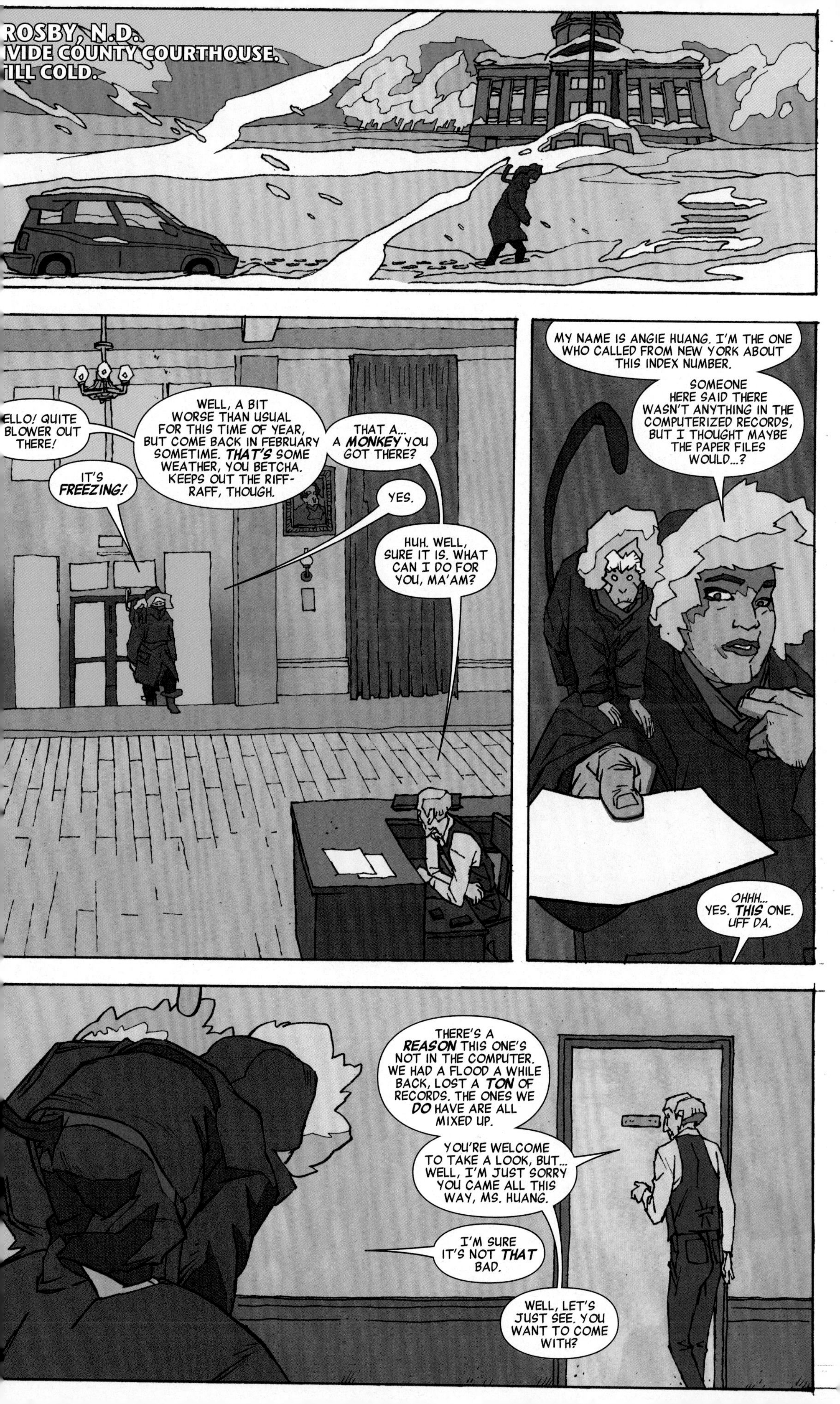

ROSBY, N.D.
VIDE COUNTY COURTHOUSE.
TILL COLD.
ELLO! QUITE BLOWER OUT THERE!
WELL, A BIT WORSE THAN USUAL FOR THIS TIME OF YEAR, BUT COME BACK IN FEBRUARY SOMETIME. THAT'S SOME WEATHER, YOU BETCHA. KEEPS OUT THE RIFF-RAFF, THOUGH.
IT'S FREEZING!
THAT A... A MONKEY YOU GOT THERE?
YES.
HUH. WELL, SURE IT IS. WHAT CAN I DO FOR YOU, MA'AM?
MY NAME IS ANGIE HUANG. I'M THE ONE WHO CALLED FROM NEW YORK ABOUT THIS INDEX NUMBER.
SOMEONE HERE SAID THERE WASN'T ANYTHING IN THE COMPUTERIZED RECORDS, BUT I THOUGHT MAYBE THE PAPER FILES WOULD...?
OHHH... YES. THIS ONE. UFF DA.
THERE'S A REASON THIS ONE'S NOT IN THE COMPUTER. WE HAD A FLOOD A WHILE BACK, LOST A TON OF RECORDS. THE ONES WE DO HAVE ARE ALL MIXED UP.
YOU'RE WELCOME TO TAKE A LOOK, BUT... WELL, I'M JUST SORRY YOU CAME ALL THIS WAY, MS. HUANG.
I'M SURE IT'S NOT THAT BAD.
WELL, LET'S JUST SEE. YOU WANT TO COME WITH?

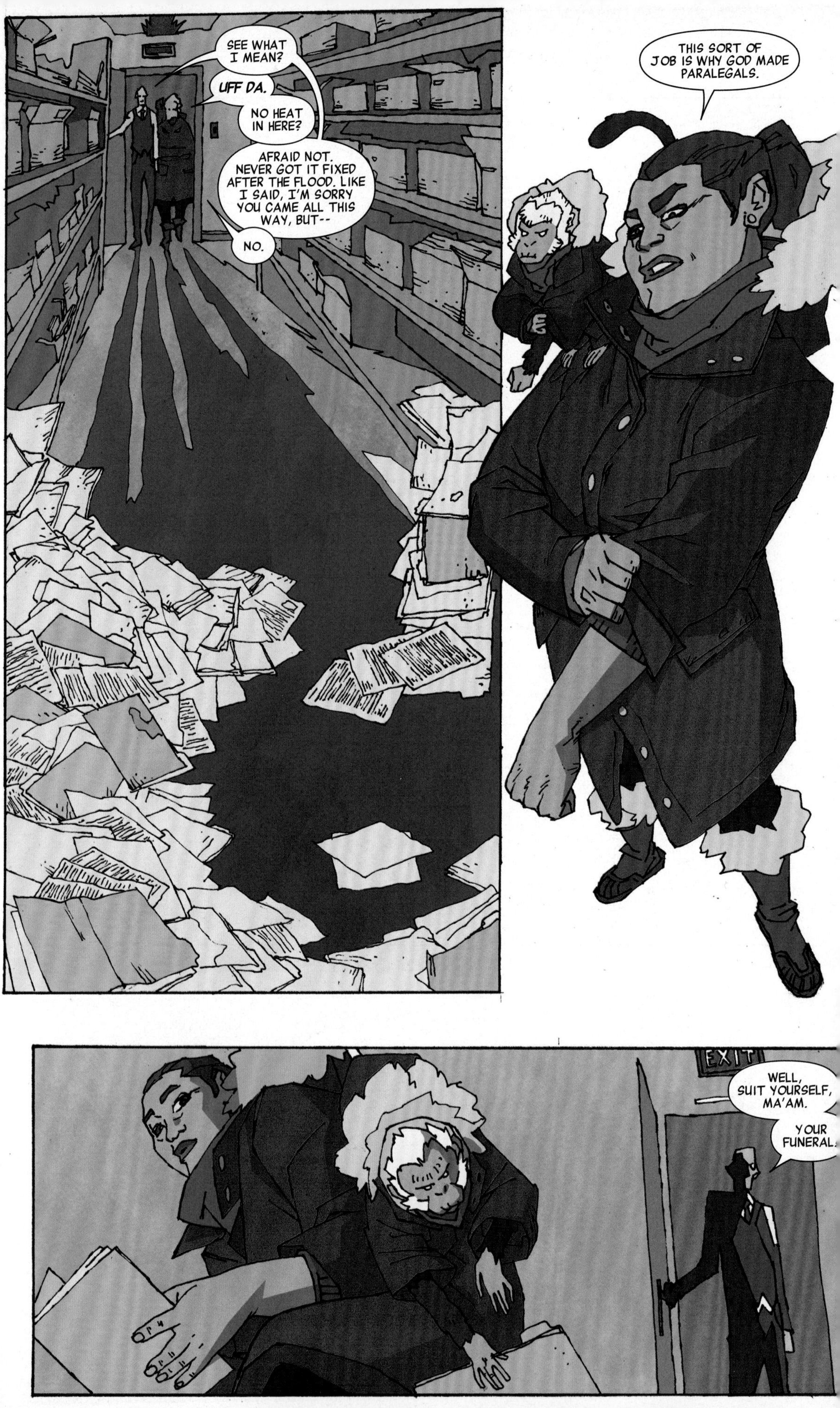
SEE WHAT I MEAN?
UFF DA.
NO HEAT IN HERE?
AFRAID NOT. NEVER GOT IT FIXED AFTER THE FLOOD. LIKE I SAID, I'M SORRY YOU CAME ALL THIS WAY, BUT--
NO.
THIS SORT OF JOB IS WHY GOD MADE PARALEGALS.
EXIT
WELL, SUIT YOURSELF, MA'AM.
YOUR FUNERAL.

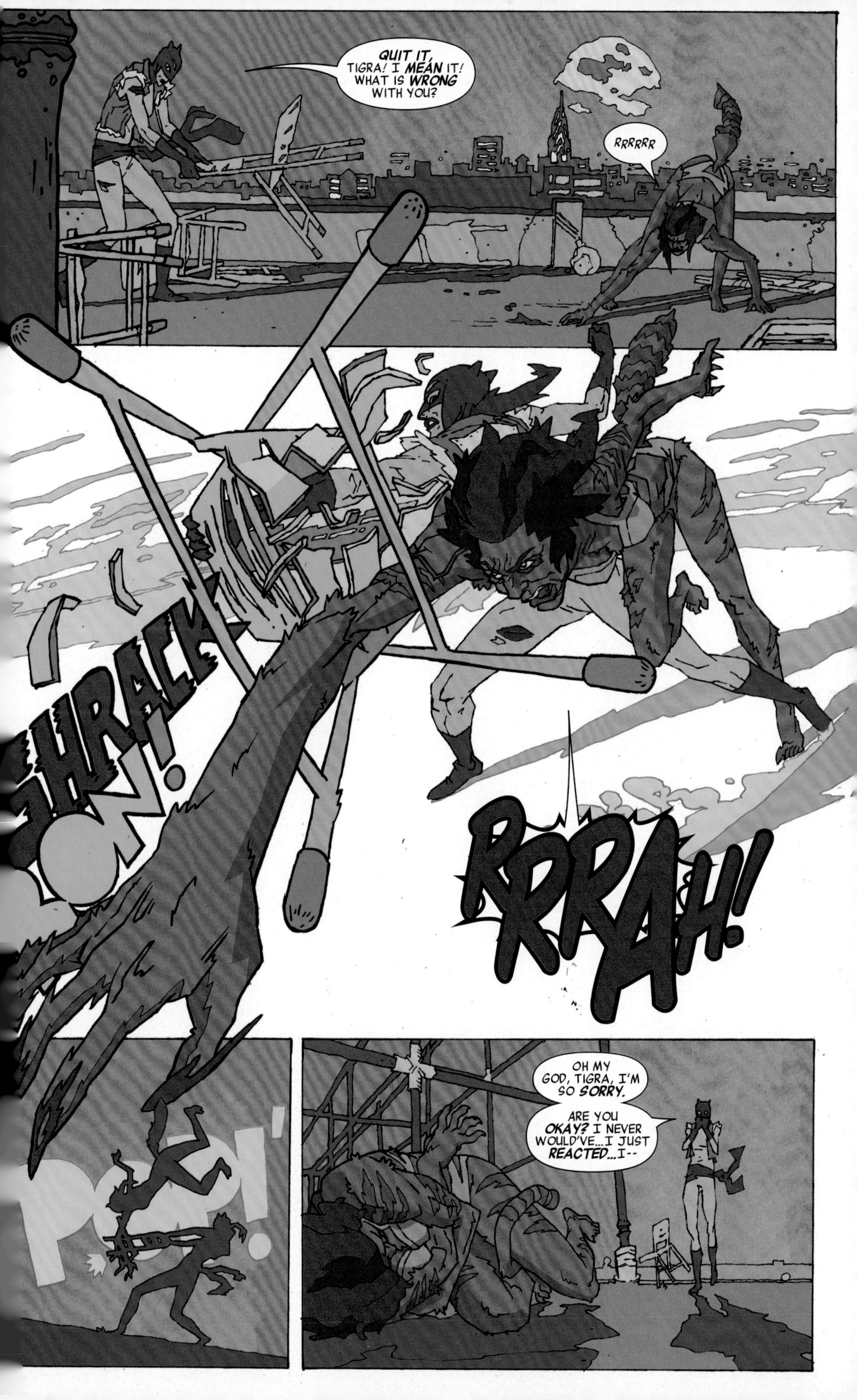
QUIT IT, TIGRA! I MEAN IT! WHAT IS WRONG WITH YOU?
RRRRRR
SHRACK!
RRRAH!
POW!
OH MY GOD, TIGRA, I'M SO SORRY.
ARE YOU OKAY? I NEVER WOULD'VE... I JUST REACTED... I--

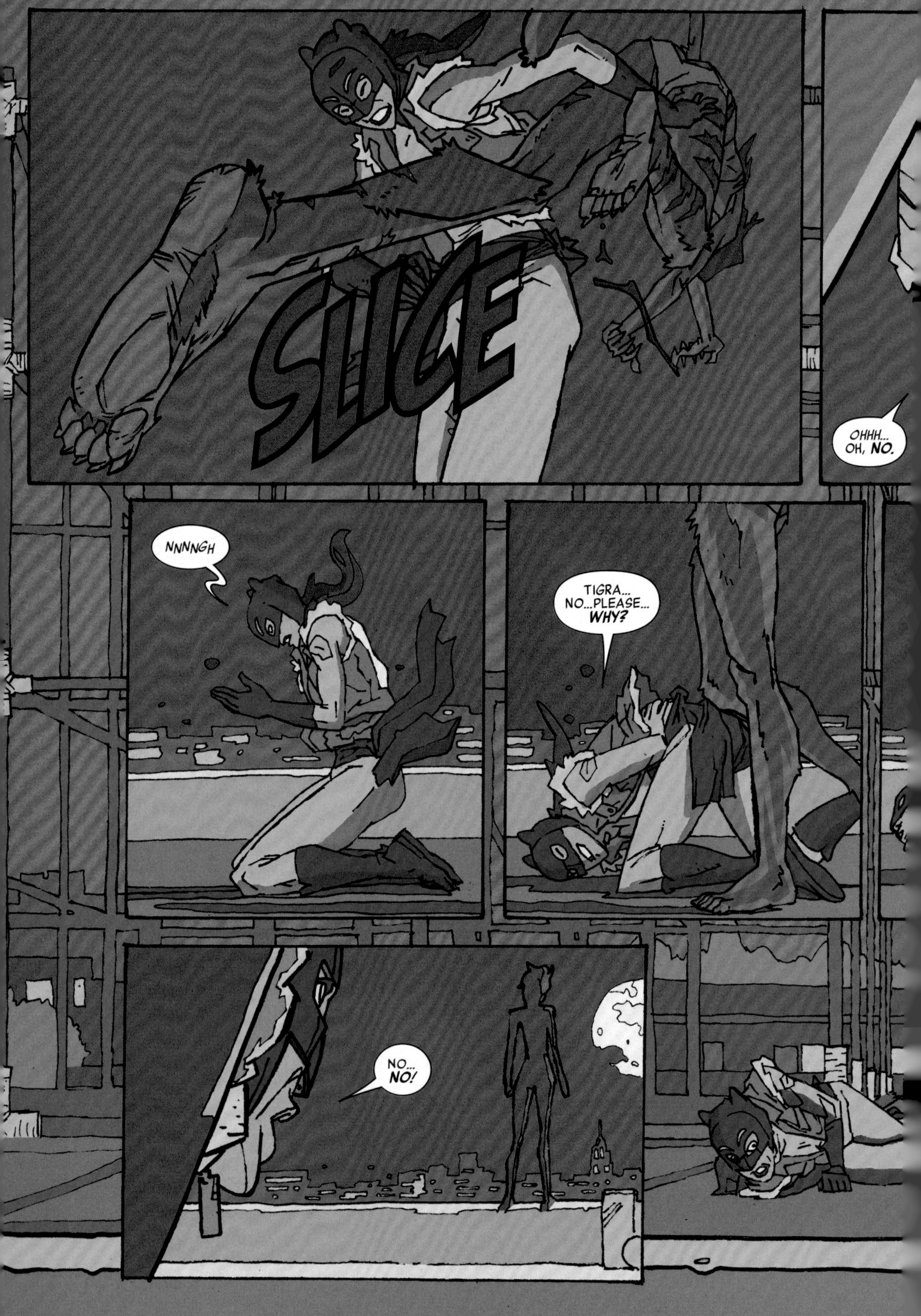
SLICE
OHHH... OH, NO.
NNNNGH
TIGRA... NO...PLEASE... WHY?
NO... NO!

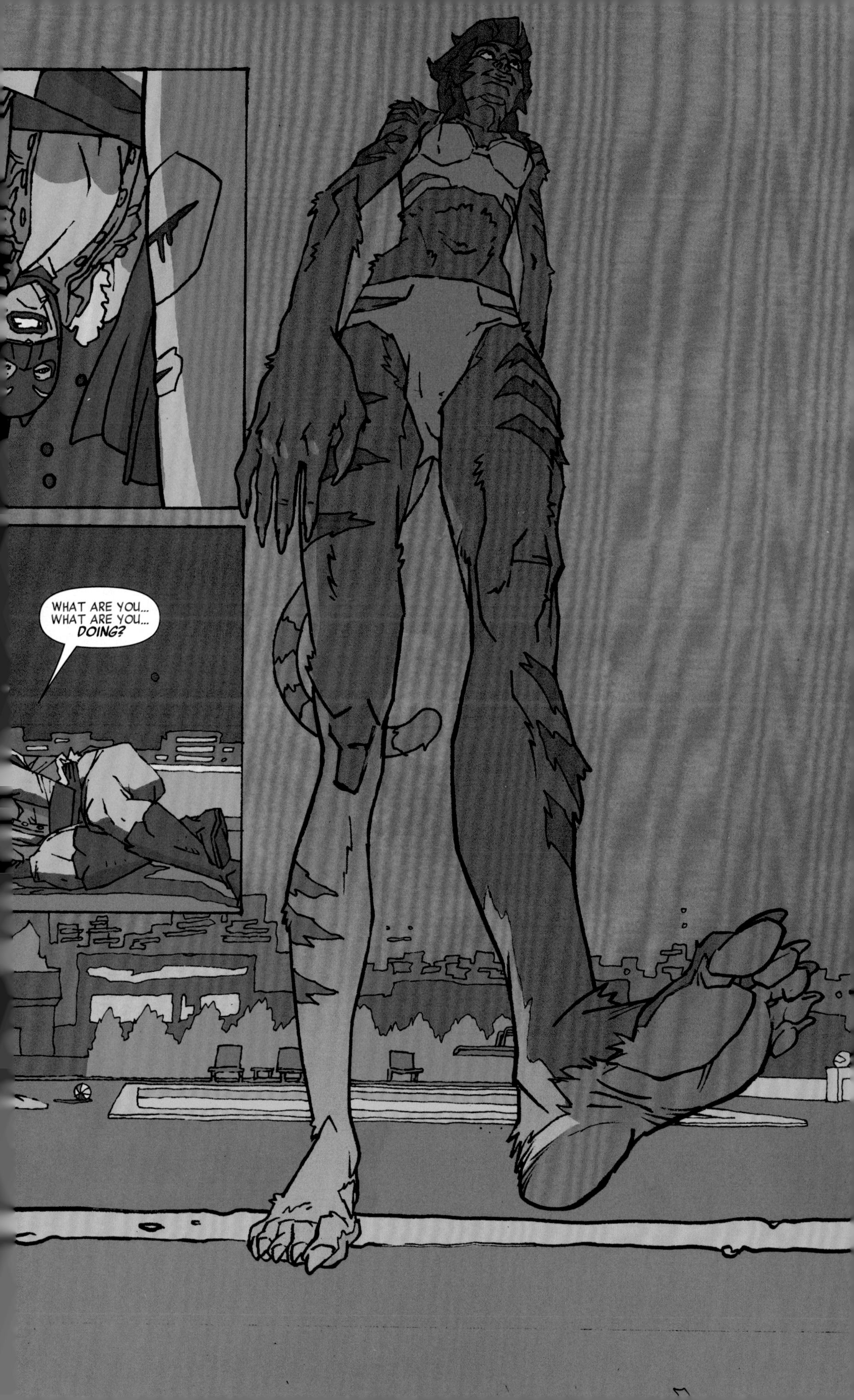
WHAT ARE YOU... WHAT ARE YOU... *DOING?*

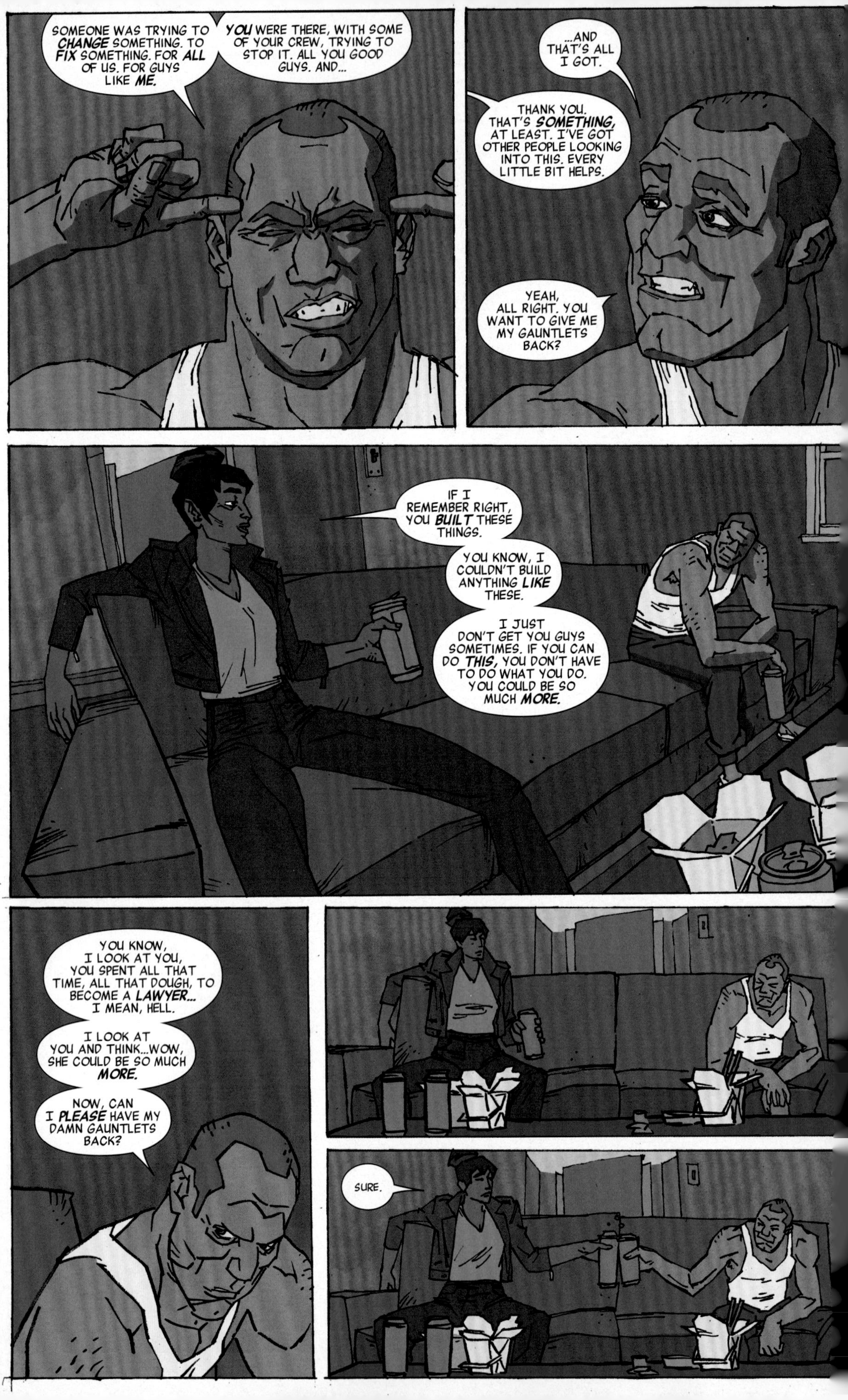
SOMEONE WAS TRYING TO CHANGE SOMETHING. TO FIX SOMETHING. FOR ALL OF US. FOR GUYS LIKE ME.
YOU WERE THERE, WITH SOME OF YOUR CREW, TRYING TO STOP IT. ALL YOU GOOD GUYS. AND...
...AND THAT'S ALL I GOT.
THANK YOU. THAT'S SOMETHING, AT LEAST. I'VE GOT OTHER PEOPLE LOOKING INTO THIS. EVERY LITTLE BIT HELPS.
YEAH, ALL RIGHT. YOU WANT TO GIVE ME MY GAUNTLETS BACK?
IF I REMEMBER RIGHT, YOU BUILT THESE THINGS.
YOU KNOW, I COULDN'T BUILD ANYTHING LIKE THESE.
I JUST DON'T GET YOU GUYS SOMETIMES. IF YOU CAN DO THIS, YOU DON'T HAVE TO DO WHAT YOU DO. YOU COULD BE SO MUCH MORE.
YOU KNOW, I LOOK AT YOU, YOU SPENT ALL THAT TIME, ALL THAT DOUGH, TO BECOME A LAWYER... I MEAN, HELL.
I LOOK AT YOU AND THINK...WOW, SHE COULD BE SO MUCH MORE.
NOW, CAN I PLEASE HAVE MY DAMN GAUNTLETS BACK?
SURE.

WELL, WOULD YOU LOOK AT *THAT.*

I THINK WE'RE DONE HERE.

DO YOU HAVE A PHOTOCOPIER?

SURE. OVER IN THE CORNER THERE. WHY? DIDJA FIND SOMETHING NOW?

I DID.

AND YOU'LL BE PLEASED TO KNOW THAT I ORGANIZED A GOODLY NUMBER OF THOSE FILES AS I SEARCHED.

NOW, I DIDN'T GET THROUGH ALL OF IT, BUT--

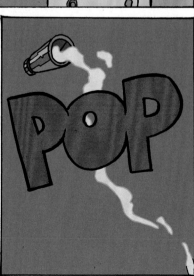

POP

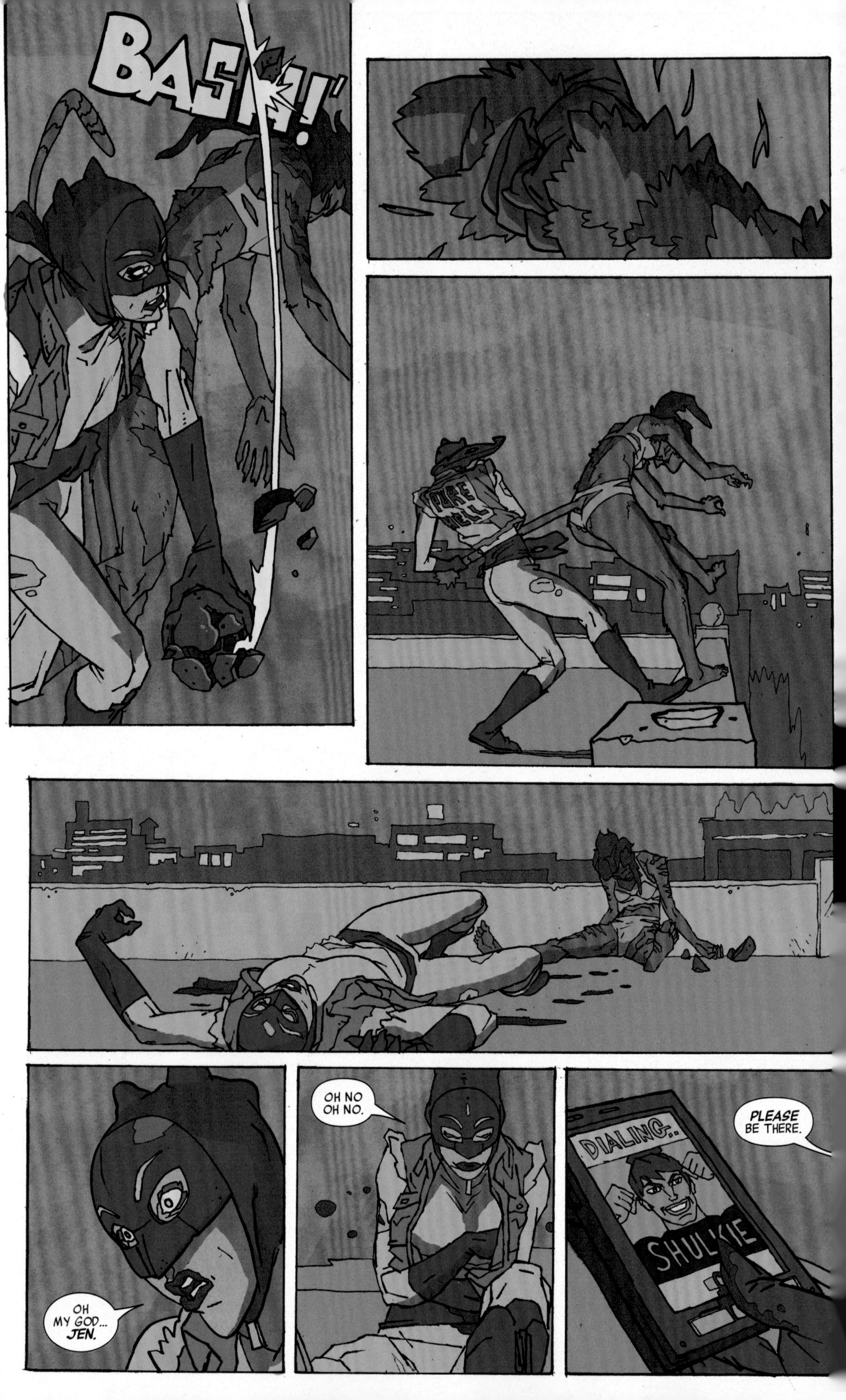
BASH!
FARE WELL
OH MY GOD... JEN.
OH NO OH NO.
DIALING..
SHULKIE
PLEASE BE THERE.

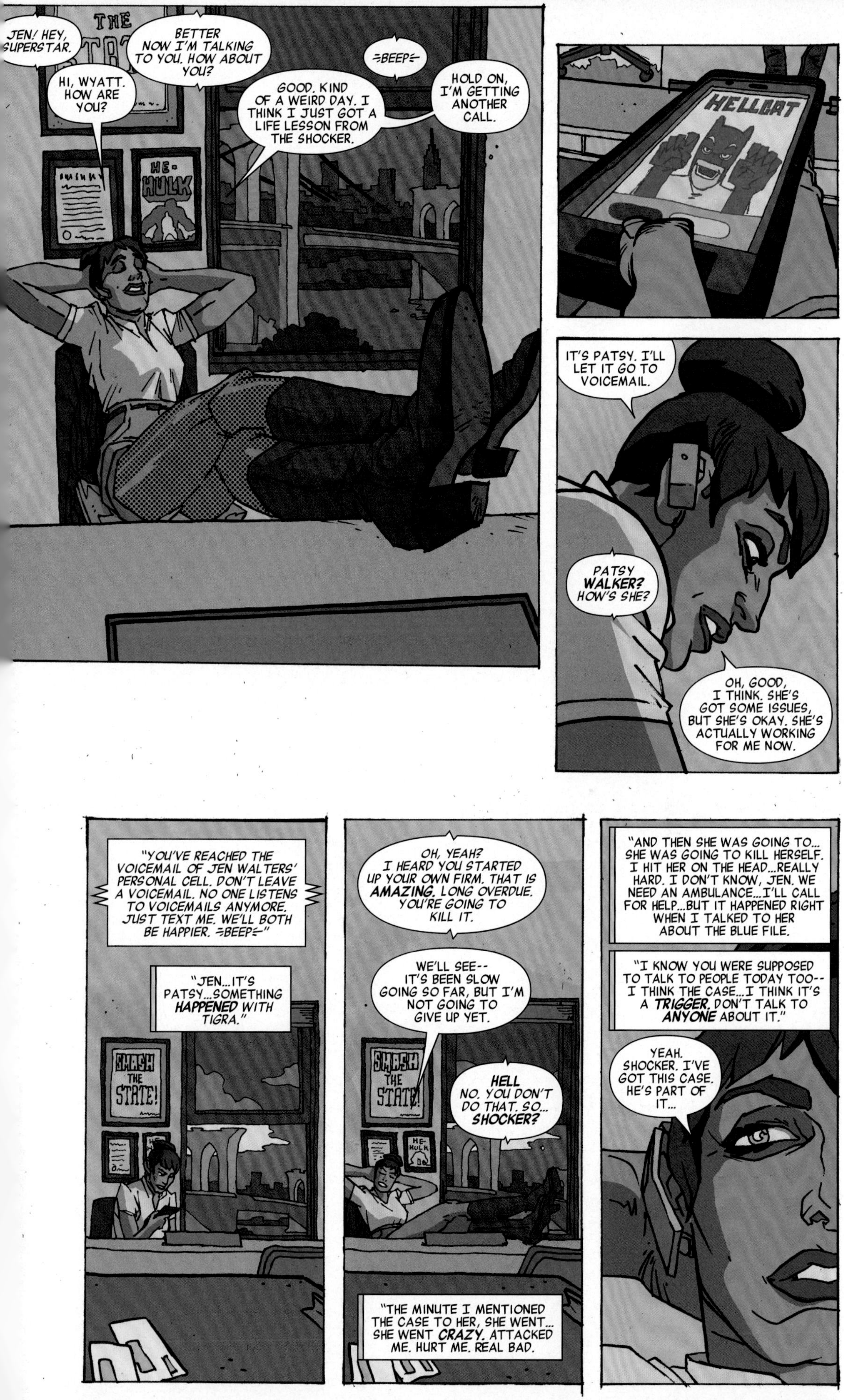
JEN! HEY, SUPERSTAR.
HI, WYATT. HOW ARE YOU?
BETTER NOW I'M TALKING TO YOU. HOW ABOUT YOU?
GOOD. KIND OF A WEIRD DAY. I THINK I JUST GOT A LIFE LESSON FROM THE SHOCKER.
HE-HULK
=BEEP=
HOLD ON, I'M GETTING ANOTHER CALL.
HELLCAT
IT'S PATSY. I'LL LET IT GO TO VOICEMAIL.
PATSY WALKER? HOW'S SHE?
OH, GOOD, I THINK. SHE'S GOT SOME ISSUES, BUT SHE'S OKAY. SHE'S ACTUALLY WORKING FOR ME NOW.
"YOU'VE REACHED THE VOICEMAIL OF JEN WALTERS' PERSONAL CELL. DON'T LEAVE A VOICEMAIL. NO ONE LISTENS TO VOICEMAILS ANYMORE. JUST TEXT ME. WE'LL BOTH BE HAPPIER. =BEEP="
"JEN...IT'S PATSY...SOMETHING HAPPENED WITH TIGRA."
SMASH THE STATE!
OH, YEAH? I HEARD YOU STARTED UP YOUR OWN FIRM. THAT IS AMAZING. LONG OVERDUE. YOU'RE GOING TO KILL IT.
WE'LL SEE-- IT'S BEEN SLOW GOING SO FAR, BUT I'M NOT GOING TO GIVE UP YET.
HELL NO. YOU DON'T DO THAT. SO... SHOCKER?
"THE MINUTE I MENTIONED THE CASE TO HER, SHE WENT... SHE WENT CRAZY. ATTACKED ME. HURT ME. REAL BAD.
"AND THEN SHE WAS GOING TO... SHE WAS GOING TO KILL HERSELF. I HIT HER ON THE HEAD...REALLY HARD. I DON'T KNOW, JEN. WE NEED AN AMBULANCE...I'LL CALL FOR HELP...BUT IT HAPPENED RIGHT WHEN I TALKED TO HER ABOUT THE BLUE FILE.
"I KNOW YOU WERE SUPPOSED TO TALK TO PEOPLE TODAY TOO-- I THINK THE CASE...I THINK IT'S A TRIGGER. DON'T TALK TO ANYONE ABOUT IT."
YEAH. SHOCKER. I'VE GOT THIS CASE. HE'S PART OF IT...

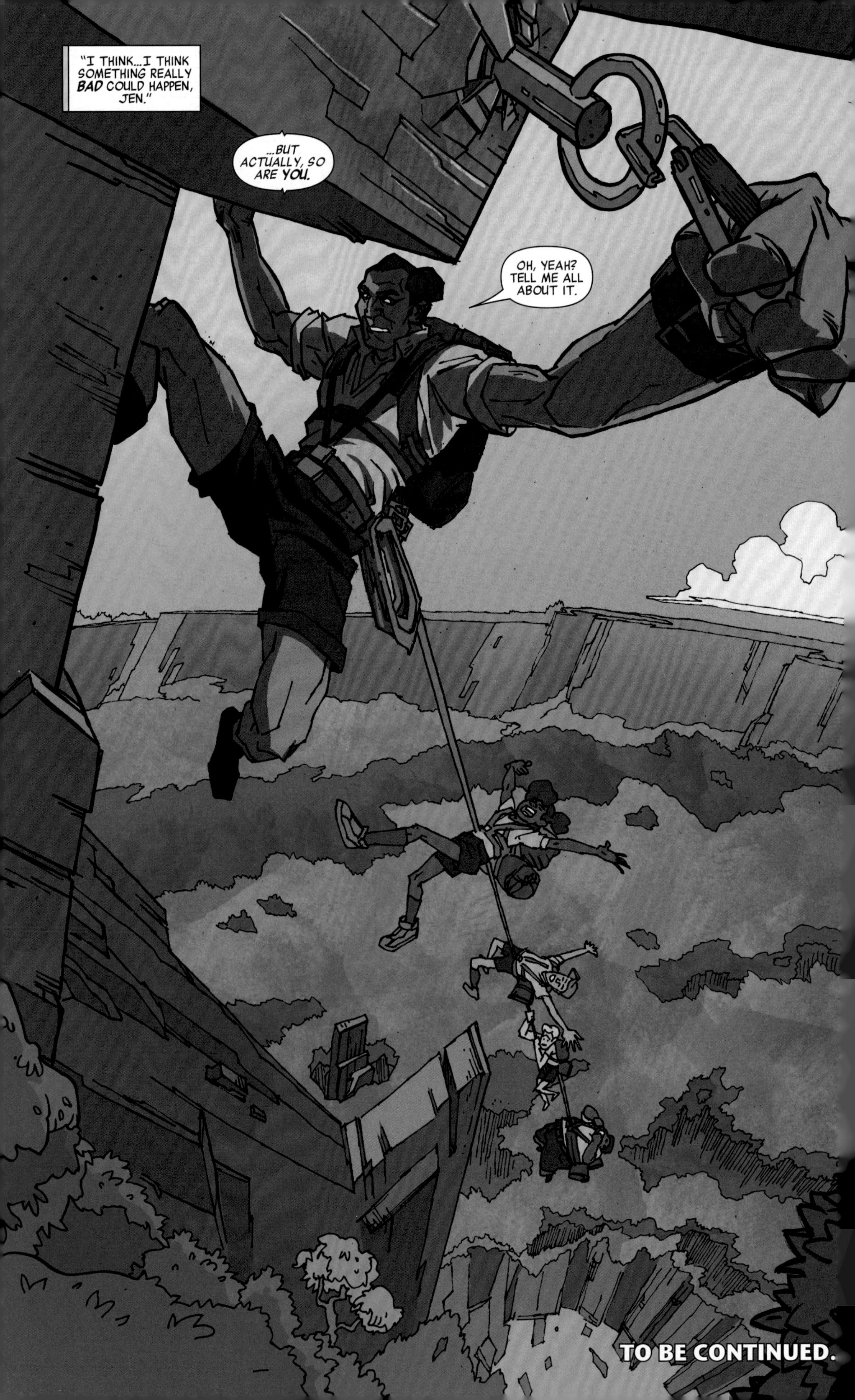
"I THINK...I THINK SOMETHING REALLY BAD COULD HAPPEN, JEN."
...BUT ACTUALLY, SO ARE YOU.
OH, YEAH? TELL ME ALL ABOUT IT.
TO BE CONTINUED.

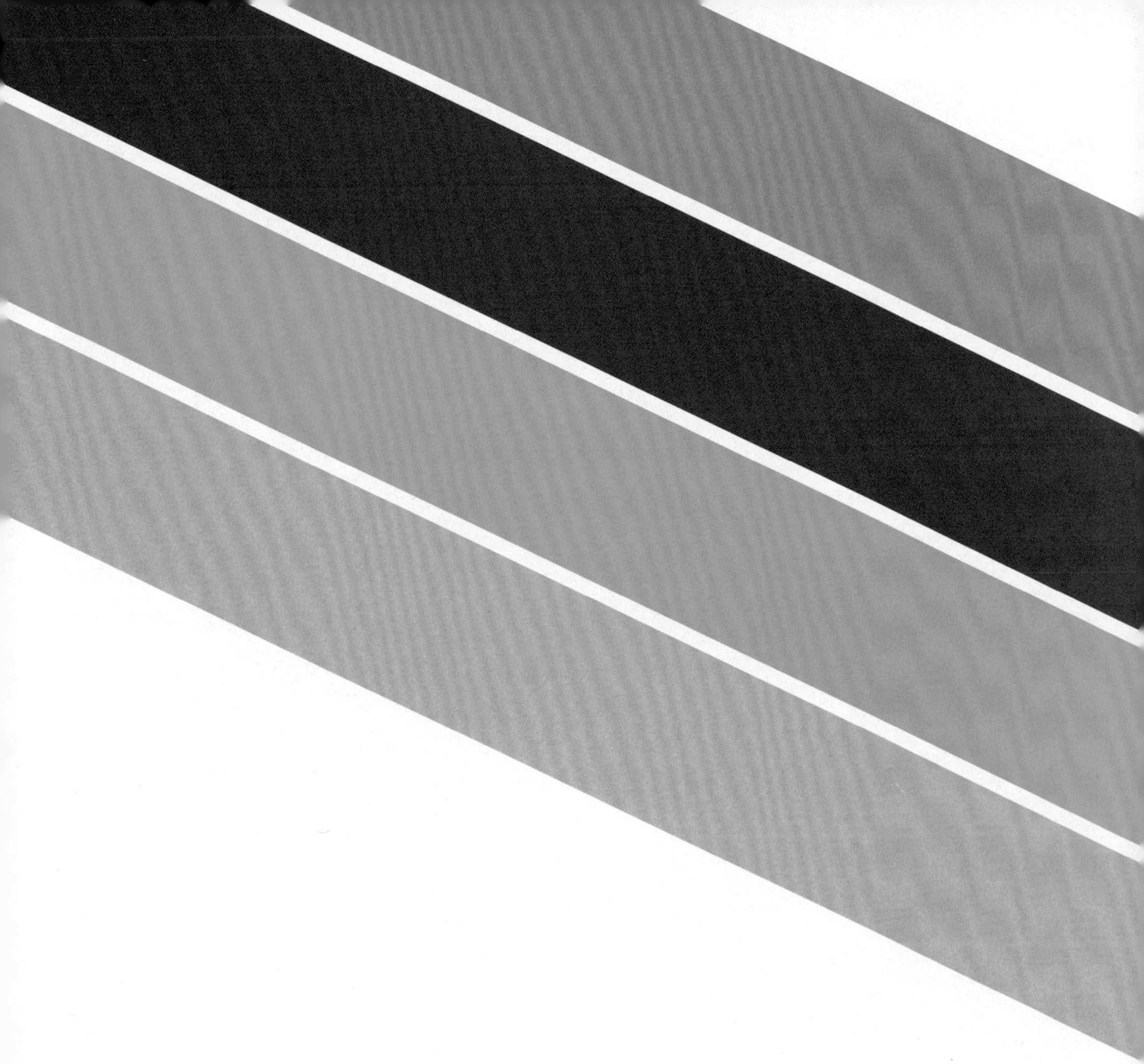

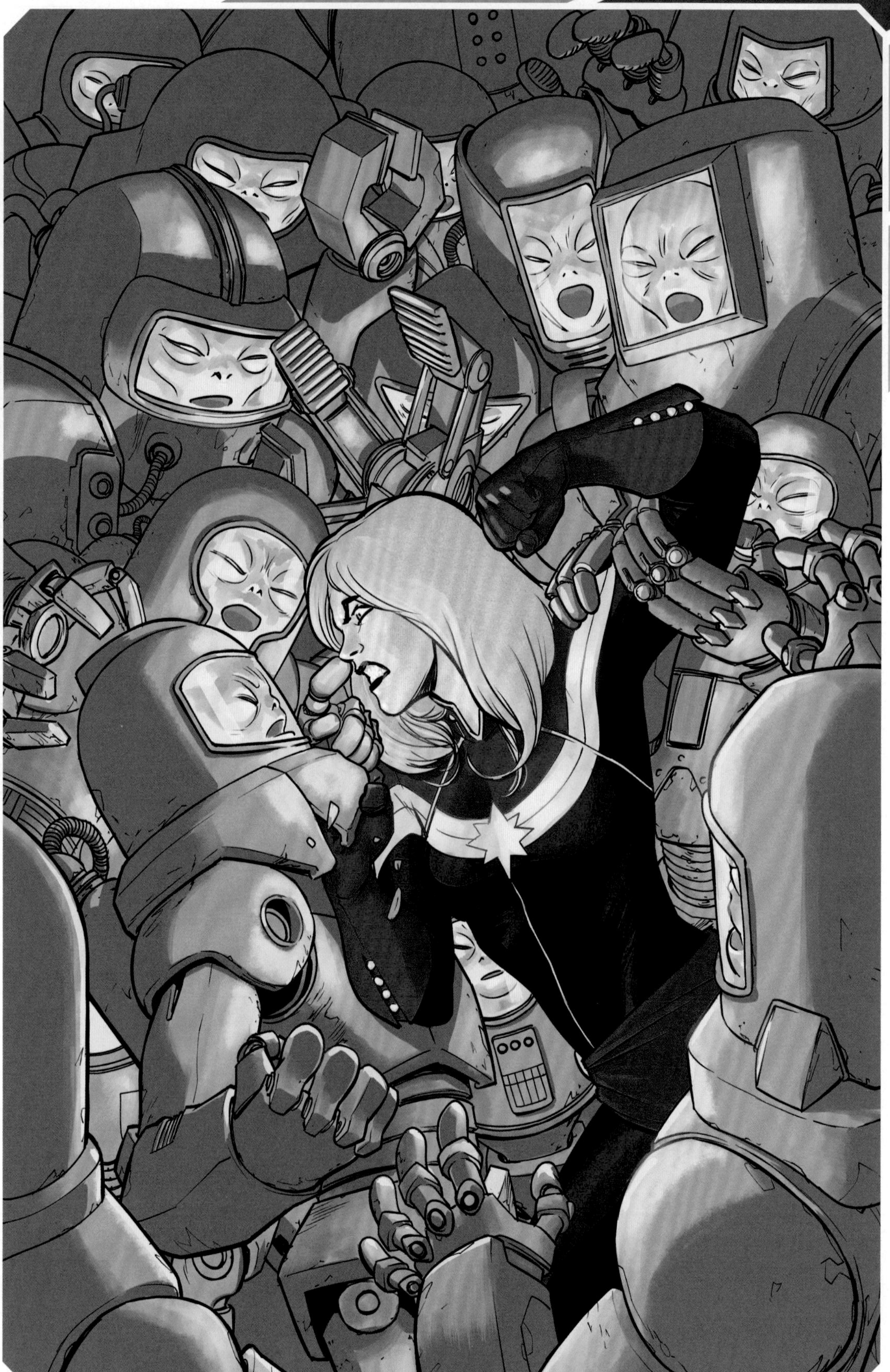

CAPTAIN MARVEL #5

When former U.S. Air Force pilot Carol Danvers was caught in the explosion of an alien device called the Psyche-Magnitron, she was transformed into one of the world's most powerful super beings. She now uses her abilities to protect her planet and fight for justice as an Avenger.
She is Earth's Mightiest Hero...she is...

# CAPTAIN MARVEL

## PREVIOUSLY

Captain Marvel has found a coalition of refugees on the poisonous planet Torfa. J'Son, ruler of the Spartax Empire, has given them three days to evacuate a small number, leaving the rest to die on the planet's surface. Unsatisfied with that option, Captain Marvel was searching for a way to save all of their lives when she and her crew, a ragtag band of extraterrestrials, were ambushed by a group of Haffensye space pirates. That begs the question – what on Torfa is valuable enough that they'd attack an Avenger for it?

# HIGHER, FURTHER, FASTER, MORE. PART FIVE

**KELLY SUE DeCONNICK**
WRITER

**DAVID LOPEZ**
ART

**LEE LOUGHRIDGE**
COLOR ART

**VC'S JOE CARAMAGNA**
LETTERER

**DAVID LOPEZ**
COVER ARTIST

**DEVIN LEWIS**
ASSISTANT EDITOR

**SANA AMANAT**
EDITOR

**NICK LOWE**
SENIOR EDITOR

**AXEL ALONSO**
EDITOR IN CHIEF

**JOE QUESADA**
CHIEF CREATIVE OFFICER

**DAN BUCKLEY**
PUBLISHER

**ALAN FINE**
EXEC. PRODUCER

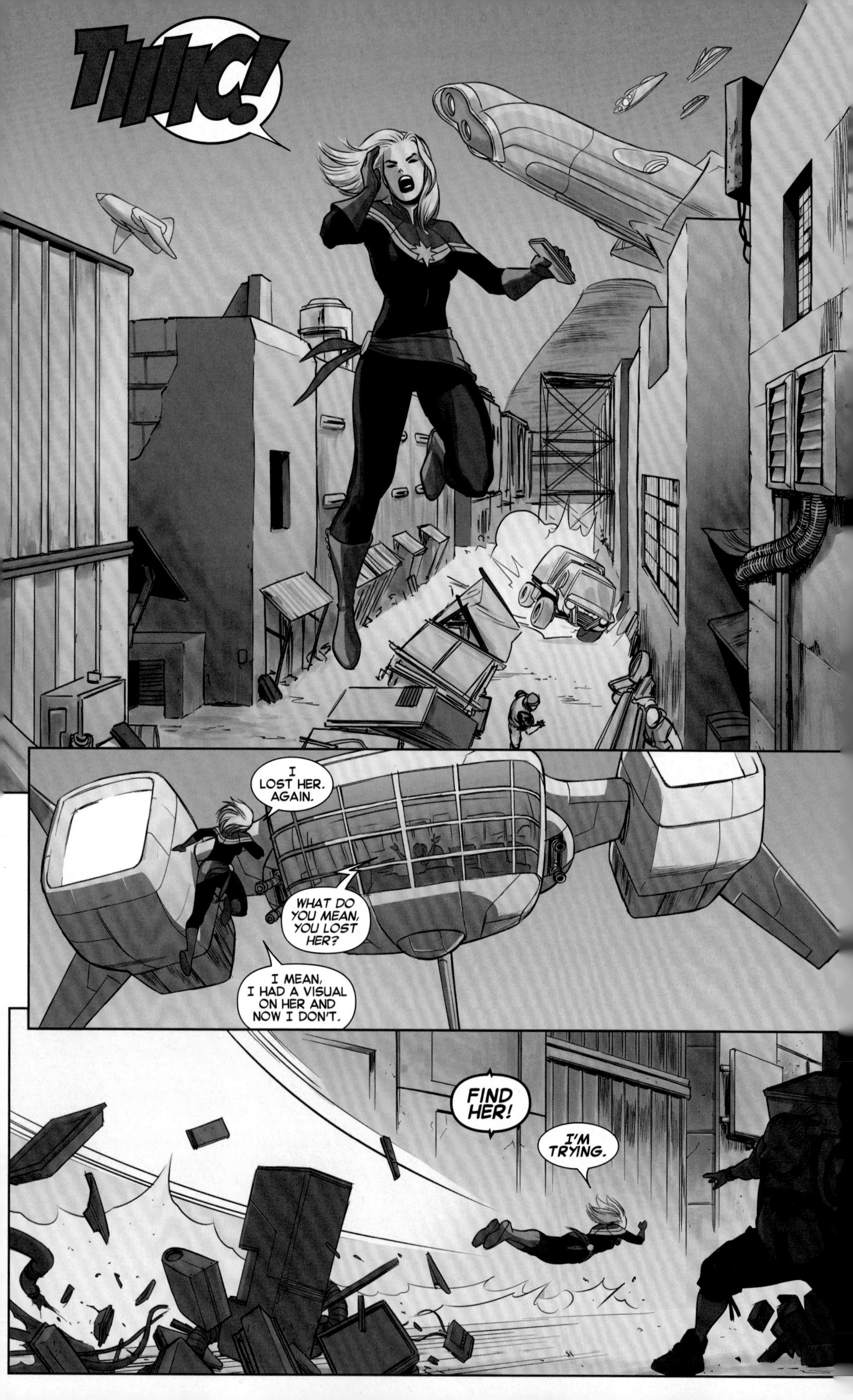
THUC!
I LOST HER. AGAIN.
WHAT DO YOU MEAN, YOU LOST HER?
I MEAN, I HAD A VISUAL ON HER AND NOW I DON'T.
FIND HER!
I'M TRYING.

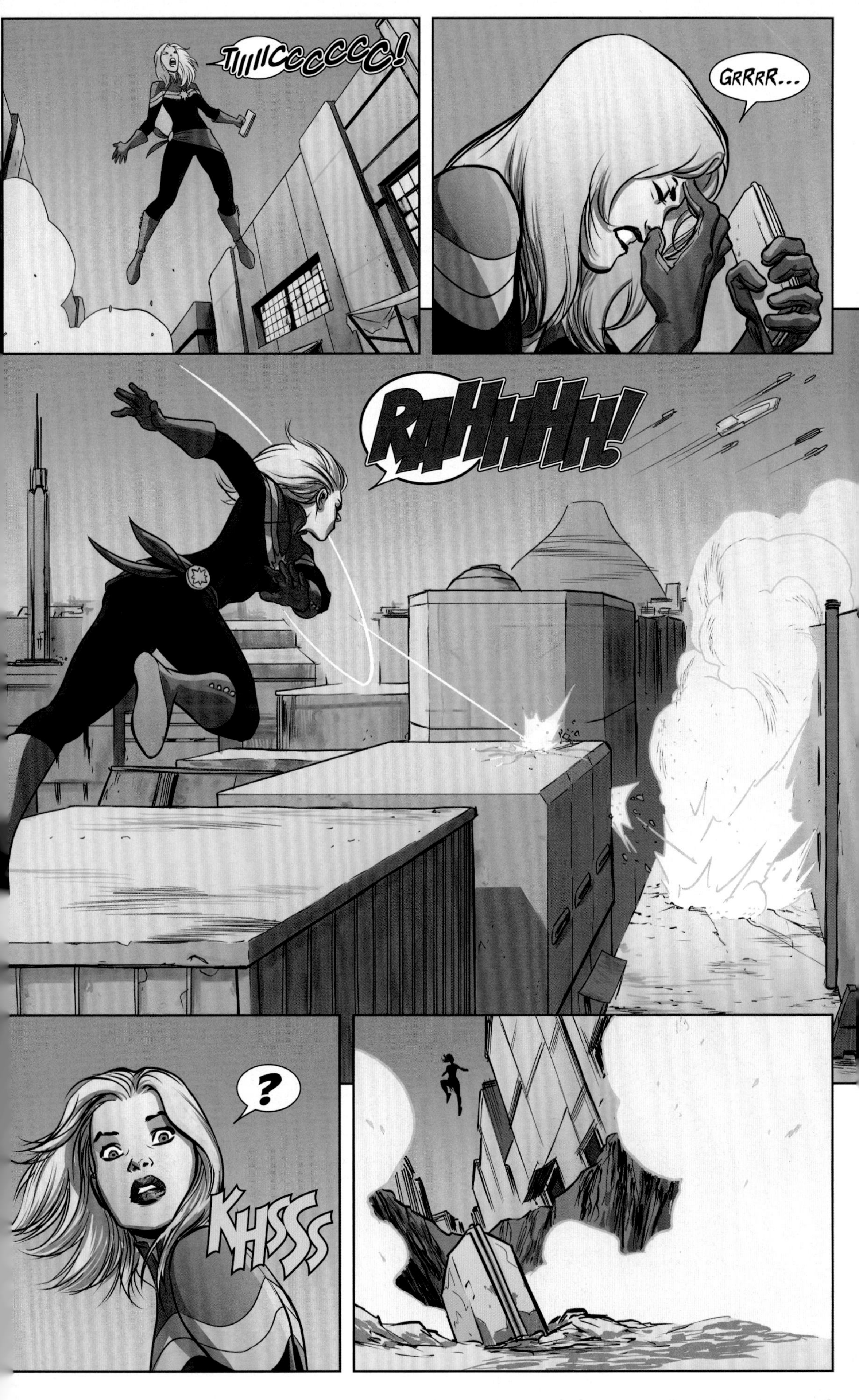
TIIIICCCCCCC!
GRRRR...
RAHHHHH!
?
KHSSS

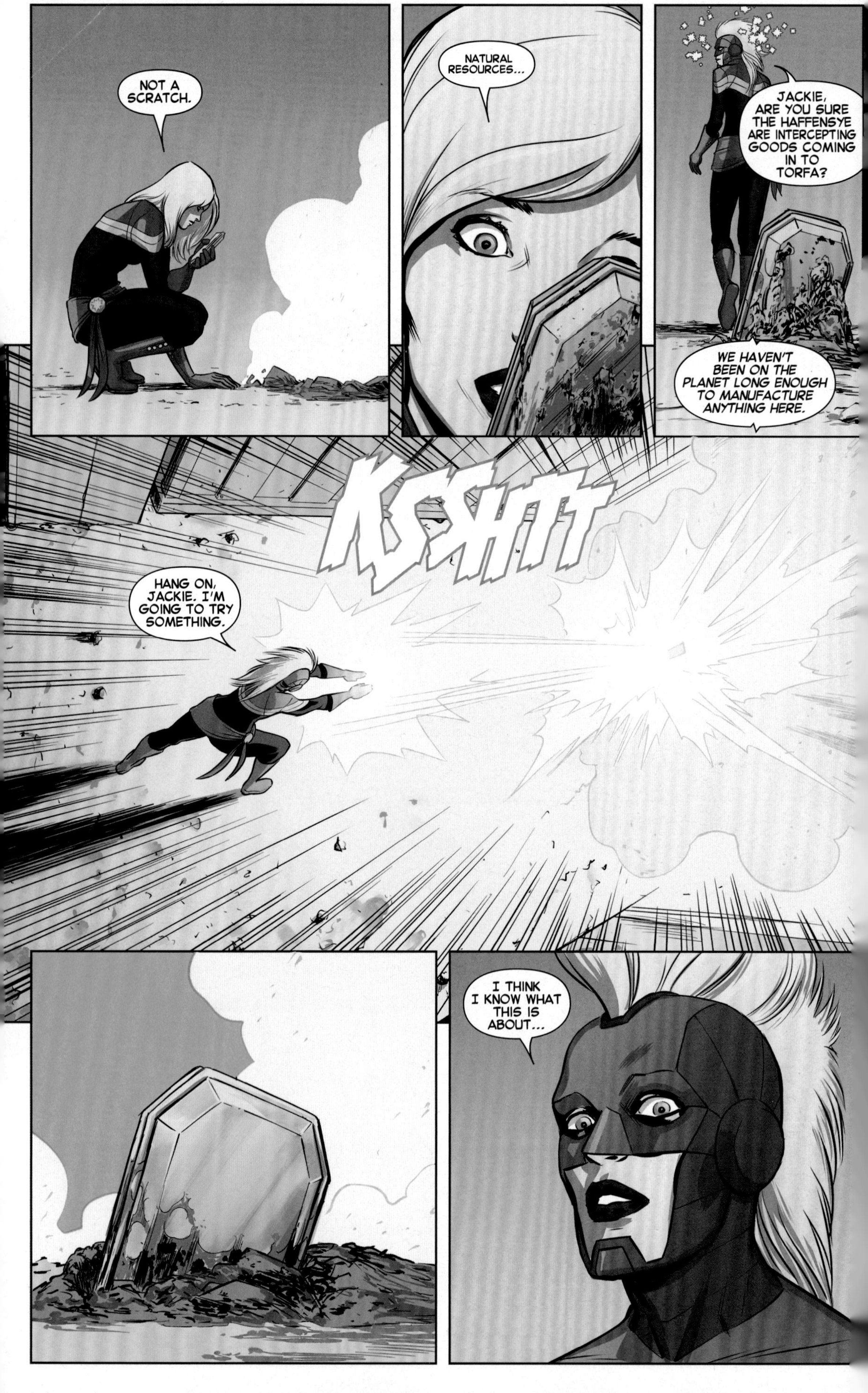
NOT A SCRATCH.
NATURAL RESOURCES...
JACKIE, ARE YOU SURE THE HAFFENSYE ARE INTERCEPTING GOODS COMING IN TO TORFA?
WE HAVEN'T BEEN ON THE PLANET LONG ENOUGH TO MANUFACTURE ANYTHING HERE.
KSSHTT
HANG ON, JACKIE. I'M GOING TO TRY SOMETHING.
I THINK I KNOW WHAT THIS IS ABOUT...

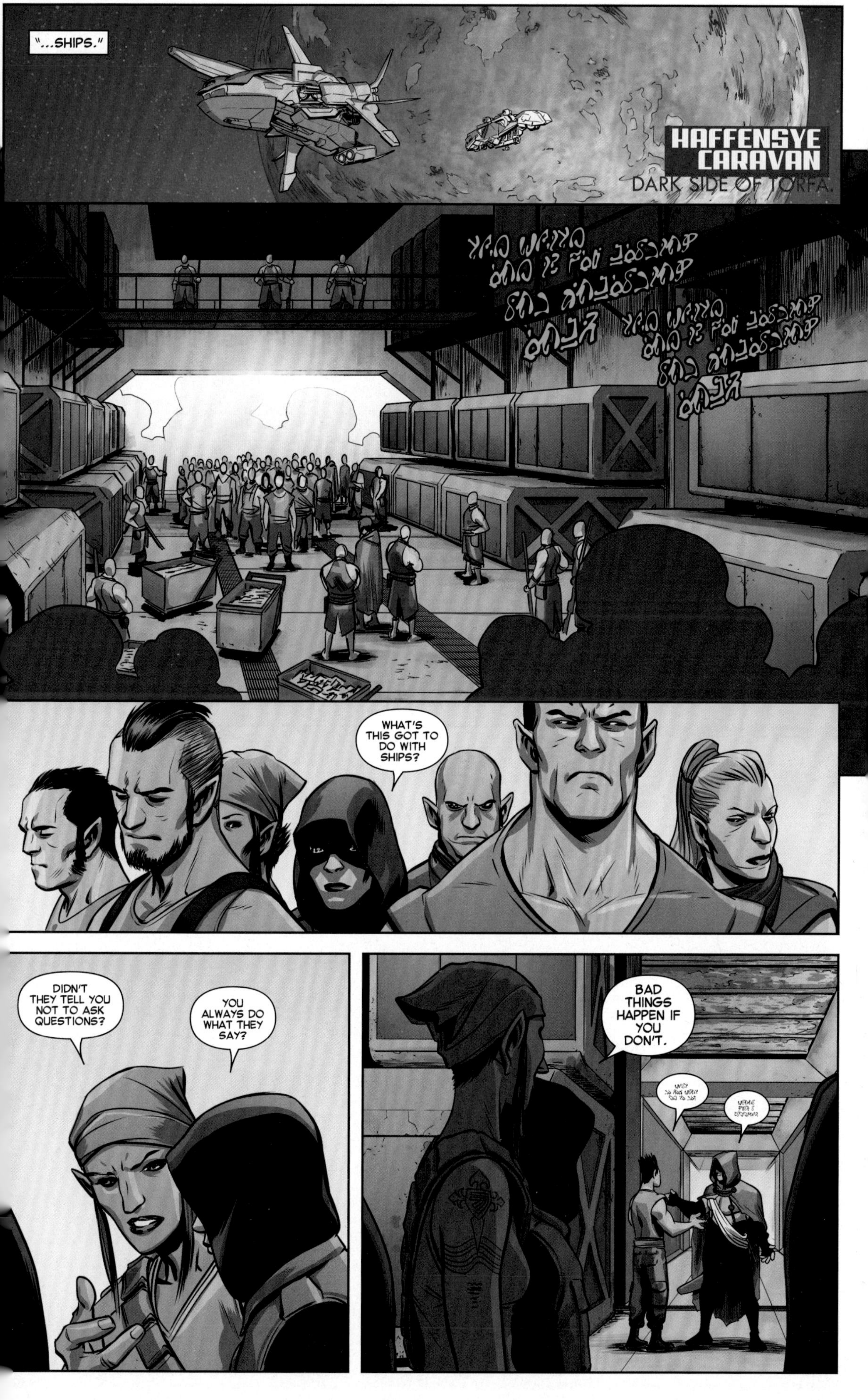
"...SHIPS."
HAFFENSYE CARAVAN
DARK SIDE OF TORFA.
WHAT'S THIS GOT TO DO WITH SHIPS?
DIDN'T THEY TELL YOU NOT TO ASK QUESTIONS?
YOU ALWAYS DO WHAT THEY SAY?
BAD THINGS HAPPEN IF YOU DON'T.

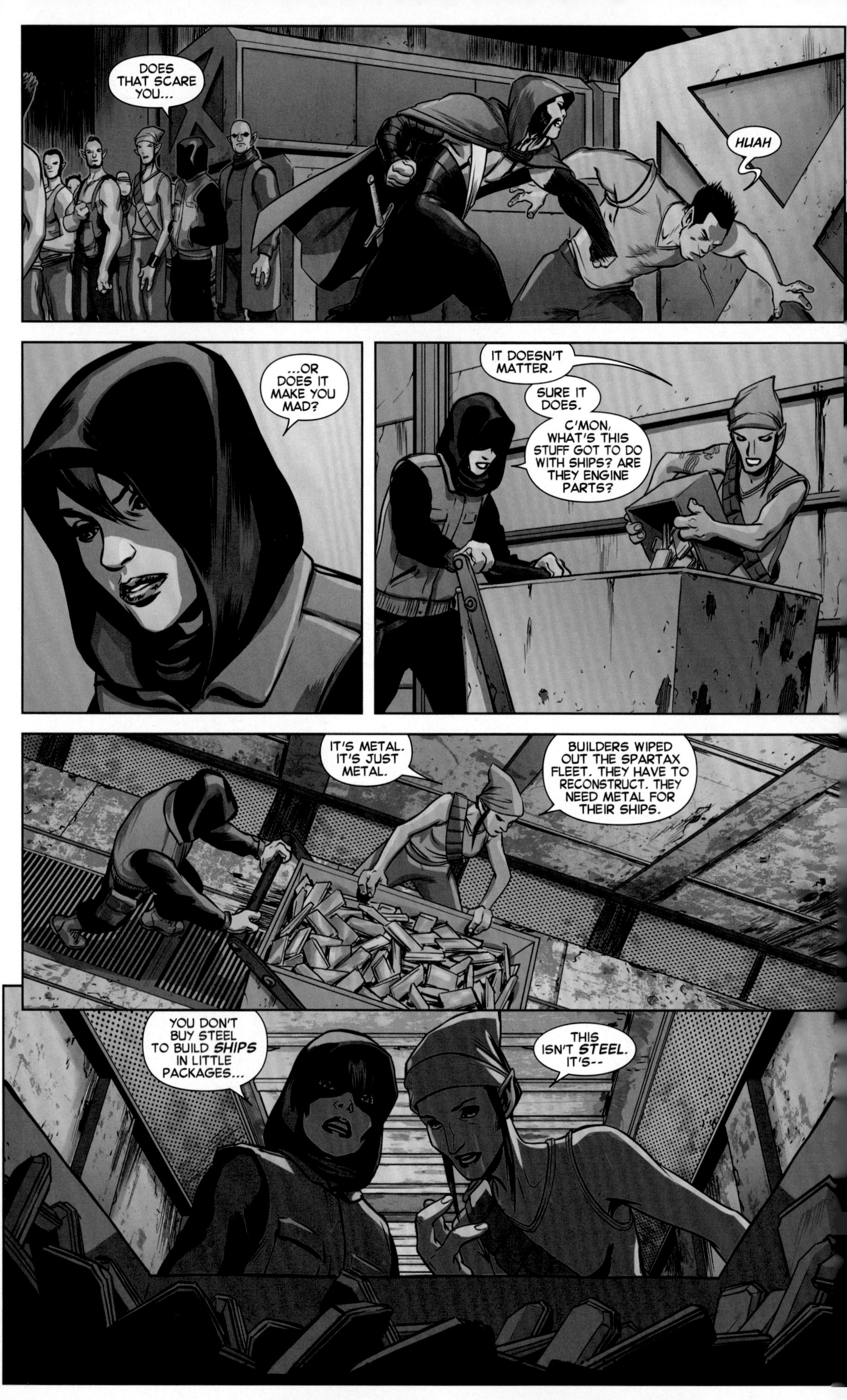
DOES THAT SCARE YOU...
HUAH
...OR DOES IT MAKE YOU MAD?
IT DOESN'T MATTER.
SURE IT DOES.
C'MON, WHAT'S THIS STUFF GOT TO DO WITH SHIPS? ARE THEY ENGINE PARTS?
IT'S METAL. IT'S JUST METAL.
BUILDERS WIPED OUT THE SPARTAX FLEET. THEY HAVE TO RECONSTRUCT. THEY NEED METAL FOR THEIR SHIPS.
YOU DON'T BUY STEEL TO BUILD SHIPS IN LITTLE PACKAGES...
THIS ISN'T STEEL. IT'S--

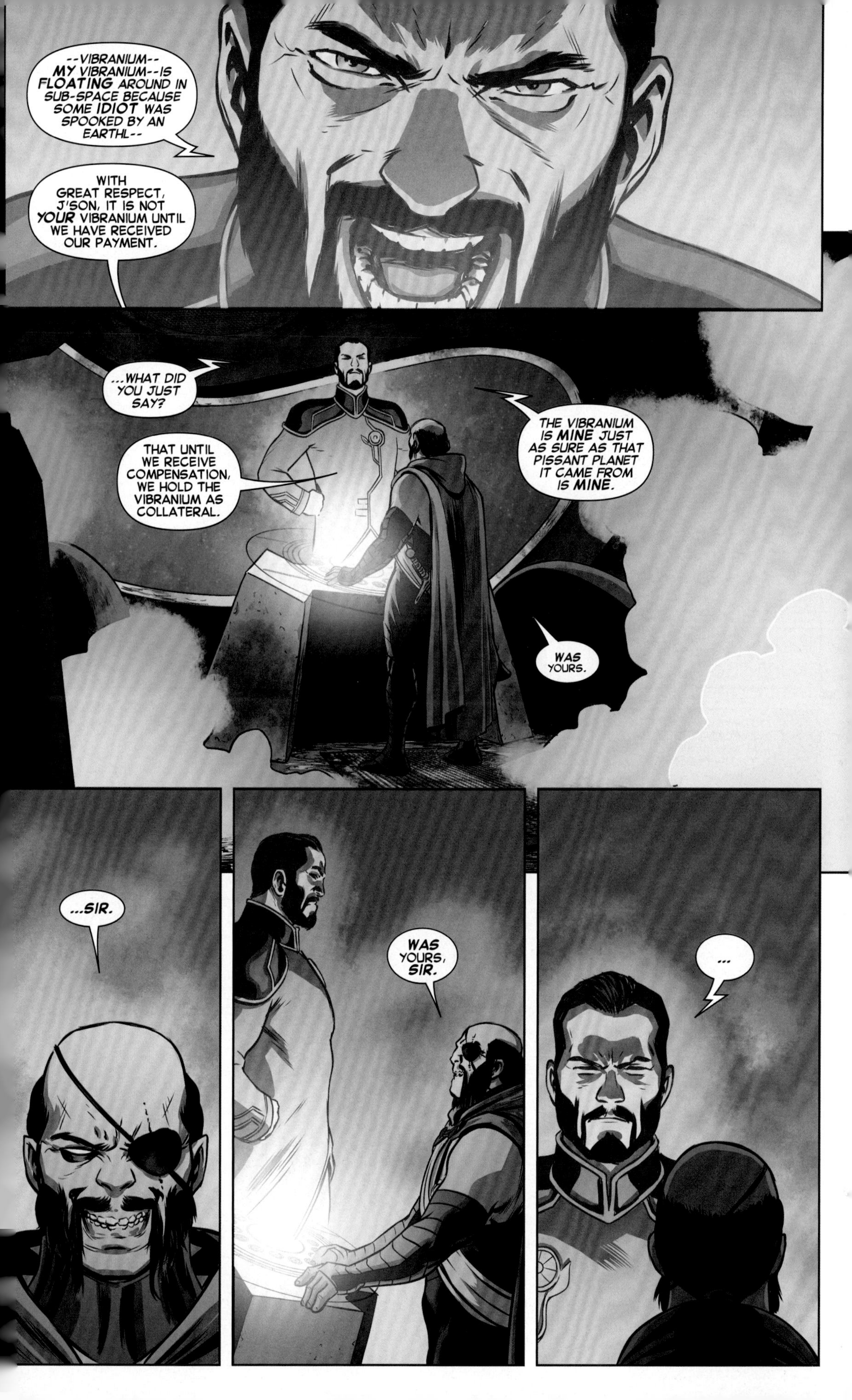
--VIBRANIUM-- MY VIBRANIUM--IS FLOATING AROUND IN SUB-SPACE BECAUSE SOME IDIOT WAS SPOOKED BY AN EARTHL--
WITH GREAT RESPECT, J'SON, IT IS NOT YOUR VIBRANIUM UNTIL WE HAVE RECEIVED OUR PAYMENT.
...WHAT DID YOU JUST SAY?
THAT UNTIL WE RECEIVE COMPENSATION, WE HOLD THE VIBRANIUM AS COLLATERAL.
THE VIBRANIUM IS MINE JUST AS SURE AS THAT PISSANT PLANET IT CAME FROM IS MINE.
WAS YOURS.
...SIR.
WAS YOURS, SIR.
...

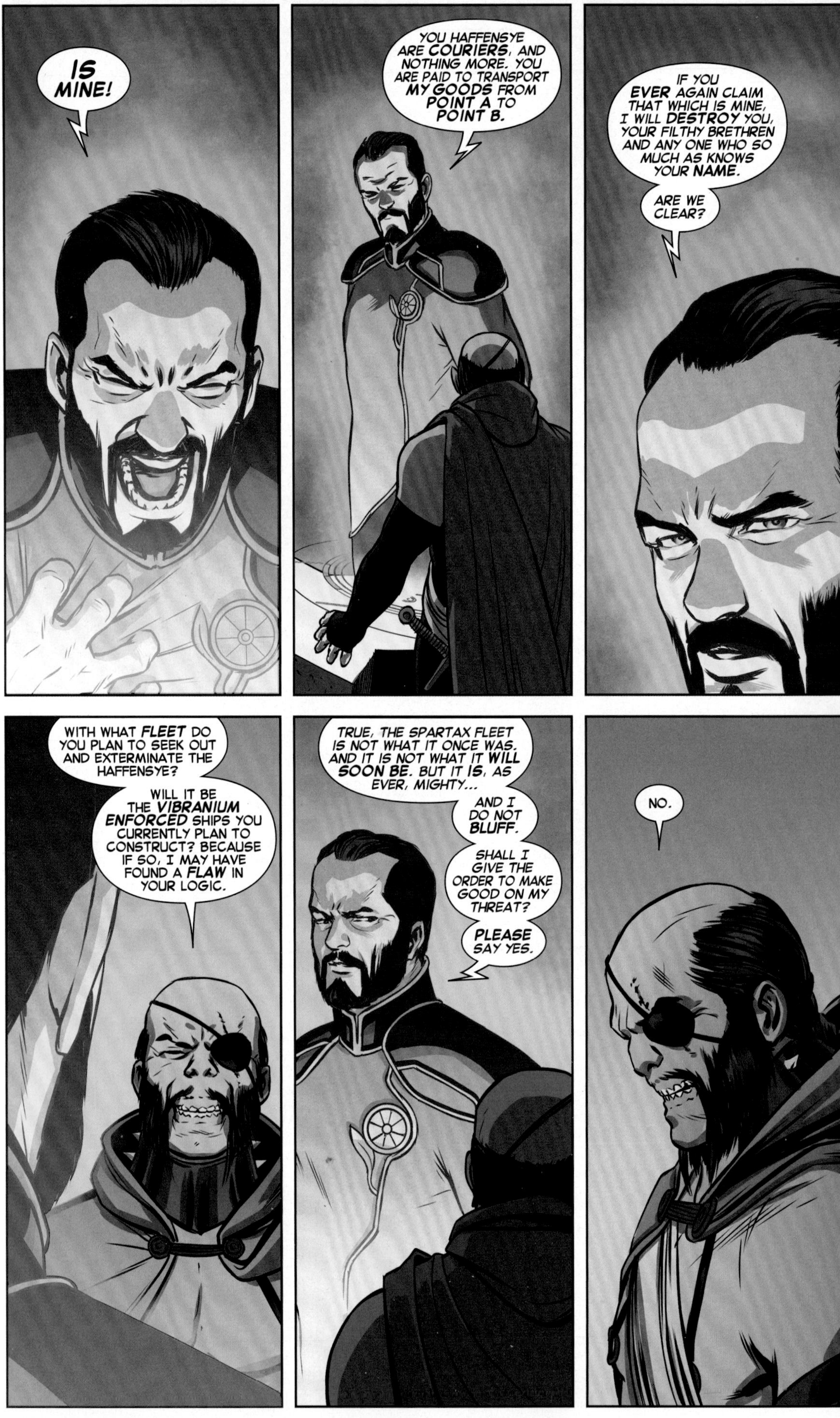
IS MINE!
YOU HAFFENSYE ARE COURIERS, AND NOTHING MORE. YOU ARE PAID TO TRANSPORT MY GOODS FROM POINT A TO POINT B.
IF YOU EVER AGAIN CLAIM THAT WHICH IS MINE, I WILL DESTROY YOU, YOUR FILTHY BRETHREN AND ANY ONE WHO SO MUCH AS KNOWS YOUR NAME.
ARE WE CLEAR?
WITH WHAT FLEET DO YOU PLAN TO SEEK OUT AND EXTERMINATE THE HAFFENSYE?
WILL IT BE THE VIBRANIUM ENFORCED SHIPS YOU CURRENTLY PLAN TO CONSTRUCT? BECAUSE IF SO, I MAY HAVE FOUND A FLAW IN YOUR LOGIC.
TRUE, THE SPARTAX FLEET IS NOT WHAT IT ONCE WAS. AND IT IS NOT WHAT IT WILL SOON BE. BUT IT IS, AS EVER, MIGHTY...
AND I DO NOT BLUFF.
SHALL I GIVE THE ORDER TO MAKE GOOD ON MY THREAT?
PLEASE SAY YES.
NO.

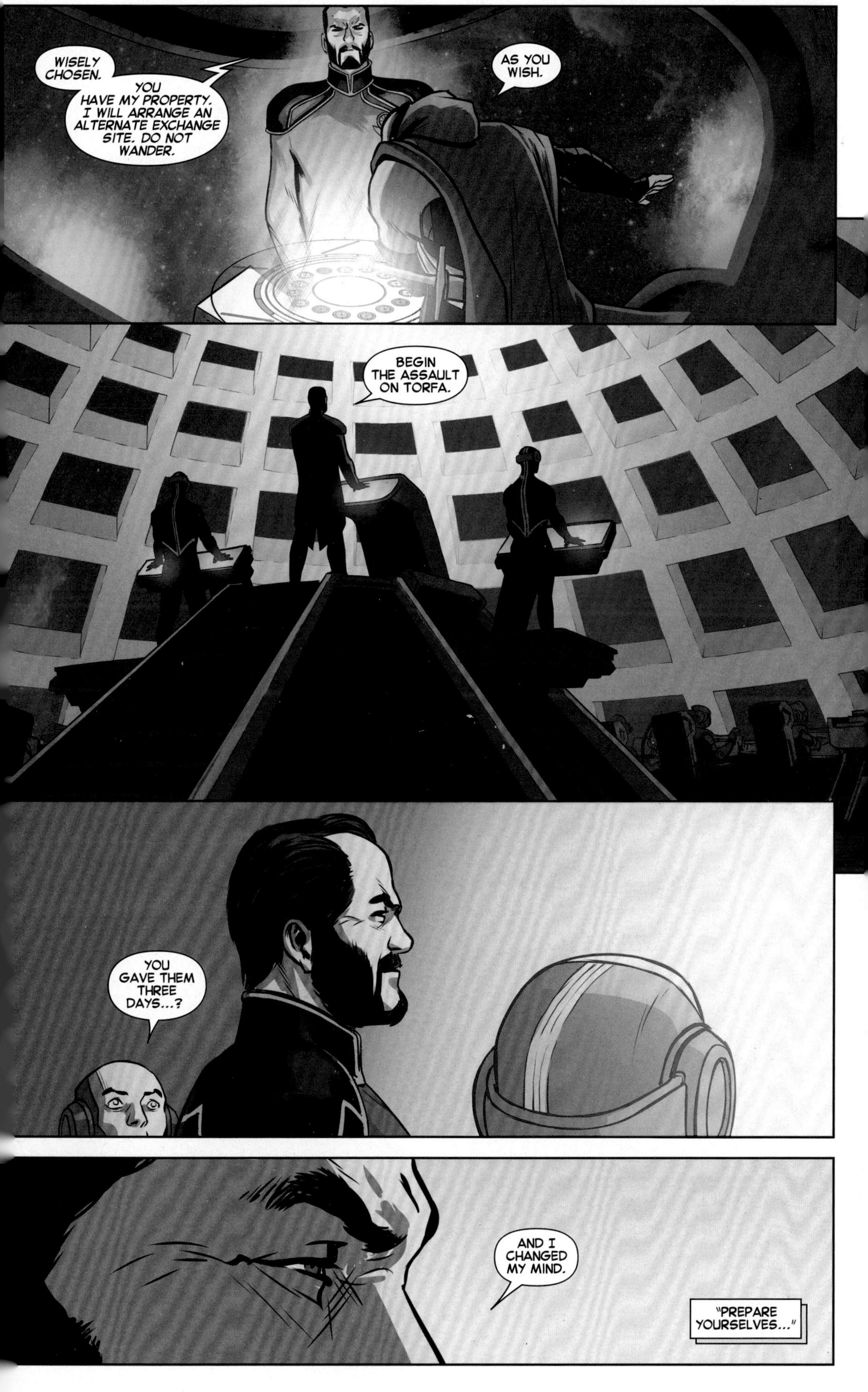
WISELY CHOSEN.
YOU HAVE MY PROPERTY. I WILL ARRANGE AN ALTERNATE EXCHANGE SITE. DO NOT WANDER.
AS YOU WISH.
BEGIN THE ASSAULT ON TORFA.
YOU GAVE THEM THREE DAYS...?
AND I CHANGED MY MIND.
"PREPARE YOURSELVES..."

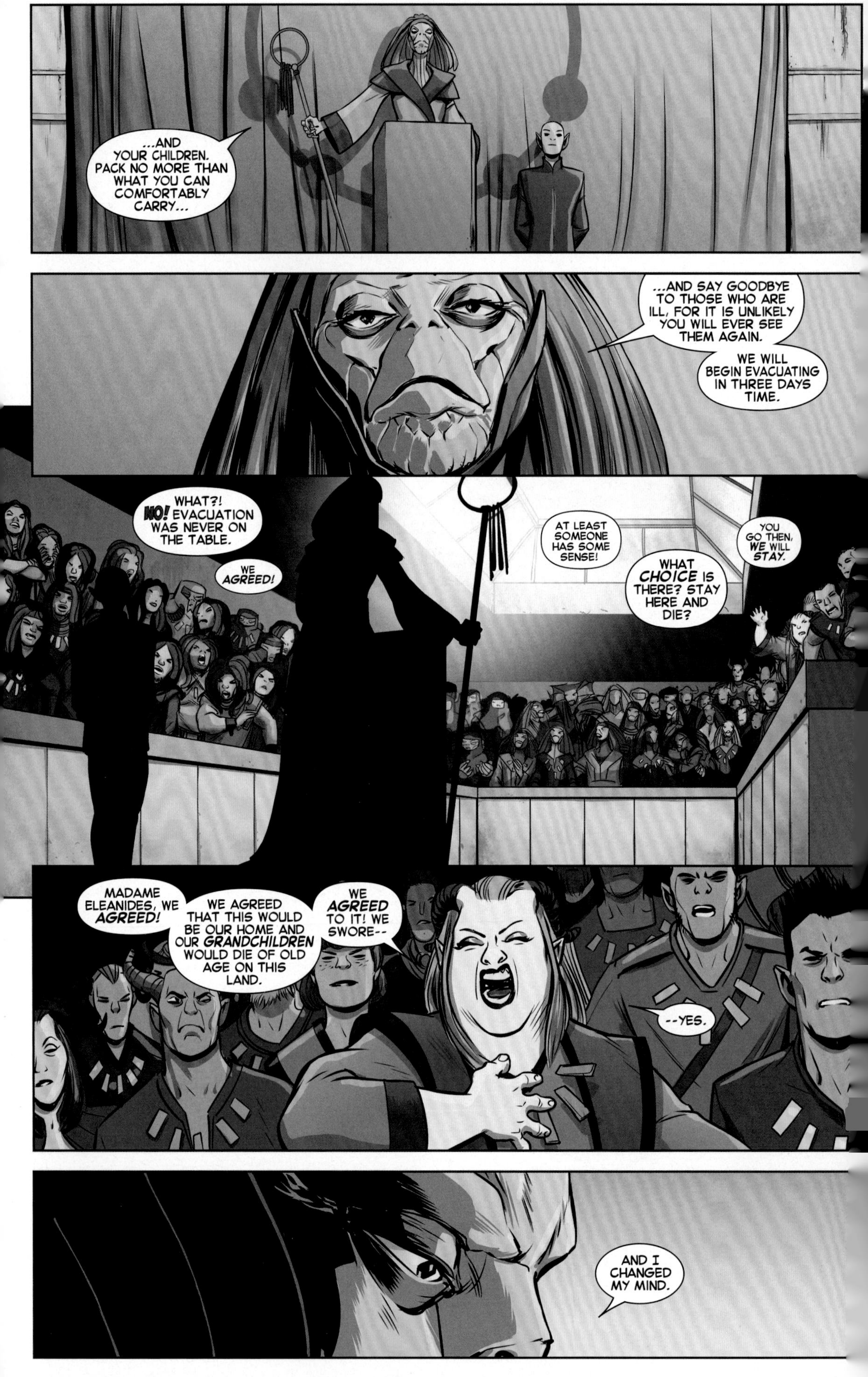
...AND YOUR CHILDREN. PACK NO MORE THAN WHAT YOU CAN COMFORTABLY CARRY...
...AND SAY GOODBYE TO THOSE WHO ARE ILL, FOR IT IS UNLIKELY YOU WILL EVER SEE THEM AGAIN.
WE WILL BEGIN EVACUATING IN THREE DAYS TIME.
WHAT?! NO! EVACUATION WAS NEVER ON THE TABLE.
WE AGREED!
AT LEAST SOMEONE HAS SOME SENSE!
WHAT CHOICE IS THERE? STAY HERE AND DIE?
YOU GO THEN, WE WILL STAY.
MADAME ELEANIDES, WE AGREED!
WE AGREED THAT THIS WOULD BE OUR HOME AND OUR GRANDCHILDREN WOULD DIE OF OLD AGE ON THIS LAND.
WE AGREED TO IT! WE SWORE--
--YES.
AND I CHANGED MY MIND.

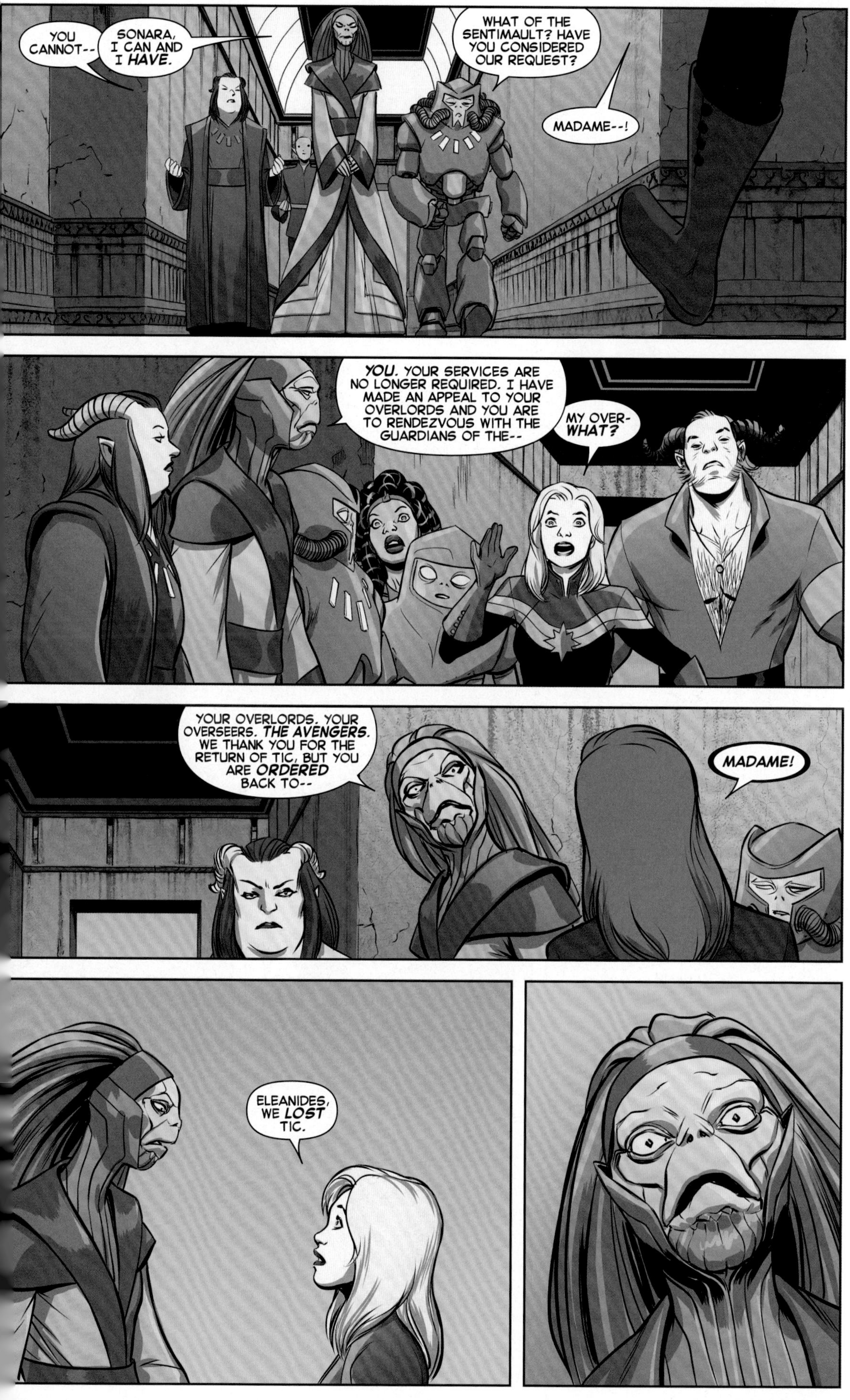
YOU CANNOT--
SONARA, I CAN AND I HAVE.
WHAT OF THE SENTIMAULT? HAVE YOU CONSIDERED OUR REQUEST?
MADAME--!
YOU. YOUR SERVICES ARE NO LONGER REQUIRED. I HAVE MADE AN APPEAL TO YOUR OVERLORDS AND YOU ARE TO RENDEZVOUS WITH THE GUARDIANS OF THE--
MY OVER- WHAT?
YOUR OVERLORDS. YOUR OVERSEERS. THE AVENGERS. WE THANK YOU FOR THE RETURN OF TIC, BUT YOU ARE ORDERED BACK TO--
MADAME!
ELEANIDES, WE LOST TIC.

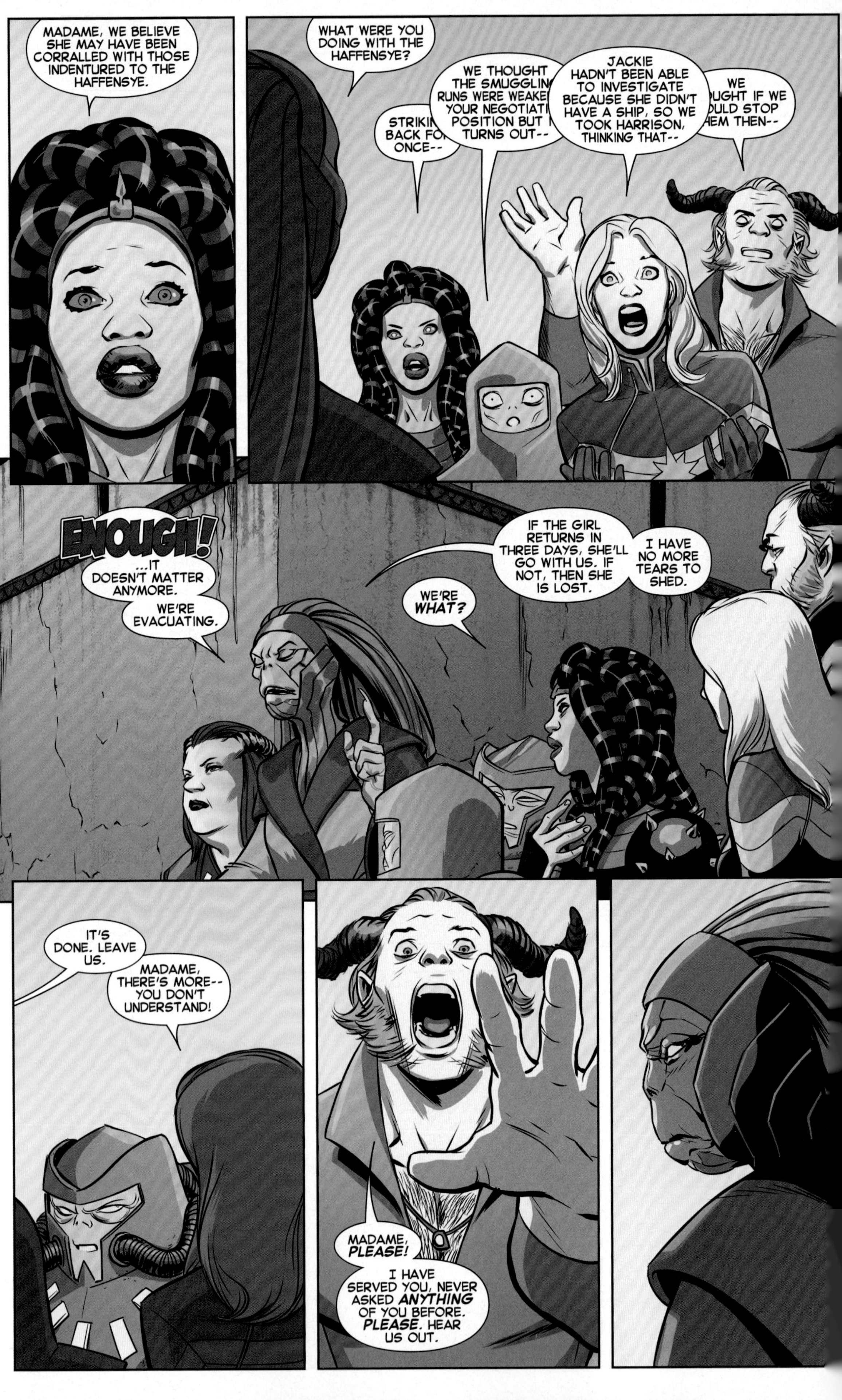
MADAME, WE BELIEVE SHE MAY HAVE BEEN CORRALLED WITH THOSE INDENTURED TO THE HAFFENSYE.
WHAT WERE YOU DOING WITH THE HAFFENSYE?
STRIKIN BACK FO ONCE--
WE THOUGHT THE SMUGGLIN RUNS WERE WEAKE YOUR NEGOTIATI POSITION BUT I TURNS OUT--
JACKIE HADN'T BEEN ABLE TO INVESTIGATE BECAUSE SHE DIDN'T HAVE A SHIP, SO WE TOOK HARRISON, THINKING THAT--
WE UGHT IF WE ULD STOP HEM THEN--
ENOUGH!
...IT DOESN'T MATTER ANYMORE.
WE'RE EVACUATING.
WE'RE *WHAT?*
IF THE GIRL RETURNS IN THREE DAYS, SHE'LL GO WITH US. IF NOT, THEN SHE IS LOST.
I HAVE NO MORE TEARS TO SHED.
IT'S DONE. LEAVE US.
MADAME, THERE'S MORE-- YOU DON'T UNDERSTAND!
MADAME, *PLEASE!*
I HAVE SERVED YOU, NEVER ASKED *ANYTHING* OF YOU BEFORE. *PLEASE*. HEAR US OUT.

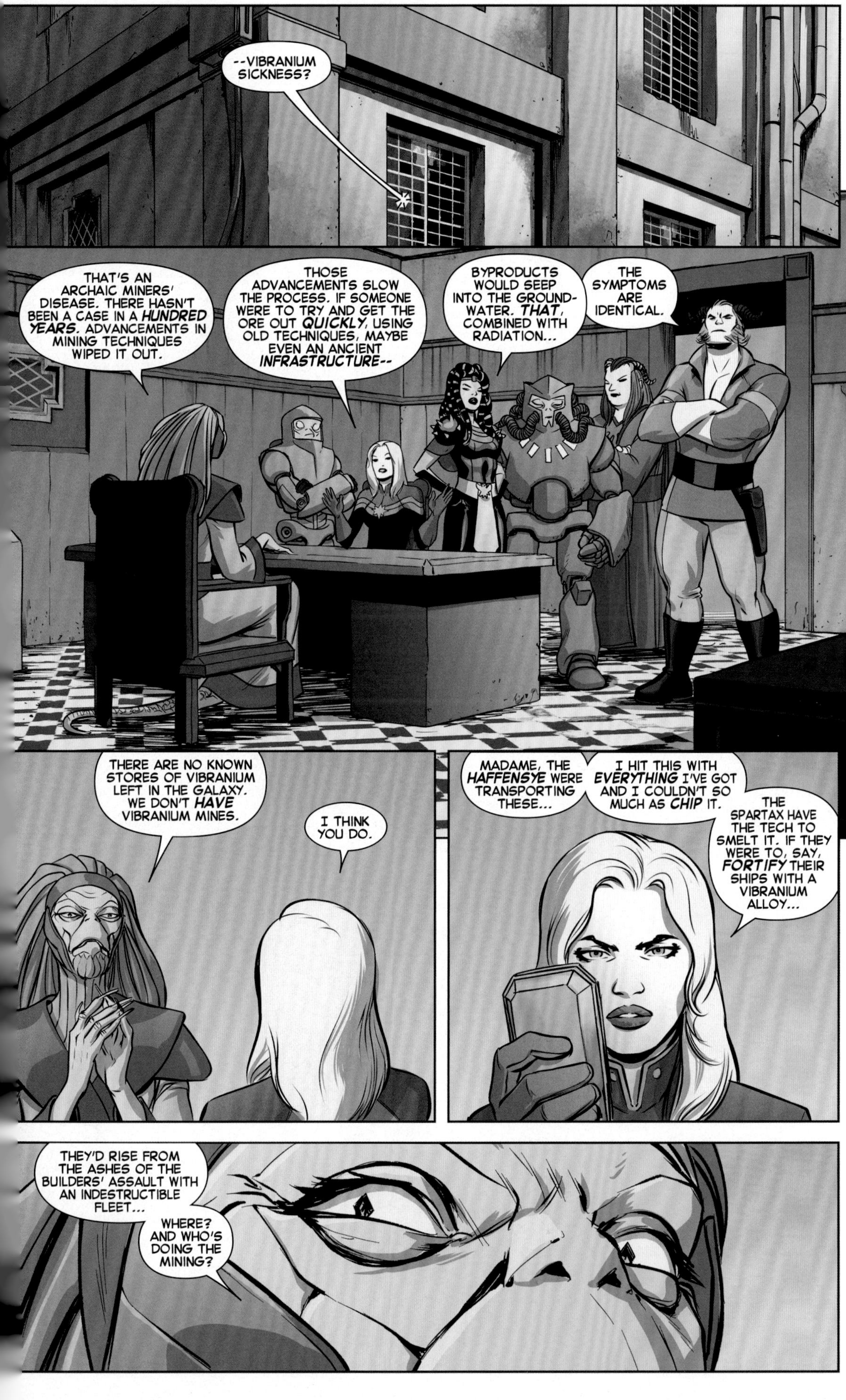
--VIBRANIUM SICKNESS?
THAT'S AN ARCHAIC MINERS' DISEASE. THERE HASN'T BEEN A CASE IN A HUNDRED YEARS. ADVANCEMENTS IN MINING TECHNIQUES WIPED IT OUT.
THOSE ADVANCEMENTS SLOW THE PROCESS. IF SOMEONE WERE TO TRY AND GET THE ORE OUT QUICKLY, USING OLD TECHNIQUES, MAYBE EVEN AN ANCIENT INFRASTRUCTURE--
BYPRODUCTS WOULD SEEP INTO THE GROUND-WATER. THAT, COMBINED WITH RADIATION...
THE SYMPTOMS ARE IDENTICAL.
THERE ARE NO KNOWN STORES OF VIBRANIUM LEFT IN THE GALAXY. WE DON'T HAVE VIBRANIUM MINES.
I THINK YOU DO.
MADAME, THE HAFFENSYE WERE TRANSPORTING THESE...
I HIT THIS WITH EVERYTHING I'VE GOT AND I COULDN'T SO MUCH AS CHIP IT.
THE SPARTAX HAVE THE TECH TO SMELT IT. IF THEY WERE TO, SAY, FORTIFY THEIR SHIPS WITH A VIBRANIUM ALLOY...
THEY'D RISE FROM THE ASHES OF THE BUILDERS' ASSAULT WITH AN INDESTRUCTIBLE FLEET...
WHERE? AND WHO'S DOING THE MINING?

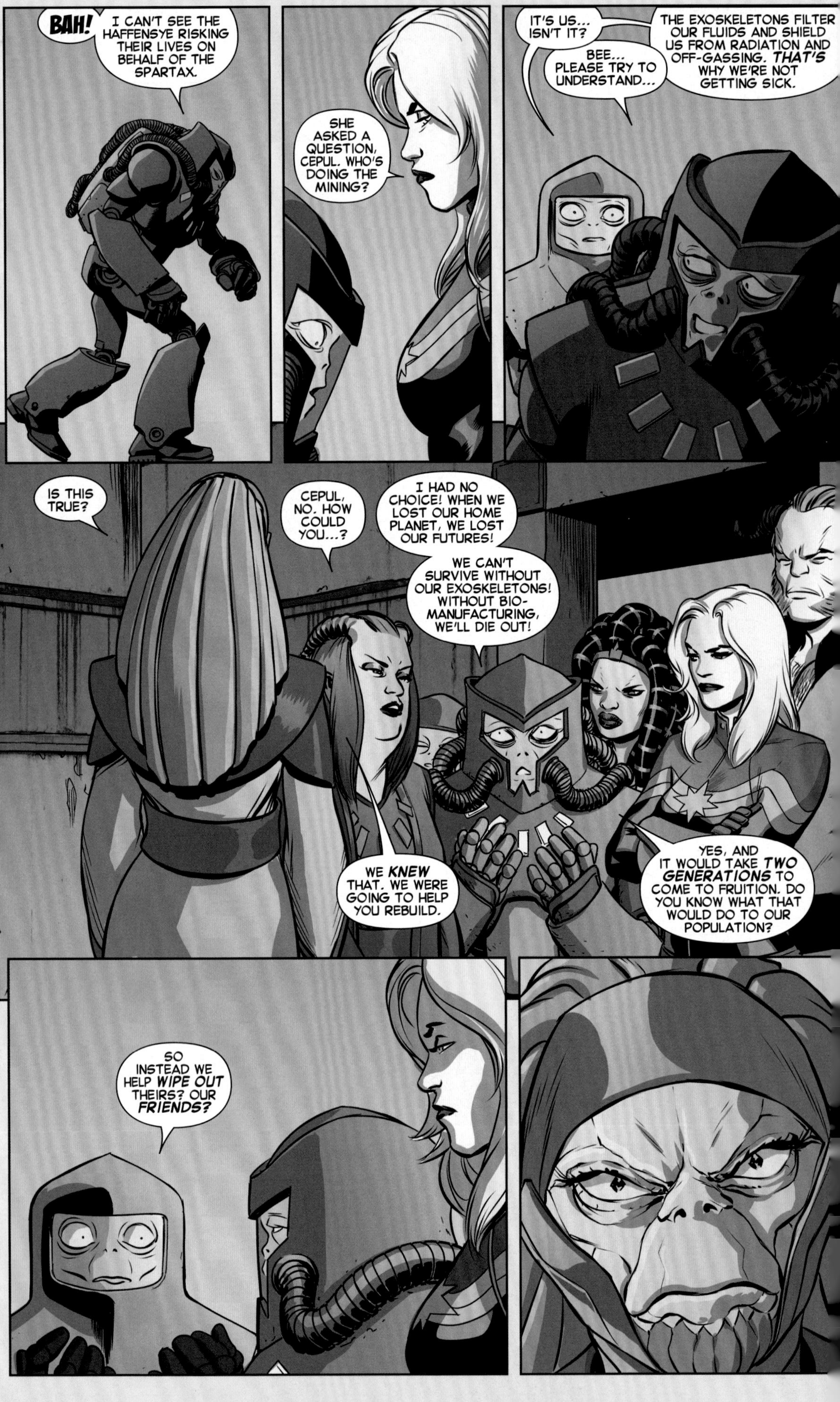
BAH!
I CAN'T SEE THE HAFFENSYE RISKING THEIR LIVES ON BEHALF OF THE SPARTAX.
SHE ASKED A QUESTION, CEPUL. WHO'S DOING THE MINING?
IT'S US... ISN'T IT?
BEE... PLEASE TRY TO UNDERSTAND...
THE EXOSKELETONS FILTER OUR FLUIDS AND SHIELD US FROM RADIATION AND OFF-GASSING. THAT'S WHY WE'RE NOT GETTING SICK.
IS THIS TRUE?
CEPUL, NO. HOW COULD YOU...?
I HAD NO CHOICE! WHEN WE LOST OUR HOME PLANET, WE LOST OUR FUTURES!
WE CAN'T SURVIVE WITHOUT OUR EXOSKELETONS! WITHOUT BIO-MANUFACTURING, WE'LL DIE OUT!
WE KNEW THAT. WE WERE GOING TO HELP YOU REBUILD.
YES, AND IT WOULD TAKE TWO GENERATIONS TO COME TO FRUITION. DO YOU KNOW WHAT THAT WOULD DO TO OUR POPULATION?
SO INSTEAD WE HELP WIPE OUT THEIRS? OUR FRIENDS?

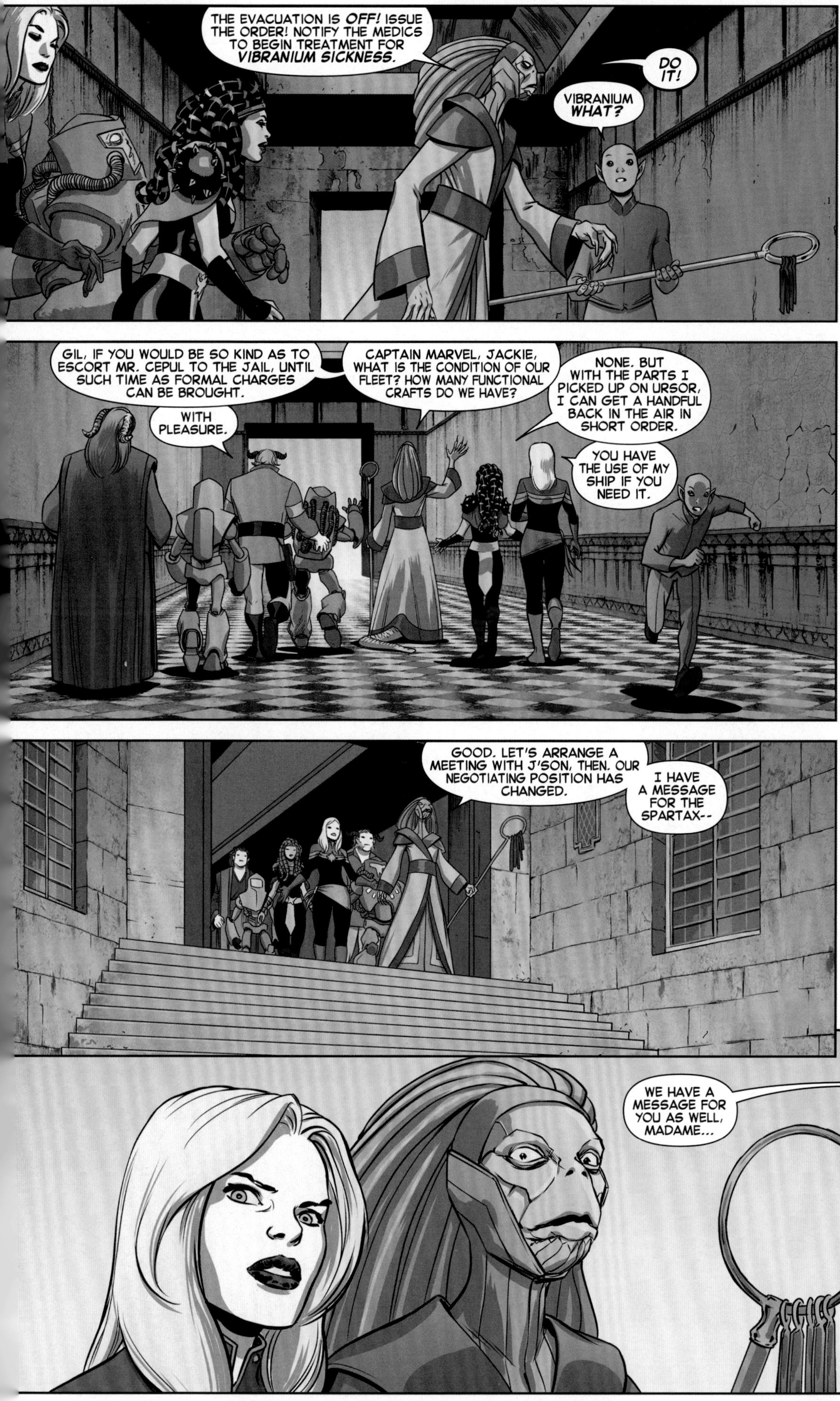
THE EVACUATION IS OFF! ISSUE THE ORDER! NOTIFY THE MEDICS TO BEGIN TREATMENT FOR VIBRANIUM SICKNESS.
VIBRANIUM WHAT?
DO IT!
GIL, IF YOU WOULD BE SO KIND AS TO ESCORT MR. CEPUL TO THE JAIL, UNTIL SUCH TIME AS FORMAL CHARGES CAN BE BROUGHT.
WITH PLEASURE.
CAPTAIN MARVEL, JACKIE, WHAT IS THE CONDITION OF OUR FLEET? HOW MANY FUNCTIONAL CRAFTS DO WE HAVE?
NONE. BUT WITH THE PARTS I PICKED UP ON URSOR, I CAN GET A HANDFUL BACK IN THE AIR IN SHORT ORDER.
YOU HAVE THE USE OF MY SHIP IF YOU NEED IT.
GOOD. LET'S ARRANGE A MEETING WITH J'SON, THEN. OUR NEGOTIATING POSITION HAS CHANGED.
I HAVE A MESSAGE FOR THE SPARTAX--
WE HAVE A MESSAGE FOR YOU AS WELL, MADAME...

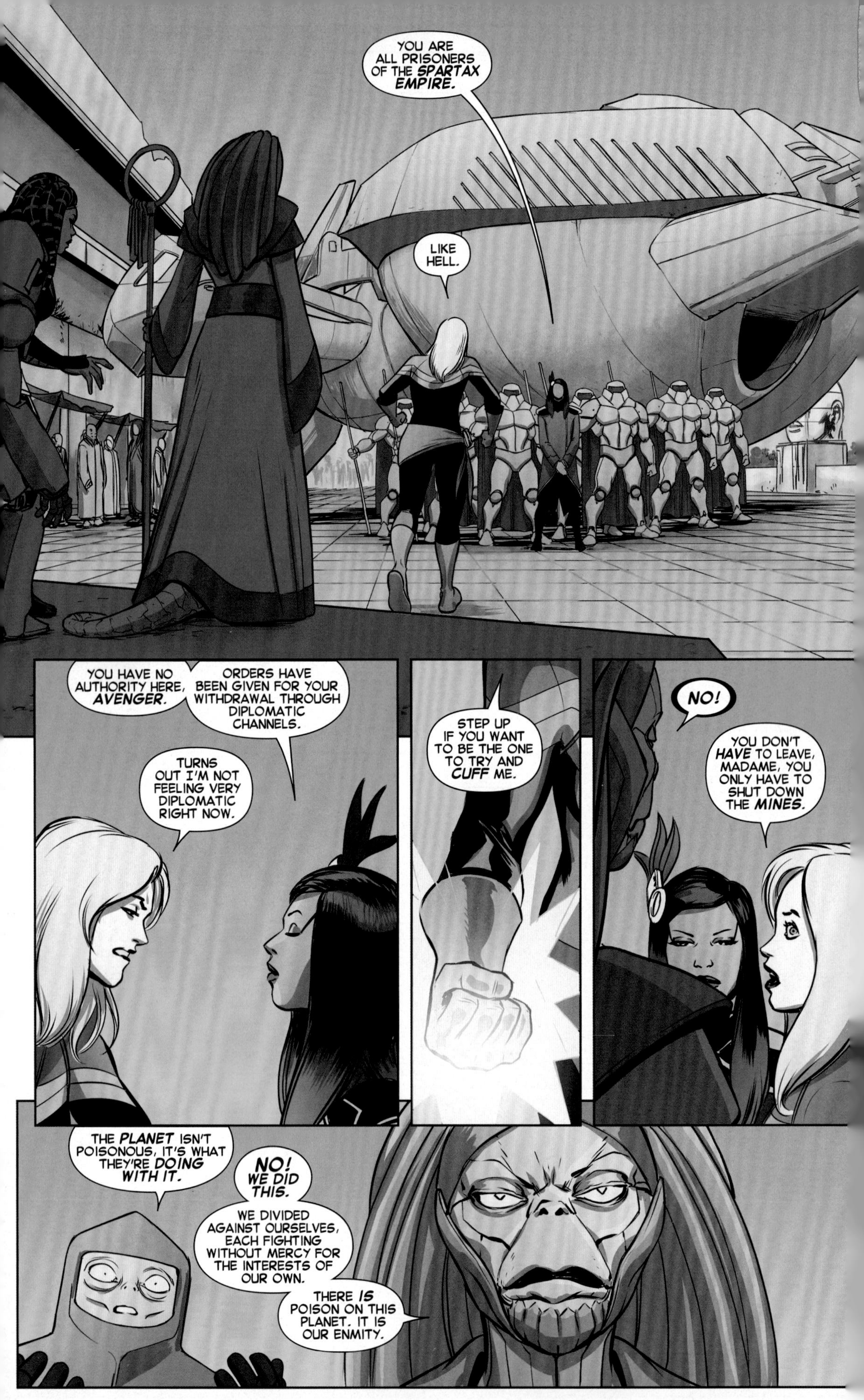
YOU ARE ALL PRISONERS OF THE SPARTAX EMPIRE.
LIKE HELL.
YOU HAVE NO AUTHORITY HERE, AVENGER.
ORDERS HAVE BEEN GIVEN FOR YOUR WITHDRAWAL THROUGH DIPLOMATIC CHANNELS.
TURNS OUT I'M NOT FEELING VERY DIPLOMATIC RIGHT NOW.
STEP UP IF YOU WANT TO BE THE ONE TO TRY AND CUFF ME.
NO!
YOU DON'T HAVE TO LEAVE, MADAME, YOU ONLY HAVE TO SHUT DOWN THE MINES.
THE PLANET ISN'T POISONOUS, IT'S WHAT THEY'RE DOING WITH IT.
NO! WE DID THIS.
WE DIVIDED AGAINST OURSELVES, EACH FIGHTING WITHOUT MERCY FOR THE INTERESTS OF OUR OWN.
THERE IS POISON ON THIS PLANET. IT IS OUR ENMITY.

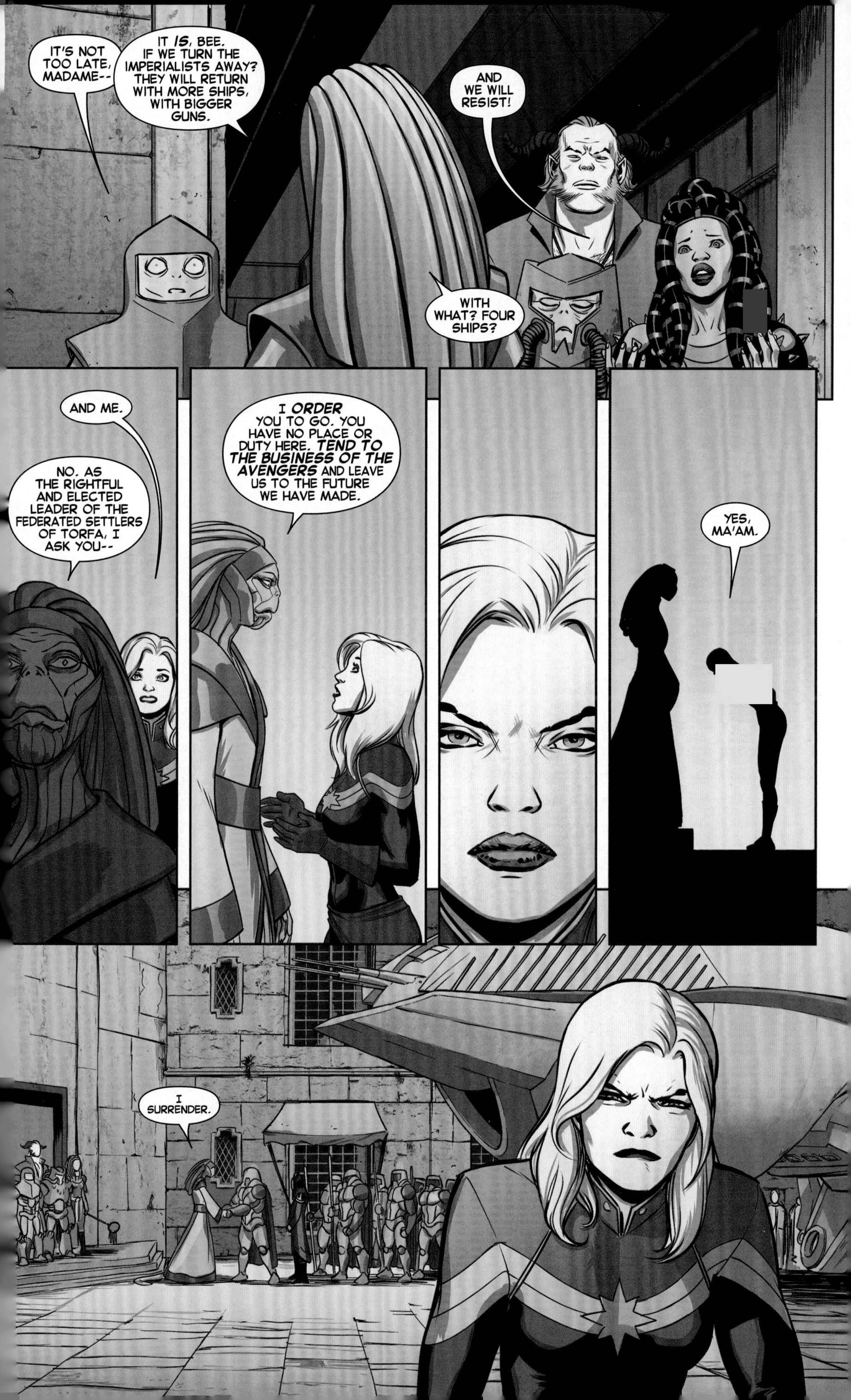
IT'S NOT TOO LATE, MADAME--
IT *IS*, BEE. IF WE TURN THE IMPERIALISTS AWAY? THEY WILL RETURN WITH MORE SHIPS, WITH BIGGER GUNS.
AND WE WILL RESIST!
WITH WHAT? FOUR SHIPS?
AND ME.
NO. AS THE RIGHTFUL AND ELECTED LEADER OF THE FEDERATED SETTLERS OF TORFA, I ASK YOU--
I *ORDER* YOU TO GO. YOU HAVE NO PLACE OR DUTY HERE. ***TEND TO THE BUSINESS OF THE AVENGERS*** AND LEAVE US TO THE FUTURE WE HAVE MADE.
YES, MA'AM.
I SURRENDER.

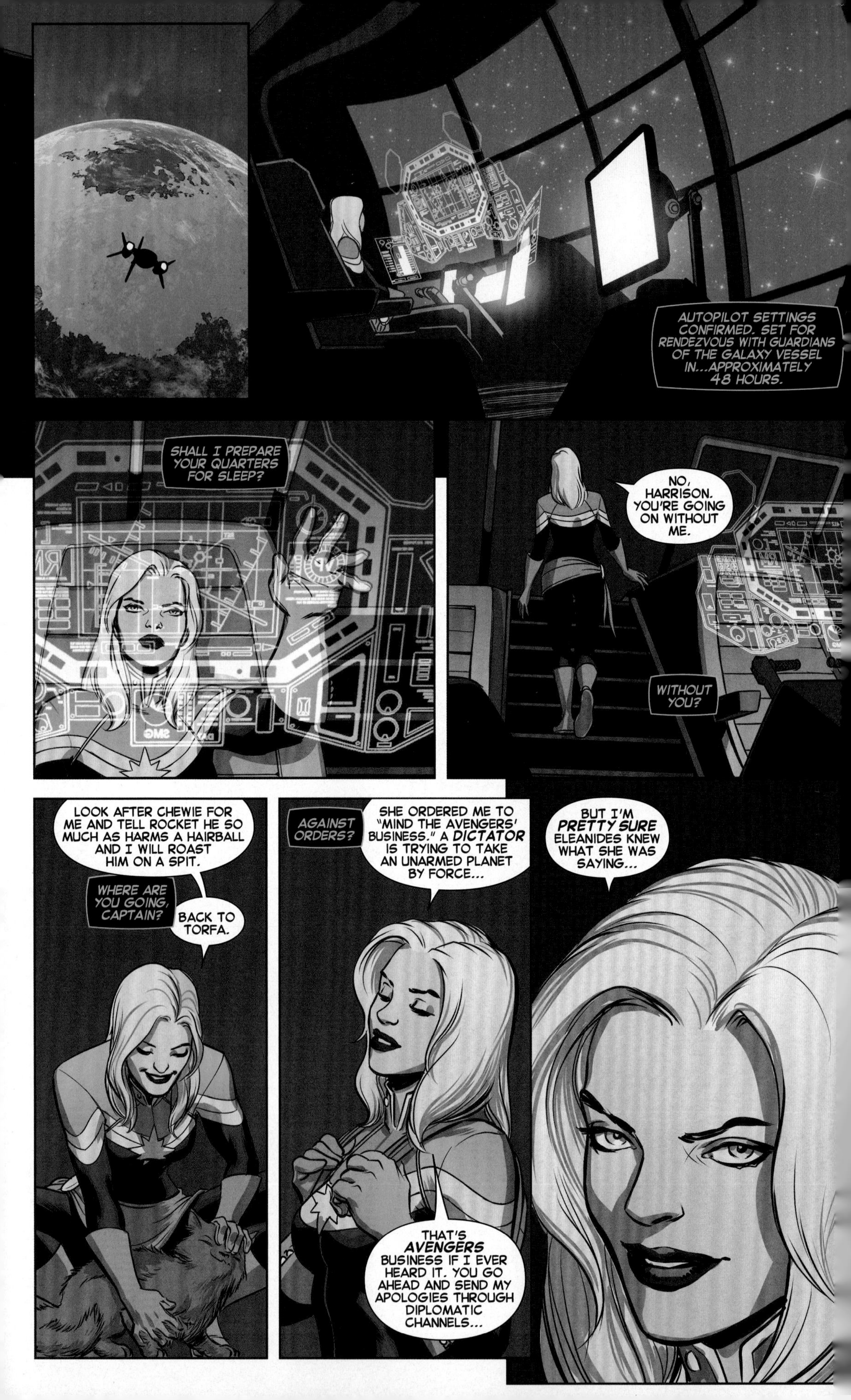

AUTOPILOT SETTINGS CONFIRMED. SET FOR RENDEZVOUS WITH GUARDIANS OF THE GALAXY VESSEL IN...APPROXIMATELY 48 HOURS.
SHALL I PREPARE YOUR QUARTERS FOR SLEEP?
NO, HARRISON. YOU'RE GOING ON WITHOUT ME.
WITHOUT YOU?
LOOK AFTER CHEWIE FOR ME AND TELL ROCKET HE SO MUCH AS HARMS A HAIRBALL AND I WILL ROAST HIM ON A SPIT.
WHERE ARE YOU GOING, CAPTAIN?
BACK TO TORFA.
AGAINST ORDERS?
SHE ORDERED ME TO "MIND THE AVENGERS' BUSINESS." A *DICTATOR* IS TRYING TO TAKE AN UNARMED PLANET BY FORCE...
THAT'S **AVENGERS** BUSINESS IF I EVER HEARD IT. YOU GO AHEAD AND SEND MY APOLOGIES THROUGH DIPLOMATIC CHANNELS...
BUT I'M ***PRETTY SURE*** ELEANIDES KNEW WHAT SHE WAS SAYING...

...AND I'M EVEN MORE SURE CAPTAIN AMERICA IS GONNA UNDERSTAND.
"MY NAME IS CAPTAIN MARVEL..."
...I AM AN EARTHLING AND AN AVENGER.
BUT TODAY I STAND AS ONE WITH THE SETTLERS OF TORFA, WHO CLAIM THIS PLANET AND ITS RESOURCES AS THEY WERE FREELY GIVEN IN THE AFTERMATH OF THE BEHEMOTH DISASTER...
THEY ARE A PEACEFUL PEOPLE, BUT I AM A WOMAN OF WAR.
IF YOU MOVE AGAINST THEM, YOU MOVE AGAINST ME.
I AM WILLING TO DIE HERE TODAY, FOR THIS CAUSE. I HAVE MADE MY CHOICE...

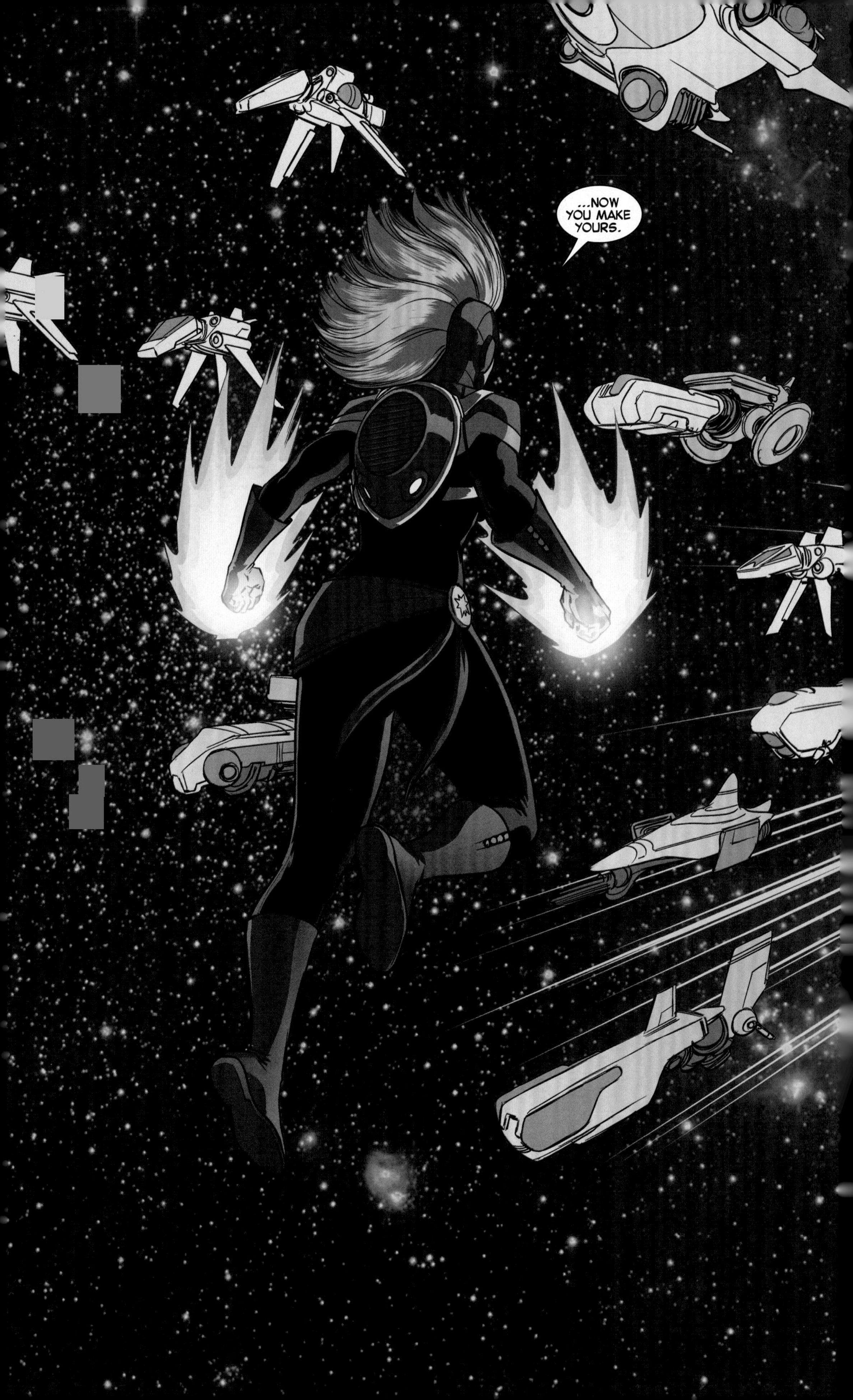
...NOW YOU MAKE YOURS.

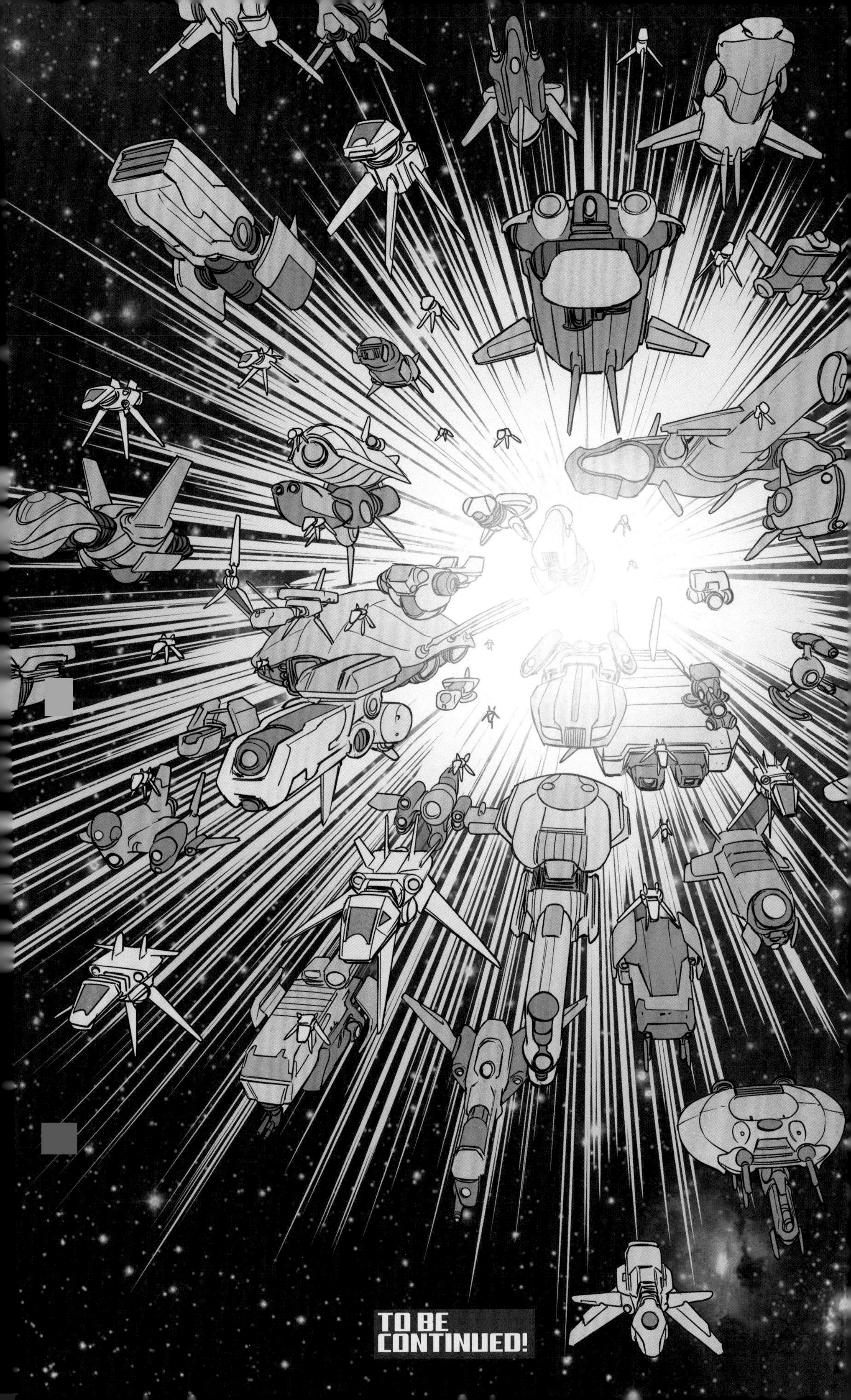
TO BE
CONTINUED!

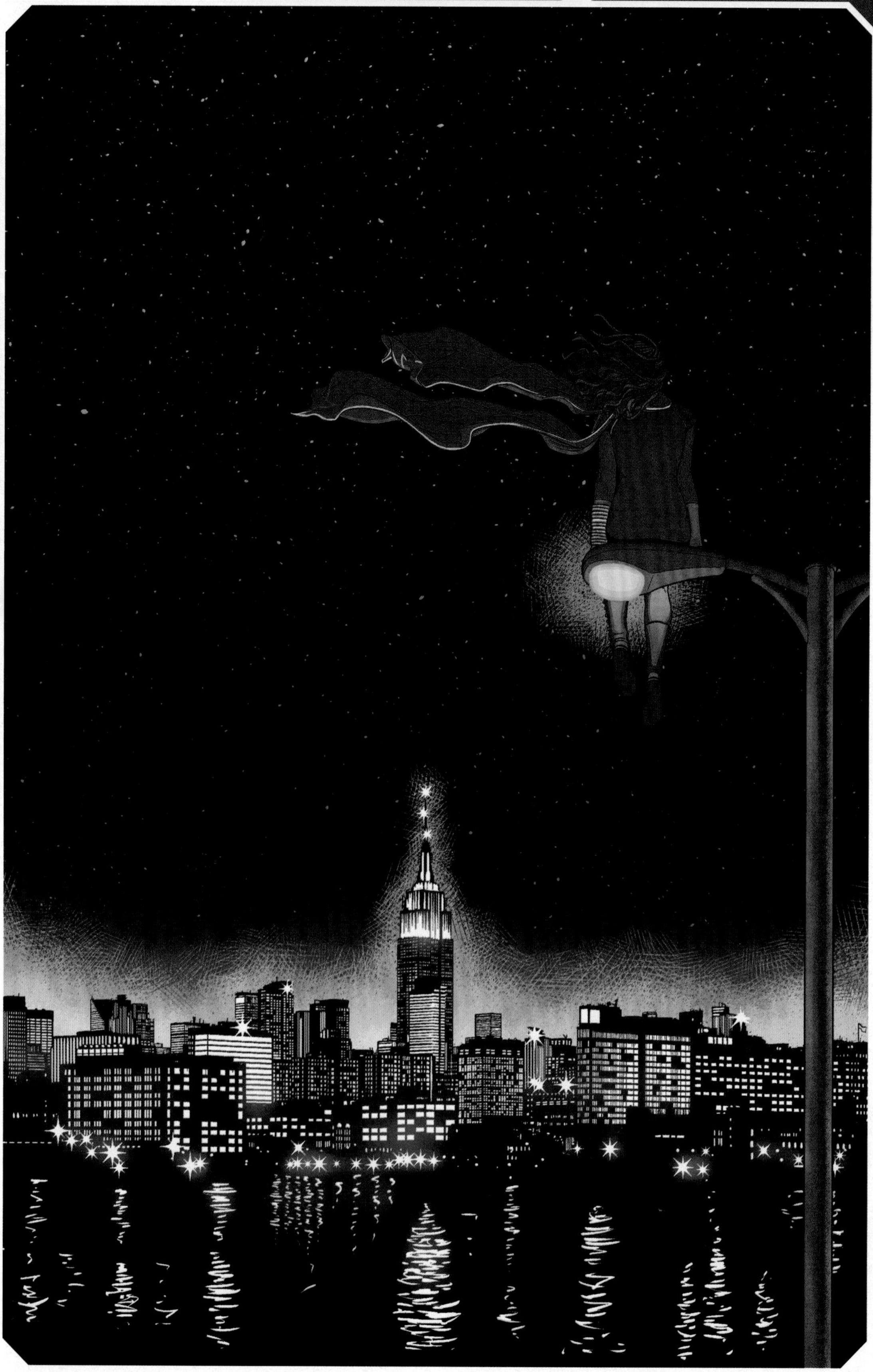

## MS. MARVEL #5

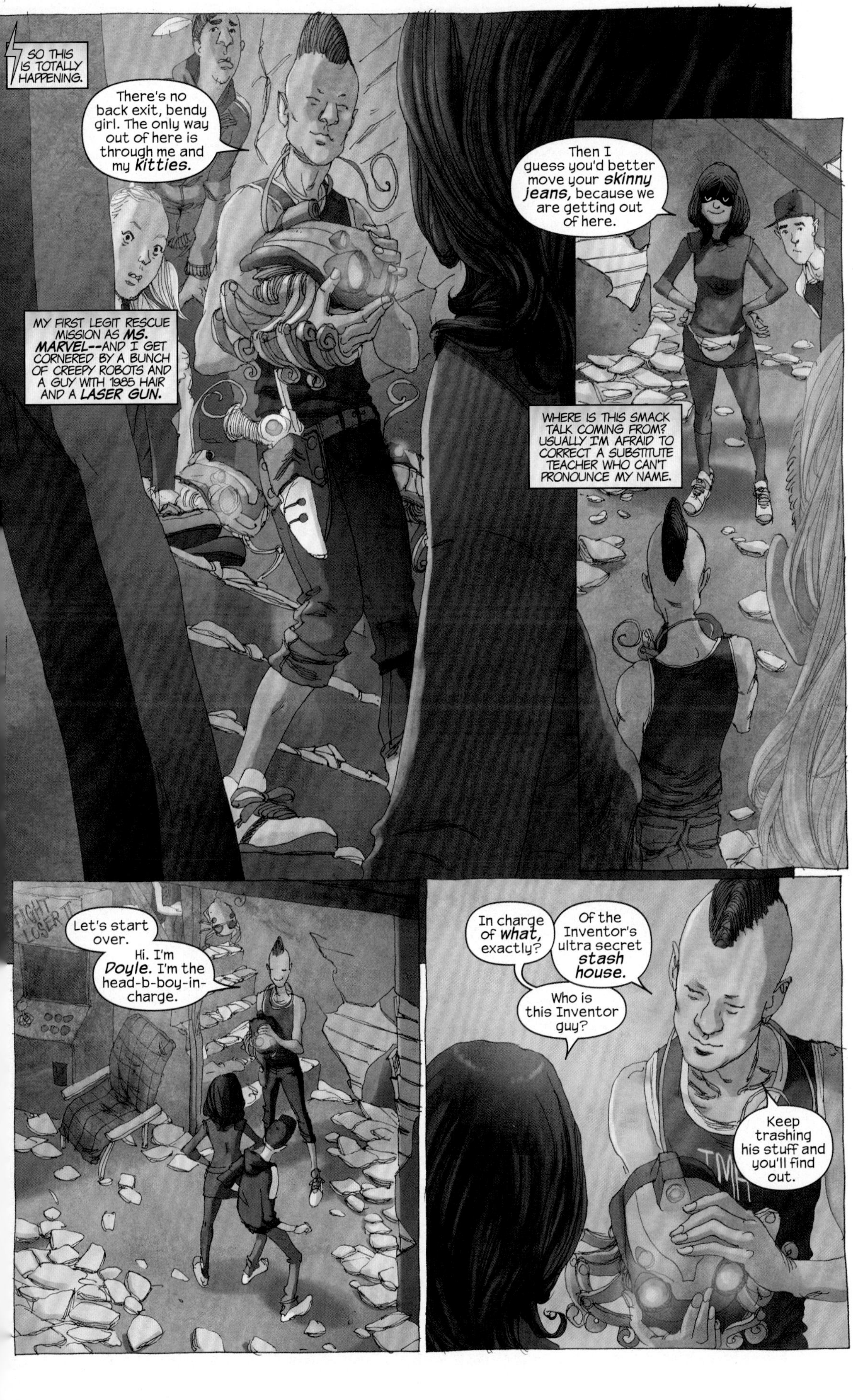
SO THIS IS TOTALLY HAPPENING.
There's no back exit, bendy girl. The only way out of here is through me and my kitties.
MY FIRST LEGIT RESCUE MISSION AS MS. MARVEL--AND I GET CORNERED BY A BUNCH OF CREEPY ROBOTS AND A GUY WITH 1985 HAIR AND A LASER GUN.
Then I guess you'd better move your skinny jeans, because we are getting out of here.
WHERE IS THIS SMACK TALK COMING FROM? USUALLY I'M AFRAID TO CORRECT A SUBSTITUTE TEACHER WHO CAN'T PRONOUNCE MY NAME.
Let's start over.
Hi. I'm Doyle. I'm the head-b-boy-in-charge.
In charge of what, exactly?
Of the Inventor's ultra secret stash house.
Who is this Inventor guy?
Keep trashing his stuff and you'll find out.

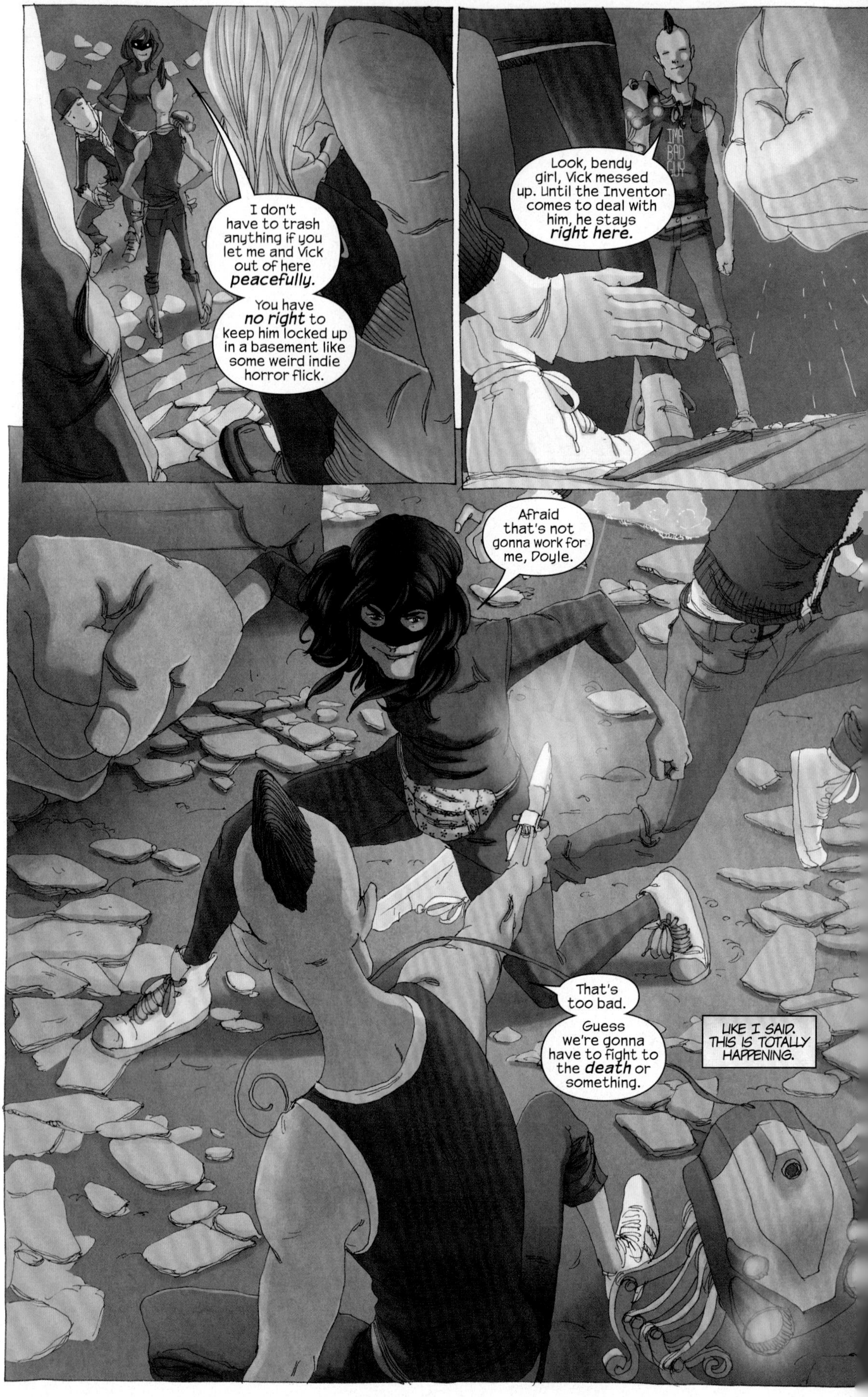
I don't have to trash anything if you let me and Vick out of here *peacefully.*
You have *no right* to keep him locked up in a basement like some weird indie horror flick.
Look, bendy girl, Vick messed up. Until the Inventor comes to deal with him, he stays *right here.*
IMA BAD GUY
Afraid that's not gonna work for me, Doyle.
That's too bad.
Guess we're gonna have to fight to the *death* or something.
LIKE I SAID. THIS IS TOTALLY HAPPENING.

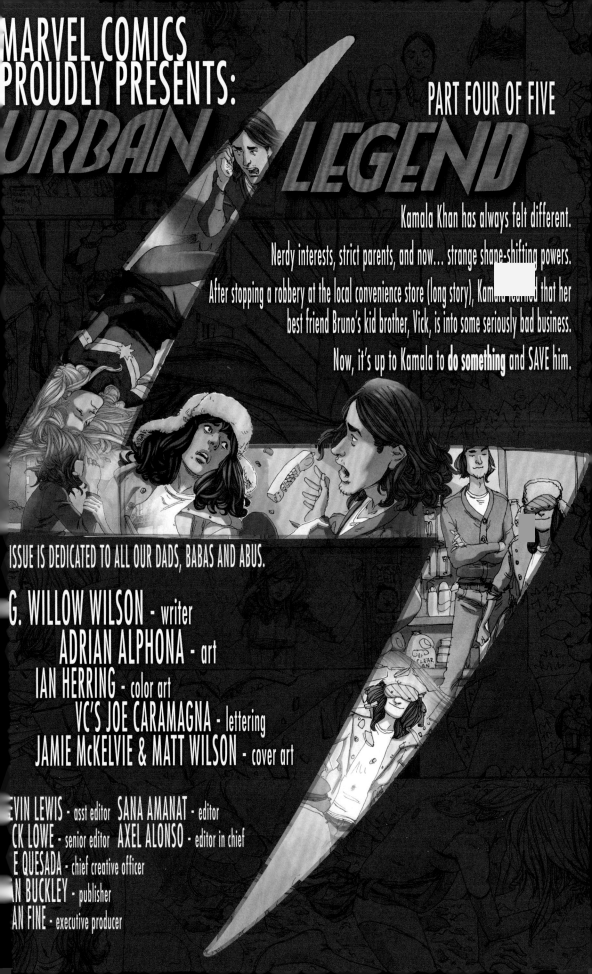

MARVEL COMICS
PROUDLY PRESENTS:

# URBAN LEGEND

PART FOUR OF FIVE

Kamala Khan has always felt different.

Nerdy interests, strict parents, and now... strange shape-shifting powers.

After stopping a robbery at the local convenience store (long story), Kamala learned that her best friend Bruno's kid brother, Vick, is into some seriously bad business.

Now, it's up to Kamala to **do something** and SAVE him.

ISSUE IS DEDICATED TO ALL OUR DADS, BABAS AND ABUS.

**G. WILLOW WILSON** - writer

**ADRIAN ALPHONA** - art

**IAN HERRING** - color art

**VC'S JOE CARAMAGNA** - lettering

**JAMIE McKELVIE & MATT WILSON** - cover art

EVIN LEWIS - asst editor   SANA AMANAT - editor

CK LOWE - senior editor   AXEL ALONSO - editor in chief

E QUESADA - chief creative officer

AN BUCKLEY - publisher

AN FINE - executive producer

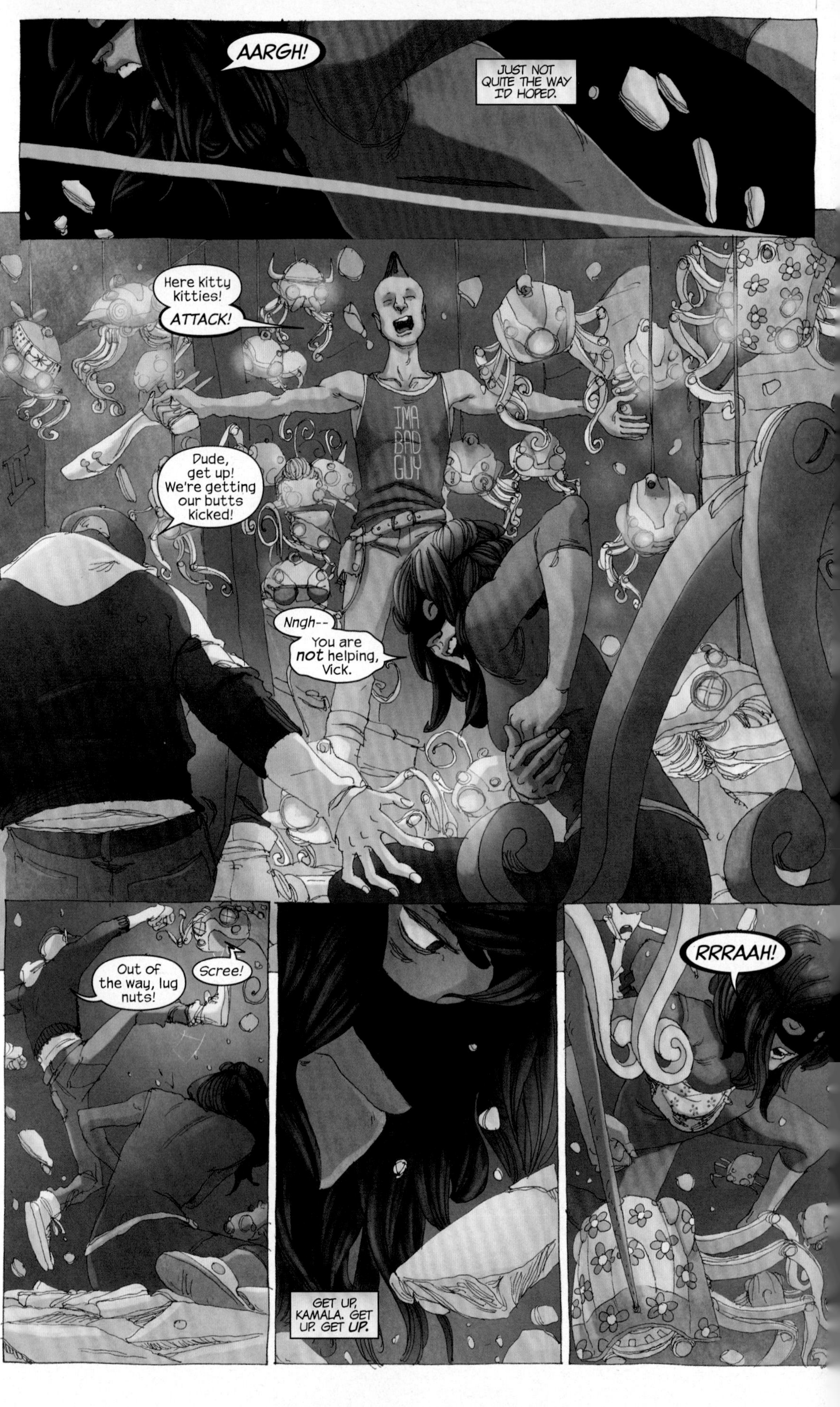
AARGH!
JUST NOT QUITE THE WAY I'D HOPED.
Here kitty kitties! ATTACK!
IMA BAD GUY
Dude, get up! We're getting our butts kicked!
Nngh--
You are not helping, Vick.
Out of the way, lug nuts!
Scree!
GET UP, KAMALA. GET UP. GET UP.
RRRAAH!

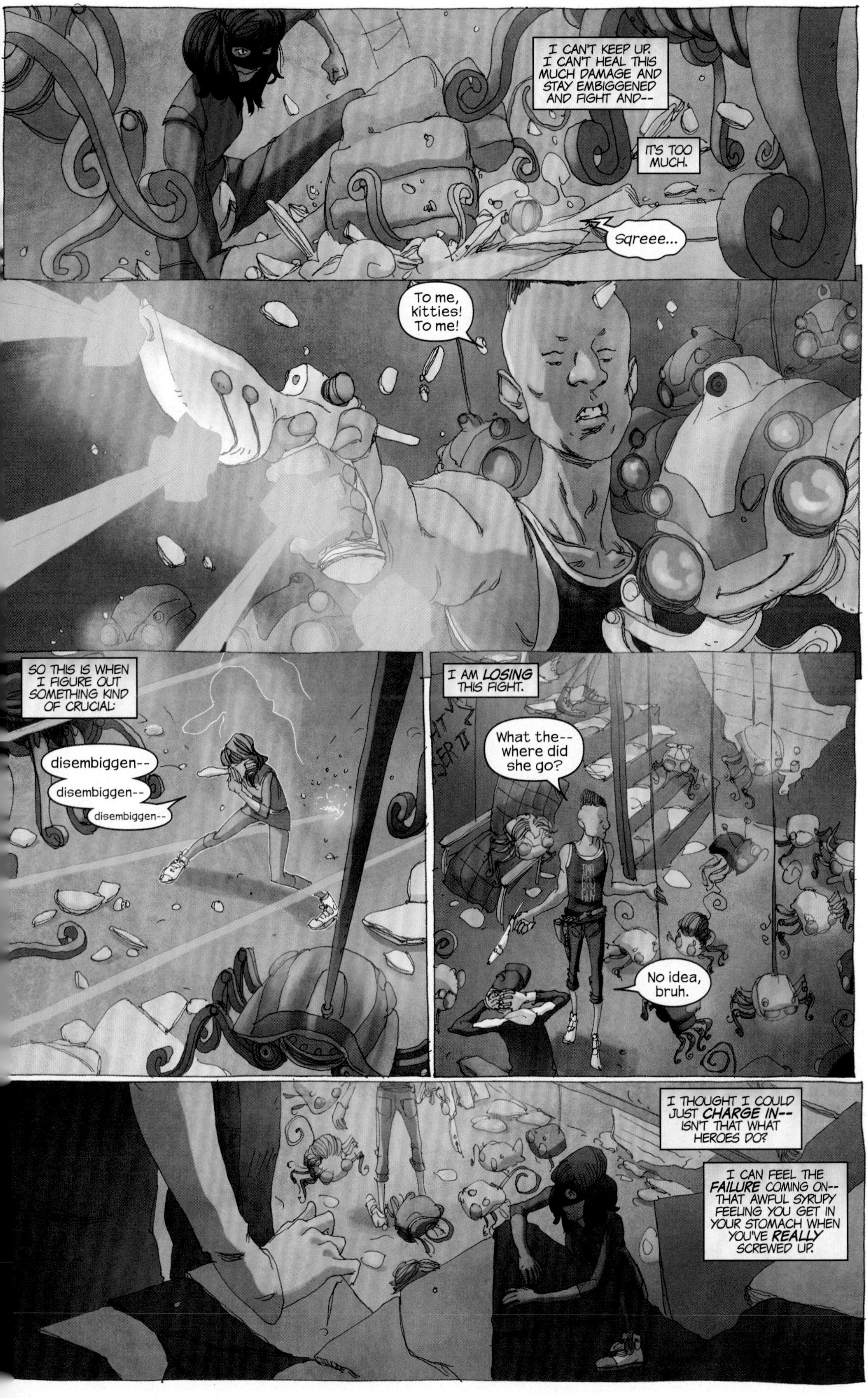
I CAN'T KEEP UP. I CAN'T HEAL THIS MUCH DAMAGE AND STAY EMBIGGENED AND FIGHT AND--
IT'S TOO MUCH.
Sqreee...
To me, kitties! To me!
SO THIS IS WHEN I FIGURE OUT SOMETHING KIND OF CRUCIAL:
disembiggen--
disembiggen--
disembiggen--
I AM LOSING THIS FIGHT.
What the-- where did she go?
No idea, bruh.
I THOUGHT I COULD JUST CHARGE IN-- ISN'T THAT WHAT HEROES DO?
I CAN FEEL THE FAILURE COMING ON-- THAT AWFUL SYRUPY FEELING YOU GET IN YOUR STOMACH WHEN YOU'VE REALLY SCREWED UP.

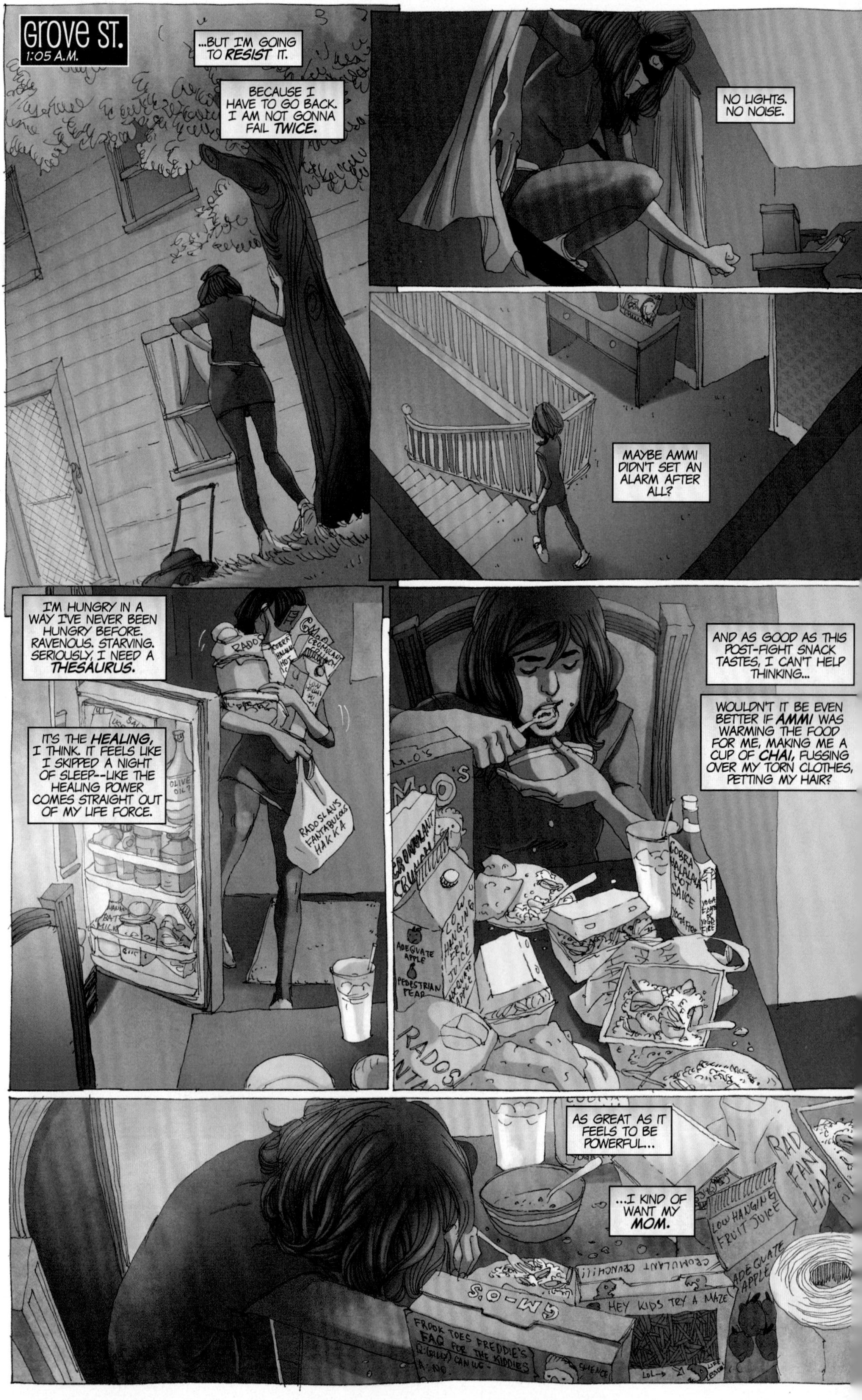

GROVE ST.
1:05 A.M.
...BUT I'M GOING TO RESIST IT.
BECAUSE I HAVE TO GO BACK. I AM NOT GONNA FAIL TWICE.
NO LIGHTS. NO NOISE.
MAYBE AMMI DIDN'T SET AN ALARM AFTER ALL?
I'M HUNGRY IN A WAY I'VE NEVER BEEN HUNGRY BEFORE. RAVENOUS. STARVING. SERIOUSLY, I NEED A THESAURUS.
IT'S THE HEALING, I THINK. IT FEELS LIKE I SKIPPED A NIGHT OF SLEEP--LIKE THE HEALING POWER COMES STRAIGHT OUT OF MY LIFE FORCE.
RADOSLAUS FANTABULOUS HAKKA
AND AS GOOD AS THIS POST-FIGHT SNACK TASTES, I CAN'T HELP THINKING...
WOULDN'T IT BE EVEN BETTER IF AMMI WAS WARMING THE FOOD FOR ME, MAKING ME A CUP OF CHAI, FUSSING OVER MY TORN CLOTHES, PETTING MY HAIR?
COBRA HALALALA HOT SAUCE
ADEQUATE APPLE
PEDESTRIAN PEAR
LOW HANGING FRUIT JUICE
AS GREAT AS IT FEELS TO BE POWERFUL...
...I KIND OF WANT MY MOM.
CROMULANT CRUNCH!!!
GM-O'S
HEY KIDS TRY A MAZE
FROOK TOES FREDDIE'S FAQ FOR THE KIDDIES

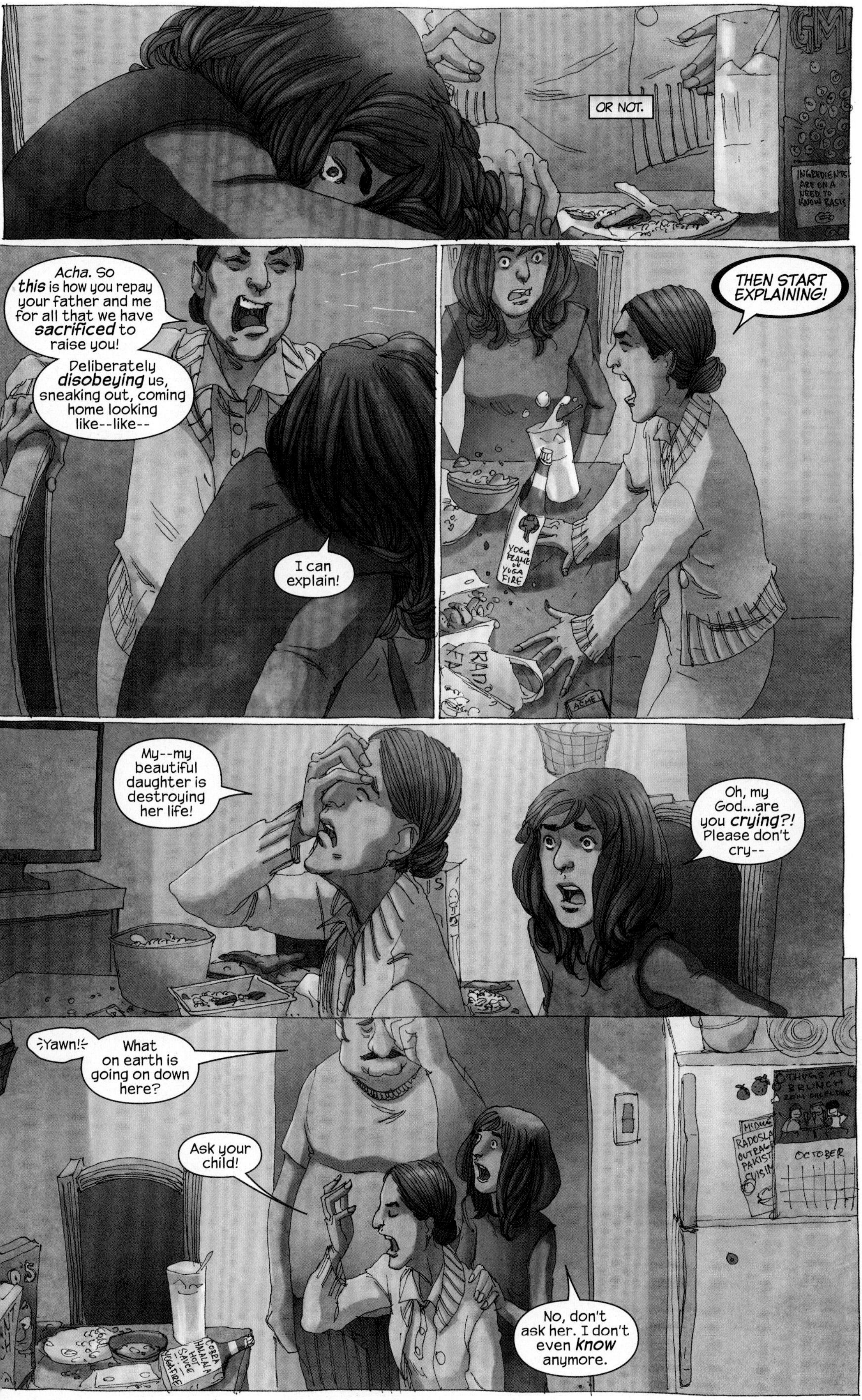

OR NOT.
INGREDIENTS ARE ON A NEED TO KNOW BASIS
Acha. So this is how you repay your father and me for all that we have sacrificed to raise you!
Deliberately disobeying us, sneaking out, coming home looking like--like--
I can explain!
THEN START EXPLAINING!
YOGA FLAME OR YOGA FIRE
ACME
My--my beautiful daughter is destroying her life!
Oh, my God...are you crying?! Please don't cry--
Yawn!
What on earth is going on down here?
Ask your child!
OCTOBER
No, don't ask her. I don't even know anymore.

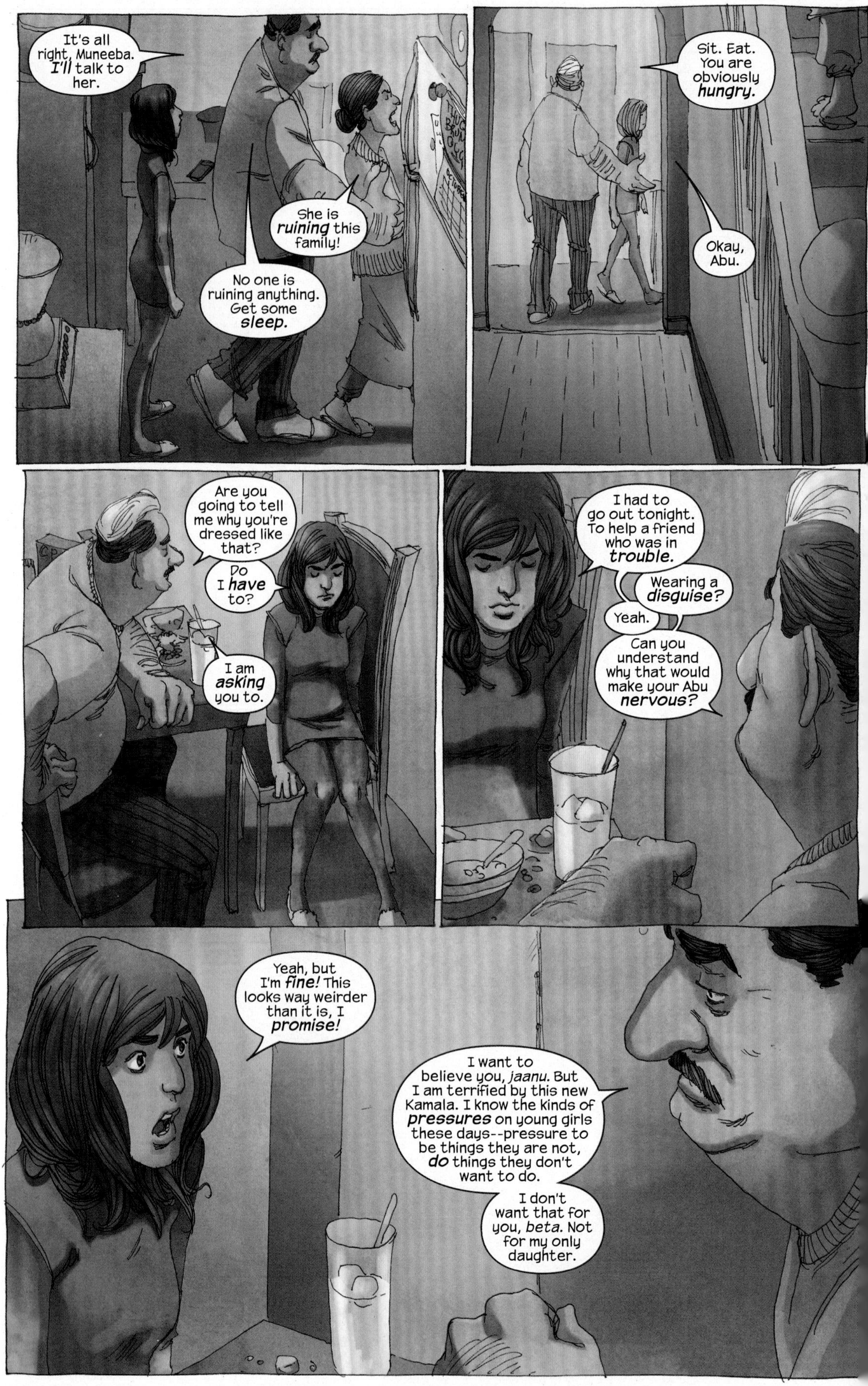
It's all right, Muneeba. I'll talk to her.
She is ruining this family!
No one is ruining anything. Get some sleep.
Sit. Eat. You are obviously hungry.
Okay, Abu.
Are you going to tell me why you're dressed like that?
Do I have to?
I am asking you to.
I had to go out tonight. To help a friend who was in trouble.
Wearing a disguise?
Yeah.
Can you understand why that would make your Abu nervous?
Yeah, but I'm fine! This looks way weirder than it is, I promise!
I want to believe you, jaanu. But I am terrified by this new Kamala. I know the kinds of pressures on young girls these days--pressure to be things they are not, do things they don't want to do.
I don't want that for you, beta. Not for my only daughter.

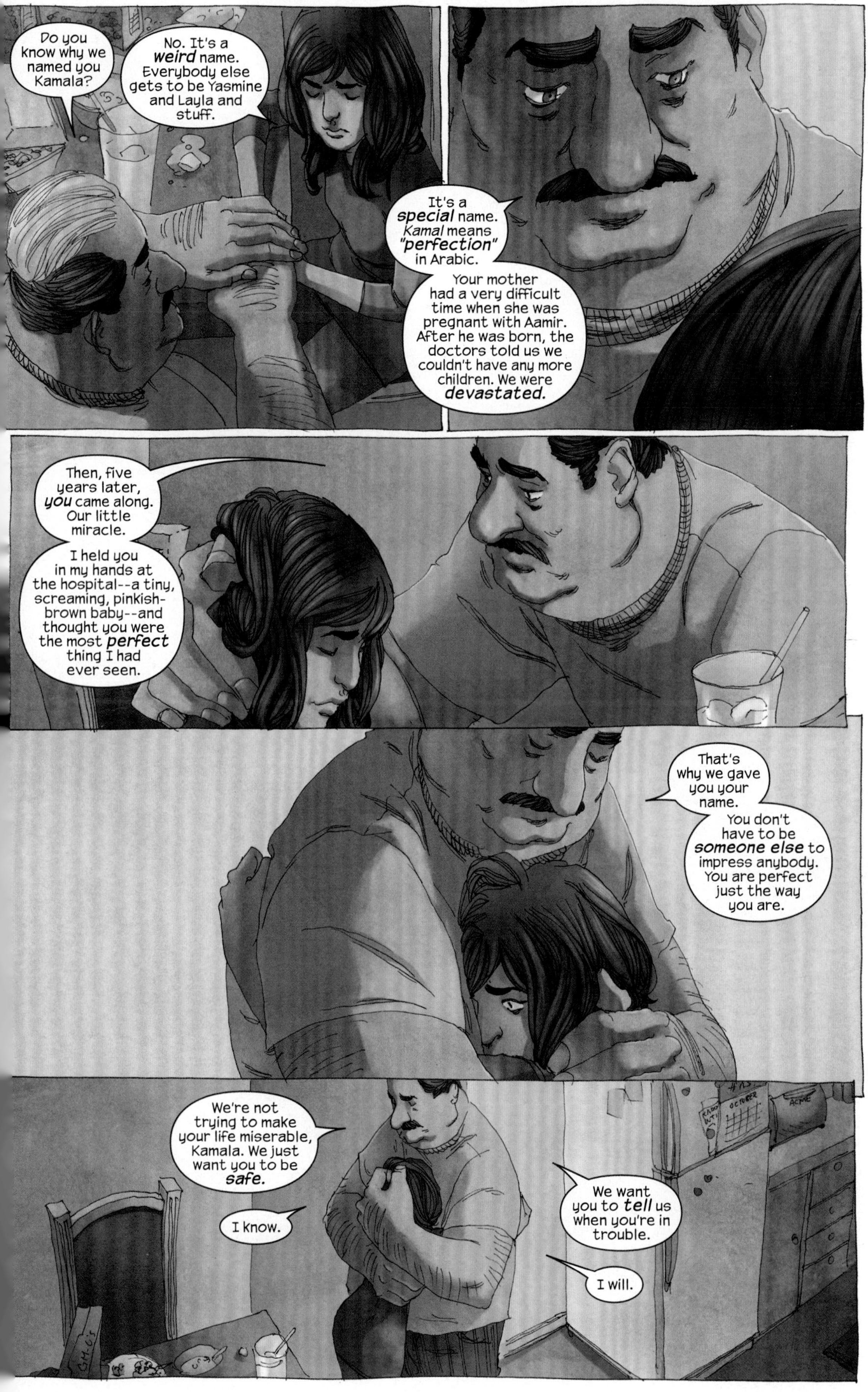
Do you know why we named you Kamala?
No. It's a weird name. Everybody else gets to be Yasmine and Layla and stuff.
It's a special name. Kamal means "perfection" in Arabic.
Your mother had a very difficult time when she was pregnant with Aamir. After he was born, the doctors told us we couldn't have any more children. We were devastated.
Then, five years later, you came along. Our little miracle.
I held you in my hands at the hospital--a tiny, screaming, pinkish-brown baby--and thought you were the most perfect thing I had ever seen.
That's why we gave you your name.
You don't have to be someone else to impress anybody. You are perfect just the way you are.
We're not trying to make your life miserable, Kamala. We just want you to be safe.
I know.
We want you to tell us when you're in trouble.
I will.

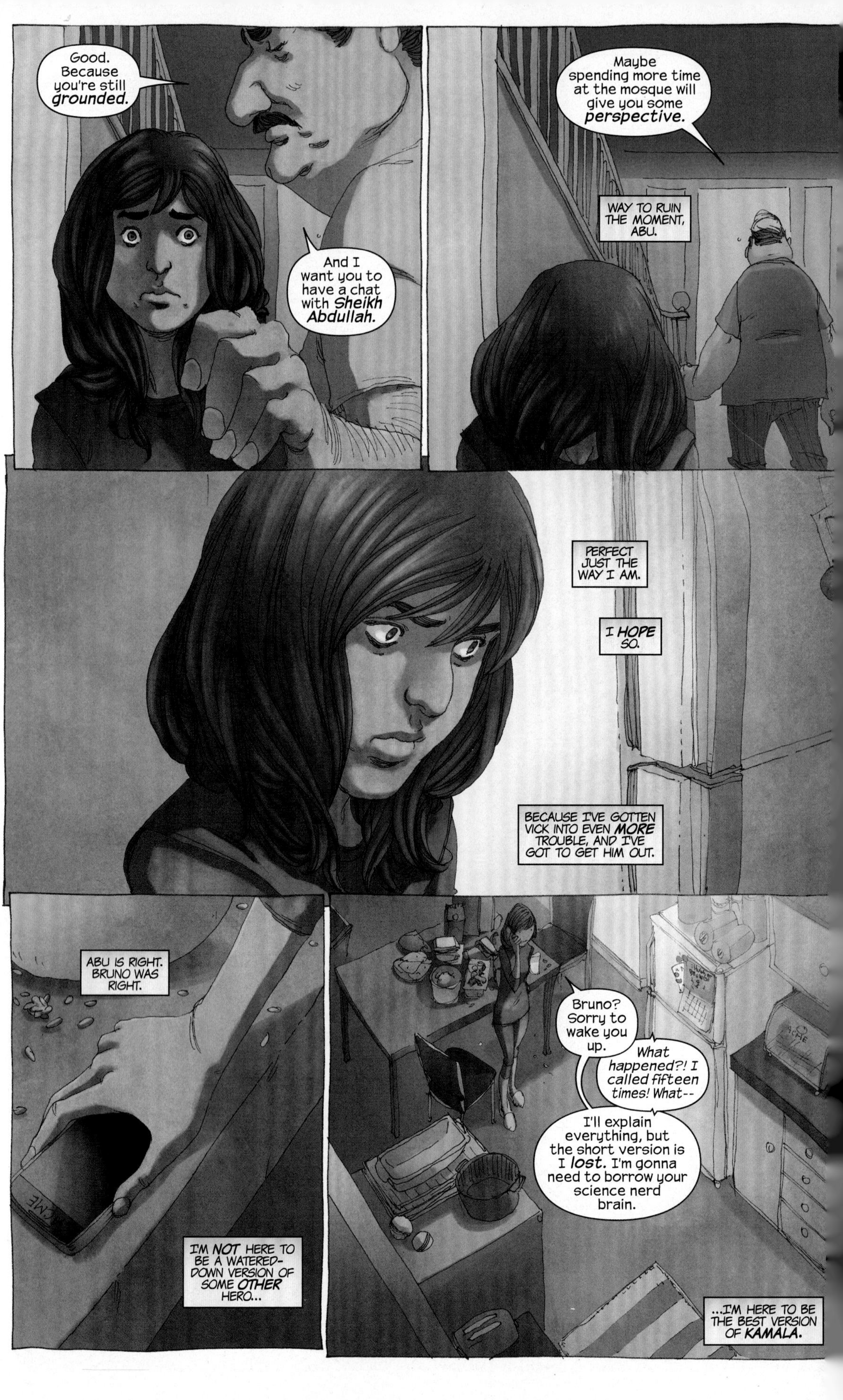
Good. Because you're still grounded.
And I want you to have a chat with Sheikh Abdullah.
Maybe spending more time at the mosque will give you some perspective.
WAY TO RUIN THE MOMENT, ABU.
PERFECT JUST THE WAY I AM.
I HOPE SO.
BECAUSE I'VE GOTTEN VICK INTO EVEN MORE TROUBLE, AND I'VE GOT TO GET HIM OUT.
ABU IS RIGHT. BRUNO WAS RIGHT.
I'M NOT HERE TO BE A WATERED-DOWN VERSION OF SOME OTHER HERO...
Bruno? Sorry to wake you up.
What happened?! I called fifteen times! What--
I'll explain everything, but the short version is I lost. I'm gonna need to borrow your science nerd brain.
...I'M HERE TO BE THE BEST VERSION OF KAMALA.

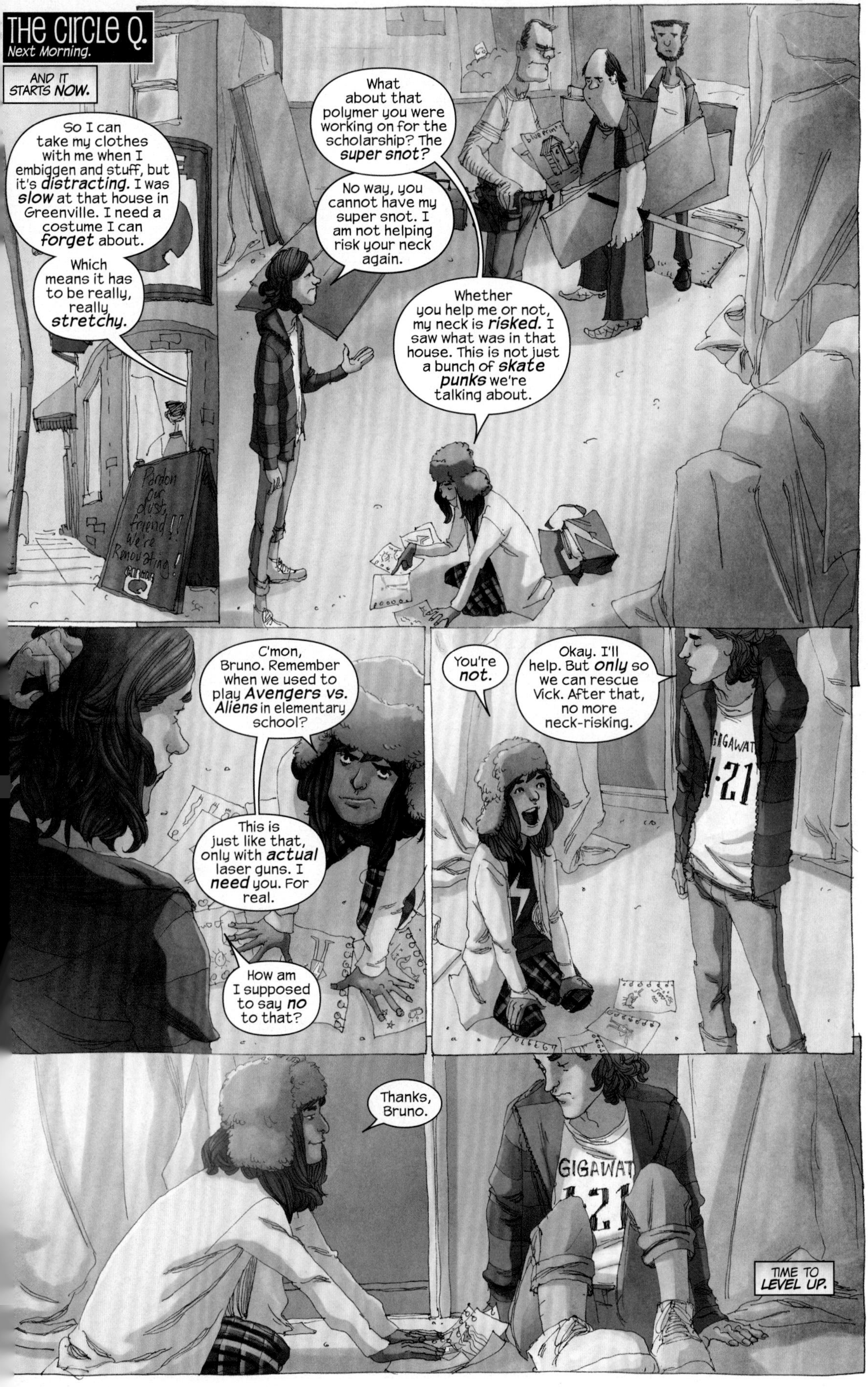
THE CIRCLE Q.
Next Morning.
AND IT STARTS NOW.
So I can take my clothes with me when I embiggen and stuff, but it's distracting. I was slow at that house in Greenville. I need a costume I can forget about.
Which means it has to be really, really stretchy.
What about that polymer you were working on for the scholarship? The super snot?
No way, you cannot have my super snot. I am not helping risk your neck again.
Whether you help me or not, my neck is risked. I saw what was in that house. This is not just a bunch of skate punks we're talking about.
Pardon our dust, friend!! We're Renovating!
C'mon, Bruno. Remember when we used to play Avengers vs. Aliens in elementary school?
This is just like that, only with actual laser guns. I need you. For real.
How am I supposed to say no to that?
You're not.
Okay. I'll help. But only so we can rescue Vick. After that, no more neck-risking.
Thanks, Bruno.
TIME TO LEVEL UP.

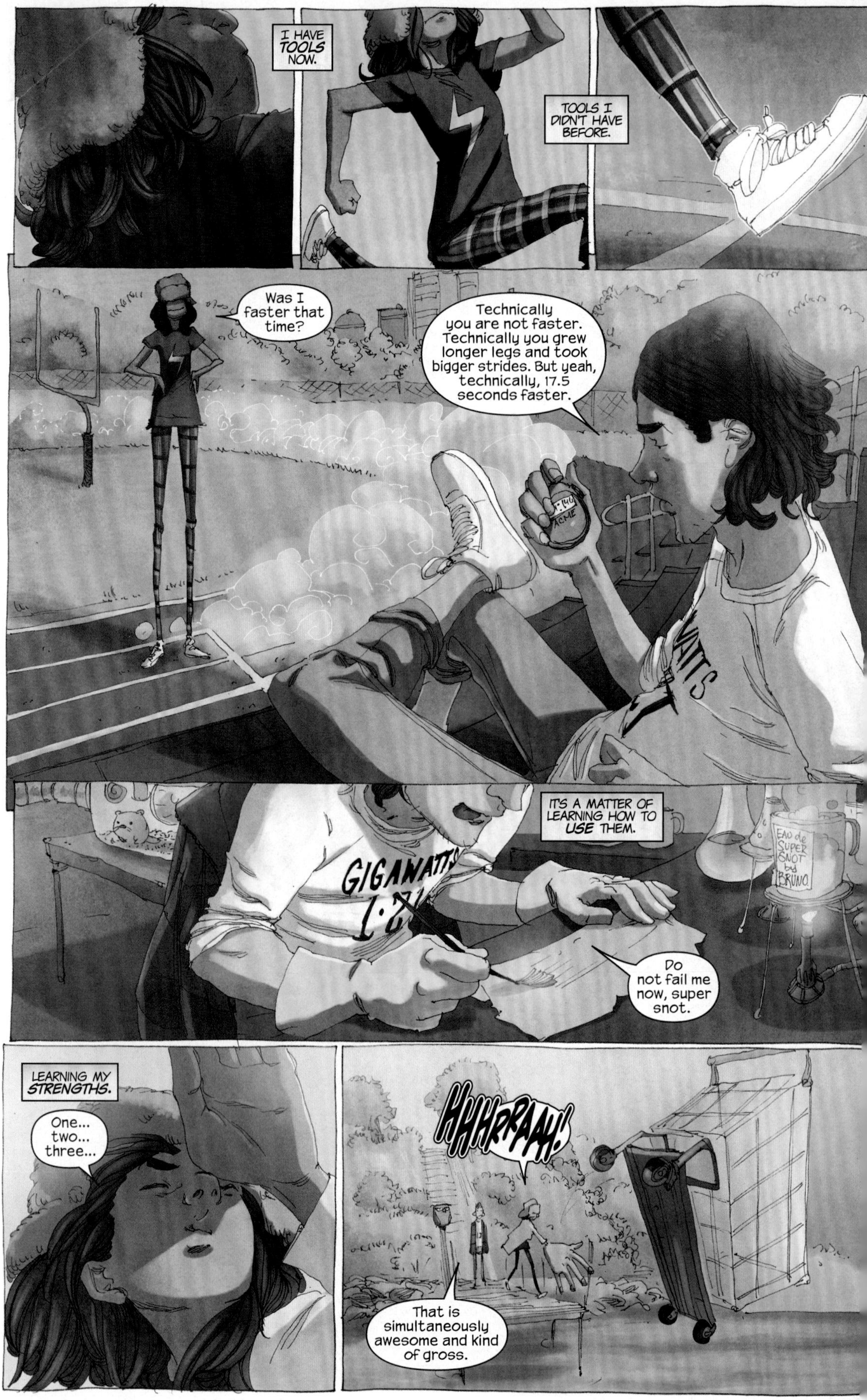
I HAVE TOOLS NOW.
TOOLS I DIDN'T HAVE BEFORE.
Was I faster that time?
Technically you are not faster. Technically you grew longer legs and took bigger strides. But yeah, technically, 17.5 seconds faster.
ACME
IT'S A MATTER OF LEARNING HOW TO USE THEM.
GIGAWATTS
EAU de SUPER SNOT by BRUNO
Do not fail me now, super snot.
LEARNING MY STRENGTHS.
One... two... three...
HHHRRAAH!
That is simultaneously awesome and kind of gross.

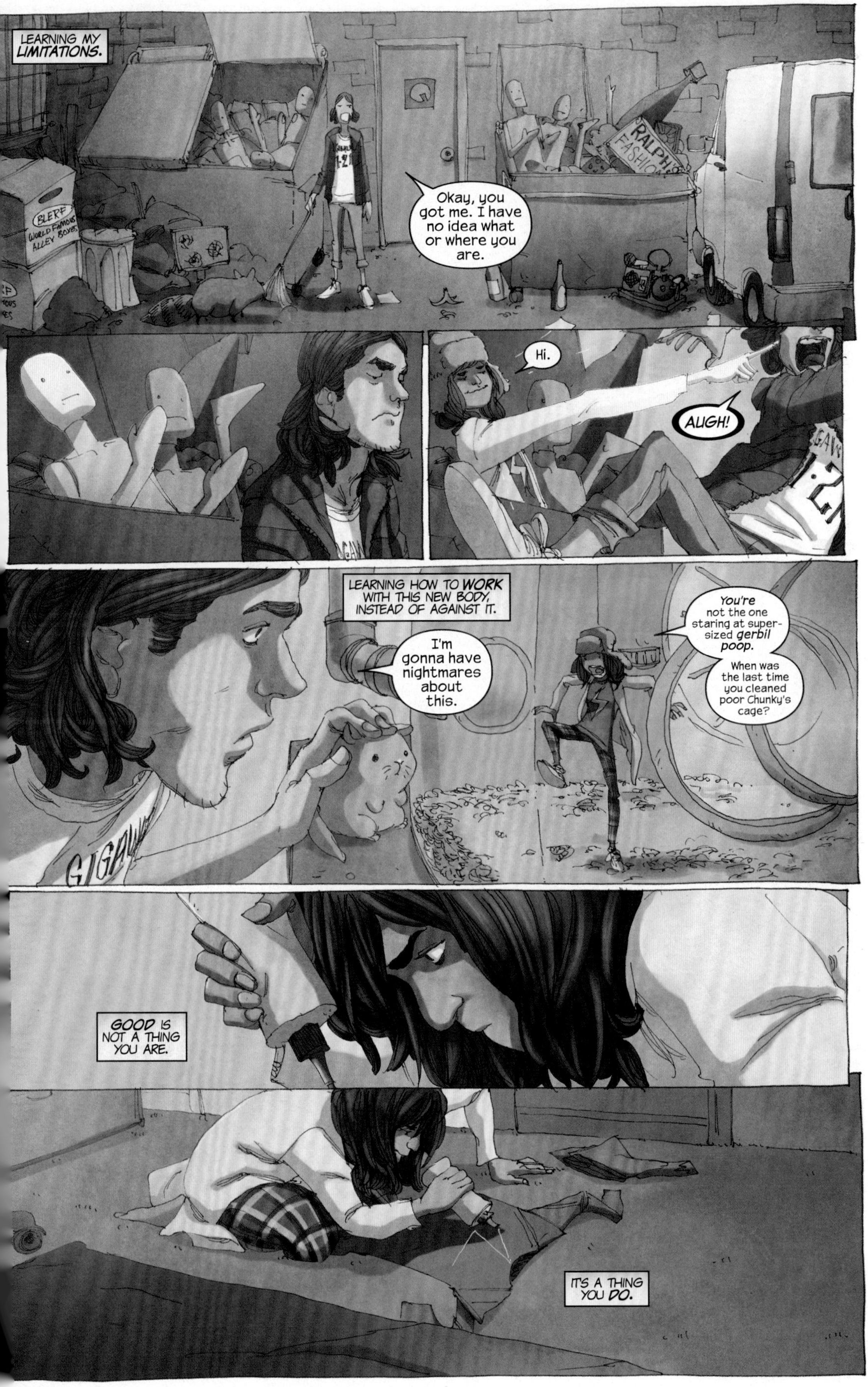
LEARNING MY LIMITATIONS.
BLERF WORLD FAMOUS ALLEY BOXES
RALPH'S FASHION
Okay, you got me. I have no idea what or where you are.
Hi.
AUGH!
LEARNING HOW TO WORK WITH THIS NEW BODY, INSTEAD OF AGAINST IT.
I'm gonna have nightmares about this.
You're not the one staring at super-sized gerbil poop.
When was the last time you cleaned poor Chunky's cage?
GOOD IS NOT A THING YOU ARE.
IT'S A THING YOU DO.

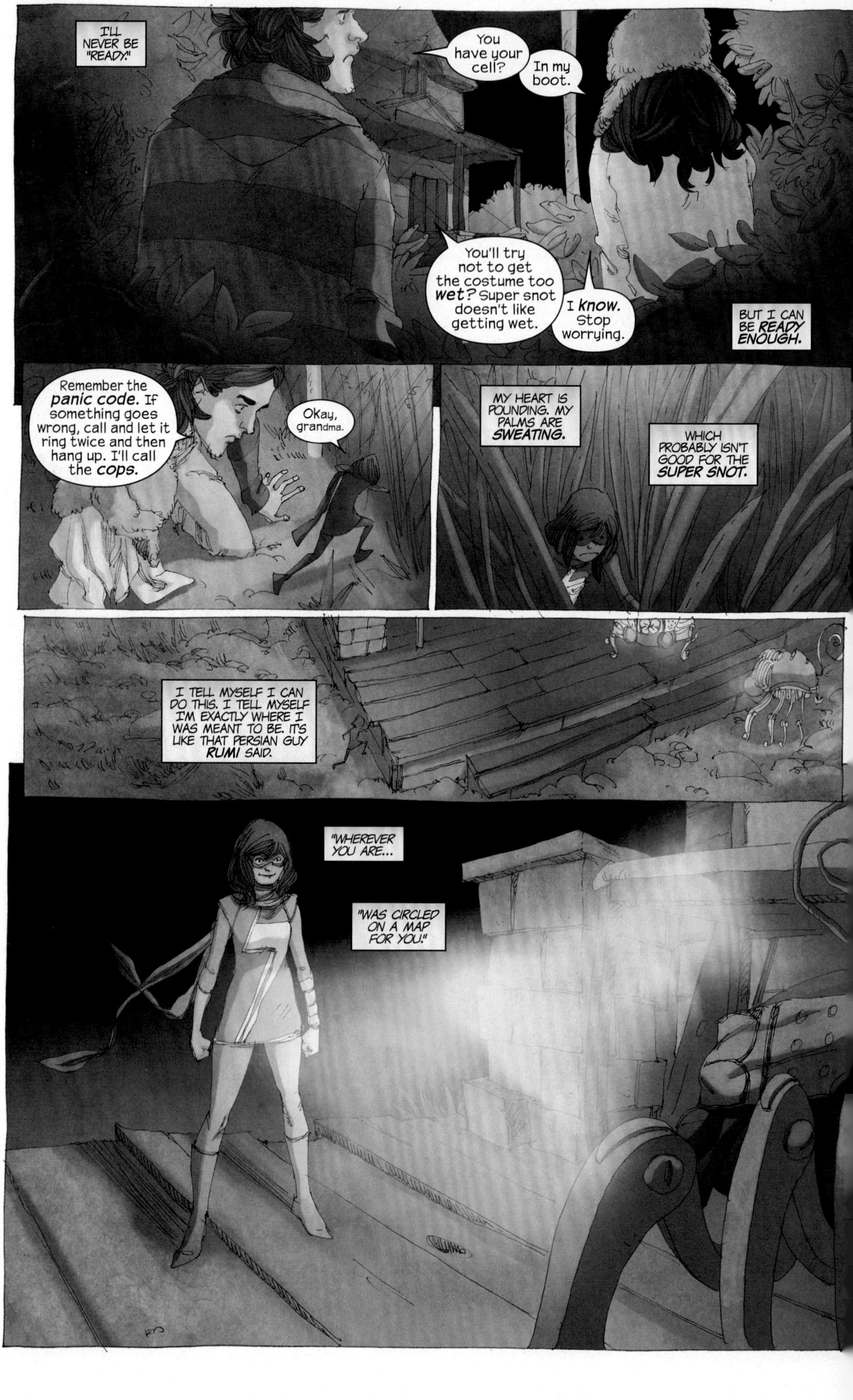
I'LL NEVER BE "READY."
You have your cell?
In my boot.
You'll try not to get the costume too wet? Super snot doesn't like getting wet.
I know. Stop worrying.
BUT I CAN BE READY ENOUGH.
Remember the panic code. If something goes wrong, call and let it ring twice and then hang up. I'll call the cops.
Okay, grandma.
MY HEART IS POUNDING. MY PALMS ARE SWEATING.
WHICH PROBABLY ISN'T GOOD FOR THE SUPER SNOT.
I TELL MYSELF I CAN DO THIS. I TELL MYSELF I'M EXACTLY WHERE I WAS MEANT TO BE. IT'S LIKE THAT PERSIAN GUY RUMI SAID.
"WHEREVER YOU ARE...
"WAS CIRCLED ON A MAP FOR YOU."

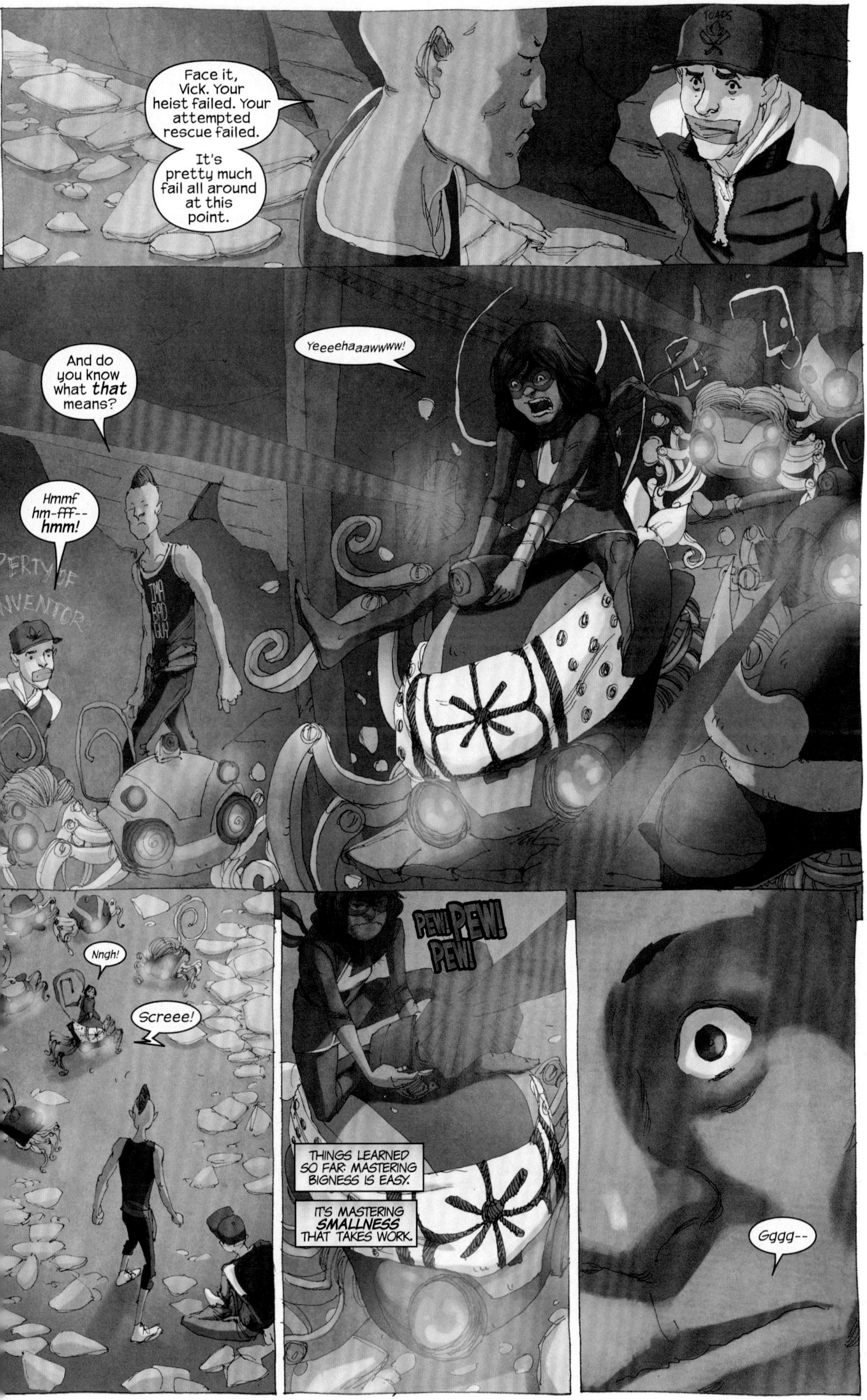
Face it, Vick. Your heist failed. Your attempted rescue failed.
It's pretty much fail all around at this point.
And do you know what **that** means?
Yeeeehaaawwww!
Hmmf hm-fff-- **hmm!**
Nngh!
Screee!
PEW! PEW! PEW!
THINGS LEARNED SO FAR: MASTERING BIGNESS IS EASY.
IT'S MASTERING **SMALLNESS** THAT TAKES WORK.
Gggg--

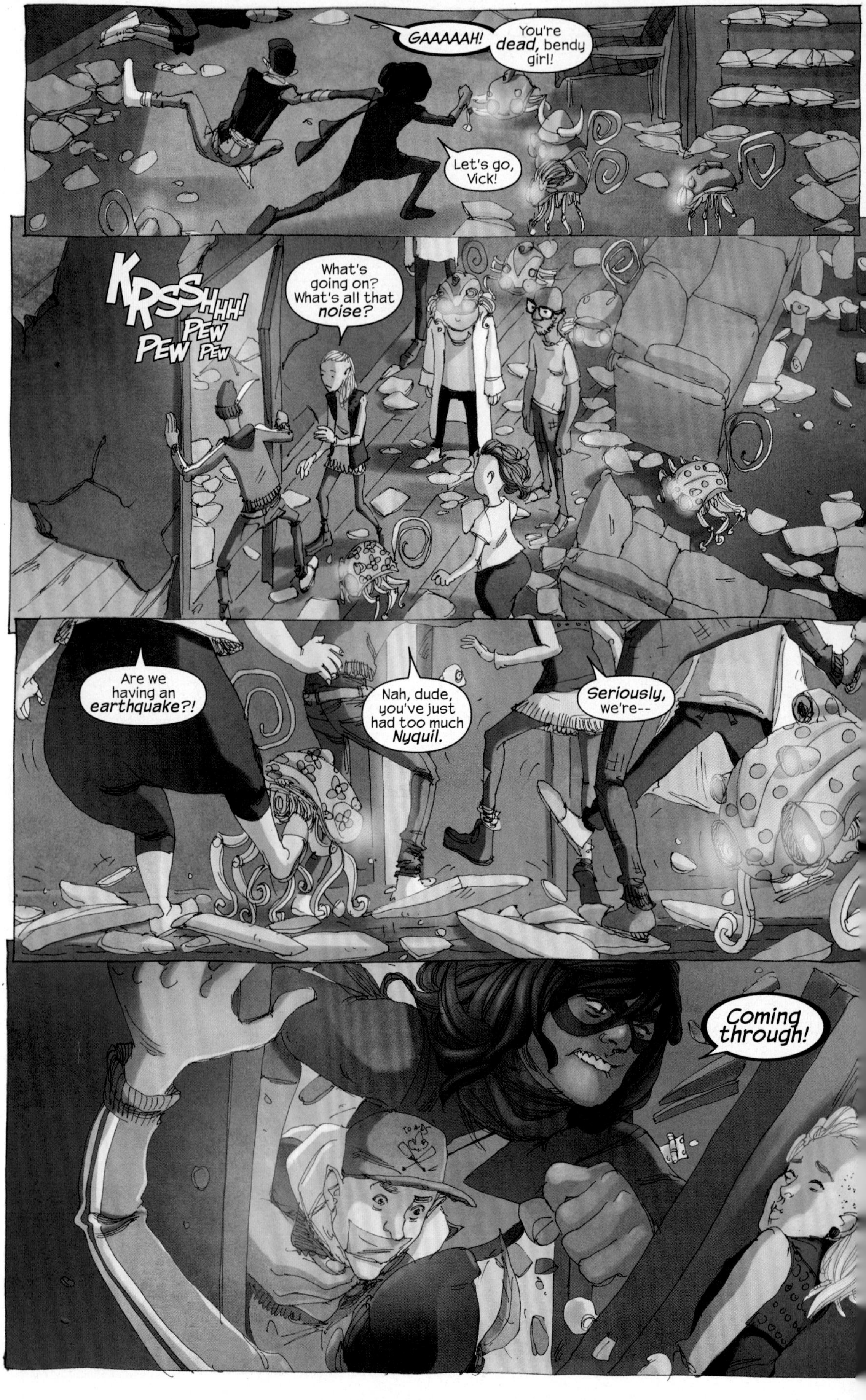
GAAAAAH!
You're dead, bendy girl!
Let's go, Vick!
KRSSHHH!
PEW PEW PEW PEW
What's going on? What's all that noise?
Are we having an earthquake?!
Nah, dude, you've just had too much Nyquil.
Seriously, we're--
Coming through!

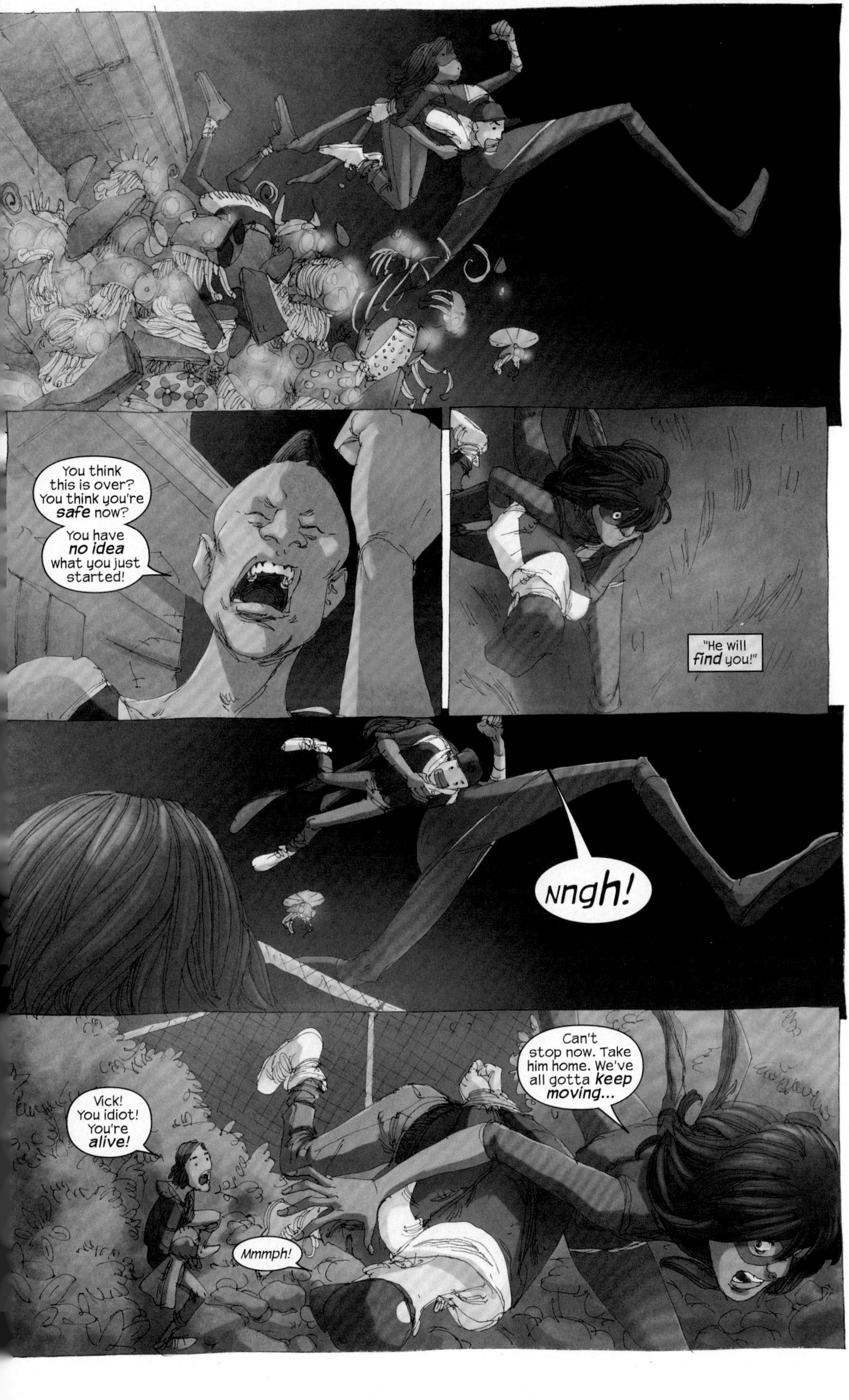
You think this is over? You think you're *safe* now?
You have *no idea* what you just started!
"He will *find* you!"
Nngh!
Vick! You idiot! You're *alive!*
Can't stop now. Take him home. We've all gotta *keep moving...*
Mmmph!

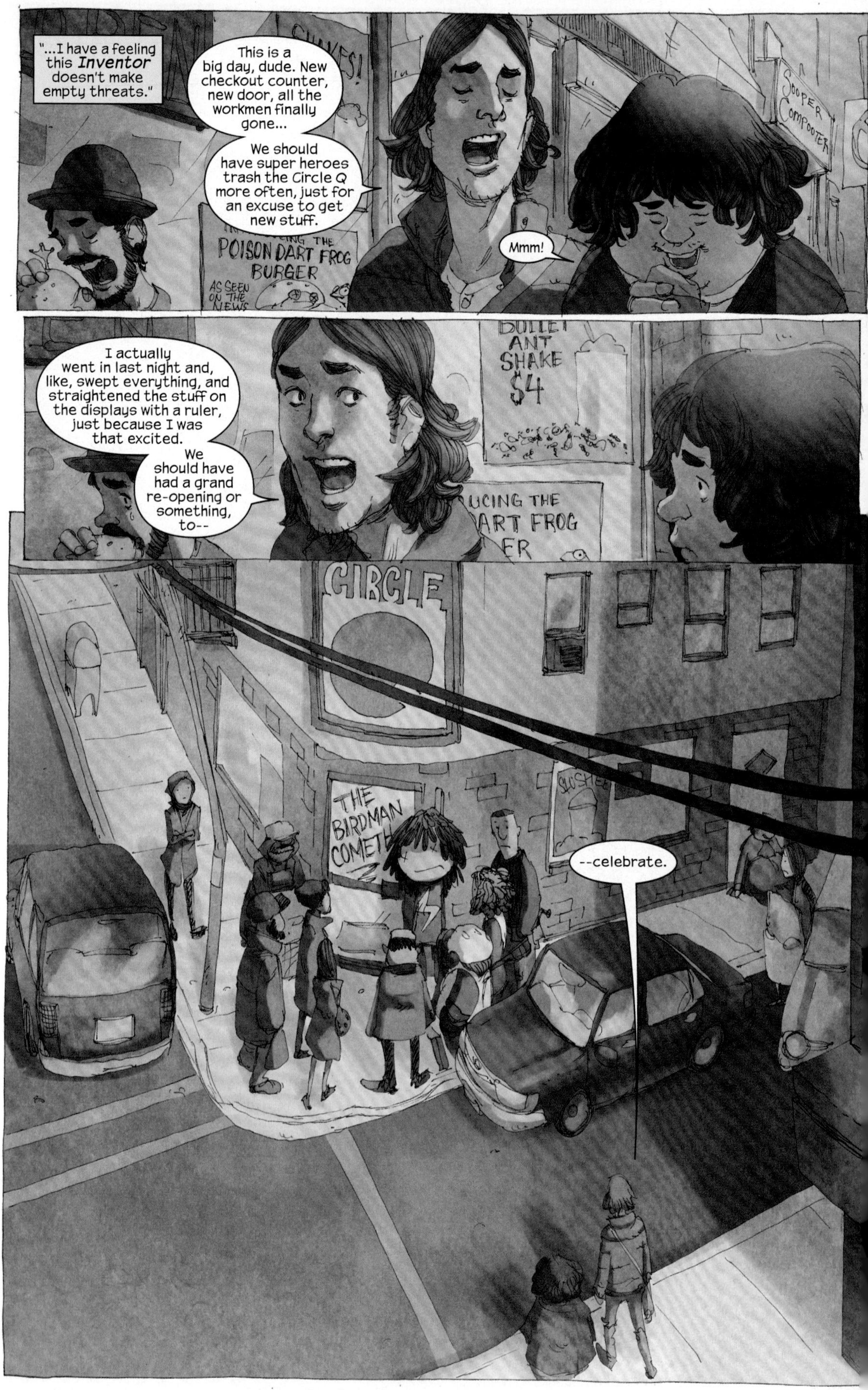
"...I have a feeling this *Inventor* doesn't make empty threats."
This is a big day, dude. New checkout counter, new door, all the workmen finally gone...
We should have super heroes trash the Circle Q more often, just for an excuse to get new stuff.
SOOPER COMPOOTER
POISON DART FROG BURGER
AS SEEN ON THE NEWS
Mmm!
I actually went in last night and, like, swept everything, and straightened the stuff on the displays with a ruler, just because I was that excited.
We should have had a grand re-opening or something, to--
ANT SHAKE $4
CIRCLE
THE BIRDMAN COMETH
--celebrate.

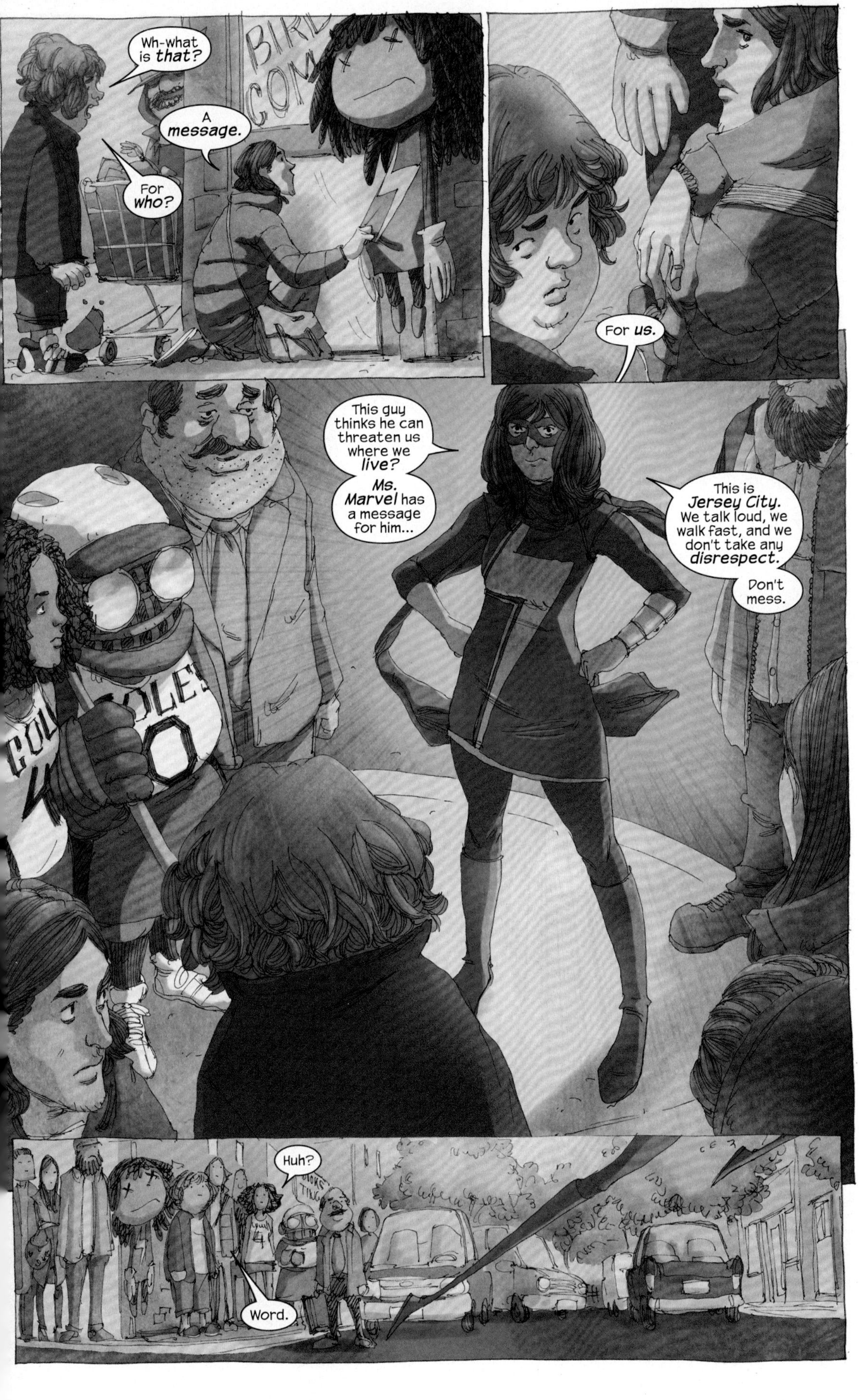

Wh-what is *that*?
A *message*.
For *who*?
For *us*.
This guy thinks he can threaten us where we *live?*
*Ms. Marvel* has a message for him...
This is *Jersey City*. We talk loud, we walk fast, and we don't take any *disrespect*.
Don't mess.
Huh?
Word.

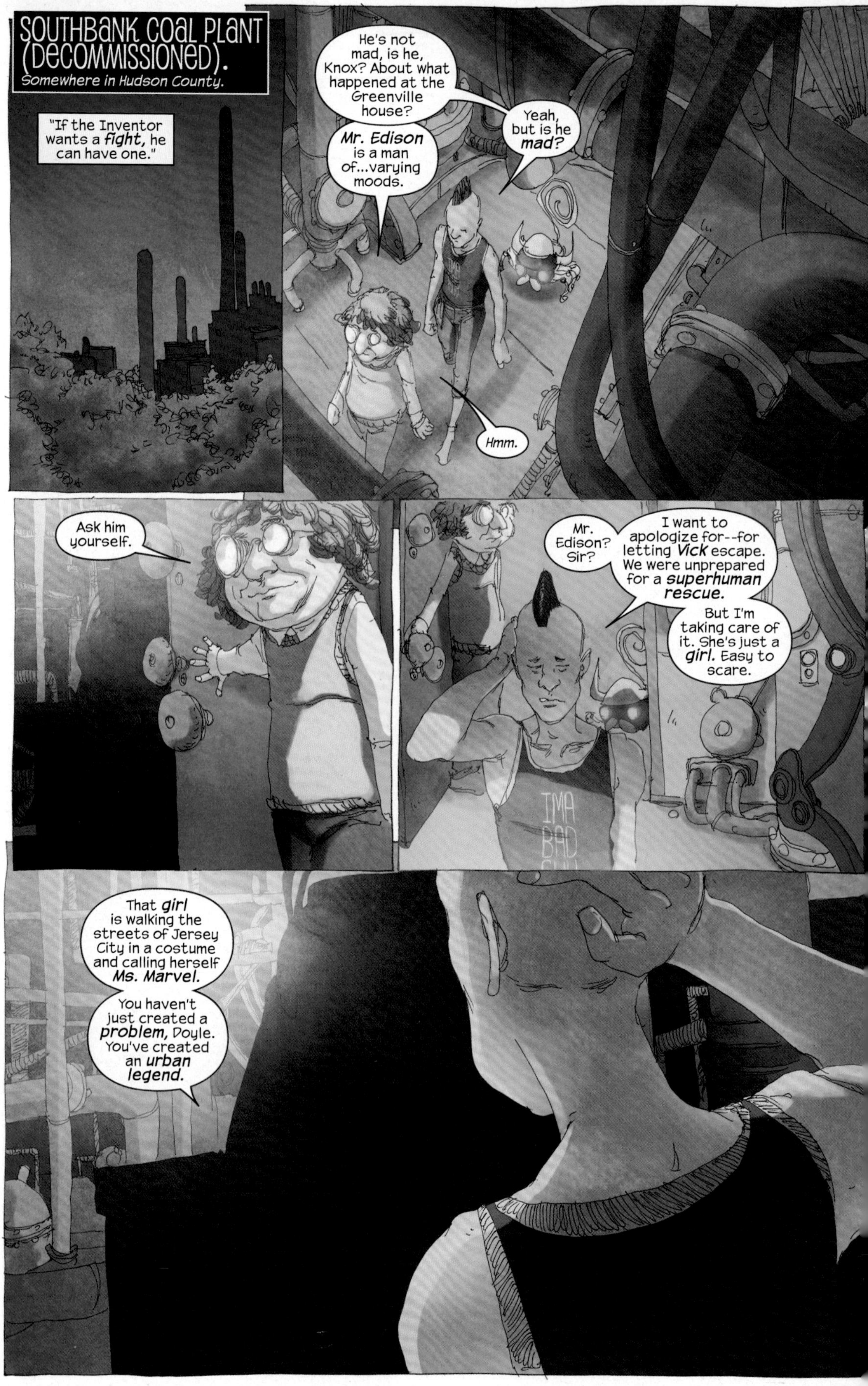
SOUTHBANK COAL PLANT (DECOMMISSIONED).
Somewhere in Hudson County.
"If the Inventor wants a fight, he can have one."
He's not mad, is he, Knox? About what happened at the Greenville house?
Mr. Edison is a man of...varying moods.
Yeah, but is he mad?
Hmm.
Ask him yourself.
Mr. Edison? Sir?
I want to apologize for--for letting Vick escape. We were unprepared for a superhuman rescue.
But I'm taking care of it. She's just a girl. Easy to scare.
IMA BAD
That girl is walking the streets of Jersey City in a costume and calling herself Ms. Marvel.
You haven't just created a problem, Doyle. You've created an urban legend.

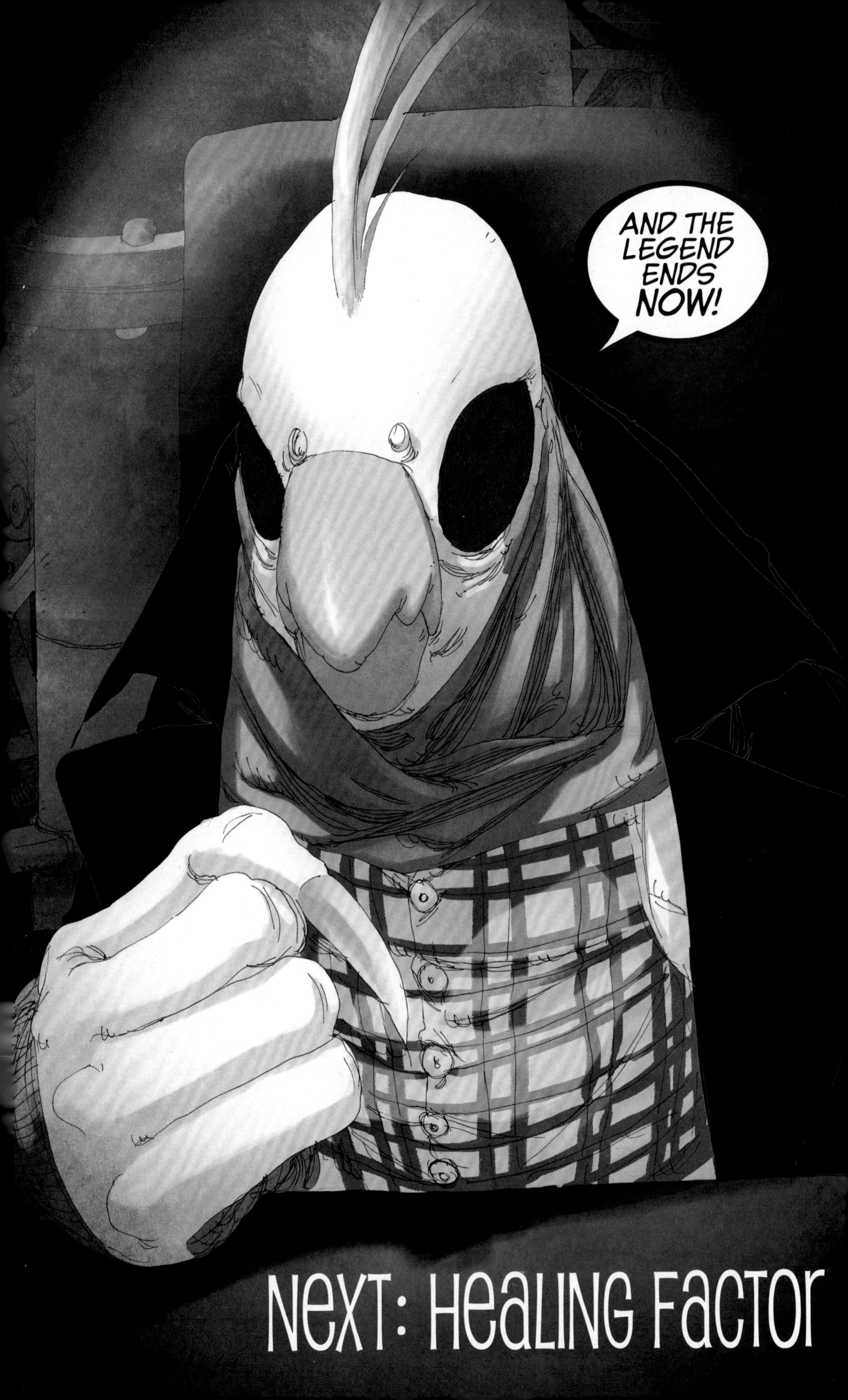
AND THE LEGEND ENDS NOW!
NEXT: Healing Factor

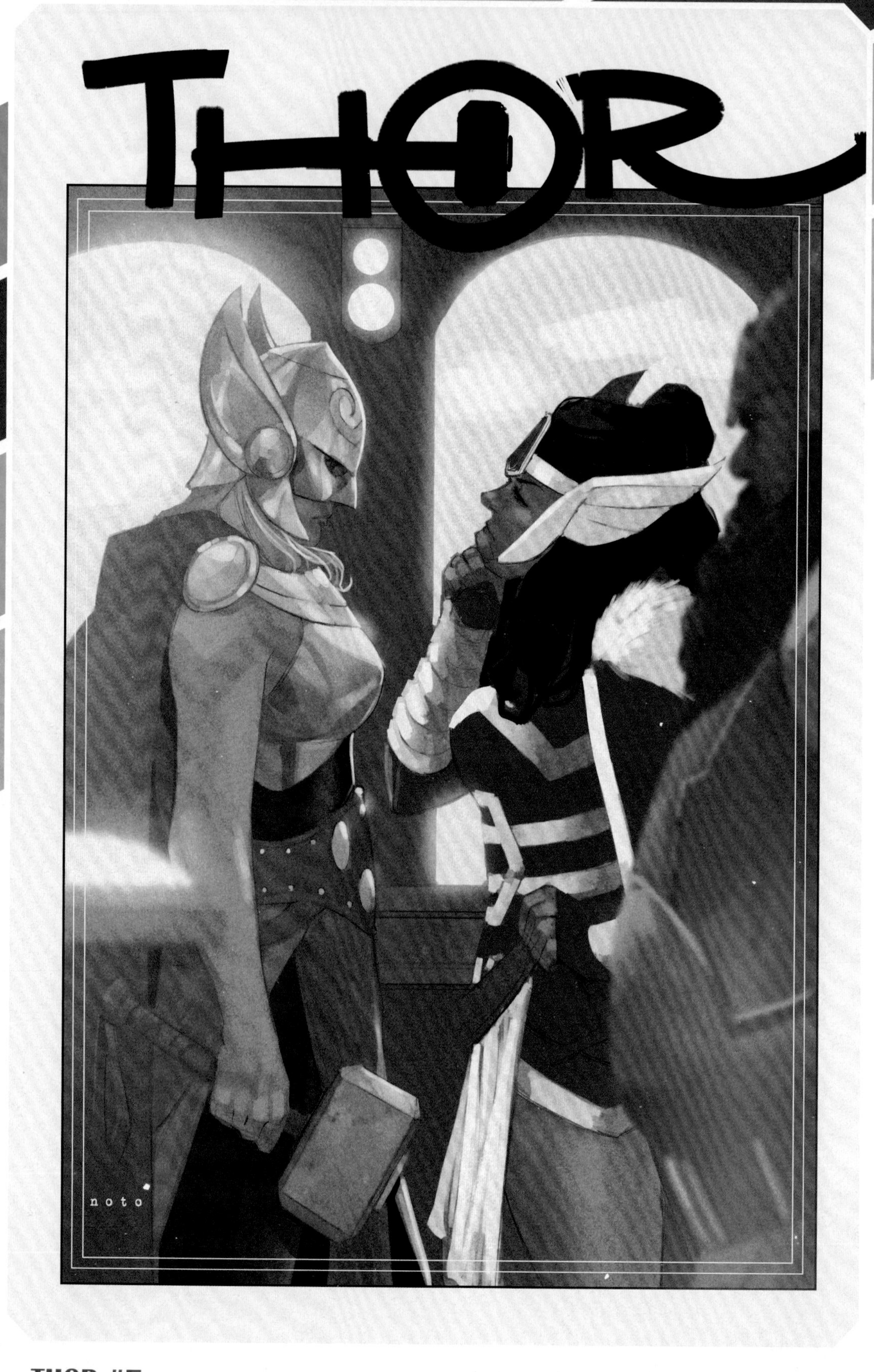
THOR
noto

**THOR #5**
Variant by Phil Noto

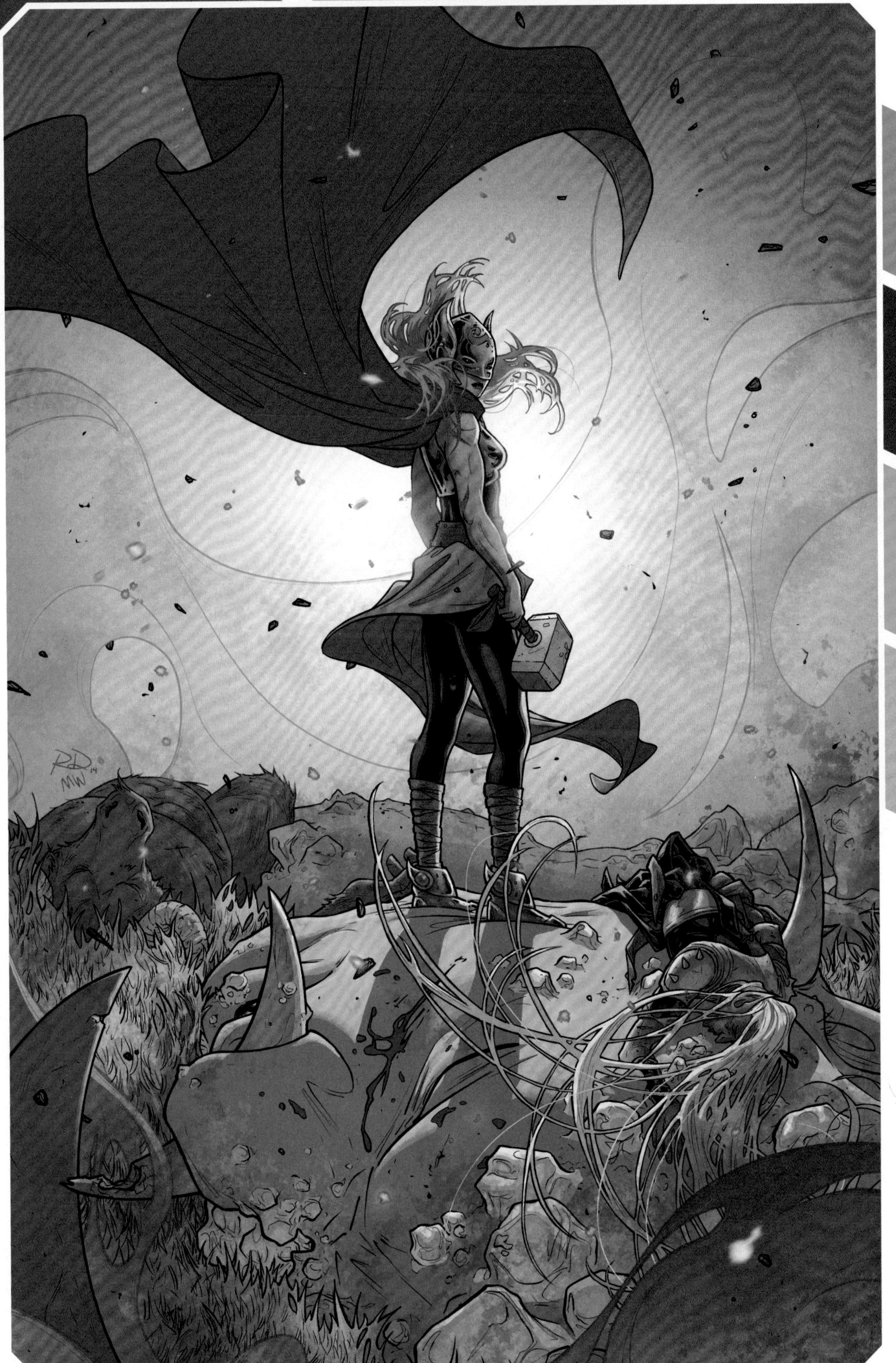

THOR #5

A NEW THOR HAS RISEN.

AFTER THOR ODINSON FOUND HIMSELF NO LONGER WORTHY OF WIELDING MJOLNIR, A MYSTERIOUS WOMAN WAS ABLE TO LIFT THE ENCHANTED HAMMER AND BECAME THE NEW GODDESS OF THUNDER.

BUT NOT EVERYONE IS HAPPY ABOUT IT. ALL-FATHER ODIN, WHO RECENTLY RETURNED TO ASGARDIA AFTER A SELF-IMPOSED EXILE WHERE HE SERVED AS HIS BROTHER CUL'S JAILOR, IS NOT HAPPY TO SEE SOMEONE ELSE USING THE HAMMER THAT HE HAD CREATED SPECIALLY FOR HIS SON.

AND THAT SON (THE OLD THOR) WASN'T HAPPY ABOUT LOSING THE HAMMER EITHER. HE WENT TO CONFRONT THE NEW GODDESS OF THUNDER, BUT AFTER A FIGHT THAT SHOOK ALL TEN REALMS, HE FINALLY WISED UP AND REALIZED THAT SHE ACTUALLY IS WORTHY.

THE TWO THUNDER GODS THEN JOINED FORCES TO TURN BACK AN ASSAULT BY THE EVIL DARK ELF KING MALEKITH AND THE FROST GIANTS ON EARTH (OR MIDGARD, AS THE ASGARDIANS CALL IT). WITH THE DAY SAVED, ODINSON OFFICIALLY HANDED OVER THE NAME OF THOR, LEAVING THE GODDESS OF THUNDER TO FORGE HER OWN PATH AS THE NEWEST CHAMPION OF MIDGARD!

# BEHOLD, A NEW AGE OF THUNDER

JASON AARON
WRITER

JORGE MOLINA
GUEST ARTIST

VC's JOE SABINO
LETTERER & PRODUCTION

RUSSELL DAUTERMAN & MATTHEW WILSON
COVER ARTISTS

PHIL NOTO
VARIANT COVER ARTIST

JON MOISAN
ASSISTANT EDITOR

WIL MOSS
EDITOR

AXEL ALONSO
EDITOR IN CHIEF

JOE QUESADA
CHIEF CREATIVE OFFICER

DAN BUCKLEY
PUBLISHER

ALAN FINE
EXECUTIVE PRODUCER

THOR CREATED BY STAN LEE, LARRY LIEBER & JACK KIRBY

When you see this: **AR**, open up the MARVEL AR APP (available on applicable Apple ® iOS or Android ™ devices) and use your camera-enabled device to unlock extra-special exclusive features!

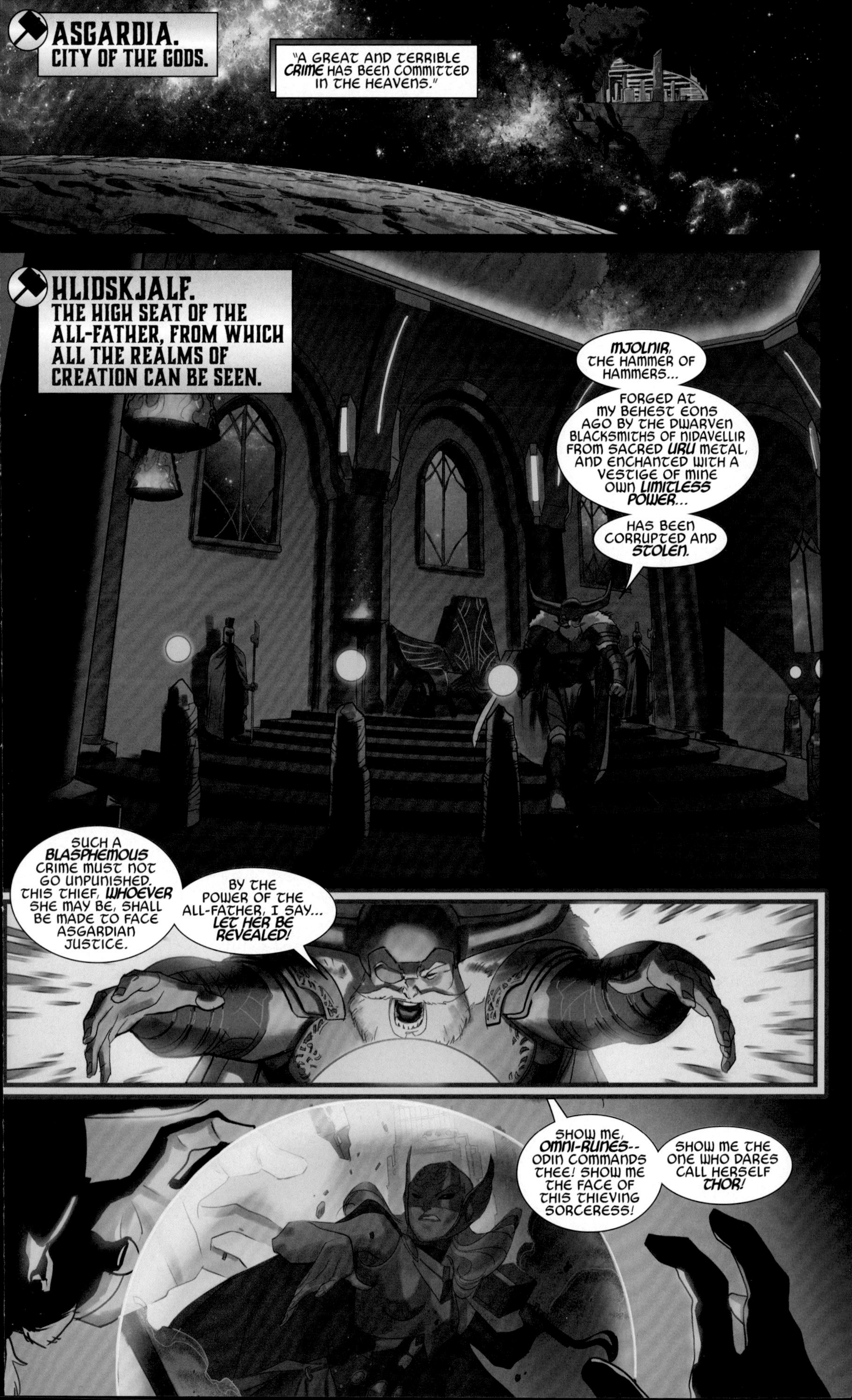
ASGARDIA. CITY OF THE GODS.
"A GREAT AND TERRIBLE CRIME HAS BEEN COMMITTED IN THE HEAVENS."
HLIDSKJALF. THE HIGH SEAT OF THE ALL-FATHER, FROM WHICH ALL THE REALMS OF CREATION CAN BE SEEN.
MJOLNIR, THE HAMMER OF HAMMERS...
FORGED AT MY BEHEST EONS AGO BY THE DWARVEN BLACKSMITHS OF NIDAVELLIR FROM SACRED URU METAL, AND ENCHANTED WITH A VESTIGE OF MINE OWN LIMITLESS POWER...
HAS BEEN CORRUPTED AND STOLEN.
SUCH A BLASPHEMOUS CRIME MUST NOT GO UNPUNISHED. THIS THIEF, WHOEVER SHE MAY BE, SHALL BE MADE TO FACE ASGARDIAN JUSTICE.
BY THE POWER OF THE ALL-FATHER, I SAY... LET HER BE REVEALED!
SHOW ME, OMNI-RUNES-- ODIN COMMANDS THEE! SHOW ME THE FACE OF THIS THIEVING SORCERESS!
SHOW ME THE ONE WHO DARES CALL HERSELF THOR!

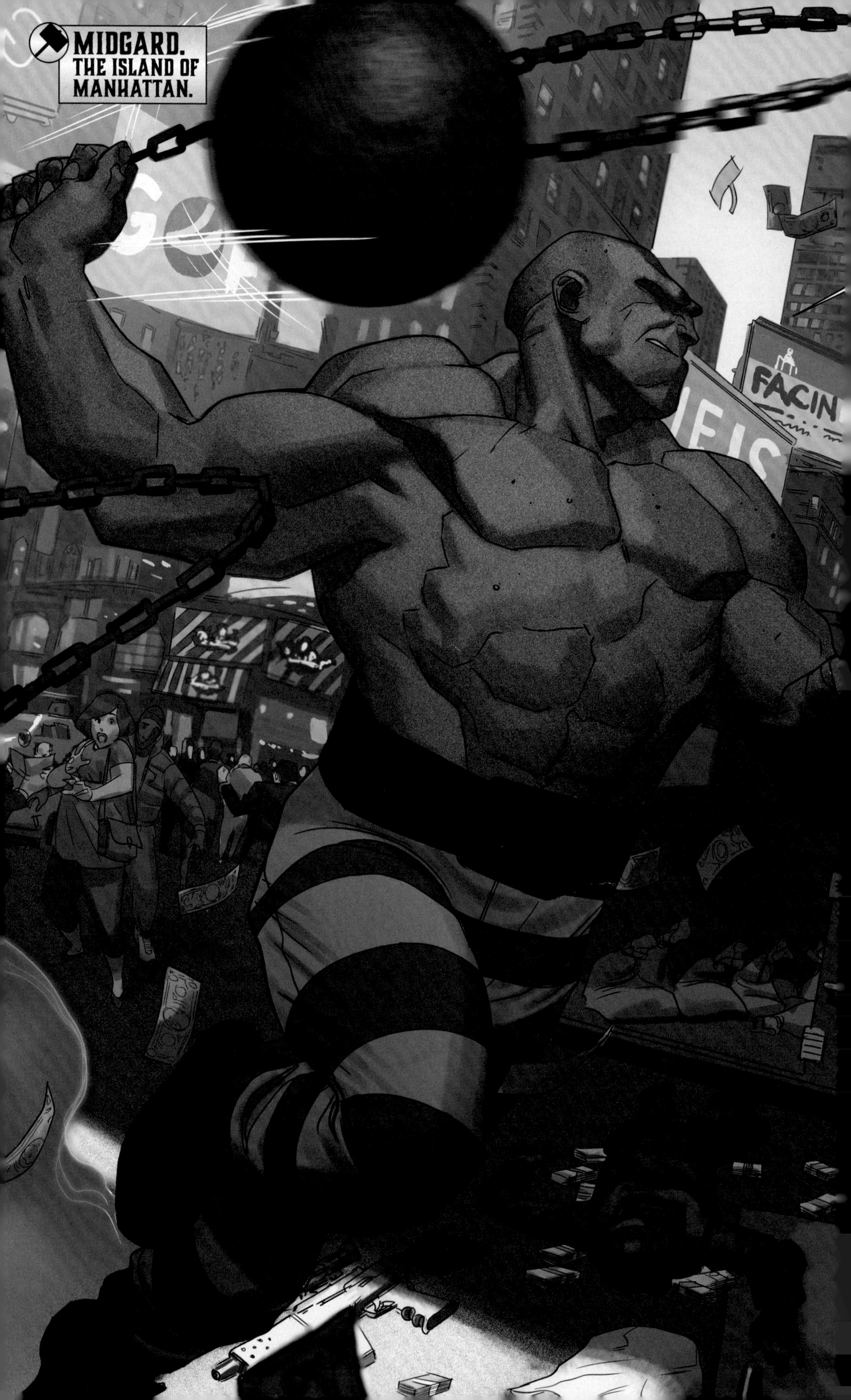
MIDGARD.
THE ISLAND OF
MANHATTAN.

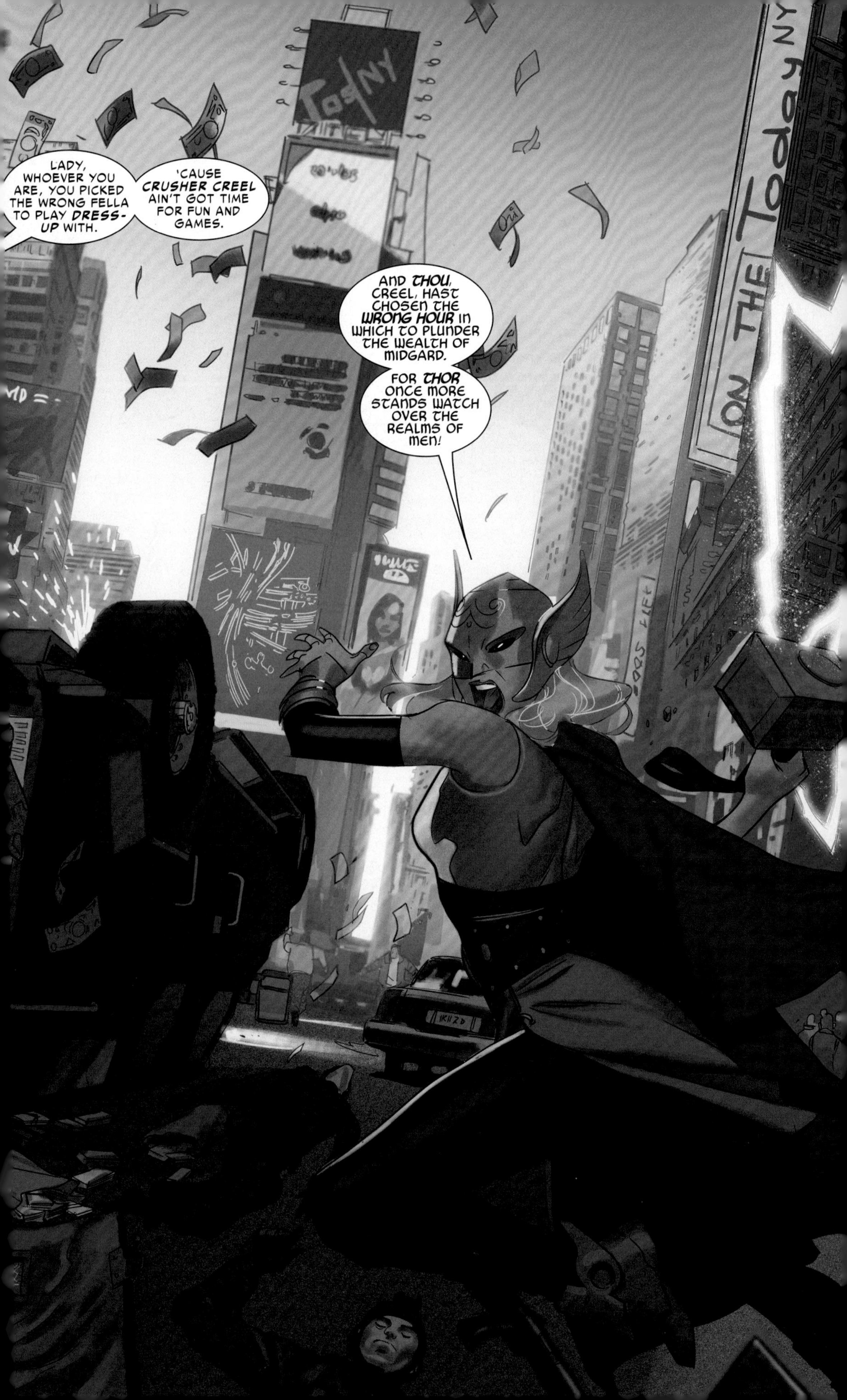
LADY, WHOEVER YOU ARE, YOU PICKED THE WRONG FELLA TO PLAY DRESS-UP WITH.
'CAUSE CRUSHER CREEL AIN'T GOT TIME FOR FUN AND GAMES.
AND THOU, CREEL, HAST CHOSEN THE WRONG HOUR IN WHICH TO PLUNDER THE WEALTH OF MIDGARD.
FOR THOR ONCE MORE STANDS WATCH OVER THE REALMS OF MEN!
ON THE Today NY

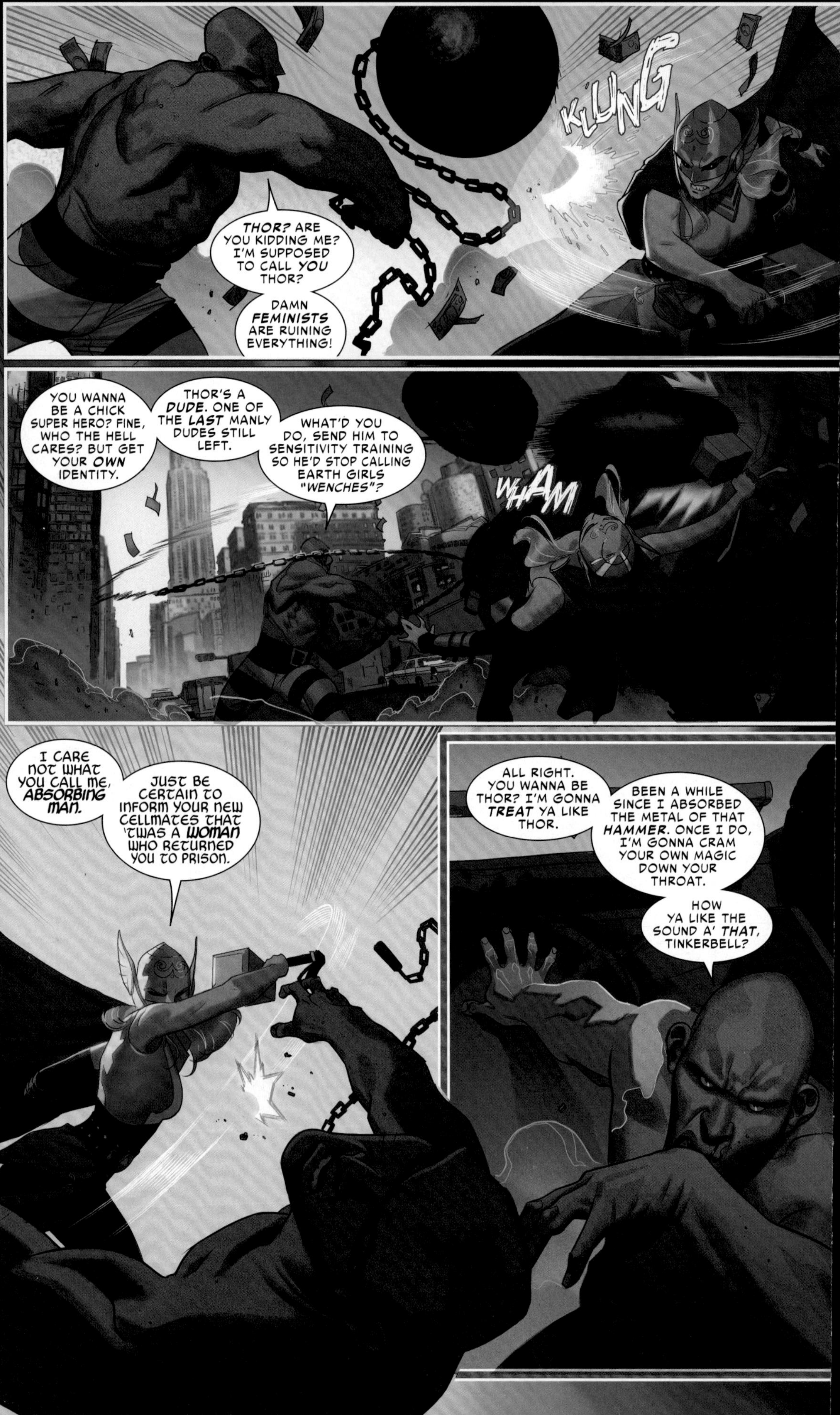
KLUNG
THOR? ARE YOU KIDDING ME? I'M SUPPOSED TO CALL YOU THOR?
DAMN FEMINISTS ARE RUINING EVERYTHING!
YOU WANNA BE A CHICK SUPER HERO? FINE, WHO THE HELL CARES? BUT GET YOUR OWN IDENTITY.
THOR'S A DUDE. ONE OF THE LAST MANLY DUDES STILL LEFT.
WHAT'D YOU DO, SEND HIM TO SENSITIVITY TRAINING SO HE'D STOP CALLING EARTH GIRLS "WENCHES"?
WHAM
I CARE NOT WHAT YOU CALL ME, ABSORBING MAN.
JUST BE CERTAIN TO INFORM YOUR NEW CELLMATES THAT 'TWAS A WOMAN WHO RETURNED YOU TO PRISON.
ALL RIGHT. YOU WANNA BE THOR? I'M GONNA TREAT YA LIKE THOR.
BEEN A WHILE SINCE I ABSORBED THE METAL OF THAT HAMMER. ONCE I DO, I'M GONNA CRAM YOUR OWN MAGIC DOWN YOUR THROAT.
HOW YA LIKE THE SOUND A' THAT, TINKERBELL?

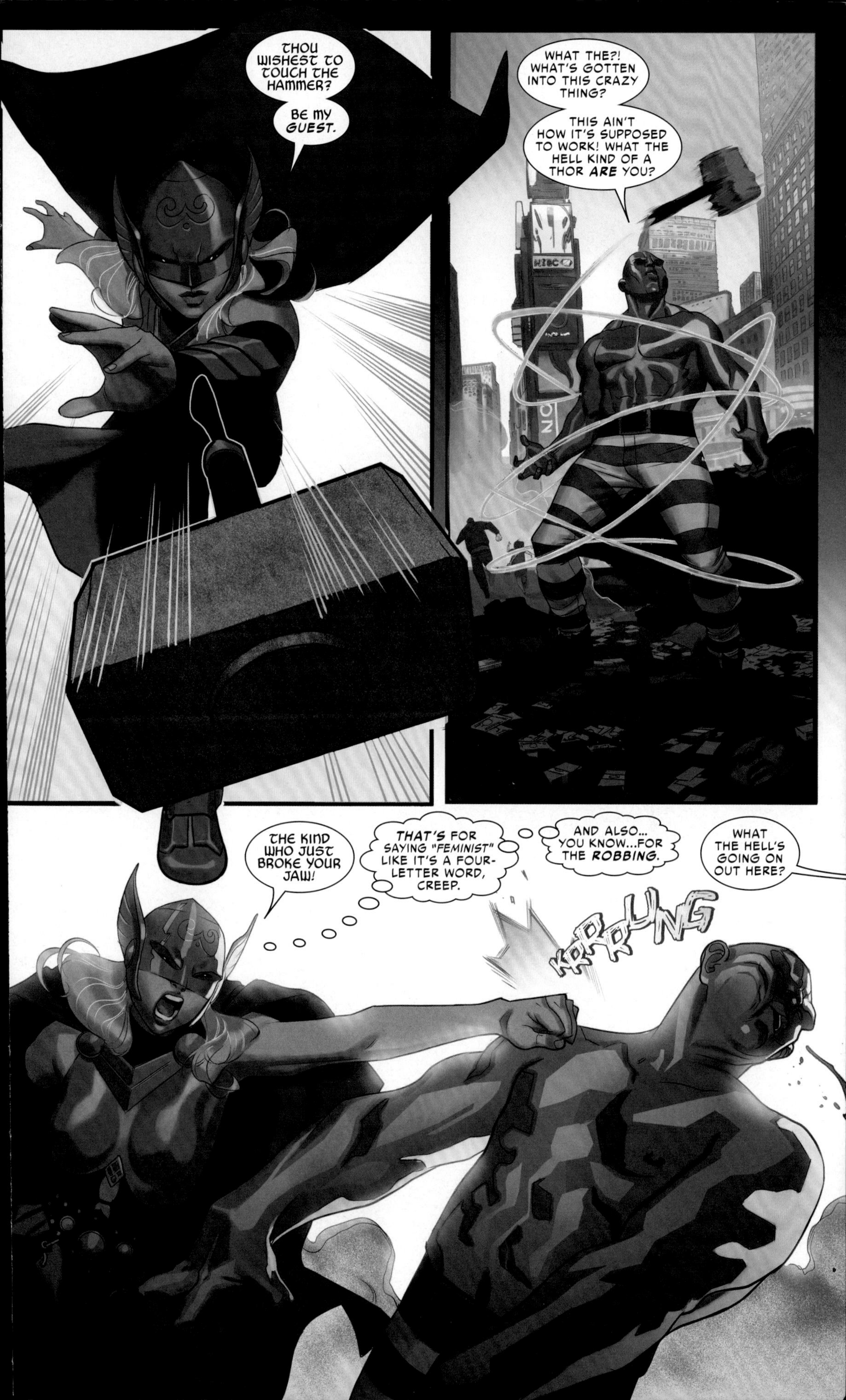
THOU WISHEST TO TOUCH THE HAMMER?
BE MY GUEST.
WHAT THE?! WHAT'S GOTTEN INTO THIS CRAZY THING?
THIS AIN'T HOW IT'S SUPPOSED TO WORK! WHAT THE HELL KIND OF A THOR ARE YOU?
THE KIND WHO JUST BROKE YOUR JAW!
THAT'S FOR SAYING "FEMINIST" LIKE IT'S A FOUR-LETTER WORD, CREEP.
AND ALSO... YOU KNOW...FOR THE ROBBING.
WHAT THE HELL'S GOING ON OUT HERE?
KRRUNG

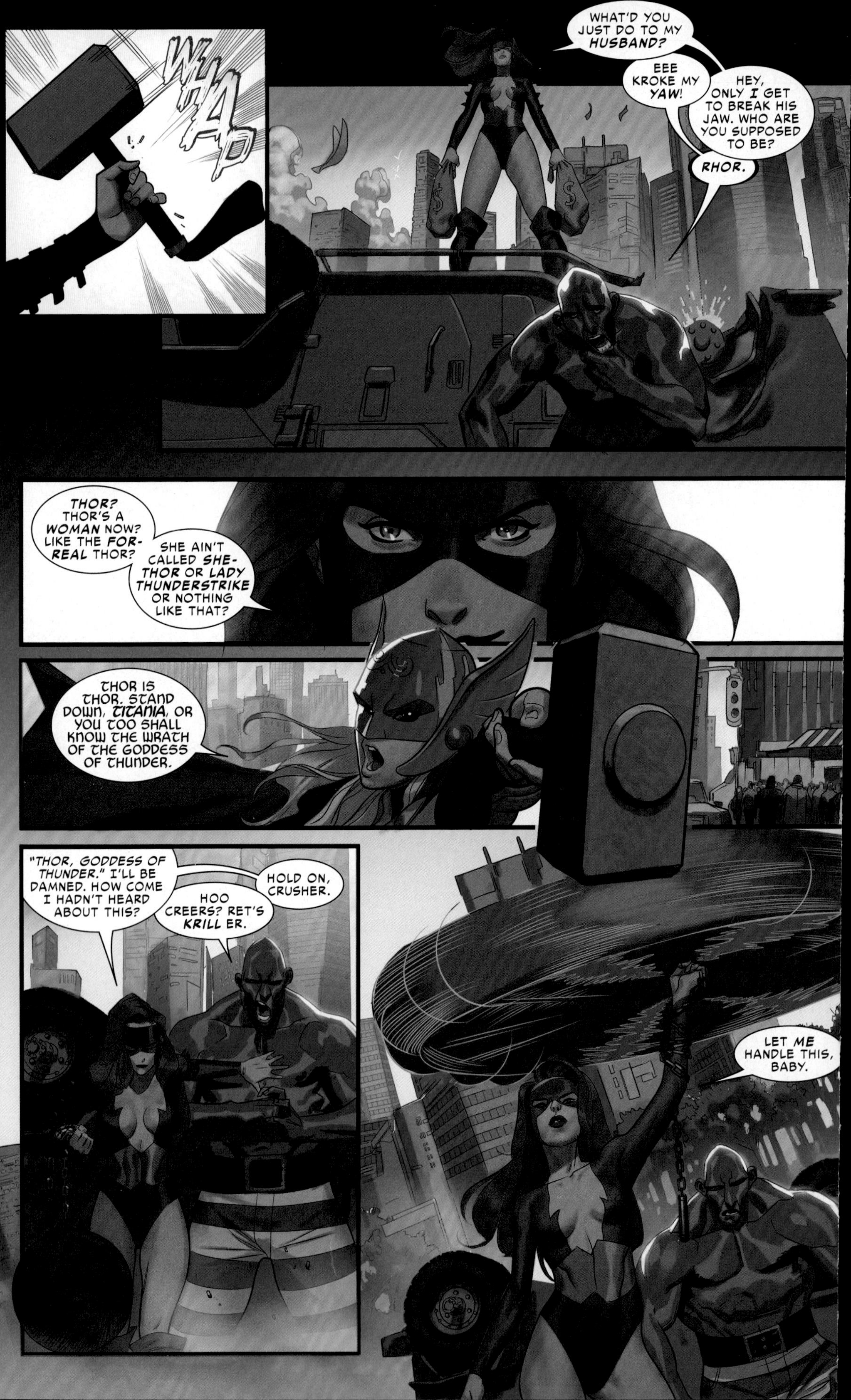
WHAP
WHAT'D YOU JUST DO TO MY HUSBAND?
EEE KROKE MY YAW!
HEY, ONLY I GET TO BREAK HIS JAW. WHO ARE YOU SUPPOSED TO BE?
RHOR.
THOR? THOR'S A WOMAN NOW? LIKE THE FOR-REAL THOR?
SHE AIN'T CALLED SHE-THOR OR LADY THUNDERSTRIKE OR NOTHING LIKE THAT?
THOR IS THOR. STAND DOWN, TITANIA, OR YOU TOO SHALL KNOW THE WRATH OF THE GODDESS OF THUNDER.
"THOR, GODDESS OF THUNDER." I'LL BE DAMNED. HOW COME I HADN'T HEARD ABOUT THIS?
HOLD ON, CRUSHER.
HOO CREERS? RET'S KRILL ER.
LET ME HANDLE THIS, BABY.

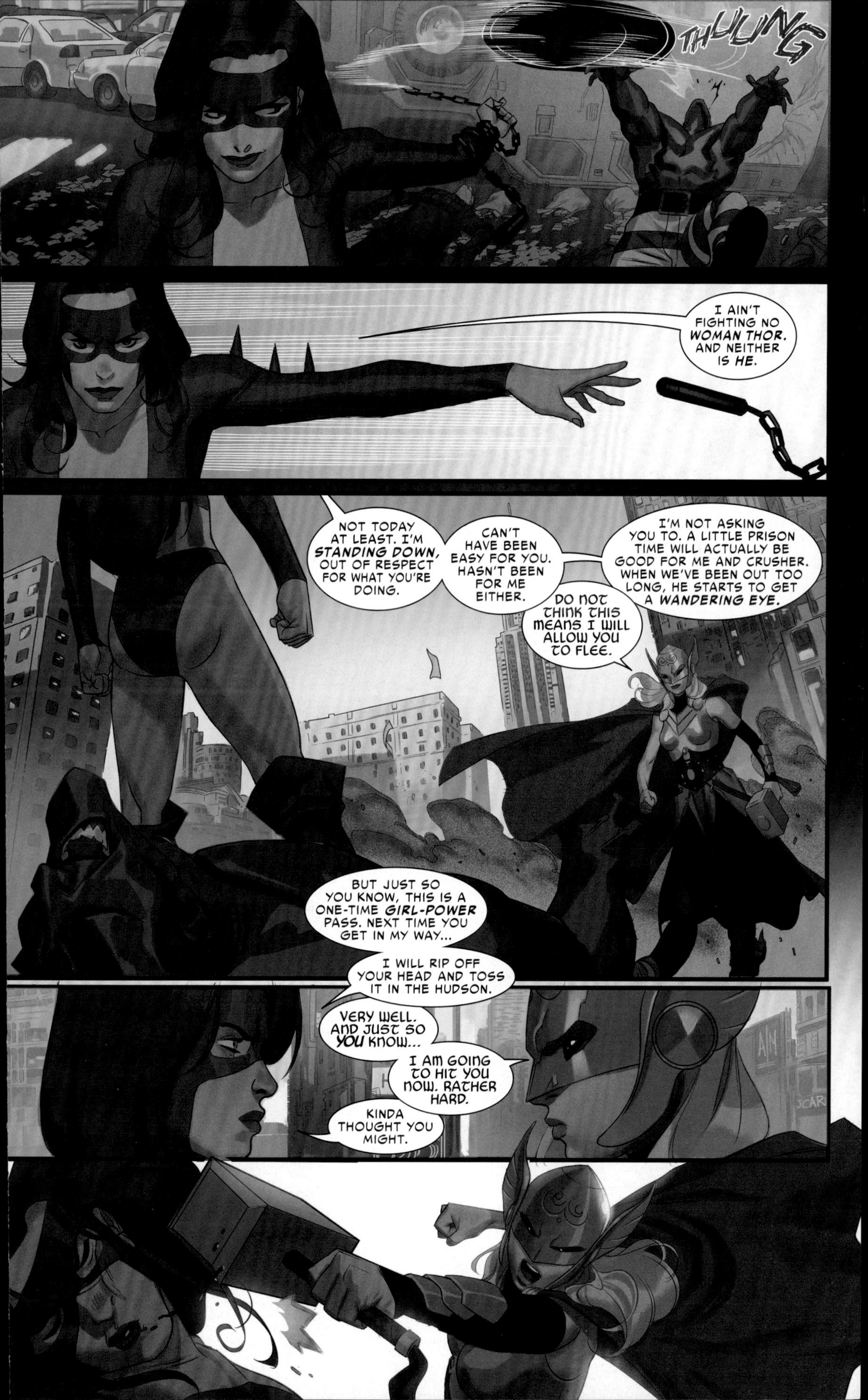
THUUNG
I AIN'T FIGHTING NO WOMAN THOR. AND NEITHER IS HE.
NOT TODAY AT LEAST. I'M STANDING DOWN, OUT OF RESPECT FOR WHAT YOU'RE DOING.
CAN'T HAVE BEEN EASY FOR YOU. HASN'T BEEN FOR ME EITHER.
I'M NOT ASKING YOU TO. A LITTLE PRISON TIME WILL ACTUALLY BE GOOD FOR ME AND CRUSHER. WHEN WE'VE BEEN OUT TOO LONG, HE STARTS TO GET A WANDERING EYE.
DO NOT THINK THIS MEANS I WILL ALLOW YOU TO FLEE.
BUT JUST SO YOU KNOW, THIS IS A ONE-TIME GIRL-POWER PASS. NEXT TIME YOU GET IN MY WAY...
I WILL RIP OFF YOUR HEAD AND TOSS IT IN THE HUDSON.
VERY WELL. AND JUST SO YOU KNOW...
I AM GOING TO HIT YOU NOW. RATHER HARD.
KINDA THOUGHT YOU MIGHT.

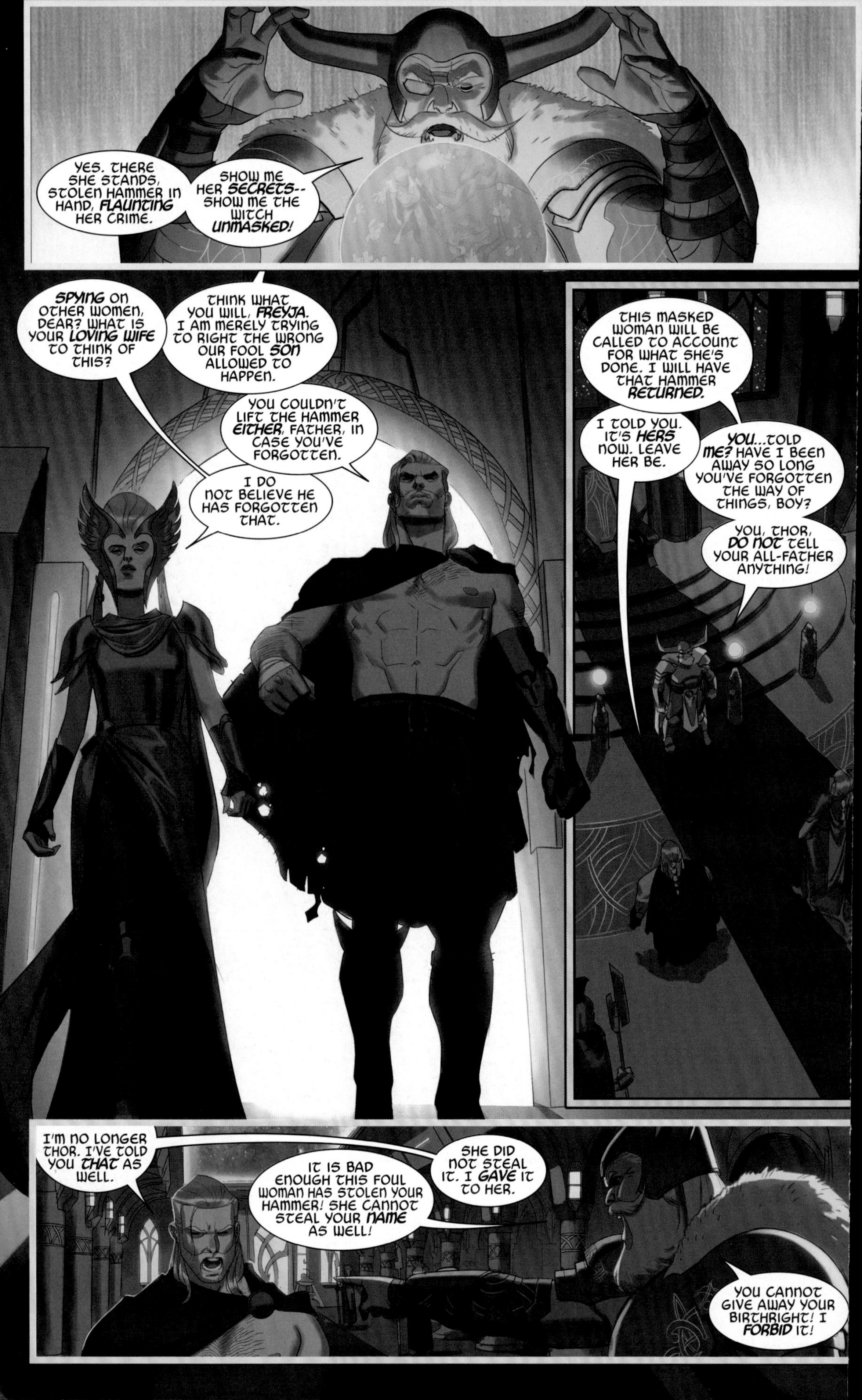
YES. THERE SHE STANDS, STOLEN HAMMER IN HAND, FLAUNTING HER CRIME.
SHOW ME HER SECRETS-- SHOW ME THE WITCH UNMASKED!
SPYING ON OTHER WOMEN, DEAR? WHAT IS YOUR LOVING WIFE TO THINK OF THIS?
THINK WHAT YOU WILL, FREYJA. I AM MERELY TRYING TO RIGHT THE WRONG OUR FOOL SON ALLOWED TO HAPPEN.
YOU COULDN'T LIFT THE HAMMER EITHER, FATHER, IN CASE YOU'VE FORGOTTEN.
I DO NOT BELIEVE HE HAS FORGOTTEN THAT.
THIS MASKED WOMAN WILL BE CALLED TO ACCOUNT FOR WHAT SHE'S DONE. I WILL HAVE THAT HAMMER RETURNED.
I TOLD YOU. IT'S HERS NOW. LEAVE HER BE.
YOU...TOLD ME? HAVE I BEEN AWAY SO LONG YOU'VE FORGOTTEN THE WAY OF THINGS, BOY?
YOU, THOR, DO NOT TELL YOUR ALL-FATHER ANYTHING!
I'M NO LONGER THOR. I'VE TOLD YOU THAT AS WELL.
IT IS BAD ENOUGH THIS FOUL WOMAN HAS STOLEN YOUR HAMMER! SHE CANNOT STEAL YOUR NAME AS WELL!
SHE DID NOT STEAL IT. I GAVE IT TO HER.
YOU CANNOT GIVE AWAY YOUR BIRTHRIGHT! I FORBID IT!

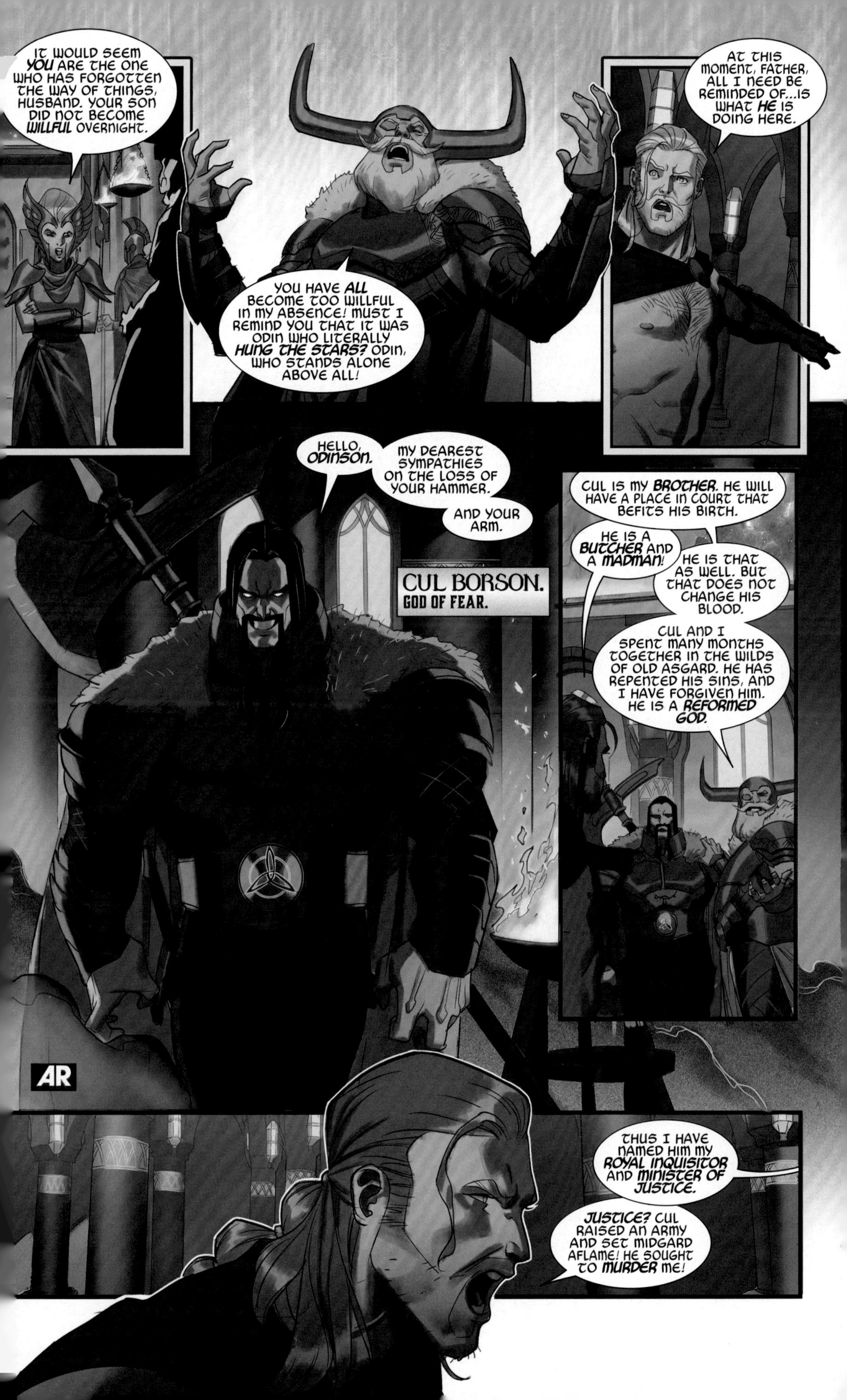
IT WOULD SEEM YOU ARE THE ONE WHO HAS FORGOTTEN THE WAY OF THINGS, HUSBAND. YOUR SON DID NOT BECOME WILLFUL OVERNIGHT.
YOU HAVE ALL BECOME TOO WILLFUL IN MY ABSENCE! MUST I REMIND YOU THAT IT WAS ODIN WHO LITERALLY HUNG THE STARS? ODIN, WHO STANDS ALONE ABOVE ALL!
AT THIS MOMENT, FATHER, ALL I NEED BE REMINDED OF...IS WHAT HE IS DOING HERE.
HELLO, ODINSON.
MY DEAREST SYMPATHIES ON THE LOSS OF YOUR HAMMER.
AND YOUR ARM.
CUL BORSON. GOD OF FEAR.
CUL IS MY BROTHER. HE WILL HAVE A PLACE IN COURT THAT BEFITS HIS BIRTH.
HE IS A BUTCHER AND A MADMAN!
HE IS THAT AS WELL. BUT THAT DOES NOT CHANGE HIS BLOOD.
CUL AND I SPENT MANY MONTHS TOGETHER IN THE WILDS OF OLD ASGARD. HE HAS REPENTED HIS SINS, AND I HAVE FORGIVEN HIM. HE IS A REFORMED GOD.
AR
THUS I HAVE NAMED HIM MY ROYAL INQUISITOR AND MINISTER OF JUSTICE.
JUSTICE? CUL RAISED AN ARMY AND SET MIDGARD AFLAME! HE SOUGHT TO MURDER ME!

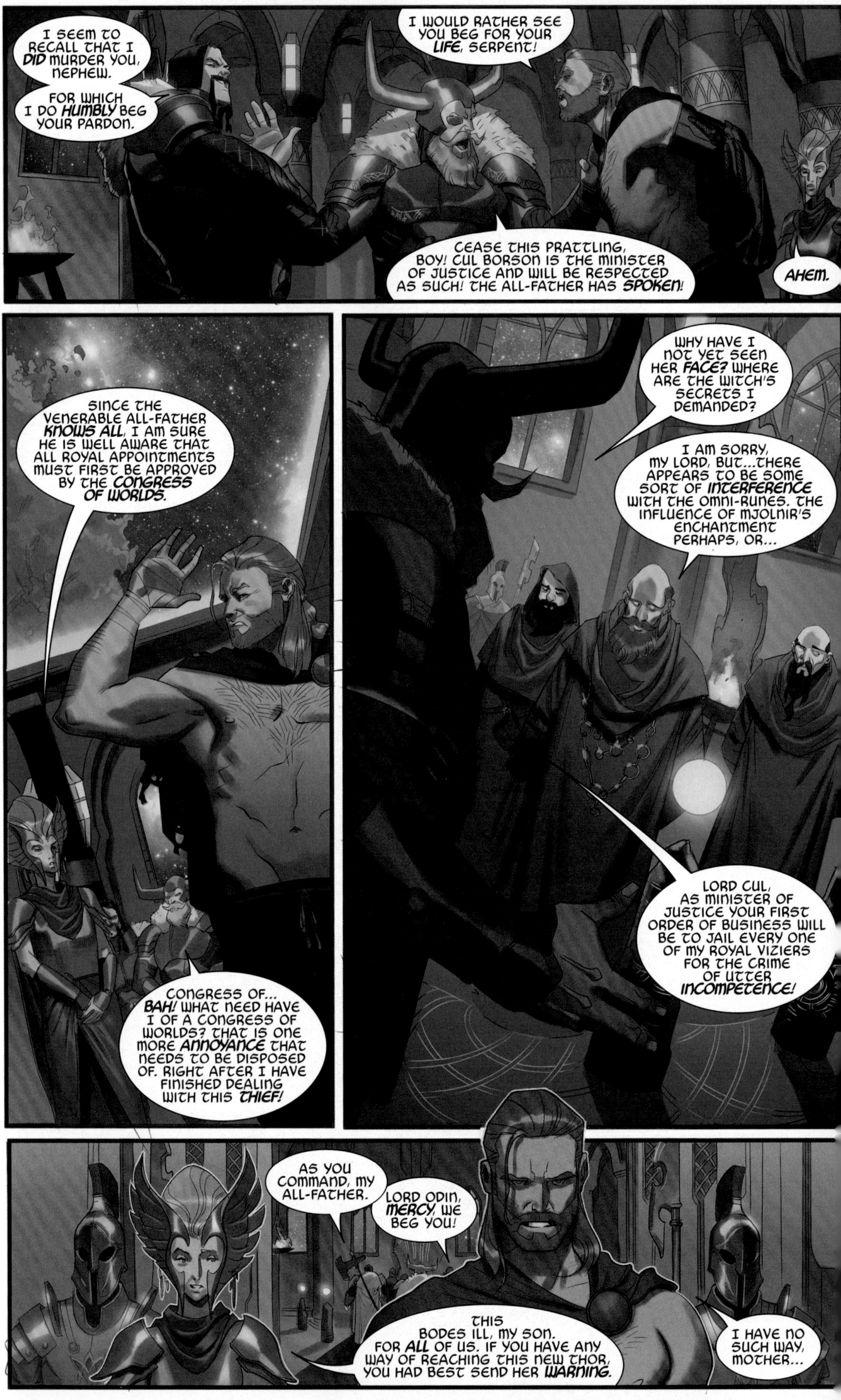
I SEEM TO RECALL THAT I DID MURDER YOU, NEPHEW.
FOR WHICH I DO HUMBLY BEG YOUR PARDON.
I WOULD RATHER SEE YOU BEG FOR YOUR LIFE, SERPENT!
CEASE THIS PRATTLING, BOY! CUL BORSON IS THE MINISTER OF JUSTICE AND WILL BE RESPECTED AS SUCH! THE ALL-FATHER HAS SPOKEN!
AHEM.
SINCE THE VENERABLE ALL-FATHER KNOWS ALL, I AM SURE HE IS WELL AWARE THAT ALL ROYAL APPOINTMENTS MUST FIRST BE APPROVED BY THE CONGRESS OF WORLDS.
CONGRESS OF... BAH! WHAT NEED HAVE I OF A CONGRESS OF WORLDS? THAT IS ONE MORE ANNOYANCE THAT NEEDS TO BE DISPOSED OF. RIGHT AFTER I HAVE FINISHED DEALING WITH THIS THIEF!
WHY HAVE I NOT YET SEEN HER FACE? WHERE ARE THE WITCH'S SECRETS I DEMANDED?
I AM SORRY, MY LORD, BUT...THERE APPEARS TO BE SOME SORT OF INTERFERENCE WITH THE OMNI-RUNES. THE INFLUENCE OF MJOLNIR'S ENCHANTMENT PERHAPS, OR...
LORD CUL, AS MINISTER OF JUSTICE YOUR FIRST ORDER OF BUSINESS WILL BE TO JAIL EVERY ONE OF MY ROYAL VIZIERS FOR THE CRIME OF UTTER INCOMPETENCE!
AS YOU COMMAND, MY ALL-FATHER.
LORD ODIN, MERCY, WE BEG YOU!
THIS BODES ILL, MY SON. FOR ALL OF US. IF YOU HAVE ANY WAY OF REACHING THIS NEW THOR, YOU HAD BEST SEND HER WARNING.
I HAVE NO SUCH WAY, MOTHER...

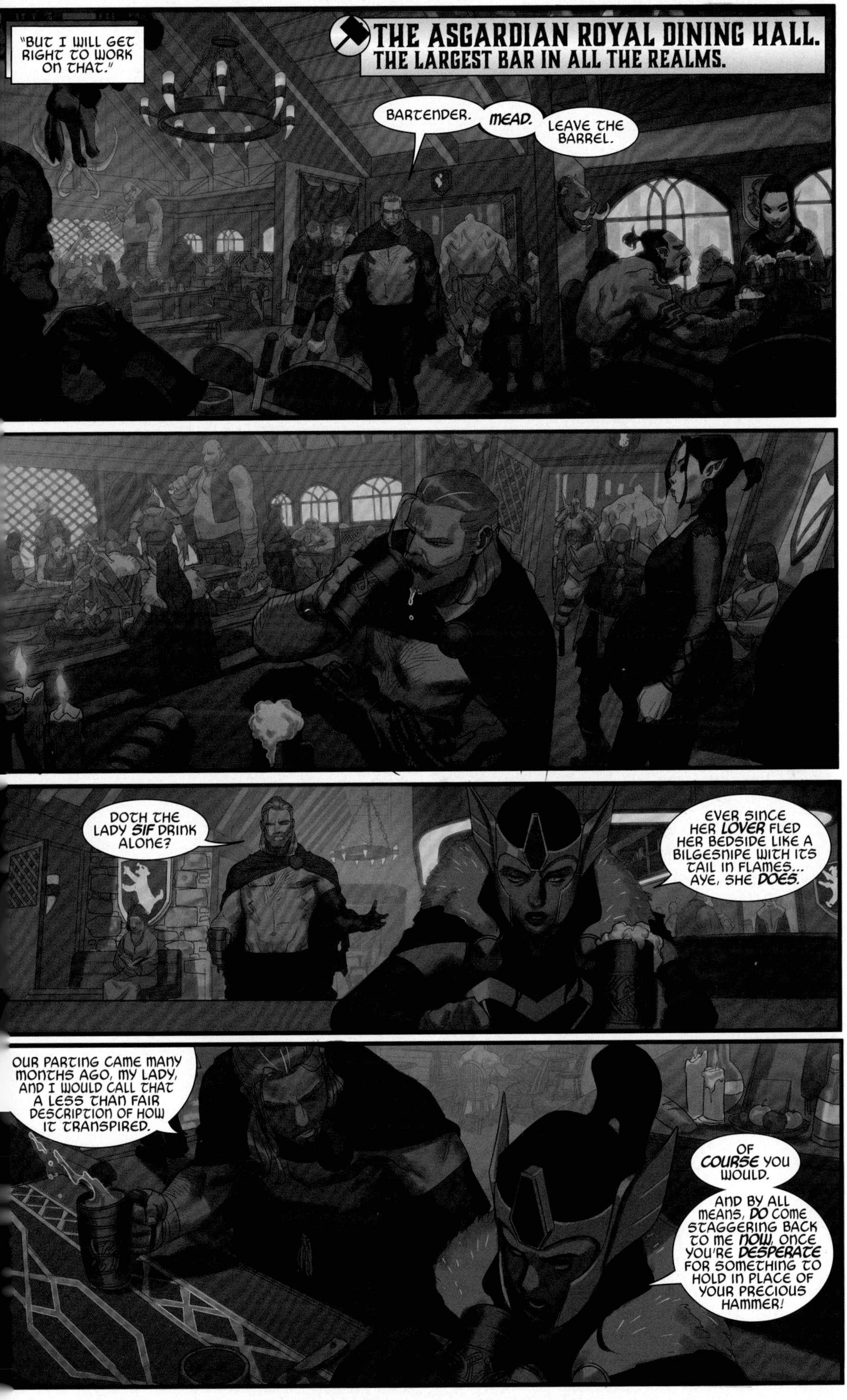
"BUT I WILL GET RIGHT TO WORK ON THAT."
THE ASGARDIAN ROYAL DINING HALL. THE LARGEST BAR IN ALL THE REALMS.
BARTENDER.
MEAD.
LEAVE THE BARREL.
DOTH THE LADY SIF DRINK ALONE?
EVER SINCE HER LOVER FLED HER BEDSIDE LIKE A BILGESNIPE WITH ITS TAIL IN FLAMES... AYE, SHE DOES.
OUR PARTING CAME MANY MONTHS AGO, MY LADY, AND I WOULD CALL THAT A LESS THAN FAIR DESCRIPTION OF HOW IT TRANSPIRED.
OF COURSE YOU WOULD.
AND BY ALL MEANS, DO COME STAGGERING BACK TO ME NOW, ONCE YOU'RE DESPERATE FOR SOMETHING TO HOLD IN PLACE OF YOUR PRECIOUS HAMMER!

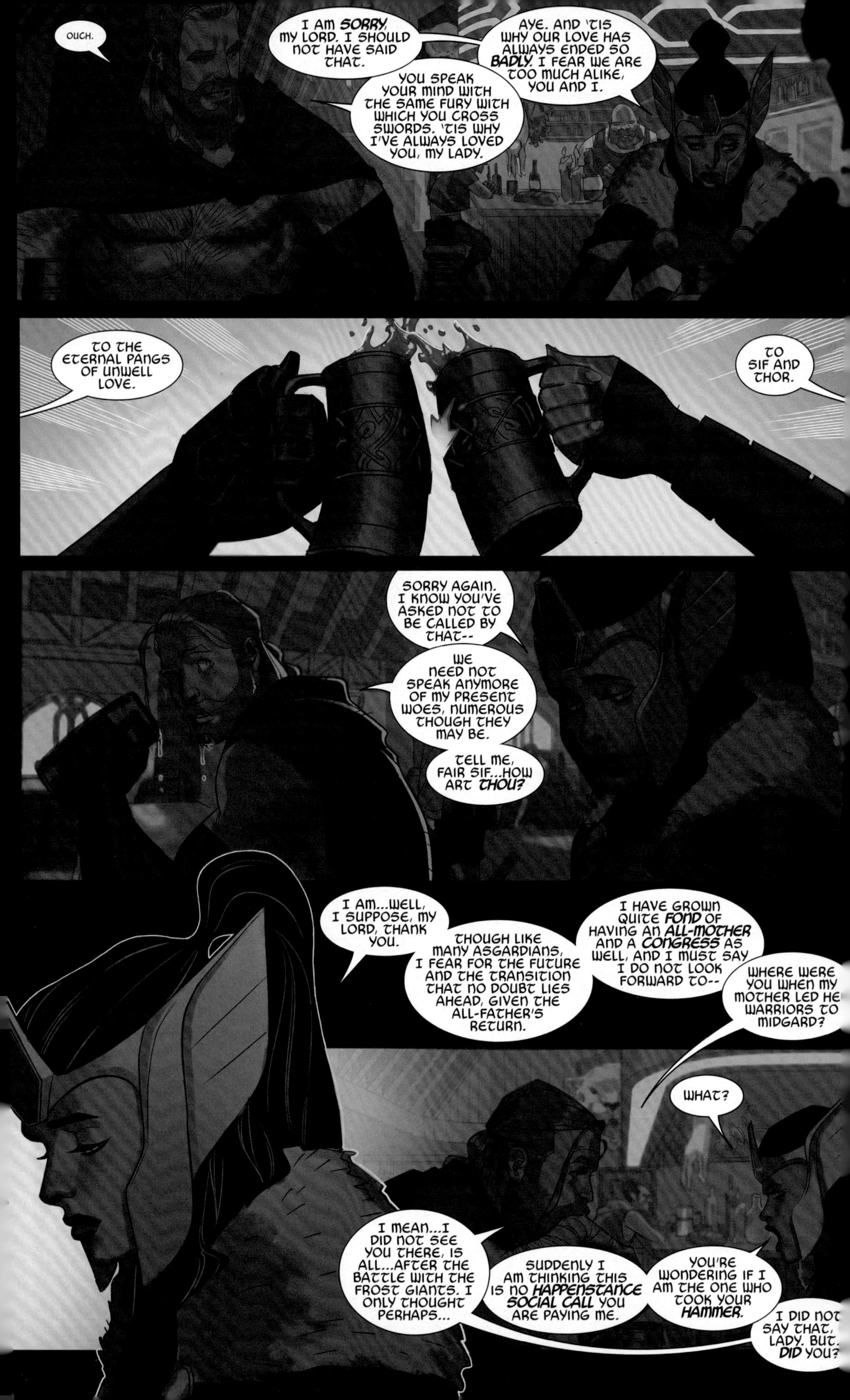
OUCH.
I AM SORRY, MY LORD. I SHOULD NOT HAVE SAID THAT.
AYE. AND 'TIS WHY OUR LOVE HAS ALWAYS ENDED SO BADLY. I FEAR WE ARE TOO MUCH ALIKE, YOU AND I.
YOU SPEAK YOUR MIND WITH THE SAME FURY WITH WHICH YOU CROSS SWORDS. 'TIS WHY I'VE ALWAYS LOVED YOU, MY LADY.
TO THE ETERNAL PANGS OF UNWELL LOVE.
TO SIF AND THOR.
SORRY AGAIN. I KNOW YOU'VE ASKED NOT TO BE CALLED BY THAT--
WE NEED NOT SPEAK ANYMORE OF MY PRESENT WOES, NUMEROUS THOUGH THEY MAY BE.
TELL ME, FAIR SIF...HOW ART THOU?
I AM...WELL, I SUPPOSE, MY LORD, THANK YOU.
THOUGH LIKE MANY ASGARDIANS, I FEAR FOR THE FUTURE AND THE TRANSITION THAT NO DOUBT LIES AHEAD, GIVEN THE ALL-FATHER'S RETURN.
I HAVE GROWN QUITE FOND OF HAVING AN ALL-MOTHER AND A CONGRESS AS WELL, AND I MUST SAY I DO NOT LOOK FORWARD TO--
WHERE WERE YOU WHEN MY MOTHER LED HE WARRIORS TO MIDGARD?
WHAT?
I MEAN...I DID NOT SEE YOU THERE, IS ALL...AFTER THE BATTLE WITH THE FROST GIANTS. I ONLY THOUGHT PERHAPS...
SUDDENLY I AM THINKING THIS IS NO HAPPENSTANCE SOCIAL CALL YOU ARE PAYING ME.
YOU'RE WONDERING IF I AM THE ONE WHO TOOK YOUR HAMMER.
I DID NOT SAY THAT, LADY. BUT. DID YOU?

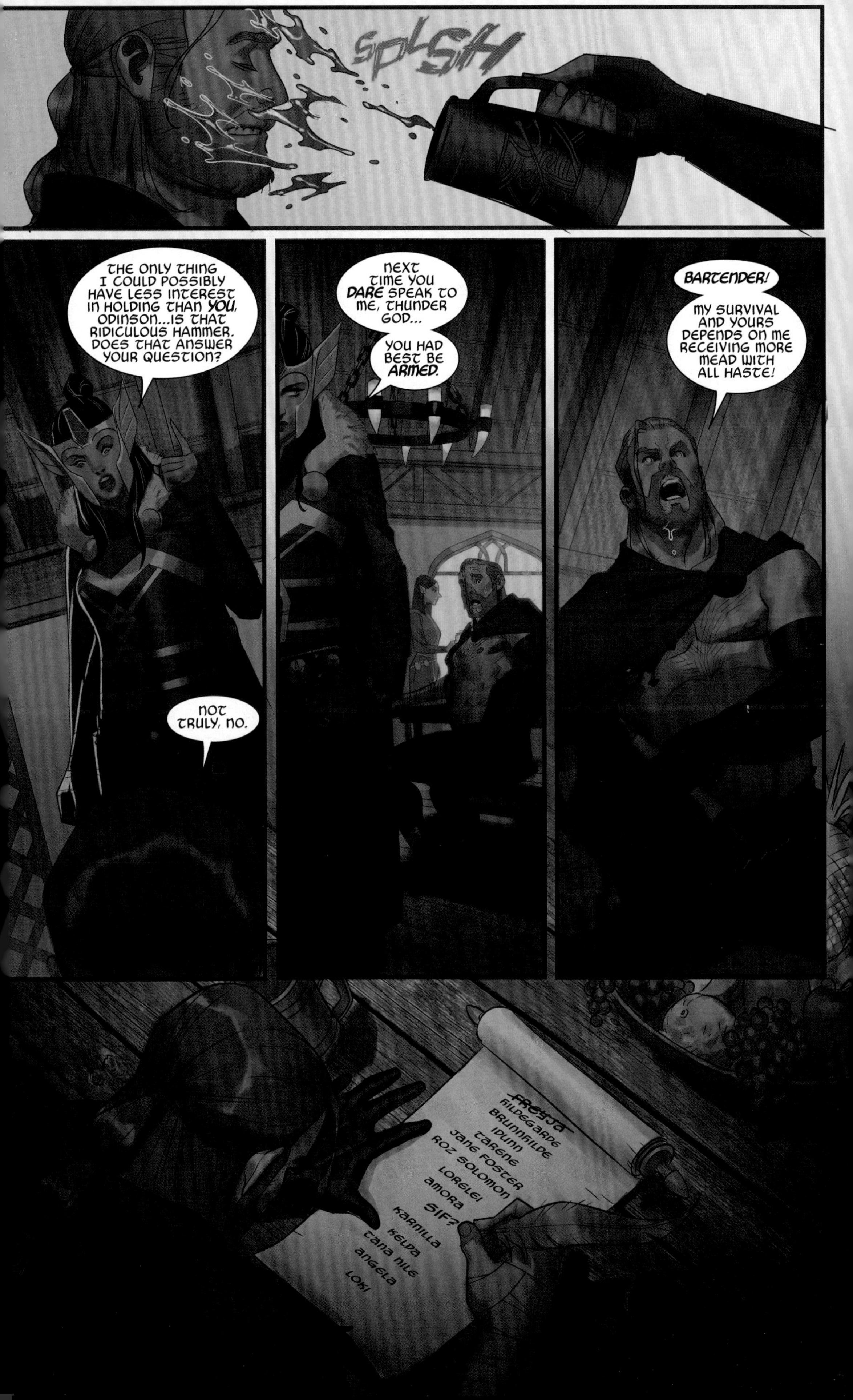
SPLSH
THE ONLY THING I COULD POSSIBLY HAVE LESS INTEREST IN HOLDING THAN YOU, ODINSON...IS THAT RIDICULOUS HAMMER. DOES THAT ANSWER YOUR QUESTION?
NOT TRULY, NO.
NEXT TIME YOU DARE SPEAK TO ME, THUNDER GOD...
YOU HAD BEST BE ARMED.
BARTENDER!
MY SURVIVAL AND YOURS DEPENDS ON ME RECEIVING MORE MEAD WITH ALL HASTE!
~~FREYJA~~
HILDEGARDE
BRUNNHILDE
IDUNN
TARENE
JANE FOSTER
ROZ SOLOMON
LORELEI
AMORA
SIF?
KARNILLA
KELDA
TANA NILE
ANGELA
LOKI

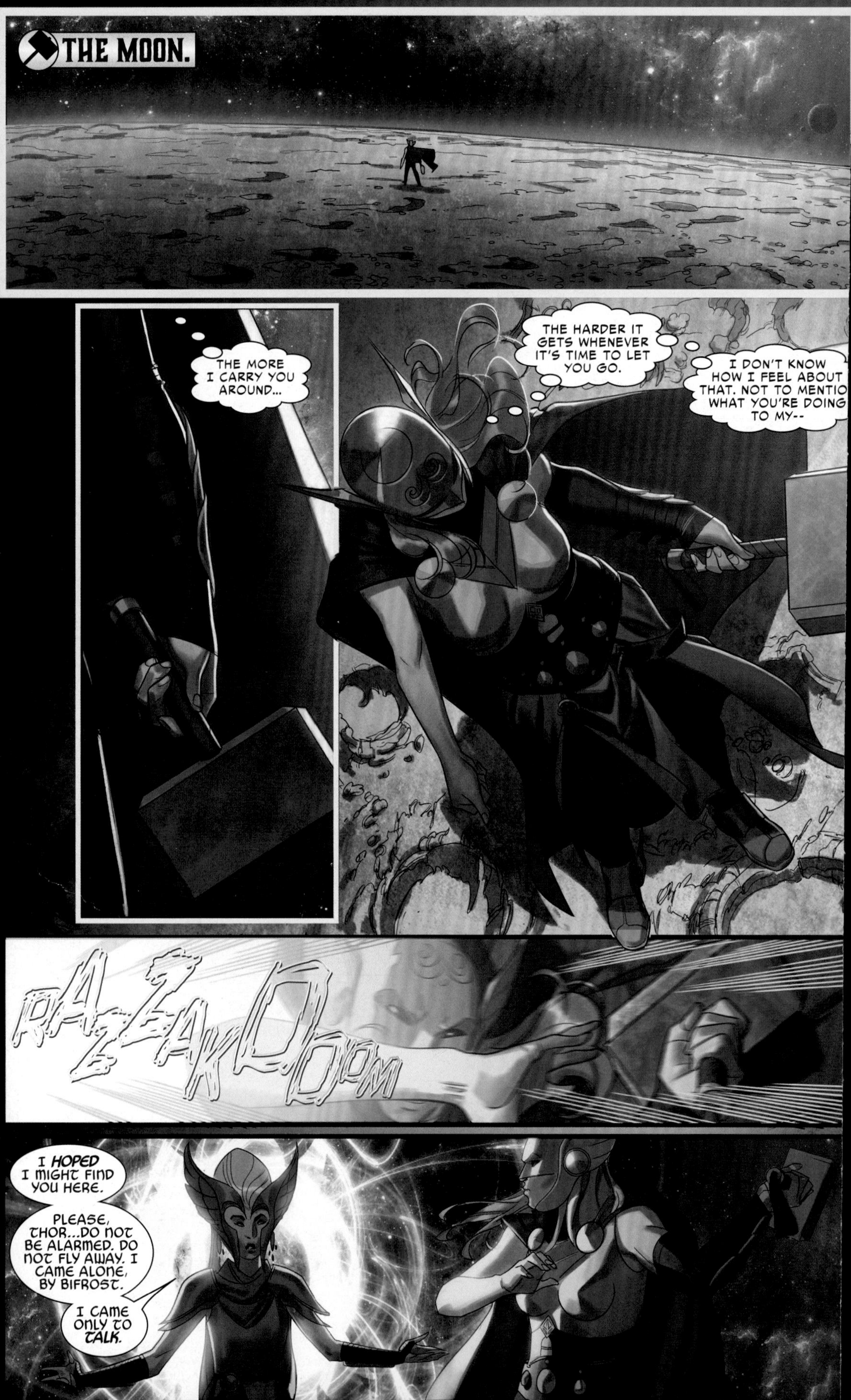
THE MOON.
THE MORE I CARRY YOU AROUND...
THE HARDER IT GETS WHENEVER IT'S TIME TO LET YOU GO.
I DON'T KNOW HOW I FEEL ABOUT THAT. NOT TO MENTIO WHAT YOU'RE DOING TO MY--
RAZZAKDOOM
I HOPED I MIGHT FIND YOU HERE.
PLEASE, THOR...DO NOT BE ALARMED. DO NOT FLY AWAY. I CAME ALONE, BY BIFROST.
I CAME ONLY TO TALK.

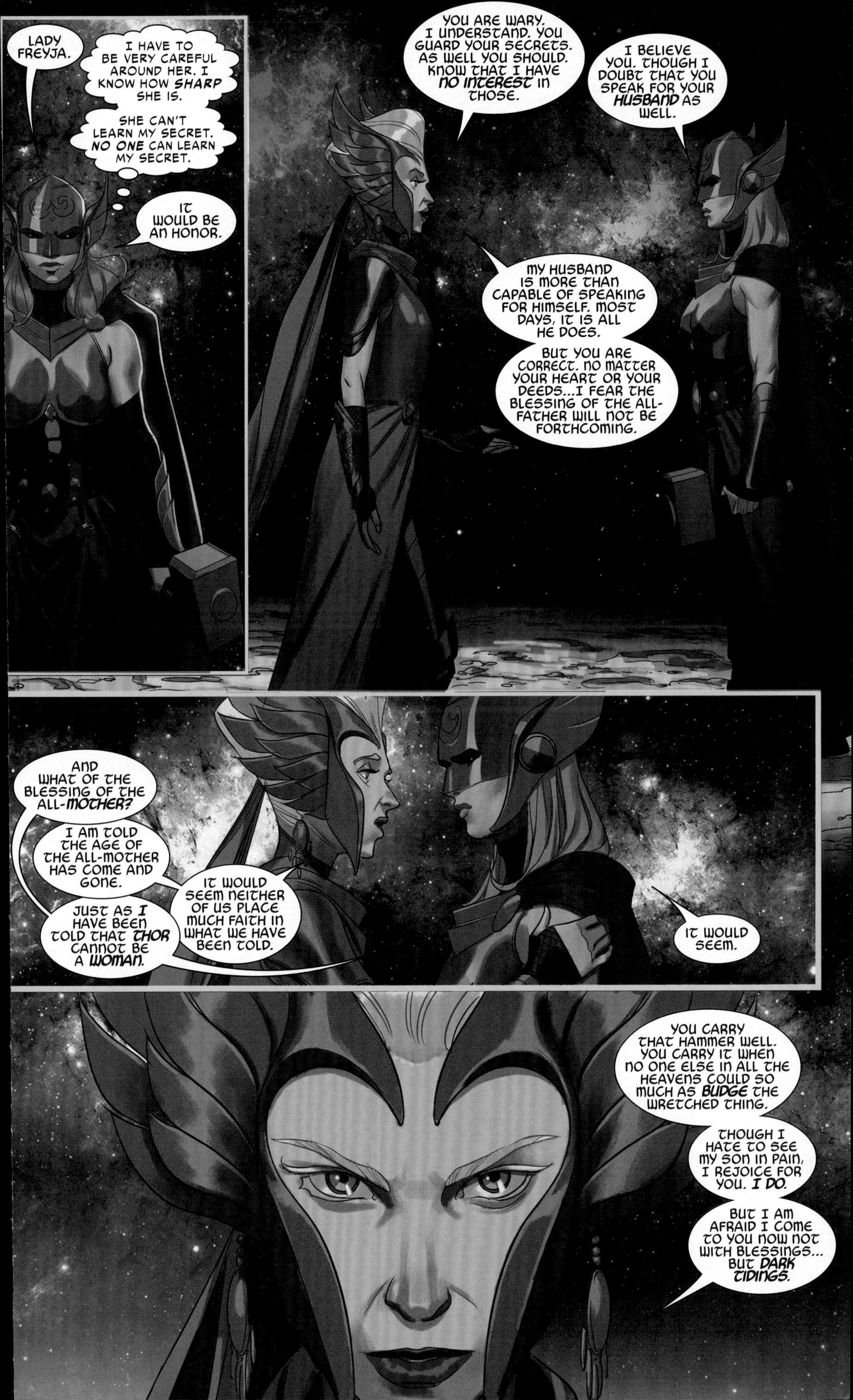
LADY FREYJA.
I HAVE TO BE VERY CAREFUL AROUND HER. I KNOW HOW SHARP SHE IS.
SHE CAN'T LEARN MY SECRET. NO ONE CAN LEARN MY SECRET.
IT WOULD BE AN HONOR.
YOU ARE WARY. I UNDERSTAND. YOU GUARD YOUR SECRETS. AS WELL YOU SHOULD. KNOW THAT I HAVE NO INTEREST IN THOSE.
I BELIEVE YOU. THOUGH I DOUBT THAT YOU SPEAK FOR YOUR HUSBAND AS WELL.
MY HUSBAND IS MORE THAN CAPABLE OF SPEAKING FOR HIMSELF. MOST DAYS, IT IS ALL HE DOES.
BUT YOU ARE CORRECT. NO MATTER YOUR HEART OR YOUR DEEDS...I FEAR THE BLESSING OF THE ALL-FATHER WILL NOT BE FORTHCOMING.
AND WHAT OF THE BLESSING OF THE ALL-MOTHER?
I AM TOLD THE AGE OF THE ALL-MOTHER HAS COME AND GONE.
JUST AS I HAVE BEEN TOLD THAT THOR CANNOT BE A WOMAN.
IT WOULD SEEM NEITHER OF US PLACE MUCH FAITH IN WHAT WE HAVE BEEN TOLD.
IT WOULD SEEM.
YOU CARRY THAT HAMMER WELL. YOU CARRY IT WHEN NO ONE ELSE IN ALL THE HEAVENS COULD SO MUCH AS BUDGE THE WRETCHED THING.
THOUGH I HATE TO SEE MY SON IN PAIN, I REJOICE FOR YOU. I DO.
BUT I AM AFRAID I COME TO YOU NOW NOT WITH BLESSINGS... BUT DARK TIDINGS.

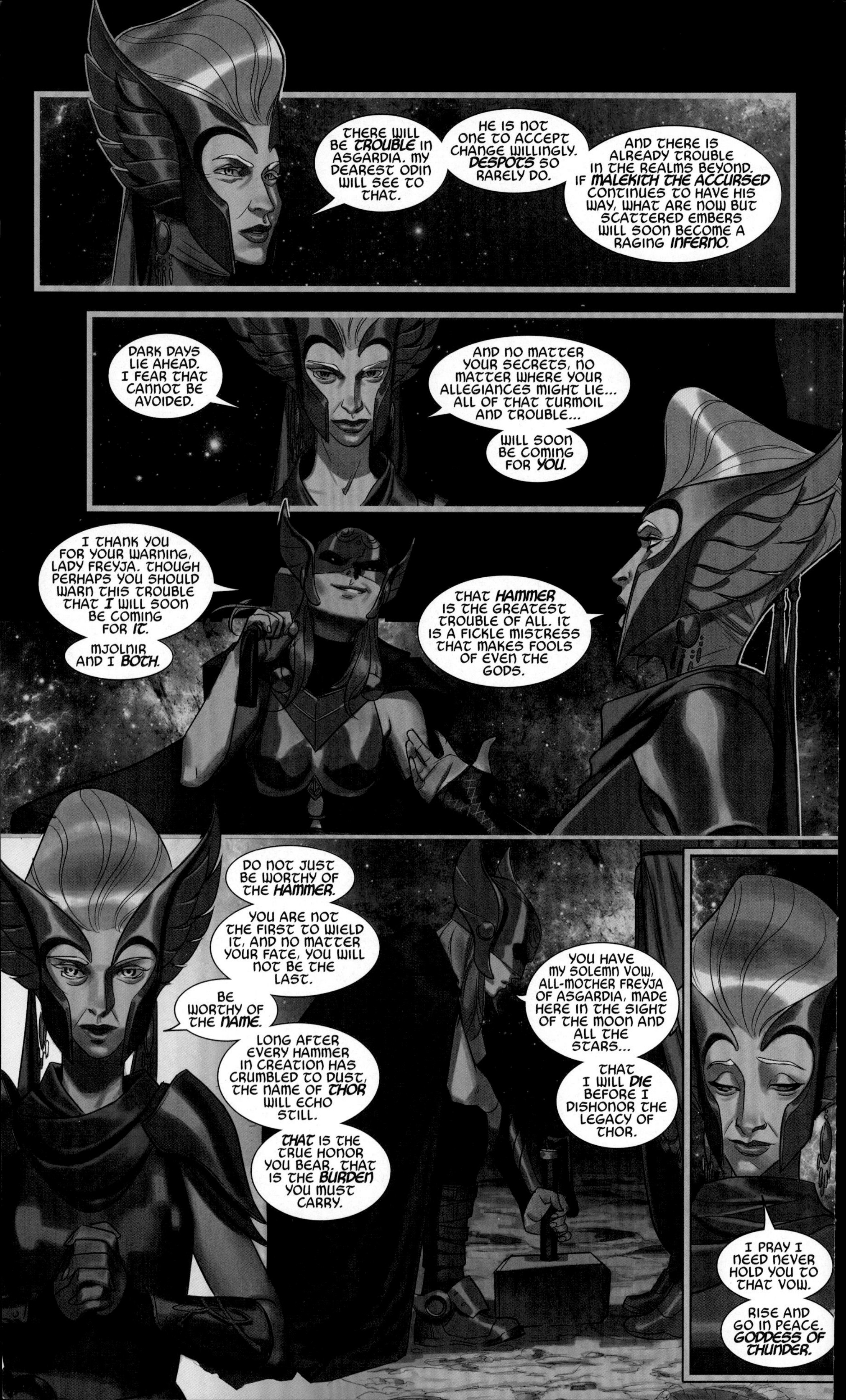
THERE WILL BE TROUBLE IN ASGARDIA. MY DEAREST ODIN WILL SEE TO THAT.
HE IS NOT ONE TO ACCEPT CHANGE WILLINGLY. DESPOTS SO RARELY DO.
AND THERE IS ALREADY TROUBLE IN THE REALMS BEYOND. IF MALEKITH THE ACCURSED CONTINUES TO HAVE HIS WAY, WHAT ARE NOW BUT SCATTERED EMBERS WILL SOON BECOME A RAGING INFERNO.
DARK DAYS LIE AHEAD. I FEAR THAT CANNOT BE AVOIDED.
AND NO MATTER YOUR SECRETS, NO MATTER WHERE YOUR ALLEGIANCES MIGHT LIE... ALL OF THAT TURMOIL AND TROUBLE...
WILL SOON BE COMING FOR YOU.
I THANK YOU FOR YOUR WARNING, LADY FREYJA. THOUGH PERHAPS YOU SHOULD WARN THIS TROUBLE THAT I WILL SOON BE COMING FOR IT.
MJOLNIR AND I BOTH.
THAT HAMMER IS THE GREATEST TROUBLE OF ALL. IT IS A FICKLE MISTRESS THAT MAKES FOOLS OF EVEN THE GODS.
DO NOT JUST BE WORTHY OF THE HAMMER.
YOU ARE NOT THE FIRST TO WIELD IT, AND NO MATTER YOUR FATE, YOU WILL NOT BE THE LAST.
BE WORTHY OF THE NAME.
LONG AFTER EVERY HAMMER IN CREATION HAS CRUMBLED TO DUST, THE NAME OF THOR WILL ECHO STILL.
THAT IS THE TRUE HONOR YOU BEAR. THAT IS THE BURDEN YOU MUST CARRY.
YOU HAVE MY SOLEMN VOW, ALL-MOTHER FREYJA OF ASGARDIA, MADE HERE IN THE SIGHT OF THE MOON AND ALL THE STARS...
THAT I WILL DIE BEFORE I DISHONOR THE LEGACY OF THOR.
I PRAY I NEED NEVER HOLD YOU TO THAT VOW.
RISE AND GO IN PEACE, GODDESS OF THUNDER.

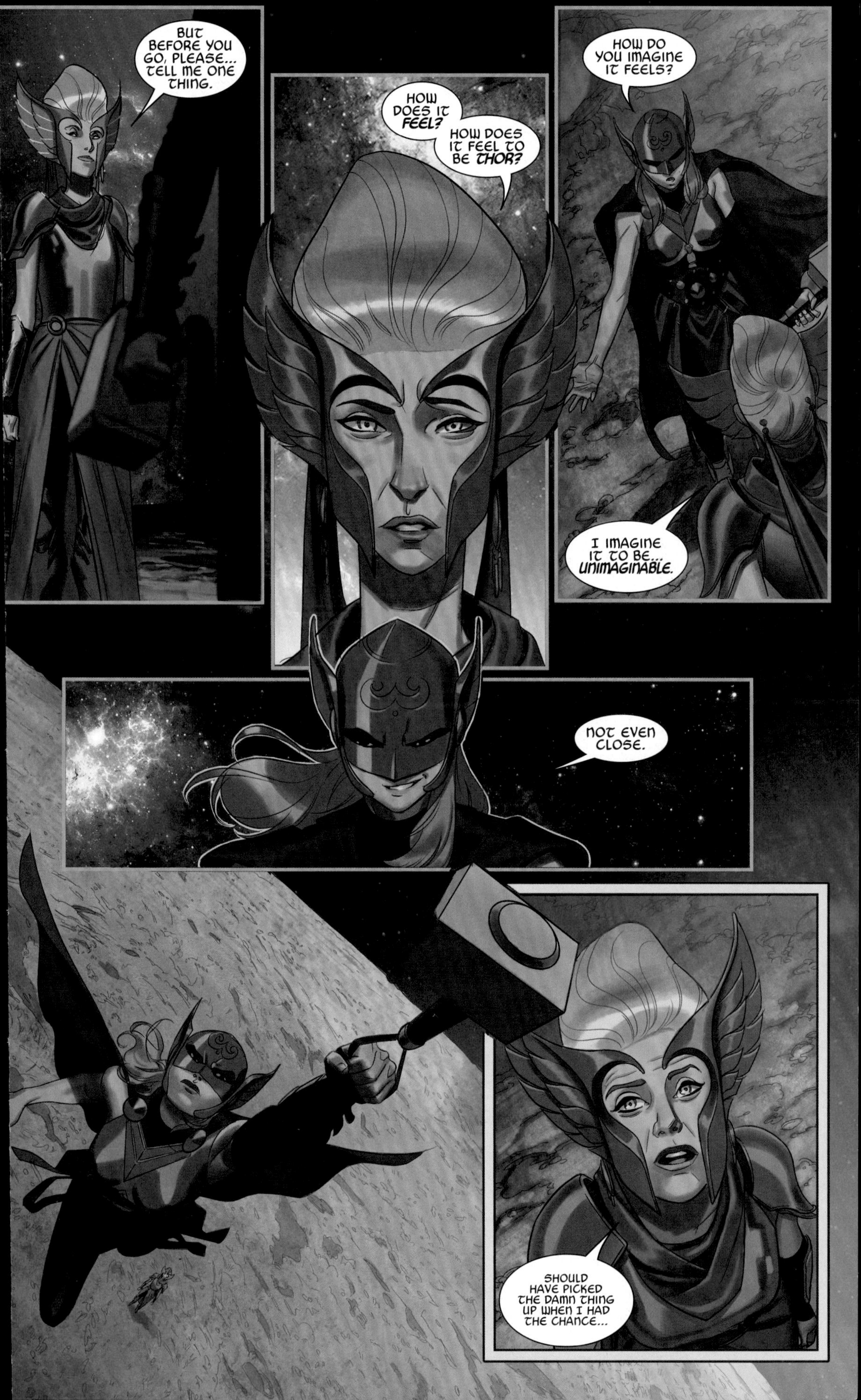
BUT BEFORE YOU GO, PLEASE... TELL ME ONE THING.
HOW DOES IT FEEL?
HOW DOES IT FEEL TO BE THOR?
HOW DO YOU IMAGINE IT FEELS?
I IMAGINE IT TO BE... UNIMAGINABLE.
NOT EVEN CLOSE.
SHOULD HAVE PICKED THE DAMN THING UP WHEN I HAD THE CHANCE...

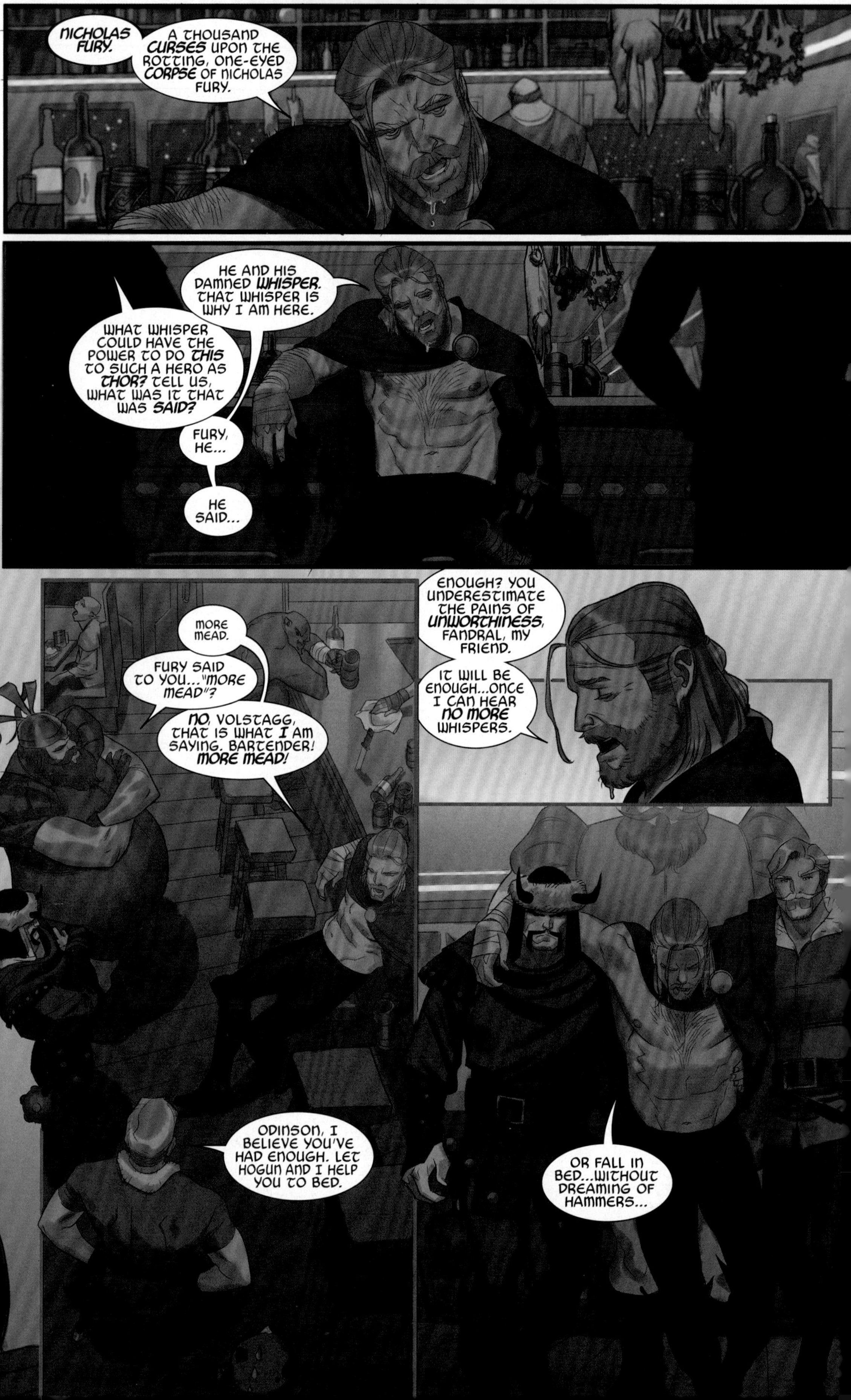
NICHOLAS FURY.
A THOUSAND CURSES UPON THE ROTTING, ONE-EYED CORPSE OF NICHOLAS FURY.
HE AND HIS DAMNED WHISPER. THAT WHISPER IS WHY I AM HERE.
WHAT WHISPER COULD HAVE THE POWER TO DO THIS TO SUCH A HERO AS THOR? TELL US, WHAT WAS IT THAT WAS SAID?
FURY, HE...
HE SAID...
MORE MEAD.
FURY SAID TO YOU..."MORE MEAD"?
NO, VOLSTAGG, THAT IS WHAT I AM SAYING. BARTENDER! MORE MEAD!
ODINSON, I BELIEVE YOU'VE HAD ENOUGH. LET HOGUN AND I HELP YOU TO BED.
ENOUGH? YOU UNDERESTIMATE THE PAINS OF UNWORTHINESS, FANDRAL, MY FRIEND.
IT WILL BE ENOUGH...ONCE I CAN HEAR NO MORE WHISPERS.
OR FALL IN BED...WITHOUT DREAMING OF HAMMERS...

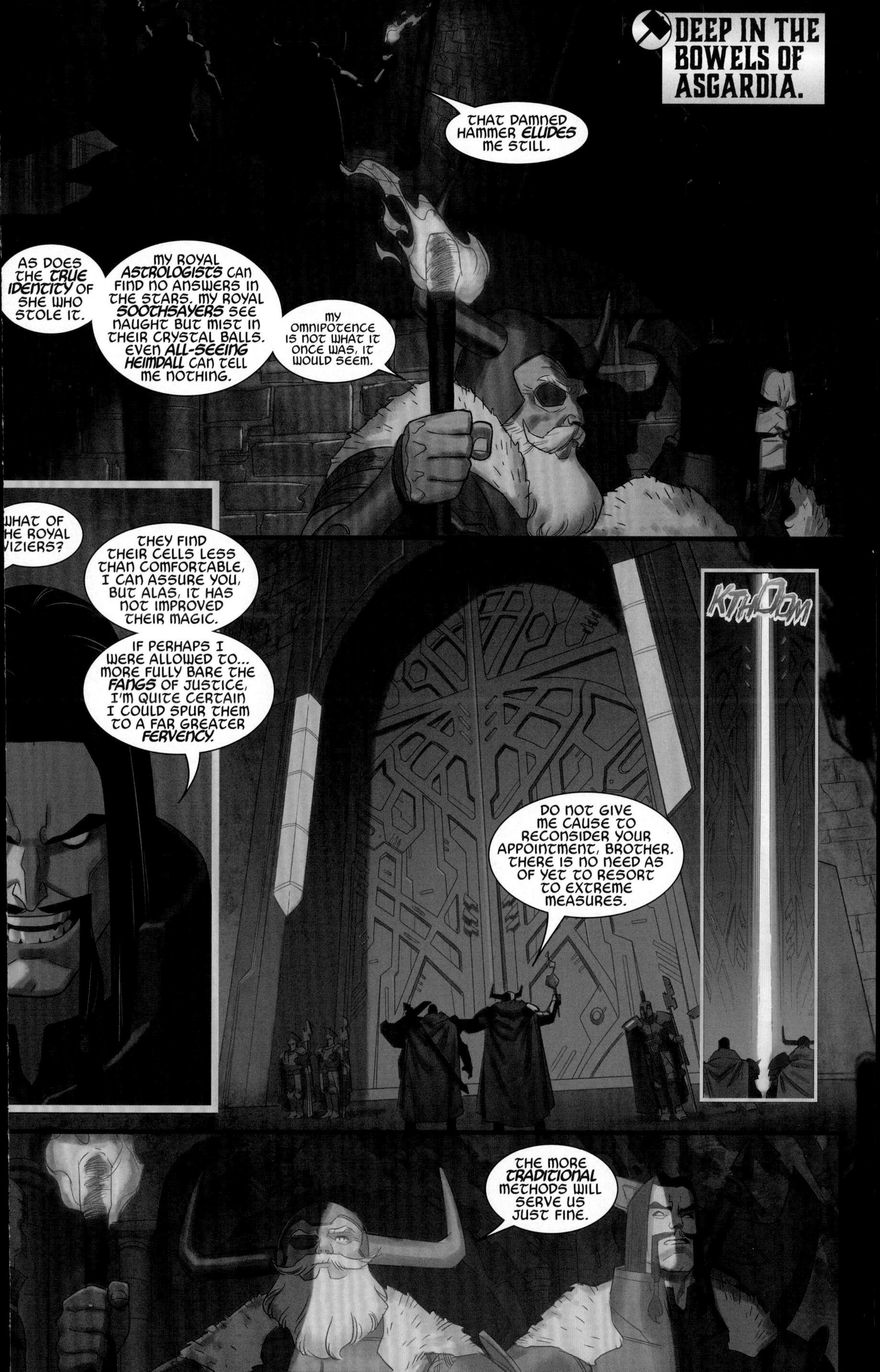
DEEP IN THE BOWELS OF ASGARDIA.
THAT DAMNED HAMMER ELUDES ME STILL.
AS DOES THE TRUE IDENTITY OF SHE WHO STOLE IT.
MY ROYAL ASTROLOGISTS CAN FIND NO ANSWERS IN THE STARS. MY ROYAL SOOTHSAYERS SEE NAUGHT BUT MIST IN THEIR CRYSTAL BALLS. EVEN ALL-SEEING HEIMDALL CAN TELL ME NOTHING.
MY OMNIPOTENCE IS NOT WHAT IT ONCE WAS, IT WOULD SEEM.
WHAT OF HE ROYAL VIZIERS?
THEY FIND THEIR CELLS LESS THAN COMFORTABLE, I CAN ASSURE YOU, BUT ALAS, IT HAS NOT IMPROVED THEIR MAGIC.
IF PERHAPS I WERE ALLOWED TO... MORE FULLY BARE THE FANGS OF JUSTICE, I'M QUITE CERTAIN I COULD SPUR THEM TO A FAR GREATER FERVENCY.
DO NOT GIVE ME CAUSE TO RECONSIDER YOUR APPOINTMENT, BROTHER. THERE IS NO NEED AS OF YET TO RESORT TO EXTREME MEASURES.
KTHOOM
THE MORE TRADITIONAL METHODS WILL SERVE US JUST FINE.

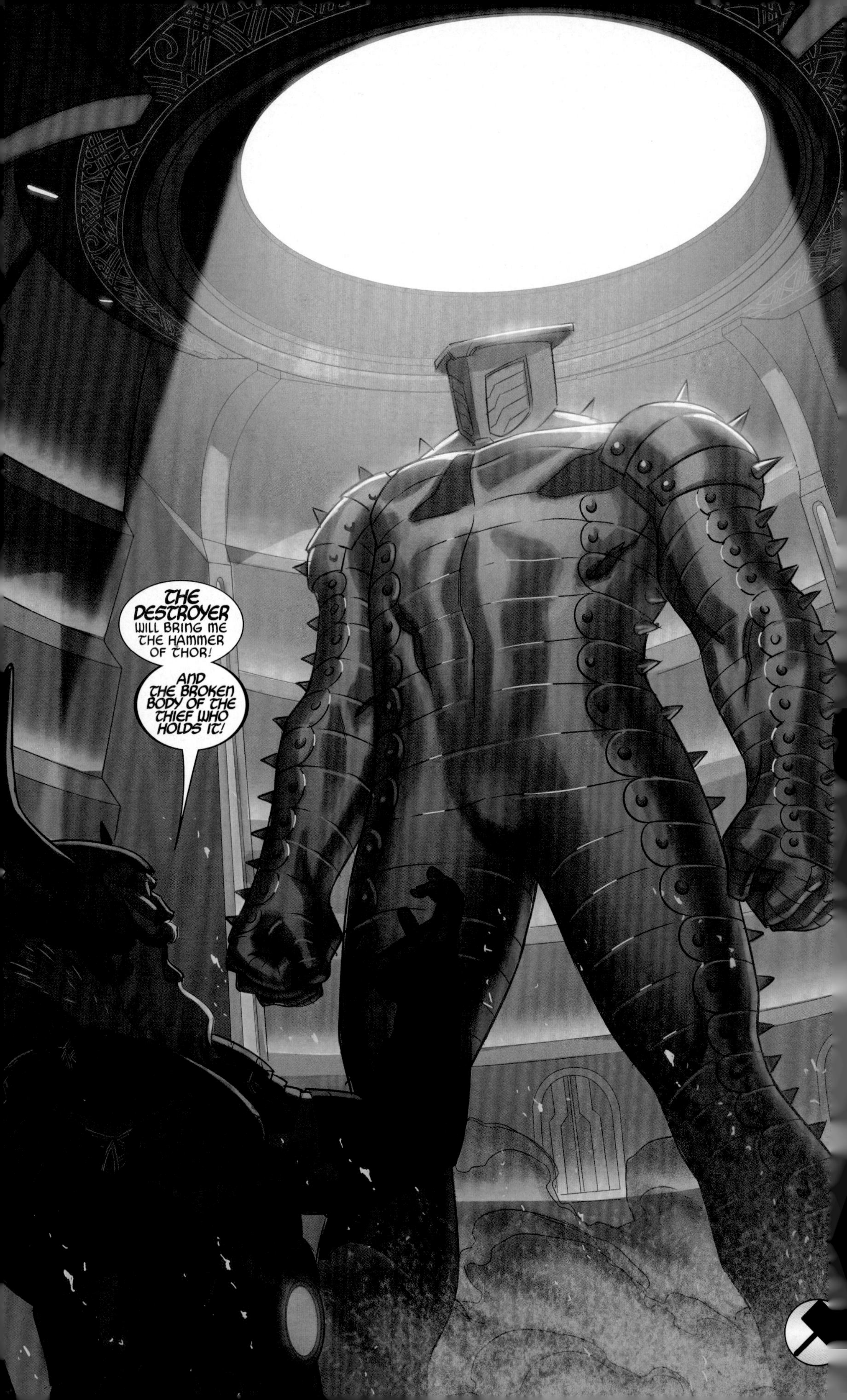
THE DESTROYER WILL BRING ME THE HAMMER OF THOR!
AND THE BROKEN BODY OF THE THIEF WHO HOLDS IT!

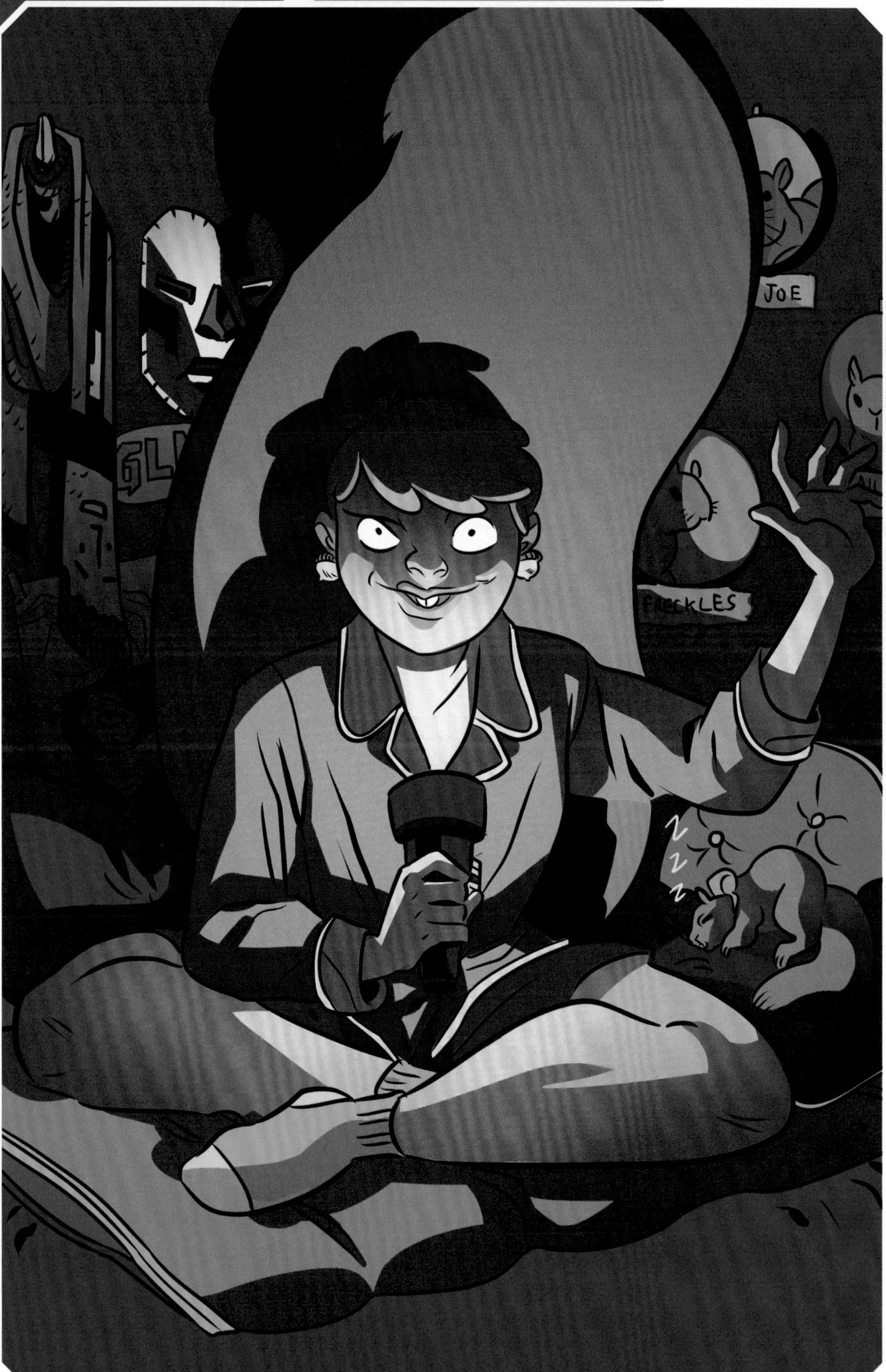
JOE
FRECKLES
Z Z Z

THE UNBEATABLE SQUIRREL GIRL #5

Doreen Green isn't just a first-year computer science student: she secretly also has all the powers of both squirrel and girl! She uses her amazing abilities to fight crime and as awesome as possible. You know her as...The Unbeatable Squirrel Girl! Let's catch up with what she's been up to until now, with...

# Squirrel Girl *in a nutshell*

**Squirrel Girl!** @unbeatablesg
@xGALACTUSx hey dude thanks for not eating the planet after all!!

**GALACTUS** @xGALACTUSx
@unbeatablesg NO PROBLEM THAT PLANET OF NUTS YOU FOUND WAS WAY BETTER ANYWAY

**Deadpool** @pooltothedead
@unbeatablesg @xGALACTUSx Wait, what? You guys weren't joking about that?

**Deadpool** @pooltothedead
@unbeatablesg @xGALACTUSx Galactus ACTUALLY came to Earth?? Yesterday? The ACTUAL GALACTUS was HERE??

**Deadpool** @pooltothedead
@unbeatablesg @xGALACTUSx dang man I spent the whole day at home watching tv in my underpants

**Deadpool** @pooltothedead
@unbeatablesg @xGALACTUSx CALL ME NEXT TIME!!

**Tony Stark** @starkmantony
A bunch of my Iron Man suit parts showed up in NYC with moon dust on them. That's actually extremely valuable, so thanks @unbeatablesg.

**Tippy-Toe** @yoitstippytoe
@starkmantony CHITT CHUK CHITTT?

**Tony Stark** @starkmantony
@yoitstippytoe I can't understand you. None of my translation algorithms can understand you. Probably because you are a literal squirrel.

**Tippy-Toe** @yoitstippytoe
@starkmantony CHUKKA.... CHITT CHUK CHITTT?

**Tony Stark** @starkmantony
@unbeatablesg Little help?

**Squirrel Girl!** @unbeatablesg
@starkmantony she's asking you if you figured out that the dust came from the new moon restaurant

**Tony Stark** @starkmantony
@unbeatablesg @yoitstippytoe What new moon restaurant?

**Tippy-Toe** @yoitstippytoe
@starkmantony CHUTT CHUK CHUKK CHITTY CHIT

**Squirrel Girl!** @unbeatablesg
@starkmantony She says "The one that just opened up! The food's good, but it doesn't have much of an ATMOSPHERE"

**Squirrel Girl!** @unbeatablesg
@starkmantony hahaha, that's pretty good actually!! good work @yoitstippytoe

**Tony Stark** @starkmantony
@unbeatablesg @yoitstippytoe You guys know I'm the head of a major corporation, right?

**Tony Stark** @starkmantony
@unbeatablesg @yoitstippytoe I shouldn't even be hanging out here as it is

**Nancy W.** @sewwiththeflo
I bet being covered from head to toe in a living squirrel suit doesn't smell as bad as you think it would.

**Nancy W.** @sewwiththeflo
IMPORTANT UPDATE:

**Nancy W.** @sewwiththeflo
So it turns out being covered head to toe in a living squirrel suit doesn't smell as GOOD as you think it would either

**search!**

#dinosaurs
#basslass
#clones
#acronyms
#nuthorde
#TIPPPPPPPY!!


Ryan North - writer
Erica Henderson - artist
Rico Renzi &
Erica Henderson - color artists
VC's Clayton Cowles - lettere
Erica Henderson - cover artist
Jon Moisan - assistant editor
Wil Moss - editor
Tom Brevoort - executive edito
Axel Alonso - editor in chief
Joe Quesada - chief creative offic
Dan Buckley - publisher
Alan Fine - exec. producer

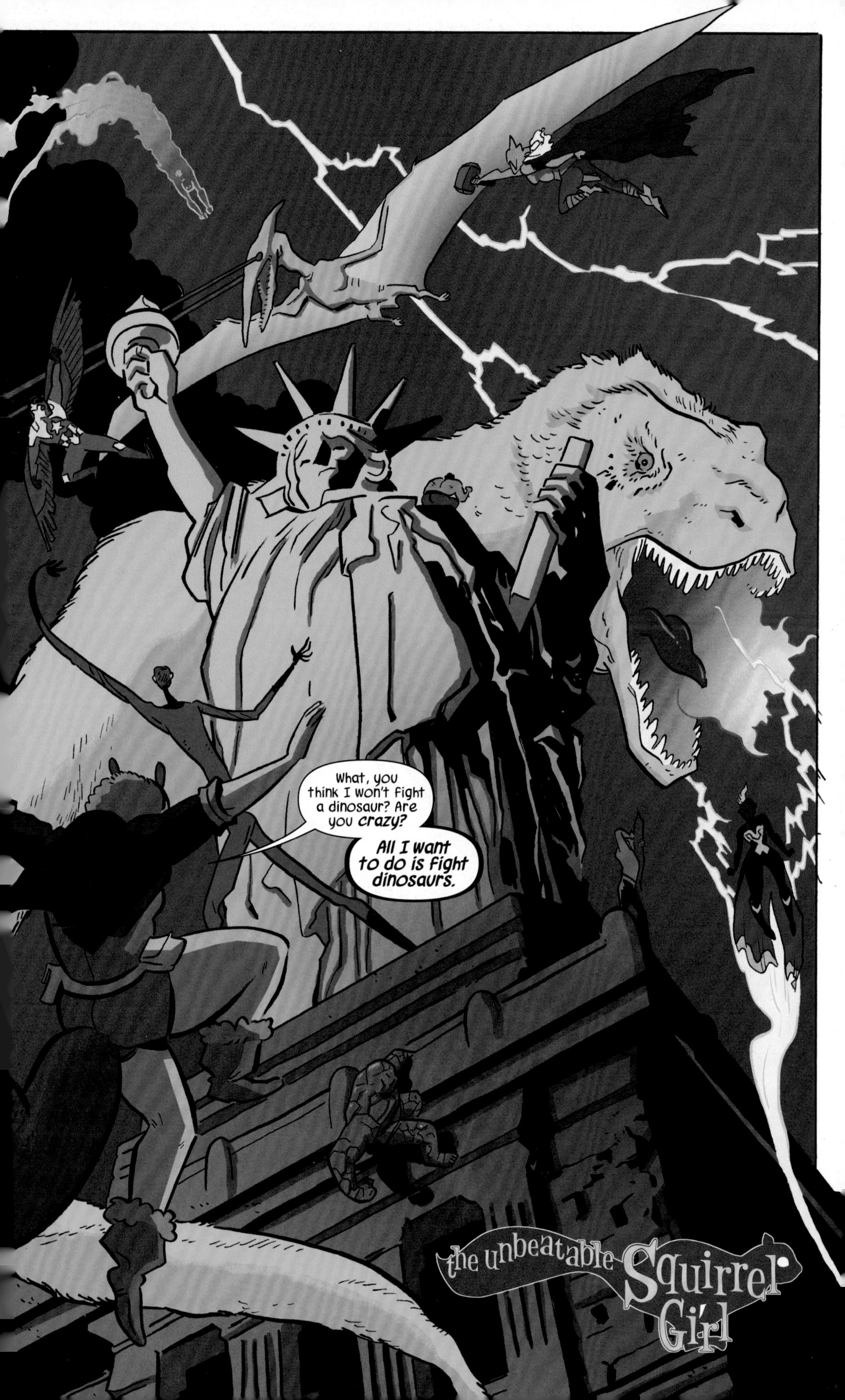
What, you think I won't fight a dinosaur? Are you *crazy?*
**All I want to do is fight dinosaurs.**
the unbeatable Squirrel Girl

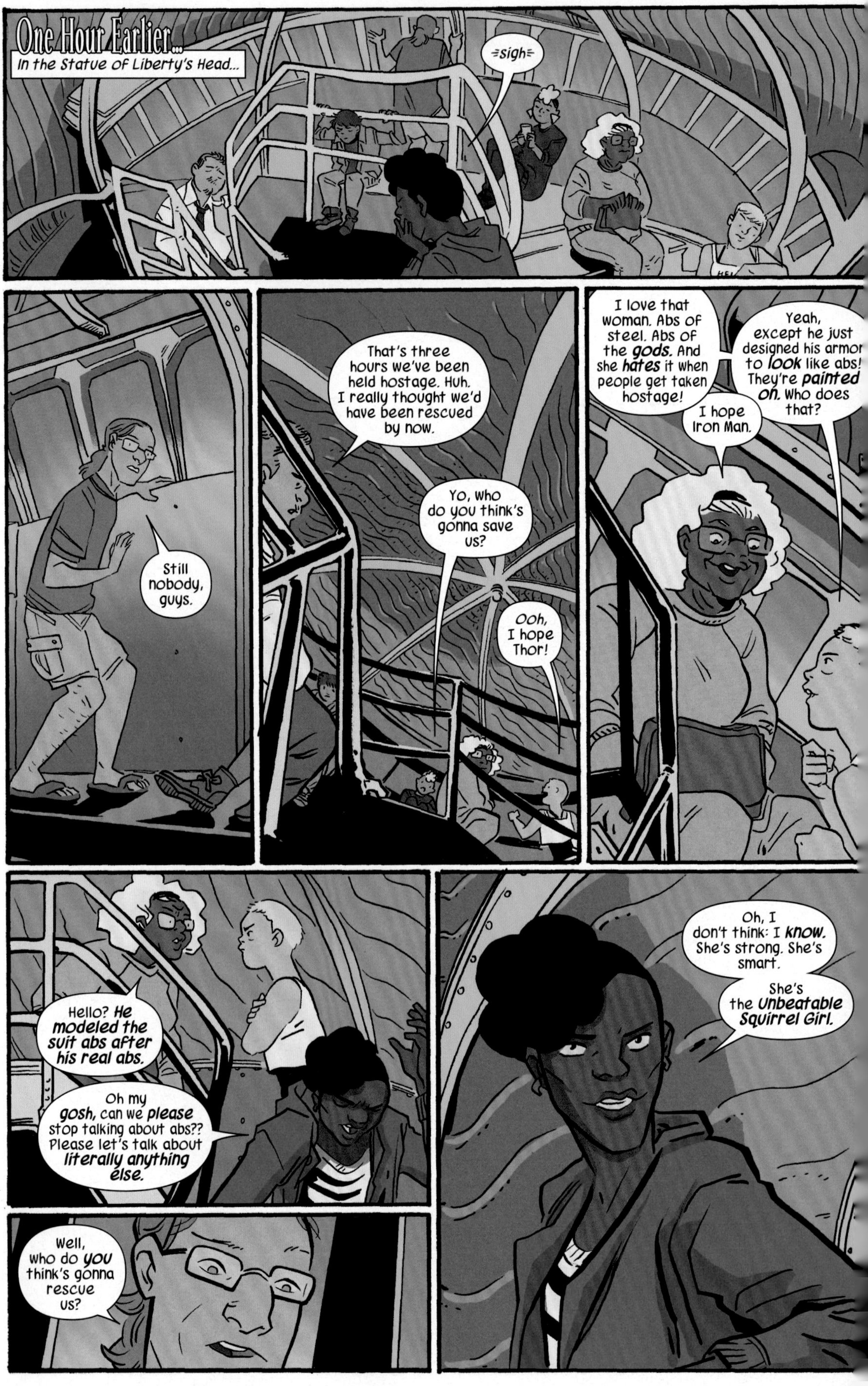
One Hour Earlier...
In the Statue of Liberty's Head...
=sigh=
Still nobody, guys.
That's three hours we've been held hostage. Huh. I really thought we'd have been rescued by now.
Yo, who do you think's gonna save us?
Ooh, I hope Thor!
I hope Iron Man.
I love that woman. Abs of steel. Abs of the gods. And she hates it when people get taken hostage!
Yeah, except he just designed his armor to look like abs! They're painted on. Who does that?
Hello? He modeled the suit abs after his real abs.
Oh my gosh, can we please stop talking about abs?? Please let's talk about literally anything else.
Well, who do you think's gonna rescue us?
Oh, I don't think: I know. She's strong. She's smart.
She's the Unbeatable Squirrel Girl.

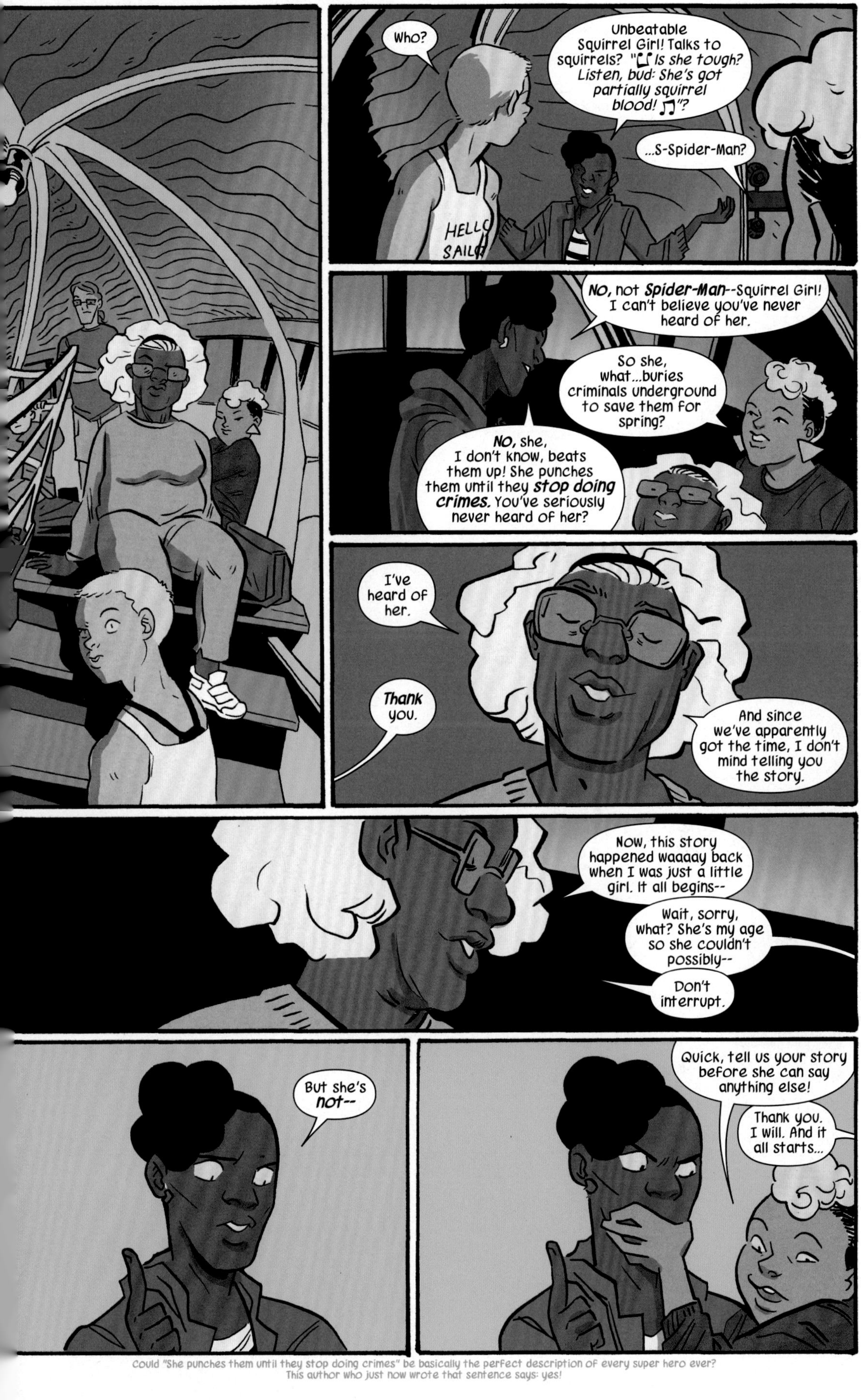
Who?
Unbeatable Squirrel Girl! Talks to squirrels? "♫ Is she tough? Listen, bud: She's got partially squirrel blood! ♫"?
...S-Spider-Man?
HELLO SAILO
NO, not Spider-Man--Squirrel Girl! I can't believe you've never heard of her.
So she, what...buries criminals underground to save them for spring?
NO, she, I don't know, beats them up! She punches them until they stop doing crimes. You've seriously never heard of her?
I've heard of her.
Thank you.
And since we've apparently got the time, I don't mind telling you the story.
Now, this story happened waaaay back when I was just a little girl. It all begins--
Wait, sorry, what? She's my age so she couldn't possibly--
Don't interrupt.
But she's not--
Quick, tell us your story before she can say anything else!
Thank you. I will. And it all starts...

Could "She punches them until they stop doing crimes" be basically the perfect description of every super hero ever?
This author who just now wrote that sentence says: yes!

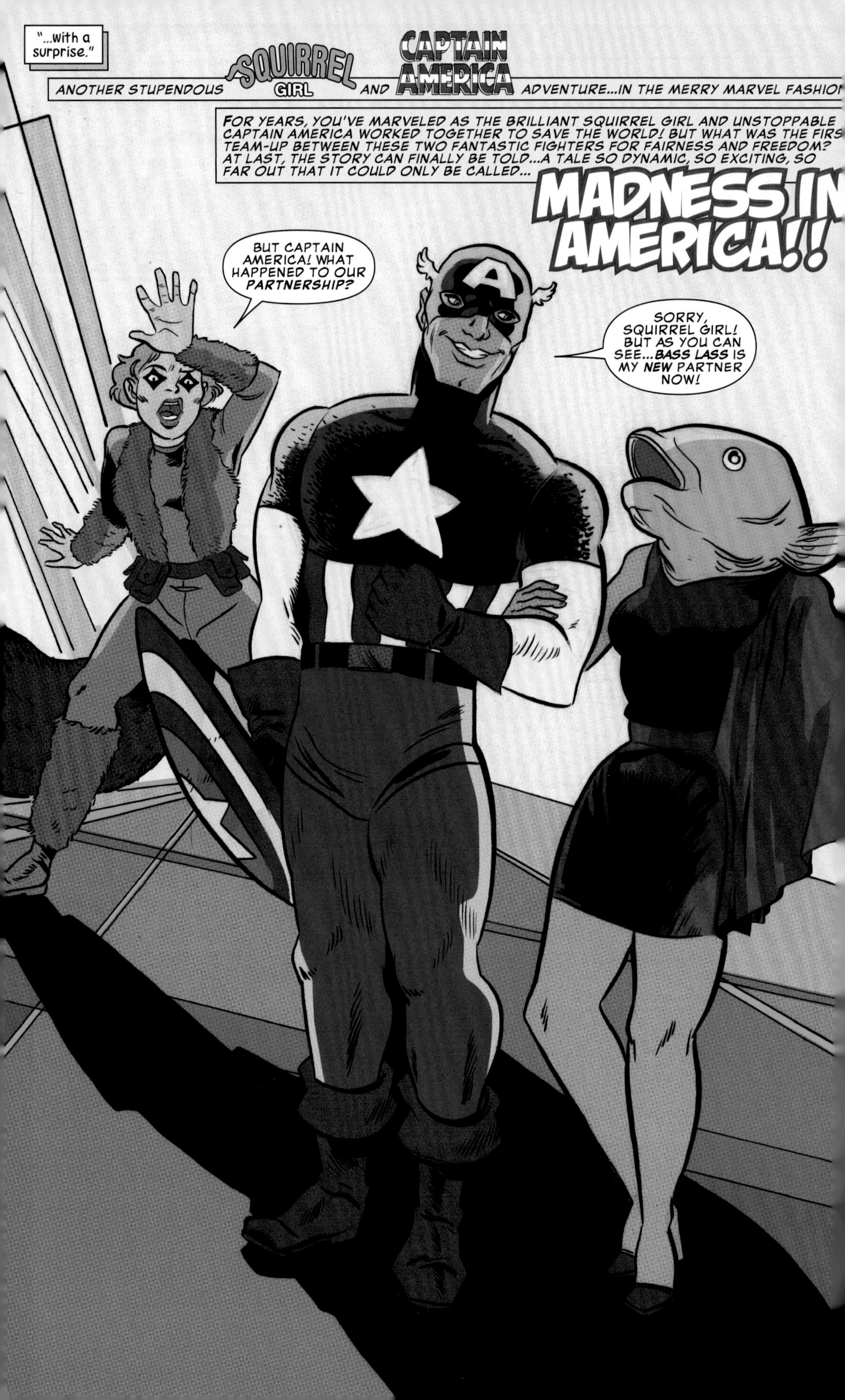
"...with a surprise."
ANOTHER STUPENDOUS SQUIRREL GIRL AND CAPTAIN AMERICA ADVENTURE...IN THE MERRY MARVEL FASHION
FOR YEARS, YOU'VE MARVELED AS THE BRILLIANT SQUIRREL GIRL AND UNSTOPPABLE CAPTAIN AMERICA WORKED TOGETHER TO SAVE THE WORLD! BUT WHAT WAS THE FIRS TEAM-UP BETWEEN THESE TWO FANTASTIC FIGHTERS FOR FAIRNESS AND FREEDOM? AT LAST, THE STORY CAN FINALLY BE TOLD...A TALE SO DYNAMIC, SO EXCITING, SO FAR OUT THAT IT COULD ONLY BE CALLED...
MADNESS IN AMERICA!!
BUT CAPTAIN AMERICA! WHAT HAPPENED TO OUR PARTNERSHIP?
SORRY, SQUIRREL GIRL! BUT AS YOU CAN SEE...BASS LASS IS MY NEW PARTNER NOW!

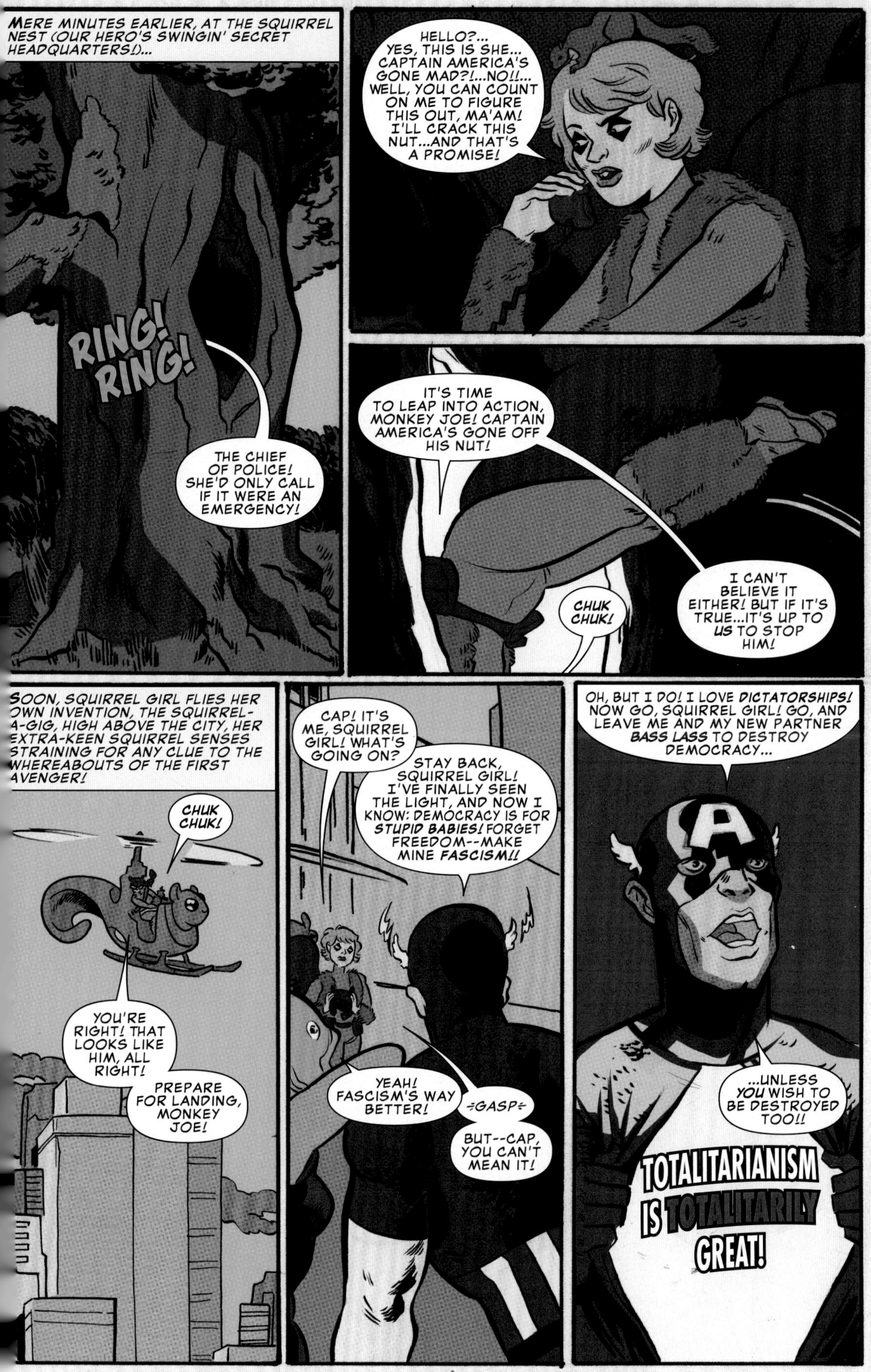
MERE MINUTES EARLIER, AT THE SQUIRREL NEST (OUR HERO'S SWINGIN' SECRET HEADQUARTERS!)...
RING! RING!
THE CHIEF OF POLICE! SHE'D ONLY CALL IF IT WERE AN EMERGENCY!
HELLO?... YES, THIS IS SHE... CAPTAIN AMERICA'S GONE MAD?!...NO!!... WELL, YOU CAN COUNT ON ME TO FIGURE THIS OUT, MA'AM! I'LL CRACK THIS NUT...AND THAT'S A PROMISE!
IT'S TIME TO LEAP INTO ACTION, MONKEY JOE! CAPTAIN AMERICA'S GONE OFF HIS NUT!
CHUK CHUK!
I CAN'T BELIEVE IT EITHER! BUT IF IT'S TRUE...IT'S UP TO US TO STOP HIM!
SOON, SQUIRREL GIRL FLIES HER OWN INVENTION, THE SQUIRREL-A-GIG, HIGH ABOVE THE CITY, HER EXTRA-KEEN SQUIRREL SENSES STRAINING FOR ANY CLUE TO THE WHEREABOUTS OF THE FIRST AVENGER!
CHUK CHUK!
YOU'RE RIGHT! THAT LOOKS LIKE HIM, ALL RIGHT!
PREPARE FOR LANDING, MONKEY JOE!
CAP! IT'S ME, SQUIRREL GIRL! WHAT'S GOING ON?
STAY BACK, SQUIRREL GIRL! I'VE FINALLY SEEN THE LIGHT, AND NOW I KNOW: DEMOCRACY IS FOR STUPID BABIES! FORGET FREEDOM--MAKE MINE FASCISM!!
YEAH! FASCISM'S WAY BETTER!
GASP
BUT--CAP, YOU CAN'T MEAN IT!
OH, BUT I DO! I LOVE DICTATORSHIPS! NOW GO, SQUIRREL GIRL! GO, AND LEAVE ME AND MY NEW PARTNER BASS LASS TO DESTROY DEMOCRACY...
...UNLESS YOU WISH TO BE DESTROYED TOO!!
TOTALITARIANISM IS TOTALITARILY GREAT!

Wait, wait!! Finish reading this comic before you run off to smash the state! There's a small chance that Captain America is wrong here!

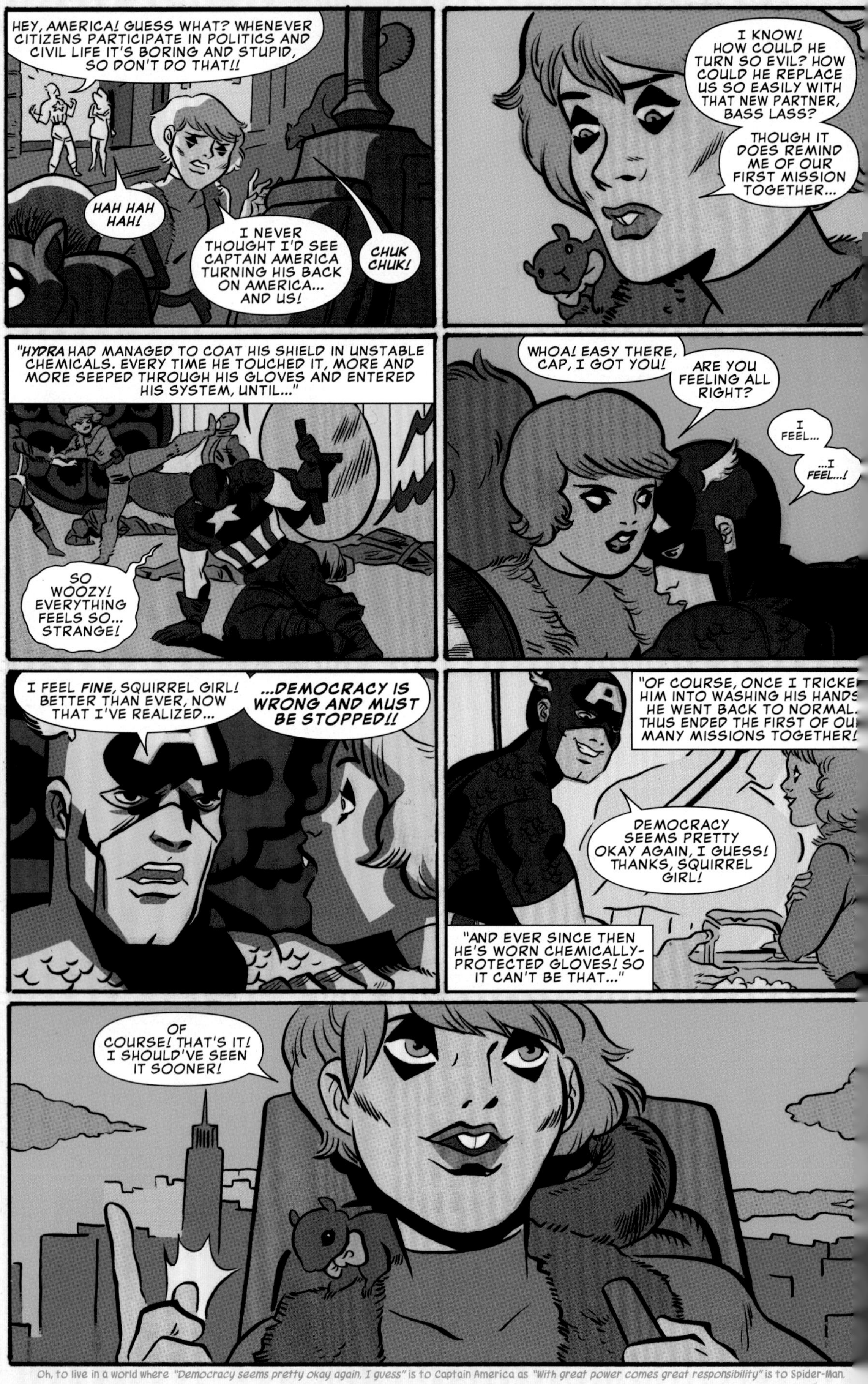
HEY, AMERICA! GUESS WHAT? WHENEVER CITIZENS PARTICIPATE IN POLITICS AND CIVIL LIFE IT'S BORING AND STUPID, SO DON'T DO THAT!!
HAH HAH HAH!
I NEVER THOUGHT I'D SEE CAPTAIN AMERICA TURNING HIS BACK ON AMERICA... AND US!
CHUK CHUK!
I KNOW! HOW COULD HE TURN SO EVIL? HOW COULD HE REPLACE US SO EASILY WITH THAT NEW PARTNER, BASS LASS?
THOUGH IT DOES REMIND ME OF OUR FIRST MISSION TOGETHER...
"HYDRA HAD MANAGED TO COAT HIS SHIELD IN UNSTABLE CHEMICALS. EVERY TIME HE TOUCHED IT, MORE AND MORE SEEPED THROUGH HIS GLOVES AND ENTERED HIS SYSTEM, UNTIL..."
SO WOOZY! EVERYTHING FEELS SO... STRANGE!
WHOA! EASY THERE, CAP, I GOT YOU!
ARE YOU FEELING ALL RIGHT?
I FEEL...
...I FEEL...!
I FEEL FINE, SQUIRREL GIRL! BETTER THAN EVER, NOW THAT I'VE REALIZED...
...DEMOCRACY IS WRONG AND MUST BE STOPPED!!
"OF COURSE, ONCE I TRICKED HIM INTO WASHING HIS HANDS HE WENT BACK TO NORMAL. THUS ENDED THE FIRST OF OUR MANY MISSIONS TOGETHER!
DEMOCRACY SEEMS PRETTY OKAY AGAIN, I GUESS! THANKS, SQUIRREL GIRL!
"AND EVER SINCE THEN HE'S WORN CHEMICALLY-PROTECTED GLOVES! SO IT CAN'T BE THAT..."
OF COURSE! THAT'S IT! I SHOULD'VE SEEN IT SOONER!

Oh, to live in a world where *"Democracy seems pretty okay again, I guess"* is to Captain America as *"With great power comes great responsibility"* is to Spider-Man.

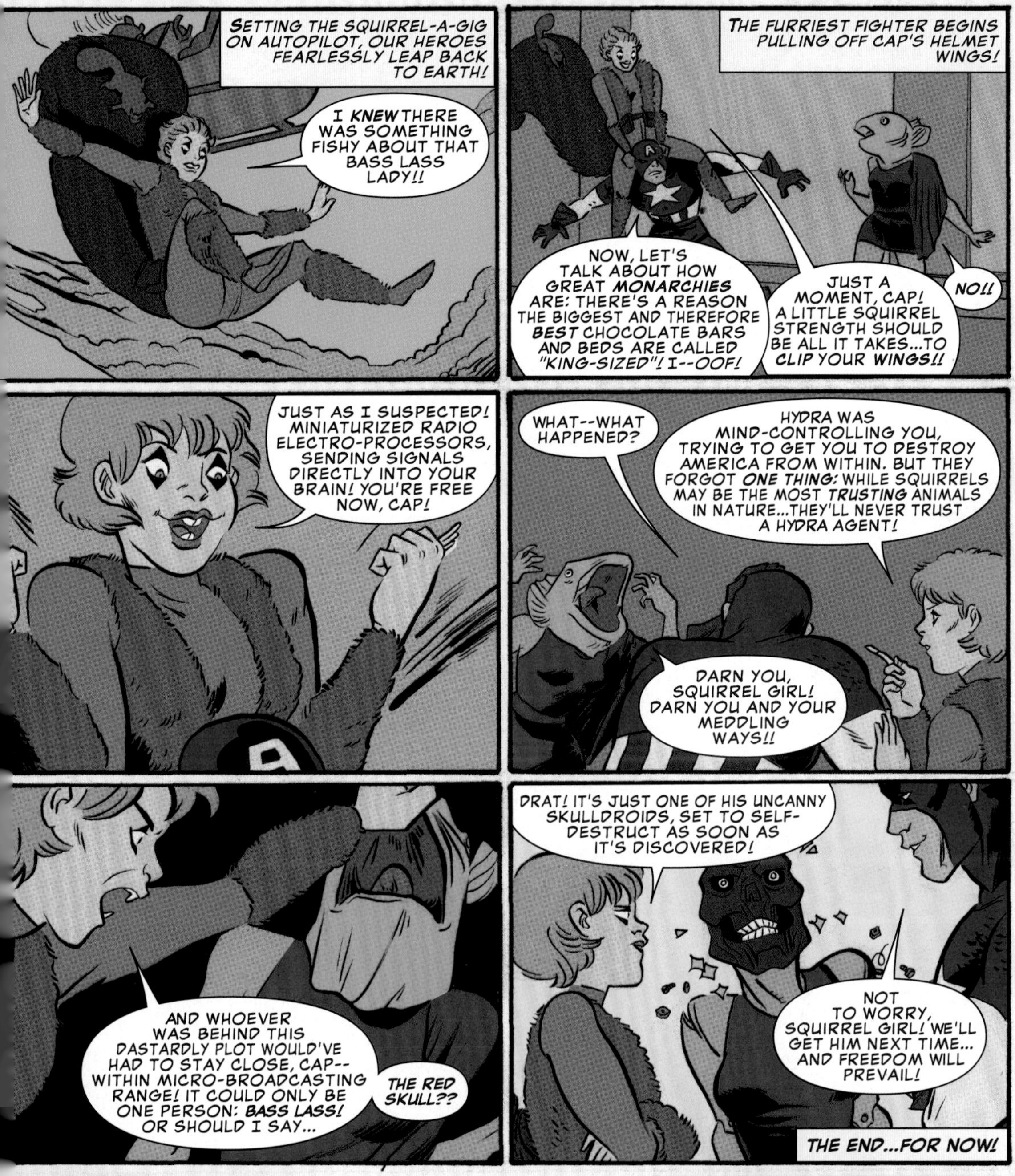
SETTING THE SQUIRREL-A-GIG ON AUTOPILOT, OUR HEROES FEARLESSLY LEAP BACK TO EARTH!
I KNEW THERE WAS SOMETHING FISHY ABOUT THAT BASS LASS LADY!!
THE FURRIEST FIGHTER BEGINS PULLING OFF CAP'S HELMET WINGS!
NOW, LET'S TALK ABOUT HOW GREAT MONARCHIES ARE: THERE'S A REASON THE BIGGEST AND THEREFORE BEST CHOCOLATE BARS AND BEDS ARE CALLED "KING-SIZED"! I--OOF!
JUST A MOMENT, CAP! A LITTLE SQUIRREL STRENGTH SHOULD BE ALL IT TAKES...TO CLIP YOUR WINGS!!
NO!!
JUST AS I SUSPECTED! MINIATURIZED RADIO ELECTRO-PROCESSORS, SENDING SIGNALS DIRECTLY INTO YOUR BRAIN! YOU'RE FREE NOW, CAP!
WHAT--WHAT HAPPENED?
HYDRA WAS MIND-CONTROLLING YOU, TRYING TO GET YOU TO DESTROY AMERICA FROM WITHIN. BUT THEY FORGOT ONE THING: WHILE SQUIRRELS MAY BE THE MOST TRUSTING ANIMALS IN NATURE...THEY'LL NEVER TRUST A HYDRA AGENT!
DARN YOU, SQUIRREL GIRL! DARN YOU AND YOUR MEDDLING WAYS!!
AND WHOEVER WAS BEHIND THIS DASTARDLY PLOT WOULD'VE HAD TO STAY CLOSE, CAP-- WITHIN MICRO-BROADCASTING RANGE! IT COULD ONLY BE ONE PERSON: BASS LASS! OR SHOULD I SAY...
THE RED SKULL??
DRAT! IT'S JUST ONE OF HIS UNCANNY SKULLDROIDS, SET TO SELF-DESTRUCT AS SOON AS IT'S DISCOVERED!
NOT TO WORRY, SQUIRREL GIRL! WE'LL GET HIM NEXT TIME... AND FREEDOM WILL PREVAIL!
THE END...FOR NOW!

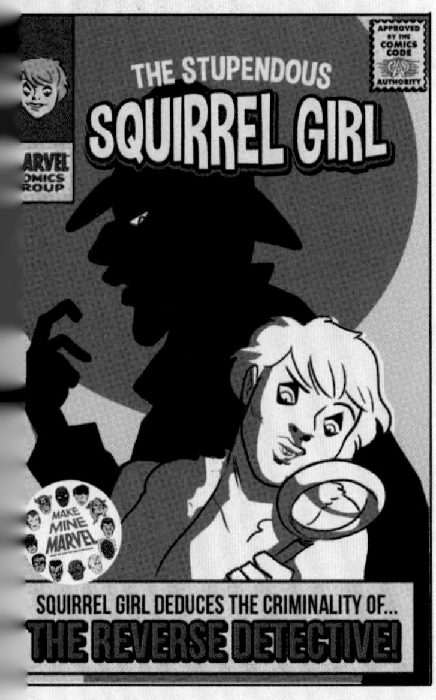
APPROVED BY THE COMICS CODE AUTHORITY
THE STUPENDOUS
SQUIRREL GIRL
MARVEL COMICS GROUP
MAKE MINE MARVEL
SQUIRREL GIRL DEDUCES THE CRIMINALITY OF...
THE REVERSE DETECTIVE!

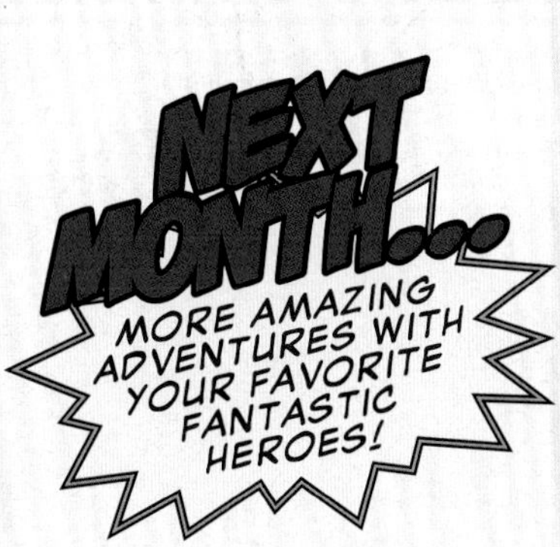
NEXT MONTH...
MORE AMAZING ADVENTURES WITH YOUR FAVORITE FANTASTIC HEROES!

In that comic, Captain America says "Stand down! That's an order, *Corporal.*" and then Corporal USA is all "Um yeah so the thing is, I think it's pretty clear we're both operating outside the traditional military chain of command here??"

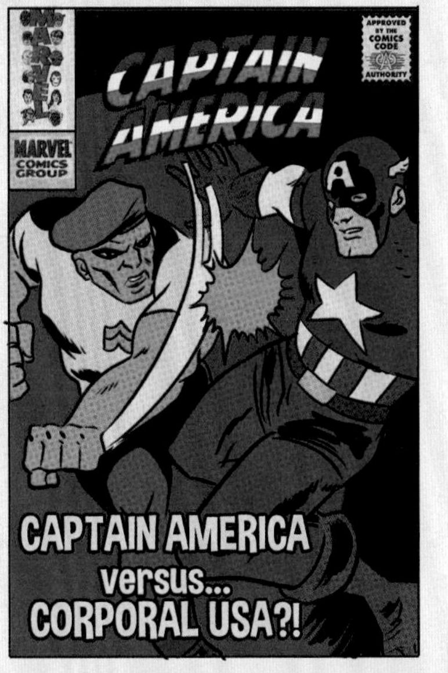
APPROVED BY THE COMICS CODE AUTHORITY
CAPTAIN AMERICA
MARVEL COMICS GROUP
CAPTAIN AMERICA versus... CORPORAL USA?!

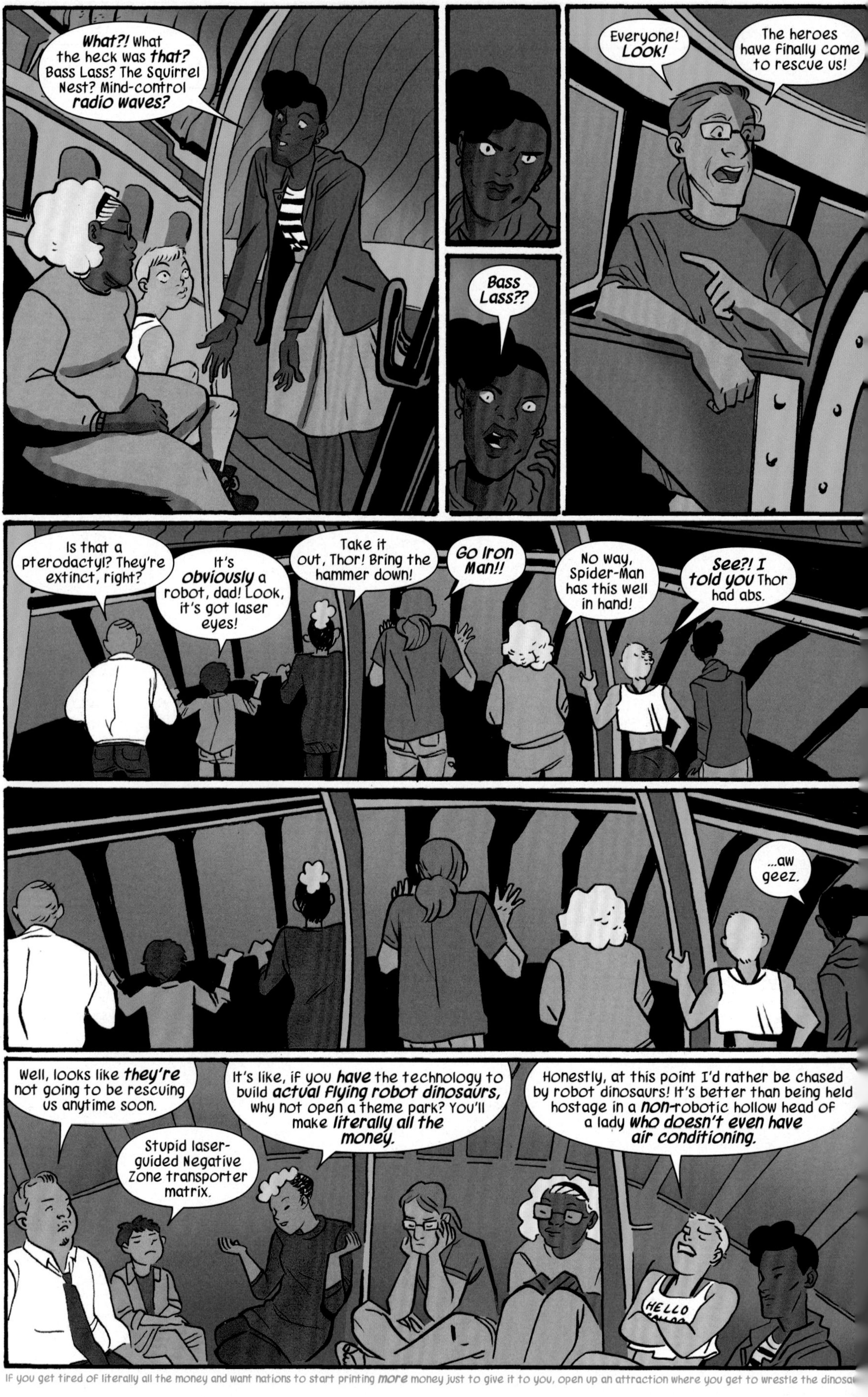
What?! What the heck was that? Bass Lass? The Squirrel Nest? Mind-control radio waves?
Bass Lass??
Everyone! Look!
The heroes have finally come to rescue us!
Is that a pterodactyl? They're extinct, right?
It's obviously a robot, dad! Look, it's got laser eyes!
Take it out, Thor! Bring the hammer down!
Go Iron Man!!
No way, Spider-Man has this well in hand!
See?! I told you Thor had abs.
...aw geez.
Well, looks like they're not going to be rescuing us anytime soon.
Stupid laser-guided Negative Zone transporter matrix.
It's like, if you have the technology to build actual flying robot dinosaurs, why not open a theme park? You'll make literally all the money.
Honestly, at this point I'd rather be chased by robot dinosaurs! It's better than being held hostage in a non-robotic hollow head of a lady who doesn't even have air conditioning.
HELLO

If you get tired of literally all the money and want nations to start printing *more* money just to give it to you, open up an attraction where you get to wrestle the dinosa

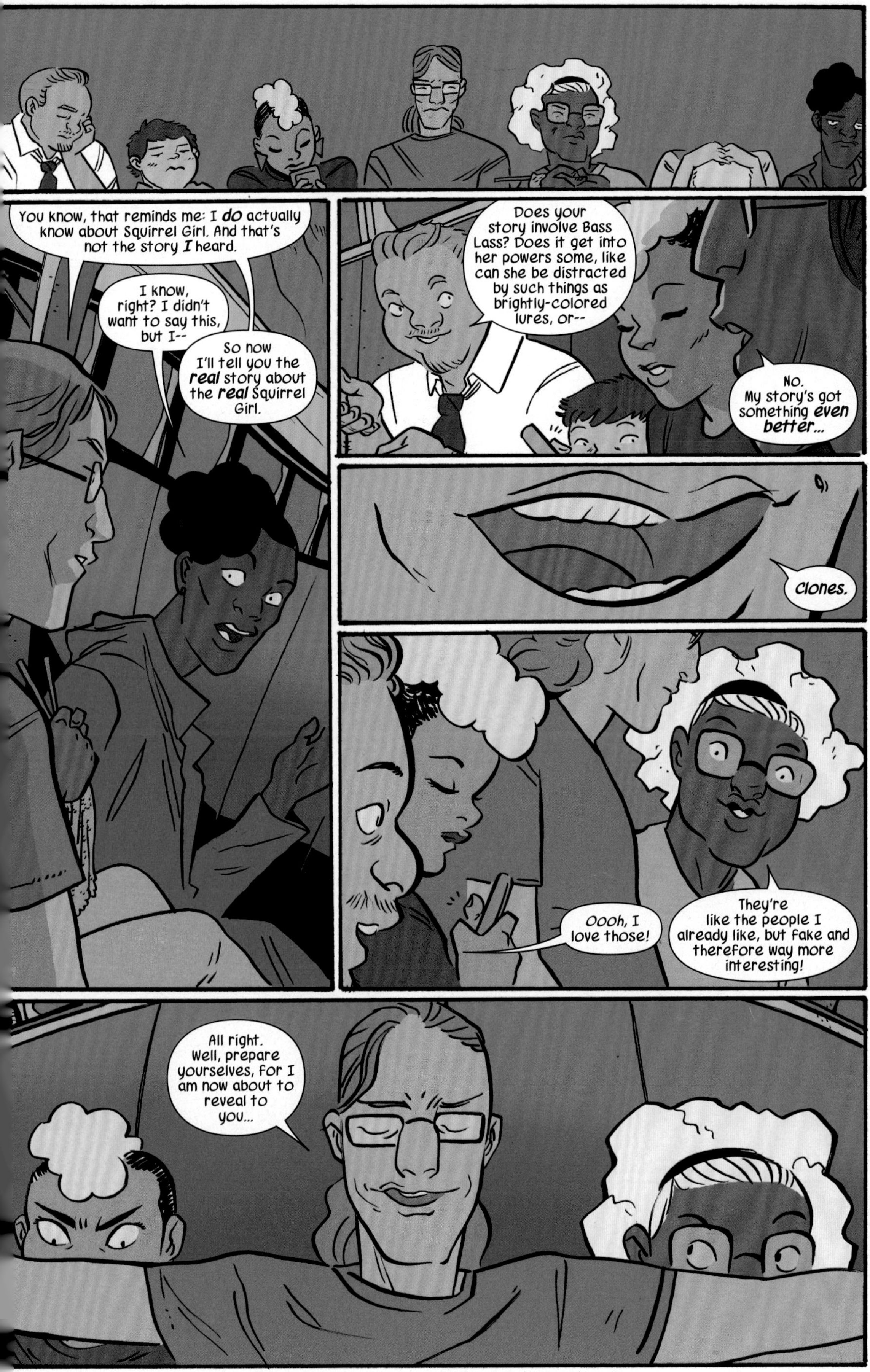
You know, that reminds me: I do actually know about Squirrel Girl. And that's not the story I heard.
I know, right? I didn't want to say this, but I--
So now I'll tell you the real story about the real Squirrel Girl.
Does your story involve Bass Lass? Does it get into her powers some, like can she be distracted by such things as brightly-colored lures, or--
No. My story's got something even better...
Clones.
They're like the people I already like, but fake and therefore way more interesting!
Oooh, I love those!
All right. Well, prepare yourselves, for I am now about to reveal to you...

...a story that if I were to give it a title I believe I would be forced to call...

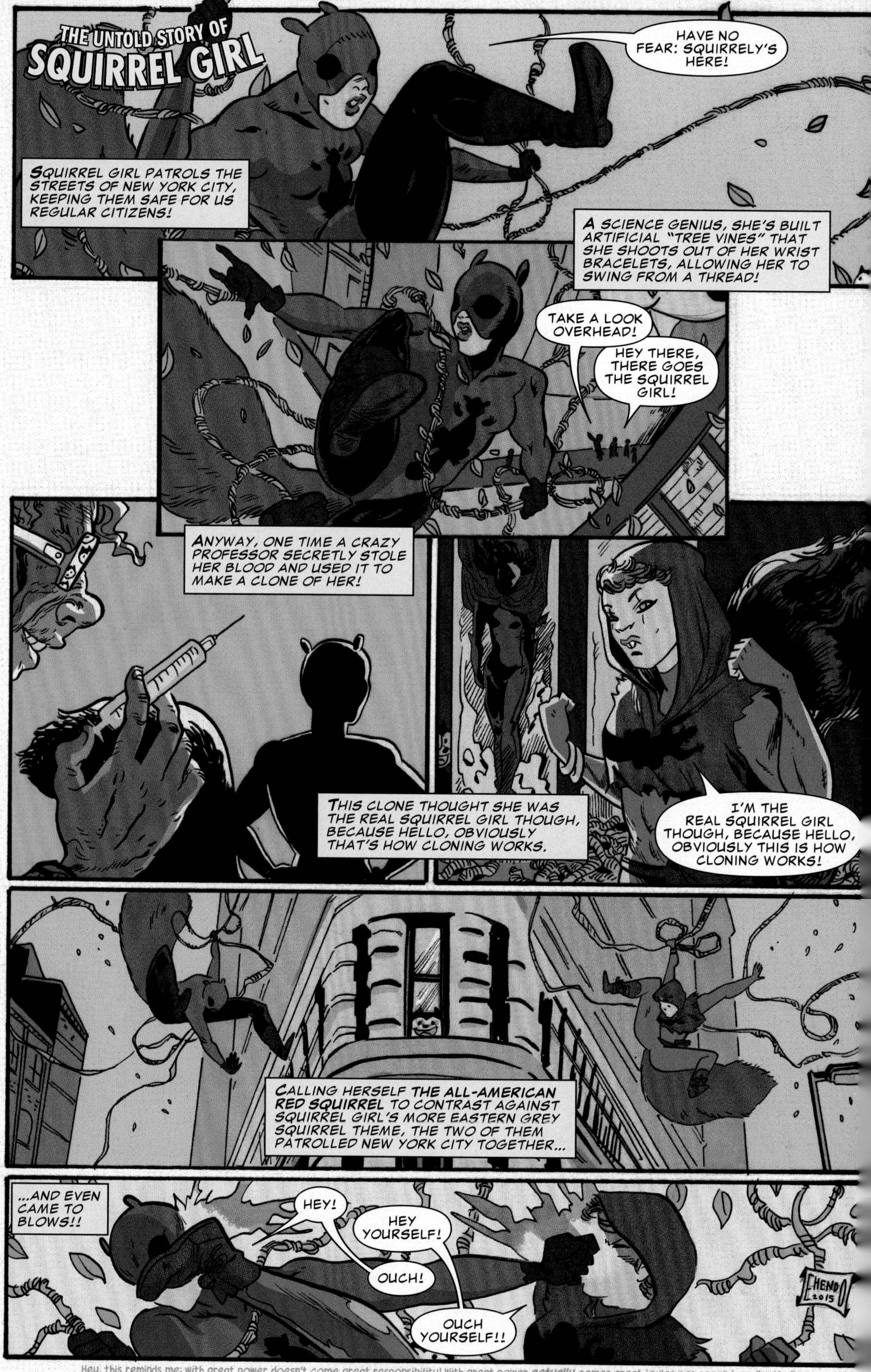
THE UNTOLD STORY OF
SQUIRREL GIRL
HAVE NO FEAR: SQUIRRELY'S HERE!
SQUIRREL GIRL PATROLS THE STREETS OF NEW YORK CITY, KEEPING THEM SAFE FOR US REGULAR CITIZENS!
A SCIENCE GENIUS, SHE'S BUILT ARTIFICIAL "TREE VINES" THAT SHE SHOOTS OUT OF HER WRIST BRACELETS, ALLOWING HER TO SWING FROM A THREAD!
TAKE A LOOK OVERHEAD!
HEY THERE, THERE GOES THE SQUIRREL GIRL!
ANYWAY, ONE TIME A CRAZY PROFESSOR SECRETLY STOLE HER BLOOD AND USED IT TO MAKE A CLONE OF HER!
THIS CLONE THOUGHT SHE WAS THE REAL SQUIRREL GIRL THOUGH, BECAUSE HELLO, OBVIOUSLY THAT'S HOW CLONING WORKS.
I'M THE REAL SQUIRREL GIRL THOUGH, BECAUSE HELLO, OBVIOUSLY THIS IS HOW CLONING WORKS!
CALLING HERSELF THE ALL-AMERICAN RED SQUIRREL TO CONTRAST AGAINST SQUIRREL GIRL'S MORE EASTERN GREY SQUIRREL THEME, THE TWO OF THEM PATROLLED NEW YORK CITY TOGETHER...
...AND EVEN CAME TO BLOWS!!
HEY!
HEY YOURSELF!
OUCH!
OUCH YOURSELF!!
HENDO 2015

Hey, this reminds me: with great power doesn't come great responsibility! With great power *actually* comes great joules per second, or "watts," the integral of which over time measures the work performed. Librarians: please go ahead and file this comic in the "WOW! SCIENCE FACTS" section of the library.

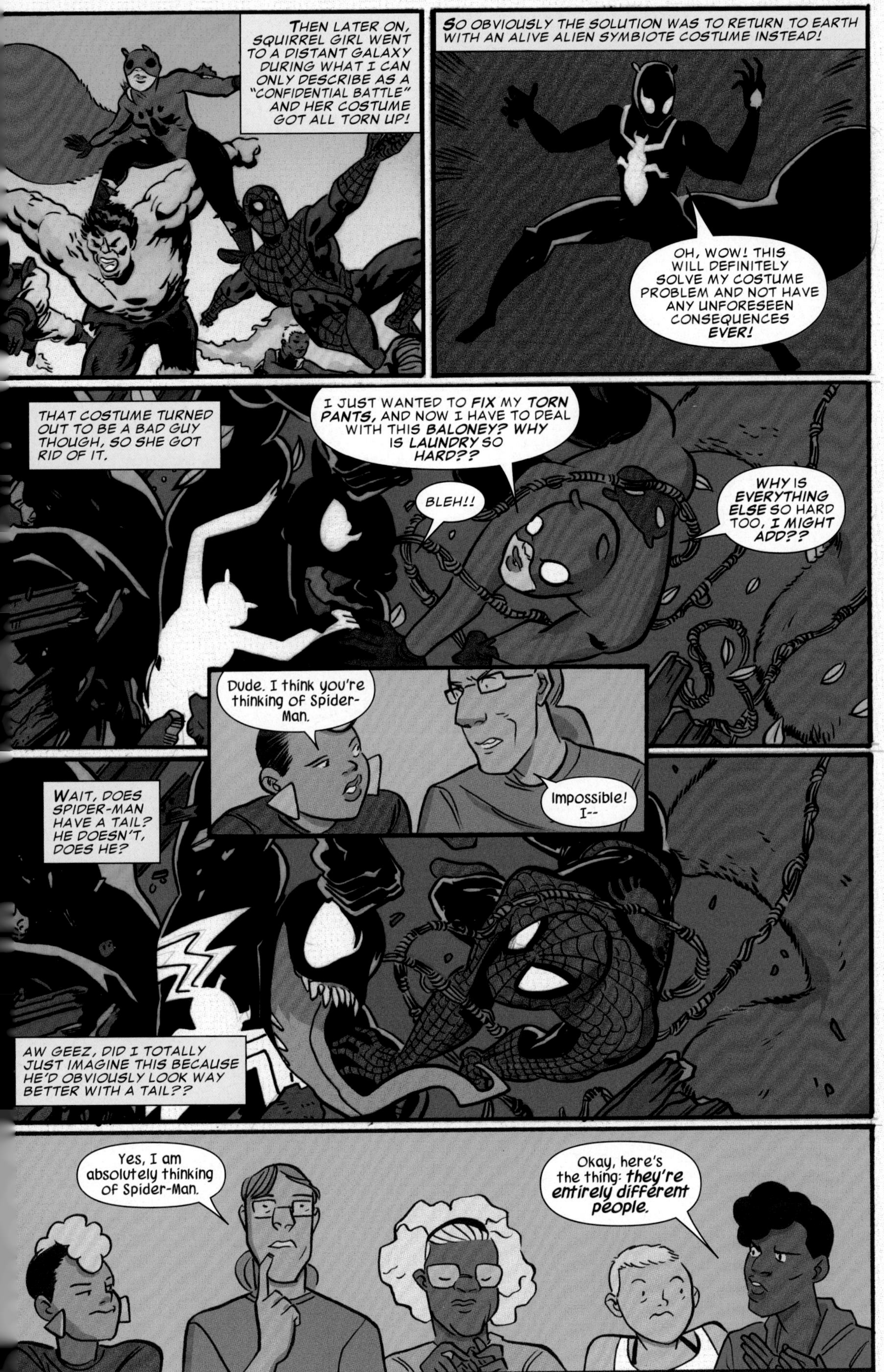

THEN LATER ON, SQUIRREL GIRL WENT TO A DISTANT GALAXY DURING WHAT I CAN ONLY DESCRIBE AS A "CONFIDENTIAL BATTLE" AND HER COSTUME GOT ALL TORN UP!
SO OBVIOUSLY THE SOLUTION WAS TO RETURN TO EARTH WITH AN ALIVE ALIEN SYMBIOTE COSTUME INSTEAD!
OH, WOW! THIS WILL DEFINITELY SOLVE MY COSTUME PROBLEM AND NOT HAVE ANY UNFORESEEN CONSEQUENCES EVER!
THAT COSTUME TURNED OUT TO BE A BAD GUY THOUGH, SO SHE GOT RID OF IT.
I JUST WANTED TO FIX MY TORN PANTS, AND NOW I HAVE TO DEAL WITH THIS BALONEY? WHY IS LAUNDRY SO HARD??
BLEH!!
WHY IS EVERYTHING ELSE SO HARD TOO, I MIGHT ADD??
Dude. I think you're thinking of Spider-Man.
Impossible! I--
WAIT, DOES SPIDER-MAN HAVE A TAIL? HE DOESN'T, DOES HE?
AW GEEZ, DID I TOTALLY JUST IMAGINE THIS BECAUSE HE'D OBVIOUSLY LOOK WAY BETTER WITH A TAIL??
Yes, I am absolutely thinking of Spider-Man.
Okay, here's the thing: they're entirely different people.

Oh, right: spoiler alert for what happened to Spider-Man two decades ago! If you don't want to know what Spider-Man was doing two decades ago, please forget this page riiiight...now. Perfect!

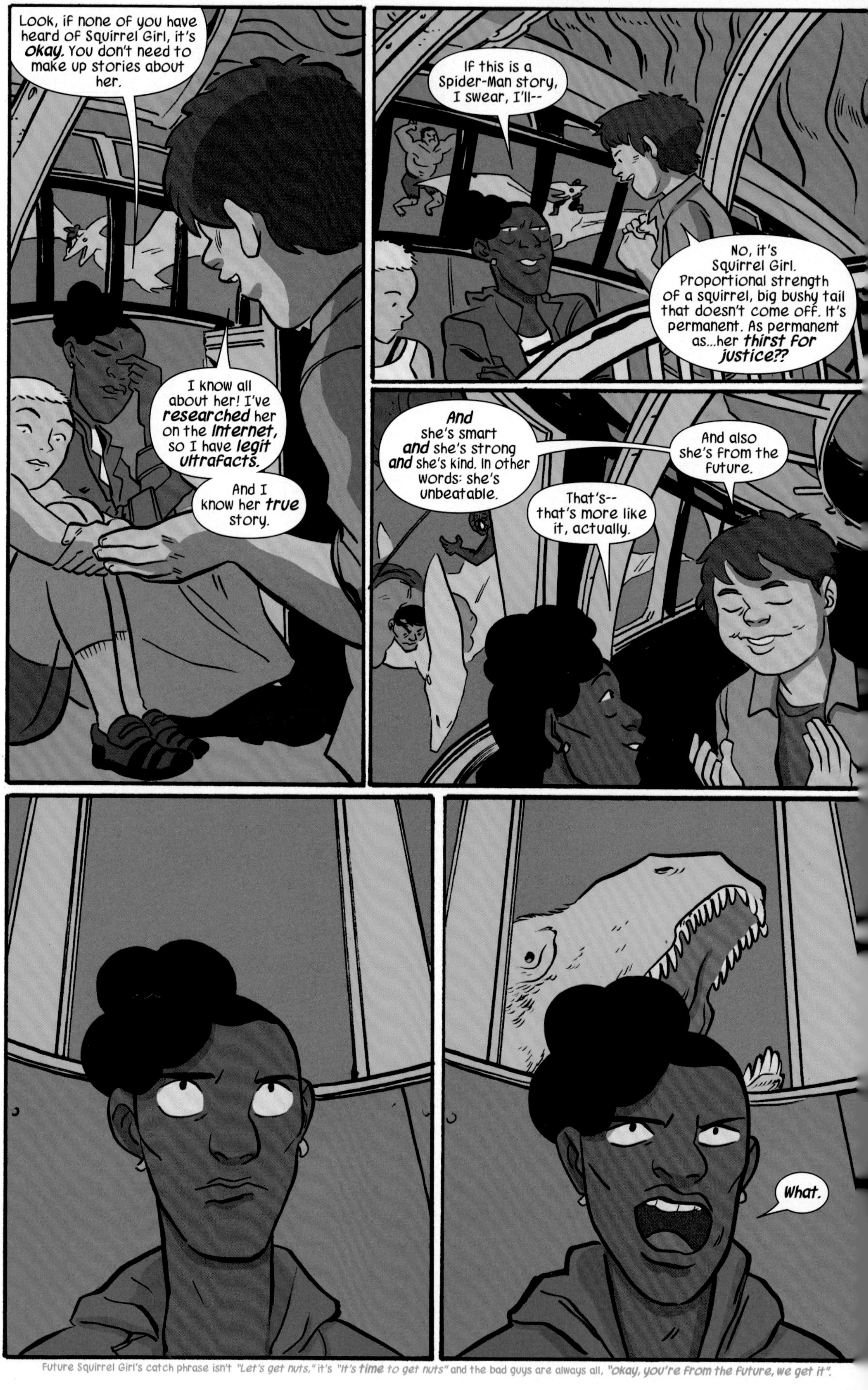
Look, if none of you have heard of Squirrel Girl, it's okay. You don't need to make up stories about her.
I know all about her! I've researched her on the Internet, so I have legit ultrafacts.
And I know her true story.
If this is a Spider-Man story, I swear, I'll--
No, it's Squirrel Girl. Proportional strength of a squirrel, big bushy tail that doesn't come off. It's permanent. As permanent as...her thirst for justice??
And she's smart and she's strong and she's kind. In other words: she's unbeatable.
And also she's from the future.
That's-- that's more like it, actually.
What.

Future Squirrel Girl's catch phrase isn't *"Let's get nuts,"* it's *"It's time to get nuts"* and the bad guys are always all, *"Okay, you're from the future, we get it"*.

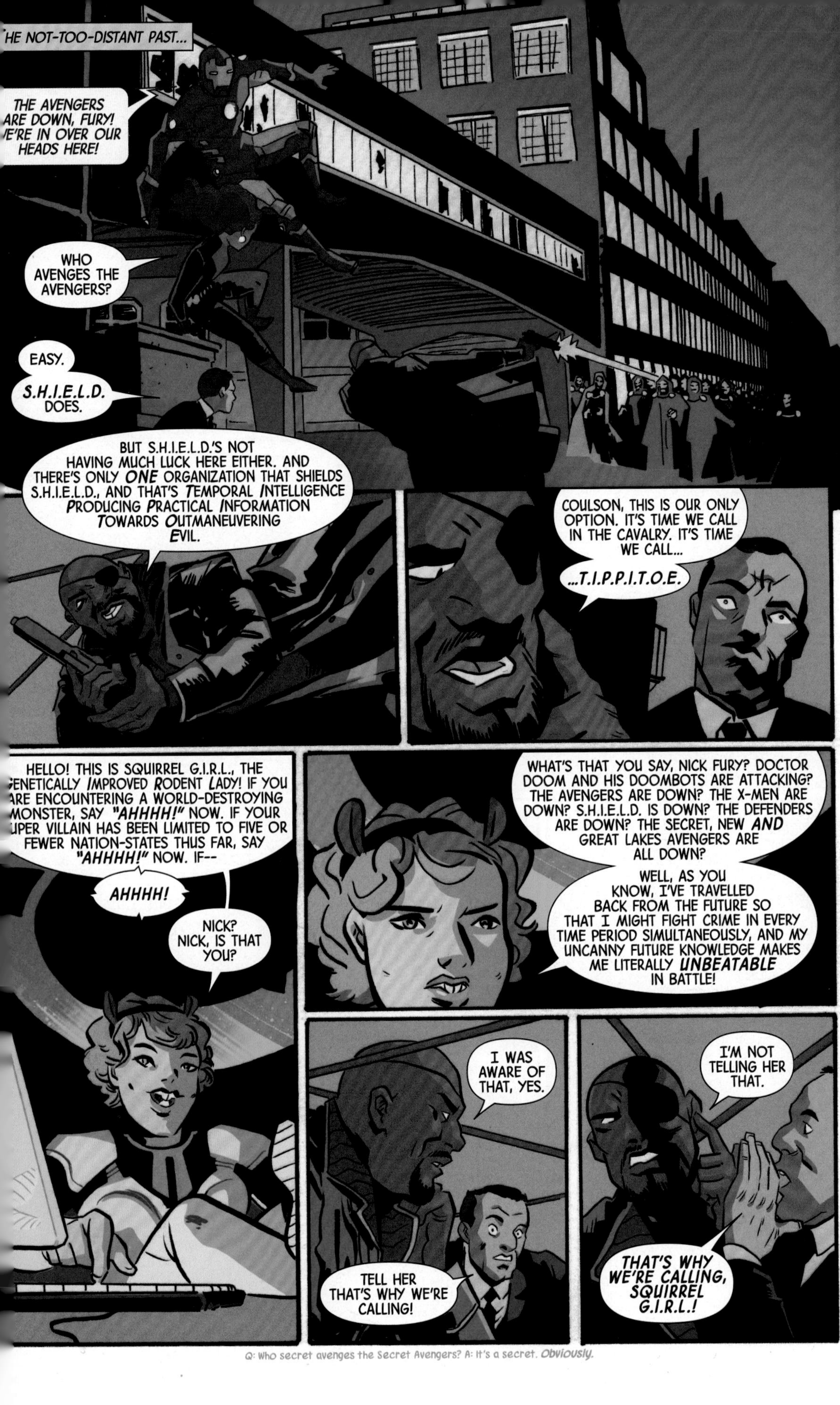

HE NOT-TOO-DISTANT PAST...
THE AVENGERS ARE DOWN, FURY! 'E'RE IN OVER OUR HEADS HERE!
WHO AVENGES THE AVENGERS?
EASY.
S.H.I.E.L.D. DOES.
BUT S.H.I.E.L.D.'S NOT HAVING MUCH LUCK HERE EITHER. AND THERE'S ONLY ONE ORGANIZATION THAT SHIELDS S.H.I.E.L.D., AND THAT'S TEMPORAL INTELLIGENCE PRODUCING PRACTICAL INFORMATION TOWARDS OUTMANEUVERING EVIL.
COULSON, THIS IS OUR ONLY OPTION. IT'S TIME WE CALL IN THE CAVALRY. IT'S TIME WE CALL...
...T.I.P.P.I.T.O.E.
HELLO! THIS IS SQUIRREL G.I.R.L., THE ENETICALLY IMPROVED RODENT LADY! IF YOU ARE ENCOUNTERING A WORLD-DESTROYING MONSTER, SAY "AHHHH!" NOW. IF YOUR UPER VILLAIN HAS BEEN LIMITED TO FIVE OR FEWER NATION-STATES THUS FAR, SAY "AHHHH!" NOW. IF--
AHHHH!
NICK? NICK, IS THAT YOU?
WHAT'S THAT YOU SAY, NICK FURY? DOCTOR DOOM AND HIS DOOMBOTS ARE ATTACKING? THE AVENGERS ARE DOWN? THE X-MEN ARE DOWN? S.H.I.E.L.D. IS DOWN? THE DEFENDERS ARE DOWN? THE SECRET, NEW AND GREAT LAKES AVENGERS ARE ALL DOWN?
WELL, AS YOU KNOW, I'VE TRAVELLED BACK FROM THE FUTURE SO THAT I MIGHT FIGHT CRIME IN EVERY TIME PERIOD SIMULTANEOUSLY, AND MY UNCANNY FUTURE KNOWLEDGE MAKES ME LITERALLY UNBEATABLE IN BATTLE!
I WAS AWARE OF THAT, YES.
TELL HER THAT'S WHY WE'RE CALLING!
I'M NOT TELLING HER THAT.
THAT'S WHY WE'RE CALLING, SQUIRREL G.I.R.L.!


Q: Who secret avenges the Secret Avengers? A: It's a secret. *Obviously.*

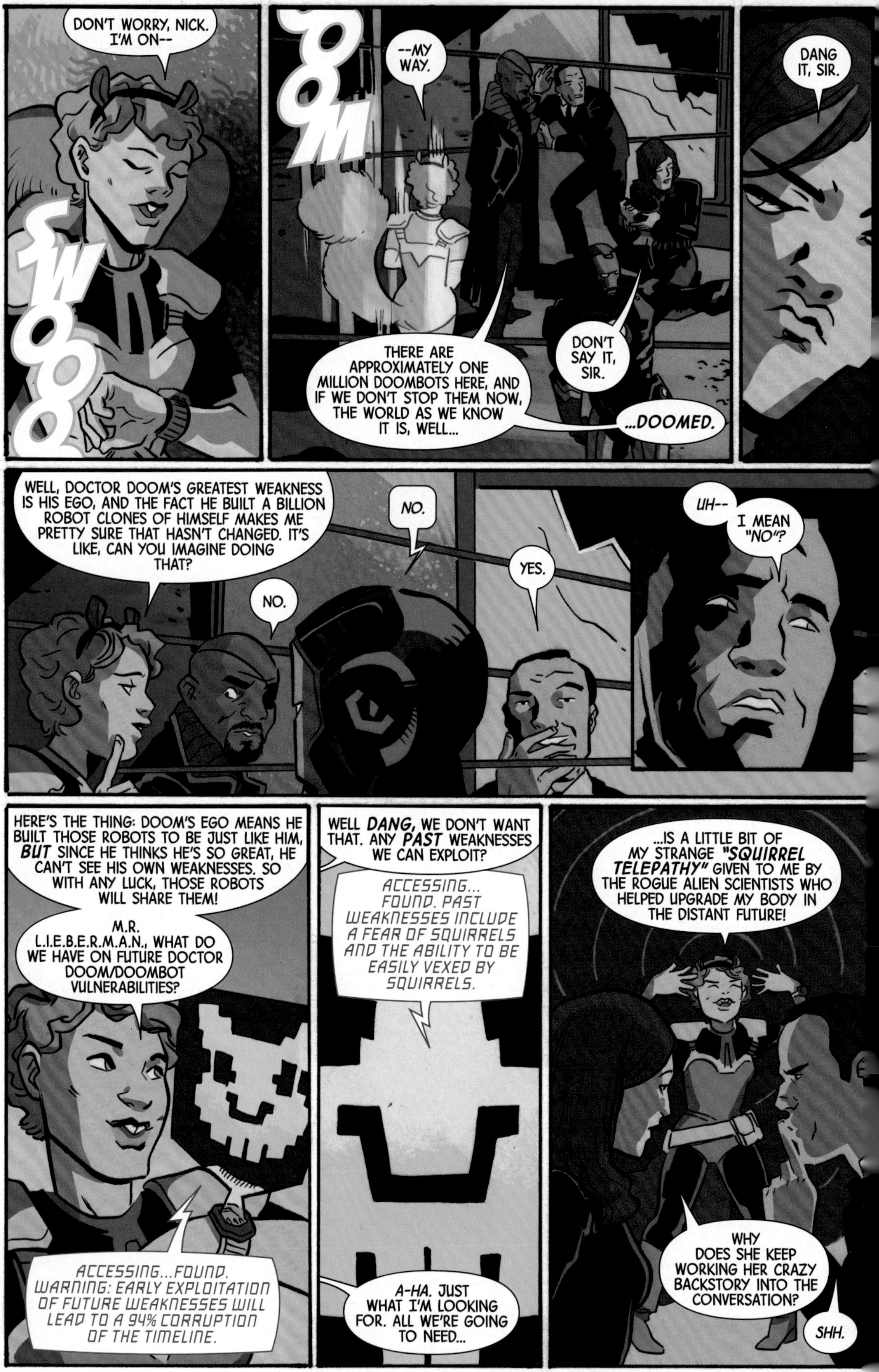
DON'T WORRY, NICK. I'M ON--
SWOOO
OOM
--MY WAY.
THERE ARE APPROXIMATELY ONE MILLION DOOMBOTS HERE, AND IF WE DON'T STOP THEM NOW, THE WORLD AS WE KNOW IT IS, WELL...
DON'T SAY IT, SIR.
...DOOMED.
DANG IT, SIR.
WELL, DOCTOR DOOM'S GREATEST WEAKNESS IS HIS EGO, AND THE FACT HE BUILT A BILLION ROBOT CLONES OF HIMSELF MAKES ME PRETTY SURE THAT HASN'T CHANGED. IT'S LIKE, CAN YOU IMAGINE DOING THAT?
NO.
NO.
YES.
UH--
I MEAN "NO"?
HERE'S THE THING: DOOM'S EGO MEANS HE BUILT THOSE ROBOTS TO BE JUST LIKE HIM, BUT SINCE HE THINKS HE'S SO GREAT, HE CAN'T SEE HIS OWN WEAKNESSES. SO WITH ANY LUCK, THOSE ROBOTS WILL SHARE THEM!
M.R. L.I.E.B.E.R.M.A.N., WHAT DO WE HAVE ON FUTURE DOCTOR DOOM/DOOMBOT VULNERABILITIES?
ACCESSING...FOUND. WARNING: EARLY EXPLOITATION OF FUTURE WEAKNESSES WILL LEAD TO A 94% CORRUPTION OF THE TIMELINE.
WELL DANG, WE DON'T WANT THAT. ANY PAST WEAKNESSES WE CAN EXPLOIT?
ACCESSING... FOUND. PAST WEAKNESSES INCLUDE A FEAR OF SQUIRRELS AND THE ABILITY TO BE EASILY VEXED BY SQUIRRELS.
A-HA. JUST WHAT I'M LOOKING FOR. ALL WE'RE GOING TO NEED...
...IS A LITTLE BIT OF MY STRANGE "SQUIRREL TELEPATHY" GIVEN TO ME BY THE ROGUE ALIEN SCIENTISTS WHO HELPED UPGRADE MY BODY IN THE DISTANT FUTURE!
WHY DOES SHE KEEP WORKING HER CRAZY BACKSTORY INTO THE CONVERSATION?
SHH.

In case you were wondering, M.R. L.I.E.B.E.R.M.A.N. stands for *"Mechanical Resource For Locating Inefficiencies, Efficiencies, Battle-Exploitable Resources, and Machinery; Also Nuts."*

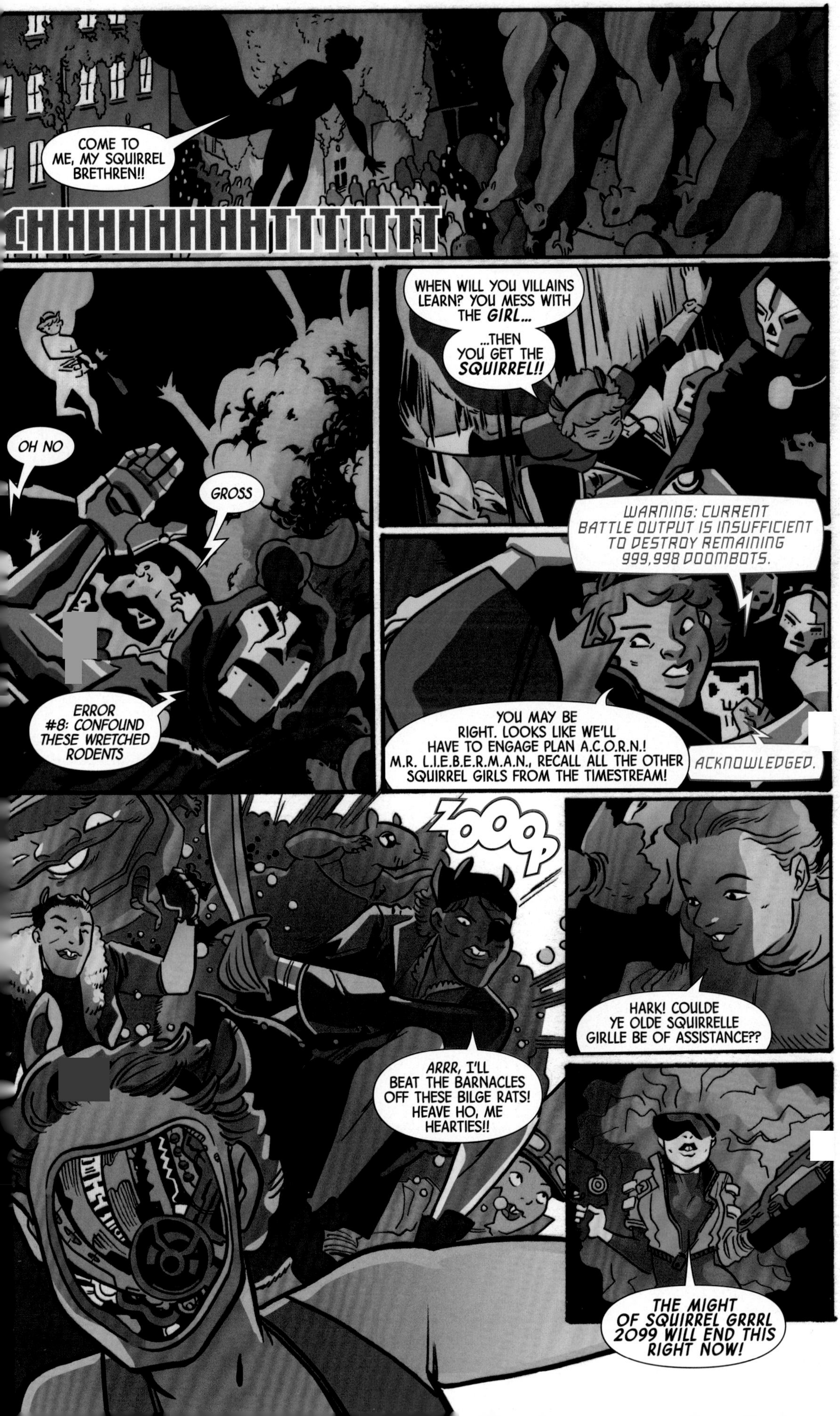
COME TO ME, MY SQUIRREL BRETHREN!!
CHHHHHHHHTTTTTTT
OH NO
GROSS
ERROR #8: CONFOUND THESE WRETCHED RODENTS
WHEN WILL YOU VILLAINS LEARN? YOU MESS WITH THE GIRL...
...THEN YOU GET THE SQUIRREL!!
WARNING: CURRENT BATTLE OUTPUT IS INSUFFICIENT TO DESTROY REMAINING 999,998 DOOMBOTS.
YOU MAY BE RIGHT. LOOKS LIKE WE'LL HAVE TO ENGAGE PLAN A.C.O.R.N.! M.R. L.I.E.B.E.R.M.A.N., RECALL ALL THE OTHER SQUIRREL GIRLS FROM THE TIMESTREAM!
ACKNOWLEDGED.
ZOOOP
ARRR, I'LL BEAT THE BARNACLES OFF THESE BILGE RATS! HEAVE HO, ME HEARTIES!!
HARK! COULDE YE OLDE SQUIRRELLE GIRLLE BE OF ASSISTANCE??
THE MIGHT OF SQUIRREL GRRRL 2099 WILL END THIS RIGHT NOW!

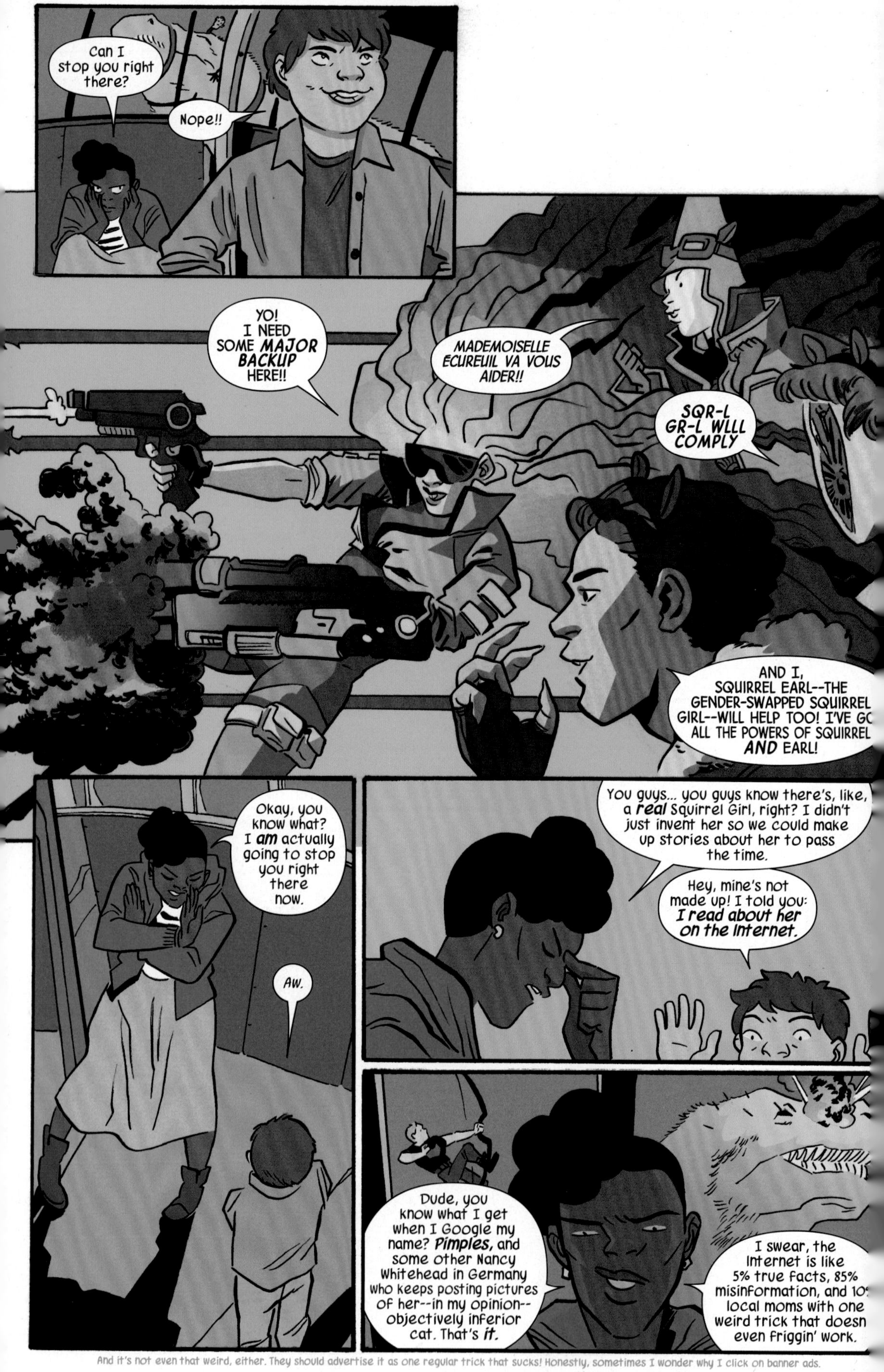
Can I stop you right there?
Nope!!
YO! I NEED SOME MAJOR BACKUP HERE!!
MADEMOISELLE ECUREUIL VA VOUS AIDER!!
SQR-L GR-L WLLL COMPLY
AND I, SQUIRREL EARL--THE GENDER-SWAPPED SQUIRREL GIRL--WILL HELP TOO! I'VE GO ALL THE POWERS OF SQUIRREL AND EARL!
Okay, you know what? I am actually going to stop you right there now.
Aw.
You guys... you guys know there's, like, a real Squirrel Girl, right? I didn't just invent her so we could make up stories about her to pass the time.
Hey, mine's not made up! I told you: I read about her on the Internet.
Dude, you know what I get when I Google my name? Pimples, and some other Nancy Whitehead in Germany who keeps posting pictures of her--in my opinion--objectively inferior cat. That's it.
I swear, the Internet is like 5% true facts, 85% misinformation, and 10 local moms with one weird trick that doesn even friggin' work.

And it's not even that weird, either. They should advertise it as one regular trick that sucks! Honestly, sometimes I wonder why I click on banner ads.

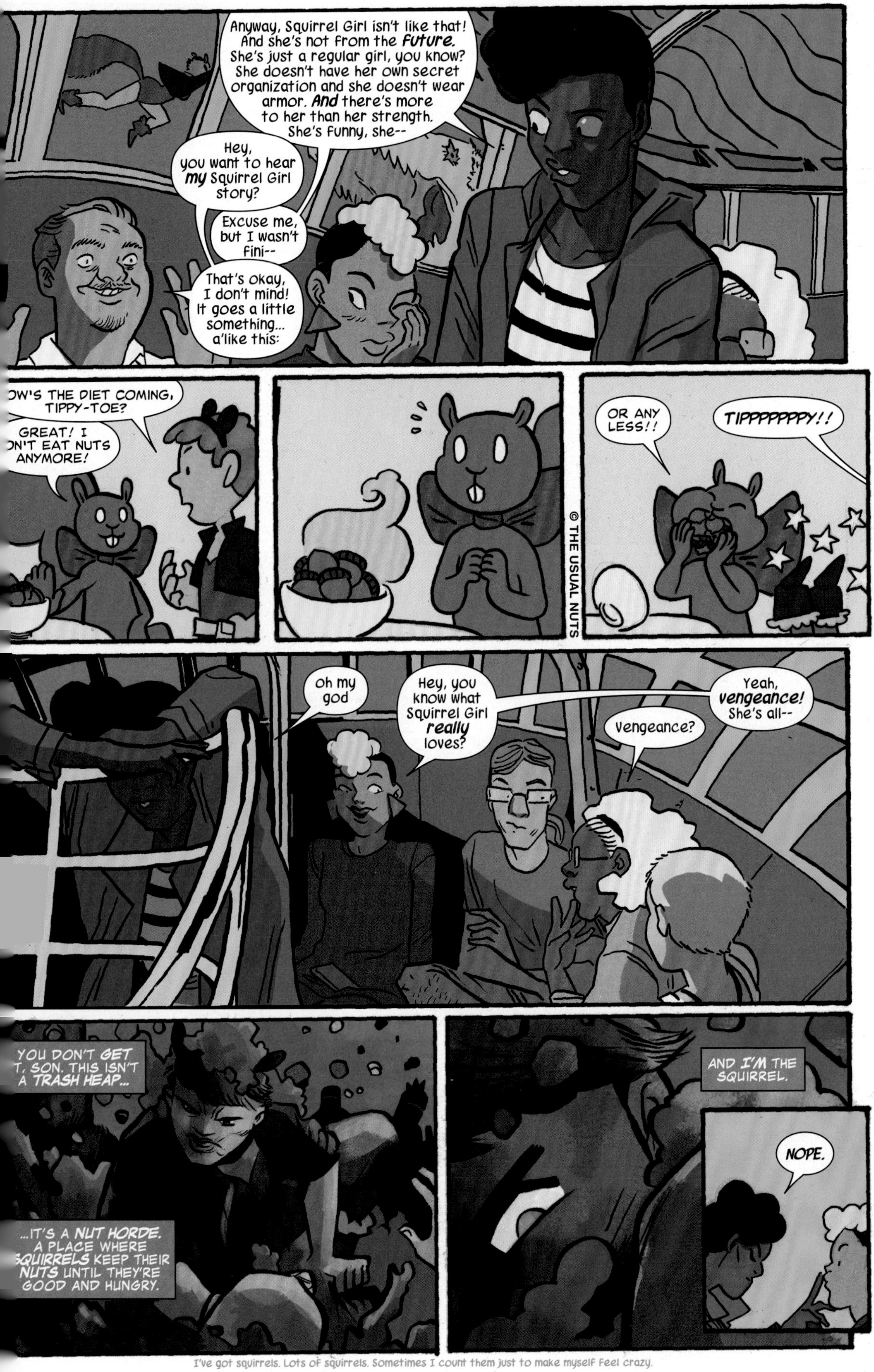
Anyway, Squirrel Girl isn't like that! And she's not from the *future.* She's just a regular girl, you know? She doesn't have her own secret organization and she doesn't wear armor. *And* there's more to her than her strength. She's funny, she--
Hey, you want to hear *my* Squirrel Girl story?
Excuse me, but I wasn't fini--
That's okay, I don't mind! It goes a little something... a'like this:
OW'S THE DIET COMING, TIPPY-TOE?
GREAT! I ON'T EAT NUTS ANYMORE!
© THE USUAL NUTS
OR ANY LESS!!
TIPPPPPPPY!!
Oh my god
Hey, you know what Squirrel Girl *really* loves?
Yeah, *vengeance!* She's all--
Vengeance?
YOU DON'T *GET* T, SON. THIS ISN'T A *TRASH HEAP...*
...IT'S A *NUT HORDE.* A PLACE WHERE *SQUIRRELS* KEEP THEIR *NUTS* UNTIL THEY'RE GOOD AND HUNGRY.
AND *I'M* THE SQUIRREL.
NOPE.

I've got squirrels. Lots of squirrels. Sometimes I count them just to make myself feel crazy.

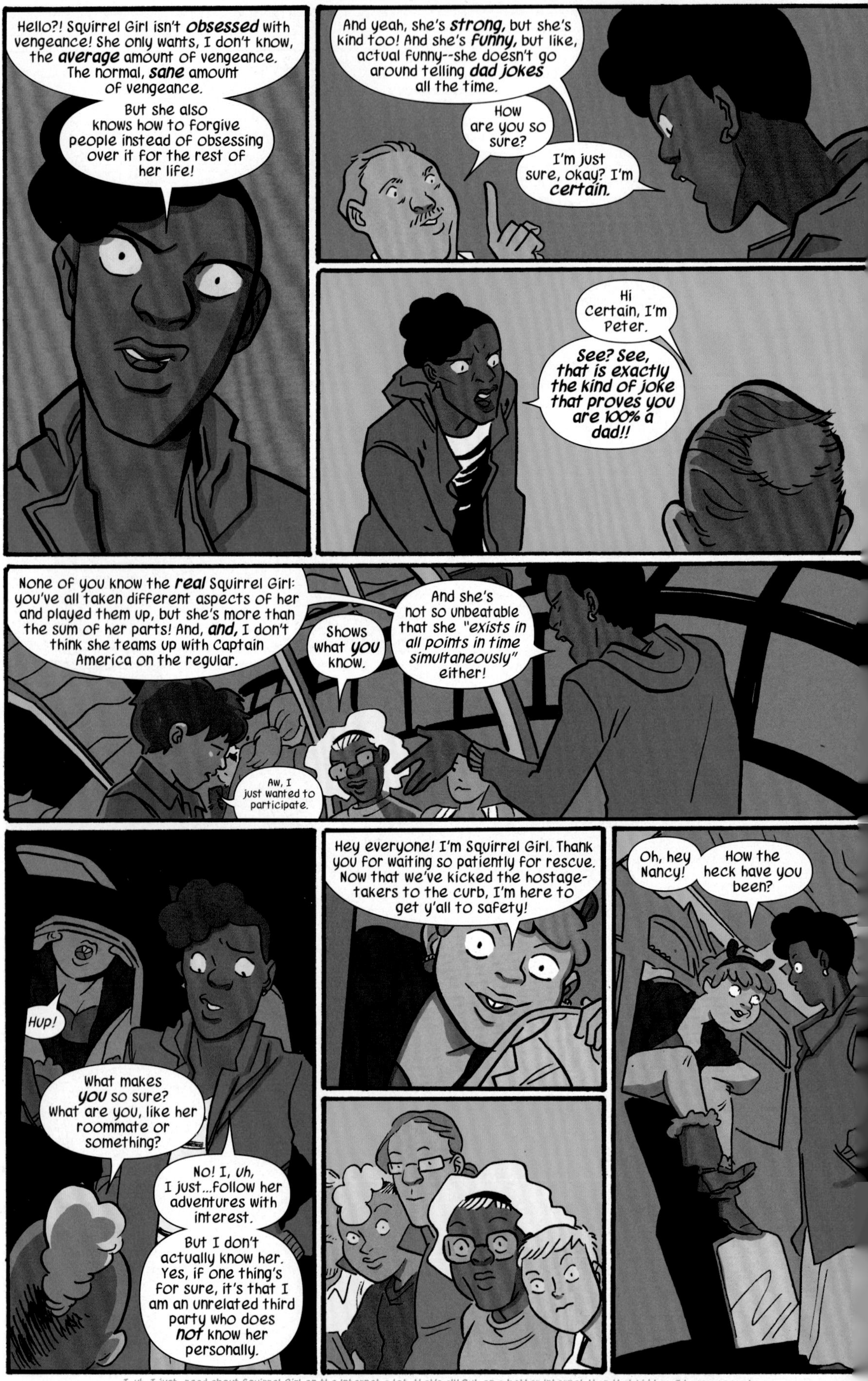
Hello?! Squirrel Girl isn't obsessed with vengeance! She only wants, I don't know, the average amount of vengeance. The normal, sane amount of vengeance.
But she also knows how to forgive people instead of obsessing over it for the rest of her life!
And yeah, she's strong, but she's kind too! And she's funny, but like, actual funny--she doesn't go around telling dad jokes all the time.
How are you so sure?
I'm just sure, okay? I'm certain.
Hi Certain, I'm Peter.
See? See, that is exactly the kind of joke that proves you are 100% a dad!!
None of you know the real Squirrel Girl: you've all taken different aspects of her and played them up, but she's more than the sum of her parts! And, and, I don't think she teams up with Captain America on the regular.
Shows what you know.
And she's not so unbeatable that she "exists in all points in time simultaneously" either!
Aw, I just wanted to participate.
Hup!
What makes you so sure? What are you, like her roommate or something?
No! I, uh, I just...follow her adventures with interest.
But I don't actually know her. Yes, if one thing's for sure, it's that I am an unrelated third party who does not know her personally.
Hey everyone! I'm Squirrel Girl. Thank you for waiting so patiently for rescue. Now that we've kicked the hostage-takers to the curb, I'm here to get y'all to safety!
Oh, hey Nancy!
How the heck have you been?

I, uh, I just...read about Squirrel Girl on the Internet a lot, that's all! But on a better Internet than that kid has. I have access to Internet 2: Internet Platinum Supreme. Yeah: invite only. You've probably never heard of it.

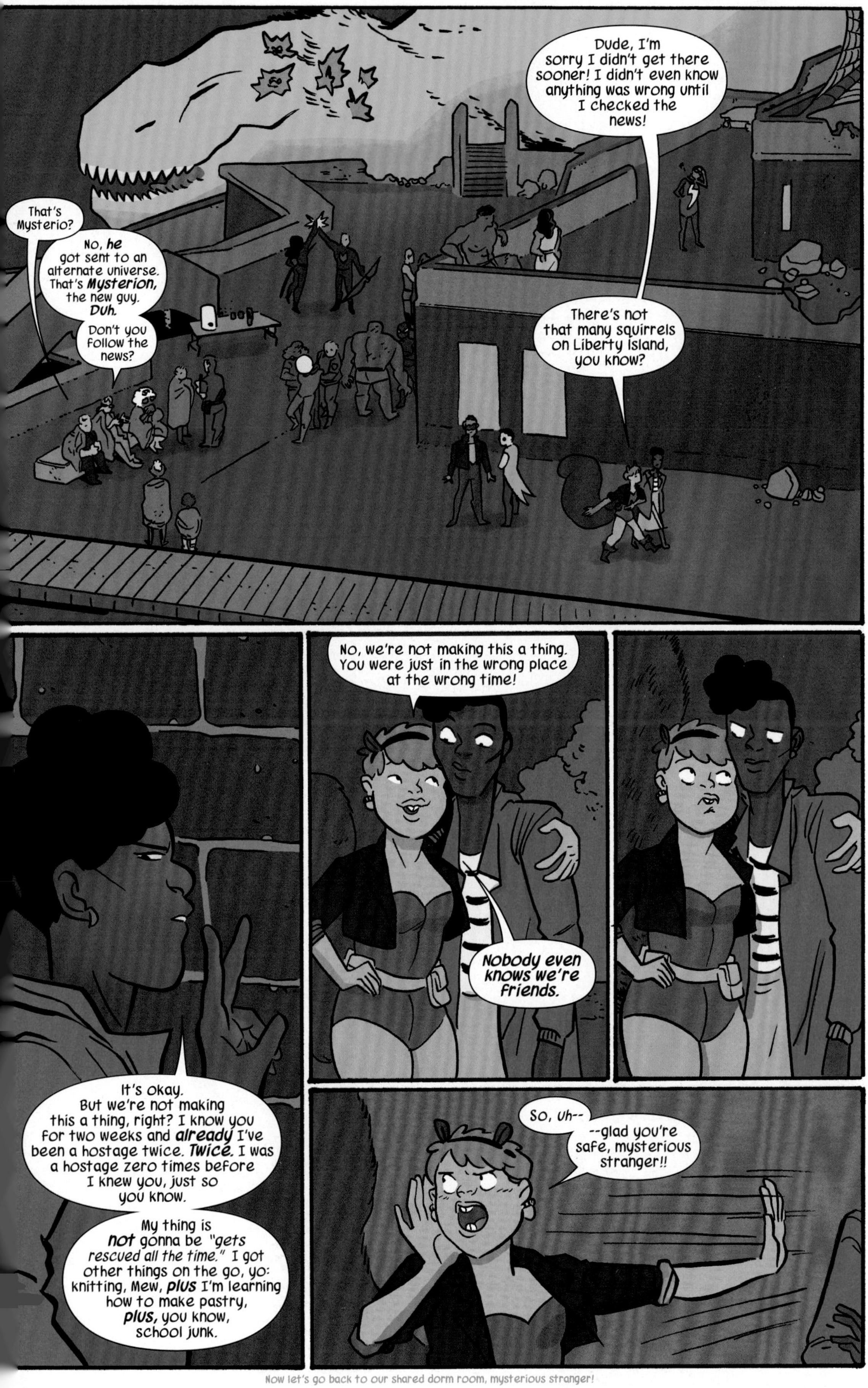
That's Mysterio?
No, he got sent to an alternate universe. That's Mysterion, the new guy. Duh.
Don't you follow the news?
Dude, I'm sorry I didn't get there sooner! I didn't even know anything was wrong until I checked the news!
There's not that many squirrels on Liberty Island, you know?
It's okay. But we're not making this a thing, right? I know you for two weeks and already I've been a hostage twice. Twice. I was a hostage zero times before I knew you, just so you know.
My thing is not gonna be "gets rescued all the time." I got other things on the go, yo: knitting, Mew, plus I'm learning how to make pastry, plus, you know, school junk.
No, we're not making this a thing. You were just in the wrong place at the wrong time!
Nobody even knows we're friends.
So, uh--
--glad you're safe, mysterious stranger!!

Now let's go back to our shared dorm room, mysterious stranger!

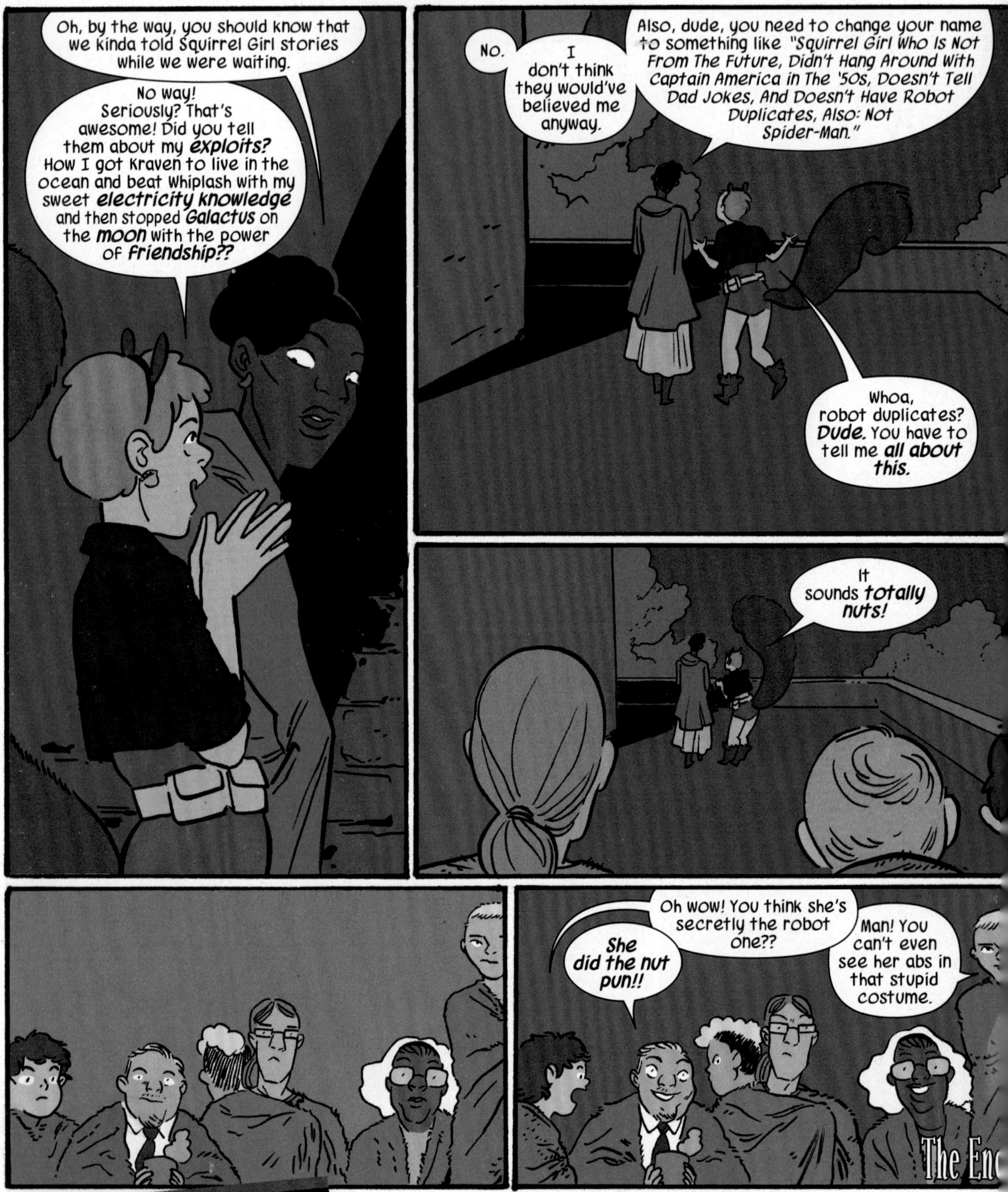
Oh, by the way, you should know that we kinda told Squirrel Girl stories while we were waiting.
No way! Seriously? That's awesome! Did you tell them about my *exploits?* How I got Kraven to live in the ocean and beat Whiplash with my sweet *electricity knowledge* and then stopped *Galactus* on the *moon* with the power of *friendship??*
No.
I don't think they would've believed me anyway.
Also, dude, you need to change your name to something like *"Squirrel Girl Who Is Not From The Future, Didn't Hang Around With Captain America in The '50s, Doesn't Tell Dad Jokes, And Doesn't Have Robot Duplicates, Also: Not Spider-Man."*
Whoa, robot duplicates? *Dude.* You have to tell me *all about this.*
It sounds *totally nuts!*
Oh wow! You think she's secretly the robot one??
*She did the nut pun!!*
Man! You can't even see her abs in that stupid costume.
The End

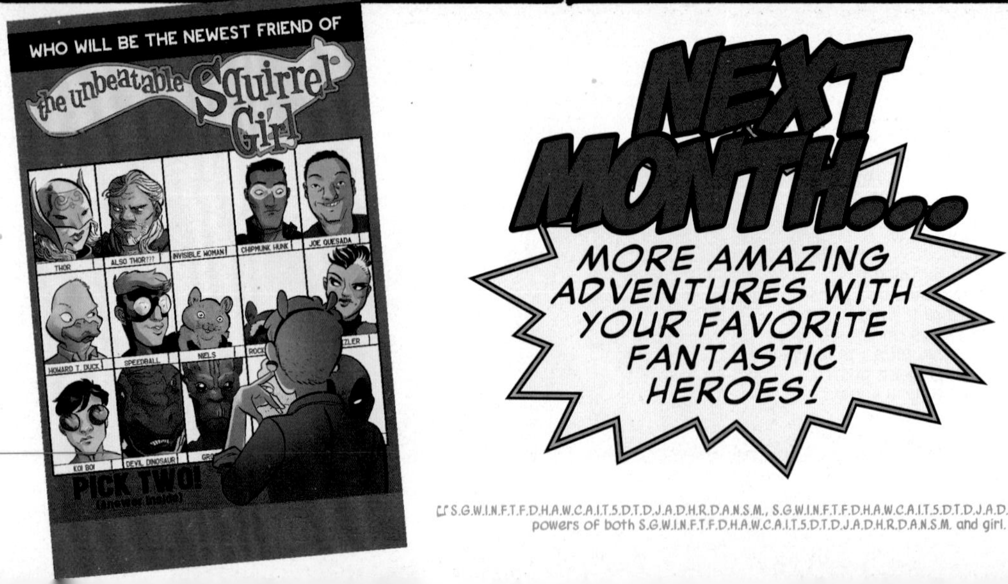
WHO WILL BE THE NEWEST FRIEND OF
the unbeatable Squirrel Girl
THOR
ALSO THOR???
INVISIBLE WOMAN
CHIPMUNK HUNK
JOE QUESADA
HOWARD T. DUCK
SPEEDBALL
NIELS
KOI BOI
DEVIL DINOSAUR
PICK TWO!
(answer inside)

# NEXT MONTH...

MORE AMAZING ADVENTURES WITH YOUR FAVORITE FANTASTIC HEROES!

♫ S.G.W.I.N.F.T.F.D.H.A.W.C.A.I.T.5.D.T.D.J.A.D.H.R.D.A.N.S.M., S.G.W.I.N.F.T.F.D.H.A.W.C.A.I.T.5.D.T.D.J.A.D.H.R.D.A.N.S.M., powers of both S.G.W.I.N.F.T.F.D.H.A.W.C.A.I.T.5.D.T.D.J.A.D.H.R.D.A.N.S.M. and girl. ♫